D0079341

Allen Tate

WITHDRAWN

Allen Tate
1923

Allen Tate

Orphan of the South

Thomas A. Underwood

PRINCETON UNIVERSITY PRESS • PRINCETON AND OXFORD

COPYRIGHT © 2000 BY THOMAS ANDREW UNDERWOOD

PUBLISHED BY PRINCETON UNIVERSITY PRESS, 41 WILLIAM STREET
PRINCETON, NEW JERSEY 08540
IN THE UNITED KINGDOM: PRINCETON UNIVERSITY PRESS
3 MARKET PLACE, WOODSTOCK, OXFORDSHIRE OX20 1SY

ALL RIGHTS RESERVED

LIBRARY OF CONGRESS CATALOGING-IN-PUBLICATION DATA

UNDERWOOD, THOMAS A.

ALLEN TATE : ORPHAN OF THE SOUTH / THOMAS A. UNDERWOOD

P. CM.

INCLUDES BIBLIOGRAPHICAL REFERENCES AND INDEX.

ISBN 0-691-06950-6 (ALK. PAPER)

1. TATE, ALLEN, 1899– 2. SOUTHERN STATES—INTELLECTUAL LIFE—20TH CENTURY.
3. AUTHORS, AMERICAN—SOUTHERN STATES—BIOGRAPHY. 4. AUTHORS,
AMERICAN—20TH CENTURY—BIOGRAPHY. 5. AGRARIANS (GROUP OF WRITERS)—
BIOGRAPHY. 6. CRITICS—UNITED STATES—BIOGRAPHY. 7. FUGITIVES (GROUP)—
BIOGRAPHY. 8. SOUTHERN STATES—BIOGRAPHY. I. TITLE.

PS3539.A74 Z93   2001

818′.5209—dc21

[B]   00-034664

THIS BOOK HAS BEEN COMPOSED IN BODONI

THE PAPER USED IN THIS PUBLICATION MEETS THE MINIMUM REQUIREMENTS
OF ANSI/NISO Z39.48-1992 (R1997) (*PERMANENCE OF PAPER*)

WWW.PUP.PRINCETON.EDU

PRINTED IN THE UNITED STATES OF AMERICA

3   5   7   9   10   8   6   4   2

Frontispiece: A 1923 silhouette of Tate, by Vanderbilt classmate James Comfort, who died of tuberculosis (Willard Thorp Papers, Manuscripts Division, Department of Rare Books and Special Collections, Princeton University Library)

PS
3539
.A74
293
2000

032000–3080 XII

_____

For my father,

and to the memory of my mother

_____

Contents

Allen Tate

Introduction

"My Terrible Family"

Not long after Allen Tate's sixty-fifth birthday in 1964, he began to
write his memoirs. The combination of his retentive mind and his literary fame, his closest associates had promised, would help him to write
an important book.[1] Anyone interested in modern American poetry
would be fascinated by his career, and many readers would already
know something of his achievements. If they did not know that he
helped found *The Fugitive*, the first significant poetry journal to emerge
from the South, perhaps they would know of his association with expatriate writers such as Ernest Hemingway and Ezra Pound. Poetry readers would recognize him as the author of *Ode to the Confederate Dead*
and other Modernist verse, or would perhaps know that T. S. Eliot once
called him the best poet writing in America.[2] Finally, there would be
those readers interested in Southern history who would remember Tate
as the leader of the Agrarian movement of the 1930s and as author of
The Fathers (1938), a critically acclaimed novel about the dissolution
of the antebellum South.

Tate was further encouraged to write the memoir when several publishers, who recognized him as a man who had both made and endured
American literary history, came knocking at his door. They knew Tate
as a critic who had occupied the Chair of Poetry at the Library of
Congress,[3] as an editor who catapulted the *Sewanee Review* into the
upper ranks of America's literary magazines,[4] and as a poet and professor whose lengthening string of prizes included those bestowed by the
Academy of American Poets, the Bollingen Foundation, and the Dante

Alighieri Society of Florence. Having published more than a hundred essays and interacted with virtually every significant American writer of the century, he was easily elected to the American Academy of Arts and Letters. Soon to become president of the National Institute of Arts and Letters, Tate had to admit that the time was ideal to write a memoir. When Charles Scribner's Sons of New York City offered him a contract for the book in June 1966, he signed happily.

Several years later, however, Tate had written very little. He was alarmed to find that the few pages he had produced contained a great quantity of factual errors. Even worse, he was finding it painful to examine his early years. "Unlike Ernest Hemingway in *A Moveable Feast*," he explained, "I couldn't bring myself to tell what was wrong with my friends—or even mere acquaintances—without trying to tell what was wrong with myself." Since discussing his own faults would mean facing "the terrible fluidity of self-revelation," he quit the memoir, having written only two parts.[5] The first part, a prologue he was almost too frightened to write, treated his childhood.[6]

In the prologue, Tate tried to show how his relationship with his parents had shaped his identity as a Southerner. He portrayed his mother as domineering and neurotic, his father as dishonorable and emotionally distant.[7] Although his parents dragged him to one city after another throughout his childhood, it was not merely the changes of place they subjected him to that left him feeling like a transient.[8] His parents' greatest wrong, he maintained, was to lie to him about his birthplace. Wanting her son to be more Southern than he actually was, Tate's mother deluded herself into thinking he was born in Fairfax County, Virginia, "among her family, who had not been wrong-sided" during the Civil War.[9] Tate's father, unwilling to challenge his wife, did not tell him the truth until after her death. Taking a car trip with his father, Tate discovered—at age thirty—that he was born in Kentucky. Pointing to a roadside house in a small town in the southeastern part of the state, his father remarked curtly, "That's where you were born."[10]

But Tate invented the story.[11] It was he who lied about his birthplace. Long before his mother's death in 1929, he knew he was born in Kentucky, not Virginia. It is difficult to determine why he made up the story for his memoirs. Perhaps he had come to believe it himself. Perhaps he was punishing his parents again for a childhood that left him unsure of their affections and ambivalent toward the South. Indeed, the angst that their Southern mythmaking produced in him during the 1920s and 1930s was far more extreme than that generated by his memoirs. In his early life, he faced the nearly impossible task of turning a negative symbol—a group of people he referred to as "my terrible family"—into a meaningful statement about himself and Southern culture as a whole.[12] Fleeing from his parents while idealizing his ancestors, he had attempted, first through politics and then through art, to replace his spiritual loneliness with ideological assuredness. Rejecting the North's celebration of progress, he altered his theory of art in order to oversee the Southern Agrarian movement, a merciless public trial of modern capitalism. Yet this coordinated effort to make American values more Southern kept him from a more personal obsession, his preoccupation with revising his parents' genealogy. It was only when he produced the final chapter of *The Fathers* in July 1938, the endpoint of this volume, that he at last gained control of his family history.

In the decades after 1938, Tate, who died in 1979, was no longer consumed by Southern history. As many Tate scholars have observed, his willingness, after being freed of *The Fathers*, to become the Resident Fellow in Creative Writing at Princeton University, and later to spend the bulk of his academic career at the University of Minnesota, suggests a man no longer exclusively Southern—or perhaps a man who was not regionally minded in the first place.[13] It is true that Tate, who went back to the South only in the twilight of his life, took more pleasure in winning the National Medal for Literature in 1976 than he did in recalling the major role he played in the Southern Literary Renaissance during the 1930s. Yet it was during the first half of his life—during the turbulent Southern period recorded in this biography—that he gained both an identity and a family by answering the question that had vexed him since his childhood: How could he be a genuine son of the South when he felt like an orphan?

Chapter One

"Mother Wanted Me at Home"

The little white house where Allen Tate was born sat near Lexington Avenue in Winchester, a vibrant town in Clark County, Kentucky.[1] Between its founding in the 1790s and Tate's birth on November 19, 1899, Winchester had grown from a cluster of several log cabins into an expanding city of six thousand residents. Although the courthouse in the middle of town was, to the chagrin of proud locals, "not gorgeous," the virgin timber, rich coalfields, and iron deposits in the surrounding bluegrass region lured businesses to the city, including sawmills, saloons, and even a music hall that featured both Shakespeare and blackface minstrels. Not long after one of the railroads crisscrossing Kentucky chose Winchester as a terminus, the adjacent hemp farms, horse ranches, and cattle ranges gave way to paved streets, electric wires, and streetcar tracks. Like many small towns in the South, Winchester was enjoying an economic boom.[2]

No doubt it was lumber that brought Allen's father, John Orley Tate, to town in the mid-1890s. Orley had entered the business in 1887, when his new father-in-law brought him into the Illinois firm he owned. But Orley, only twenty-five years old at the time, took neither to the marriage with Nellie Varnell nor to the business—or for that matter to anything that interfered with his freedom to come and go as he liked. Having spent his youth living off an inheritance from his grandfather, he soon found that he was unable to get the few timber stands, mills, and farms he had taken over to generate much profit. He was well on the way to squandering the land he inherited, and had already begun bitterly—and falsely—claiming that his own uncle stole an enormous tract of mountain timber from him. The harder it became for Orley to earn a living, the more itinerant he became; soon he was dragging his growing family around the country in search of business opportunities. Before arriving in Winchester, he and Nellie had not only produced two sons, Varnell, in 1888, and Benjamin, in 1890, but had wandered as far as Washington, D.C., and Texas, and back. In 1901, when Allen was two years old, Orley moved the entire family to Ashland in order to be closer to his lumber firm and to the business contacts he needed in an ill-fated job as a salesman for an Indianapolis tool company.[3]

Though Allen sometimes found himself sympathetically recalling his father as an innocent young man whose uncle swindled him and betrayed the family by fighting against the South in the Civil War, he more frequently remembered his father as brutal and unpredictable, as someone given to explosive fits of violence, philandering, and drinking. Long after Orley's death, Allen stood in awe and terror of this power-fully fisted man, whose elegantly tailored suits and gentle blue eyes belied a volatile personality. Whenever Allen and his brothers misbehaved, he disciplined them with "the razor strap."[4]

Orley had once been forced to resign from a local men's club for casting aspersions on the character of another member's wife, yet he played the role of an antebellum Southern gentleman anxious to defend his honor at any opportunity. Allen often described the horror he felt as a child of six when, at lunch with his parents, he watched his father attack a waiter in a hotel restaurant. When a young black man serving them spilled soup on the table, Orley jumped to his feet, lifted a nearby chair, and crashed it over the waiter's head, killing him—or so Tate came to believe.[5] "I was afraid of him, and never ceased to be afraid of him," he reflected later.[6]

For obvious reasons, Nellie Tate lived on the run from Orley. A short, tiny-footed, prim woman who wore white kid gloves and frowned upon Sunday entertainment and card-playing, she did her best to insulate herself and her three sons from a husband she differed from in every way imaginable. She probably sensed that he had married her for her beautiful dark eyes and sartorial splendor—and she may now have regretted the plumed hats and luxurious fur collars she had worn seductively in her youth. Both of her parents had opposed her marriage to him because he had a reputation for being a gambling rich boy who "followed the horses and women," and before long many of their fears were confirmed.[7] In religion, Nellie found that Orley considered himself a Robert Ingersoll freethinker, whereas she assiduously studied the

Bible, choosing to divide her loyalties between Presbyterianism and Episcopalianism. Although Orley's father was a pious schoolteacher, Orley never developed any interest in studying, and when it came to intellectual matters, Nellie found him dull in comparison to her father, who had attended law school. Nellie herself lacked an analytical mind, but she read voraciously, devouring novels from Thackeray to Twain to the sentimental works of Augusta Evans. Having once studied briefly at a convent in Georgetown that resembled a finishing school, she thought she was her husband's social and intellectual superior.

Next to their intellectual differences, the greatest source of tension between Allen's parents lay in the romantic feelings Nellie nurtured for her Southern ancestors. Conveniently overlooking the fact that she and Orley were of Scotch-Irish ancestry and were both born in Illinois, she tried using her family ties to Virginia and the Old South as a buffer against her husband.[8] Nellie, whose full name was Eleanor Custis Parke Varnell Tate, claimed to have been born in Fairfax County, Virginia, June 7, 1865, on the Varnell's ancestral farm, Chestnut Grove. So inflated was the myth she attached to this estate and the surrounding land, known as Pleasant Hill, that while she herself had moved to the border state of Kentucky, she referred to Yankees who had been in Virginia for the forty years since the Civil War as "those new people."[9] Claiming a distant relative in Robert E. Lee, she set up a rigid dichotomy between her own side of the family, the Varnells and Bogans, and Orley's relatives, the Allens and the Tates. She told her husband in frequent diatribes that he had sprung from a family of Yankee extraction. It did not seem to matter to her that his relatives on both sides were descended from old Virginia families or that Oak Grove, the Kentucky estate where the Allens settled, was not much different from Pleasant Hill.[10] "My mother," Tate reflected in later life, "had a strong if undisciplined imagination. I am sure she knew in a sense, which I could not fathom, that much of what she said was not true; but she said it so often, with such richness of accumulated detail, that she came to believe it."[11]

Years later, Tate speculated that the reason for his mother's "high-handed disrespect for history" and her self-image "as a heroine of parthenogenesis in Virginia" lay in her need to separate herself from Orley and his roving life in the New South.[12] Orley, perhaps recognizing the difficulty of the frequent moves he made in an effort to make a better living, tried to avoid arguments with her. He rarely mentioned his forebears and refrained from challenging her lectures on genealogy. But Nellie found her marriage to him unbearable. Since the restrictive social conventions of the era prevented her from getting a divorce, she spent little time with him.

Orley Tate accepted his wife's decision to lead a nomadic life, traveling from summer resort to mountain health spa, and Allen suspected that his father wanted it that way. Though she went on her peregrinations in order to get away from Orley, she blamed the stifling weather. "It's so sticky," she would complain on the coolest of spring days, and, gathering up her copious belongings into enormous trunks big enough to hold Grandfather Varnell's wedding waistcoat and Great-Grandmother Bogan's black lace, off she would go, in search of peace of mind and idle recreation.[13] She inherited land from her father, an unhappily married lawyer who once had eighty-one slaves and 200,000 acres of timber in several states, but she seemed determined to sell everything she owned in order to finance her seasonal expeditions.

By the time Allen was born, in Nellie Tate's thirty-fifth year, she had identified a winter escape route, too. As soon as he was old enough, she whisked him away to Nashville. Her cousin taught mathematics at Vanderbilt University, and Allen's two older brothers, Ben and Varnell, enrolled there in the fall of 1906. She was, Tate later observed, "one of the few mothers who felt that she had to follow her sons to college."[14]

I

Nashville that autumn was showing the first signs of the uncontrolled urbanism and boosterism that would anger Tate during his Agrarian period in the 1930s. In 1906, the large farm estates on the fringes of the city were no longer self-sufficient and were threatened by suburban development. The city was swallowing every community nearby and had, just that September, in a carnival-like ceremony during which the Board of Trade handed over to the mayor an oversize key to the city, annexed the area surrounding the Vanderbilt campus. Intending no mockery, Nashvilleans referred to their town as "the Athens of the South," and unapologetically constructed a full-scale replica of the Parthenon in Centennial Park, across from the university.[15] Strings of horseless carriages, such as the new Model F Packard and the Cadillac runabout, were common features on the streets. While local developers dreamed of building a giant railroad terminal to connect the great Illinois Central and Southern Railroads to Nashville, town businessmen made plans for the city's first movie theater and first lighted Christmas decorations. Into this environment of commercialism and urban expansion, Nellie brought her three sons, installing them in the less-than-elegant Tulane Hotel, a residential inn near the university.[16]

Despite the flurry of activity in Nashville, Allen lay bedridden his first winter there and was tended to almost constantly by his mother. Perhaps the death of her two-year-old daughter, Annie Josephine, ten years earlier had made her so fearful of losing her youngest son—fears no doubt heightened when she observed that Allen was born with an enormous head. Although he had his mother's fair skin, high forehead, and thin hair, his cranium was so large that people were soon speculating he was hydrocephalic (his relatives, in fact, wondered if he was "all there").[17] Fortunately for him, a large tuft of wispy blond hair sprouted on his bulbous brow, and by the time he arrived in Nashville he had become a precocious-eyed, if sickly, six-year-old who parted his slicked tuft of hair in the middle and wore tightly laced black boots.

Tate never forgot that winter with his mother. "After chicken pox," he recalled, "I had in succession measles and scarlet fever, which kept me in bed—where my mother seemed to like having me—and I read or she read to me *Grimm's Fairy Tales*, Hans Christian Andersen, G. A. Henty's *With Clive in India* and *With Lee in Virginia*, and best of all Page's *Two Little Confederates*, the little heroes of which I envied the blue, double-barrel guns sent to them after the War by the wounded Yankee soldier they had helped nurse back to life."[18] When Nellie was not reading to him from American classics like *Tom Sawyer* and *Huckleberry Finn*, she seemed to relish playing a role in the formation of his Southern identity, and told him stories—some true, others not—about the slaves and Civil War heroes in her own family. She was especially proud of her father, who fought at Gettysburg in Pickett's charge. Since she had no other way to spend her time, she made a career out of lecturing Allen on his genealogy. "Mother wanted me at home," he remembered.[19]

Yet there was an increasing selfishness in the way she clung to her son. In the summer of 1907, she took him to Dawson Springs in Kentucky, but she probably had her own leisure in mind rather than his precarious health. By Christmas, when his health had deteriorated instead of improved, it was not clear whether her full-time ministrations were helping or hurting. She brought him to a local doctor, who began treating him for "nervous indigestion" and expressed to her his fears that the disorder might be related to the unusual childhood illness known as St. Vitus' dance, a disease caused by rheumatic infection in the brain and characterized by involuntary movements of the face and tongue, followed by heart disease, and, finally, respiratory-tract problems. With such a gruesome prognosis, Allen was immediately put on a liquid and dry toast diet. It was not until two years later, when Nellie took him to the Louisville doctor she saw for her neurasthenia, that they discovered the misdiagnosis. After a brief examination that included thermometer, stethoscope, and an old-fashioned thumping on the chest, the white-haired physician, dressed in the traditional Prince Albert of the day, turned to Mrs. Tate and announced, "Madame, what this boy needs is a good square meal."[20]

Though Allen believed that his life had been saved, he never ceased to be afraid of his mother's smothering care. "The sight of her," a friend of his recalled, "could make Allen turn pale."[21] Even after forty years, when he was going through the first of three divorces, his "very bad mother fixation" continued to haunt him.[22] He confessed to his first wife, the Southern novelist Caroline Gordon, that he had neurotically identified her with his mother, on whom he wanted "to take revenge because she menaced him when he was young and helpless."[23] He had come to empathize with George Washington, whose mother, he read, had "tried and humiliated" him. After learning from Julia Cherry Spruill's *Women's Life and Work in the Southern Colonies* that Washington's mother, a distant relative of Nellie's, was indomitable and domineering and interfered with Washington's career, he wrote a note to his brother Ben in the book's margins: "Thus, after five generations 'blood will tell.' Isn't she just like Mama?"[24]

When Allen was finally well enough to begin formal schooling in late 1908, he was still trying to escape from Nellie's attentions and was suffering a variety of humiliations. She had begun dressing him in Windsor ties and sailor suits, in Buster Brown outfits, or, worse, as Little Lord Fauntleroy. He resisted by jumping into the gutter on the way to school and rolling around in the dust so he would be scruffy enough to look more masculine.[25] Swearing his allegiance to the great Confederate generals and pretending he was John Pelham, he fought off "imaginary Yankees" with a wood saber.[26] His classmates picked on him anyway, bullies beat him up from time to time, and everyone teased him about his "small voice" and Yankeeish Kentucky accent, rude to their ears in comparison to Nashville's soft drawl.[27]

Since the community surrounding Vanderbilt was now within the city limits, Allen was eligible to enroll as a second grader in the well-known grammar school the Tarbox, on Broad Street. A red brick building of three stories, the school had become the best elementary school in West Nashville and was attracting children from the most distinguished families. Classes, however, were run in a militaristic fashion, and students were required to march to their performance-ranked seats to the tune of live piano music. It was possible to advance to the preferred seating area only by reciting lessons before the entire class. Miscreants were subjected to public humiliation by a paddle-brandishing principal, a Mr. E. S. Brugh, who seemed to enjoy eliciting shrieks of pain from his students. The upper grades met on the top floors, the lower grades on the bottom, and boys and girls were kept completely apart from one another even on the playground, where administrators erected a special barricade. Since the school was also segregated racially, the blacks at Tarbox were not students but the custodians who tended the potbellied stoves and an old woman who ran the concession stand outside.[28]

Casting about for ways to prove his manliness in the midst of this alien urban environment, Allen made friends with a few boys his age and joined a neighborhood football team known as the Little Vanderbilts. Though he never made a tackle, he did learn how to pass the ball and was allowed to pose as center in a newspaper photograph. But just when his health seemed to be mending, he suffered a relapse and had to withdraw from school, this time staying at home for a full year, during which his father rejoined the family in Nashville and set up another short-lived business. Allen was confined to bed again. Images from this period in his life would haunt him and later appeared in his poetry: "At nine years a sickly boy lay down / At bedtime on a cot by mother's bed / And as the two darks merged the room became / So strange it left that boy half-dead."[29]

No doubt to get away from her husband, Nellie took Allen to Louisville, Kentucky, a city she had run to periodically since the mid-1890s. The two of them arrived in town with so little advance planning they had to stay at Galt House, an antebellum hotel on the banks of the Ohio River. But Louisville was a bustling metropolis of a quarter million inhabitants and plenty of housing, and they were soon ensconced in an apartment on Floyd Street. When Allen's health improved enough for him to continue his schooling, Nellie enrolled him in a boarding school run by an elderly couple she had befriended.

The Cross School became one of the few happy settings of Tate's childhood. For the next three years, the Crosses served as his surrogate parents, offering him emotional stability, parental approval, and a classical curriculum comparable to those offered by European preparatory academies. Mrs. Cross, who held a doctorate from the University of Pennsylvania, founded the school in 1895 over the objections of her husband, W. O. Cross, who called her a "foolish woman" for buying a twenty-seven-room mansion for delinquent taxes.[30] The heavy stone building boasted an arched entryway, ceilings nineteen feet high, French chandeliers, imported stained glass, finely crafted woodwork, a wide sweeping staircase, and bulging bookcases. On South Fourth Street, the old mansion was not far from the center of town.

In pedagogical principles, atmosphere, and curriculum, the Cross School was entirely unlike the riotous Tarbox School in Nashville. The Crosses had only sixty students enrolled during the school's heyday, and even then classes were small, informal, and conducted around tables. Recitations were made before even smaller groups of students of various ages, each of whom followed an individually tailored program. Mrs. Cross, who had grown up in a large family that lived on a farm, applied the lessons she had learned when she and her siblings were held accountable for individual chores. She stressed the development of character and monitored her students for "indications of natural inclination and aptitude."[31] Her husband, despite his initial resistance to the school, soon began teaching there himself, applying what he had learned in his long career as public school principal. Though he taught arithmetic and Latin, his approach was not especially systematic. He was conscientious about the assignment of vocabulary words and required the students who ate lunch with him to speak in Latin when they asked for a second helping of biscuits, but he taught without a textbook. It was little tribute to Mr. Cross's teaching techniques when Allen finally learned how to decline and conjugate Latin verbs and read a part of Cornelius Nepos's *Lives*.

Perhaps because she listened to children rather than lecturing them, Mrs. Cross was a more successful teacher. In the very first week of class, she went around the room calling on students to see what poems they knew well enough to recite. Allen, who came into the school with the advantages of a bedridden child who had learned how to read long before his peers, raised his hand and volunteered *The Chambered Nautilus* and *To Helen*. When a few of the other students snickered, Mrs. Cross looked about sternly and said, "We will ask Allen to recite 'The Chambered Nautilus'."[32] He recited so beautifully that Mrs. Cross presented him with a little edition of Lewis Carroll's *Through the Looking-Glass* and thereafter took a special interest in him. She soon gave him his first exposure to the old-fashioned field of study known as "rhetoric," long a popular course of study in the South.[33] Each week, he and his peers were required to spend time reading, to turn in a single-page essay, and to work through tedious exercises in grammar. Though he had trouble with his prepositions, he never had difficulty finishing novels, and by the end of the year had read *Ivanhoe* and *A Tale of Two Cities*.

Allen's mother soon decided to ask the Crosses to admit him as a boarding student. She had been unable to locate a good nurse to watch over him, and because she found it difficult to walk with him between their new apartment and the school, she hoped the couple would take him in. Since she also wanted the freedom to travel whenever she felt like it, she was no doubt delighted when the Crosses agreed to her plan. Now she could spend the winters looking in on Allen's older brothers in Nashville, visiting relatives in Illinois, or, if absolutely necessary, accompanying Orley on his own aimless travels.

Allen had not escaped Nellie's interminable trips to watering places and mountain resorts, but living with the Crosses lent stability to his life. There were only two other boarders there, and he had the opportunity to become a member of a small family. In the new environment, his physical appearance improved markedly: color returned to his face; his oversize forehead became slightly less misshapen; he began parting his hair on the side and started wearing a sport coat and necktie instead of a sailor's suit. But if the three idyllic years he spent with the Crosses strengthened his self-confidence and bolstered his intellectual abilities, living with the old couple gave him with a false sense of domestic tranquility. His newfound happiness came to an abrupt end in 1912, when Nellie brought him to Ashland to rejoin his father.

II

Ashland must have looked no different to Allen than Louisville had. With the Ohio River nearby, the town grew steadily from its settlement in the eighteenth century until 1854, when it was spurred to exponential growth after the Kentucky Iron, Coal and Manufacturing Company laid out plans for a city. By 1912, Ashland was a thriving industrial hub. Automobile traffic, movie houses, and scores of small associations, including the YMCA, Elks, and the Merchants Club, contributed to a commercial environment similar to those Allen had witnessed in Nashville and Louisville.[34] But the frenzied local economy could not have been as disturbing to Allen as the turmoil within his own home.

Allen must have observed the growing disparity between his parents' way of life and their shrinking financial resources. Even though they had been living off of their assets for years and were on a course to financial ruin, they seemed neither to realize nor to care that they were exhausting their land holdings. They continued to live beyond their means, and after reuniting in Ashland, they moved to 314 East Winchester Avenue, a large and comfortable home in an upper-middle-class residential area. These carefree financial attitudes had their effect on Allen. Raised by a father who paid little attention to household expenditures and by a mother who claimed the family had descended from the gentry, Allen not only became a poor manager of his own money, but learned to think of himself as a member of the genteel class. He compensated for the shame he felt over his parents' financial condition by carrying himself as something of a Southern aristocrat.

The reunification of Allen's family under one roof also presented him with the challenge of getting reacquainted with his father. Until departing Louisville, Allen had only periodically been forced to deal with Orley, who seemed a distant figure, frequently absent and rigidly Victorian. Though Orley continued to describe himself either as a lumberman or a traveling salesman, and was supposed to have come to Ashland to start a new business, he spent much of his time taking naps in the dusty backroom office of their new home. Each night after dinner, he made Allen come shake his hand in gratitude for the evening meal. In earlier years, his father had spoken to him rarely, and then only to offer such platitudes as "You know, every American boy can be president if he wants to."[35] But now he began lecturing Allen.

The occasion for such a lecture might be an indiscretion, like the time Allen pilfered a bottle of liquor from Orley's private cabinet. Allen had smuggled the bottle out to his friends waiting inside the stable, taken a swig, refilled the bottle from the tap, and quietly returned it. Complacent in the belief that he had cleverly covered his tracks, he continued shaking his father's hand each night, until several days later Orley interrupted the rite to remark coldly, "Son, the next time you steal the whiskey don't ruin it for other people by putting water in it." Orley, who attributed such behavior to blacks and poor whites only, was not bothered by his son's intemperance but by the social significance of the behavior.[36]

His father also lectured him on the facts of life, warning him flatly, "Never go with a common whore."[37] It is altogether likely that Allen, who had reached puberty and was developing an interest in girls, had begun to suspect his father's unfaithfulness to Nellie. He already knew something of his father's cruelty to her because just a few years earlier, in Nashville, he burned a letter Orley wrote that made her cry. Though in time Allen took a less critical view of his father's philandering and was amused that even on his death bed in 1933 Orley found the energy to compliment the attending nurse on her fine proportions, he felt humiliated for his mother. He must have been upset that throughout her marriage to Orley, he was rumored to be "chasing other women, having champagne suppers and drinking champagne out of ladies' shoes."[38]

Since Orley was orphaned at the age of eleven, he probably understood little about bonding between parents and children, and even less about being a role model for an adolescent.[39] Yet Orley's incapacity for emotional intimacy with his own sons only deepened Allen's desire for a strong father, and at times Allen felt affection for and—especially after his death—empathy with Orley. After all, he had been named after his father: his full name was John Orley Allen Tate. Through most of Allen's childhood, he was called both Allen and Orley, and until his college classmates started teasing him with the nickname "Oily," he had even signed his name, in carefully crafted letters, "Orley A. Tate." Distancing himself in a warmhearted way, he tried calling his father "Poo," but there was something contrived about the affection manifest in such a nickname. "I didn't greatly enjoy my father's society," he confided to a friend after Orley's death, "and I saw him only once or twice a year, for a few days; but I was greatly attached to him by those mysterious ties that I hope we shall never understand. In the most important respects he was a perfect father, but there was never a way for me to tell him so. He had no understanding of the modern world, but he had fixed points of reference for his ideas and conduct; and I think one of his perfections lay in the imperfection of both his ideas and conduct. In other words his code was perfect and his conduct erratic— the formula for a 'gentleman' of his era."[40]

In his own way, Orley did show a certain loyalty to his three sons. Once Ben beat up two boys near Winchester and one of the boy's fathers came to the door complaining. Orley, whom Allen later described as "having the pioneer psychology and carrying a gun until he was forty," challenged the man to a duel and waited in vain for him on the street the next morning.[41] Yet while Orley seemed physically powerful to his sons, Allen sometimes found himself worrying that his father would die and he would be left behind. His fears were probably heightened whenever his father teased him for dragging in back "like a cow's tail."[42] Soon Allen began having a recurrent nightmare in which he was left alone in an enormous deserted house where every so often a vaguely recognizable woman or man would walk in from one of the many doors and stare at him threateningly. He began repeatedly envisioning his father lying in a casket, an image that terrified him in childhood and made him feel "unmanned" as he grew older.[43]

Allen's brothers, Ben and Varnell, were living in Ashland, but they were of little comfort to him. While Allen admired them, they were some ten years older than he was and had not spent much time with him. Ben and Varnell were only two years apart in age, had attended the same high school in Ashland, entered Vanderbilt in the same class, and joined the same fraternity. Both had recently married, and after abandoning their study of law at Vanderbilt, they returned to Ashland to start a wholesale tobacco business together.[44] Though they had known their parents in the early years of their marriage, they told Allen little of what they knew about Orley and Nellie. As a result, Allen grew up as if he were an only child, often feeling like an orphan with an overbearing foster mother.

When his older brothers were younger, they had suffered their own humiliations from their mother, and undoubtedly felt a degree of sympathy for Allen. Nellie made both older boys wear knickerbockers, double-breasted jackets, and high collars. She dressed Varnell in delicate lace, in medieval-looking robes with rope belts, and once in full Scottish regalia, including a plaid kilt, an oversize tartan bow tie, and a black velvet vest. (With his blond hair and blue eyes, he could have passed for Allen without a large cranium.) Viewing her first two sons as ornaments, she was of little help with their education. She insisted on following them to Nashville when they entered Vanderbilt, but spent all of her money on her summer travels and saved nothing for their tuition. The two boys, who were forced to work long hours in order to get through school, harbored resentments toward her for years afterward.

Ben and Varnell learned to take care of themselves. Ben, for example, used to say, "We were brought up with silver spoons in our mouths and were expected to eat the spoons."[45] Reacting against his father's financial instability, he resolved to become a millionaire. He had absorbed enough of his mother's genealogical preoccupations to make him worry about the the family name. "I'm not going to be a pauper with an honored name," Ben proclaimed, adding, "—by God, I'm going to make it!"[46] Since his new wife came from an affluent family, it was easy for him to establish the business that eventually made him the breadwinner for the entire Tate family. He learned to distance himself from his parents, and later remarked of their mother, "She'd tell me what to do and I'd say 'Yes, m'am,' and I'd do what I goddamn-well pleased."[47]

Varnell, who would soon move west to make his fortune, became equally independent. "We did not have parents of the mental type, to point out much of anything to us," he explained later, "so we more or less 'growed up,' and had to take some hard knocks."[48] Varnell turned out to be a gentle and thoughtful young man who was less intellectual than Allen and less successful with money than Ben. Years later, his son described him as "sort of half way in between" Ben, who was "all business," and Allen, who was "all arts."[49] Though Varnell developed some insecurities about having accomplished less than had his two younger brothers, his experience with their parents made him feel genuine kinship with Ben and Allen. He came to value all the things their parents had failed to provide for them: "happiness, a family, the respect of your fellow-men, absence of financial worries, your own self-respect."[50] As his wife observed in later years, he and his two brothers had "inherited much intelligence, but little love and understanding."[51]

Unable to elicit much emotional support from his parents, Allen looked around for substitutes. Presently he encountered an elderly and obese Southern lawyer who had fought for the Confederacy and retired to a life of Jeffersonian yeomanry. The old man spent most of his time reading or distractedly tending to his farm, and soon took Allen under his wing, lending him books, coaching him in the Greek classics, and lecturing him on philosophy. No doubt bored by the teachers in the local junior high school in Ashland, Allen was taken by the Confederate's demeanor, especially by his worn panama hat and habit of looking disappointed when a person did not immediately recognize quotations from Plato's *Phaidros*.[52] Certainly he was the opposite of Allen's anti-intellectual father, who proclaimed that he "did not read books."[53]

It was in Ashland that Allen developed his lifelong habit of taking refuge from emotional conflict by reading in private. His brothers had assembled an impressive book collection at Vanderbilt, and since their parents' small library contained more than minor novels by John Esten Cooke, Augusta Evans, and E. P. Roe, Allen began reading in the back room of the house.[54] In addition to Shakespeare, Scott, and Dickens, he found popular history books, a rare two-volume edition of Wordsworth's *Lyrical Ballads*, and, of special interest, a worn multivolume edition of Edgar Allan Poe, once owned by his mother's grandfather, Major Benjamin Lewis Bogan.[55] The set included not only Poe's poetry and tales, but also a biography of him by James Russell Lowell. Allen spent hours reading through the biography and staring at a "desperate and asymmetrical" picture of Poe, hoping—not unrealistically—that he might one day resemble the writer. Allen enjoyed the first literary criticism he read, Poe's *Marginalia*, and soon tried writing on his own. Since Allen had also been reading astronomy and was fascinated by the notion of a universe perfectly and hierarchically ordered, he found Poe's *Eureka*, a bizarre metaphysical essay applying the laws of Newton to criticism, especially appealing. Inspired, he tried to construct a scale model of the planets by lining up a volleyball and various pieces of fruit in his backyard on Winchester Avenue.[56]

As Allen became more bookish, his relationship with his mother became more strained. Unable to elicit any intellectual encouragement from her, he soon decided that she was showing him a new indifference—the first signs, he mistakenly concluded, of a permanent withdrawal from him. She seemed unequipped to respond to his blossoming interest in poetry. Though she reminded him that his Great-Grandfather Bogan, a "poet" who was also editor of the *Alexandria Gazette* and had known "Mr. Poe" personally, she began warning him: "You are straining your mind and you know your mind isn't very strong."[57] Allen found that she viewed the intellect not as a device for sifting evidence and evaluating beauty, but as a reservoir for the romantic images she had appropriated from the literature of nineteenth-century Southern writers. Yet he had discovered that he did not like for her to ignore him, and continued trying to win her approval. "At the age when most boys were turning blackflips to impress the girls," he admitted later, "I was quoting poetry to them as surrogates of my mother, to whom I had to prove that I was not an imbecile."[58]

Nellie had hardly withdrawn from him. Hauling him with her to summer resorts like Sweet Chalybeate Springs in Virginia and Estill Springs in Tennessee, she took on a renewed interest in encouraging his ties to the South. When she brought him to Washington, D.C., to be near her surviving descendants, the surroundings encouraged her in her mission to educate him in the history, actual and legendary, of the Varnell and Bogan families. She dutifully brought him to Fairfax to see the the disintegrating foundations of Pleasant Hill, burned to the ground by Union troops en route to Manassas; she took him to Georgetown to visit elderly relatives; and she ceremoniously introduced him to an ancient "mulatto" woman she claimed had been her grandfather's slave. These excursions left a permanent impression on Allen. Some of his mother's family history contributed to the passionate defense of Southern culture he articulated in the 1930s, and Pleasant Hill itself reappeared many years later as the physical setting of his novel, *The Fathers*.

As his mother foisted her Southern legends on him, Allen felt a mixture of hatred and love for her. On the one hand, he appreciated her strong will and even enjoyed seeing her pretend to be a Southern belle. But he came to resent the effect of her delusions on his intellectual development. In time, he saw her as pathetic. After her death, Tate confided to Ellen Glasgow, the famed Virginia novelist, that the code-obsessed Southern belle of her novel *Virginia* was just like his mother, a social artifact—a "Southern woman of the past generation—a generation caught between two fires." A Woman of his mother's era, he explained, "had a training to which the world no longer responded, and a courage that was equal to every ordeal except that of facing the fact that her courage was irrelevant."[59]

Throughout 1914, Allen was unable to escape Nellie. He spent the summer with her in a Maryland chautauqua known as Mountain Lake Park. Trying to avoid her, he developed an infatuation with a boarding-school girl from Kentucky. He recited poetry to the thin young woman and played tennis with her, but his flirtations led nowhere. To make matters worse, the mood at the park became oppressive in August after guests learned of the German invasion of Belgium and the beginning of World War I. Allen returned home with his mother, and she enrolled him in Ashland's Central High School, a bloated, Victorian building erected at the turn of the century to accommodate the town's growing population of young people. The instruction there was probably poor in comparison to that of the Cross School, but Allen performed well during the 1914–15 school year. In algebra, in English literature, and in English composition, he received grades of 90; in ancient history and Latin, 85. His withdrawal from his family into the world of books had yielded positive results.

III

In 1915, Orley Tate's business failed and the Tates were forced to give up their home on Winchester Avenue. Allen often referred to his father's "financial collapse" as a turning point in his life. After editing a biographical sketch of himself years later, he contemplated adding a reference to the event, a piece of information he believed would "throw light on the uncertainties and perhaps some of the aberrations of my life up to about 1925."[60] Since his parents now had only a few parcels of land to sell and no prospects in Ashland, they packed up again.

Orley took the family farther west along the Ohio River to Evansville, Indiana, directly across from Owensboro, Kentucky.

"What I remember most about my boyhood," Tate once told an interviewer, "was being moved around."[61] Until he entered college, he rarely stayed more than a few years in one place. Though most of those places were Midwestern or Northern rather than Southern, the urban growth he observed during his brief residences in cities in the Ohio Valley stimulated his interest in Southern Agrarianism, his hatred of Northern industrialism, and his firm belief that America was permanently and negatively transformed by World War I.

Certainly industrial values were ubiquitous in Evansville, Indiana, between 1915 and 1917. These values seemed more threatening since the border city was situated in an agricultural region with strong Southern influences. The same year that the Tates moved to Evansville, Theodore Dreiser returned to see the city of his adolescence and was struck not only by the Evansville's intensely Germanic culture, but also by its distinctive regional affiliation. Evansville, Dreiser observed, "has all the characteristic marks of a Southern city—a hot, drowsy, almost enervating summer, an early spring, a mild winter, a long, agreeable autumn. . . . Darkies abound, whole sections of them, and work on the levee, the railroad, and at scores of tasks given over to whites in the north. You see them ambling about carrying packages, washing windows, driving trucks and autos, waiting on table. It is as though the extreme South had reached up and touched this projecting section of Indiana." Evansville, which boasted it had the world's least expensive soft coal, also ranked as the second largest producer of hardwood lumber. Yet even as steamboats ferried out products from more than three dozen furniture factories, Orley Tate seemed unable to translate his townsmen's insatiable appetite for growth into personal profit.[62] After only a few months, he moved the family back along the river to Cincinnati, Ohio.

Like the other Ohio Valley cities where Allen had lived, Cincinnati was an industrial mecca surrounded by farmland.[63] Almost twenty railroads served the city from the South. Cincinnati's proximity to the river, its transportation channels, and its vast fields of bituminous coal explain why its machine-tool and metal manufacturers became major suppliers of materials during World War I. Just as the Tates were arriving in town in 1916, the Chamber of Commerce was launching a campaign to double the size of its membership, and pamphlets appeared touting the town's superiority as a manufacturing center. Recently the

Industrial Department had lured seven major industrial firms to town and both the Business Men's Club and the Main Street Merchants' Association were hard at work advertising the city. They joyously welcomed the new hospital and medical college buildings, bragged about the new jitneys, and gloated over the city's growth in population to more than 400,000.

Yet Cincinnati was already experiencing the problems associated with urban industrialism. The coal industries emitted great quantities of smoke, tuberculosis infection was a problem, and residential areas and public parks seemed increasingly threatened by industrial developers. To make matters worse, the city was struggling to emerge from a dark political era under the infamous machine politician "Boss" George Cox, and was still suffering from years of labor unrest and social strife. Many of the city's native-born whites were venting hostilities toward blacks who had recently emigrated from the South in search of work.

If the problems of industrial growth left a permanent impression on Allen, they had no direct bearing on Orley Tate's business interests. Certainly they do not explain why Orley failed to make a living selling saws and axes in cities with such immense lumber and manufacturing interests. The most generous way to explain his failure is to portray him as an example of the tragedy his son later ascribed to Northern victory in the Civil War: Orley was a Southern gentleman deprived of his land and forced to make a living by trading off of the commercialization and industrialization of his own region. He was a victim of the doctrine of mindless progress sweeping the Middlewest and the "New South." Yet while Orley no doubt would have been more comfortable as a Kentucky landowner than as a traveling tool salesman, his troubles may have been due to laziness. Most mornings he was apparently unable to get dressed before noon.

The real victim as Orley shuttled his business back and forth between Evansville and Cincinnati was Allen, whose recent intellectual growth was held in check by the repeated changes in his educational environment. He changed secondary schools half a dozen times as Orley's fleeting businesses pulled him out of Kentucky into surrounding cities. During the war years alone, Allen was enrolled in four public schools; not long after he settled into one, he would be removed to another, only to be returned eventually to the first. As a result, he had neither the opportunity to build friendships with children his age nor the opportunity to follow a single course of study from beginning to end.

This instability was unfortunate because the two schools Allen attended in Evansville and Cincinnati were excellent. Evansville High School offered an especially challenging program. The school had strong ties with the University of Chicago and boasted one of the best high school libraries in the Ohio Valley. There was even a monthly literary magazine sponsored by the English department. But the antiquated building, which opened its doors on Seventh Avenue in 1868, was not big enough for its one thousand students. Perhaps it was all the moving around and the overcrowded classrooms that accounted for the drop in Allen's grades when he attended the school for a few months late in 1915. Though he made a respectable 85 in mathematics and an 84 in English, he barely passed history and Latin.[64]

Allen's performance at the Walnut Hills High School in Cincinnati was even worse. The school, located in a residential area near Cincinnati's medical college, offered an ideal environment for learning. When it was completed in 1895, the granite and sandstone building was viewed as "a model structure." It had the latest heating and ventilation systems, a finished hardwood interior, and sixteen classrooms, all gaily decorated and equipped with adjustable desks. There were physics and chemistry laboratories, an auditorium, a gymnasium, a map collection, and a library stocked with history, science, and literature books, including a special grouping of Roman and Greek classics. Allen's grades during the 1916–17 school year nevertheless continued their downward spiral. He received a 72 in zoology, 70 in Latin, 68 in physics, 65 in elocution; even in English, his average was less than 80. And while he could have joined a variety of organizations, such as the Drama, Spanish, and Debate Clubs, he participated in no extracurricular activities.[65]

IV

The one area where Allen expressed his creativity was in music. At Nellie's urging he had taken up the violin, and in the fall of 1916, shortly after he entered the Walnut Hills High School, he began violin lessons at the nearby Cincinnati Conservatory of Music. The Conservatory was founded in 1867 by Miss Clara Baur, a serious-minded matron who wore a large crucifix around her neck and dedicated the school "to the praise of God and the study of music."[66] When she died in 1912, her temperamental but shrewd niece, Bertha Baur, took over, and by the time Allen began lessons there, the school was enjoying its most prosperous year. Housed in an Elizabethan-style estate purchased from the Shillitos, an early Cincinnati merchant family, the Conservatory had expanded its faculty in number to sixty-one. Since the faculty was internationally recognized, students who normally would have been studying in Europe but were diverted to American conservatories because of the war were assured of the most rigorous training available.

Although the five faculty members in the violin department were doubtless overworked, it was a common practice for them to take on additional students from the community and to tutor them for pay. Allen, who never actually lived at the Conservatory, arrived just as two of the best violinists in the world had begun taking on outside students. The first of them, Jean Ten Have, a native of Lyon, France, was the son of a prominent Dutch composer and violinist and joined the violin department that September. A lean, balding man with a bushy black moustache and dark liquid eyes, he spoke English with some proficiency but had not yet learned many American idioms. Though he was already in his midforties by the time he began to instruct Allen, he was still considered a developing artist and made his American debut at Emery Hall in Cincinnati just as Allen arrived. "His tone is clear and clean," a reviewer noted afterward, adding, "his virtuosity is of the kind which seeks its aim by legitimate means rather than by any sensational display."[67] At the Cincinnati Conservatory of Music, Ten Have quickly lived up to his reputation as a master of chamber and ensemble music, impressing everyone with his personal sincerity and his professional poise. After working with Allen for four months, he turned him over to his own teacher, Eugéne Ysaÿe, the internationally acclaimed violinist and conductor.

Allen was justifiably proud of studying under Ysaÿe, who would come to be known as "the pioneer of twentieth-century violin playing." A child prodigy who earned a brilliant record at the Conservatory in Liège in the mid 1860s, Ysaÿe studied first under Wieniawski at the Brussels Conservatory and then under the master, Vieuxtemps, in Paris. By 1879, he was conducting the Bilse Orchestra in Berlin, where he and his younger brother Théo, a piano virtuoso, became friendly with Jules LaForgue, the French symbolist poet known for vers libre. By the time Eugéne Ysaÿe arrived in Cincinnati, he was already well known in the United States. He would soon conduct the Cincinnati Symphony and play before vast audiences at hippodromes across America. As an interpretive artist with an eclectic repertoire running from Debussy to Bach, he believed that violinists should be intellectual, poetic, and passionate, all at once. Students at the Conservatory of

Music worshiped him, not only because of his strict standards, but also for the polite way he interrupted their playing to make corrections. A practicing Catholic who had an air of worldly wisdom about him, he was heavyset with plump cheeks, a wide, pudgy face, and a double chin. Though he was almost sixty years old, his hair, which he greased straight back, was jet black.[68]

Ysaÿe was remarkably modest given the magnitude of his successes—and possessed none of the intimidating characteristics of Allen's father—but Allen was terrified of the violinist and spent two months in the spring of 1917 preparing a program for him around Tartini's *Devil's Trill Sonata.* When the day of the recital arrived, Allen found that his audience consisted only of Ysaÿe and a pleasant young woman enlisted to play the piano in accompaniment. Allen was so nervous that he fumbled through the piece. When Ysaÿe did not stop him in his usual manner and said nothing afterward, Allen finally had the nerve to ask, "Mr. Ysaÿe, how was it?" Ysaÿe replied merely, "Your left hand is good, but it is all very uninteresting."[69] It may have been Allen's recital that prompted Ysaÿe to comment soon afterward that "a boy of eighteen can not expect to express that to which the serious student of thirty, the man who has actually lived, can give voice. If the violinist's art is truly a great art, it can not come to fruition in the artist's 'teens."

Though Allen's parents had kept him on an emotional roller coaster, he was not yet capable of meeting Ysaÿe's requirement that to be a master violinist, a musician must have "known hope, love, passion and despair" and "must have run the gamut of emotions in order to express them all in his playing." When Allen finally did come to understand Ysaÿe's dictum ("La musique ne se comprend pas, elle se sent; elle est l'émanation de l'âme et du coeur"),[70] he had lost his technical control and overcompensated by exaggerating the emotion in his playing. Many years later when Eric Bentley accompanied him on piano in a Mozart violin sonata, the playwright observed, "I discovered Allen was not a classicist after all, but madly romantic: he played like an impetuous teenager."[71] If Ysaÿe deflated his ambition to become a well-known concert violinist, Allen was only mildly disappointed—for in failing, he not only achieved a small victory over Nellie but complied with his father's wish that the Tate boys undertake traditionally manly activities only. Orley did not want him to study the violin to begin with because he "didn't think it went with Kentucky."[72]

Allen's failure at the Conservatory meant his return to the public schooling he haphazardly began in Ashland. He spent several months back at Evansville High School, until Nellie, who no doubt sensed what lay ahead for them as Orley's bankruptcy unfolded, brought Allen to Northern Virginia and Washington, D.C., to be near her cousins and Pleasant Hill. Attempting to satisfy her ancestral pieties, in October 1917 she enrolled him in the Georgetown Preparatory School. Her father had attended the school in the early 1850s, and her great-grandfather was an in-law of the Reverend Francis Neale, S.J., Georgetown's second president.

Allen had entered America's oldest Jesuit school, founded in 1789 by Reverend John Carroll, the first Roman Catholic bishop in America. Classes were held on the Georgetown University campus, known as "the Hilltop." Though Allen and many other students were "day scholars," who paid an annual tuition of three hundred dollars, others paid an additional room and board fee and lived in dormitories such as Healey, an enormous stone building with a high clock tower and spires. There were only about twenty students in each of the school's four grades, and discipline was strict; attendance and punctuality were cardinal virtues. Only one-hour lunch breaks interrupted the daily routine of four discrete classroom periods beginning at 9:00 A.M. and ending promptly at 2:45 P.M. Afterward, every student was expected to stay on campus until 5:00 P.M. for such activities as drama, chorus, orchestra, and altar Guild. Tobacco use was expressly forbidden, and the faculty, almost all of whom were members of the Society of Jesus, aimed "to cultivate habits of industry and carefulness."

Allen apparently had no difficulty in meeting the admission requirements, but his new school was demanding. The Jesuits taught a carefully prescribed curriculum over two academic terms, with examinations falling after Christmas and Easter recesses. Each student followed a course of study predetermined for the entire class, and the boys in Allen's grade faced the toughest one. Eight of the twenty-five hours of instruction each week were devoted to Latin; five to Greek; four to mathematics; three to modern languages; two to English and two to history; and a half hour apiece to elocution and instruction in Catholicism—an allotment that gave some of Allen's weakest subjects priority. The Latin and Greek instruction, worlds apart from the casual teaching Allen received at the Cross School, was especially rigorous. Now he was expected to master Latin etymology, syntax, and grammar; to read extensively in Virgil and Cicero; to know both Greek syntax and Homeric dialect; and to be able to read with equal proficiency from *Cyropædia* and the *Iliad*. Courses in American history included civics training and field trips to the Supreme Court, Congress, and the Senate. In addition to receiving extensive instruction in English composition, narration, exposition, argumentation, rhetoric, and essay writing, students in Allen's grade read Shakespeare (*The Merchant of Venice*); Addison (selections from the *Spectator*); Macaulay (on Samuel Johnson); Webster (*White Murder Trial*); and Bacon (*Essays*). In their spare time, the boys were expected to read from a combination of work that included William Makepeace Thackeray, Bulwer-Lytton, George Eliot, and Benjamin Franklin. And for the first time since the days he had spent reading his family's library in Ashland, Allen returned to poets like Tennyson, Wordsworth, and Pope.

During the 1917–18 academic year, Allen also received instruction in Christian doctrine. The guiding principle at Georgetown was always explicit: "There is no solid morality without religion." Although Allen was exempt from examination in religion, an entrance bulletin warned, "Religious Instruction is considered of the first importance. Catechism forms one of the class recitations and a weekly lecture is given on moral subjects." The prefect of discipline, Reverend Vincent S. McDonough, S.J., taught from an English translation of Father Joseph Deharbe's catechism, a popular question-and-answer book containing detailed Catholic interpretations of Faith, the Ten Commandments, and the Means of Grace—interpretations that were, of course, new to Allen. In the public schools, he had been among students from a variety of religious backgrounds, and though Nellie was pious, she attended church infrequently and brought him along rarely. Since she allowed him to stop his sporadic attendance at Presbyterian Sunday school altogether in 1916, he was never indoctrinated into any particular religious faith. Georgetown adhered to an educational philosophy that was strictly Catholic, but Tate recalled how Nellie had put him there "not for an education either religious or secular," but because his grandfather "went there and was perfect."[73] Tate's conversion to Catholicism late in 1950 was a long time in the making.

Allen's grades at Georgetown Prep were uneven. The midyear examination he took in January and the final in June of 1918 showed that he was having serious difficulty with classical languages. In the first semester exam, he correctly answered an average of fewer than two-thirds of the questions. His examinations were impressive in some areas—he scored 90 on each of the four English tests—but his miserable failure in the Latin and Greek sections ruined his overall performance. The following semester, his work was equally inconsistent. He maintained his superior grades in English but received zeros on all three segments of the Greek examinations. Though this difficulty with classical languages was nothing new, and dated back to Mr. Cross's poor teaching, it was doubtless humiliating to Allen, especially since every month at Georgetown the faculty gathered all four classes and read each student's grades out loud.

About the time of Georgetown's commencement exercises in June 1918, Allen applied for admission to Vanderbilt University. His parents had wanted to send him to Princeton, then known as the most Southern of the Northern universities, but Orley's bankruptcy brought an abrupt halt to the plan.[74] The tuition at Vanderbilt was relatively low, and since both of Allen's older brothers had attended the school, it seemed a logical alternative to Princeton. Orley and Nellie may also have had to respect the wishes of Allen's older brother Ben, on whom they were now dependent financially. By the time Allen was ready for college, Ben was manager of the Ajax-Elkhorn Coal Company in Ashland and was earning a good enough living to help the family during the bankruptcy.

Having two brothers who were Vanderbilt alumni was no guarantee that Allen would be admitted to the university, for he had changed schools so frequently that his transcripts baffled the admissions officers. His record showed that he had the requisite number of credits for matriculation, but that he lacked the correct distribution of subjects. When the school accepted him, it was with two conditions: that he be examined beforehand in third-year Latin and in solid geometry. The reasons for these provisos must have been apparent to him. His first semester Latin grades were so abysmal he could not have complained fairly when the admissions committee wanted reassurance about his preparation in the language. And while the curriculum at Georgetown had included a course in solid geometry, Allen was never examined in the subject and had no grades to present for evaluation.

To satisfy the geometry condition, Nellie took Allen to Nashville and hired a charismatic Vanderbilt undergraduate named Dorothy Bethurum to tutor him. She was not a math major, but was an excellent student who later became an important medievalist; since she was several years older than Allen, she had already mastered freshman math. At first Dorothy dismissed her new situation as "a business arrangement," but she soon discovered that Allen was a "very apt student." The two became fast friends as they spent the month of August in her home reviewing for the geometry exam.[75]

Allen passed geometry, but the Latin examination worried him. As autumn approached, the test loomed large in his mind, especially since it would be administered by Professor R. B. Steele, an eminent Virgil scholar who taught Latin at the university. But "Tootsie" Steele, as students called him, was under the hold of his own academic biases and misread Allen's transcript. Instead of examining him in the usual Cicero, he asked him to translate a passage from book 2 of Virgil's *Aeneid*. Allen must have been delighted since he had read and memorized book 2 less than a year earlier. He had failed "Latin Memory" that semester at Georgetown, but remembered the passage about Hector's shade so well that he finished the translation in less than fifteen minutes. Steele, suspecting that Allen somehow had cheated, looked at him quizzically until he realized that it would have been impossible. After a pause, he had to say, "Mr. Tate, you have satisfied the entrance requirement in Latin."[76]

Allen was greatly relieved to have gained admission to any college. Since neither his father, who briefly attended Centre College in Danville, Kentucky, nor his brothers, both of whom dropped out of Vanderbilt to go into business, had completed their degrees, the admission was undoubtedly a relief to his mother. She was so excited, in fact, that when Allen began his first semester at Vanderbilt, she decided to stay with him in Nashville.

Chapter Two
"Unlike a Natural Mother"

Many years after Tate graduated from Vanderbilt, he returned to Nashville to deliver a lecture before an alumni gathering. Still bitter about his mother's refusal to let him enter college alone, he told his audience that Vanderbilt had been "unlike a natural mother" to him. Instead of evoking the combined feeling of "love and hate that, according to Freud, is the normal emotion of the adolescent for his mother," Vanderbilt, he explained, made him feel like "a perpetual child." His undergraduate days at the school, Tate believed, provided him with the happy childhood he never had.[1]

To a degree, Tate's memory was accurate. It is true that Vanderbilt offered him the intellectual encouragement he sought in his own family and the tutelage of a remarkable group of teachers and poets. Few dispute that his professors and classmates helped transform him from a fragile and sensitive teenager,[2] insecure about his intellectual abilities, to a rising poet and critic. Yet the euphoria he would soon feel in creating a haven from his mother, in making friendships that did not depend upon parental love, and in entering his first genuine romance— all of these joys exacted a secret toll Tate would have to repay later. Vanderbilt might have helped him to construct a new family of his own design, but it also allowed him to leave unresolved the conflicted Southern identity his parents had given him.

I

When Allen entered Vanderbilt in the fall of 1918, the university was no longer the pious college founded in 1873 by Methodist Episcopal bishops who captured the money of Cornelius Vanderbilt.[3] The enrollment was still relatively small—there were 700 students in the university and some 250 in Allen's class; and since most of these students were from Tennessee and neighboring states, the school had a distinctively regional quality. But Vanderbilt was fast becoming a large nonsectarian university known throughout the South for its classics, English, philosophy, and modern language departments. Graduate programs in dentistry, divinity, engineering, law, medicine, and pharmacology were thriving.[4]

The growth of the university was due largely to the influence of Chancellor James Kirkland, who wrested the school away from the church in 1914. A South Carolina Latin teacher who had abandoned his own Methodism, Kirkland was determined to build the most powerful independent college in the New South. At a time when many colleges in the South had small endowments and undistinguished faculties, or were run by clerics who were inexperienced in financial matters, Kirkland devoted his energies to fund-raising and economic development. Before long, however, he was worshiping the doctrine of "progress" and ruling the university with an iron hand. During World War I, students considered him to be "more a dictator than the Kaiser."[5]

Since Allen was of draft age and was thinking about enlisting in the military if he was denied admission to college, he was relieved when his acceptance at Vanderbilt allowed him to avoid the decision. But even if he had attempted to join the army, he probably would have been rejected. Dorothy Bethurum, his friend who had tutored him in geometry, saw that it "would have been an idle gesture" for him to enlist, since he was "sickly" and "on the verge all the time."[6] Though Allen's looks had improved and he now possessed a delicate nose and piercing eyes, his shoulders were narrow and unathletic, and his classmates observed that he was "almost a runt."[7] Already he had been threatened by respiratory problems, and he was lucky to escape the Spanish influenza raging across campus that fall.

At Georgetown, Allen had already seen something of the effects of World War I on American campuses, but now he was witnessing a complete transformation: Vanderbilt had become a military encampment. The administration had recently decided to allow a unit of the Student

Army Training Corps (SATC) to move onto the college grounds, and soon the peaceful tree-lined campus was overrun by five hundred boys wearing ill-fitting uniforms of tunics, breeches, and puttees. The Gothic dormitories became barracks, reveille was called at 6:00 A.M., and a strict 9:00 P.M. lights-out policy was instituted. Most campus publications were suspended, and even the powerful Greek-letter fraternities, which monopolized the social life at Vanderbilt, were temporarily displaced by the military. Yet the mobilization of the university ground to a halt when the armistice was signed in November, and by December the campus had returned to normal.

Having his mother around did not help Allen adjust to his first year in college. Though he and Nellie had settled in a neighborhood he remembered from his days at the Tarbox School, it is unlikely that he found the accommodations very congenial. In all probability he and his mother returned to the shabby Tulane Hotel or moved into one of the boardinghouses nearby. Since most of the boys lived in Vanderbilt's dormitories or with the other boys in the fraternity houses, Allen was probably cut off from a good part of the campus social life. What was worse, he could take only limited comfort in the knowledge that Nellie had no say in determining his course of study. The curriculum for entering students was prescribed. Like other freshmen, he was expected to take Latin and Greek, mathematics and chemistry, and freshman English.

Allen's Latin class, which included instruction in composition as well as readings from Cicero and Livy, was taught by R. B. Steele, the Latin professor who examined him for admission to Vanderbilt. Steele, who had reddish gray hair, had earned his doctorate from the Johns Hopkins University and was active in the American Philological Association.[8] He emphasized the art of translation in his rigorous classes. While Allen enjoyed learning Latin poetry, his grades descended from B to C over the academic year. Previous students had annotated the textbooks so that the students who followed them could anticipate Steele's jokes, but Allen never figured out when to laugh. Once when the entire class revealed its ignorance by laughing after Steele skipped over the joke in his recitation, the annoyed professor remarked: "Young gentlemen, you should emend your texts from generation to generation." Allen knew "Tootsie" Steele was "a great scholar in his own way," but also concluded that he was not only "a deadly example of German scholarship" but "the worst teacher in the world."[9] Steele must have been astonished when the brilliant young translator he had examined just a few months previously did so poorly.

Allen also took the required courses in mathematics. At first, he was able to avoid Nellie's cousin, William Pinkerton Ott, a professor of mathematics and enrolled in a course with a charismatic professor named Charles Madison Sarratt. But the plan backfired. Perhaps because Allen believed that it "was beneath the dignity of a literary young man to study mathematics," he received E's in the subject during the fall and winter trimesters and an F in the spring.[10] These failures meant that he would have to retake the course the following semester with Professor Ott. (Of his brief encounter with Professor Sarratt, Allen joked, "He taught me the graph of a function, / That was as far as I got, / But he flunked me one day in a most casual way, / An' I learned Mathematics from Ott.")[11]

Allen made an equally poor showing in chemistry. The course was generally recognized as one of the most difficult in the Vanderbilt curriculum; in addition to two lectures and a recitation, students were expected to attend a separate three-hour laboratory session and to spend another three hours preparing their assignments. Allen was unable to concentrate on the material, found the lectures boring, and, after breaking "a lot of test tubes" in the laboratory, dropped both parts of the course after only one term.[12] He was so put off by chemistry that he avoided the subject for the remainder of his college career and wound up having to satisfy the requirement at a nearby teacher's college.

Every week, Allen and his classmates met in room 23 of Science Hall for freshman English. Though he earned an A in this course, his success was no doubt due to his long-standing interest in the subject matter and not to any affection for his instructors, both of whom he found deficient. The first, John Thompson Taylor, was young and inexperienced. For two meetings each week, Taylor instructed the class in composition before turning it over to Professor Edwin Mims for a third meeting, on Fridays. Allen no doubt found the Friday meetings more engaging, since they were devoted to English literature. At first he even liked Professor Mims, who spoke in a "mighty, dramatic, and sonorous voice" and balanced his "posed eccentricities" with an enormously entertaining lecturing style.[13] Mims also showed a genuine interest in each student in the class. He lived on campus with his family in a big Victorian house, and whenever he saw students he knew walking across campus, he would stop them to see how they were getting along in their courses.

But it soon became apparent that Allen and "Eddie," as the students liked to call Dr. Mims, were not going to hit it off. Part of their failure to get along was irrational. Another student later explained, "Allen was just set against him from the beginning, and I think Eddie was a little bit set against Allen, too."[14] Behind their personality clash, however, lay some identifiable stresses. Mims was accustomed to "a kind of traditional culture that necessitated politeness," and though he appreciated his new student's ear for poetry, he found Allen's undisguised dislike for him disturbing.[15] Soon he decided that what Allen needed was disciplining. At the same time, Allen thought he recognized a kind of smugness in Mims, who sported a moustache and a goatee, dressed a bit too elegantly, and tapped a cane on the brick sidewalks as he walked along the campus reciting poetry to himself. Although Mims was hard at work that year trying to understand the new poetry he kept hearing about and was reading selections from Amy Lowell's *Tendencies in Modern American Poetry* (1917) and Louis Untermeyer's *Modern American Poetry* (1919), he loved the Romantic and the Victorian poets and expected all of his students to memorize large chunks of their work.[16] Every year, he required the entire class to recite the end of Tennyson's *Ulysses* from memory and in unison. Allen was annoyed by such practices; it seemed to him that Mims ruined even the most subtle verse with his emotionalism, that he was recklessly substituting evangelical fervor for explication.

Allen was equally annoyed by the way Mims seemed to ingratiate himself with Chancellor Kirkland and the other progressives in the administration. After attending the Chicago World's Fair in 1893, Mims decided that science and technology would redeem mankind.[17] Although he was originally from rural Arkansas and had attended Vanderbilt during its Methodist heyday, he had studied briefly at Cornell University, taught for many years in North Carolina, and returned to Nashville in 1912 as a prominent scholar. He openly supported Kirkland's beliefs in progress through economic growth, and the chancellor, who had recruited him for the faculty, allowed him into his inner circle of right-thinking men.[18] Before long, Mims was running the English Department. Although he made the surprising move of adding nonacademic writers to the department, he developed a reputation as a traditionalist rather than an innovator. Allen immediately identified him as a professor who toed the administrative line.

In contrast to Allen's disdain for Edwin Mims was his reverence for his Greek professor, Herbert Cushing Tolman.[19] A classical scholar brilliantly accomplished in Latin, Greek, Sanskrit, Ancient Persian, and Babylonian cuneiform, Tolman was a New England–born graduate of Yale and an ordained Episcopal minister. He was appointed to Vanderbilt's chair in Greek in 1894 after a stint at the University of North Carolina. By 1914, Tolman was considered the preeminent scholar at Vanderbilt. He had also become prominent in Nashville, where local residents enjoyed his engrossing public lectures on the history of Ancient Greece. His powers of gentle persuasion made him popular with students, who affectionately referred to him as "Tollie." Kirkland shrewdly appointed him dean of the College of Arts and Science.

Allen was awestruck by Tolman and admitted to being a "young barbarian" in comparison.[20] Proclaiming that Tolman was smarter than he "by a darn sight," Allen put his nose to the grindstone in Greek A, a beginner's course that promised "Easy selections from Plato, Xenophon, [and] Herodotus."[21] In an effort to meet Tolman's exacting standards, Allen lined the inside cover of his Greek textbook with mysterious notes such as "Ostracism of Hellenic character from glossaries and lexicons impracticable for etymological scholars."[22] As the year progressed, he built Tolman into a kind of modern-day classical hero and found confirmation for the professor's mythic stature in his "divinely broad and sculptured brow."[23] Once Allen spotted Tolman lounging on a hammock in his yard. "Some boyish impulse moved me to approach and speak to him," he recalled. "In my self-consciousness, and in a clumsy effort to impress him, I made up a Greek sentence to surprise him with. . . . I said, 'KAIRE HE ATARAXIA TON PHILOSOPHON ECHEI.' ["Greetings. Calmness has the philosopher]." "No," Tolman replied, smiling, "not has me—had me from the beginning, I was born taking my ease. So your verb should be in the second aorist."[24] From then on, Allen enrolled in Tolman's classes every year. Allen was so taken by him that he decided to major in Greek and Sanskrit.

Allen earned an A in Greek, but his newfound interest in the classics barely sustained his interest in academic matters. He found that most of his courses were dull, and though he was no doubt hampered by the presence of his mother, he began looking to his classmates for relief from the boredom. He joined the literary organization for underclassmen, the Blue Pencil Club, and sang second bass in the Glee Club. Joining these clubs must have been difficult for him, since he was still rather unsure of himself socially. Later he described himself as a "bashful and green" freshman, as "the most innocent boy who had ever entered Vanderbilt."[25] But he seemed to have little difficulty in making friends.

Since Allen now attended "the fraternity school of the South,"[26] it would have been virtually impossible for him to avoid the enormously powerful Greek-letter societies, and he joined Phi Delta Theta, the oldest and most prestigious fraternity on campus. The Phi Delts, who lived in a three-story mansion with four neoclassical columns in front, arrogantly thought of themselves as "the aristocracy of the Greek world."[27] Though the fraternity still reverberated with memories of Allen's older brothers, most of the boys who belonged to Phi Delta Theta were natives of Nashville, and they harbored suspicions toward outsiders. They tried to make Allen "feel the high honor" because he was a Kentuckian elected as a freshman.[28] Though the boys seemed to like him, they teased him with nicknames such as "Oily" and "Greasy."[29]

But Allen had an advantage over the other new fraternity members who were outsiders. He had known many of the boys as playmates in childhood or as classmates at the Tarbox School and still felt comfortable among them. He was pleased to discover that two of his former teammates on the "Little Vanderbilts" football team, Elliott Adams and Robert McNeilly, were now members of the fraternity. Allen became especially friendly with a local boy named James Waller, an immature, pint-sized freshman who taught himself to win at poker by reading from the encyclopedia. Waller, who would later become an eminent economist, had a nickname almost as annoying as Allen's; he was called "Bulldog." Before long, Greasy, Bulldog, and a third pledge, Jesse Wills, whom Allen remembered as "tall, awkward, shy, and sensitive," began spending their time together.[30] Since Allen and Jesse, who were more literary-minded than Waller, had not yet established themselves as campus poets, the three boys probably spent their time like other students, who relaxed by seeing movies, walking downtown to the student emporium, or frittering away the hours in the fraternity house.

As Allen tried to carve out a niche at school, he was still subject to the whims of his mother, who remained firm in her command over the family. As soon as the academic year ended, she accompanied him to her beloved Virginia so that he could enroll in the University of Virginia summer school in Charlottesville. After moving into a local hotel, they were joined by Orley, who was rarely employed and now let Nellie order him around. Since she owned what few assets they had and controlled "the purse strings,"[31] he seemed content to remain inconspicuously in the background as she divided her time between hotels in Cincinnati and Washington, D.C. Nellie had no difficulty walking, but she now spent most of her time sitting in a wheelchair and had to be drawn up to the dinner table when she ate.

Despite the presence of his mother, Allen tried to lead a leisurely existence in Charlottesville. Each day when he came back from his classes, he would play ball with his nephew, Varnell's son Bob, who was spending the summer with them. Although Allen knew that his postponement of mathematics and chemistry would come round to haunt him when he returned to Vanderbilt, he spent his days savoring Virginia's advanced literature courses and working on a sequence of sonnets in his spare time. Meanwhile, in Nashville, his fraternity brother Jesse was feeling jealous. "I again envy you your studies," he wrote. "Modern Poetry, the history of art, Restoration drama—why you are not going to school there for there is no boredom in your course."[32]

Before arriving in Charlottesville, Allen had also confided to Jesse his conviction that "Romance was everywhere,"[33] and his hopes were realized when he met a young woman named Alice Lee. Allen and Alice spent hours in rapt conversation beneath the magnolia trees on the green in front of Thomas Jefferson's Rotunda, or sitting at Alice's house on Rugby Road. They sometimes stayed up talking so late that her mother would grow irritated and call down to them with lines from "Romeo and Juliet" such as: "Parting is such sweet sorrow I fain would say goodbye until the Morrow."[34] Sensing that Allen had strayed from his academic pursuits, Jesse wrote to ask, "How does the moon shine in Virginia?"[35]

II

When Allen returned to the Vanderbilt campus in the fall of 1919 for his sophomore year, he came alone. For the first time in his life, he was completely free of his mother. Because his years under her care had instilled in him a deep need for intellectual encouragement, it was not surprising that he began forming unusually strong attachments to some of the older professors who taught his courses. From these professors he received not only the intellectual guidance denied him by his parents, but also his first systematic training in poetry, criticism, and aesthetic theory.

Allen exercised his new freedom in the way he approached the curriculum during his sophomore year. Ignoring both of his unsatisfied requirements in chemistry and mathematics, he signed up only for courses that interested him. Brimming with confidence from his successes under Professor Tolman, he enrolled in Tolman's advanced Greek class and succeeded in earning A's all three terms. Allen had done so well in the graduate courses he took at Virginia that he indulged his interests in literature and signed up for two English courses at once.[36] One was an overview beginning with Beowulf and ending with Kipling; the other, a hybrid course divided between American literature and Shakespearean plays. Allen was excited enough by the prospect of studying such an array of literature that he was willing to overlook the fact that half of each course was taught by Edwin Mims.

Mims divided his course in American literature between New England authors and Southern authors. In addition to assigning a popular poetry anthology containing large representations of the work of Emerson, Longfellow, and Whittier, he made students read from his own anthology, *Southern Prose and Poetry*. "The principal purpose of this collection," Mims explained in the preface, "is to inspire the youth of the South to a more earnest and intelligent study of the literature of that section." While Mims claimed that he was not trying to glorify the South, he argued that the region's "boys and girls should begin to acquaint themselves with some of the fine spirits who have endeavored to record in beautiful language the emotional experiences peculiar to the section in which they dwell."[37] The anthology was a somewhat sentimental collection that included the work of Joel Chandler Harris, George Washington Cable, and John Esten Cooke, Nellie Tate's favorite. The book also included more contemporary Southerners like the Virginia novelist Ellen Glasgow, yet Allen later recalled that Mims's "emphasis as a teacher was on the New England writers of the past century, and there was not much said about Southern letters since Sidney Lanier. The necessity to import 'culture' was the doctrine I heard in Dr. Mims' classes."[38]

In Allen's opinion, whenever Mims discussed Southern literature, he seemed to be more concerned with its role in the South's social and political history than with its aesthetic value. It was true that Mims was no longer a productive literary scholar, and that his interests had turned to the problems faced by the New South. He would shortly publish *The Advancing South* (1926), frequently spoke out for social and economic modernization, belonged to the Law and Order League, and referred to himself as "a citizen with a capital 'c'".[39] As a consequence of his political views, Mims's Southern literature anthology also contained Henry Woodfin Grady's *The New South*, essays on educational progress by liberals like Benjamin Harvey Hill and Walter Hines Page, and even L. Q. C. Lamar's *Eulogy on Charles Sumner*, the Massachusetts antislavery senator who enraged Southern politicians before the Civil War.

Allen's artistic needs were satisfied by another English professor named Walter Clyde Curry, whose Shakespeare class was "the talk of the campus."[40] Even though Curry was a native of South Carolina, many of his students swore that he spoke in an affected Chaucerian accent. He was a specialist in Early and Middle English and was equally adept in the work of Milton and in late-Elizabethan and Jacobean drama. After receiving his doctorate from Stanford, he came to Vanderbilt for his first teaching job. He was younger and more energetic than many of the other professors in the department, was producing scholarly articles on Chaucer, and had already published his dissertation, *The Middle English Ideal of Personal Beauty.*

When Allen arrived in Curry's class as a nineteen-year-old sophomore, he took an immediate liking to the professor. Since Curry was still in his early thirties and was a conspicuous bachelor who dated Vanderbilt coeds, he seemed less remote to Allen than Mims or even Tolman. Curry's spectacles gave him an air of scholarly innocence, and though he was a dapper dresser, his unpretentious manner invited Allen's trust. At the same time, Curry sensed an air of brilliance about Allen and took special interest in him. He began lending him books and encouraged him to write. Curry's bachelor suite in Kissam Hall had become a kind of mecca for undergraduates interested in literature, and before long Allen was virtually living there, using the typewriter or passing the hours with Curry talking about literature. Many years later, Allen remembered Curry as a kindly confessor who showed "infinite patience" with him.[41]

It was under Curry's tutelage that Allen produced his first publishable poem. Curry was himself an aspiring poet, and had set his sights on the *American Poetry Magazine*, a fledgling journal published in Milwaukee by the American Literary Association. The purpose of the magazine, as stated by its editors, was to "bring to the front the unknown American poets."[42] If the majority of the magazine's contributors probably deserved to remain unknown, early issues did feature the work of modestly talented young poets like Thomas Hornsby Ferril, Howard Mumford Jones, and Oscar C. Williams. Soon Curry was contributing, and as his poems began appearing with some regularity, he passed on news of the journal to his better students. Allen soon had poetry accepted by the magazine also.

Allen's first poem, *Impossible*, appeared in the March 1920 issue. Although he dismissed the poem in later life and refused to add it to any editions of his collected work, it showed early evidence of his ability to mimic the style of other poets. The poem derived from Allen's reading in *The Mabinogion* , a collection of Welsh myths, and was modeled after Keats's *I Stood Tip-Toe upon a Little Hill.*[43] Allen wrote the poem in free verse:

> Do you remember how last year we walked
>   Against the purple sun through pearly shade,
>   And stopped all breathless—lingered there and talked,
>   And heard swift pyrotechnics nature played?[44]

While not a very distinguished poem, *Impossible* was better than a sonnet by Curry that opened the same issue of the magazine. The editors had already criticized Curry for the unevenness of his verse and for trying "to put too much into a small vessel."[45] The professor wrote to protest the uncharitable tone of their criticism—"this is not constructive criticism, it is merely a pleasant variety of whip-lash"[46]—but before long he had to admit that Allen was a better poet than he. Recognizing his new mentor's weakness, Allen began feeling intellectually superior to Curry and took on rather a patronizing tone toward him. In later years, he observed that Curry "could write good lines but he was not committed to poetry."[47] Curry accepted his own shortcomings, however, and when he eventually collected his verse, he titled the unpublishable volume, "Futility, a Volume of Useless Verse."

Dr. Curry was not the only talented teacher to influence Allen during his sophomore year. That autumn, Allen enrolled in a course in deductive logic taught by Charles Herbert Sanborn. Sanborn, who was in his mid-forties and was chairman of the Philosophy and Psychology Department, taught every course Vanderbilt offered in the two subjects. He was operating at the peak of his ability when Allen met him. A transplanted New Englander who profited by a rigorous German education, he quoted freely from the Dante he had memorized as a young man and kept up not only with the scholarship in his own field but with that in several other disciplines.[48] In an effort to integrate the works of the classical philosophers with theories of contemporary psychologists, Sanborn fell back on a highly abstract, theoretical vocabulary in his lectures. Although he had a weakness for sentimental poetry and warned students against placing too much faith in science, he considered himself a positivist and promised students that he would teach them "the art of thinking."[49] Sanborn expressed his academic and political opinions with such complete self-assuredness that students gave him the nickname "Cocky."

After attending only a few sessions of Sanborn's logic course, Allen grew frightened by this erudite professor. Allen's friend Dorothy only made him feel more intimidated when she told him about her own experience with the professor: "When Cocky looks down his nose at you, it is more terrible than a direct rebuke." Adding to Allen's fears was Sanborn's threatening physical presence—he was a powerful athlete and coach whose prowess in football, baseball, and fencing was legendary throughout Nashville.[50] But even though Allen knew that Cocky demanded "letter perfect" work, he resolved to prepare his assignments religiously.[51] Not even the difficult work of the philosopher George Boole deterred him from his new interest in logic, a subject easily as difficult as the chemistry and mathematics courses he kept avoiding.[52]

As demanding as he found Sanborn's course, Allen was attracted to the professor's self-confidence and to his willingness to defy the administration. Allen had noticed that the faculty at Vanderbilt was divided between professors who rallied behind Kirkland and Mims and those who found their progressive spirit insufferable. During the war, Kirkland and Mims had done everything in their power to unify the campus behind Woodrow Wilson, and they were dismayed when Sanborn began airing his extreme criticisms of the Allies. Eventually, Sanborn had to be muffled by the local police. Whether Allen knew about Sanborn's sympathy with the German imperialists is not clear, but he had no doubt heard that Sanborn was a notorious "thorn in Kirkland's side," and this would have been enough to build the professor up in his eyes as an antiestablishment hero.[53]

Allen, in fact, was so swayed by Sanborn's logical approach to the study of art that he considered changing his major to philosophy and aesthetics.[54] But in the end, his desire to write poetry won out over his newfound affection for Sanborn. When it came time to declare a major, he put himself down as an English major minoring in Greek. His decision meant that he would have to take three yearlong courses in English and one year-long course in Greek, and he could rest secure in the knowledge that he was already well on the way to satisfying these requirements.

In the meantime, as Allen's sophomore year progressed, his literary interests were reinforced by new friendships. Suddenly he found that there were other students who enjoyed writing and had talents matching his own. Across the street, in the Sigma Chi fraternity, he found a distracted seventeen-year-old named Merrill Moore, who was well on the way to becoming the most prolific sonneteer in history. Moore's friends remembered him as "an odd, gangling youngster well along in his 'teens, uncertain of his arms and legs, a little hollow-chested and spindling, with a sparse reddish beard just sprouting on his chin to match the shock of red hair on his head."[55] Allen decided that Moore was "a mischief maker" the moment he saw him, but he was impressed by his energy.[56] In Moore's fraternity Allen also rediscovered Matt Wigginton, another childhood playmate, who would soon be elected class president. Although Allen's dislike for the administration grated on Wigginton, who was more traditionally minded, both were members of the Blue Pencil Club and the two became friends. Perhaps because its small membership included Wigginton, Robert McNeilly, and Jesse Wills, the Blue Pencil Club elected Allen as president. Encouraged by such successes, Allen joined the editorial staff of the *Jade*, a campus humor magazine founded by the Calumet Club the previous year and fashioned after the Harvard *Lampoon*. On the staff of the *Jade* he met Bill Bandy, a tall, dark-haired boy from Nashville who had just abandoned the engineering program to major in French literature. Bandy was quickly developing the interests that transformed him into a major Baudelaire scholar. Though he was a year younger than Allen, the two soon became friends.

After winning over so many of his classmates, Allen found the courage to join the Drama Club. Almost immediately, he was selected to play a major role in *Man Proposes*, a one-act play staged in the Vanderbilt chapel. Allen's membership in the Glee Club and his training in music no doubt helped him to land the part, which required singing. The role was perfectly in keeping with the aristocratic image Nellie had inculcated in him during his childhood. Dressed immaculately in a tuxedo, he played "Mr. Reginald De Lancey Van Tromp," a character described in the program as "a man with ancestors."[57] It was ironic that throughout Allen's college career he would use the self-image given him by Nellie in order to gain his emotional independence from her.

Allen also used this aristocratic image to disguise his dire financial straights. Matt Wigginton recalled that while "Allen talked quite a good game about family wealth," no one ever saw any of it.[58] His classmates wondered why he was under continuous financial pressure when tuition was only about $125 a semester. They could conclude only that most of what he told them about his family amounted to fantasy. He took on work playing the violin with local jazz bands to bring in a few extra dollars,[59] but pride would not allow him to admit that he was having a hard time. Later, he realized that he had felt ashamed of his father's bankruptcy, and bitterly explained: "my father had humiliated us; and now that I was in college there was not enough money to see me through."[60] After college, Tate advised his friends to accept support from their parents whenever it was there for them to take, "because when you need it, it won't be."[61]

In all probability, it was Allen's financial condition that motivated him to accept his first job, a teaching position at the Wallace University School. Situated on West End Avenue directly across from the Catholic Cathedral, the Wallace School was just a stone's throw from the Vanderbilt campus. The ramshackle three-story brick building housed about a hundred students. Mr. Clarence B. Wallace, a talented Latin teacher who came to Nashville from Virginia in the 1870s, founded the school Nashville boys remembered as having had but one aim: "to prepare you to enter Vanderbilt." Mr. Wallace "barely eked out a living" and offered his teachers paltry remuneration, but each academic year he was successful in recruiting a few Vanderbilt undergraduates to teach for him.[62] Some of the students who taught in the school thought they were unqualified, but Allen apparently had complete confidence in his pedagogical skills and in his new employer. He included Mr. Wallace among his new role models, later calling him "a bulwark of the classical and humane tradition in teaching."[63] In 1920, Allen began teaching an English class for him. Although he patiently read Shakespeare to his unruly students, he occasionally made the mistake of lecturing above their heads. One boy admitted that it was not until "years later that the answers dawned on us."[64] But Allen's students were impressed by the degree of their new teacher's tolerance; he refrained from putting them down for demerits when they misbehaved.

As the summer of 1920 approached, Allen was still in need of money. He had become uncomfortably dependent on Ben, whose business talents had grown so much that he was able to found his own coal company in Cincinnati. Ben's new venture quickly blossomed into a major enterprise, and while he and his wife, Bessie, still spent time in Ashland, they moved to Cincinnati so he could run the operations. Ben continued to help his younger brother, but encouraged him to cultivate financial independence. Not long after Allen arrived in Cincinnati for a summer visit, he found a job for him on the assembly line at the local Ford Motor plant. The job was disastrous. Allen purchased expensive matching overalls and shoes, reported for duty, and was assigned to a position that required him to lie flat on his back all day. After six hours in the supine position, during which time he repeatedly excused himself by feigning an urgent need to use the toilet, he finally walked off the job. Although his employers at Ford conscientiously paid him a day's wages, the money did not even cover the cost of the uniform.[65]

III

Although he was still broke, Allen returned to campus in the autumn of 1920 eager to begin his junior year. If anything, his enthusiasm was too great. Looking for ways to satisfy his literary interests without sacrificing his popularity, he overextended himself by signing up for a host of extracurricular activities. In addition to renewing his membership in the Calumet Club and the *Jade*, he took on greater responsibilities in the Drama Club and became its publicity manager. He even joined the staff of the *Commodore*, Vanderbilt's yearbook.

The people Allen met in these organizations tugged his personality in two different directions, toward scholarship and away from it. On the staff of the *Jade*, he worked under an editor in chief named Ralph E. McGill, who would later run the *Atlanta Constitution* and make a name as one of the South's most articulate liberals. Allen concluded that "Mac" was just "a big extroverted football player" who was unable to understand "the difference between literature and propaganda."[66] At the same time, Allen wanted to be accepted by boys like Ralph McGill, and before long he was assuming a posture of intellectual apathy. He was seen lying around on the grass as he read or sitting on the steps of the Phi Delta Theta House looking bored to tears.

The harder Allen tried to repress his burgeoning intellectual interests, the more difficulty he experienced in convincing some of his friends that he was not a scholarly introvert. They began to think that his literary interests were setting him apart from the rest of the class and that he should be more happy-go-lucky. Students who did not know him personally but had heard about his literary talents dismissed him as a bookworm or, worse, as a "teacher's pet."[67] Even his childhood friend Matt Wigginton, known on campus as "a wheeler-dealer" and "the man you had to see," soon concluded that Allen was "pure scholar" and that the two of them were "miles apart."[68]

Some of Allen's fraternity brothers developed suspicions about his suitability as a Phi Delt. Many of the boys were serious athletes and after Allen made sophomore honor roll they viewed his intellectual achievements as an embarrassment to the fraternity. Perhaps in response to his academic success, they took to barreling drunkenly into his room every night at 10 o'clock. Allen had to barricade his doors.[69] Only the few intellectuals in the fraternity, boys like William Vaughn, a Phi Delt who later won a Rhodes Scholarship, appreciated having someone like Allen around. "It seemed to me," Vaughn later observed, "that Allen had read everything before ever he entered Vanderbilt."[70]

Allen's desire to be accepted by the other Phi Delts soon led him into self-destructive behavior. Perhaps in an effort to prove his manliness, he began drinking with his fraternity brothers.[71] Prohibition was in effect in 1920, but to the consternation of Chancellor Kirkland, who disliked fraternities to begin with, the fraternity boys ignored the laws. Crudely produced bootleg alcohol was available in large quantities, and students drank it ritualistically by holding their noses as they swallowed. Undaunted by such ceremony, Allen soon earned a reputation among the other students for his ability to consume vast quantities of liquor without showing any change in his behavior. Although his own fraternity and a few others were dominated by hard-drinking football players, Allen was "known as the Phi who could drink anyone in any fraternity under the table."[72] He even joined in fraternity stunts. One night, he and a friend stole onto the front porch of the home of Wilbur F. Tillett, dean of the Divinity School, and painted the words Beer for Sale in large white letters.[73]

Allen also began exhibiting a disrespect for professors he did not like. Once during his junior year, he was in class with Pierre E. Briquet, a Romance languages professor from Switzerland known by Vanderbilt students for having "a very low opinion of the erudition of American students and a very high opinion of his own."[74] Briquet called on Allen and asked, "Mr. Tate, do you know who Dante was?" "Yes Mr. Briquet," replied Allen. "Do you know who Jesus Christ was?" Briquet was livid and went to Dean Tolman to insist that Allen be removed from the university. In the resulting meeting, Tolman, who had already had the opportunity to size up Allen's youthful excesses, came up with a brilliant compromise. "Allen," he said gently, "go to the man and apologize to him. But you *don't* have to mean it!"[75]

Dorothy Bethurum, who had recently graduated summa cum laude and was now a conscientious graduate student, took Allen's new behavior in stride. Since returning to Vanderbilt for graduate work, she had renewed her friendship with him and occasionally let him take her out on dates. Allen enjoyed the time he spent with her because she never made him feel like a boy. He never forgot the time the two of them were about to enter her sorority, and she called inside, "There's a man with me." It was the first time any young woman had called him a "man." [76]

But Allen did not always act responsibly when he was out with Dorothy. Dorothy's mother was not pleased with their plan one evening to go to a dance; she not only disliked Allen but "suspected him of something; suspected he was drinking too much." At first, Dorothy was miffed by her mother's apparent prejudice against Allen, who seemed to her to have "punctilious manners." "I would have thought that Allen was just the kind of man to bring over," Dorothy recollected. She soon found, however, that some of her mother's suspicions were valid. Much later in the evening, it became apparent that Allen was unable to see her home safely, so she bade him farewell and called her brother, who agreed to meet her. When the two siblings arrived at their home without Allen, Doug first climbed up the drainpipe and quietly reentered the house. In the meantime, Dorothy shouted out to the empty street, "Goodbye, Allen, I had an awfully nice time—goodnight! No, don't come in—it's late." When her mother confronted her with "Doesn't the young man want to come in and say 'goodnight'?" Dorothy replied, "Yes, I suppose he did, but I just didn't want to be bothered."[77]

Although Dorothy and he were just friends, Allen soon developed a reputation for "chasing girls and partying."[78] He had already had one short-lived relationship with a Kappa Alpha Theta sorority sister named Ella Mai Wilson, a brunette whose father was a Nashville pharmacist.[79] Ella was older than Allen, and nothing serious ever became of their relationship. Soon she had graduated and departed Nashville for Cuba, where she became a schoolteacher. But her departure barely interfered with Allen's interest in members of the opposite sex. His classmates had no trouble in guessing the author of a poem that appeared in the yearbook that spring:

> Hear the sighing of the girls,
>> Soulful girls!
> What a melancholy fancy lies entangled in their curls;
>> What affection in their eyes,
>>> Languid luring in their glances;
> Ah, the action they devise
>> As they welcome love's advances!
> Idolize
> With their eyes
> Him who tells them pleasant lies;
> Always softly, sweetly sighing, always lying, lying, lying—
>> Oh the girls, girls, girls, girls,
>>> Girls, girls, girls,
> Oh the lying in the sighing of the girls![80]

Some of Allen's female classmates seemed bored by such open flirtations. "Allen Tate didn't interest us at all," one woman recalled.[81]

Allen found many of the coeds he met to be puritanical. One time, he and Ralph McGill and a few other literary-minded boys were invited to a sorority house to read their poetry and drink coffee. On the walk over to the house, Tate practiced the poem he planned to recite that evening. When he got to the last line—"They bore on high the phallic symbol bold"—one of the boys asked, "Gee Allen, don't you think you might embarrass them?" "No," Allen replied, "all these girls come from Middle Tennessee high schools. They won't have the vaguest idea what a phallic symbol is." Apparently, Allen was correct. Not even the house-mother seemed to object to his histrionic recitation of the poem.[82]

As Allen's junior year came to a close, his uneven grades reflected not only his newfound social interests but a curious pattern of attachment and rejection in his relationships with his teachers. He seemed to thrive only in courses in which his professors both encouraged him intellectually and nourished him emotionally. For obvious reasons, his grades under Professor Briquet dropped from A to D. And while Allen was deeply interested in English Literature, neither Curry nor Mims came close to serving as father figures. Now that Allen had surpassed Curry as a poet, he was rather bored by the professor, and after struggling through his tedious course in Anglo-Saxon grammar, his grades in the class tumbled. By the final term of the year, he was so bored by the course that he dropped it and switched into Mims's course on the Romantic poets. But Allen soon concluded of Mims: "Too much bull was his trouble, / He didn't know when to cease, / An' I wouldn't do such, 'cause he rode me too much, / But I learned about bulling, at least."[83]

By contrast, Allen performed brilliantly under Professors Tolman and Sanborn. He not only mastered Tolman's difficult course in Ancient Persian, but continued moving up the ladder as a student of Greek, earning straight A's in an advanced course in Greek drama that required him to read from *Œdipus Tyrannus*, *Antigone*, and *Prometheus Bound* . After earning equally high marks in Cocky Sanborn's history of philosophy course, Allen determined to take every class the professor offered. He claimed that Tolman and Sanborn did more for him than anyone else at Vanderbilt.[84]

IV

Allen's need of a motivating figure in his English courses was finally satisfied in the beginning of his senior year. In the autumn of 1921, he walked into a course called the Literature of Our Own Age and took a seat in the back row of the classroom. He was surprised to see that he had already met the junior professor who was teaching the course. One day about a year earlier, Allen had been loitering in Dr. Curry's office when Professor Ott walked into the room in the company of a rosy-cheeked young man fresh from a tour of duty in France with the AEF. He was fair-skinned and blushed easily, appeared to be in his early thirties, and spoke in a high monotone modulated only by his Southern vowels and his perfectly constructed sentences.[85] Although the new teacher said very little to the group assembled in Professor Curry's suite that day, Allen was struck by the man's unassuming manner.[86] Later the two met again in the Calumet Club, the literary organization for students and faculty. He learned that John Crowe Ransom was the son a Methodist minister from Tennessee, and that he was a Rhodes Scholar who had already published *Poems about God*, a widely reviewed volume of verse that Robert Graves, the English poet, called "the greatest book of poems that has come out of America since Robert Frost's *North of Boston.*"[87] Ransom eventually became, next to T. S. Eliot, the greatest influence in Allen Tate's life.

Allen and John Ransom would become close friends, but their relationship at Vanderbilt was complicated and trying for both of them. On the one hand, Ransom, who was more than ten years older, did not quite know what to make of this ambitious and frequently egotistical young man. The first term Ransom had him as a student, he concluded that Allen was immature and impatient. But soon he realized that his course was not challenging enough for such a talented student. He was impressed by the level of Allen's commitment to writing, and later observed that Allen "had a native sense, or at least a very early sense, of being called to the vocation of literature." He found that Allen was unwilling to write the kind of critical papers expected of students in the course. Instead, he submitted "essays about the literary imagination, with corollary excursions into linguistics and metaphysics," essays Ransom admitted were "slightly bewildering" to him, both in their content and their style.[88] He gave Allen a D for the first term.

If Ransom was bewildered by Allen, Allen was equally frustrated with this inscrutable professor. Though Allen condescended to Professor Curry, he had grown accustomed to his explicit criticism of poems and his informal style in the classroom. Now he encountered a professor who motivated his students by gaining their admiration and then withdrawing from them. Disappointed by the lack of explicit criticism of his work, Allen marched into Ransom's office carrying a paper recently returned to him. "Mr. Ransom," he began, "why did I—if you don't mind, would you tell me why I got an A minus?" Taking the paper in hand, Ransom casually leafed through a few pages, and finally pointed to the last sentence in a paragraph. "Why do you always put your best idea at the end of a paragraph where nobody will see it?"[89] Ransom asked. Pointing to a word on another line, he calmly inquired, "Why is that there?"[90] Allen was so startled by the casual and detached tone of Ransom's criticism that he said nothing when Ransom returned the paper to him without changing the grade.

While Ransom's frustrating pedagogical technique and reserved manner worked surprisingly well in motivating Allen, he frequently found Ransom's style as maddening as it was effective. Many years later, Tate concluded, "There was nothing inspirational in John Ransom's teaching; it was analytical, tentative, and understated; it assumed that we were men, not boys; and the civility of his demeanor was a gentle but severe reminder that we must try to behave like gentlemen, even when we were not. His role was that of *par inter pares*, a character to emulate but not to imitate."[91] Before long, Allen began attributing to Ransom hostility that he himself possessed. Only after Ransom's death more than fifty years later did Allen admit his true feelings. "I thought him cold, calculating, and highly competitive. I can say this because I, too, was calculating and competitive, and I was arrogant enough as his student . . . to think I was a rival! But I was not, like him, cold: I was *calidus juventa*, running over with violent feelings, usually directed at my terrible family."[92]

Allen's general rebelliousness was in some measure inspired by the books he was reading. Not long before Allen's senior year, H. L. Mencken, the Baltimore journalist and humorist, had attracted increasing attention for his indictment of arts and letters in the South. That year Mencken republished *The Sahara of the Bozart*, a sarcastic essay playing on the French phrase "beaux arts" that mocked the South for its cultural backwardness. "Down there," Mencken remarked, "a poet is now almost as rare as an oboe-player, a dry-point etcher or a metaphysician."[93] Such sarcasm appealed to Allen's new iconoclastic mood, and before long he was observed walking around the Vanderbilt campus carrying a copy of Mencken's essays. Mencken's disrespect for the traditions of the past was especially appealing to Allen, who was already developing his argument that Southern literature before World War I was of no use to Southerners his age because "there was nothing there."[94]

Since Allen found the work of Virginia novelist James Branch Cabell, then one of the South's few nationally known writers, unreadable, he turned elsewhere for literary inspiration. The *American Poetry Magazine* ran a section called "Paris Notes," which mentioned distant but alluring literary personalities such as Sylvia Beach and Ezra Pound. At the same time, Allen's friend Bill Bandy was encouraging his growing interest in the poetry of Mallarmé and Baudelaire, and their poetry led him into study of the Symbolist poets, about whom he had read so much in the avant-garde literary magazines sprouting up all over Europe and America. Allen was especially struck by Ezra Pound, whose difficult-to-decipher verse had been appearing in the *Little Review*, the *Dial*, and *Poetry* magazine for some years. Certainly it was a far cry from the classics like *The Divine Comedy* and *The Fairie Queene* Allen had been reading in his classes.[95]

In the midst of all this reading, two more of Allen's poems were published. *Red Stains*, which appeared in the *American Poetry Magazine* in the fall of 1921, was the first of his poems to display the images of violence and death manifest in much of his work. Later readers wondered whether the "red stains" referred to in the title were those of hymenal fluid on a mattress and whether the poem might be a highly intellectualized review of an evening of sexual intercourse:

> In a pyloned desert where the scorpion reigns
> My love and I plucked poppies breathing tales
> Of crimes now long asleep, whose once-red stains
> Dyed stabbing men, at sea with bloody sails.
>
> . . . .
>
> The poppies fainted when the moon came wide;
> The cur lay still. Our passionate review
> Of red wise folly dreamed on. . . . She by my side . . .[96]

Red Stains was a marked contrast to a satirical piece Allen published simultaneously in the *Jade. A Ballade of the Lugubrious Wench* was styled after François Villon, the fifteenth-century French poet, and showed another side of Allen's personality:

> Here is the virgin with cheeks aglowing,
> Beside her the hag with shriveled thighs,
> The maiden wots not of Grief's trousseauing—
> Scorching all laughter to ashy sighs.[97]

At the minimum such contradictory images suggested that Allen's emotions toward women were becoming complicated as he grew older. Perhaps it was to be expected that many of his new poems would be filled with images of decaying old women at the same moment his mother's health was declining. But his juvenilia also reflected the freedom of his social life away from Nellie; the counterposed images of

virgins were a natural product of his interest in the young women surrounding him at school. He would later conclude that every mother
must eventually know "the rivalry of other and younger women in her
sons' affections."[98]

One reason for Allen's attention to themes such as the loss of virginity
was that he had entered the first serious romance of his life. Although
he had shown interest in a number of women since coming to college,
in the middle of his senior year he suddenly found that he was head
over heels in love with a bright young woman who had transferred
from Hollins College in Virginia. Eleanor Hall, who entered Vanderbilt
in her sophomore year, was also strikingly beautiful. She had a milky
complexion, mirthful eyes, and thick wavy brown hair resting above
her high cheekbones and delicate brow. She belonged to the Tri Delta
sorority, but lived on Twenty-First Avenue, near the university. She and
Allen probably met in Drama Club when Allen was serving as publicity
manager. He began writing love poems to her, and before long they
were regularly seen sitting together on campus, talking. After Allen
began bringing Eleanor to dances, he even revealed himself to be "an
enthusiastic and graceful terpsichorean."[99] As they became an increasingly conspicuous couple on campus, the most intimate details of their
relationship somehow became public knowledge. Even though Dorothy
and the rest of Allen's friends were convinced that he was in love, they
were astounded when he and Eleanor went to bed together. "Nobody
had ever heard of anybody doing such a thing at Vanderbilt," Dorothy
recollected later. It may not have been the behavior itself that Allen's
friends found objectionable. Perhaps they were shocked because
Eleanor and Allen made no secret of their commitment to one another.
But now when Eleanor walked by, Dorothy remembered everyone
thinking, "this is a strange creature here on campus."[100]

V

Allen's relationship with Eleanor coincided with a burst of academic
recognition. That autumn a number of professors in the Calumet Club
had begun to think that he was not an ordinary college English major,
and they elected him president. He seemed more motivated, more intellectually alive, and more academically productive than many of the
senior faculty. Even students and professors who disliked him were
admitting his brilliance. Years later, Ransom remarked, "At twenty his
mind was further on its road than mine when I had passed thirty."[101]

In November of 1921, as Allen stood talking with him on the steps of College Hall, Donald Davidson, a young M.A. who taught in the English department, asked Allen to join a small group of amateur poets who were meeting periodically to discuss poetry and philosophy.[102] Davidson knew Allen in the Calumet Club and had pleasant memories of Ben and Varnell Tate, who used to lend him books from their library when they had attended Vanderbilt a decade or so earlier. When Allen entered Vanderbilt, he also became friendly with Davidson, whose darting coal-colored eyes and his nervousness, a product of his overseas duty during World War I, made him strangely likable. Allen readily accepted the flattering invitation to join the poetry gathering.

Allen knew nothing of the poetry circle Davidson described to him, yet the group had been meeting off and on for about six years. In its early years, the group had consisted of Walter Clyde Curry, John Ransom, and Davidson, as well as three Vanderbilt undergraduates: Stanley Johnson, a forceful and cynical philosophy major; Alec Stevenson, the scholarly son of Vanderbilt's Semitic languages professor; and William Yandell Eliott, a bright, big-boned young man headed for a Rhodes Scholarship. But it was a rather bizarre man named Sidney Hirsch who gave the group both its identity and a place to congregate. Hirsch was a polymath with no formal education. His rambling discourses on linguistics and matters of the occult were counterbalanced by his modest fame as a playwright, his genuine expertise in Greek drama, and his astonishing—though occasionally suspect—command of etymology. Under Hirsch's aegis, the group met every couple of weeks until the war intervened. When Ransom and Davidson returned from Europe, they retrieved Curry, and though they were minus a few members, reconvened the group. Hirsch had since moved into the large brick house of his brother-in-law, a Nashville clothier named James Frank, where every second Saturday evening, members of the group exchanged carbon copies and verbal criticism of their latest poems.

Allen's pride in having been invited to join the group increased when he entered living room of the Frank's home on Whitland Avenue and found that he was the only undergraduate present. Hirsch lay convalescing in a chaise lounge and was soon pontificating on various and obscure etymological issues. Allen was by now studying a variety of classical languages under Tolman, but even his recent exposure to Sanskrit did not help him to decipher Hirsch's remarks. Yet as eccentric as Allen found Hirsch that evening, he was intoxicated by his proximity to so many older intellectuals and began attending the meetings regularly. All through the autumn of 1921 and the winter of 1922, he joined the half-dozen aspiring poets in their deferential ring of seats around Hirsch.

Not long after Allen joined the group, he noticed that their real leader was John Ransom. Without fail, Ransom arrived at the meetings with a carefully wrought poem in hand and read it to the group in his detached, even tone of voice. Like Hirsch, Ransom was faultlessly, and sometimes stiflingly, polite. Hirsch continued to call the meeting to order, and to call on each poet to read his offering, but Ransom had become the one to whom everyone looked for acceptance or rejection. One reason for the group's deferential behavior toward Ransom was their respect for his tangible literary accomplishments—it was Robert Frost who had recommended that Henry Holt and Company publish Ransom's *Poems about God*. But the real source of Ransom's influence was the way he mixed restrained criticism with ironic humor to gain the group's admiration and respect. It must have seemed to Allen that Ransom was manipulating the older men the same way he had been manipulated.

In the beginning, the poems Allen brought to the meeting met with little or no reaction. When he read poems that many members found rather unintelligible, Hirsch sat patiently with his head down, making only an occasional, too-generous comment. But the apathy Allen encountered only spurred him to try harder to win the group's approval. His poetic successes under Dr. Curry had given him just the amount of self-confidence he needed to continue producing poems every other week. For models, he turned not only to the poets he had been reading in Mims's class but also to the exciting new poetry appearing in the little magazines. Modern poetry especially appealed to him since he was beginning to dislike many of the traditional poets worshiped by Mims, who, it was said, "burned to bring the glories of Browning and Tennyson and Matthew Arnold to the South."[103] Allen began telling his friends that it was the " 'sweetness and light' school" that he was protesting in his own poetry, and the group came to expect a "tightly-seeded lyric" from him.[104] Before long, Ransom noticed a consistent voice emerging in Allen's contributions; his young student seemed to be coming "unerringly into his poetic identity."[105]

Accustomed to shocking his professors in order to get their attention, Allen found that his mixed feelings for authority figures found a natural and acceptable outlet in the ruthless verbal criticism expected after each poet read his newest poem. Since everyone was expected to join in the close textual readings of the poems presented at the meetings, Allen was emboldened. It must have been apparent to him that having read a greater number of literary magazines than other members, he was much better versed in recent trends in poetry. In later years Ransom recalled, "I think we all coveted his judgment of our poems as being the most instant, and about the best, that we were going to find."[106]

Concluding that Allen "was much more advanced than anyone in the group,"[107] Ransom, like the others, soon was rushing up to him to get his reaction to poems before they were read out loud in the meetings. Allen's friend Merrill Moore, also a Calumet Club member, heard of Allen's celebrity and approached him with a poem.[108] As Allen stood on Dudley Field reading it, he decided that Moore's talent was significant.[109] It was surprisingly easy for him to convince the group to allow another undergraduate to join.

By February 1922, the group had written so many poems that Sidney Hirsch suggested that they ought to attempt to publish their best work in magazine form. Allen and the others were enthusiastic about the idea, and the group quickly settled on the *Fugitive* as a title for the proposed magazine. A poem of Hirsch's about an outcast poet bore the same name, which reflected the group's difficult relationship with the administration at Vanderbilt. Their fears were temporarily exacerbated when Mims, who had hired Ransom, Davidson, and Curry, tried to dissuade them from going ahead with publication. If their poems were any good, he argued, they "could be published in the Eastern journals."[110] In spite of this reaction, the group perversely asked Allen to drum up enthusiasm on campus. As one of his first assignments, Allen went to see Chancellor Kirkland to sell him a subscription. Kirkland responded even more negatively than Mims, and turned him away rudely. In the face of such a lukewarm reaction on their own campus, the group decided that it would be unwise to use their real names in the journal, and each found a pseudonym to fit his personality. Ransom became "Roger Prim," Hirsch "L. Oafer," and Allen "Henry Feathertop."

Since the other "Fugitives," as they soon took to calling themselves, were unfamiliar with Allen's efforts to emancipate himself from his mother, none of them understood the significance of his pseudonym. He took the name from a short story by Nathaniel Hawthorne. In the story, a "cunning and potent" witch fashions a scarecrow from a pumpkin and a meal-bag. After dressing her own creation as a nobleman in aristocratic finery and silk stockings, she brings her son to life. But the old witch's "motherly affection" soon turns to scorn. Warning Feathertop that he must puff continuously on the pipe she has stuck in his mouth or he will revert to a bag of straw, she endows him with half a million acres of vineyard in the arctic circle and sends him on a doomed mission to meet a maiden in small village. When Feathertop finally meets the damsel, who is "of a soft round figure, with light hair and blue eyes," and possesses a "fair rosy face," the simple girl thinks he is an aristocratic nobleman and, finding him irresistible, falls hopelessly in love with him. But she faints after catching a glimpse of him in the mirror and seeing that he is only a scarecrow. Returning home to the witch, Feathertop announces, "I've seen myself, mother! I've seen myself for the wretched, ragged empty thing I am!" Untouched by Feathertop's suicide, the old witch concludes that her son's feelings were "too tender; his sensibilities too deep."[111]

When the first issue of the *Fugitive* appeared in April of 1922, the small blue booklet, five hundred copies of which were published at the personal expense of the contributors, included two poems by "Henry Feathertop." Although Tate's two contributions were voted in with the rest of the poems, he later described them as "preposterously bad."[112] The first, titled *Sinbad*,[113] began as a long poem about Sinbad the Sailor, but Allen lost the energy to complete it, and the truncated poem, written in the style of Browning, stood as a pathetic monument to Allen's failure to share in Eddie Mims's enthusiasm for the poet. The other poem, *To Intellectual Detachment*, was also imitative, but even the obvious influence of Edwin Arlington Robinson did not obscure the fact that Allen was mocking himself:

> This is the man who classified the bits
> Of his friends' hells into a pigeonhole . . .

"God give him peace!" the poem continues, "He gave none other peace. / . . . And as his art, disjected from his mind, Was utterly a tool, so it possessed him . . ."[114] There was nothing in either poem to suggest that "Henry Feathertop" was on the verge of becoming a well-known Southern poet, but Allen wrapped up a copy of the first issue and shipped it off to H. L. Mencken, who was now editing the *Smart Set* in New York City. "So far as we know," Allen wrote to Mencken, "this is the only Southern Magazine devoted exclusively to verse."[115] Although Mencken publicly responded to the first issue of the *Fugitive* with one of his traditional backhanded compliments (the magazine, he commented, constituted "at the moment, the entire literature of Tennessee,"[116]) privately he was more encouraging. Commending the group's "remarkable uniformity of mood and outlook," Mencken admitted to Allen that the issue "contained some excellent stuff."[117] The ultimate compliment was Mencken's closing request that Allen send him something for the *Smart Set*.

But reactions to the first issue of the magazine were far from uniform. A reviewer for the *New York Times* announced that the poetry in the first issue was "extremely mediocre."[118] Local reviews, though more charitable in tone, were mixed. Reviewers in the Nashville newspapers cited the poems as being of "real literary value" and heralded the magazine as "a cultural asset to the city." One Nashville reviewer admitted that the *Fugitive* would "fill a very much-needed want in the literary life of the community." But readers had trouble understanding what the poems were about. Even as they admitted that the verse was "marked by considerable breadth and scope of imaginative imagery," they also noted that the poems were "somewhat smothered in the technicalities of verse writing." One reviewer concluded that the *Fugitive* would never "appeal to the great mass of people who use poetry as a means of more or less light diversion."[119] Only more sophisticated European readers seemed to appreciate the new journal. With some exaggeration, Allen later recalled, "While the Fugitive poets were read in the editorial offices of the NOUVELLE REVUE FRANÇAISE in the heart of Paris, they were gently ridiculed in the suburbs of Nashville; while they were well known at the Universities of Oxford and Cambridge, they were a petty nuisance on the campus of Vanderbilt."[120]

Fortunately, Allen was enjoying other successes besides those related to his work on the *Fugitive*. In April, the *Double Dealer: A National Magazine from the South*, accepted his poem *Euthanasia*. The poem, which Allen considered the one good poem he had written during the previous winter, drew on his now familiar themes of romance, physical decay, and death:

> The graceless madness of her lips,
> Who was the powder-puff of life,
> Cannot rouge those cheeks nor warm
> His cold corpuscles back to strife.[121]

The *Double Dealer*, recently founded in New Orleans, billed itself as an organ of the Modernist movement in America, and was publishing a wide range of rising poets. Since its first issue in January of 1921, the magazine had published poetry by Hart Crane, Babette Deutsch, and Oscar Williams, as well as prose by Carl Van Vetchen, Matthew Josephson, and Sherwood Anderson. By late May 1922, the editors were so astounded by the poems Allen was submitting that they wrote to tell him he was one of "the white hopes of the South." "Absolutely anything that you do will be met very hospitably here," one editor remarked. "We are betting on you."[122]

But just as Allen began to enjoy greater notoriety than any other senior in the university, his health failed. Only a few weeks after the first issue of the *Fugitive* appeared, a doctor ordered him hospitalized for observation. His physician suspected that he had pneumonia or—still worse—tuberculosis. For months, in addition to carrying on a passionate affair with Eleanor Hall, Allen had been reading voraciously outside of class, producing poems for the Fugitive meetings, working on a complicated translation of some Greek verse by Sappho,[123] and struggling with his regular course work. Having failed trigonometry and managing only a D in algebra, he must have known that as the final term of his college career approached, he had still not fulfilled his mathematics requirement. He had also been ignoring the chemistry requirement.

Though Allen's respiratory problems were partly a psychosomatic withdrawal from his various responsibilities, he was genuinely in poor health. His lung problems seem to have developed in his childhood around the time he was thought to be suffering from St. Vitus' Dance, and the problem was still plaguing him when he entered Vanderbilt. To make matters worse, in order to bolster his new image as a Bohemian, he had taken up cigarette smoking with a fury. Although the fictional Feathertop's mother ordered her son to explain his chain smoking as a doctor's prescription, even someone with persuasive powers as strong as Allen's could not have convinced the people around him that there was anything healthful about his new habit. Allen's hospital stay did little to improve his condition, since he was unable to relax after the whirlwind of the previous few months. A fraternity brother who visited him in the hospital was shocked to discover the patient paying absolutely no attention to his surroundings. The Phi Delt reported later, "He was reading Homer, in the Greek, of course!"[124]

It may have been during Allen's hospitalization that he collected all of the poems he had written at Vanderbilt. It was not just his desire to compete with John Crowe Ransom that motivated him; he was also propelled by Eleanor, who had become his muse. Gathering his contributions to the *American Poetry Magazine*, to the *Fugitive*, and to the *Double Dealer*, and adding them to the poems he had written for Eleanor, he was able to bring together thirty-one poems he liked. After dividing the poems into four sections, which he titled, "Poems," "Poems in Realism and Satire," "Sonnets," and "Last Sonnets," Allen had them typed into a fifty-page manuscript and bound in soft brown leather.[125] Titling the booklet *Parthenia and Other Poems*, he prepared a separate handwritten edition for Eleanor, and after tying it together with lace, he adorned the cover with a passage from Shakespeare and a drawing of a heart.[126] He presented her with a copy of each edition, inscribing one, "For Eleanor, June 3, 1922," and signing it "O.A.T.," a rare use of all three of his initials. In the printed edition, the title page read,

TO M. E. H.

These poems, written by a young Scholar
for his Lady, the author knows to be
nothing, yet he has hope that the sentiment
of the gift may bring to it some value.

Allen was correct in downplaying the verse, for the poems that followed were uneven in quality. Although many of the poems in the volume had already been published and showed evidence of his later skills, some of the poems addressed obliquely to Eleanor were adolescent in style and in content. These contained undeveloped themes in his work: female innocence and decadence, fertility and death, fear and human mortality.[127] Lines in *Parthenia and Other Poems* repeatedly juxtaposed sterile or experienced women with fertile young virgins, widows with maidens, old maids with flappers, goddesses with slave girls, or fused the two in some contradictory mix. There were angels who undressed, "Lesbian puritans," "a grandmother on ice-skates," and harlots making white lace for virgins. The poems also made explicit reference to "psychoanalytic lust" and to "the psychology of Sigmund Freud." One poem in the volume, *The Flapper*, had as its subject a rebellious young woman who dances the night away under the scrutiny of her mother, who fears that she might end up a prostitute. In the young woman's undulations on the dance floor, Allen later explained, he was reminded of "the most primitive religious ceremonies—phallic worship, etc."[128]

The poems in *Parthenia and Other Poems* also contained references to a relationship between young lovers who eventually part. "Who will remember how they loved? Who will remember happiness?" one poem asks. Allen opened the volume with a simple request—"Give me, Lady, your heart; then I'll be going"—and ended with the themes of separation and abandonment, expressed in poems with titles such as *You Left*. It is perhaps significant that the last poem in the volume is titled

Suicide, a poem in which Allen referred to "the untold part" of his personality. "I have felt darkness lead me by the hand," he confessed.

The gift apparently marked the end of Allen's six-month relationship with Eleanor, the first woman in his life to win his unconflicted affection. In professing complete loyalty to Eleanor, Allen held in abeyance painful and ambiguous feelings for his mother (whose first name, one might pause to consider, was also Eleanor). Although years later he said that "an unhappy love affair"[129] made him disconsolate during the Fugitive era, he met Eleanor Hall at a moment when his mother's lack of confidence in his intellectual prowess might have deflated his ambitions as a poet. In addition to being beautiful, Eleanor was a well-adjusted and literate young woman, well on her way to becoming an editor of the society page in the *Nashville Banner*.

By late May, Allen's physician had ordered him to take an extended cure in the mountain air of North Carolina. Although his name was listed in the program with the other graduates of the Class of 1922, Allen was unable to finish the final term of his senior year, and he received no degree. He was gone by commencement, and the only evidence of his recent presence on campus was a mocking advertisement someone had tucked into the back pages of the Class of 1922 yearbook: "LOST, STRAYED OR STOLEN—One 'Lugubrious Wench.' Please return to Allen Tate."[130]

Chapter Three

"O Poet, O Allen Tate, O Hot Youth!"

Valle Crucis, North Carolina, was an unlikely setting for Allen Tate's conversion to Modernism. Nestled in the mountains of western North Carolina, the village was as pastoral and remote a place as he could have imagined. The nearest town was Boone, a community almost as small, and the winding, narrow roadways made passage into Valle Crucis difficult. Though the natural beauty and tranquility of the valley convinced the Episcopal Church to establish a mission there in the 1840s, Allen christened the area "the land that God forgot." By the time he arrived in June 1922, the "Vale of the Cross" boasted only a seminary and a general store, a dairy farm, boardinghouse, and church school. Mail arrived by buggy, and many of the hundred or so inhabitants of the community still lived in log cabins.[1]

After moving into one of several boardinghouses catering to tourists and "lungers," Allen began a regimen of exercise designed to expand his breathing capacity and to strengthen his physique. His friends in Nashville had been pleading with him to stop smoking, and soon he was writing letters to them reporting on his aerobic conditioning. To his fraternity brother Jesse Wills he bragged that he was "out of doors from six to six."[2] During those hours, he swam and fished in the local streams, rode horseback through the rolling hills, and hiked into the surrounding mountains. He was eating and sleeping so well that only a few days after he arrived, he announced, "I feel like a new man already, and I'm damned if I believe I have TB."[3]

Even though Allen had suddenly become "an apostle of the vigorous life," before long he felt "boxed in by the hills" and was painfully aware of "the world lost beyond them."[4] The boardinghouse was oppressive. "From my two windows, always I see a green land and mountainy," he wrote in a poem.

> And in this house but lately death
> Found one young and got his breath.[5]

Since he found the fire-and-brimstone sermons in the local chapel equally stifling, to lessen his boredom he spent more and more time writing. He was homesick for Nashville, and he began the first sustained correspondence of his life. Besides writing to Jesse Wills and Merrill Moore, he was soon turning out lengthy letters to Don Davidson. The two men shared so many ideas about aesthetic theory that it was only natural when they became intellectual soul mates. Allen also knew that in his isolation, correspondence with Davidson and the rest of the Vanderbilt group would prevent him from spending more time convalescing than writing poetry.

Allen devoted many days to submitting poems to little magazines. If a poem was rejected by one journal, he sent it to another on "a regular route." "I don't know what the emotion of discouragement is like," he boasted.[6] Before long, he had placed two more poems in the *Double Dealer* and one in the *Wave*, an avant-garde journal published in Chicago. He also set his sights on the *Reviewer*, published in Richmond, and on the *Smart Set* and the *Dial*, both published in New York. He began revising verse from *Parthenia and Other Poems*, the volume he had collected for Eleanor Hall. Many of the volume's poems were new to the Fugitives and met with their admiration. The group especially liked the title poem, *Parthenia*, which they said was "one of the best things" he had ever written.[7] Motivated by such praise, Allen was able to crank out poetry at a faster rate than ever. "You are going at a fine clip, and must keep on hammering out poems by the car-lot," Davidson urged, adding, "Produce! Produce!"[8]

Allen's modest fame had begun to press beyond the borders of the Vanderbilt campus. Not only had his verse in the *Fugitive* received critical attention in the *Nashville Banner* and in several other Southern papers, but the two poems he had recently published in the *Double Dealer* were creating ripples of interest across the country. If he was thrilled when a *New York Times* review of the *Double Dealer* singled him out as "a new personality from whose pen interesting things may be expected," he was astounded when the editors of the *Double Dealer* not only called him "a poet with a new tang" but ranked him with writers like H. L. Mencken, James Branch Cabell, and Willa Cather.[9] "Pretty good for Feathertop, eh?" Allen joked to Davidson.[10]

Allen's affiliation with the *Double Dealer* brought him into contact with younger American writers interested in Modernism, the revolutionary aesthetic movement incubated overseas and now wreaking a self-satisfied, and not always appreciated, havoc in American art, literature, and poetry. By encouraging extreme experimentation with traditional forms, by taking on social and psychological subjects previously avoided, and by jettisoning simple depictions of human reality, American Modernists—who were no more unified in their ideas about the new movement than were the Europeans—were fighting tooth and nail over the idea of language and the meaning of contemporary culture.[11] In the *Double Dealer*, where Allen appeared with verse by a blossoming literary critic named Edmund Wilson, with a letter to the editor from Ezra Pound, with a satirical skit about God by a young writer who signed himself Ernest M. Hemingway, and with a translation from the work of Jules LaForgue by Hart Crane, Allen found himself entering the quarreling Modernist camp.

When Crane, a Ohioan who was Allen's age and already well on the way to becoming one of the chief American poets of the century, received his copy of the *Double Dealer*, he was so struck by Allen's poetry that he sent him an admiring letter. "I see you've been reading T. S. Eliot," he teased.[12] Allen had already noticed Crane's interest in Modernism and was flattered by the attentions of a like-minded poet. Both poets had read and been influenced by poets of the French Symbolist movement of the nineteenth century. In Rimbaud and LaForgue, in Mallarmé and Baudelaire they discovered poets who mixed perfect craftsmanship with cryptic imagery. Allen decided that Crane was "a brilliant devil" and the two of them struck up an affectionate correspondence.[13]

Now Allen hungered to read all of the "Moderns"—and he began distancing himself from older, conventional poetry. Announcing that his new aim was to combine "lyrical beauty and the satirical touch," he concluded that many of the traditional rhyme schemes and meters employed by the major British poets were hackneyed and formulaic.[14] "Of course there is much traditional gushing in English Poetry— Wordsworth, Shelley, Keats—," he observed, ". . . but I can see no reason for my being a liar even to emulate my great predecessors."[15] Newer poets like T. S. Eliot were more exciting to him. In *Poems* (1920), Eliot's first collection of verse to be published in America, Allen found

The Love Song of J. Alfred Prufrock and *Gerontion*. He was stunned by the unconventional style of these poems and decided that he had found a new mentor. "T. S. Eliot," he told Merrill Moore, "has done only four or five fine poems, but in the past five or six years these few have established a school."[16] "Eliot," Allen announced, "goes straight to the real thing; this is of course his 'modernity,' and I am with him."[17] Allen was, in fact, so taken by Eliot that he resolved to learn all that he could about the movement that surrounded him in Europe. In magazines such as the *Little Review*, Allen traced the origins of Modernism to writers like James Joyce, whose banned novel, *Ulysses*, had created an uproar when it appeared in serial form several years earlier. By August, Allen had recast his poetic style to conform with the Modernist revolution, and Davidson had to admit that his friend's new poetry was "quite as good, as far as method and style go, as any of Eliot's stuff."[18]

Allen recognized that there was a practical advantage in mimicking the Modernists. After the *Double Dealer* began accepting his verse with regularity, he concluded that they did so because the tone of his poems was "in unison with Eliot, Pound, and Company."[19] He began to see himself as working on the cutting edge of a great movement that would change literary history. Soon he was using expressions like "us Moderns" and "those of our calling."[20] "Whatever the limitations of us Moderns," he told Davidson, "we are certainly exploring, and giving voice to, a vast neglected field; others may do it better in years to come—but so much for the originators."[21] When Allen learned from Hart Crane that his verse had pleased Gorham Munson, Kenneth Burke, and Matthew Josephson, editors of a new ultramodernist journal named *Secession*, he was thrilled. "It is really exhilarating," he confided to Crane. "Though many miles separate me, a Southern barbarian, from you all, I can't help but feel that I am one of you—in the making anyway."[22] (The editors at *Secession* were a bit less enthusiastic than Crane let on. Burke remarked to a friend, "A man by the name of Allen Tate, a poitrinaire in North Carolina, has been sending us stuff, strongly Laforguian, and we have taken one thing in which the adolescent disillusion was at a minimum.")[23]

The problem with Allen's deliberate conversion to Modernism was that it made the subject matter of his poetry less intelligible—even to his most sympathetic and learned readers, the Fugitives. Although Allen's friends recognized that his obscurity was due in part to the advances he was making in his poetic style, the Vanderbilt group had begun questioning the value of poems that were unintelligible to readers. Local reviewers had attacked the first issue of the *Fugitive* for having been so "wrapped in the mists of poetical technique" that no "ordinary mortal" could "be very certain what they were all about."[24] Another reviewer accused the group of coldness and academic stuffiness, of writing poetry that identified them as "men who have lived their lives and experienced their emotional crises in pretty strict accord with colleges and universities and their dicta."[25] Even Professor Edwin Mims warned them that their poems lacked "humanness."[26] The Fugitives were still licking wounds inflicted by such criticism, and Davidson no doubt spoke for them all when he gently warned, "You are getting to be too brilliant and intellectual for me, Allen—I can't follow you." He blamed Allen's obscurity on the little Modernist magazines he had been reading: "I fear you are stepping a little too far in the direction of Secessionism and Eliotism and Dialism."[27] Even Jesse urged Allen to slow down. "May your intellectual Muse unbend a trifle in the serenity of the wilderness and forget a little sophistication," he pleaded.[28]

But much of Allen's obscurity derived from his conversion to Modernist principles regarding the relationship between human emotion and artistic expression. He discovered in T. S. Eliot's little book *The Sacred Wood*, first published in 1920, a passage that seemed to sum up the problems he encountered whenever he attempted to put his feelings directly into his poetry: "The only way of expressing emotion in the form of art," Eliot wrote, "is by finding an 'objective correlative'; in other words, a set of objects, a situation, a chain of events which shall be the formula for that *particular* emotion; such that when the external facts, which must terminate in a sensory experience, are given, the emotion is immediately evoked."[29] After reading this passage, Allen announced that he had located in the writings of "the demi-god T. S. Eliot" the single "best statement of the problem of the artist." Eliot, he decided, "is a greater critic than he is a poet; the professors accuse the modern poets of superficiality; well Eliot is the most learned man writing now and the least musty."[30] Perhaps it was to be expected when Allen started producing poems that, as Louise Cowan later observed, made "use of a new ironic mask and a new indirection, wherein a state of mind is suggested, rather than described, by the images and allusions in the lines."[31]

Armed with Eliot's *Sacred Wood* in one hand and Kant's *Critique of Judgement*—which stressed the cognitive and logical aspects of art—in the other, Allen decided that it was impossible to write poetry without emotional detachment.[32] Explaining his new style to Davidson, Allen wrote, "I can't understand how emotion is put into a poem . . . emotion as I try to understand it psychologically, is not a real division of the mind, but only an aspect of it, inseparable from any mental state, however 'intellectual' that state may seem."[33] He began voicing strong objections to poetry based explicitly on the personal experiences of the poet. In the mind of the reader who demanded that poetry satisfy him emotionally, Allen argued, "the emotional content of the poem appeals *only* because it strikes a note in the personal experience of the reader; thus it is the content and not the art which is important to such a mind."[34] In Allen's opinion, the Modernist poet's revolt against traditional form in poetry allowed intellectuals like himself to express themselves in a medium that more closely approximated the complexity of their thoughts. "Just as the emotions of a girl of fifteen may inevitably find artistic expression in the shallow mould of the triolet, so the terrible and devastating attitude of Eliot can be honestly conveyed only in the form he has chosen."[35] Soon Allen considered himself a champion of Eliot's doctrine of "objectivity in art" and proclaimed that form and design, not feelings, were the proper object of study for a poet.[36] "I don't think that one poem is better than another at all because of bigness of themes, i.e. philosophy," he remarked. "It is all style, method, diction, and a hundred other things."[37]

These Modernist ideas worked perfectly for Allen. His parents had taught him to feel a great deal about the South, but they had never taught him much about expressing emotions directly. Now he had finally identified a way to intellectualize feelings of all kinds. It is no wonder that his poems from this period increasingly had as their protagonist an artist detached from the events, objects, and people around him. Behind the man in Allen's poems—the artist who cannot act on events but who is instead preoccupied by the way they act on him[38]— was a child who had been subjected to the emotional unpredictability of conflicting parents. He had observed the way his father used formality to distance himself from turmoil in the family, yet he had also been frightened by Orley's violent outbursts, which were evidently not unlike those W. J. Cash attributed to poor whites of the Old South. "To lie on his back for days and weeks," Cash explained, "storing power as the air he breathed stores power under the sun of August, and then to explode, as that air explodes in a thunderstorm, in a violent outburst of emotion—in such fashion he would make life not only tolerable but infinitely sweet."[39] And if Allen had witnessed his mother's periodic withdrawals from him and her deliberate manipulation of his father, he had also witnessed her unregulated emotionalism. With such a family, it was natural for Allen to feel comfortable with an aesthetic theory that not only allowed him to attend to style rather than express feelings, but also to hide his identity as a Southerner.[40]

In Modernist poetry, Allen also found a way to capture his feelings about love and sex. He had been disturbed by the contradictory behavior he observed in his father, whose open philandering substituted sex for romantic love. It was no accident that the poetry Allen wrote during this period infrequently explored love.[41] Although the volume he had given to Eleanor Hall was an expression of affection, many of the poems it contained were concerned with the the loss of moral purity in men and women and the impossibility of recapturing sexual innocence. (In one poem of this period, Allen urged his female protagonist: "Hide your pink knees from the gaze of other men. You must be pure . . .")[42] Now he was writing another series of poems that carefully juxtaposed images of old women, whose fertility was withering, with portraits of pure virgins destined to become otherwise. It was not just Allen's separation from his mother and the spectacle of her physical decline that accounted for this preoccupation. His separation from Eleanor Hall was still weighing heavily on his mind. Of his new poem *Horatian Epode to the Duchess of Malfi*, for instance, he admitted, "The death of the Duchess finds a parallel in my own life. In my train of free association the two events, her death and the loss of a beautiful woman, are inextricably mixed."[43]

As Allen began showing the Fugitives these poems, they questioned him about the sexual references, and he went to great lengths to explain them. After sending off one poem to Davidson, Allen asked, "By the way, do you get 'eluding fallopian diagnosis'? Rather obscene, but rather expressive of the physiological interpretation of emotion, in this case erotic emotion."[44] In another poem, Allen explained that the male protagonist "is sex-crazed, and has made his Lady's fingers a fetish."[45] The Fugitives tried humor in response to Allen's allusions—and to the genre he playfully called "the poetry of sex."[46] On reading his poem *Nuptials*, Alec Stevenson asked, "Any phallic significance to 'climbing the greasy pole'?"[47] Davidson already knew the answer. "Gosh," he teased Allen, "you're a dirty poet!!!"[48]

In part, Allen's frequent sexual allusions were a reaction against the prudishness he perceived in traditional poetry. The Victorians, he believed, had catered to women and men who refused to read of "thighs and ruby lips and tempestuous passion" unless such images had been "sentimentalized into a scheme of pretty flowers and birds." The Moderns, on the other hand, were brazenly throwing "the bare flesh into sharp contrast with [the] mind."[49] "No glory for your breasts and thighs shall my poor verses advertise," Allen wrote.[50] Instead, he proudly referred to himself as "the youthful harbinger of guts, ovaries, and death."[51] He had begun to think that he could become a greater realist by counterbalancing images of sexual beauty with those of physical decay and death.

While Modernism helped Allen to control his emotions, it opened him to new conflicts with the Fugitives. In his absence, Ransom, Davidson, Merrill Moore, and Bill Elliott, who were at least sympathetic to Modernism, had lined up against the more Victorian-minded Fugitives such as Stanley Johnson, Alec Stevenson, James Frank, and Sidney Hirsch, who rejected the movement entirely. Allen knew he had helped create this rupture among his friends and later boasted that it was through him "modern poetry made its first impact upon the doctors who gathered fortnightly in Mr. Frank's house."[52] The more his friends criticized his conversion, though, the more he looked forward to defending his views when he returned to Nashville. "The report of the last meeting was as thrilling as a western movie!" he told Davidson. "Darn those conservatives! I'll harangue 'em till five A.M."[53]

Yet for all of Allen's aesthetic disagreements with other members of the group, he enjoyed, for the first time in his life, playing the role of the youngest child in a large family. Now that he had tested a new family and managed to preserve his independence, his only worry about returning to Nashville was the thought of seeing his original fraternity brothers. He asked Don Davidson to put him up when he returned, explaining, "I don't relish much staying in the damn frat. house, even for a few days." He no longer felt the need to impress the rowdier members of Phi Delta Theta. Having replaced one set of surrogate brothers with another, he was brimming with affection for the Fugitives, whom he now called "the brothers."[54]

By the autumn of 1922, Allen's health was better than it had been in all his years in college, and it seemed possible that he might be able to leave Valle Crucis. But he did not have the money to pay the tuition for his final semester of college, and he could not return to Vanderbilt. New York City was alluring, but moving there was equally impossible. If he was physically stuck in the South, he did find one consolation: he had escaped his mother. Years later, he would make cryptic references to his time away from Vanderbilt: "I was out for a year, supposedly on account of my health. It wasn't my health at all."[55] Ultimately, it is unknown whether his problems were academic, financial, or psychological. But what Tate clearly gained during his leave was a much-needed opportunity to recover his happiness without his mother's ministrations.

I

In November, Allen left Valle Crucis for Cincinnati, where he was forced to rejoin his parents. But since no word had come from the Southern Teachers Agency, an organization that was helping to find him a job, his only option seemed to be to defer his return to Vanderbilt indefinitely and to accept a job working in the Ashland, Kentucky, office of United Collieries, Ben's new coal concern.

Allen found Ashland, the city of his childhood, even more depressing than Cincinnati. "I am marooned," he reported to Don Davidson.[56] He had not been in his "dirty little town" since he was fourteen years old, and he self-consciously noted that he was returning "unheralded and unsung."[57] Although the office of Ben's company was located in the Second National Bank Building, the workplace was grim. Before long, even Allen's food seemed to taste like coal.[58] The only distraction he could see was the stenographer, a young woman whose "penchant for brutal-looking men" he found fascinating. Later he wrote a poem about her, and titled it *Mary McDonald*.[59]

In the middle of such an unliterary environment, Allen still found a way to maintain his prolific output of words. He was expected to put in regular hours at the office, but in the evenings he had no responsibilities, and if he was not reading Balzac's novels, Taine's *History of English Literature*, or Chaucer's *Tales of Canterbury*, he wrote poetry. When he did not have to go in to work the next day, he would write into the early hours of the morning, composing letters or lines of poetry. Some poems he turned out after only an hour; others he spent days or even weeks working on. He was soon regularly selling his poems to a number of avant-garde journals.

Allen was also developing talents as a prose stylist. Writing so many letters to Davidson and other friends helped him to develop his skills, and when he produced a few book reviews and editorials, he became increasingly attentive to his style. He decided that he wanted to be a critic and writer in addition to being a poet, and began praising other professional writers wherever he could find an open forum. Obviously preoccupied with his own situation in Ashland, he mailed a small sum of money to a starving German writer after reading of the man's plight. In the accompanying letter, Allen noted that American authors had lives just as difficult. "They seldom attain to the dignity of starvation," he added, "usually becoming financially independent hacks or mere failures in life, that is, unsuccessful businessmen; but this state of things is hardly due to free choice."[60]

Allen spent much of his time in Ashland helping to run the *Fugitive*. Though he lived hundreds of miles from Nashville, he took charge of advertising and circulation for the magazine and counseled the group on a variety of business matters. After ordering advertisements from a local printer, he promoted the magazine to every Ashland resident he could corner, and even sold subscriptions to his mother and to Ben in Cincinnati. He also continued to participate in the editorial decisions of the *Fugitive* by reading and criticizing poems, writing editorials, and corresponding with other magazine editors. And since the Fugitives had finally abandoned their pseudonyms, his name now appeared prominently below his poems.

Although he later came to believe that the poetry he wrote during this period was "nearly all bad," Allen was thrilled to hear from Jesse Wills that his new work had "fed the flames of a rather violent discussion at the last *Fugitive* meeting."[61] One poem, *Nuptials*, Allen's first poem to offer a critique of the values associated with urban industrialism, left the group baffled but certain of his genius.[62] Alec Stevenson called it "damnably good," while Davidson told Allen he had displayed "almost a perfect technique."[63] The poem, he explained to Allen, had "the proper balance between the modern and the traditional," a style he believed would allow Allen to write his finest poems. And as much as he disliked the influence of Eliot in Allen's work, Davidson confessed that Allen's poems now had "a quality of cleanness and sureness, like the lines of fine statuary."[64]

Allen resolved to publish a volume of poetry. John Ransom's *Poems about God* served constantly to remind him of his teacher's tangible achievements and made the possibility of publishing a collection of poetry seem less remote. Driven to see his own work in print, Allen had completely reworked *Parthenia and Other Poems* by adding new poems and revising or deleting others, The makeshift book that began as an expression of his affection for Eleanor Hall could now become his first book-length manuscript. Cynical about his image as a passionate young man, he retitled the volume *Calidus Juventa?* (Latin for "hot youth?"). The title poem, Tate explained, would follow an epigraph "from Horace (Odes III, xiv)" and consist of two stanzas:

We are afraid that we have not lived
Yet we know no dying.
Toss an image to the indifferent morning
Amid laughter and crying—
Amid fitful buffetings of all strangled hearts
While they are dying.

Draw tight the words of death shivering
On the strictured page—
The goblet of Morgan Fay is shattered;
Life is a bitter sage,
And I am a weary infant
In a palsied age.[65]

After shipping his manuscript off to Lieber and Lewis, a small publishing house in New York City, Allen was encouraged by the news
that the editors at the firm were keeping his verse for further
study.

Allen's ambitions had been fueled when T. S. Eliot's newest long
poem, *The Waste Land*, overtook the November 1922 issue of the *Dial*.
The poem's demanding style appealed to Allen. Edited severely by
Ezra Pound, it nevertheless remained lengthy and complex, making
difficult and obscure allusions to poets and novelists, to songs and
myths, and to personal facts intelligible only to its author. Allen recognized not only that Eliot had overturned traditional form and meter in
poetry, but that he had mastered the diction and technique he had been
wrestling with himself since he left Vanderbilt. The late-nineteenth-
century Modernism Allen found so alluring in the work of the British
poet Arthur Symons and in the French symbolists now seem recapitu-
lated and intensified in *The Waste Land*. The subject matter of the
poem also attracted Allen. Eliot's counterpoised images of fertility and
sterility seemed a fittingly grim commentary on the postwar malaise
and urban anomie Allen was observing even among the residents of
Ashland.

Allen became an outspoken critic of any poem or essay that did
not conform to Eliot's ideas about art. He began presenting many of
Eliot's opinions as definitive and took it upon himself to correct devia-
tions from the master wherever he saw them. "Just now," he told Davidson, "I am working on a review, or it may be a short essay, on the
current vulgar errors (!) so prevalent concerning the Waste Land—
notably Conrad Aiken's review in the *New Republic*. . . . That gentle-

man is somewhat misguided."[66] Yet it was not just Allen's admiration of Eliot that made him question everything that was traditional. He had begun to enjoy literary feuds in themselves and had discovered that when he played the role of an enfant terrible people paid attention to him. Davidson kept trying to convince him to control his temper. "My dear boy," he asked in dismay, "what will you do next?"[67] But Allen was proud of what he called his "polemic custom" and freely admitted his "freshness, vituperative spirit, weakness for condemnatory generalization."[68]

In his contrary mood, Allen began to object to the way John Ransom was running the *Fugitive*. Ransom, for instance, had recently promised to let James Frank, the one Fugitive who was more of a businessman than a poet, publish a poem called *Pegasus*. Allen read the modest poem and was so mad over being "frozen out" of the editorial process that he threatened to resign if Ransom published it. "I don't care to be identified with such artistic policies," he explained. "GUTS are the sine qua non of art. Art is a grim dominion, and personalities have no place in it. Is the purpose of artistic creation merely the satisfaction of vanity?" "There is only one thing in life to me," he insisted, "and that is the continual possibility of pursuing literature as an art, and I can therefore countenance no compromise in a matter which is of the utmost vitality to me." "If Jesus Christ should come upon earth and present me a poem I sincerely thought inferior," Allen fulminated, "I would tell him *just that* to his teeth if the issue at stake were as vital as this one."[69]

Never having enjoyed the privilege of speaking back to his own father, Allen relished criticizing a man who possessed if not Orley Tate's violent disposition, his emotional distance. "John Ransom could be hardboiled if he wanted to," Allen concluded. "The trouble with him is that he is so damn prissified with his Oxford culture that he won't bat his eye for fear it isn't good manners. Imagine a man past thirty-five still self-conscious!"[70] Ransom tried to defend his choice by citing Frank's "unusual modesty as an author," but Allen had taken such a strong stand that the poem was struck from the issue.[71] Since Davidson did not much care for the poem either and was equally unhappy with Ransom's passivity, he rejoiced in Allen's victory. But he could not help but observe the pattern in his friend's relationships and gently rebuked him for his repeated confrontations with authority figures. "O Poet, O Allen Tate, O Hot Youth," he taunted, "I salute you."[72]

II

In later life, Tate would say that he became a writer because he was unable to keep his mind on anything else.[73] Certainly he hated working at his brother's coal firm, for as much as he tried, he was unable to find even the vaguest romantic aura about the workplace. Jesse Wills, who had recently heard that T. S. Eliot was employed by a British bank, passed on this bit of news and tried to play up the similarity of Allen's predicament in Ashland. "I, the hard working clerk," he wrote to Allen, "have been rather comforted by the thought that *you* were a coal dealer on a *Main Street*, working by day, and at night, in your spare time, retiring secretly into the cloister of your mind to meditate upon 'The Waste Land' and build rhythms of your own around a like irony."[74] But Allen became so distracted in his role as a suffering artist that his performance on the job began slipping. One day he was brooding over his literary controversies when he should have been thinking about anthracite coal, and he made an error that apparently cost the company seven hundred dollars, an enormous sum in 1923. When Ben discovered that Allen had ordered a boxcar full of coal to Duluth, Minnesota, instead of to Cleveland, Allen's three months of working in a world he despised came to an end.[75] But Allen had apparently saved enough money to complete his undergraduate degree, and he immediately returned to Vanderbilt for the spring term.

As soon as he arrived on campus in February 1923 he regretted coming back, but his classmates thought him "more relaxed and carefree" than ever. They especially noted his healthy glow and "more sportive outlook."[76] Behind his happiness, however, lay a new arrogance and impetuosity. Many years later, Tate explained that the "several varieties of snobbishness" he exhibited on returning to school were the product of his nine successful months publishing poetry. "My conceit must have been intolerable," he confessed. "Had not the editors of *The Double Dealer* written me a letter saying that they saw in me the White Hope of the South? Add to that the easy lesson in shocking the bourgeoisie that I had learned from reading French poets, and was relearning for American use from Ezra Pound, and you have before you the figure of a twenty-two year-old prig as disagreeable as you could possibly conjure up."[77]

Allen soon discovered that he was so burdened by "a lot of damn university routine" that he could not get to his poetry.[78] He had left a half dozen literature and language courses unfinished when he departed Nashville in the spring of 1922, and now they consumed all of his time. But the more he saw his recent poetic achievements fading, the harder he found it to discipline himself to attend classes and to prepare his assignments. His academic boredom began expressing itself in a familiar pattern: in classes he found relevant to his literary interests, he earned A's; in everything else, D's. Under professors who liked him, men like his old mentor Walter Clyde Curry and philosophy professor Charles Sanborn, he enjoyed noteworthy academic successes. But under those who expressed any reservations about him—Edwin Mims, for instance, or science professors—Allen responded by cutting their classes and lectures. In search of familiar ground, he again began loitering in Curry's suite in Kissam Hall. There he could borrow the typewriter and would be sure to meet others who were interested in poetry and literary matters.

It was in Dr. Curry's suite that Allen would meet a boy who changed his life. One February day, Allen sat in front of Curry's typewriter banging out a poem that was not turning out to his satisfaction. Sensing someone else's presence in the room, he turned around in his chair and saw the most unusual young man ever to cross his path. Tall and gawky with a disheveled mop of red hair, the boy had a thin, homely face and a pointy nose. He seemed both physically uncoordinated and socially awkward.[79] Approaching Allen nervously, he asked, in a voice barely audible, "Have you written a poem?"[80] When Allen replied that he had, the young man, who called himself "Red," produced a poem of his own and offered to trade. Allen read the poem and learned that this sixteen year old from Guthrie, Kentucky, was Robert Penn Warren.

Soon the aspiring poets had become fast friends and were spending all of their time together. Red introduced Allen to his roommate, Ridley Wills, a cousin of Jesse's who, like Allen, had recently come back to Vanderbilt to finish his degree. Ridley's education had been interrupted by World War I, and during his years away he had worked as a journalist and enjoyed the notoriety of publishing a novel called *Hoax*. Although he and his cousin Jesse were good enough poets to have been invited into the Fugitive circle, the two boys were opposites. Jesse was gangly in appearance and bashful in manner, while Ridley was not only short, but irreverent. Some people found him to be both immodest and sarcastic.[81] Allen was annoyed by Ridley's "spurious pretensions," but he apparently sensed that Ridley shared his iconoclasm, his disrespect for some of the older professors in their midst, and—most of all—his reputation as a "hot youth."[82] Impressed by the flattering reviews Ridley's novel had received, he decided that Ridley was worth knowing

Ridley, Allen, and Red got along so well that they were soon rooming together.[83] The university assigned them to quarters on the third floor of Wesley Hall, a monstrously Gothic dormitory that also served as headquarters for Vanderbilt's Methodist Seminary. Although the room was only about forty feet square, the boys had enough space for two bunk beds, several typewriters, and their miscellaneous personal belongings. To negotiate their way through the clothing, food, and books, they stacked everything on the beds during the day and tossed it all on the floor at night to make room to sleep. Every day at 5:30 in the afternoon, the local "literary migrants," as Red called them, appeared in their room for conversation.[84]

Since Red was the youngest of the trio and stood in awe of his roommates' literary accomplishments, Ridley and Allen treated him like a freshman. They made him sleep in the upper berth and sometimes pricked him with a needle to make him jump out of bed and tell them his dreams. Red also reported having endured "the rather painful privilege of having Wills and Tate leave some manuscript" of his "in bloody tatters."[85] But soon Allen and Ridley brought Red to a meeting of the Fugitives, and before long, Allen told the group "that boy is a wonder, or I'm much mistaken, and deserves election to the Board."[86] He began promoting Red's work not only to the Fugitives, but also to the editors of the *Double Dealer*, who immediately recognized his talents and began publishing his verse along with Allen's.

In April, Maxim Lieber, a principal in the publishing firm that had been considering Allen's book of verse, wrote to accept *Calidus Juventa*.[87] Lieber, who would later become a prominent literary agent representing an array of novelists from Alvah Bessie to Thomas Wolfe, was developing a reputation as an aggressive and successful publisher and was full of praise for Allen's poetry. He scheduled five hundred copies of the volume for release on the fifteenth of September 1923 and priced them at $1.50 apiece. Allen was so excited that he began signing his letters "Calidus Juventa."

As it turned out, however, Allen's first collection of verse was a thin pamphlet written in collaboration with Ridley Wills and titled *The Golden Mean and Other Poems*.[88] The project began one evening early in the spring term when Allen and Ridley were sitting in a diner. They stayed up all night in the restaurant to write most of a manuscript of twenty-two poems: eleven by Allen honoring Ridley and eleven by Ridley honoring Allen. Each poem was matched with another poem of the same title; the poems written by Ridley used traditional Victorian verse forms and made fun of the Modernists, while Allen's contributions used experimental techniques to satirize the Victorians. The title they chose for the volume mocked Edwin Mims, who had been urging the Fugitives to find a "golden mean" between Victorianism and Modernism.

Ridley and Allen also designed *The Golden Mean* to satirize T. S. Eliot. They called one pair of poems *The Chaste Land* and poked fun at Eliot's most memorable lines. They attached comic footnotes to the volume in further satire of Eliot, who had added a series of scholarly references to the bound edition of *The Waste Land* after early readers of the poem complained that many of the allusions were obscure.

Allen's contributions to *The Golden Mean* reinforced the image he was cultivating as an impetuous young man bent on shocking traditionalists with his morbid themes and sexual puns. In one poem, titled *In Defense of Suicide*, he wrote,

> In the ultra-violet midnight, when the heart
> remembers what the mind cannot forget,
> I walk, chased by Furies, and I stagger
> Simultaneously withdrawing my rubber dagger
> and hypnotize grief with histrionic art
> which satisfies the average woman yet.[89]

Ridley found such sexual horseplay infinitely amusing and teased, "You are a wild foal, Allen."[90] In a biographical sketch appended to the volume, Ridley tried to define Allen's new style and called him "a bright and snickering figure" who deserved "to be congratulated for having so adequate a medium of vent."[91] Allen joined in the mockery of his own arrogance and admitted in his biographical sketch that Ridley had "a very bright future behind him, because he is more than successful in his collaboration with me."[92]

The two boys had Merrill Moore write an equally flippant preface to the manuscript; after adding some humorous verse Allen had written a month or so earlier, they dedicated the pamphlet to the Fugitives and ordered two hundred copies from a printer in town. But as soon as the book appeared, Allen apparently began worrying about being linked so closely to Ridley, who was essentially a humorist, and he downplayed the volume to his serious-minded Modernist friends. "A word about that absurd book, *The Golden Mean*," he remarked to Hart Crane. "We shall make a little money out of it from the local public, and that is the whole point of publishing it, so far as I'm concerned. Wills is inclined to think it is clever."[93]

The Modernist controversy so frivolously treated in *The Golden Mean* had become increasingly troublesome for Allen. He was still trying to persuade the Fugitives of Eliot's importance, but also wanted to answer their charge that many of his recent poems derived from his readings in *The Waste Land*. When Davidson warned him that he was "distinctly limiting" his potential "by the Eliotish manner" he was adopting,[94] Allen initially ignored this advice and submitted some of the new poems to Edmund Wilson, an editor at *Vanity Fair*. Wilson, however, returned them with a brief note: "I look forward to something extraordinary from you. But do try to get out of the artistic clutches of T.S. Eliot."[95] "Now say 'I told you so,' " Allen remarked sheepishly to Davidson, adding, "I answered it forthwith explaining my dilemma— that of having to avoid, consciously, Eliot's idiom and viewpoint, which in the nature of me are also mine."[96] Of his "Eliot taint," he finally admitted, "it's hard for me to detect it in my own stuff unless it is very pronounced."[97]

While Allen feared what he called "the dangers of ultra-modernism," he was simply too worked up to abandon Eliot completely.[98] He continued to derive the utmost personal pleasure from *The Waste Land*, and when the poem was reissued as a book he did everything he could to advertise it to his friends. Ransom remembered that Allen told him about the poem "with as much agitation" as he "ever knew him to register."[99] A Phi Delta Theta brother recalled being "unceremoniously grabbed by Allen, taken upstairs to his bedroom, seated in the only chair provided while he sat on the bed," and then read to from what "he declared to be a superb new poem." "I'm not quite sure whether, at that time, even Allen comprehended the poem," the Phi Delt remembered, "but I am quite confident that he apprehended it: the one poet speaking to another."[100] Allen was equally excited when he returned to his room in Wesley Hall one day and discovered that Red Warren had covered the gray plaster of their walls with art gum and painted four wall murals of *The Waste Land*.[101] Any reservations Allen may have been developing about Eliot's technique were further eroded in mid-1923 when Eliot himself wrote a letter to one of the Fugitive poets singling out Allen's verse in particular for praise. "I feel like putting a record on the gramophone," Allen remarked, alluding to the typist who did so in *The Waste Land*.[102]

III

As the spring term progressed, Allen's selective studying habits drew him farther and farther from the academic goals he had set for himself. In May he admitted to feeling "the drunkenness of a sentimental depression," and suddenly he found that he was reliving the academic nightmare of his freshman year.[103] He was simply not capable of satisfying his requirements in mathematics and chemistry.

At first, he had made a concerted effort to conquer his problems with mathematics. He stopped writing poetry entirely and spent his first month back at school preparing for a special examination in trigonometry that, if he passed, would allow him to forgo taking the course. At the same time, he bravely enrolled in a course in analytic geometry, a subject he found equally difficult. Determined to rid himself of both subjects once and for all, Allen impressed his classmates with his resolve. On the first day of class he took a seat "directly before the professor and stared at him, listening to every word with profound and theatrical attention."[104] But even this concerted effort soon met with failure; a Vanderbilt classmate observed that "Allen's cortical synapses consistently displayed a vacuous dead-spot when confronted with the mysteries of $a^2 - b^2 = (a - b)(a + b)$."[105] His repeated failures in mathematics were so astonishing to his classmates that rumors started circulating that Professor Ott had it out for him and planned deliberately to delay his graduation by failing him. Allen scraped by with a passing grade on the trigonometry exam, but the Administrative Committee put him on academic probation. His brief conscientiousness undone, he began cutting geometry class.

Allen's attempt to satisfy his chemistry requirement also met with disaster. It was not simply that he found it impossible to study the subject matter. He was also unable to get along with his new chemistry professor, Dr. James Miller Breckinridge, a Canadian-born research scientist educated at the University of Wisconsin. Allen almost immediately fell foul of Breckinridge, no doubt because Allen considered his new teachers a "crew of dolts" and was not very good at hiding his disdain.[106] After completely alienating Breckinridge and failing to convince the administration to give him an unearned credit for chemistry, Allen concluded that his situation was hopeless. The conferring of his degree, he told Hart Crane, would have to be "a gift by special action of the faculty on the ground of 'brilliant record' in all work but Chemistry."[107] In mid-June, however, Allen was told what he already knew: he would receive no degree since his mathematics and chemistry requirements remained unsatisfied. Since he could not possibly have returned for a third senior year, this news presented him with the choice of leaving Vanderbilt permanently without his diploma or enrolling in summer courses at the nearby Peabody Teachers' College.

To make matters worse, Allen was suffering from an increasingly strained relationship with his brother Ben, who provided his principal means of financial support. In previous years, Allen had been able to supplement the tuition money he received from Ben with a small income from tutoring and other jobs. Allen's conscientious efforts to help pay his way through college apparently impressed Ben. But now Ben worried about supporting him indefinitely. The more Ben studied his younger brother's behavior, the more he was troubled by it; he wondered whether Allen was drinking and whether he could ever be trusted to finish his degree.

Allen's financial condition deteriorated further when he became estranged from his parents. Orley Tate, who had been reduced to trudging through the streets of Cincinnati selling supplies to gasoline stations, now lived with Ben, who supplemented his income with a small stipend. In Allen's eyes, Orley had become rather a pathetic and shadowy figure, a old man who had an enormous belly, wore a rupture belt, and flirted with young ladies. He did nothing for Allen. Nellie Tate, whose psychosomatic debilities grew worse each year, was equally unsupportive. Although she remained feisty enough to pressure Allen about his degree, she provided him with little of the financial help that might have helped him earn it more comfortably. As he spent less and less time at his poetry, and more and more time worrying about the difficulties of studying under financial duress, Allen's resentments grew. He concluded that his own family had little understanding of his artistic aspirations. When asked why he no longer spent much time with his poetry, he complained, "I have to consider the social dignity of the family who encourage me only when I satisfy the concept of a deserving young man." By May, he was convinced that both Ben and his parents were shortly to abandon him financially. "My sure failure to get the damn degree cuts me off from family sustenance," he confided to Hart Crane.[108]

When Allen failed to earn his degree in June 1923, Ben responded to his letters with stony silence. Finally, Allen was forced to ask Don Davidson, who had been a classmate of Ben's at Vanderbilt, to intercede. Davidson was older, and since he was a faculty member, he had a better chance of reasoning with Ben. Arguing that the math department had that spring made "a general slaughter" of seniors "as an example to future generations," Davidson succeeded in convincing Ben to pay tuition and fees so Allen could make up the lost credits in summer classes at Peabody. But Davidson scolded Allen privately for his devil-may-care attitude, and argued that there was "more than an atom of justice" in his older brother's anger. "As it stands," Davidson told Allen, "he probably looks at you as a rather bad gamble, and will be skeptical until you demonstrate the efficiency which the business man admires." Ever the pragmatist, Davidson convinced Allen to write to Ben "in such a tenor that it will make the way smooth for you to get a similar assistance from him next fall, in case you decide to work for a Master's."[109]

At first it seemed that Allen's classes at Peabody would be the death of him. "After four hours chasing hydrogen atoms round a fetid chemical laboratory, it is pretty hard not to indulge in a little adolescent pessimism," he complained.[110] But he thought that a degree might enable him to land a job to finance his career as a writer in the North. The romantic appeal of New York City had grown so strong in his mind that he finally admitted that he was "browbeaten at last" to "get the damn degree."[111] It helped that he had settled into a routine.[112] From eight A.M. until noon, he attended classes at Peabody; after breaking for lunch he then spent two hours writing business letters for the *Fugitive*. Following a late-afternoon class, he would spend a couple of hours reading, playing tennis, or swimming with Stanley Johnson, another Fugitive who was around for the summer. Finally, after eating dinner in Wesley Hall, Allen would retire to Professor Curry's suite in Kissam Hall, where he had lived since the beginning of the summer. Amid the cockroaches that infested Curry's rooms, he either worked further on the *Fugitive* or wrote poetry and personal letters. Only the promise of moving to New York, a plan that filled him with an excitement he described as "somewhat pubic," kept him from entirely ignoring his mathematics and chemistry assignments.[113]

Despite all of the financial and academic pressures he was facing that summer, Allen found time for a social life. Since he was still recovering from his breakup with Eleanor Hall, he tried to distract himself by courting other women at Vanderbilt. He was especially struck by an "opulent" female graduate student, a native of Corinth, Mississippi, who had recently moved into the home of a retired Vanderbilt professor and his wife, but he failed to win her over.[114] He met other women through Lyle Lanier, a Vanderbilt senior whom he knew from one of Professor Sanborn's philosophy courses.[115] A farm boy from rural Tennessee, Lanier grew up working in the fields or helping out at his father's general store. As a former English major, he shared Allen's enjoyment of poetry, and soon the two boys were good friends. Together they attended a series of summer parties held in fraternities on West Side Row and occasionally double-dated Vanderbilt coeds.[116] Allen was quick to revitalize his reputation as a ladies' man, and his friends enjoyed teasing him about it. Failing to find him in Professor Curry's suite one summer evening, Jesse Wills left a message for him on the typewriter: "Still philandering at 6:30? I'm ashamed of you."[117]

IV

Allen had now twice experienced the humiliation of watching his classmates graduate and leave Nashville without him. And since most of the Fugitives were out of town for the summer, he felt lonely and abandoned. Yet as more and more of the responsibilities of running the *Fugitive* were turned over to him, he found a welcome distraction in retiring to Curry's offices in order to work on the magazine. "There is no work I enjoy more than this editorial work," he remarked with satisfaction.[118]

For much of the summer, Allen ran the *Fugitive* almost single-handedly. As the magazine's business manager, he spent hours sending out circulars, soliciting financial support from local businessmen, and trying to market the magazine to bookstores. Since May, he had been helping to oversee the *Fugitive* poetry contest, an event that drew hundreds of entries. He was especially conscientious in his handling of the large volume of correspondence with the entrants; perhaps it had been his own experiences with poetry editors that nurtured his remarkable sensitivity to the egos of other young poets. "I never saw anyone who enjoyed writing letters as he does," Jesse Wills told Don Davidson. "He's carrying on a personal correspondence with several of our contestants of both genders."[119]

Allen had also amassed a significant amount of editorial power in Ransom's absence. Before the summer was half over he was proclaiming, "It is practically up to me what may go into the next issue of *The Fugitive*."[120] In the meantime, he was forming connections with many of the most promising younger poets outside of Nashville. Allen alone was responsible for convincing the group of the genius of Hart Crane, who with Allen's encouragement was already at work on one of his most important long poems. Other poets brought into the Fugitive circle by Allen included Virginia Lyne Tunstall and Laura Riding, two of the prominent female poets of the 1920s. By the middle of the summer, the Fugitives recognized that Allen was indispensable to the success of the magazine.

Allen's new power had emerged at the most auspicious moment. Subscriptions were arriving from all over the country, and though most copies of the magazine were still distributed free, the print run of the *Fugitive* had more than doubled since the first printing of five hundred magazines. That year, the editors of the *Braithwaite Anthology*, a popular collection of contemporary verse, cited the *Fugitive* for showing "more character and originality during the last year than any poetry magazine in the country" and concluded that poets "John Crowe Ransom, Allen Tate, Donald Davidson, Stanley Johnson, and Merrill Moore, give to its pages a succession of brilliantly individual work."[121] Within a year of the magazine's founding, the *Fugitive* had worked its way into the canon of contemporary poetry.

All the time Allen was enjoying the fruits of such publicity, his jealousy of Ransom was growing. For some time after winning the argument over Frank's poem, Allen accepted the hierarchy and sullenly deferred to his former professor. But when Don Davidson began urging him to join him in gentle resistance to Ransom's hold over the magazine, Allen looked for ways to put "the Tatian taint" in his editorials—even if the final product was not "sufficiently jesuitical to please even John Ransom."[122]

The tensions between Allen and Ransom were exacerbated in July when Christopher Morley, editor of the *Literary Review*, a publication of the *New York Evening Post*, made the mistake of using the phrase "John Crowe Ransom's 'Fugitive'" in his literary gossip column.[123] Allen, who probably remembered with annoyance that readers of the first *Fugitive*, in which the group used pseudonyms, had misattributed every poem in the volume to Ransom, sent a heated letter to Morley. "*Allen Tate*, acting managing editor of *The Fugitive*," Morley wrote in a published correction, "informs us that the paper is not *John Crowe Ransom's*, 'nor mine even, nor truly anybody else's.' It seems that no one is ever likely to be the editor of it; it is handled by a board of some thirteen editors, each of whom has as much to say about it as any other."[124] To Davidson, Allen confided, "You know that I've never had any illusions about John's modesty. This sort of nonsense makes me sore as *hell*." He believed Ransom had finally revealed his enjoyment in having people think the magazine was his. "What sickens me about the whole matter," Allen added, "is his refusal to admit that self-interest—in this case, self-exploitation—has any part in his motives at all. I can forgive a man for being vain and egotistical, but I can't forgive him for being dishonest."[125]

Just when it seemed that the estrangement between the two poets could not possibly have been worse, Ransom placed his famous critique of *The Waste Land* in the *Literary Review*.[126] Allen, who had been trying for months to publish his own flattering review of the poem, pre-pared for a showdown. He crafted a condescending letter to the *Literary Review* to damn Ransom for abandoning "free critical inquiry" and for resurrecting "superannuate theories." The pompous letter also accused Ransom of misunderstanding the form of *The Waste Land*, and of Modernist verse in general. The one bit of justice, Allen's letter concluded, was that Ransom's attack was "not likely to give T. S. Eliot much concern."[127]

Ransom, who had been up to this point tolerant of Allen's frequent rebellions against him, had lost his patience. He sent Allen a devastating rebuttal and deviously made it appear that he had written it only to blow off steam. Shortly afterward, however, Ransom had it published. "The truth is," Ransom said, "Tate has for two years suffered the damning experience of being a pupil in my classes, and I take it his letter is but a proper token of his final emancipation, composed upon the occasion of his accession to the ripe age of twenty-three." Ransom knew exactly where to strike: "I always gave him due credit on the grade books for having a brilliant mind, though I was not in possession of the magic formula for putting it to work." Perhaps thinking of the D he had handed Allen in advanced composition, Ransom concluded, "Mr. Eliot's critical prose is vitiated by precisely the same quality that marks in greater degree the prose of Mr. Tate's letter. . . . it abhors the academic (*i.e.*, the honest and thoroughgoing) method, and is specious after all, using its glittering scraps of comment and citation without any convincing assurance that the subject has been really studied."[128]

Although Allen was still convinced he had won the controversy, he was livid—for Ransom now opposed his being named associate editor of the *Fugitive*. "I am through with John for good," he vowed, "but will make no public avowal of it for the sake of *The Fugitive*."[129] Davidson was horrified by the actions of both his friends. On the one hand, it seemed to him that Ransom's rebuttal was "grievously wrong and unjust."[130] Yet he told Allen that his own attack against Ransom "bit deep." "You might have been a *leetle* more tactful," he chided.[131]

In the meantime, Allen had almost finished his summer classes. Although he claimed that his days had become "all alike," his dull routine offered him rewards.[132] Before long he was not only on top of his chemistry assignments but had made the best mark in the class on a mathematics examination. His financial condition had also improved after his reconciliation with Ben, and he made a little money by tutoring a few students. At the end of August 1923, he at last passed his two remaining academic requirements and was told he could expect his degree to be conferred in the fall.

The more Allen studied his options for the future, he grew reconciled to teaching "in some college."[133] Yet if he stayed on at Vanderbilt to pursue a needed credential such as a master's degree in classics, he had to have a fellowship—something difficult to acquire given his academic record. He could depend on Charles Sanborn and Herbert Tolman to recommend him, but he feared that in the eyes of the more traditionally minded members of the scholarships committee, his literary achievements might not make up for his erratic grades. "They don't follow the current movement." he complained. "Literature, to most of these Profs, is about as remote as Timbuctoo."[134] Undeterred, he applied for the scholarship and began looking for a politically powerful professor who would argue his case before the committee.

Unfortunately for Allen, the most logical person to speak on his behalf was Edwin Mims. Davidson, who was closer to Mims in age, urged Allen to approach the professor. "Tell Dr. Mims, if you want to," Davidson added, "that I, as Allen Tate's trusty watch-dog, vouch for that young man's discretion as a dignified graduate student. The Dr. will help you, I think."[135] Although other students had noticed that Mims was "a little envious"[136] of Allen's success, the tension between the two had lessened considerably during Allen's convalescence in Valle Crucis. Not long after Allen left town, Mims delivered a public lecture in which he not only praised the Fugitive poets, but hailed Allen's poetry for its "remarkable power of phrasing" and for being "graphic and amazing with audacity." After reading two of Allen's poems to his audience, Mims graciously concluded, "The success which Allen Tate has gained extends even beyond *The Fugitive* circle."[137] Encouraged by Mims's generosity of spirit, Allen decided to speak to him.

But both Allen and Don Davidson had forgotten about the satire Allen had inflicted on Mims in *The Golden Mean*. Allen's disrespectful appropriation of Mims's phrase "golden mean" apparently caused the professor to suspend any renewed affection he was feeling for his former student. When Allen went to speak with him about the scholarship, he discovered that Mims had been stewing for months. The meeting ended in disaster. "I'm sorry to say," Allen reported of Mims afterward, "that he is, of all men, the most dishonest, and that I am driven into a like dishonesty, for practical reasons, because he happens to be in academic power. He wouldn't recommend me for the scholarship until I offered him some sort of apology for past irreverences! Imagine confusing personalities with scholarship!"[138] Irritated by the rejection, Allen thought for a while he might try teaching in the philosophy department at the College of the City of New York. But then he came up with an even more ambitious plan: he would apply for a graduate fellowship in the Yale University Department of Classics.

Davidson, who by now had grown accustomed to Allen's outbursts, responded with his characteristic objectivity. "Remember that I am, as always, on your side," he told Allen, "and yet in this case I should have to be on Dr. Mims' side, too. As I have told you before (and so believe has Curry) you and Ridley weren't quite fair in your attitude toward Dr. Mims last spring. I am sure that he felt very much hurt and bothered by a belief that you and Ridley were in the ranks of the enemy, and that you were on occasion not losing opportunities to make sport of him . . . You say 'Imagine confusing personalities with scholarship.' Yet that is exactly what you and Ridley did." No one seemed to understood Allen's pattern of behavior better than Davidson. "Young man," he scolded, "if you wish others to be charitable to you, you must be charitable to others. Thus do I moralize, and damme [*sic*] if it isn't true. You are having lots of troubles these parlous days, aren't you, and no one grieves more than I for that. But look back and ask yourself, if stones have bruised you, whether that is not often because you have, forsooth, deliberately butted your head against them."[139]

Allen's fear of being abandoned by his professors grew worse when Dean Herbert Tolman suddenly died in November 1923. His response to Tolman's death also revealed his new habit of grouping the professors in his environment into two camps. If Allen vilified Mims, he worshiped Tolman, who, he said, "gave every man his love" and thus deserved unqualified praise. "I should have missed an attitude Of mercy, and a finer mood," Allen wrote in self-deprecating elegy to the Greek professor,

> Without this happy gentleman—
> I, the young barbarian![140]

Not only had Tolman kept the administration from expelling him, he had personally loaned him tuition money. Never once had he rejected Allen.

Allen's idolatry of Tolman resurrected behavior that went back to his childhood. Whenever his own father ignored him, betrayed him, or lectured him, he searched for older figures whose characters were free of any moral ambiguity. To be encouraged by his professors, Allen needed to believe that they had unchanging affection for him. If Allen had become the "hot youth" Davidson claimed he was—or the "child of wrathful detachment"[141] others believed him to be—he was in some measure combating fears that he had been orphaned. Having self-absorbed parents, Allen had frequently to prove to himself that he was a son to somebody.

Allen's grief over Tolman was no doubt intensified by the fact that he and Red Warren had been tenants on the professor's property for about a month. In the back lawn of Dean Tolman's house sat a tiny but cozy bungalow that had once served as servants' quarters. The little house, known as the Tolman cottage, had but two rooms and a fireplace and was apparently not well insulated. As fall began turning to winter, the cottage got colder and colder. In the mornings, Red and Allen would lie bundled up in their beds and argue over whose turn it was to get up and stoke the fire.[142]

But there was never a shortage of socializing in the cottage. Allen's friend Lyle Lanier, who decided to attend Peabody College for graduate work in psychology, was one of many visitors. Lyle's fiancée, Katherine Nichol, lived with her parents on the other side of the fence at the edge of the Tolman's property line. It was easy for Lyle to cut over to the cottage, where he enjoyed just sitting and listening to Allen and Red read selections from the poetry of William Blake, A. E. Housman, and T. S. Eliot. When Lyle and the other boys were not around for literary conversation, Red and Allen entertained their female friends. Dean Tolman's widow, a cranky old woman who spent a good part of her time spying on the boys through her back window, complained of the frequent parties being held in the cottage; she also claimed to have observed a number of unescorted young women leaving the cottage in the early hours of the morning.[143]

Although Allen's social activities were highly amusing to his friends, his intellectual achievements were finally being recognized by the university. After his graduation in October, the Alumni Office publicly pronounced him to be "one of the finest student poets" in the school's history, and shortly afterward he was elected to Phi Beta Kappa.[144] Despite his abysmal grades in the sciences, the professors on the selection committee of the Vanderbilt chapter recognized that his transcript showed genuine brilliance in literature and in languages. Allen also knew Greek, a prerequisite for election to the society. After being inducted into the society in a ceremony presided over by Professor Mims, the chapter's new president, Allen adopted a new scholarly pose. He began wearing gray three-piece suits so that he could string his Phi Beta Kappa key across his vest.

V

In the wake of his graduation, Allen found himself lingering in Nashville with little else to do but write poetry and work on editorial correspondence at the *Fugitive*. He was relieved to have earned a degree, yet he was feeling somewhat revolted by the South. These feelings of repulsion had been growing since the moment he returned to Vanderbilt the previous spring, and they were exacerbated by the confrontation with Mims. As Allen reexamined Nashville, his thoughts kept migrating North. If he was not accepted to Yale, he would establish himself as a freelance writer in New York City. Ransom had warned him for months about the unlikelihood of "any good man's making his way there by literature pure and undefiled," but Allen refused to change his plans.[145] He was prepared to wait on tables by day and to sleep on Hart Crane's sofa if he was unable to find work as a writer in New York.

In the meantime, he felt so cut off from the mainstream of literary life that even his colleagues had begun to bore him. "The Fugitives," he had confided to Hart Crane, "are the sorriest gang I've yet seen, and the rather lurid romanticism that hangs about me down here is somewhat irritating; so everything considered, the South will see little of me after I have done with the present compromise."[146] Allen's damning of the Fugitives for being sentimentalists was surprising in light of their hatred of the maudlin literature of the Old South. Even in the first issue of the *Fugitive*, the entire group had made it clear that they were in revolt against local tradition. "Southern Literature," they had proclaimed, "has expired, like any other stream whose source is stopped up. The demise was not untimely: among other advantages, *The Fugitive* is enabled to come to birth in Nashville, Tennessee, under a star not entirely unsympathetic. *The Fugitive* flees from nothing faster than from the high-caste Brahmins of the Old South."[147]

Most local reviewers recognized that the Nashville group was bringing notoriety to their city and prestige to the South. As more issues of the magazine appeared, hometown newspapers typically heralded the publication as "an advertising instrument for this city and this state."[148] One journalist observed, "There are a good many people in different parts of the world who, a year ago, if the word 'Nashville' had been mentioned would have had a vague image of a city somewhere or other in the South, but who, today, at the mention of the name would say, 'Oh yes; Nashville. That's the city in Tennessee where *The Fugitive* is published.' "[149] Allen and the others tried using these local insecurities to their advantage—in a fund-raising leaflet, for instance, they made a direct appeal to all "Southerners interested in the national success of a local periodical."[150] They shrewdly pointed to the increasing amount of praise they were receiving in New York newspapers. After all, the *Herald* had cited the magazine as "an encouraging sign of the growing preoccupation of the Southern people with literature," and the *Times* singled out the publication as "representative of the renascence of letters that the South is undergoing."[151] It was not surprising that the Fugitives began to think of themselves as an answer to H. L. Mencken's call for a new Southern literature.

But Allen was growing increasingly frustrated by the way Northern literary critics grouped the Fugitives with other Southern poets, as if all Southern artists were the same. He had correctly observed that the renaissance in Southern letters was a fragmented movement, splintered not only by geographical subdivisions in the South, but also by aesthetic differences. It seemed to him that Southern writers were put in the uncomfortable position of having to defend a movement whose membership not even Mencken could have agreed upon. When, for instance, a popular journal called the *Southern Literary Magazine* emerged out of Atlanta, Allen criticized the publication because certain "groups in the South . . . do not feel themselves adequately represented by such an organ."[152] The challenge for a member of the Fugitive group, as Allen saw it, was in learning how to reap all of the benefits of being a Southern writer without being grouped in with the mawkish traditionalists. "Obviously," Allen wrote that autumn, "there are only a few of us in the South, and I should think none of us wants to go on record with our Georgia contemporaries as champions of the dear 100% Sentimentalism of the Section."[153]

As if attacking his own mother, he began rejecting any piece of Southern literature or poetry in which he detected the faintest trace of anything "saccharine and grandmotherly."[154] The strongest show of loyalty a Southern writer could make, he now argued, was to write about the South objectively and realistically—warts and all. He redoubled his efforts to win over Mencken and sent him poem after poem for the *Smart Set*. His prose began echoing with Menckenesque phrases. "Here I am," he complained, "a fungus on a decayed magnolia stump."[155] Nashville, he decided, was simply a "bog of Methodism and ante-bellum sentimentality."[156] While local critics praised the Fugitive group for writing " 'Nashville' in large letters on the literary map,"

Allen told poetry editors that of his two identifying traits—his youth and his residence in Nashville—the second trait was "perhaps the more damning."[157]

To attack the South was difficult for Allen, since his strongest identity was not as a Modernist but as the Southerner his parents had, truthfully or not, taught him to be. What was more, he genuinely wanted to advance Southern literature. If he held contradictory feelings for the South, they were in keeping with the mixture of love and hatred that seemed to be governing his attitudes toward the people around him—from his own parents to his professors and his literary idols. He wanted to believe that the South would help him to control his alternating feelings of anger and emotional detachment; "the South," he concluded, "is as good a correlative of emotion as any place else."[158] But if he saw that Southern society, like his own family, was treating him not as a favorite son, but as an orphan, he would reject it as it had rejected him.

Chapter Four

"They Used to Call Me 'the Yankee'"

Throughout the autumn of 1923 and into the early months of 1924, Allen remained trapped in Nashville, where his routine reinforced his malaise. He continued to meet with the Fugitives and to edit the magazine, but he had begun to feel that members of the group were hostile not only to his work but to him personally. Nothing seemed to be going right for him. His financial condition deteriorated even further, his application for a graduate fellowship at Yale elicited no immediate response, and his dream of moving to New York City faded again. The future seemed so uncertain that when he was offered a temporary position in a West Virginia high school, he accepted it.[1] He left Nashville quickly and in late February 1924 found himself in the mountains of West Virginia.

Moving to West Virginia made Allen think further about his regional identity. Like him, the state was divided between Northern goals and a Southern personality.[2] During the Civil War, residents of northwestern Virginia remained loyal to the Union and voted to secede from their own state to form West Virginia.[3] Wedged between a Unionist stronghold in Ohio and solidly Confederate Virginia to the east, the new state was tugged in opposite directions. An area that had condoned slavery since the 1780s would soon be scarred both by Confederate raids and Union invasions. Northern victory settled West Virginia's legal status, but its cultural affiliations remained Southern. Only the state's preoccupation with industrial progress betrayed its Northern influences. Living in West Virginia reminded Allen not only of the differences between urban and rural life, but of the contrast between the New York writers he had begun to emulate and the Fugitives he left behind. He seemed to have found the appropriate setting for his difficult transition from the South to New York.

I

Allen was especially struck by the growth that was taking place in Lumberport, the town where he was to live and teach.[4] Excited by "the prospect of solitude for three months," he perhaps expected to find in "the wilds of West Virginia" a bucolic mountain village similar to Valle Crucis, North Carolina.[5] Instead he found a buzzing town of fifteen hundred people who moved about in trains, automobiles, and streetcars. For years the local farmers had been boring into the area's forests and sending timber down the precipitous mountainside waterways on rafts.

Allen already knew from witnessing his father's business ventures along the Ohio River the effects of the timber business on border towns in the South. But he had probably never seen a town so small industrializing so quickly. In addition to the lumber operations, there were more than two dozen thriving coal mines and some two hundred gas wells. The local economy never slowed down after its explosive growth during the First World War and, since wages remained high, small businesses were still sprouting everywhere. A local periodical boasted: "There are now two churches, one school, twelve grocery and clothing stores, one drug store, four garages, two meat markets, one bank, two restaurants, three hotels, three barber shops, four pool rooms, a postoffice, theatre, hardware store, confectionery, dance hall, public library, glass factory and over five hundred dwellings."[6] All of this commercialism inspired Allen with as much cynicism as awe. Sarcastically, he reported to his friends that the streets in town were actually paved.

But Allen was genuinely impressed by the resolve of the townspeople. Since many of the students in the Lumberport High School were children of the town's civic and business leaders and were expected to attend college, the school board lured in qualified teachers from universities such as Vanderbilt by offering them relatively high wages for the era, $175 a month. Allen used a portion of his new salary to move into the home of a man named Carson Hess, who owned a planing mill and a thriving lumber business. Hess and his wife lived in a spacious two-story home, where they let rooms to schoolteachers. Allen undoubtedly recognized how unfavorably his own father, a failed lumberman, compared with Mr. Hess, and soon he was speaking of "the honor" of living with the town's "leading citizen."[7] It was probably not a coincidence when, shortly after arriving at the Hesses, Allen published *Poem for My Father*, about a pauper who was sixty years old, the same age as Orley Tate.[8]

At first, Allen threw himself into his new job. He arrived in the middle of the school year, less than a month after the school building had burned down, and though he and the other nine faculty members had to meet about 150 students in temporary facilities ranging from a partitioned gymnasium to the local opera house, Allen agreed to teach four courses—one Latin and three English. He also promised to direct a play, and he took on the responsibility of advising the entire junior class. He wasted no time in letting his students know what he expected of them; as the president of the senior class later explained, when he gave them their lessons, "he meant for us to get them."[9] If the students admired their new teacher's immaculate manner of dress, his thin frame, and his fair complexion, they were somewhat frightened by his top-heavy brow, his Phi Beta Kappa key—which he continued to wear prominently—and his intellectual intensity. "He always seemed to walk with his head down," one student remembered, and "must have been in serious thought of some kind."[10]

But students also noted that when Allen taught, there was a twinkle in his eye, even when he was severe with them. They were grateful that someone who was obviously highly literate "didn't get sickening with it," and that he used humor to correct their errors. "We weren't allowed to say 'I ain't,' " the mayor's daughter remembered. "He'd just look at us and say, 'What was it? I didn't hear it.' And if we said 'ain't' again, he'd say, 'I didn't hear that.' "[11] Allen took increasing pleasure in mixing intimidation and theatrics in the classroom. "My seniors," he reported to Don Davidson, "are taking 'The Rape of the Lock,' and I don't know when I've had so much fun. I rouse 'em in the approved Mimsian fashion; and would you believe it? They seem to be getting something out of it besides *lessons!*"[12]

As Allen began to feel more comfortable in the classroom, his students recognized that as long as they turned in their assignments, they could get away with teasing him. They gossiped about him after school, and in class noted with glee that behind this apparently well educated Southerner was a city slicker who seemed just a bit helpless when he ventured beyond the field of literature. The local farm boys would puzzle him with questions that were remote from his own experience. "Mr.

Tate, do you plant or sow potatoes?" they asked. Since Allen had not been raised on a farm, he would stumble in his reply, offering something like, "Are there any members of the agriculture class present?"[13] But all of this teasing was in good fun. While the students knew that he viewed his job only as "a stepping stone" to the "career that he hoped for in New York," they concluded he was a "good fellow" and the "smartest teacher" in the school.[14]

II

Allen soon discovered that he could teach without preparing in advance, and he began spending a great deal of time sitting in front of his new typewriter. Putting aside his poetry, he wrote more prose in West Virginia than he had ever written before. He was delighted to find a ready outlet for book reviews when Davidson began editing the book page of the *Nashville Tennessean*.[15] During the five months Allen spent in Lumberport, he reviewed almost two dozen volumes of poetry, fiction, and nonfiction, including the work of DuBose Heyward, Edwin Arlington Robinson, J. E. Spingarn, and Jean Toomer. Though these reviews amounted to his first sustained effort at literary criticism, Allen called them "hack writing" and told his Vanderbilt classmate Bill Bandy how happy he was that "these things will never be collected."[16]

The greatest problem with Allen's early prose was its complexity. "I *simply* can't *simplify* that first paragraph," he said of one piece for the *Fugitive* . "I know they are rotten sentences, but I wasn't thinking about style; it is a very difficult point and to make it completely lucid I should have to write it out in a very long article."[17] He looked for and found a justification for writing in an inaccessible style. It was, he decided, "the megaphone of popular education" that he was fighting; his obscure phrasing would "help educate the populace."[18] Davidson, who was apparently under pressure from his editor to make Allen eliminate some of the philosophical terms and Modernist jargon in his articles, pleaded with him to write more intelligibly. But Allen refused to dilute his ideas. In a review of E. E. Cummings, he explained, "It's going to be very much like playing Leo Ornstein [a Modernist composer and pianist popular in the 1920s] on an accordion to try to render a just account of E. E. Cummings' first volume of poetry in terms of a popular review."[19]

Allen might have received less criticism for his prose if he had not been so inexperienced. He had published only a couple of reviews and editorials, one in the *Fugitive* and one in the *Double Dealer*, and was simply not comfortable with newspaper and magazine writing.[20] John Ransom, having read a few of his early efforts, asked him in exasperation, "Why are you not more provisional, tentative, qualified, disparaging, as you contemplate the Stream of your Ideas?"[21] Allen knew that Ransom was the superior writer and confessed his lack of experience. "As I re-read my article," he said of a representative review, "it *does* seem a bit hectic—and very bad prose, but indeed much better than I wrote a year ago." He wanted "to improve with age, like Bourbon."[22]

Yet as much as Allen recognized the difficulty of his prose style, he was unwilling to abandon the Modernist aesthetic theories that produced its obscurity. In both poetry and prose, he was looking for a style that captured his own thought processes rather than stock emotions or easily identifiable feelings. Cummings had achieved "perfection" in Allen's view for the simple reason that his work "translates thought completely."[23] Such a goal fit in neatly not only with T. S. Eliot's "objective correlative," but also with the notion of "direct intuition," a related idea Allen found in the philosophical works of George Santayana. More and more, Allen cited ideas like these in response to the argument that poets were supposed to be concerned with "rational exposition, rather than with the pure presentation, of intuition or ideas." Modern poets, he argued, "can't write like Homer or Milton." While the ancient Greeks and the Classical poets could rely on their simplistic notions about "Heaven, Hell, Duty, Olympus, Immortality," a Modern poet like himself could only draw "a distracting complexity" from the "data" of his life experiences. Such a writer could "be happy only in the obscure by-ways of his own perceptive processes."[24]

Allen continued applying these aesthetic theories in his own emotional life. Perhaps because his emotions could change both radically and quickly—and because he did not often understand his own feelings—he was attracted to a philosophical system that assigned a positive value to ambiguous and changeable feelings. Throughout the five months that he spent in Lumberport, he found that his moods ranged from euphoria and anger to melancholy. When he first arrived in town, he announced, "My *heart* is rather light all the time."[25] Before long, however, he was depressed. Using these fluctuations to his advantage, he took pride in describing himself as an artist prone to vacillation "between gaiety and bitterness."[26]

Behind Allen's moodiness in Lumberport were some genuine disappointments, not the least of which was the frustration he experienced trying to get his volume of poetry published. When Albert Boni took over Lieber and Lewis in 1923, he seemed uninterested in the manuscript Maxim Lieber had accepted from Allen. This misfortune was no doubt as humiliating to Allen as it was disappointing, for he had been publicly describing himself as the author of *Calidus Juventa: A Book of Verse*. What was worse, Davidson, now Allen's best friend, was bringing out his own first volume of poems with Houghton Mifflin in Boston. Redoubling his efforts, Allen returned to his poetry manuscripts and made a new selection, dropping the title Calidus Juventa. He sent the revised manuscript to Thomas Seltzer, an independent publisher in New York, but entertained few delusions as to the the book's popular appeal. "Indeed," he admitted, "the more I look at my copy of the ms., the worse—or rather the more absurd even the best of it seems."[27] When Seltzer, as predicted, promptly rejected the volume, Allen asked Davidson for a letter of recommendation so he could send the poems to Houghton Mifflin, who refused them. "As I thought," Allen concluded in dismay, "they were afraid of the modernism; they said the poems were brilliant and original, and that they'd like to see my collection a year from now if I hadn't placed it elsewhere."[28] Having all but lost hope, he sent the manuscript to another Boston firm, the B. J. Brimmer Company, publishers of *Braithewaite's Anthology*, a contemporary verse collection published annually. But Brimmer also rejected the volume. Adding to Allen's despair, Boni and Liveright returned the manuscript they had inherited from Lieber and Lewis, and he discovered that the new owners of the firm had never even seen the improved version of the book Maxim Lieber once promised to publish. Boni agreed to look at the later version, but Allen felt dejected. "The demand of intelligibility," he explained, "has about undone me."[29] It seemed to him that nobody appreciated his emotionally unrevealing poems. "I repeat again a bit wearily," he told Davidson, "that perhaps poems aren't literally *about* things; *that* sort of aesthetics was held naive even before Kant, who discusses the point specifically."[30]

Allen would have had an easier time handling these rejections if his relationship with the Fugitives was not so strained. He had grown self-conscious about how the group might respond to his relentless efforts to publish his poems. "I am as deeply self-interested as any of them," he tried to explain, "and at this time have good practical reason to be, this being the particular stage of my life where I am fighting, as it were, for my very existence."[31] Davidson reassured him that there was no reason to believe "that anybody felt hostile" toward him, but Allen remained unconvinced.[32] Some of his fears stemmed from his argument with Ransom over Eliot's *Waste Land*. If Allen was satisfied that "peace" had been "established over last summer's corpse," he still found Ransom's attitude condescending.[33] Fearing the magazine was doomed to failure under Ransom's leadership, Allen sent in his resignation with the explanation that his permanent departure from Nashville made it impossible for him to continue as an editor. But he could not keep from revealing his insecurities about the group's feelings for him. "First of all," he told them, "ever since we began publication, and before, my verse has been met with violent opposition; it has never received other than severe criticism, often ridicule."[34] Allen condemned the group for their indifference, and for ignoring everything he had done to keep the magazine in the limelight.

Allen's letter elicited the reassurance he craved. "I wish you could have listened in on our meeting last evening," Ransom wrote. "In the first place, you would have been able to renew your slipping confidence that you had cast in your lot among friends."[35] Presented with reassurances like this one, as well as the news that the group had rallied and was confronting its financial and managerial problems, Allen sheepishly admitted, "We all have the inferiority complex, every artistic person has it." He was pleased to know that his letter drew the poets out of their apathy, and conceded "it *is* devilish hard not to get twisted up in looking at one's own self."[36]

In the midst of Allen's increasing insecurities about the loyalty of his friends and teachers at Vanderbilt, he was rejected for graduate study at Yale. Many of his friends knew of his application, and Davidson, Ransom, and Warren were eagerly awaiting news of his acceptance. When a rejection letter arrived instead, Allen was so distraught that he immediately wrote to Yale and asked them to return not only his completed application, but all letters of recommendation. Yale complied with the request but followed what was undoubtedly standard procedure and refused to return one letter that had not accompanied his application. Allen was convinced that Edwin Mims had written an unsolicited letter. Since neither the content nor the author of the letter was ever revealed, it is hard to know whether Allen had correctly identified his saboteur, if indeed he had one. "No explanation was required, my dear Don," Allen insisted. "If your throat isn't cut in front, why, then it's easily done behind your back, and with less noise."[37] Red Warren, who shared Allen's dislike for Mims, fueled Allen's suspicions. "I have not the slightest doubt," he wrote Allen, "but that it was the viperous letter of the Dr. that did the mischief."[38]

Just when it seemed that Allen's mistrust of the Vanderbilt administration could increase no further, Dean Tolman's widow threatened to publicize her accusation that women visitors had occasionally left the Tolman cottage early in the morning when Red and Allen were living there the previous autumn. This charge, Allen decided, was "the climax" in "a series of rank injustices."[39] Without considering the matter carefully, he sent a full-scale letter of rebuttal to the old woman and threatened her with a libel suit. When news of the letter reached a number of Allen's friends and teachers, reactions were mixed. Red Warren, who was still on campus, naturally approved of Allen's great "gusto" and greeted the letter as "masterful of its kind." "I am quite delighted," he added, "that Mrs. Tolman has been adequately 'told.' "[40] He began jokingly to refer to the episode as the "fornication in the cottage" scandal—or as "love among the ruins."[41] Faculty members like Charles Herbert Sanborn, however, were less amused. Even though Sanborn suspected that many of Allen's countercharges against Mrs. Tolman were true, he thought Allen's letter had "transgressed the bounds of strict courtesy."[42] Dr. Mims was equally perturbed. Perhaps because his own daughters were known to socialize with Red and Allen, he exerted some effort to help the boys out of their scrape. But privately he put word out that he believed Mrs. Tolman was telling the truth, and he criticized Allen for writing the letter.

Allen was only mildly contrite. "I hated to do it," he said halfheartedly, "but I'm cornered, nearly desperate; I've got to do something to curb this hostility toward me in certain quarters."[43] After sending the letter, he began joking about what he called his "epistolomania," and he evidently enjoyed the sensation he had created;[44] for the rest of his life he excelled in writing censorious letters to his enemies. While he knew these letters were "diabolical," he explained to his friends that they fulfilled his need for a certain amount of conflict in his day-to-day activities. "What is life," he asked, "without war?"[45]

III

As the school year drew to a close in the late spring, Allen began thinking about his immediate future. The fear that many of his friends were turning against him only strengthened his desire to leave the South, which he now termed "a region none too friendly at best."[46] Southern newspaper reviewers were attacking Davidson's first volume of poetry, and Allen could only comment, "No wonder we all get disgusted and want to leave. Some of us can't leave, though," he added, referring to his own financial predicament.[47] The principal of the Lumberport High School had offered to raise Allen's salary an additional thirty-five dollars a month if he stayed on, but Allen told his friends that he "wouldn't stay for a thousand!"[48] He still harbored desires to "go to some place like Yale," but he could not bear the thought of having to accept any further financial assistance from his brother Ben.[49] In Allen's view, Ben offered to pay for his graduate training only because he was likely to earn a higher salary when he finished. "Naturally," Allen observed sardonically, "I'd rather not accept further assistance from any one who is hostile to my conception of the intelligent life to the extent of thinking me insane!"[50]

Allen was completely certain that in New York he would be greeted with open arms by kindred spirits and like-minded Modernists—and there was a good measure of truth in his belief that a favorable reception awaited him there. Hart Crane had been urging him for months to move there as quickly as possible, and now a young poet from Harvard named Malcolm Cowley was pushing for him to come.[51] Cowley, formerly one of the editors of the Modernist journal *Secession*, had offered to include some of Allen's poems in an anthology of verse by "Secessionist" poets. Since this meant that his work might appear next to poetry by Crane, Cummings, and William Carlos Williams, Allen was ecstatic—and even self-deprecatory: "Whatever we may think of these people I personally am pleased that my work has been esteemed without my actual presence on the scene to boost it—or detract from it, as the case may be!"[52] Even more exciting, Cowley, who was employed by *Sweet's Architectural Catalogue*, reported that he was working to convince Boni and Liveright to publish Allen's poems. Only Allen's finances held him back; he did not want to waste what little money he had saved in Lumberport on a hasty and ill-fated trip to New York. Instead, he thought about taking a summer job with Red Warren as a day laborer in Guthrie, Kentucky, Warren's hometown. He even considered returning to Nashville temporarily, where he might be able to earn money as a newspaper reporter.

Toward the end of May, however, a near tragedy made Allen's return to the South a necessity: Red Warren attempted suicide in his room at Vanderbilt.[53] A friend found him lying flat on his bed, unconscious after he had draped a towel soaked in chloroform over his face. Next to his bed lay a note in which he explained that he "would not make a poet."[54] After a brief stay in the local hospital, he left for Kentucky with his parents. Unexpected though Warren's actions were, all of his friends had been worrying about him for months. He had put himself under tremendous academic strain and, to make matters worse, had injured his eye in an accident. There was a chance that he would lose sight in both eyes. Allen, who had downplayed a warning from Lyle Lanier several weeks earlier that their friend seemed to be affected with "a regular organic disorder,"[55] was overcome with grief, anger, helplessness—and perhaps guilt. He was certain that Warren would never have made the attempt if he had been with him in Nashville. "I am MAD," he wrote Davidson, "—mad as hell."

Allen and Red had always been in deep sympathy with one another. Allen had from the beginning taken on the role of an older brother, and helped Warren to revise and publish his poetry. Warren, on the other hand, deferred to his friend and showed him enormous gratitude. In several senses, they were soul mates. Both boys had greater poetic talents than emotional maturity—Allen was twenty-four and Red a mere nineteen—and both were conscious of oddities in their physical appearance. "I am sure," Allen told Davidson, "that I am the only person who doesn't look on Red as a merely interesting monstrosity mostly to be avoided." Describing his friend as a "palm tree planted in Labrador," Allen blamed Red's depression on the hostile forces he thought he had observed at Vanderbilt and advised Red's friends to "keep Mims away from him in any form."

Throughout Warren's crisis, Allen showed not only a remarkable concern for his friend but revealed an unusual knowledge of the emotional aftereffects of a suicide attempt. He discounted the romantic reason Warren gave for trying to take his own life and warned Davidson not to "be so naive as to put any worth in Red's later feeling that it was a bit ludicrous; such an attitude is always compensatory, it is despair's weapon against itself." Allen urged his friends to treat Red's feelings as if they were "old china cups that have nitro glycerine in them." "His spiritual loneliness," he explained, "and his thirst for companionship and genuine affection are back of this; he's in a social order where men are afraid to love each other."[56] Soon Allen wrote a poem for Warren and titled it *Young Classicist to a Younger and Romantic Friend*.[57]

Perhaps because Allen believed that Warren's family was as emotionally insensitive as his own, he decided to spend the summer visiting with Red in Guthrie. Red was elated by Allen's decision and immediately began planning their summer; he worried that Allen might become bored in the small town. "For more trivial diversion," Red promised, "there is a very beautiful arrival in our midst, a young female from Clarksville, who has moved to Guthrie. So your summer may not have to be wholly ascetic."[58] But Red's letters also indicated that he had rebounded and that Allen need not appear in Guthrie until late June.

<h1 style="text-align:center">IV</h1>

Despite his financial worries, Allen was unable to resist the temptation to make a run up to New York City. After leaving Lumberport in what he called a "very splenetic" mood, he arrived in New York in early June 1924.[59] He found a powerful and intimidating metropolis, but this "big and desolate and hectic" place appealed to his senses.[60] "I'm greatly thrilled at the mere *physique* of this great city!" he told Davidson. At first Allen even rejoiced in the industrialization that made the city into a noisy iron fortress. "Fancy going under a huge river at the rate of 40 miles an hour!" he said of the subway. "The sheer wonder of it is almost atonement for its significance as a phase of the Triumph of the Machine."[61]

Hart Crane had been busily preparing for Allen's visit and found a room for him in a building at 65 Columbia Heights, in Brooklyn. The two poets, who had now been trading letters for almost two years, hit it off immediately. "Crane is a peach of a fellow," Allen decided, "and is treating me royally. He's a 160 pounder, strong as an ox, looks like an automobile salesman (at a slight distance) and is proud of his looks; talks incessantly of trivialities and laughs all the time; but confessed to me late last night that he was a mystic!"[62] Although Allen held some reservations about his overly vivacious manner—and may have detected and disliked Crane's sexual preference for men—he did not doubt the young poet's sincerity and brilliance. For his part, Hart liked Allen immediately, and the two of them were soon wandering through New York's colorful Greenwich Village, a Bohemian maze of ethnic restaurants, small theaters, art galleries, and speakeasies.

Crane took Allen round to meet each of the Modernists Allen knew so well by reputation. To the names of each of the half dozen New York poets he had come to admire, he was finally able to attach personalities and faces, which he described in exaggerated detail to Davidson. First, there were the Secessionist poets, Malcolm Cowley, Gorham Munson, and E. E. Cummings. Cowley, who took Allen on a long walk through the Bronx Zoo, turned out to be "a mess of a person, the type of snob that becomes a snob himself by giving one to understand that he deprecates all other snobs." Though Cowley was a Phi Beta Kappa graduate of Harvard, Allen thought that he looked "like a truck driver" and was astounded to find that he was completely unwilling to "talk literature."[63] To make matters worse, Allen was embarrassed when Cowley looked at his vest and said, "We no longer wear our Phi Beta Kappa keys."[64]

But the two men became friends anyway. Cowley promised Allen that he would be included in the Secessionist anthology and counseled him on his troubles with the Bonis; he suggested that Allen sue them for five hundred dollars if they refused to honor the contract they inherited. Touched by these acts, Allen had to admit that Cowley was "a very keen and refreshingly unpretentious person withal."[65]

Cowley's friends Gorham Munson and E. E. Cummings also elicited mixed reactions from Allen. If Allen disliked Munson's writing style and his shyness, he also noted Munson's obesity and his "excessively fantastic" appearance—his "petite spiked mustaches and a huge tuft of hair on the back of his head." He was willing to overlook Munson's physical appearance only because the poet was "very precise in his statements—no fumbling; he knows his own mind." Cummings Allen remembered as the poet whose first volume he found virtually flawless. Yet when Allen met him over dinner one evening, he was amazed and disappointed to find that in conversation Cummings exhibited an infuriating self-control reminiscent of John Ransom. What was worse, Allen observed, Cummings "never talks literature, unless he introduces the subject." Allen was also annoyed to discover that he was morally opposed to all "Poetic Theories" and claimed to write poetry just "the way it seems good to him."[66]

The circle of poets Allen encountered in New York seemed rather alien to him, but the group welcomed him warmly. All of these men regularly socialized with other writers and theater people in Greenwich Village. Within a week, both artistic sets were entertaining Allen. In the company of a friend of Crane, a young writer named Susan Jenkins who was also secretary for the Provincetown Players, Allen attended a production of Eugene O'Neill's *All God's Chillun Got Wings*, staged at the Provincetown Theatre on Macdougal Street. Another evening, Cowley and the others took him out for a night on the town that concluded with a long hike down to look at the barges below the Brooklyn Bridge. The young poets could see the murky water slapping against the pier and the immense ships passing below New York City's skyline. In the distance loomed the giant letters of a sign advertising Waterman's Fountain Pen. Here was a city that suggested the end-stage in the commercialism Allen had been observing throughout the Upper South. It seemed like another world.[67]

The excitement proved too much for Allen, and before long he was "hankering to leave."[68] It was not just the distraction of being surrounded by so many ambitious and successful young poets or his worries about Red Warren; the bustle of urban life was difficult. He was still a Southerner at heart, and he held on to the less demanding pace he had learned in the border towns and Southern cities where he was raised. Crane, who saw him off at the train station, thought he departed "in a frightfully feverish state."[69] Exhausted and confused, Allen took a meandering, two-week-long train ride to Kentucky, taking in "a few creaky towns in Virginia" along the way and puzzling over his reactions to New York, which seemed "stalwart and noisy" in retrospect. Observing the dramatic differences between the Northern metropolis and the Southern towns he had come to know in childhood, Allen mused "there is no America," only sections and localities.[70]

V

Guthrie, Kentucky, offered Allen far more than he expected. Although the town was only a little more than an hour's ride from Nashville, it was a sleepy Southern town and soothed his nerves immediately. He found Red Warren robust and happy, better than he remembered seeing him in a long time. The two of them abandoned their writing projects and turned to the outdoors. Allen admitted to feeling "very primitive" as he and Red fished, swam, and rode horseback. "I am having a wonderful time here," he wrote Davidson, "and the quietness is not the least charming phase of it, after the grimy noise of urban life."[71]

The main attraction for Allen in Guthrie was the young woman Red had mentioned a month earlier.[72] Her name was Carolyn Gordon, and she was visiting her mother at the family farm in Clarksville, Tennessee—only a stone's throw from Guthrie.[73] It may very well have dawned on Allen, when he heard this young woman's name, that she was the same Chattanooga journalist who had written a highly complimentary newspaper article about the Fugitives just a year earlier. Ransom had written excitedly to Allen, promising to send him an article by "one Miss Gordon, who has developed quite a fondness for us."[74] When Allen received the clipping, he could only have been flattered and pleased. In the article, titled "U.S. Best Poets Here In Tennessee," Gordon praised the Fugitives for helping the state to gather "the highest poetic laurels." She also made special mention of Allen's success publishing in the nation's poetry journals and—no doubt to Allen's great satisfaction—correctly identified him as "the most radical member of the group."[75]

Perhaps it was Carolyn who prompted her mother to call Red Warren's mother and suggest that the two young men pay a visit. When Allen and Red turned in to the dirt lane leading to Merry Mont, the Gordon farm, Allen spied a striking woman with curiously arched eyebrows, dark eyes, and long brown hair. "You know," he told a friend years later, "I pissed in my pants. She was the most beautiful girl I had ever seen."[76] Allen and Red took Carolyn for a long walk in the woods and in no time at all Red saw that the young woman had completely captivated Allen. "After that," Warren recalled, "I rarely saw my guest."[77]

Although Carolyn Gordon was four years older than Allen, the two had much in common. Carolyn's family was every bit as eccentric and emotionally tumultuous as Allen's. Like Allen, Carolyn was subject to mood swings; she claimed to have attempted suicide at the age of four. Years later, she would explain her lifelong urge for geographical rootedness and emotional security as a reaction to her "father's constant moving around."[78] Both she and Allen also spent significant amounts of time in small Southern preparatory schools that stressed the classics. Like Allen, Carolyn taught for a year in a public high school. After attending Bethany College in West Virginia, she returned to Tennessee in 1919 and signed on as a writer for the *Chattanooga News*. Though her lucid and intelligible prose style lacked the theoretical and philosophical underpinnings of Allen's, her ambition to become a professional writer rivaled his own. It must have seemed to Allen that Carolyn was meant for him.

Yet by 1924, Allen had developed a kind of cynicism about women. It was an attitude that drew not only from the pathetic example of his own parents' marriage, but also from his inability to sustain a long-term romantic relationship. He had lost confidence in himself after his relationship with his college sweetheart Eleanor Hall ended. "I am quite an expert in making things worse," he told a Vanderbilt classmate experiencing troubles in love, "and I am sure that all you need now is my advice in order to produce the desperation requisite to a properly romantic tragedy. You see my long experience has made it impossible for me to succeed in the little transaction of which the soubriquet is love. If first you succeed, try, try again and in the end you will achieve the most picturesque failure."[79] It was symbolic that, in preparing a revised edition of his poems for the publishers in New York and Boston, he eliminated a sonnet about the end of his relationship with Eleanor. He no longer viewed himself as the tender young artist suffering from unrequited love—he had converted his feelings of woundedness into a flippant contempt for romance.

Allen learned that he could hide his hurt feelings by incorporating a tone of self-mockery and satire in his poetry. "Of course, you may not like this serio-comic person I put in my poetry," he told Davidson, "but that's what I am, and I can't change it."[80] He admitted the problems of having a mind "that always more or less looks upon itself with the satire of suspicion"[81] and that avoided anything sentimental or traditionally feminine. In a poem about the eighteenth-century poet Alexander Pope, whose ugliness and hunched back caused women in London to avoid him on the street "more out of fear than pity," Allen attempted to explain how Pope became both a hater of women and a talented satirist.[82]

But Allen's cynicism about women also drew from the misogyny that sometimes emerges in tightly knit male groups such as the Fugitives. He took mischievous pleasure in denouncing all bad poetry submitted to the *Fugitive*, but when any such verse had been written by a woman, there was an added dimension to his criticism. "Damn that woman!" he said of a Miss Cartwright from California. "I've insulted her three or four times, and still she insists on telling me in Zolaesque detail the color of her eyebrows. Next time she'll venture that she has a shapely leg, and I'd rather miss the confession."[83] After meeting a *Fugitive* contributor named Helene Mullins, Allen advised Davidson, "I'm in favor of rejecting all verse henceforth by this piece of baggage! She's the vulgarest, rudest wench I've yet graced with my presence. She also has a voice like the taste of a persimmon. Pretty if chorus girls are beautiful."[84] Of Harriet Monroe, the editor of *Poetry* who offended the Fugitives by urging Southern writers to look to the antebellum past for inspiration, Allen concluded: "Her journal at best is a saccharine orgy of feminine emotion."[85] It did not soften any of his attitudes to know that one of the most popular poets in the South was the sentimental Edna St. Vincent Millay, whose verse the Fugitives despised.

There was only one female contributor to the *Fugitive* that Allen had any genuine respect for, and she was an "intense, unhappy woman" named Laura Riding, the daughter of an outspoken Socialist tailor in New York City.[86] Although Allen at first thought the bulk of her poetry "nearly worthless," he was convinced that he had discovered a "volatile genius."[87] "You are the one," he told her, "to save America from the Edna Millays!"[88] On the way to Lumberport in February 1924, he stopped in Louisville to meet Riding, and ended up spending sixteen hours straight with her. He was enchanted. "Her intelligence is pervasive," he reported afterward, "it is in every inflexion of her voice, every gesture, every motion of her body."[89] He also admitted that he found her to be "exceedingly belle."[90] But she was married to a young historian named Louis Gottschalk. Though Allen began sending lengthy letters to her—letters in which, she recalled years later, "he wrote with fervor as one most seriously committed to me personally"[91]—Allen probably recognized that it was impossible to have any sort of romantic involvement with her.

Then Allen met Carolyn Gordon, who not only rivaled Riding intellectually, but who was beautiful and unattached. Carolyn, who had dated a number of boys in college, held the attraction of being romantically experienced while appearing to be a complete innocent. If Allen continued populating his verse with fallen women, he insisted that his own muse be a traditional woman—a kind of antebellum Southern belle—with an aura of innocence and purity. He damned anyone who wrote "like a repressed spinster,"[92] but was shocked when he met a woman in New York who openly professed to be a lesbian. Carolyn not only fulfilled Allen's ambiguous ideals but fell for him at once. In an irony that perfectly captured both his morbidity and his conflicted feelings about sex, Allen later reported that he and Carolyn made love for the first time in a Guthrie graveyard.[93]

Allen was in heaven that summer. "I've never felt lazier and better," he told Don Davidson early in August 1924. "My life for the last month has been the living song of the Lotus-Eaters."[94] But some of his friends in Nashville began worrying about the rapid changes they observed in his mood. His classmate and fraternity brother, Jesse Wills, who was still jittery after Warren's suicide attempt, was upset by Allen's sudden euphoria. "Your mental state as depicted in your letter, made me ponder a little," he told Allen. "But I am optimistic enough to consider your mood just the lies of love." Jesse, who had been Allen's confidant since their freshman year at Vanderbilt and had witnessed each of his infatuations, was a bit cynical about the permanence of this latest romance in Guthrie. Perhaps in reference to Allen's flirtation with a University of Virginia coed during the summer of 1919, Jesse slyly suggested that "a fresh draught from the springs of the Venusberg at Charlottesville" might bring him to his senses.[95]

VI

At the end of the summer of 1924, the only thing standing between Allen and his return to New York City was loyalty to his mother. Although he found her periodic interference in his life maddening, he felt guilty about abandoning her. Accordingly, after he left Guthrie, he went to Cincinnati in order to help her move to Washington, D.C., where she could be near the Virginia relatives she worshiped. "My mother," he explained after he arrived in Washington, "will be here all winter, alone; and I suspect pretty strongly I ought to be as near her as I can."[96] Allen had agreed to meet Carolyn Gordon in New York that fall, but he mentioned her in none of his letters. It was as if the affair had never taken place.

For two months that autumn, Allen lived with his mother in the Bancroft Hotel, on 19th Street in northwest Washington. The living arrangement—an unfortunate throwback to Allen's years with Nellie in Nashville and Louisville hotels—was apparently subsidized by Allen's brother Ben. No doubt to get away from Nellie, Allen began looking for a job. He devoted a great deal of his time and energy to applying for an instructorship at the nearby George Washington University, but he was convinced that "the hostility of certain Vanderbilt people"— most notably Edwin Mims—doomed his application.[97] When Allen failed, for unknown reasons, to secure the teaching post at George Washington, he broadened his contempt for Mims into a lifelong bias against anything remotely connected with the academic world. Professors, he decided, wrote "not for literature, but in order to get a better job."[98] His desire for a doctorate was gone forever.

By the end of October, Allen was miserable. Though he was making inroads as a reviewer for magazines like the *Nation* and the *Saturday Review*, his social life consisted of little more than occasional get-togethers with unknown local poets. But it was not just the "constant isolation among imbeciles"[99] and his mother's neurasthenia that contributed to his discontent. He was also "very impecunious" and found his dependence on Ben for living expenses humiliating.[100] Although he had heard from a friend in New York that a job awaited him—a position as an assistant editor for a small publishing house—his filial obligations discouraged him from accepting it.

But when the job was offered to him a second time, he decided to take it. By accepting the position in New York, Allen knew that he was breaking with his mother, perhaps forever. At first, he felt little guilt over his withdrawal from her and justified his departure by explaining to his friends that his "effectiveness" in Washington was "about over" anyway.[101] He even took for granted Ben's willingness to pay the expenses that would now allow her to live on her own. Years later, however, Allen admitted that his life would have turned out differently without Ben's generosity toward their parents, "I might have had to give up my career to add a few pennies," he explained to his brother. "I should have forfeited whatever prospects I had in the literary world without doing them any real good."[102]

While the break in 1924 ended the pattern of attachment and withdrawal that had governed Allen's relationship with his mother, for the rest of his life he would be troubled by his mixed feelings for her. Despite his guilt-ridden loyalty to her, he was never able to recover from his sickly childhood under her care. He would visit her from time to time during the next several years, but he apparently found even these fleeting interactions to be quite painful. She had a way of making him feel like a child even after he was a grown man. It was not long after he broke with her that he wrote one of his most powerful poems, *Death of Little Boys*, a poem whose effect on readers the critics have since debated—but which, for Tate himself, might have been another effort toward personal liberation.[103]

VII

When Allen finally moved to New York City in early November, he took pleasure in returning to the anonymity afforded by a city where "nobody, fortunately, is his brother's keeper."[104] Unlike large Southern cities, where Victorian morality was still everywhere apparent, in New York Allen discovered that "it isn't important whether you drink liquor or are a virgin." He stayed with Hart Crane, but only until he could find a small apartment in the Village. After settling into his new job at the Climax Publishing Company, Allen began exploring the city, not in the company of his friends, but by himself. He found something deeply satisfying in an enormous city that allowed a man time to himself. "One can be utterly alone," he explained, "—in some cheap Italian restaurant, dining alone for seventy cents, with a sense of intimacy with oneself that I have never felt before; one feels independent and, at the same time, humble."[105]

But Allen's withdrawal from people lasted only as long as it took him to recover from the emotional claustrophobia he suffered living with his mother in Washington. Before long, he had reentered the community of writers he met the previous summer and was "swamped in the maelstrom of literary N.Y." "I've seen at least 4,976½ persons since I got into New York a month ago," he reported.[106] Surrounded by all of these sympathetic artists and writers, his mood reversed. "It's great," he announced, "to get up at eight and feel so good you have to take calisthenics to calm yourself." He gained ten pounds, explaining, "There's nothing like being happy."[107]

Allen entered an even wider literary and social circle than the one he joined the previous summer. In the company of his new friends Crane, Cowley, Munson, and Cummings, he met other young writers of the day. In a young poet from Boston named Louise Bogan, a contributor of verse to the *New Republic*, he found "a sweet lady with star-eyes and hopeless literary preferences."[108] Later Allen would call her "the most accomplished woman poet" of her time.[109] He also took an immediate liking to William Slater Brown, a young writer who had been an ambulance driver during World War I. Suspected of being pro-German, Brown and Cummings had been imprisoned together overseas, and afterward Cummings had immortalized Brown as "Mr. B" in his novel *The Enormous Room*. After meeting Brown, Allen concluded, "There is no wittier, more charming, more learned person."[110] Allen also met Edmund Wilson, the brilliant but temperamental literary critic who had warned him away from T. S. Eliot in 1923. Allen was a bit intimidated by Wilson, who seemed both physically striking and intellectually threatening. When Allen went on his Saturday afternoon walks through Washington Square, he stole glances up at the tired brownstone where Wilson lived. Wilson, Allen remembered years later, was usually sitting "by the large window, typing busily or looking down through his pince-nez at the book open on his knees."[111] He was so absorbed in his work that he never responded when Allen waved hello.

Most of Allen's new friends seemed to like him immensely and especially appreciated his "wit, his critical spirit, and his individual poetic style."[112] He was invited to attend their parties, to join them on day trips to Connecticut to visit the Eugene O'Neills, or to come with them to Andover, New Jersey, to see Kenneth Burke, the brilliant young literary critic who helped Malcolm Cowley edit *Secession*. A typical afternoon in the city might consist of sitting in a Greenwich Village café or speakeasy. On Saturday evenings, the entire group would meet for dinner in the basement of John Squarcialupi's little Italian restaurant in the Village. "I think we were drawn together by three things," Tate said of his New York friends. "We were young, we were poor, and we were ambitious. That is, we thought that the older generation was pretty bad, and we were later going to replace them."[113]

Allen felt less kinship with Matthew Josephson, a sickly Brooklyn boy educated at Columbia University and recently back from Europe. Josephson, another of the Secessionist poets and a founding editor of the Modernist magazine *Broom*, had loitered among the Surrealists in Paris. He was "a thin, dark, intense-looking man, with a moustache and deep-set, thoughtful eyes."[114] Allen objected to Josephson's "humorless egotism" and to the way he designated himself leader of the small circle that included Allen, Burke, and Crane. Josephson was equally skeptical about Allen.[115] Years later, he remembered his first meeting with Allen, "a wispy, blond young man with an enormous cranium and diminutive and delicate features." Though Josephson was impressed by Allen's exhaustive knowledge of European literary movements, he was immediately struck by his discomfort with his Southern background. "He used to ridicule the pretensions of Southerners to culture," Josephson recalled, "holding that all they did was 'second rate'; and even tried to suppress his Southern accent." "At Vanderbilt University they used to call me the 'Yankee,' " he told Josephson proudly.[116] (Years later, Tate admitted, "Back in the Twenties, Southerners in New York almost had to pretend they weren't Southerners.")[117]

Nowhere was Allen's uneasiness with his Southern past more pronounced than in his ambivalent attitudes toward the *Fugitive*, which was almost defunct. He wanted the magazine to continue, but he also recognized that it "set out to introduce a group of new poets and, that done, it has no more to say."[118] As he built a reputation among the New York writers, it became easier for him to sever his ties with the Fugitives. Finally deciding never to return to Nashville, he asked the group to print the following statement with his notice of resignation: "Living in N.Y., he feels that his absence from Nashville keeps him from active participation in editorial policies and attitudes, and that the continuance of his name on our masthead implies an agreement with our policies which does not exist in his mind."[119] It was ironic that Allen was abandoning the magazine just as a number of major Northern periodicals had begun to canonize the *Fugitive* as an "extraordinary Southern magazine of verse."[120] But such recognition only reminded Allen of his disgust with the South for ignoring the Fugitives. He had little interest in affiliating himself with a region and a people who seemed not to care about him. When Davidson told him about this nationwide praise of the magazine, his cynical reply was, "Any of it from the South? I doubt it."[121]

As much as Allen continued to fight off his Southernness, he was equally resistant to becoming a New Yorker. Following his first meeting with the Modernists in New York, he had been surprised to discover that they were missing a few traits he had assumed all poetry groups held in common. These young writers, he discovered, were every bit as talented as those he had left behind in the South, and in many ways they appeared more worldly. Yet he noticed how little interest any of them had in the complicated philosophical and asthetic ideas that propelled discussion in the Fugitive meetings and that dominated his own thinking. And while he had discovered "a thousand groups in New York," he found that the New York poets he met cared little about the group ethos the Fugitives had used to their professional advantage.[122] Being around people who lacked the Southern sense of fraternity made Allen pause to consider his roots.

VIII

Allen's confusion over his regional identity was exacerbated by the reappearance in his life of Carolyn Gordon, who was—next to his own mother—the most unapologetically Southern woman he would ever know. Carolyn met up with him almost the moment he arrived in the city, but it was difficult for them to spend time together. She had landed a job as a feature writer for a newspaper syndicate, but was paid only $160 a month and was sharing an apartment with a woman she had known back in Tennessee. Allen's friends recognized that Carolyn was out of her element. "She wasn't 'one of us,' " Cowley later observed. " 'We' were mostly poets and intellectuals and men. Carolyn was a newspaper woman from Chattanooga."[123] Allen, who was still trying to impress these New Yorkers, in all probability felt awkward in a relationship with someone who, unlike himself, made absolutely no excuses about being Southern. When he and Carolyn had a falling out in late 1924, they stopped seeing one another. The relationship would have been over permanently if not for the fact that Carolyn was pregnant with Allen's child.

Even as Carolyn's condition became visible in early 1925, Allen refused to marry her. The reason for his refusal is not entirely clear, but it may have been a product of his cynicism about love. He was drawn to maternal women like Carolyn, yet when asked to make a commitment, he began to feel that he was suffocating—in fact, that he was experiencing some kind of emotional death. What was worse, for all of his compatibility with Carolyn, he was not in love with her. Their relationship had grown quickly and seemed to be based more on physical attraction than on mutual understanding. A poem of Allen's that appeared shortly after he met Carolyn was appropriately titled *Prothesis for Marriage* and offered, "It is a weariness you wed, / An impaired languor for a staggering bed: / The crazy pinnates of an autumn lust." It was only by extracting Carolyn's promise for a divorce after the birth of the child that Allen consented to marriage. They were wed in a bleak civil ceremony in New York City in mid-May 1925. Within a week, Tate was backdating the marriage to explain Carolyn's condition. He perhaps meant for Don Davidson to read between the lines when he wrote, "I have been busy telling my friends here how I was married to a Miss Carolyn Gordon on December 27th."[124]

Allen's views toward Carolyn began to change after they were married. First of all, the thought of becoming a father set his poetic juices aflow. "You shall discover all the reasons why a child is the best of poems," a friend told him. "Your son (for it will be a son) will be the pet of all the crowd."[125] The entire day Carolyn was in labor, Allen loitered around the hospital repeating poetry to himself until he "was ordered to depart as being ludicrously useless."[126] After the delivery, he was so excited that he was even willing to overlook the fact that the baby was not a boy. "It is a girl," he told Edmund Wilson. "I was slightly depressed for a moment, but now I am thoroughly convinced that only girls are worth having."[127] When Allen saw his daughter, whom he and Carolyn named Nancy Susan Tate, he was genuinely moved. "She has fine blue eyes," he wrote Davidson, "a perfect chin, and amazingly prehensile fingers. What more could one wish?"[128] Having a daughter even made Allen question his two neat categories for women. "She will not be a poet," he insisted of little Nancy, "she will be a society lady or a chorus-girl, and the choice will not be between extremes, the same qualities being requisite to both!" The baby not only brought Allen closer to Carolyn, but helped Carolyn to be accepted by his New York friends. Hart Crane agreed to be the godfather and Edmund Wilson arranged for the young couple to receive an emergency grant of $250 from a writer's relief fund; Wilson and his wife, Mary, even passed on some of their own baby furnishings. All of little Nancy's things, Allen reported proudly, came from "various literati whose children have outgrown them."[129]

Just as Allen's fatherhood was bringing him into a more permanent relationship with Carolyn, Laura Riding, who had recently divorced Louis Gottschalk, showed up in New York City. Soon Allen was again reading and criticizing Laura's poems, and promoting her work to the Fugitives. She became "a constant visitor to the Tates" and was seen around Greenwich Village helping with their new baby. Allen enjoyed Laura's company, but Carolyn, was understandably chilly toward this aggressive young woman, whom she found "very charming, if strenuous."[130] Before long, Carolyn picked up Hart Crane's nickname for Laura and began referring to her as "Laura Riding Roughshod." It was later rumored that Allen and Laura had an affair when she was in New York and that afterward Tate called her "All right from the neck down," a remark she termed a "clubroom pornographic reference."[131]

Whatever the nature of Tate's relationship with Laura Riding, her brief stay in Greenwich Village strengthened his marriage to Carolyn and cemented his growing dislike for New Yorkers. Riding was a native of Brooklyn who never quite understood his Southern side. Except for her brief stint in Louisville, Allen explained, "She never had any connection with the South."[132] He told Davidson that she "could never forgive me for the fact of most of my ancestors having been Virginians, while her people lived in an East Side tenement!"[133] Shortly after she left New York, Allen called her "the maddest woman I have ever met."[134]

IX

It was no accident that the mixture of love and hatred that Allen felt for all of the women in his life—Laura Riding, Carolyn Gordon, and his own mother—would also appear, albeit in a more diffuse fashion, in his reemerging views of the South. By 1925, he was devoting more and more time to reexamining the conflicted identity given to him by his parents. As a Southerner in New York he tried to embrace Modernist artistic values without renouncing his affiliation with the Fugitives. He could not easily reject the Fugitives' pride in the literary renaissance just beginning to flourish in the South. As a result, his career began to turn in on him; he had become a Modernist poet repressing his Southern identity. With two sets of friends, Modernist aesthetes and group-minded Southerners, he was, as many scholars have observed, "divided against himself."[135]

One event that caused Allen to question his attitudes toward the South was a disastrous meeting with H. L. Mencken, whose attacks against Southern culture continued to agitate many intellectuals from the region. For more than a year Allen had been promising Davidson to write a series of articles for the *Tennessean* with titles such as "What Is a Southern Poet?" "Function of Poetry Criticism in the South at the Present Time," and "Social Insignificance of the Arts in the South."[136] As these Menckenesque topics festered in his mind, he determined to publish a single essay on the South in the *American Mercury*. Since Mencken edited the magazine from New York, Allen arranged to meet him for drinks. The rendezvous was a disaster. As soon as Allen mentioned the article, Mencken grew somewhat condescending in tone and apparently warned him that he would have to write the piece in the sarcastic style typical of the *American Mercury*. Annoyed, Allen ended the evening abruptly and Mencken, by now somewhat inebriated, hailed a cab and went home.

From that evening onward, Allen was not a devotee of Mencken, but an enemy. "While he is doubtless a great man, and can kill my literary reputation with one vulgar blow." Allen concluded, "He is ultimately an ass." Mencken, he added mockingly, "is the flapper of Amer. Lit., i.e., he gives typical expression to female sophomores in Southern and Middle Western universities." It further enraged Allen that Mencken was attacking not only Southern writers but also the New York Modernists in his new circle of friends. The first issue of the *American Mercury* ran a vituperative satire of Cowley, Cummings, Crane, and others. Previously one of the journals Allen most respected, the magazine was now in his eyes "a two-ring circus of which the squeamish intelligence, which is often mine, grows extremely bored."[137] To Paul Green, the brilliant North Carolina playwright then editing the *Reviewer* in Chapel Hill, Allen posed a rhetorical question about Mencken: "Don't you think we should have had the Southern 'renascence' without him? And don't you think there are certain things he should wake up to himself? Literature, for instance."[138]

That summer Mencken acted as a principal in an event that further alienated Tate from him. In July, John T. Scopes, a high school teacher from Dayton, Tennessee, was brought to trial for teaching the theory of evolution in a biology class. Mencken, who not only helped plan Scopes's defense but covered the event for the *Baltimore Evening Sun*, used the trial as a forum for publicizing his indictment of the South. Since Clarence Darrow was defending Scopes and the aging evangelical Populist William Jennings Bryan was prosecuting him, tensions ran high throughout the nation. Allen's interest was piqued: he asked the editors of the *Nation* to send him down to Tennessee to cover the trial. Allen never made it to the "Monkey Trial," but the episode in Dayton added to his ambivalent feelings about the South.[139]

Throughout 1925 Allen continued to wrestle with the long essay on arts and letters in the South he had proposed to Mencken. Finally, in October, Allen's "Last Days of the Charming Lady" appeared in the *Nation*. In the essay, which foreshadowed most of the ideas he would articulate during the Nashville Agrarian movement in 1930, he attacked both the mindless industrialism and the "secular and vulgar" religious beliefs that emerged in the South after the Civil War. Although he bemoaned the "disintegration" of culture and the destruction of "the graces of living" that took place when the South, and particularly old Virginia, fell, he damned the Old South for its rampant anti-intellectualism.[140] But if he criticized the South, Allen was annoyed when, shortly afterward, "some son-of-[a]-bitch from the South" described him in print "as a 'somewhat Menckenesque literary crusader.' "[141] Distinguishing himself from Mencken, who in his view attacked Southerners without understanding them, Allen argued that he had the right to strike back against his own people when they interfered with his artistic development. As a result, Allen's criticisms resembled those of a child criticizing a parent.

Certainly there was a personal dimension to Allen's essay. Anyone who had ever known his mother would have had no trouble identifying the model for the "charming lady" in the essay. "The charming lady," Allen explained, "will most likely be where you would have her, under the lilacs, with magnolias, if it is spring (and it is sure to be), heavy on the air not far away. She will not fail, being what she is—the typical Charming Lady—to talk quietly about the age at once heroic and golden in the history of the States of the Secession. Her conversation will be deft and serious but not too serious, because it will be cast in a whimsicality of fortitude before the intimate rumor of raped magnificence: It is certain to be an elegy of the perished amenities of the Old South." The charming lady's grandfather, like Nellie Tate's, honored the traditional values of antebellum Virginia.

In effect, Allen had chosen for his allegorical figure of the Old South the kind of sentimental woman he had grown to dislike so much. The few people who read books in the Old South, he explained, were, like his own mother, devoted fans of a mawkish literary tradition that began with Walter Scott and ended in the "shallow" books of Thomas Nelson Page. Though Allen carefully avoided any explicit mention of slavery, he attributed the fear of ideas and the disdain for the intellect that governed literary tastes in the antebellum South to the region's doomed commitment to "the permanence of a special politico-economic order." To save the South from such sentimentalism would require a "sensitive person from the South"—a man such as himself.

The essay was Allen's first major attempt to encourage Southerners to take a hard look at themselves in order to change their self-destructive behavior. The South, he contended, had lost the ability "to look at itself critically." He reproved Southerners for having let "an outsider" like Mencken attack them "with much vehemence, considerable acumen, and little justice."[142] Of the handful of insiders looking at the South, even the most prominent—none other than Edwin Mims—misunderstood the region's history. Allen was deeply disturbed by the New South ideas about material progress that informed a series of essays Mims wrote in reply to Mencken. (When Mims's popular book *The Advancing South* appeared the following year, Allen dismissed the work as a "monument of vulgarity"—"probably the worst book ever written on any subject." The book was further proof to him that Mims had a "clubwoman's mind.")[143] Allen did not think any more highly of Mencken than he did of Mims, except for the fact that Mencken "is honest and Mims isn't: neither is intelligent."[144] In a single essay, Allen succeeded in putting down three people—his mother, Mims, and Mencken—who had at one time or another rejected him.

Yet just as Allen had always shown an abstract devotion to his mentors even as he turned against them, he was unable to reject the South. If he wanted the South to advance, he wanted the region to do so neither by the doctrines of material and industrial progress he ascribed to Mims nor by the cheap journalistic tactics he attributed to Mencken. Allen objected not to the liberalism espoused by these two men, but to their debasement of artistic standards and their anti-intellectualism. People like Mims and Mencken simply did not understand the Modern Southerners who began writing after World War I.[145]

X

Even before Allen arrived for his first day of work at the Climax Publishing Company in New York, he had decided that the job was destined to be "a rotten grind."[146] His salary was only thirty dollars a week, and the only consolation was that he would be working under someone he liked, Susan Jenkins, the woman he had accompanied to *All God's Chillun* the previous July. The company's chief venture was a magazine called *Telling Tales*, hotly in competition with another New York-based magazine called *Snappy Stories*. Both magazines, Tate explained, "were supposed to be filled with sex," but they were tame by later standards.[147] Contrary to his expectations, Allen found that the job responsibilities were hardly onerous; he was able to spend a good portion of his time working on his correspondence and taking three-hour lunch breaks. It was only after Susan Jenkins quit and Allen had assumed her post as managing editor that his responsibilities grew. But his promotion was short-lived. In November 1925, after trying to correct an error in one of the boss's memos, Allen was either fired or he quit.[148] He told his friends that his employer had attempted to make him do "extra work without extra pay."[149]

Allen, whose finances were even more strained after his marriage, was growing weary of the expense and grim urbanism of New York. The city, he concluded shortly after his arrival, "is all a cold winter for the tender Southerner."[150] Since coming to New York, he and Carolyn had been forced to live in a series of tiny apartments in Greenwich Village. (Carolyn's mother had been so horrified by their poverty in New York that autumn that she brought their baby back to Kentucky.)[151] When Susan Jenkins told them about Patterson, New York, the idyllic little community where she and and her fiancé Slater Brown were living together in an eighteenth-century farmhouse called Robber Rocks, Allen and Carolyn were understandably enchanted. The village, surrounded by rocky and wooded hills, sat close to Connecticut. Malcolm Cowley and his wife, Peggy, had settled in the same locale, and Allen thought he had found a writers' colony in the making. Since he was beginning to make a small income as a freelance writer and Carolyn had abandoned her job in order to work on a novel, the two of them decided to join their friends in the foothills of the Berkshires. But they could not afford their own place—"We couldn't buy an extra Woolworth dinner plate," Carolyn remarked wistfully as they surveyed one house in Patterson[152]—so they rented the downstairs of a house close to Robber Rocks. The landlady, Mrs. Addie Turner, who lived on the second floor, Allen remembered as "a New England farm woman, and extraordinarily stupid, but motherly and kind—just a 'character.' "[153]

That winter turned out to be one of the happiest periods in Allen's life. Though he and Carolyn were snowed in for most of the time and had to get around on skis and sleds, they felt as if they had been freed of responsibilities. Friends like Slater Brown noticed that the young parents "never mentioned the baby."[154] Instead, they entertained numerous literary visitors who, Allen explained, brought "the only good part of New York" to their doorstep.[155] They also took to the rustic life. "I can't believe I've ever been anything but a woodsman," Allen reported after his shotgun and leather boots arrived from the Sears, Roebuck catalog.[156] He was enormously content in his new routine: "I saw wood an hour and a half every day; get up and make the fires; write all morning (eight to twelve); have lunch; go hunting in the afternoon for partridge, pheasant, rabbits, squirrels, etc., or go skating on the lovely lake a mile away; come into dinner (or supper, in the country); smoke happily for half an hour; then read 18th century novelists (Richardson at present) until nine-thirty when I go to bed!"[157] Before long, Allen put on eleven pounds and was happier than ever. He looked back at his life in New York with disdain. "I was never made for the town," he concluded.[158]

Allen and Carolyn asked Hart Crane to come stay at their new homestead. Otto Kahn, a venture capitalist, had recently awarded Crane a large grant, and Crane was anxious to join the Tates in Patterson so he could work on *The Bridge*, his epic poem. Allen was thrilled to have Crane living in the house. Since becoming a correspondent of Crane's in 1922, he had developed a deep affection for him and signed letters to him with "love." From New York, he wrote everyone of Crane's brilliance and went to great lengths to help him to place his verse with various poetry editors. When Crane arrived in Patterson in December 1925, the two young poets took long walks together, and Allen told Davidson that Crane was "one of the finest men alive."[159] But Crane was also an emotionally needy young man whose mood swings, egotistical outbursts, and incipient alcoholism could be trying. Although he was soon hard at work on *The Bridge*, he seemed unable to write more than a few lines without emerging from his study to make Allen a sounding board. "There were times," Susan Jenkins remembered of Crane and his poem, "when his friends felt as though they were the anvil on which he was hammering it out. His fellow-poet Allen bore the brunt."[160] Allen grew increasingly perturbed as Crane began to interfere with his own work.

It was chiefly Crane's relationship with Carolyn, however, that led to the showdown he had with the Tates in April 1926. Hart seemed to be getting along splendidly with Carolyn, and he cheerfully joined in the preparations for a Christmas feast. But before long he was trying to make conversation with her when she was concentrating on her work. Carolyn responded with tact at first—and tried showing him subtle indifference. But when he persisted, she bolted her door shut. Hurt, Crane returned her behavior with a surliness of his own. He would eventually write to his family about Carolyn's "malicious nature" and of the "cankerous bile" of her "narrow, jealous mind."[161] "My poem," he later concluded, "was progressing so beautifully until Mrs. Tate took it into her head to be so destructive!"[162]

Allen, who was harboring his own resentments, shared Carolyn's anger toward Crane. Thinking mistakenly that Mrs. Turner and Hart were gossiping about him, he opened the door to his room and shouted (Crane recalled), "If you've got a criticism of my work to make, I'd appreciate it if you would speak to me about it first!" That evening, he and Carolyn both wrote to Crane, and the following morning Crane reported finding "a couple of the nastiest notes under my bedroom door that I ever hope to get from anyone."[163] Carolyn's letter to Crane did not mince words. "Any social life which we all might have enjoyed together," she wrote, "has been prevented by the feeling that we have to *protect ourselves from you.*" Allen, who called Crane egotistical, warned his friend, "Negativity is simply the term you apply to any force not directly sympathetic to your own personal aims; and these aims include, incidentally, your poetry as well as your merely moral situations." While Crane considered both letters to be "indiscriminate slanders," he offered his apologies[164]—but Allen and Carolyn agreed that their friend's days in Mrs. Turner's farmhouse had come to an end. "We had to put him out," Tate later wrote.[165]

Later that summer Tate made peace with Crane by writing the introduction to *White Buildings*, Crane's first volume of poetry.[166] But from the time of their argument in Patterson, Tate was extremely careful to separate his abiding commitment to Crane's career from his opinion of him as a man. "Before I ever saw him," Allen said of Crane a month after his suicide in 1932, "he had convinced himself—like many homosexuals—that I was one of the tribe, and after he discovered his error, he felt it, with the fantastic logic which such a malady often induces in people, as a kind of personal betrayal."[167]

XI

Even though Tate lived outside of New York, his reputation as a book reviewer and critic was growing so quickly that he found himself being pulled back toward the city. One day that winter, he had "hobbled down from Patterson on frostbitten toes" to meet Mark Van Doren, literary editor for the *Nation*.[168] Van Doren, an aspiring poet and an English professor at Columbia University, was charmed by Allen as he sat with him in Times Square talking about Wordsworth. And as a direct result of a similar friendship he cultivated with Edmund Wilson, Allen was made a regular contributor to the *New Republic*—"all but a member of the staff!" he announced gleefully.[169] In the meantime, he had also become a contributor to the *Saturday Review of Literature*, the *Guardian*, and the *Reviewer*. Overseas, his prose was welcomed into the *Calendar of Modern Letters* and into T. S. Eliot's prestigious *New Criterion*. Although Allen was writing little in the way of new poetry, his earnings as a writer of book reviews and magazine articles went from only a hundred dollars in 1925 to more than six hundred in 1926.[170]

Yet for all of his successes, Allen seemed dissatisfied. His creative impulses had weakened, and he craved the polemical and the controversial. When editors pared down his book reviews and essays, he admitted feeling as if he had been "emasculated."[171] "Writing for *The New Republic*," he told Malcolm Cowley, "is like having coition with a corpse; one masturbates in the presence of a dead image: the orgasm appears, but the initial erection is never complete."[172] He was frightened by the capriciousness of New York reviewers, by the ease with which they could inflate, and then deflate, a young writer's reputation. He never did much care for the *Saturday Review of Literature*, whose editor, Henry Seidel Canby, he decided was "a fool and dishonest."[173] Tate was so disillusioned by the *Dial* that he entertained the idea of starting up a Southern magazine with Davidson—a magazine that would allow neither journalists nor academicians to contribute and that would counteract what another Fugitive called "the dominance by New York of American letters and publishing."[174]

Some of Allen's brewing hatred for New York literary politics stemmed from his continuing inability, even after he had moved North, to interest a publisher in his volume of poems. Frustrated that his reputation as a freelance writer was beginning to overshadow his reputation as a poet, he observed, "I can't get my own poems published, but I write Introductions to other books!" Trading on his connections at the *New Republic*, he got a reading of his poems by Macmillan and Company. When the manuscript came back, he gave it to Edmund Wilson, who agreed to approach the Bonis again. When that plan

failed, Tate submitted four copies of his manuscript—simultaneously—to four more publishers, including Simon and Schuster and
the Viking Press. "After these," he vowed, "four more, four more, four
more, possibly until I include the Scandanavians."[175] It did not make
him feel any better when Eliot kept a few of his poems under consideration for months, only to return them with a brief but courteous letter
declining to print them in the *New Criterion*. The poetry, Eliot explained, "overreaches itself" and betrays "a certain stridency and over-
emphasis." "But," he added, "it is a poetry in whose future I am most
interested."[176] Allen was hurt but took the criticism in stride. Eliot,
he admitted after reading the letter, "put his finger precisely on my
defects."[177]

For the remainder of the summer of 1926, Allen was subdued. Even
in a spot as beautiful as Patterson, old problems were reappearing;
financial concerns, especially, loomed on the horizon. Carolyn's mother
returned with Nancy in July, and while the couple seemed united in
their renewed affection for their daughter, they had grown accustomed
to their freedom. "She and Allen, more than ever," Malcolm Cowley
observed at the time, "give the impression of babes in the wood, unable
to cope with the complexities of modern life. When the grocer refuses
to extend them further credit, Allen writes an article, then settles back
into inertia."[178] If Allen found something languid and romantic—something vaguely suggestive of an old Virginia farmer—about his life in
Patterson, he looked out of place in the village. Carolyn noted how
lackadaisical he seemed, especially when he was outside in the garden.
"I think," Carolyn wrote a friend, "Allen feels toward Nature as I do
toward mathematics—respectful indifference. He walks about the garden hailing each tomato and melon with amazement—and never sees
any connection between planting seeds and eating fruit." But, she concluded, Allen had "changed a lot in the last year. He's certainly a more
integrated personality."[179]

The problem was that Allen's intellectual and emotional tranquility
was superficial. Even as he began arguing for a "poetry that integrates
emotion with intellect"—for verse that allowed "the expression of a
whole mind"[180]—he must have known that these aesthetic theories
were at odds with his personality. In childhood, his intellectual life had
always been a response to the emotional strife in his family. Both his
creative ambition and his feelings for the South began as a reaction to
conflict, as an effort to please his parents and conquer his surroundings. But now that he was freed from his mother's presence and married

to Carolyn, he faced a dilemma. In order to remain artistically productive, he needed to feel that he was somehow in opposition to his environment. In Patterson, no one made him confront his regional identity; since he had no authority figures to criticize and no audience to impress, he had to choose neither the South nor the North. It was a peaceful existence, but an emotionally deadening one.

Chapter Five

God the Father and the South

In the autumn of 1926, Tate slowly began to emerge from the intellectual cocoon he had entered after moving North. The greater his separation from Orley and Nellie Tate, the greater his need to explore the Southern identity they had foisted on him in childhood. "I'm one of those people," he later observed, "who must stand a long way off before I can see what is under my nose."[1] Though he was still angry at Southern society for turning its back on its artists, he saw little point in continuing to attack other Southerners. He began wondering instead whether Northern values dating back to the Civil War era were responsible for the feelings of emotional fragmentation that were plaguing him—and whether those values had caused the disintegration of his own family. Although he had never been pious, he was beginning to feel not only a need for religion in some form, but also for a hero for the South.

I

One explanation for Tate's changing attitude toward the South was the difficulty of his life in the North. In October, he and Carolyn abandoned their rural retreat in Patterson. It would have been difficult to face the wintry Berkshire woods with an infant—not to mention the inconvenience of being cut off from New York City's literary culture for another year. Yet the moment the Tates returned to an urban setting, they were once again forced to endure the abject poverty they had known in the first year of their marriage. They arrived in the city penniless and had to accept a custodial position in a small brownstone home at 27 Bank Street in Greenwich Village. Their apartment consisted of two basement rooms and an alcove they used as a guest room. In exchange for a relatively small amount of janitorial work, which included minding the furnace and carrying out garbage, they paid no rent and received a stipend of fifty dollars a month. Since Tate's income from reviewing books for the *Nation* and the *New Republic* added little to the hundred or so dollars he received each month as a manuscript reader for Minton, Balch, and Company, he welcomed the new living arrangement. But friends like Hart Crane were appalled. "Think of it," he mused. "Allen a janitor!"[2]

Carolyn, who had been hard at work on her novel about "upper class" Southerners, was reduced to doing clerical work.[3] After a brief stint as a typist for the radical American Society for Cultural Relations with Russia, she landed a job as an assistant to the eminent British novelist Ford Madox Ford. By 1926, Ford had written a long series of novels—including *The Good Soldier*—and was enjoying unprecedented fame. He was also the powerful editor of the *transatlantic review*. Carolyn began by helping him type the manuscript of his latest novel, *The Last Post*. After working for a while in his tacky little room on West Sixteenth Street, she succeeded in convincing him to move into the apartment above Allen and her in the Village. Though Ford thought the way they lived "something terrible," he began eating his meals with the Tates and before long grew quite fond of both of them. He found Allen to be "such a nice fellow and a good poet" and Carolyn an "extraordinarily well educated" Southern belle.[4] He was already falling in love in with her. But she was undoubtedly distressed by Ford's personal habits. Clad in his underwear and perspiring heavily, the obese Englishman sat dictating his novel to her without a trace of self-consciousness.

Matthew Josephson, the Secessionist poet who had sensed the Tates' insecurities about New York, looked for a way to draw attention to their penury so that some philanthropist might come to their aid. Finally he came up with the idea of asking an editor at a New York newspaper to dispatch a reporter to Bank Street to write a feature story that could be titled something like "Poet-Janitor Composes Sonnets While Stoking Boiler." When the journalist arrived, however, Tate was not grateful but enraged. He used his frightening air of formality to dissuade him from writing a story. Although Josephson later dismissed the entire episode as "a Dadaist prank," Tate never forgave him. "I was a poet," he said proudly, "and I would not consent to let an accidental fact of my life be used to draw attention to the poetry."[5]

The Tates' poverty was so extreme that Allen's twenty-seventh birthday passed in November without celebration. He was depressed and dissatisfied with New York City. Yet it was in this state of mind—and to some degree because of it—that he conceived and wrote his most famous, and perhaps his finest, poem, *Ode to the Confederate Dead.*[6] By Christmas of 1926, he had completed a first draft of the poem, originally titled *ELEGY for the Confederate Dead.* The earliest version began:

> Row after row with strict impunity
> The headstones barter their names to the element,
> The wind whirrs without recollection;
> In the riven troughs broken leaves
> Pile up, of nature the casual sacrament
> Against the sinkage of death,
> While in uncertainty of their election,
> Of their business in the vast breath,
> They sought the rumor of mortality.

"Figure to yourself a man stopping at the gate of a Confederate graveyard on a late autumn afternoon," Tate explained many years later. "The leaves are falling; his first impressions bring him the 'rumor of mortality.' " But the poem, Tate added, was not simply about the modern Southerner's difficulty in coming to terms with his own traditions and bringing them back to life. It was, he said, " 'about' solipsism or Narcissism, or any other *ism* that denotes the failure of the human personality to function properly in nature and society." Although set in the South, the poem's larger theme was "the cut-off-ness of the modern 'intellectual man' from the world." Such a man, who was obviously Tate, was trapped between a need for religious faith and the reality of the "fragmentary cosmos" surrounding him.[7]

In an article Tate thought "the best" ever written about him, critic Lillian Feder observed that the *Ode*, rich in allusions to the ancients, must be interpreted within "the framework of the classical world." Tate's poetry, she observed, "speaks of the present only in relation to the past, and his view of the past is the epic view, heroic, exalted, the poet's past rather than the historian's."[8] For Tate, the *Ode* not only explored these complex views of the present but marked the beginning of the twelve-year period recognized by many scholars as the era in which he was absorbed by Southern culture and the history of his own family. Indeed, he told Davidson that writing the poem had been so wrenching for him personally that it dredged "up a whole stream of associations and memories, suppressed, at least on the emotional plane, since my childhood."[9] Years later he still believed he had let go emotionally "only once: in the Ode."[10] In the first published version of the poem, later to be revised considerably, he asked

> What shall we say who have knowledge
> Carried to the heart? Shall we take the act
> To the grave? Shall we, more hopeful, set up the grave
> In the house? The ravenous grave?
>
> Leave now
> The turnstile and the decomposing wall:
> The gentle serpent, green in the mulberry bush,
> Riots with his tongue through the hush—
> See him what he knows—he knows it all![11]

In time, the final line would become "Sentinel of the grave who counts us all!"[12]

Tate's Southern friends were mystified. Davidson admired the poem, but was annoyed at his friend for reducing the grand themes of Southern history to "personal poetry."[13] "Your *Elegy*," he observed, "is not for the Confederate dead, but for your own dead emotion." It did not appear to Davidson that the poem had much to do with Confederate soldiers. "Where, O Allen Tate," he asked, "are the dead? You have buried them completely out of sight—with them yourself and me."[14] Even Robert Penn Warren referred to the poem as "the Confederate morgue piece."[15] Yet after the Fugitives examined the *Ode* more closely, they abandoned their early reservations. They came to agree with subsequent critics who placed the *Ode* among the major poems of the century. It would be reprinted countless times.

Meanwhile, the instability of the Tates' life in New York seemed to grow each month. Perhaps in revolt against their janitorial labors, in the summer of 1927 they left Bank Street for Hudson Street and moved into a dilapidated eighteenth-century building that had served as an inn during the American Revolution and had once housed criminals. The walls were scarred by bullets and the plumbing was poor. It was no place for children, but since they had agreed to letting Carolyn's mother keep Nancy with her in Kentucky for half of each year, they were able to move in without too much concern.[16] They named their cold-water flat "the Cabinet of Doctor Caligari," after the terrifying avant-garde film directed by Robert Wien.

The Tates' social life was beginning to reflect their disaffection with the North. Their circle still included many New Yorkers, and recently they had become better friends with Louise Bogan, the poet; her new husband, Raymond Holden, who was an independently wealthy man of letters; Irita Van Doren, literary editor for the *Herald-Tribune*; and Léonie Adams, a young Barnard graduate Tate once called "a distinguished minor poet."[17] After moving to the Cabinet of Dr. Caligari, however, Tate and Gordon increasingly substituted Southerners living in New York for these Northern friends. They became close with the diminutive Katherine Anne Porter, an aspiring novelist born in Texas and raised in Louisiana, who moved into the apartment below them. They also opened their home to recent graduates of Vanderbilt who were trying to establish themselves as writers in the North. The Vanderbilt contingent included Red Warren, now a graduate student at Yale University; Stanley Johnson, a Fugitive poet who had written a novel satirizing the Vanderbilt English department; and Lyle Lanier, Tate's college friend who now taught psychology at New York University.

But it was Andrew Lytle, a lanky blond Vanderbilt graduate a few classes behind Allen, who became the favored houseguest. Although Lytle was then taking the Yale courses of George Pierce Baker, the famous New England drama professor, he was a devoted Southerner from Murfreesboro, Tennessee. John Ransom, Lytle's mentor at Vanderbilt, urged him to go meet Tate in New York. Lytle never forgot the day he knocked on Tate's door. He recalled being greeted by "a severe and courteous formality"—even Tate's eyes seemed like mirrors.[18] While Tate at first thought Lytle "a professional aristocrat" who could have been "a little stronger in the intellect," the two men quickly found themselves analyzing the Tennessee "Monkey Trial" of 1925. Both men were incensed at the Darwinians for launching a "Liberal attack" against the conservative Christian values prevalent in the South.[19] Years later, Lytle remembered Tate's early conviction that "the failure of belief" was a critical problem for all people.[20]

Carolyn complained that she was unable to get any work done around "these young poets from the South," who telephoned "as soon as they hit the Pennsylvania Station" and then stayed "anywhere from a week to a month."[21] But being around a group similar to the Fugitives helped renew Tate's appreciation for the distinctive characteristics of Southern life—such as its emphasis on socializing. Surrounded by these Southerners, he began to feel even more out of place in a Northern metropolis. He took to appending the same defiant note to everything he published: "Allen Tate (1899–) is a Southern poet and essayist living in New York."[22] Only half in jest, he signed his letters to Davidson, "Yours for States Rights and death to the Yankees."[23]

Tate's Northern friends and acquaintances noticed his withdrawal from them. "Formerly," Matthew Josephson observed, "he had been as a Yankee among Yankees; he used to assure me that most of the so-called aristocratic families in the South were descended from British indentured servants or deported criminals convicted of having stolen a sheep or something of that sort."[24] But now, as Carolyn worked on her novel about her family, the Meriwethers—whom Allen considered "the landed gentry of Southern Kentucky"[25]—he gave an increasing amount of thought to his own family history. He took new pride in the South's distinguished families and set about proving his mother's claim that he, too, was descended from aristocrats. Soon he was digging through genealogical records in the New York Public Library and writing letters to his relatives in an attempt to piece together the family history.

As Tate pored over his genealogy, he began feeling a deep need to cull from the history of his Southern ancestors some explanation for the nomadic, rootless lives he and his parents had come to lead. Soon he began theorizing that Union depredations during the war were to blame. "This quest of the past," he explained to Davidson, "is something we all share, but it is most acute in me—more so than in you, I suspect. You, for example, have never changed your scene; your sense of temporal and spatial continuity is probably more regular than mine; for since the Civil War, my family has scattered to the four winds, and no longer exists as a social unit."[26] He determined to take a trip to Virginia to search for lost relatives and family records.

Though his genealogical researches allowed him to distance himself somewhat from the Southern myths inculcated in him by his mother, he discovered that she had drawn the family tree with greater accuracy than he had imagined. He had always been fascinated by her maternal ancestors, the Bogans, but now he identified with them more closely than ever before. Just before moving back to New York City, he wrote a poem called *Obituary*, in memory of his grandmother Bogan, who lived through the Civil War into the twentieth century.[27] Next he made a kinship chart for his older brother Varnell that began with George Washington, wound its way through the Bogans, and culminated in the birth of the three Tate boys: Allen, Ben, and Varnell.[28] Speculating that the poet Louise Bogan was a cousin, he sent her a letter. "We are surely related," he wrote with excitement, "if you are descended from the Virginia family of your name. They lived in Spotsylvania, Shenandoah, and Fairfax Counties from the beginning of the 18th century, and intermarried with the other leading families of the section."[29] So fervent was his interest in the aristocracy of antebellum Virginia that he began to lie about his birthplace. Although he knew that he was born in Kentucky, on official documents he now said he was born in Fairfax County, Virginia.

Tate had difficulty fitting his father's side of the family into his schema of aristocratic Virginians. He knew his father's maternal ancestors were the Allens, who moved from Kentucky to Illinois, but he could trace the Tates, his father's paternal ancestors, only as far back as a James Johnston Tate born in Orange County, North Carolina, in 1821. At first, he concluded that his difficulties were simply the difficulties faced by all Southerners whose families were pulled apart by the Civil War. "Our past," he told Davidson, "is buried so deep that it is all but irrecoverable."[30] But the absence of records did not keep him from concluding, on skimpy evidence, that his father's side of the family was descended from "one of the oldest and finest Southern families."[31]

Tate was aching to talk about the South. He had recently met John Gould Fletcher, a wealthy Arkansan who had moved to Europe following study at Harvard. After underwriting the *Egoist* and trying to conform to the Imagist poetry movement, Fletcher rejected the company of Ezra Pound for Amy Lowell and was now back in the United States. Tate was pleased to encounter another Southerner wrestling with his Modernist identity. Although Fletcher was almost a generation older and a severe depressive, Tate had much in common with his new friend. Both may have sensed they shared controlling mothers and both men held strong, if contrary, theories about aesthetics. Most of all, however, the two poets shared a fascination with regionalism. Fresh from his initial encounter with Tate, Fletcher made the following diary entry: "The Southern spirit is national; The Northern is mystic."[32] He was keenly interested in writing for "the Southern symposium" Tate had begun mulling over.[33] "Our self-knowledge," Tate explained to him, "has been forced upon us at the point of bayonets that now rest in museums."[34]

Tate doubted whether "a typical citizen of the South" would comprehend, let alone agree with, his new theories about Southern culture.[35] Yet as angered as he was by what he called "the stupidity of our people," he now reserved his venom for "the Yankees who battered them into what they are."[36] His research into his family history had left him certain of one thing. "I've attacked the South for the last time," he resolved, "except in so far as it may be necessary to point out that the chief defect the Old South had was that in it was produced, through whatever cause, the New South."[37] Although Tate denied having had a "Southern reversion," he was beginning to talk like a neo-Confederate.[38]

II

In the very early months of 1927, the Bonis asked Tate to write a biography. Since he had come to believe that were few heroes for Southern intellectuals, and since he personally was searching for a historical figure embodying his new theories about the South, he was attracted to the idea of writing a biography. The problem was that the Bonis wanted him to write a life of Cotton Mather, the New England minister of the Colonial era. "I wish there were some Southern character that would yield himself to the kind of treatment modern biography seems obsessed with," Tate lamented. The problem was that "modern methods" of biography were of no use when it came to Southerners. They were not easy subjects for psychological biography because most of them were "either dull or brilliant, while the Colonial New Englanders were pathological" and therefore "pleasant to the contemporary taste."[39] But in April, Tate's problem was solved when Minton, Balch and Company offered him a contract to write a biography of the legendary Confederate general, Thomas J. ("Stonewall") Jackson. Tate was ecstatic and began his research immediately. The project turned out to be the first stage in his decade-long quest for a new Southern father.

Although Tate had been reading about the South for two years, he immediately dug into a stack of histories, memoirs, and military narratives of the Civil War. His mother had raised him to believe that the entire conflict had taken place in Virginia, among her ancestors exclusively, and though he took some pride in these stories, he was anxious to understand the war in its larger aspects. He started spending twelve hours a day reading, and before long admitted to having "become a perfect fanatic" about the war as well as "a formidable bore in conversation."[40] After realizing that he was more interested in the war than in Stonewall Jackson, he lobbied for Minton, Balch to title his book

Stonewall Jackson, A Narrative of the Civil War. But they insisted that it would be a financial disaster to publish the book without the word *biography* in the title.[41]

Tate conducted an equal share of his research outside of the library. Since he had never seen a battlefield, on the Fourth of July 1927 he and Carolyn set out on a two-week motor tour of the Shenandoah Valley. They wanted to visit relatives in Virginia, but the principal goal of the trip was to inspect some of the battlegrounds where Jackson had led troops. Stopping first in Gettysburg, Pennsylvania, where Tate's grandfather Bogan and two other relatives fought, Tate reconstructed the battle mentally as he roamed the battlefield. He was especially captivated by the indoor "cyclorama," an immense mural of the battle painted on the wall of a round room. ("The picture alone" was worth the trip, he concluded.)[42] At subsequent stops in Virginia, he tried to visualize the events his mother had described to him in childhood. In Woodstock, he encountered the widow to one of Stonewall Jackson's officers. The old woman, whose daughter published a newspaper founded by Major Bogan, regaled him with stories about "Old Jack" and showed him hair cut from Jackson's horse. Outside of Port Republic, Tate found a flattened minié ball in a dusty cornfield.[43] "At the old scenes blood speaks from the earth, in a forgotten tongue," he observed.[44]

Tate had agreed to complete the biography by January 1, 1928, and after returning to New York, he had no choice but to write hurriedly. By November, the first section of the book was ready for the typist. He spent most of the winter writing and revising, sometimes churning out as many as forty thousand words in ten days. By early March, he had finished all fourteen chapters of *Stonewall Jackson: The Good Soldier* (subtitled in honor of Ford Madox Ford) and the galleys were ready to be proofread. Yet he was disappointed with the finished product and dismissed it as his "little bread-and-butter opus."[45] "I wish I could get out an injunction against the reading of it by my friends," he told Mark Van Doren, "— and an injunction to compel the General Public to read it."[46]

To construct his narrative, Tate relied on published sources almost exclusively. His major sources of information about Jackson included Roy Bird Cook's *The Family and Early Life of Stonewall Jackson* (1924); G. F. R. Henderson's massive two-volume study, *Stonewall Jackson and the American Civil War* (1898); and Mary Anna Jackson's worshipful account of her husband's career, *Memoirs of Stonewall*

Jackson (1891).[47] For background information on the war, he mined detail from the popular four-volume work *Battles and Leaders of the Civil War* (1884).[48] Because he was self-conscious about his heavy reliance on these accounts, he chose not to annotate the biography. In his bibliographical essay, he explained that in order to keep from disrupting the story with "references to authorities," he had "almost invariably paraphrased" quotations from the work of other scholars.[49] (After the book was published, one annoyed critic announced that "Mr. Tate's failure to cite sources clearly" made the book ". . . useless for reference purposes.")[50]

Since many of the sources Tate used contained exhaustive accounts of Stonewall Jackson's campaigns, the biography he produced was almost a work of military history. He assumed too great a familiarity on the part of the reader with the geography of the South and with the theaters and battlegrounds of the war. Complicating matters even further, he weighed down the narrative with statistics on troops and supplies, with blow-by-blow accounts of battles, and with the names of a variety of military figures. He did his best to transform some of this technical material into literature. "I am putting powder, blood, dirt, stink and sweat in the story," he told Davidson, "and I am going to try to give it the unity of a novel by passing it through Jackson's own mind." Though he barely needed to supplement his already morbid imagination, he asked Davidson, who was the veteran of a hardening tour of duty in France during World War I, to help him by describing "the atmosphere and feeling of a battle."[51] Instead of depicting the painful experiences of individual soldiers, however, Tate dashed off war scenes in which ruined artillery, horse carcasses, and corpses blanketed the battlefield.[52] As "the sweet odor of scorched flesh stuck in the men's nostrils," surgeons worked amputating limbs of fallen Confederate soldiers. Great "piles of arms and legs" rose four or five feet in height while "groans and shrieks still rose from the field."[53]

Before Tate began writing, he knew what he wanted to say about Stonewall Jackson: "had Jackson been in chief command" of the Confederate armies from the start of the Civil War and not been accidentally shot by his own men in 1863, the Confederate states would not only have won the Battle of Gettysburg, but the war itself. "We should now be a separate nation," he told Davidson.[54] Tate would tell the story of a brilliant general deterred from his mission by the stupidity of Jefferson Davis, president of the Confederacy. Reined in by Davis, Jackson was never allowed to realize his "one fixed idea: the success of the Southern cause."[55]

Tate's vindication of General Jackson gave him an opportunity to vent his hostility toward Northerners who wrote Southern history. While most historians of Tate's day spoke in terms of a Southern "rebellion," Tate described a "revolutionary party growing up in the North" that was bent on destroying "democracy and civil liberties in America by freeing the slaves."[56] By substituting Southern names for battles—Sharpsburg for Antietam, Manassas for Bull Run—and by calling the Southerners "Constitutionalists" and the Northerners "Rebels," he managed to tell the story of the war from the geographical and the political perspective of a Southerner living in the 1860s.[57] He was barely able to contain the glee he felt in being able to reverse the Northern point of view that informed most histories of the Civil War. "I'm doing a stirring partizan account," he told Davidson proudly. "The stars and bars forever!"[58]

Perhaps because Stonewall Jackson's life story was that of a man who overcame trying family circumstances to become a major figure in Southern history, Tate showed remarkable empathy with his subject.[59] Descended from Scotch-Irish emigrants, born and raised in Virginia, the young Jackson portrayed by Tate was a cryptic and serious-minded young man who spent hours reading history books, possessed intense powers of concentration, and had little interest in material wealth. He had trouble with mathematics, suffered from nervous indigestion, and rarely revealed his emotions publicly. He was raised by his mother, whom he praised for being "mindful" of him when he was "a helpless, fatherless child."[60] Like Tate, he was distraught because his "relatives were scattered." He was, Tate wrote, "almost painfully aware of his social predicament."[61] Although Jackson had come from respectable ancestors, his "illusion made it out that the whole family had gone into a decline: it thus became his self-imposed duty to restore it."[62] It was noteworthy that Tate sent copies of the completed biography to more than two dozen relatives.

Tate's portrayal of Jackson suggested that he was especially preoccupied by the relationship of men to their fathers. Though both Tate's father and Stonewall Jackson were orphaned as children, Jackson turned out differently. A childhood without parents helped transform Tate's father into the worst sort of parent, but a similar experience made Jackson into a devout Christian, a faithful husband, and a loving father. Tate depicted him as a compassionate Southerner who bowed respectfully to elderly blacks who greeted him on the street, founded a church school for slaves, and purchased those who were mistreated by their masters. Though uncertain how it might be achieved, he believed in the abolition of slavery. Jackson was a far cry from the irreligious Orley Tate, whom Allen frequently portrayed as a Simon Legree in his relationship with blacks.

Tate was bewildered by Stonewall Jackson's willingness to forgive his father, who was—like Orley Tate—a spendthrift who played cards, who borrowed money from his friends, and who squandered his land and fortune, leaving his wife with nothing. Although Tate had long ago stopped using his full name, John Orley Allen Tate, he praised Stonewall Jackson, also named for his father, for having shown the courage to sign an official document "Thomas *Jonathan* Jackson." Jackson "was evidently willing to take the name of an unsuccessful parent and vindicate it."[63] Perhaps inspired by Jackson's charitableness, Tate dedicated the biography to his father and his mother. He also drew a series of battle maps for reproduction in the book and boldly signed them "J.O.A.T."

The book received mixed reviews in Northern periodicals. While Herschel Brickell of the *North American Review* called it "eminently fair and readable," Daniel Robert Maué of the *Outlook* called it "a book for Virginians" written with "an abruptness that is disconcerting."[64] An anonymous reviewer in the *Bookman* sarcastically announced that while the book fell "somewhere between the proper provinces of the character study and pure history," it was "valuable as neither." Its narrative power, the reviewer continued, was marred by "breathless, choppy" prose.[65] By contrast, in a review for the *Nation*, Tate's friend Raymond Holden singled out the book for being "well written," and A. W. Vernon of the *New Republic* praised the book's "lapidary style."[66]

Yet Tate's thesis about Jackson was well received by conservative Southern intellectuals. William E. Dodd, the prominent historian at University of Chicago, wrote a major review of the biography for the front page of the book section of the *New York Herald-Tribune*. Though critical of Tate's vindication of Jackson at the expense of Jefferson Davis, Dodd concluded, "It's a good book Mr. Tate has given us, one of the very best of new biographies."[67] Almost immediately, he wrote Tate that he had "the touch of a literary master and also a sense of historical values," traits that ensured him "a future of great influence and power."[68] When Dodd asked him to write a biography of another Southern figure for a new series, Tate was "flabbergasted" by the attention of this "hardboiled professional historian."[69]

Only Donald Davidson, who remained closer to Tate than anyone else, recognized that the biography reflected Tate's growing need for a system of thought more emotionally satisfying than Modernism. "One would think him more concerned about the French symbolists, say, than the battle of Chancellorsville," he wrote of Tate in a review for the *Nashville Tennessean*. But Davidson saw that Modernism had failed to provide Tate with a way to combat the spiritual ills he was suffering in the North. "Not whim, but inner necessity and conviction brought Allen Tate to Stonewall Jackson," he explained. Tate was a "troubled modern" who had turned "with relief to a figure that wears no uncertainty of the heroic." At last, he had found "a cause to cleave to."[70] What attracted Tate to Jackson was the way the general used his religious beliefs to stand his ground against encroaching Northern values. Although Tate conceded that Jackson's incessant praying, Bible reading, and deference to ministers were the products of "a diseased mind," he found it remarkable that the general had maintained his piety in the midst of defeat and adversity—something impossible for the modern Southerner.[71] Tate said that the Jackson biography originated in his *Ode to the Confederate Dead*, but at least one later critic of the book would observe that in writing about Jackson, Tate had begun to disassociate himself from the twentieth-century Southerner frozen before the entrance to the Confederate cemetery and unable to understand the values and traditions of his ancestors. Tate wanted Jackson, who expressed his religious faith through a life of action, to inspire Southerners facing the dilemma he described in the *Ode*.[72] As Davidson concluded, Tate was "the first Southern biographer of the younger generation who has had the courage to worship an old hero and to remember his fathers."[73]

III

Tate's life of Stonewall Jackson sold well. Before the book even made it to the shelves of bookstores, it had earned back its advance. More than half of the five thousand copies printed in the first run were exhausted in just a few weeks. To capitalize on this success, Earle Balch urged Tate to begin another biography immediately. Since Tate had a large quantity of unused notes on Jefferson Davis, he decided to write "a psychological narrative" of the Confederate president's career between 1860 and his arrest by the Union Army in 1865. "If I don't do it now," he told his friends, "the war fever will cool, and I never will."[74] He began the book in March 1928 and planned to have it finished by the following September.

The enthusiasm Tate had shown when researching the life of Jackson reached even greater heights as he began work on the Davis biography. In early June, the Tates and three-year-old Nancy, back from Kentucky permanently, departed on another Southern tour, this one more elaborately planned than the last. They brought along Katherine Anne Porter, who needed a ride to Pennsylvania, and Andrew Lytle, who was just starting a biography of Nathan Bedford Forrest, the Confederate general. Tate knew that Lytle, whose biography would also be published by Minton, Balch, was the one friend who would enjoy touring battlefields as much as he would. They left town in a rattletrap 1921 Ford Tate grew to love and hate both.[75]

Tate insisted on doing most of the driving in the thirty-five-hundred-mile trip. Carefully mapping out their route, he decided they would drive west from New York City through Pennsylvania, where they would stop first at Gettysburg, followed by the Virginias, Tennessee, Kentucky, the Lytle home in Huntsville, Alabama, and finally back to New York through Virginia. Oil fumes permeated the Ford, and many of the back roads they took were unpaved. But Tate was hypnotized by his mission. When he was not the driver, Lytle recollected, an "excruciating look of pain" came over his face. Every seventy-five miles or so, they stopped to set up camp, pitching their modest tent on the land of a farmer willing to let them eat vegetables growing in his fields. Making periodic trips into town, they found copies of *Stonewall Jackson* on display in local bookshops.[76]

Many years later, Lytle explained the real meaning of the trip to the two men—it was, he explained, a "quest for our common historic past." Although Tate evinced a military historian's obsession with Antietam, seeing the battlefield also helped him and Lytle to understand the intellectual fragmentation they felt as displaced Southerners. When Tate walked up to a fence surrounding the field where the Union Army made its famous charge, he stood hushed, as if he were in a church. The "enemy" died here by the thousand, he whispered to Lytle. So happy were her companions that Carolyn could not help bursting into laughter. Yet Tate was genuinely moved.[77]

Tate found it virtually impossible to do much substantive work during the trip. After a brief rendezvous in Harper's Ferry with Red Warren, who was researching a biography of the radical abolitionist John Brown and who shared Tate's new interest in Southern history, the group left for Alabama. By the time they made it to the Lytles' in late July, they were exhausted. As they pulled in the drive, Nancy, by now schooled in military history, asked, "Is this Uncle Andrew's camp?"[78]

Then, not long after their arrival, Tate noticed that the Lytles had "started drinking whiskey after breakfast."[79] Fearing that he would get no work done is such an atmosphere, he cut short their stay in Alabama and drove the family to Richmond so he could work in the state library each morning. He tried writing in the tiny tent at night, but found that he was "surrounded by millions of flies and assailed from the rear by a nation of ants."[80] When at last he made it back to New York City, he admitted, "I feel like the Confederate States—still alive but not the man I was."[81]

IV

As Tate began forming stronger loyalties to the South, he reconsidered the Modernism in his poetry. His Modernist technique had helped him to sell a substantial number of poems to little magazines and poetry journals, but it had not attracted a publisher for his volume of verse, and now it seemed as if this technique was also interfering with his interest in history. Although he persisted in criticizing Southern poets who injected "magnolias, niggers, and cotton fields" into their verse in order to please "a foreign audience,"[82] the poetry he began writing in the late 1920s suggested that he was less afraid of being identified as a Southern poet.

Ever since first reading the works of Eliot in 1922, Tate viewed poetry as an ahistorical enterprise; poems were carefully constructed art objects. In early 1927, for instance, he finally published his first extended essay on poetic theory, "Poetry and the Absolute," in the *Sewanee Review*, where he argued that "all great poets are absolutists" because "there is nothing beyond their poetry." It was, he elaborated, "the absolute intensification of perception beyond its moral situation" that explained "the unique quality of poetry." By concentrating on the composition of a poem rather than on its historical or moral dimensions, the poet demonstrated the "absolute" or objective value of poetry.[83] The essay met with varying degrees of approval. While Phelps Putnam, a young poet born in Boston and educated at Yale University, called it "the best stuff on poetry" he had read "since Jesus was a little boy," William S. Knickerbocker, editor of the *Sewanee Review*, saw the essay as confirmation that Tate wrote poems with no historical message simply to prove the validity of his Modernist theories.[84]

Charges such as those made by Knickerbocker motivated Tate to reconsider Eliot's emphasis on the form rather than the content of poetry. "I possess considerable power as a poet," he told another young poet named Yvor Winters, "but I have never exhibited it completely." He explained that this failure was due to his "lack of something to write *about*."[85] Tate had long believed with Eliot that there were no longer any major themes to engage modern poets. But then Tate developed an interest in Southern history. Years later, Matthew Josephson, still fascinated by Tate's regional conversion, explained: "To be a good poet, Allen now believed, one must put down his roots in the ideas of his ancestors."[86] Tate went back to Eliot's *The Sacred Wood* for justification of his new interest in the traditions of the South. To his immense pleasure, he found a passage in which Eliot commented, "Tradition cannot be inherited, and if you want it you must obtain it by great labour. It involves . . . a perception, not only of the pastness of the past, but of its presence."[87] Echoing these words, Tate now said that his own poetry aimed "to see the present from the past, yet remain immersed in the present and committed to it."[88] If this was an intellectual cartwheel of sorts, the fact that Tate resorted to it suggests the seriousness of the dilemma he faced: he was a Southerner conscious of his region's history, but trained in the theories of Modernist movements of New York and Europe.[89]

If Modernism had shown Tate a way to avoid his emotions and insecurities, a poetry more Southern in theme promised him an opportunity for personal catharsis. "You know," he told Davidson, "my poetical theory used to keep me from approaching 'life' directly."[90] It had always seemed easier to him to deny any loyalties to the South. "From my eighteenth to my twenty-fifth year," he explained, "I tried to suppress those views, or emotions." He finally gave in to them because he was no longer able to "pretend to believe in any others."[91]

After Tate wrote the first draft of his *Ode to the Confederate Dead*, he began devoting more time to a long poem he had begun writing in Patterson, New York. He intended the poem, titled *Causerie*, to demonstrate "that climaxes in experience are dead, killed off by the thing variously called science, naturalism, industrialism, cosmopolitanism"—forces of modernization he associated with the North.[92] Like the *Ode*, *Causerie* suggested an emerging theme in Tate's poetry: that of the modern Southerner in a hostile, industrializing society struggling with Faith. After returning to New York City, Tate decided to expand *Causerie* into a ten-part poem "dealing with the cultural situation of an American in the industrial age."[93] In both the first part of the poem, shortly to be renamed "Retroduction to American History," and in the second, which appeared in the avant-garde magazine *transition*, he tried to adhere to Eliot's philosophy of using the past as a frame for discussing the present. He described "an age of abstract experience," where men like John Ransom, Red Warren, and Jesse Wills—all of whom he mentioned by name—were faltering because they "lacked doctrine."[94] He planned additional sections of the poem that would mention other Modernists by name and place them side by side with Southerners of earlier centuries—men like Thomas Jefferson and Jefferson Davis. Though modern in technique, the poem would be populated by Southerners.

By 1928, Tate had also begun reevaluating the poetry written by the Fugitives. For years, he had been arguing that the Fugitives should first be identified as craftsmen, and then, and only then, as Southerners. He had especially objected to the term "Southern Poetry."[95] But after moving to New York, he became defensive about the group's Southern origins. After trying for about two years to interest a publisher in an anthology of their poetry, he decided that it could never be published without an introduction by a prominent New York literary critic. "It means nothing whatever," he commented at his lowest point in the negotiations, "to the back-slapping, log-rolling fraternities here that a group of good poets wrote out their hearts in Nashville, Tenn."[96] After being turned down by five publishers, however, the book was finally accepted by Harcourt, Brace in late 1927.

Critical reactions to *Fugitives: An Anthology of Verse*[97] reminded Tate that talented Southern poets were a novelty to Northerners. Critics cited the Fugitive anthology not as an example of the Modernist movement in America, but as evidence that H. L. Mencken had been wrong about the South. (Edmund Wilson, for instance, greeted the anthology as testimonial to "the new awakening of creative activity in the South.")[98] Tate took another look at the Nashville movement. "Fugitive poetry," he explained in a new essay, "turned out to be profoundly sectional in that it was supported by the prejudices, feelings, values, into which the poets were born." If poets across the country wanted to avoid "the all-destroying abstraction, America," as the Fugitives had, they would have to be "brought back to contact with the local cultures from which, in each instance, they originally sprang." He tried to explain how the Fugitives' poetry had been Southern even though it infrequently mentioned the South. Their Southernness, he explained, was reflected not in the subject matter of their verse, but in their emphasis on poetic technique. Their carefully crafted poems were an expression of a peculiarly Southern preoccupation with "form and style."[99]

Tate underwent a similar conversion during his exhausting efforts to publish his first book of poetry, titled *Mr. Pope and Other Poems*, which finally came out in the summer of 1928.[100] Publication of the poems had not come easily. After almost five years of failed efforts to interest American publishers in a volume they found too obscure, he had turned to European firms. But when Ford Madox Ford sent the poems to a British publisher, they fared no better. Shortly afterward, T. S. Eliot asked Faber and Gwyer to publish the volume—even though he believed his American protégé was "a little tied up" in his "own tail."[101] Though the firm agreed to bring out the poems, they wanted help with the cost of publication, and Tate refused.

It may have been these rejections that motivated Tate to alter the manuscript he had assembled in 1923, for the collection that Minton, Balch published in 1928 now contained the *Ode to the Confederate Dead*, *Causerie*, and other poems that emerged as Tate's childhood memories fought with his Modernist aesthetics. Although angered when a reviewer of for the *New York Tribune* identified him as Stonewall Jackson's biographer instead of as a poet,[102] Tate had to admit that without the biography, he never would have been able to publish the poetry in the United States. Minton, Balch and Company agreed to bring out the poems only after the Jackson biography had sold enough copies to offset the financial loss of publishing the verse. "Old Jack did it all," he told Davidson.[103]

Reviews of *Mr. Pope and Other Poems* confirmed that Tate's reputation as a Southerner was of greater interest to critics than his Modernism. Although the book was not widely reviewed and seven years later had sold only 330 copies,[104] those critics who did review it recognized a brilliant, if troubled, poet still under the hold of Modernist ideas but captivated by Southern themes. Morton Zabel, soon to assume the editorship of *Poetry Magazine*, criticized Tate's "tortured syllogistic design" and his "deliberate obscurity," but hailed the "beautiful solemnity" of the *Ode to the Confederate Dead*.[105] Similarly, John Gould Fletcher condemned the "thwarted obscurity" and "portentous incoherence" of Tate's modernism, but praised him as a "considerable poet" from the "insurgent South" who was carrying out an "agonized search for absolute values."

Fletcher saw what Tate himself had been reluctant to admit; that he was best when he deserted Eliot to write poetry about the historical imagination of modern Southerners. "Whenever he deliberately narrows his range of knowledge to that of the past alone," Fletcher elaborated, "as in the impressive Ode to the Confederate Dead, he is a major poet."[106] A year later, the Poetry Society of South Carolina awarded Tate the Caroline Sinkler Prize for the best poetry book to have been published by a Southerner in the previous year. Although Tate still viewed himself as a Modernist poet criticizing the modernization of America, he had learned a valuable lesson. Shortly after the book appeared, he concluded, "The good in all poetry has a provincial origin, no matter how much it may be disguised. The contemporary menace to poetry lies in the complex causes that force us into an exile from which we can't return."[107]

V

Before getting entangled with his biography of Jefferson Davis in 1928, Tate tried seizing an opportunity to complete his ten-part poem about the industrial age. He had heard about grants being offered by the Guggenheim Foundation to writers interested in spending a year abroad and decided to apply for one—although he evidently knew in advance that Ford Madox Ford was going to get the "sinecure" for him.[108] The application Tate submitted to Henry Allen Moe, director of the foundation, was no less impressive for being pro forma. Stressing his affiliation with the *Fugitive*, which he now considered "one of the most important literary forces in recent years," Tate called himself a self-educated freelance writer who had "never been employed by an institution." Writing in the third person, he added: "He would abhor the reputation of a specialist: it is his wish to be considered a man of letters."[109] Tate's references suggested that he was well on the way to achieving his goal: besides Ford and John Crowe Ransom, his supporters included Henry Seidel Canby, editor of the *Saturday Review*; Mark Van Doren, literary editor of the *Nation*; Edmund Wilson, at the *New Republic*; and John Gould Fletcher.

But Tate's year in Europe went awry shortly after he set sail on September 29, 1928. Surrounded by a "mist of alcohol" and followed by his wife and their three-year-old daughter, he made his way to the gangplank at the pier in Hoboken, New Jersey. Toting the memoirs of Jefferson Davis, *The Rise and Fall of the Confederate Government*, and a walking stick once owned by his grandfather, he was in the highest of spirits.[110] Once the ship left port, Tate's mood grew even better. He was surprised not to feel seasick. It was not until the ship encountered one of the largest storms ever recorded in the Atlantic Ocean that he began to worry. He looked out the portal in amazement as "waves like mountains" crashed over the ship's stern and onto the deck. Winds of ninety miles per hour whipped around the boat.[111] Fearing the worst, he stayed dressed for three days straight.

The Tates found that London did not satisfy their Southern tastes. Shortly after they landed, they began visiting tourist spots like Westminster Abbey but quickly grew bored and homesick. They left for Oxford in order to be close to its libraries, and ended up liking the community so much that they moved into a house on Hilltop Road big enough for the two of them, their daughter, and their friend Léonie Adams, who had become their traveling companion. Each day, Tate rode his bicycle between the house and the library, but he found it difficult to work on the long poem he had promised the Guggenheim Foundation.[112] Instead, he wrote an article titled "American Poetry since 1920" and revised a draft of his famous essay on Emily Dickinson.[113] (He told Malcolm Cowley that the Dickinson essay would refute critics who argued that she "would have been better off if she had indulged occasionally in sexual intercourse.")[114] He also spent a good portion of his time visiting with Red Warren, who had won a Rhodes Scholarship and was in residence at Oxford finishing his biography of John Brown. But all of these diversions came to an end in November, when Tate came down with a terrible case of the flu. To make matters worse, he had already spent much more money than expected and had no choice but to petition the Guggenheim Foundation for special permission to write a few book reviews—work that would only lead him farther from the project he had planned.

In the meantime, he discovered that his new Southern allegiances prevented him from feeling comfortable among the British Modernists he had wanted to know since the early 1920s. One day, he met Herbert Read, a shy literary critic from Yorkshire, and pronounced him "the best mind in England." Read brought Tate to a pub in London where the writers and editors of the *Criterion* gathered each week for lunch. At last Tate was introduced to T. S. Eliot, who focused all of his attention on him and began politely asking his opinion on a variety of subjects. Although Tate liked Eliot, he was somewhat put off by his affected British accent and found his reticence about personal matters both intimidating and baffling. He wrote Donald Davidson that Eliot was a "really a nice man," but that he was "a Sphinx." Instead of looking like an exotic Modernist, he resembled "a New England Divine."[115] Many years later, Tate explained, "The difference of age seemed insuperable; he was forty years old and had published a small, but formidable, body of work while I, a provincial young man from the South, had published one small volume of verses."[116] Herbert Read seemed slightly less alien to Tate. "I felt closer to rural Yorkshire and to Herbert's grandmother Jane Tate," he explained, than to Eliot's Bostonian demeanor and New England relatives.[117]

Tate's Southernness made him feel equally self-conscious among other prominent writers living in Britain. He was early on invited to a party in the apartment of Harold Monro, the bohemian English critic and poet who edited the influential magazine *Poetry Review*. Monro also operated the famous Poetry Bookshop on Great Russell Street, where young writers and critics met to discuss literature. Tate, who was unfamiliar with social customs in England, took it for granted that Carolyn was invited to the party, which was to be held in Monro's apartment above the bookstore. Yet when the young couple arrived at the flat a little after the scheduled time, they discovered only men in the room and were greeted with "dense silence."[118] Mercifully, F. S. Flint, one of England's early practitioners of free verse, walked to the end of the room to engage them in conversation. Then Monro himself came toward them in the company of a stout man with steel-colored hair, whom he presented as Robert Frost. Even in 1928, Frost's fame was so great that Tate, who already felt uncomfortable, was stupefied. Seeing Tate's discomfort, Frost turned to the group and said, "Tate's vowels are different from mine. Just listen: 'The murmurous haunt of flies on summer eves.' "[119] He asked Tate to repeat the phrase and when the assembled Englishmen perceived no difference, he told them that the "insensitive English ear" was not capable of distinguishing his own New England vowels from Tate's Southern accent.[120] Though Frost was trying to be friendly, Tate "disliked him instinctively."[121]

Toward the end of November, the Tates decided to cut short their stay in England. Though both Carolyn and Léonie were working efficiently at Oxford, Allen suffered from a wracking cough, and he was unable to work. He had planned to coedit a scholarly edition of the poems of John Skelton with Red Warren, but Warren was distracted by his own work. Overcome by feelings of gloom, Allen and Carolyn moved to Paris with Nancy and Léonie. After spending three months in a two-room pension at the Hotel de Fleurus, they relocated to Ford Madox Ford's flat at 32 rue de Vaugirard, just a few minutes walk from the hotel. Ford had gone to New York City for the winter and spring and left the apartment to them in exchange for Carolyn's help typing a five-hundred-page manuscript. The move eased their financial predicament, but the new quarters were too small. Carolyn and Allen slept in the living room on a divan, Nancy on a smaller bed across the room, and Léonie in a tiny closet by the door.

Tate was happy enough at first in Paris. Not fluent in French, and not particularly eager to meet any Parisians, he passed the hours in cafés, frittering away his stipend money on lemon bitters and tinkering with his long poem. Soon he discovered that every time he picked up the manuscript of *Causerie*, he was unable to understand what he had already written. To make matters worse, the Jefferson Davis biography was largely unwritten and the manuscript lay untouched since the previous summer. Paralyzed by the vast quantity of work that lay before him, Tate began wiling away his time drinking. "If I stuck a pin in my leg," he wrote to Mark Van Doren, "alcohol would spurt, with the unerring purpose of lemon juice, into Nancy's eye."[122] By February of 1929, Carolyn, Léonie, Nancy, and Allen had again come down with the flu, and while they were able to take turns nursing one another, illness continued to debilitate them for the duration of their stay in Paris. As they spent more and more money on visits to the doctor and prescriptions, their finances began to collapse. There was nothing to do but petition the Guggenheim Foundation for a six-month extension of the fellowship—the only plan that seemed to offer the possibility of salvaging their year abroad.

In the meantime, Carolyn was unable to get any work done. Her mother had died in January, Allen had been unable to interest the editor of the *Virginia Quarterly Review* in her short stories, and the novel she had been working on for several years was at a standstill. Although she had placed Nancy in the care of a governess, she still spent hours looking after the little girl—and worrying about Allen, who was depressed and intemperate. She kept warning him that he was going to die of "auto-intoxication"[123] and told her relatives in dismay that he was unable to get out from under the Davis book. Finally, he began trudging to the American Library in order to use their multivolume set of *The Official Records of the Union and Confederate Armies.*[124] But as the deadline drew nearer, Carolyn saw no choice but to drop her own work and take on some of the research and writing for him.

Tate might have spent his Guggenheim year more productively had he been able to assume the role of the typical expatriate writer living in Europe. But he felt uncomfortable around the transplanted Americans whose World War I experiences prompted Gertrude Stein to call them "the Lost Generation." It was not that he denied their artistic achievement, for many years later he insisted, "No generation is lost that could produce with devotion and dedication the work that these young men had produced."[125] But Tate's Southern reversion had led him in the opposite direction geographically and philosophically. In search of historical facts that would help him to understand his origins, he berated members of the Lost Generation for pursuing "a fantasy" and for trying to change their identities by ignoring their heritage and living abroad.[126] They chose expatriation, he later hypothesized, because they were afraid that without it, they would "remain sorry provincials."[127] Though he thought them selfish and egotistical, Tate cultivated friendships with some of these writers after his arrival in Paris, and tried to convert them to a Southern point of view. "It is our job," Tate told another Southern Modernist, "to create a foundation for thought; not to move to France and give up the ghost with Gertrude Stein."[128]

Tate had known and admired the work of Ernest Hemingway for several years before he met and became friends with Hemingway in Paris. After reviewing three of Hemingway's early novels for the *Nation*, Tate decided that he was "one of the great stylists of English prose."[129] What appealed to him in Hemingway was his "careful rejection of 'ideas,' " a central tenet in Tate's Modernist credo. Describing *In Our Time* (1925) as "the most completely realized naturalistic fiction of the age," he praised Hemingway for never commenting "in excess of the immediate value of the object as thing seen."[130] A year later, Tate called *The Torrents of Spring* (1926) "a small masterpiece of American fiction."[131] Only when *The Sun Also Rises* appeared in the same year did Tate find anything to criticize. Though he called it "a successful novel," Tate thought it less impressive than his earlier work and dismissed many of its characters as cardboard figures.[132]

Even after Tate's aesthetic theories began to bend under the weight of his interest in Southern history, he looked for ways to justify his admiration for Hemingway's fiction. Apart from Hemingway's stylistic genius, Tate argued that his work revealed "that sense of a stable world" missing from "modern life." When Davidson expressed some misgivings about Hemingway's value to Southerners, Tate warned, "We must not get so lost in our vision of what novelists should do to the Southern scene that we reject the version of 'reality' given us by writers who are not Southern." For all of Tate's dissatisfaction with Modernism, he was unwilling to abandon his belief that literature should be written and studied first as an object of art—as a linguistic and formal text free of any hidden didacticism. Only Hemingway, it seemed to him, had integrated his ideas with the form of his fiction.

Tate told Davidson that if Hemingway "were a Southerner he would be just the novelist we were looking for."[133]

In the autumn of 1929, Tate and Hemingway met in Paris. With his second wife, Pauline, and their infant son, Hemingway had recently moved into an apartment near the Tates. Tate was standing inside Shakespeare and Company, the bookstore operated by Sylvia Beach, patron of James Joyce and other early Modernists, when he noticed "a big dark fellow" next to him.[134] Without bothering to introduce himself, Hemingway turned to Tate and said that he had not been influenced by Defoe and Marryat as Tate had claimed in a review. In a moment, the two men were walking off to a café to get a drink. They liked one another and by October were spending their Sunday afternoons together at the Veladrome d'Hiver bicycle races. Though Tate disliked Hemingway's unwillingness to show any gratitude to his friends, a shortcoming that especially upset his Southern sensibilities, he was charmed by Hemingway's "boyish, sheepish smile" and decided to overlook his egotism for the time being.[135] It helped matters when Hemingway told him with some degree of mystery that the defeat of the Confederacy was "a great calamity for all men" because it raised the price of life's "ordinary pleasures."[136]

A large part of their relationship, however, was based on male ribaldry. "Ford's a friend of yours," Hemingway said to Tate shortly after meeting him. "You know he's impotent, don't you?" Silent for a moment, Tate told Hemingway that this piece of information was of no interest to him since he was not female. But Hemingway persisted, and he warned Tate not to have sex too frequently as a young man or he ran the risk of exhausting the limited supply of orgasms he and all men were endowed with at birth.[137] After reading *The Pit*, a poem Tate was working on that began "There is a place that some men know, / I cannot see the whole of it, / Nor why men come there," Hemingway told him it was obviously about the vagina. Tate was willing to accept this as "a good interpretation" since the problems of Modern Man generally began "that way."[138]

Yet for years Hemingway had been extremely sensitive to Tate's opinion of his work. After reading Tate's lukewarm review of *The Sun Also Rises*, he told Maxwell Perkins, his editor at Scribner's, that he was anxious to publish work that would placate "Tate, and the other boys who fear I'm on the toboggan." Critics like Tate, he wrote Perkins in exasperation, "have a habit of hanging attributes on you themselves—and then when they find you're not that way, accusing you of sailing under false colours."[139] Annoyed at Tate for describing his male and female characters as "puppets," he tried to revive an unpublished short story that would "set Mr. Tate's mind at rest as to my always avoiding any direct relation between men and women because of being afraid to face it or not knowing about it."[140]

Hemingway's preoccupation with Tate's opinions grew after the two men became better acquainted in Paris. When the earliest copies of *A Farewell to Arms* reached him, Hemingway appeared at Tate's door, bearing a copy of the book for him to read and approve. Afraid that he might catch Tate's flu, he refused to come into the room where he lay convalescing and handed the book through the door to Carolyn. He returned the following day pleased to hear that Tate had read the book overnight and pronounced it "a masterpiece."[141] Though privately Hemingway said that the *Ode to the Confederate Dead* contained "the lifeless-est lines to Dead Soldiers ever read," for the rest of his life he referred to Tate as "a good critic" who was not only "damned intelligent," but "a very good fellow."[142] He even forgave Tate for having a frail physique, "because what it came down to was guts." "And moral guts," Hemingway added, ". . . Allen had."[143] Before the Tates left Paris, Hemingway tried to persuade them to settle with Pauline and him in the South, where Pauline had family in Arkansas. But Tate never felt entirely comfortable around Hemingway, and after their time together in Europe, he made no serious effort to rekindle the friendship. Much later, after reading Hemingway's *A Moveable Feast*, a nonfictional account of writers in Paris in the early 1920s (in which Hemingway wrote that Fitzgerald was insecure about his penis), Tate dismissed him as a "complete son of a bitch."[144]

Tate's friendship with F. Scott Fitzgerald was equally troubled.[145] Tate and Fitzgerald had a mutual friend in John Peale Bishop, the poet from West Virginia. After discovering the Tates in Paris, Bishop's wife, Margaret, invited them to a dinner party so they could meet the Fitzgeralds. When the Fitzgeralds finally showed up, Scott immediately disappeared into the kitchen, where he spent a good portion of the evening mixing martinis. Tate was left standing with Fitzgerald's wife, Zelda, who was born and raised in Alabama and had a great uncle who had been a Confederate general. When she discovered that Tate was also a Southerner, she mistakenly concluded that they had danced together at the University of the South in Sewanee, Tennessee. But Tate easily forgave the error. Put off by her husband's aloofness, he was relieved to find that she had "the Southern woman's gift for conversation that made people feel that she had known them for years." "Not a beautiful woman," he mused, "but immensely attractive."[146]

Scott Fitzgerald was not enamored with Carolyn Tate, even though her Southern style rivaled Zelda's. "Met your friend Allen Tate," Fitzgerald wrote Edmund Wilson afterward, "liked him and pitied him his wife."[147] Perhaps because Carolyn had gained fifteen pounds and was preoccupied by the death of her mother, Fitzgerald asked Tate if he actually enjoyed sleeping with her. "It's none of your damn business," Tate replied, turning away. He was further put off by Fitzgerald's obsession with his own reputation and his vain interest in knowing how Americans were receiving his new novel, *The Beautiful and Damned*.[148]

Although Tate socialized with Fitzgerald a number of times during his stay in Paris, and came to think of him as "the best American novelist of his generation," he was bored by his "self-pity and self-hatred" and concluded that he was a "fatuous" drunk.[149] But he did manage to lecture him about the evils of Northern industrialism, and at least one of Fitzgerald's biographers speculated that these conversations helped persuade Fitzgerald to live in Maryland after he came back from Europe.[150]

Tate's impatience with the Lost Generation turned to resentment when he met the group's spiritual leader, Gertrude Stein. One evening after Ford Madox Ford returned to Paris, the Tates were invited to Stein's literary salon at 27 rue de Fleurus. After being shown in by Alice B. Toklas, Stein's companion, they joined the Hemingways, the Bishops, Ford, and Fitzgerald in the half circle of chairs that had been arranged around Miss Stein, who was pontificating on the progress of American literature. The abstraction in the work of Ralph Waldo Emerson, she explained, had shown promise. Later, the novels of Henry James foreshadowed the revolt of American writers against conventional forms. Tate thought he was being polite by saying, "How interesting," but Stein turned to him angrily and said, "Nonsense, my dear Tate, nonsense."[151] She then concluded her lecture by explaining that her own Modernist fiction represented "the culmination of American literature." On the way home with the others, Tate decided that Stein was not only an egomaniac and a snob, but that she was "mad as the March Hare."[152] Walking behind Fitzgerald on the moonlit, rain-soaked sidewalk, Tate heard him mumble in disgust, "I have seen Shelley plain."[153]

The worst aspect of Stein's behavior was something Tate found bothersome in all Lost Generation writers: they knew little of the ways of the South and did not hesitate to air their regional prejudices. Once, for instance, when she saw Tate on the street, she began mumbling the words "Presidential timber" over and over until, seeing Tate's unresponsiveness, she explained: "That refers to presidents of the United States after the Civil War, Harrison and the others. Of course, no Southerner can afford to know any history." Tate, who had spent the last several years reading almost exclusively in history, was only able to conclude to himself in silent anger, "You ignorant old bitch."[154]

Tate ended up spending most of his year in Europe with other Southerners. He felt more comfortable around men like John Bishop, who had grown up on the border between North and South and who he believed understood his preoccupation with history. He could even overlook Bishop's Princeton education in light of his poetic ability and his aristocratic Southern style. Tate also spent a good deal of time with Julian Green, a shy novelist from Virginia who shared his fascination with genealogy; and with Bill Bandy, a Vanderbilt classmate now an American Field Service Fellow interested in Baudelaire. With these Southerners and the Jefferson Davis biography as distractions, Tate never developed any close ties to the expatriate writers. Years later, he explained that he had been "as oblivious of France as if I had been in Montgomery, Alabama, in 1861, to report the organization of the Confederate government."[155]

VI

In July 1929, Tate finally mailed the completed manuscript of *Jefferson Davis: His Rise and Fall* to Minton, Balch and Company.[156] The book, which would not appear for a few months, was one of the least original works Tate ever produced. He claimed to have consulted some one thousand individual primary sources, but he did not cite them because he wanted the book to be seamless. ("I could have appended a bibliography that would have staggered a congress of historians," he boasted, "but what the devil is bibliography?")[157] In a postscript, however, he admitted that his book was largely a synthesis of William E. Dodd's political biography, *Jefferson Davis*, and Hamilton James Eckenrode's *Jefferson Davis: President of the South*.[158] Tate also relied heavily on the work of two Vanderbilt history professors: Frank L. Owsley, a former student of William E. Dodd's who wrote a study called *State Rights in the Confederacy*, and Walter Lynwood Fleming, whose several monographs on Davis Tate found invaluable.[159] For descriptions of the South, he gleaned material from books like Mary Boykin Chesnut's *A Diary from Dixie*, J. B. Jones's *A Rebel War Clerk's Diary*, and Dodd's *The Cotton Kingdom*.[160]

The prose in Tate's *Jefferson Davis* was not entirely his own either. Carolyn not only aided in the research on the relationship of the Confederate government to England and France but wrote three entire chapters, which Tate called "the best" in the book. "I arranged the notes and provided an outline," he told Davidson, "and she did the rest."[161] Determined not to invest any more time working on the project, and believing that his critical interpretation of Davis was at odds with the celebratory approach expected of "a publisher's book," Tate also copied passages verbatim from Varina Howell Davis's two-volume memoir of her husband, *Jefferson Davis* (1890).[162] "I embedded in my text at least twenty-five pages (pages in my book) directly lifted, without inverted commas, from that book," he admitted proudly.[163]

Tate succeeded in producing the unapologetic attack of Davis he imagined. He did find things to praise in Davis: he was a man of personal integrity; his debating skills in Congress were almost unequaled; he was "possibly the best educated man in the United States Senate" and perhaps "the best Secretary of War the United States ever had." What was more, he treated his slaves with compassion and was the only Confederate leader immediately to recognize the brilliance of Robert E. Lee. But Tate's Jefferson Davis was also "a chronic neurotic," an inept Mississippi planter "emotionally bound to the Union," who was personally responsible for the defeat of the South. Because he expected men to behave according to prescribed rules, Davis pinned all of his hopes for victory on the unrealistic possibility of Europe intervening in the war. His rise to power was simply "a miracle of good fortune." He was a slave to logic and possessed an overly theoretical and legalistic mind that lacked "emotional subtlety." Calling Davis "the most disinterested statesman in American history," Tate offered him as the perfect example of the Southerner suffering from a "separation of his intellect and his feelings."[164]

The biography revealed Tate's growing distrust of Southerners who refused to express their religious beliefs through action. In his conduct of the war against the Union, Davis made the mistake of thinking that faith alone could save the South. Unlike Stonewall Jackson, he put "more upon the will of God than God is ever willing to bear." If Tate could agree there was "an ultimate point, doubtless, in human affairs where God alone may act," he censured Davis for thinking that the Confederacy had reached that point by 1863. "It was to his lasting credit," Tate said of Davis, "that he wished to display the Christian virtues of charity and forbearance; but what his country needed was the Machiavellian virtue of policy."[165]

Tate's life of Jefferson Davis received the attention and praise of several important American historians. Allan Nevins, who was already becoming one of the greatest Civil War scholars in America, criticized Tate for ignoring Davis's early political career and for devoting too much space to unimportant matters, but he praised Tate for effectively synthesizing the work of other biographers into a book he found "both useful and stimulating," one that filled "a place all its own."[166] Similarly, Henry Steele Commager, also on his way to a distinguished career, commended Tate for his "consummate skill" in weaving together his sources into a "brilliant mosaic of historical interpretations." Although Commager criticized Tate's heavy reliance on secondary sources, he called his book "a strikingly thoughtful and artistic work" bound to "excite the admiration and the wonder of the more professional historian."[167] Finally, Frank Owsley, whose ideas appeared throughout the biography, called it "a very clear-cut job" that, while popularized, was useful "to the scholar because of its keen and correct insight into the major problems of the period."[168]

The biography, however, raised a few eyebrows among reviewers who were not historians. One Southern reviewer, who called himself "an informed survivor of the Confederate era," deemed the book "fairly repulsive." Tate had taken "a patient martyr" and ruined his life story with a book that was sloppy and inaccurate.[169] Another reviewer described Tate as one of those "consciously Confederate Southern writers, who bear themselves with something of the air of royalty in exile," and "who resent the loss of the Civil War because it deprives them" of their "aristocratic" self-image.[170] But none of these accusations hurt the book's sales. Robert Penn Warren noticed that immense stacks of the book in bookstores in his neighborhood were "melting like that snowflake in hell."[171]

VII

In the 1960s, four decades after the publication of his Confederate biographies, Tate would vehemently oppose a plan by G. P. Putnam's Sons to reprint them. He feared that he would be labeled an apologist for slavery. An editor at Putnam's assured him that no one would reach that conclusion—though a few passages "expressive of general thought about the Negro in the 1920's" would have to be deleted.[172] Tate had populated both biographies with demeaning caricatures whose physical features included drooping jaws and frightened eyes. These "good old" Negroes made awe-inspired remarks such as, "My stars, but the gineral is jus' mad this time. Mos' like lightnin' strike him!"[173] Although Tate described the horrors of the slave ship and the brutality of the slave-traders, he wrote that the slaves who made it to the South lived in homey cabins with their "young pickaninnies" and received excellent medical care. To educate these happy-go-lucky slaves beyond their "station," Tate argued, would have been to ruin their happiness. Drawing from legends about slaves in his own family, Tate described antebellum blacks as "docile, and for the most part devoted to the cause of the Confederacy."[174]

Other passages in the biographies suggested that Tate believed that blacks differed in intelligence according to their tribe of origin in Africa. Without caveat, he described white slave-traders who had "learned to distinguish enormous differences" in the intelligence and temper of the Africans they enslaved: While the Nagoes, Pawpaws, and the Whydahs made "ideal slaves," the Coromantees "were proud, haughty and fierce." "The Congoes and the Angolas from the far south were tractable," he continued, "but they were stupid and shiftless. The Eboes were even stupider." No experienced slave-trader would purchase a Gaboon, for "he was too likely to die on the voyage."[175]

Tate would undoubtedly have attributed his early racism to his upbringing. He was born in a town that once housed a slave market, raised in a state with one of the highest lynching rates in the South, and educated almost exclusively in segregated schools. What was worse, he had seen his own father attack a black man and walk away without repercussions. Witnessing this event may explain why Tate, at the age of ten, thought nothing of allowing a black boy named Henry, the son of his parent's cook, to receive a whipping for an infraction he had committed himself. Then, about a year later, as Tate walked along a road in Mount Sterling, Kentucky, in the company of four playmates headed for a swim in a local creek, he came upon the mangled corpse of a black man who had been lynched. Though the horror of these events festered in Tate's mind and would erupt painfully in his middle years, they remained buried in his subconscious throughout the 1920s and most of the 1930s.

Referring to the racist schema in Madison Grant's infamous *Passing of the Great Race* (1916) as "Nordic moonshine,"[176] Tate turned to other books for the view of blacks he put forth in the biographies. A good portion of his ideas on slavery came from Ulrich Bonnell Phillips's *American Negro Slavery* (1918), the first exhaustive study of slavery in the American South and still the definitive work on the subject when

Tate began the biographies. Phillips, who changed his name from Ulysses to Ulrich so as not to suggest any relation to the Union general and president, Ulysses S. Grant, argued that slavery was a paternalistic system not harmful to blacks.[177] Many of his conclusions about "the peculiar institution" would not be called into question by revisionist historians until years later.[178]

Tate also drew ideas from nineteenth-century proslavery theorists such as Thomas R. Dew, a professor at the College of William and Mary, and William Harper, of the University of South Carolina—"We must revive these men," he told Davidson.[179] Though Tate did not cite it in his bibliographies, he apparently also read George Fitzhugh's *Cannibals All! or Slaves without Masters* (1857). Like Fitzhugh, Tate contrasted the slavery of the Old South to the horrors of modern industrialism and asked if there was any difference.[180] Southern slavery, Tate explained, "took the form of benevolent protection: the White man was in every sense responsible for the Black," who if freed would have been subject to wage slavery, a worse form of exploitation by Northern industrial capitalists. Because Northerners were already exhibiting "a fatal confidence in the powers of machinery," they "required a different kind of slave" who would be given "the illusion of freedom."[181] Unlike these Yankee capitalists, Southerners "were bound by their responsibility to a definite physical legacy—land and slaves—which more and more, as Southern society tended to become stable after 1850, checked the desire for mere wealth and power."[182]

Tate believed that these theories were confirmed in works of the doctrinaire states' rights advocate John C. Calhoun.[183] "The institution of slavery," Tate explained in *Stonewall Jackson*, "was a positive good only in the sense that Calhoun had argued that it was: it had become a necessary element in a stable society."[184] He elaborated on this idea in the Davis biography. "No slavery system is good simply because it involves slavery," he admitted. But "out of the great evil of slavery, had come a certain good: the master and slave were forever bound by ties of association and affection that exceeded all considerations of interest." There were two unjust aspects to slavery: "the first was the humiliation of the name—slavery; the other was that it gave the talented individual little chance to rise. Only in these two respects is the modern industrial laborer better off than the Negro slave: as a class he has no more than the slave's chance to better himself." The industrial worker, Tate continued, "has the feeling, which the Negro lacked, of not belonging to an institution or class—a void that he fills with cheap luxuries, cheap automobiles, cheap radios, cheap literatures; so that because he is the major consumer of mass production, the production is diluted to his wants, and the higher values of all society are degraded." All things considered, Tate concluded, "the modern system is probably inferior to that of slavery; the classes are not so closely knit; and the employer feels responsible to no law but his own desire."[185]

Yet Tate's defense of slavery was not as spirited as his attack against the Northerners who fought to abolish it.[186] He especially deplored the self-righteous millennialism of the abolitionists who rallied around antislavery writers like Harriet Beecher Stowe, author of *Uncle Tom's Cabin*. "These privy-to-God people," Tate wrote "were sending little pamphlets down South telling the Negroes, whom they had never seen, that they were abused." Abolitionists not only ignored the United States law that required them to return fugitive slaves to their Southern owners, they laughed in the face of the Dred Scott decision, in which the Supreme Court upheld slavery in the new territories. The problem with abolitionists—and all Northerners—was that they "thought God had told them what to do." The Southerner had better sense because he "knew that God only told people to do right: He never told them *what* was right."[187]

VIII

After mailing off the manuscript of the Davis biography, Tate and Gordon left Paris for what they hoped would be a relaxing summer vacation in Brittany. But their tranquility was short-lived. On July 19, 1929, Allen was on the Grand Hotel de Cornouailles terrace when a cablegram arrived from his brother Ben in America: their mother was dead. While spending the summer at a spa in Monteagle, Tennessee, Nellie Tate had come down with pneumonia and died within three days. Tate was stunned. For minutes he sat speechless, staring at the ocean in front of him. Out on the water, he could see the sardine boats propelled by multicolored sails. He wanted to return to the South immediately, but knew that by the time he made it back, he could do little for his relatives anyway. He attempted to write a letter to his father but words failed him. He was overwhelmed with guilt as he remembered his rebellion against his mother in 1924.[188] The more he thought about having been absent "in Mama's last hours," the deeper he sank into depression.[189] He was undoubtedly thinking about his rudeness to her the last time he saw her. During his trip South the previous summer with Carolyn, Nancy, and Andrew Lytle, they had run into her in Monteagle.

"My God!" Tate had uttered in shock. "There's Mama!" Expressionless and dressed in black, she was sitting on a porch at the retreat. Although Nellie had never met Carolyn before, Allen was visibly uncomfortable and cut short the visit after repeatedly interrupting with, "Mama, we got to go now."[190]

Perhaps Tate would have felt less guilt if he had not spent so many hours in Europe thinking about the relationship of men to their mothers. Only days before he learned of his mother's death, he was at work revising a poem he titled *Mother and Son*, one of the most intensely personal poems he had ever written. The poem, which the literary critic Louis Untermeyer thought "without reservation, the best thing" he had read of Tate's so far, made an analogy between a son and a "cuttlefish." Tate selected the small marine animal as a symbol because of its ability to blind prey with a dark ink and then hide in it. The parallel, he later explained, was that "a man in emotional danger withdraws into his private mind where not even maternal love can follow him and where he becomes mysterious and menacing."[191] It may not have been coincidental that the poem took final shape shortly after Hart Crane visited Paris and confided in Tate about his traumatic childhood. Although Tate later concluded—perhaps thinking of himself—"that many young men have had parents like the Cranes but did not become homosexual," he was moved by the experiences of another poet who grew up listening to "the constant quarreling of his mother and father."[192]

Spending so much time thinking about his mother made Tate reflect on the destruction of his family. Living in Europe, he explained to Edmund Wilson, was "like going back to some scene of one's childhood."[193] As he studied the farming towns in France, he not only felt nostalgia for the places his mother had taken him to as a small boy, but reached the conclusion that the Civil War was responsible both for the ruination of the Ohio Valley, where he grew up, and for "the defeat of independent agrarian communities" all over America.[194] Owing to John Gould Fletcher, he had come to value a book called *The American Heresy*, by Christopher Hollis, a British Catholic who argued that the two distinct nations that once existed within America were transformed by the Civil War into a single country.[195] The North's industrial obsession had destroyed the European values of feudalism and in doing so had replaced "agrarian aristocracies" with "middle class urban impulses."[196] Having an opportunity to see the stable agrarian communities in Europe helped convince Tate that his own family had dispersed as a direct result of this industrialism. "My hatred of the 'Yankees,' " he wrote to Mark Van Doren, ". . . is only personal in the most extreme sense—that is, I hate the force that destroyed the background of my family and ultimately set me adrift in the world."[197]

Tate and Gordon began seriously considering a plan to purchase the farm where her father was born in Louisa County, Virginia, outside of Charlottesville. They asked Red Warren, Andrew Lytle, and Katherine Anne Porter to join them so they might establish a Southern literary community. Carolyn would raise chickens and finish *Penhally*, her novel about the history of a Southern family from 1800 to the industrialization of the South. Allen would write two new books: a complete history of the South and a biography of Robert E. Lee, the only Southerner he could think of who was perfect. Everyone in the community would write novels, poems, and reviews. "Think of the encouragement and support we could feel if we worked as neighbors," Tate wrote Lytle when he presented the idea.[198]

But Tate was looking for something beyond supportive friends and a comfortable physical environment. Just before leaving for France, he told John Gould Fletcher that while he had always been "an enforced atheist," he was "willing to be convinced."[199] It was not a belief in the afterlife he craved, but "some ultimate discipline of the soul" for everyday life. Davidson was shocked to receive a letter in which Tate confided, "I am more and more heading towards Catholicism." He had "reached a condition of the spirit where no further compromise is possible."[200] Then his mother died, and though his intellectual interests had always interfered with his ability to share her religious feelings, now especially he felt the absence of religion in his life. His poem *The Pit* now explored the battle between the intellect and faith—and bore a new title, *The Cross*. It was unclear whether the cross represented a symbol of salvation or an intellectual burden to twentieth-century man.[201] Depressed and out of sorts, Tate was looking for a philosophy to live by, an entire system of thought, with ordered and hierarchically arranged values.

He rejected the only contemporary philosophical movement that offered a value system structured enough to check his feelings of intellectual fragmentation. Neohumanism, which was presided over by several academic literary critics a generation older than Tate—Irving Babbitt, a professor of comparative literature at Harvard; his colleague Paul Elmer More; and Norman Foerster, an American literature professor at the University of North Carolina—was fundamentally opposed both to literary Modernism and to religion. Though Tate could not help being attracted to the Humanists' neoclassicism, he concluded that it was "a great mistake to suppose that Humanism is a real substitute for religion," for in their critique of Romanticism, the Humanists had given in to science, which helped to produce modern industrialism.[202] Studying the Humanists showcased in some of his favorite publications and the attack against them T. S. Eliot launched in the *Criterion*, Tate set to writing his own indictment of the movement. In his essay "The Fallacy of Humanism," Tate criticized the Humanists for creating a value system without investing it with any identifiable source of authority. "Religion is the sole technique for the validating of values," he explained.[203] Eliot, who had only two years previously joined the doctrinally conservative Church of England, called the essay "a brilliant article" and agreed to publish it as soon as possible.[204] Bursting with pride, Tate told his friends that the essay was merely the first step in a campaign he was about to launch.[205]

The campaign would be the most important of Tate's life. Several years earlier, as he was beginning to abandon his Menckenesque attitudes toward the South, he had proposed that several of the Fugitives contribute to a symposium defending Southern culture against Northern industrialism, commercialism, and materialism. Now, back in Tennessee, Ransom and Davidson had suddenly become enthusiastic about the idea and wanted to organize a dozen Southerners to contribute to an anthology. But when the two men wrote Tate asking him to participate, he unveiled ideas larger than they had imagined. Tate explained his plan to Davidson:

1. The formation of a society, or an academy, of Southern *positive* reactionaries made up at first of people of our own group.
2. The expansion in a year or two of this academy to this size: fifteen active members—poets, critics, historians, economists— and ten inactive members—lawyers, politicians, private citizens— who might be active enough without being committed at first to direct agitation.
3. The drawing up of a philosophical constitution, to be issued and signed by the academy, as the groundwork of the movement. It should be ambitious to the last degree; it should set forth, under our leading idea, a complete social, philosophical, literary, economic, and religious system. This will inevitably draw upon our heritage, but this heritage should be viewed, not in what it actually performed, but in its possible perfection. Philosophically, we must go the whole hog of reaction, and base our movement less upon

the actual old South than upon its prototype—the historical, social, and religious scheme of Europe. We must be the last Europeans—there being no Europeans in Europe at present.[206]

The movement Tate proposed, which he told Andrew Lytle should emerge from "a society something like the *Action Française* group," was not simply an effort to reverse the outcome of the Civil War.[207] Although he had finally come to believe that "the Old South might be made into a convenient symbol of the good life for everybody," he had lost "sympathy with all designs merely to restore the ruins."[208] Like Davidson, he believed that the group ought to "leave the gate open for an appeal to any of the parts of the country that may be suffering from the invasion of the metropolitan, industrial, business mind and that may be restive under the yoke of progress."[209] In Tate's words, they should attempt to promote "a sectionalism of the mind."[210]

There was no need to search for contributors. Tate, Davidson, and Ransom would each write essays, and would have no difficulty recruiting kindred spirits. Many of their friends from Vanderbilt had also undergone Southern conversions in recent years. Andrew Lytle and Red Warren had written biographies that had radicalized them; Frank Owsley's work in Southern history was confirming him in a hatred for Northern industrialism; H. C. Nixon, a friend of Ransom's who wrote a doctoral dissertation on the Populist movement, had become convinced of the value of an agrarian economy; and Lyle Lanier reported that his psychological training had shown him the illness of the industrial mind. In the Vanderbilt English department, the group found two more Southern conservatives: John Donald Wade, a professor who had written a biography of Augustus Baldwin Longstreet, the Georgia writer; and Henry Blue Kline, a graduate student studying for his master's degree. Only two Southerners not affiliated with Vanderbilt would be asked to contribute: John Gould Fletcher, who would write an essay on education in the South; and the Mississippi novelist Stark Young, drama critic for the *New Republic*, who would write a general essay on the group's philosophy.

Tate had long been formulating the idea for the essay he would contribute to the anthology. In *Stonewall Jackson*, he argued that Northerners had always enjoyed the advantage of believing that they lived in a culture where "God was never wrong."[211] Southerners, on the other hand, lacked religious beliefs strong enough to endow them with the will to win the war. Similarly, in the Jefferson Davis biography, he argued that antebellum Southerners represented "the forlorn hope, of

Conservative Fundamentalist Christianity and of civilization, based on agrarian, class rule," but the vagueness of their Protestantism destroyed them.[212] "The remote source of the old Southern mind," Tate elaborated in a letter to John Ransom, "was undoubtedly Catholicism or at least high Church-ism." He proposed writing an essay to prove that "the old Southerners were historically Catholics all the time."[213]

"Agrarianism," as the new movement would come to be called, was the natural culmination of all Tate's thought since he left the Fugitives in the early 1920s. But the idea had not crystallized in his mind until after his move to Europe and the death of his mother. What attracted him the most to the movement was that it promised to fill the voids in his spiritual life. "I am an atheist," he told John Gould Fletcher, "but a religious one—which means that there is no organization for my religion."[214] The obvious solution was to make the South, its culture and its history, into an organized religion. Agrarianism, Tate insisted, would be "a whole religious, philosophical, literary, and social program, anti-industrial on the negative side, and all that implies, and, on the positive, authoritarian, agrarian, classical, aristocratic."[215] He refused to make the mistake of the Humanists, who tried to develop a system of thought for the modern world but ignored the needs of the human spirit. "Only God," he insisted, "can give the affair a genuine purpose."[216]

1. Despite the fact that she and her husband were both born in Illinois, Tate's mother, Eleanor Custis Parke Varnell Tate, claimed to have been born in Fairfax County, Virginia. (Courtesy of Ben E. Tate, Jr.)

2. Long after Orley Tate's death, Allen stood in awe and terror of his powerfully fisted father, whose elegantly tailored suits and gentle blue eyes belied a volatile personality. (Courtesy of Ben E. Tate, Jr.)

3. Tate's mother dressed him in Buster Brown outfits, as Little Lord Fauntleroy, or, as in this portrait made on Tate's sixth birthday, in sailor suits. (Caroline Gordon Papers, Manuscripts Division, Department of Rare Books and Special Collections, Princeton University Library)

4. Allen's brothers, Varnell (left) and Ben (right), were some ten years older than he was but had suffered their own humiliations from their mother. (Courtesy of Robert V. Tate)

5. Tate when he was seven. (Courtesy of John Prince)

6. Tate's parents continued to live beyond their means, and after reuniting in Ashland, Kentucky, in 1912, they moved into 314 East Winchester Avenue, a comfortable home in an upper-middle-class residential area. (Courtesy of Arnold Hanners)

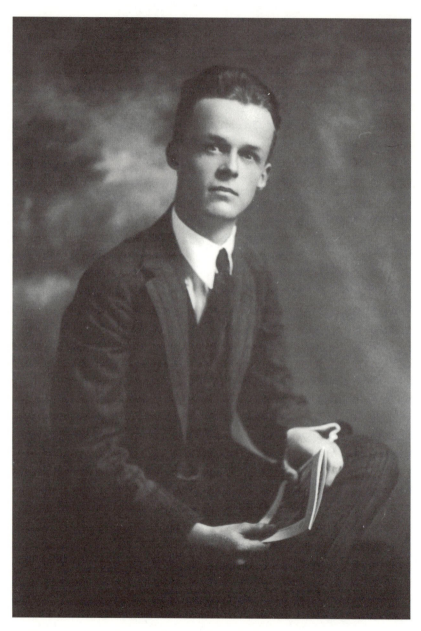

7. Tate, shortly before graduating from Georgetown Preparatory School in June 1918. (Courtesy of Robert V. Tate)

Dramatic Club Recital Consists of Three Clever Comedies

—Photo by A. J. Thuss.

A scene from "Man Proposes," one of the three short plays which will be presented Friday night by the Vanderbilt Dramatic Club. The participants are, reading from left to right: Miss Emma Alexander, John Bell Keeble, Edgar Tate, Miss Mary Pepper, William G. Downs, John E. Frazier, Miss Christine Waterfield.

Practically all arrangements have been completed for the annual performance of the Vanderbilt Dramatic Club, which will be held in College Hall next Friday night, and the indications are that this will be one of the most successful years the club has ever known.

Three one-act plays will be given by the club instead of the usual one long play, as it was thought by Mrs. Harry Anderson and the officers of the club that this would suit the public much better. These three plays are: "If Morning Glory Wins," "Man Proposes" and "All in the Game."

The tickets have been placed on sale at Joe Morse and Porter clothing stores and in College Hall at the university. Practically half of the entire house has already been sold, it is reported.

The chapel at College Hall is being rapidly fitted up for the performance. The first three rows of seats have been taken out and the stage more than doubled. Curtains are being strung and footlights installed. Scenery from the Princess has been secured for all three of the plays.

"If Morning Glory Wins" is a short play containing only three characters. The plot centers around the will of a rich old bachelor. The cast is as follows:

Mr. Putnam (an elderly bachelor).. ....Robert Alexander, Jr.
Sylvia (his niece) ....Miss Leslie McCarty
Archie (his nephew) ....Adley Lyles

"Man Proposes" is the longest of the three plays and is considered one of the best. The plot is laid around a race track and betting on the horse Morning Glory. The cast is:

Miss Agnes Wortley (a winner of hearts) ......Miss Emma Alexander
Mrs. Van Tromp (a widow to be won) ....Miss Christine Waterfield
Polly (a serving maid who serves).. ....Miss Mary Pepper
Mr. Stuart (a theoretical bachelor) ....John E. Frazier
Mr. Reginald De Lancey Van Tromp (a man with ancestors)....... ....Orley Allen Tate
Mr. Charlie Newbank (a man with money) ....W. G. Downs
Mr. Frederick Steens (a man with neither) ....John Bell Keeble

"All in the Game" is the play written by Mrs. Harry Anderson especially for the club and the plot is not being made known. It is sufficient to say that it is a promising situation between two men and a girl. Cast:

The man ....H. Herbert Corson, Jr.
The girl........Miss Leah Belle Levy
The friend .....Kenneth McKenzie

8. In *Man Proposes*, a one-act play staged in the Vanderbilt chapel in 1921, Allen played "Mr. Reginald De Lancey Van Tromp," or "a man with ancestors." (Allen Tate Papers, 5:5, Manuscripts Division, Department of Rare Books and Special Collections, Princeton University Library)

9. Most Nashville, Tennessee, reviewers recognized that the Fugitive poets were bringing notoriety to their city and prestige to the South. (Courtesy of Photographic Archives, Heard Library, Vanderbilt University)

FACULTY OF LUMBERPORT HIGH SCHOOL

Viola Peterson, A. B. ....L. H. S. 1922-24
Lillian G. Martin, A. B. West Virginia University.................L. H. S. 1923-24
Vivian Ligget, A. B. Wesleyan, A. M. Columbia.....................L. H. S. 1923-24
J. H. Wallace, Cumberland College...L. H. S. 1923-24
Allen Tate, A. B. Vanderbilt University.................................L. H. S. 1923-24
Grace Payne, B. S. Agr., West Virginia University.................L. H. S. 1923-23
Elizabeth Cavendish, Chicago University................................L. H. S. 1921-24
R. T. Gray, B. S. Agr., University of Maryland.....................L. H. S. 1922-24
E. B. Whaley, A. B., West Virginia University.......................L. H. S. 1921-24
A. B. Sharps, Fairmont Normal...L. H. S. 1922-24

10. If Tate's students at the Lumberport (West Virginia) High School admired their new teacher's immaculate manner of dress, they were somewhat frightened by his intellect. In this 1924 yearbook photo, Tate (back
right) wore his Phi Beta Kappa key prominently. (Courtesy of Randal
Strother)

11. In Stella Bowen's 1929 painting, in which all three of the Tates gaze in different directions, the couple seems preoccupied by matters other than parenthood. (Caroline Gordon Papers, Manuscript Division, Department of Rare Books and Special Collections, Princeton University Library)

Benfolly

Bottom land

River

12. Situated on a hill at the top of a dirt road, "Benfolly" dated to the Jacksonian era. The back of the house, shown in this photo annotated by Tate, overlooked a bluff above the Cumberland River. (Courtesy of Marcella Comès Winslow)

13. After reading the completed manuscript of Caroline Gordon's *Penhally*, Maxwell Perkins of Charles Scribner's wrote to say that there was not a "false note in the whole length of it." Here, Gordon appears in a promotional photograph for the book. (Caroline Gordon Papers, Manuscripts Division, Department of Rare Books and Special Collections, Princeton University Library)

14. In June 1933, Malcolm Cowley, the "Yankee," and Tate, the "Rebel," stood in front of a war monument and posed as peaceful representatives of the Union and Confederate armies. (Courtesy of Audio-Visual Archives, Special Collections and Archives, University of Kentucky Libraries)

15. From their college days, Tate and Robert Penn ("Red") Warren, shown here in 1933, were in deep sympathy with one another. Tate took on the role of an older brother and helped Warren to revise and publish his poetry. (Courtesy of Audio-Visual Archives, Special Collections and Archives, University of Kentucky Libraries)

16. Tate in 1934. (Courtesy of Helen Tate; photograph by Thompson Studio, Clarksville, Tenn.)

17. Altering the names of his mother's ancestors, Tate was able to generate an extensive genealogical background for the characters in *The Fathers*. His great-grandfather on his mother's side, Major Benjamin Lewis Bogan (1795–1870)—the Virginia secessionist shown here—became "Major Lewis Buchan." (Courtesy of Ben E. Tate, Jr.)

18. In his adolescence, Tate and his mother visited a very elderly former slave in Washington, D.C. "Aunt Martha Jackson," Tate was told, was the half-sister of Major Bogan and had apparently been willed to the major by his father and hers, John Armistead Bogan. Her descendants appear in this photo. (Allen Tate Papers, 48:6, Manuscripts Division, Department of Rare Books and Special Collections, Princeton University Library)

19. During a 1937 trip to Georgetown, Tate revisited the brick-and-stone ancestral home he described in "The Immortal Woman" and found the 1797 structure abandoned. In *The Fathers*, he reinhabited the house with the Posey family. (Courtesy of University Archives and Manuscripts, Jackson Library, The University of North Carolina at Greensboro)

20. In having been so preoccupied by the parents who produced him, Tate had given little thought to Nancy, shown here in 1937. But as he finished *The Fathers*, he began to reexamine his role as a father to her. (Caroline Gordon Papers, Manuscripts Division, Department of Rare Books and Special Collections, Princeton University Library)

Coming on September 23rd

ALLEN TATE'S

long-awaited novel

THE FATHERS

21. A postcard soliciting orders for *The Fathers*. Tate wrote friends, "I finished the novel on the night of the 21st: the last incident was on July 21st 1861. Nancy became a woman on the 21st. The book will appear on Sept. 23rd, her birthday." (Courtesy of University Archives and Manuscripts, Jackson Library, The University of North Carolina at Greensboro)

22. The Cross School in Louisville, Kentucky, provided one of the few happy settings of Tate's childhood. Revisiting the school in 1956, Tate found it overgrown by weeds. (Courtesy of *The Courier-Journal*; photograph by Al Blunk)

Chapter Six

An Agrarian and "the Brethren"

Although the Tates grew fonder of Paris in the remaining months of their stay, the Guggenheim Fellowship expired in late December, and by New Year's Day 1930 they were on an ocean liner bound for New York City. Taking up temporary residence at the Hotel Carteret on Twenty-third Street and Seventh Avenue, they began hunting for an apartment. At last they located a cramped studio on West Twenty-sixth Street. The apartment, which Carolyn described as "a two by four furnished place," was not large enough for two people, and before long she and Allen were quarreling.[1] It was annoying to be trapped in New York again, especially when both of them were at work on Southern projects. Carolyn was preoccupied trying to finish her novel about her ancestors, while Allen was distracted by his plans to help lead an anti-industrial movement. Their plan to settle an agrarian community in Virginia had fallen through, but the couple soon decided to return to the South. Early in March, they moved to Merry Mont, Carolyn's family farm, where they planned to stay as long as it took them to find a piece of property in Tennessee.

Tate's return to the South created quite a stir among Southerners who remembered his vociferous criticisms of the region during the early 1920s. Not much time passed before William S. Knickerbocker, editor of the *Sewanee Review*, wrote an editorial about Tate entitled "The Return of the Native." "What did New York do to him?" he asked rhetorically. "He could find no good in his native region," Knickerbocker observed, "but fled to what he thought were more congenial surroundings in the city of the purple towers." Then "a miracle happened." The more time Tate spent away from Tennessee, "the fiercer became his Southern loyalties and his Northern antipathies." Although Knickerbocker censured Tate for "certain tendencies to irascibility," he seemed pleased to have him back in Tennessee. Tate's reputation as a poet, critic, and reviewer had grown so much that it was a victory for the South to have retrieved him.[2]

But the Tates still lacked a permanent home and any sense of family stability. With no Guggenheim stipend to fall back upon and with Nancy back in their care, they had no money to purchase a house. Knowing that his brother Ben, who was well on his way to becoming a millionaire, would understand their need for rootedness, Allen made a trip to Cincinnati. "Fortunately for us," Carolyn reported afterward, Ben "followed the coal business rather than literature."[3] Although the Great Depression had already begun, Ben's company was yet to be affected and he did not balk when Allen asked for eleven thousand dollars to buy a farm near Merry Mont. Not only did Ben agree to put up the money, he asked only for interest—a token sum he never intended to collect. Awed by his brother's generosity, Allen cheerfully overlooked the possible hypocrisy of using money earned in the coal business to live on a farm. "When I went up to Cincinnati to see my brother," he joked to Malcolm Cowley, "I found that Industrialism had been profitable beyond my best nightmare."[4]

I

Occupying an eighty-five-acre tract of land adjacent to Clarksville and some fifty miles from Nashville, the Tennessee compound that Ben Tate purchased for the Tates provided an inviting meeting ground for the group soon to be known as the Vanderbilt Agrarians—a group that would try for six years to recast Southern culture as the proper prototype for American life. A poor tenant farmer lived on one corner of the property, where he tended to crops ranging from tobacco to watermelon, but mostly the grounds consisted of unspoiled forest land populated by a variety of birds and woodland animals. Ponds and creeks, teeming with pickerel and bass, dotted and crisscrossed the landscape. The Cumberland River ran along one side of the property line, and Tate planned to build a dock and a raft from logs and discarded barrels so that he and his visitors could swim, fish, and canoe.[5]

The Tates came to call the old house on the edge of this idyllic estate "Benfolly"—a tribute not only to Ben Tate's generosity but to his want of wisdom in trusting anything to their financial future. In appearance and size, the house rivaled the antebellum mansions of the Lower South. Situated on a small hill at the top of a dirt road, the two-story mansion dated back to the Jacksonian era. Up close Tate thought the house looked "like a big-bellied tetrahedron," but he took pride in its two neoclassical columns, eight rooms, and two baths.[6] The back of the house, which overlooked a bluff above the river, opened onto a spacious porch.

While the Tates were delighted when rumors reached their New York literary friends that they had "a dining room big enough to seat Stonewall Jackson's staff," Benfolly was totally lacking in amenities when they moved in during late June 1930.[7] There was no electrical service and the plumbing system consisted of a single cistern. There was no furniture. When the household items Tate inherited from his mother finally arrived in enormous shipments, he and Carolyn distributed these oddities as best they could around the house. Boxed, tied with string, and packed into large trunks, Nellie Tate's possessions consisted mostly of knickknacks—buttons from long-forgotten political campaigns, daguerreotypes of her Bogan ancestors, silverware, a pitcher once owned by the family of George Washington, and a bottle of 1912 bourbon.

In this new setting, Tate viewed himself not so much as a farmer, but as a cultivated country squire—as one of the gracious plantation owners he associated with the antebellum era. He insisted that writers like himself were most emotionally content and artistically productive when they lived in an ordered, preindustrial community like that of the Old South. ("The South," he insisted, "is not a section of geography, it is an economy setting forth a certain kind of life.")[8] He had long believed that the Old South had failed to produce an important body of literature, but now he began to admire its genteel men of letters for their elaborate hospitality to visitors. Likening Benfolly to the country estates of earlier Southern writers like Thomas Holley Chivers, Sidney Lanier, and William Gilmore Simms, he took pleasure inviting his friends to visit him.[9] Sojourners included not only Tate's father and two brothers, but Ford Madox Ford, Malcolm and Muriel Cowley, and Red Warren and his new wife, Cinina.

The residents of nearby Clarksville, Tennessee, were unaccustomed to having writers in their midst and were suspicious of the Tates' Bohemian appearance. Although the couple owned a large home, they were worse off financially than ever before, and the condition of their clothes suggested abject poverty. One gray afternoon, a townswoman saw two hoboes standing before a storefront. They looked so destitute in their mud-caked shoes, matching skullcaps, and torn overcoats that she moved to give them some pocket change. She stopped in her tracks, however, when she saw that the two figures were the Tates.[10]

The Tates were equally shocked by their new neighbors. After learning of a ceremony to be conducted in the local Confederate cemetery, the young couple hurried off, thinking that they would hear "a becoming eulogy of the soldiers and a proper understanding of the principles for which they fought." Instead, they encountered a self-righteous Baptist preacher railing against the evils of the Confederacy and ballyhooing the New South. "Northern capital," the preacher proclaimed, "is moving here, and soon the blessings of industrial prosperity will be with us." He concluded his sermon by urging his listeners to forget "the South of oppression and slavery" and to "build up the South of Henry W. Grady," a leading proponent of industrialism.[11] The Tates were livid. After the speech, Tate proudly reported that his wife had marched up to the minister "and told him before all the smiling ladies, who though it 'wonderful,' " that his sermon was "an insult to the South, an insult to the old veterans, and a perversion of the Southern spirit."[12]

Believing that industrial values were ruining even his own "quiet agrarian town,"[13] Tate applied himself more fervently to the movement he and his Vanderbilt friends had conceived the previous year. His interest in the project was both political and personal. The Vanderbilt group had always served as a surrogate family for him, and after his spiritual crisis in Europe, he found that he needed the group more than ever. Fortunately, they were happy to have him back. Remembering his success in placing the anthology of Fugitive poetry with a publisher, they asked him to negotiate a contract for the new prose symposium. He set to work on this task and, just before leaving New York, succeeded in convincing Harper's to publish the book.

Yet as the group began working on their essays for the anthology, Tate was dismayed to see old conflicts from the Fugitive era reappearing—the group was not the family unit he hoped it would be. The essayists, he discovered, were divided in their aims.[14] At the beginning, Tate viewed the movement in more abstract terms than the others. Although he himself lived on a farm, he saw the new movement not as an agricultural crusade, but as a defense of a threatened philosophical tradition. In his mind, the anthology was another opportunity to attack the Humanists, or for that matter anyone who promoted a value system that ignored religion.[15] He worried that some of his fellow essayists saw the anti-industrial movement as exclusively political and economic.

Tate was especially perturbed by the title they selected for the anthology. Uncomfortable with the term "Agrarian," he suggested a variety of titles that omitted the word, such as *Articles of an Economic Reform of the Spirit* and *The Irrepressible Conflict*.[16] When at last the group settled on *I'll Take My Stand*, the defiant phrase from the Confederate marching song *Dixie*, he was furious. Red Warren agreed that the title was "the god-damndest thing" he had ever heard.[17] Tate complained that it "reduces our real aims to nonsense." By choosing such an anti-intellectual phrase, he warned—by stressing emotions rather than broad philosophical issues—they would be sending readers the wrong signals about the movement. Critics would portray them "plowing or cleaning a spring" and would "make hash of us before we get a hearing."[18] When the group refused to change the title, he insisted on adding a disclaimer to his essay: "The writer is constrained to point out (with the permission of the other contributors) that in his opinion the general title of this book is not quite true to its aims. It emphasizes the fact of exclusiveness rather than its benefits."[19]

To unify their essays, the group signed a "manifesto" written by John Ransom and attached it to the book as a preface. All of the articles that followed, they announced, would "support a Southern way of life against what may be called the American or prevailing way." It was not just the "New South" proponents of industrialism and mercantilism the group damned in the preface. They also denounced the welfare statism and progressive materialism of the North. To them, mechanization brought on by the applied sciences meant the wholesale destruction of religion and the arts—and the victory of mass culture over individualism. "Modern man," the manifesto announced, "has lost his sense of vocation."

But the manifesto made the group out to be more interested in agricultural economics than they were at that stage. Although the contributors freely admitted they did "not intend to be very specific in proposing any practical measures," they were "happy to be counted as members of a national agrarian movement." Their ideas would be united in "the phrase, Agrarian *versus* Industrial." "The theory of agrarianism," they elaborated, "is that the culture of the soil is the best and most sensitive of vocations, and that therefore it should have the economic preference and enlist the maximum number of workers." They criticized the labor-saving machinery being introduced throughout the South because it had "reduced the part of the population supporting itself upon the soil to a smaller and smaller fraction."[20]

The essays that followed this introduction reflected little of the unity evident in the preface. Tate's essay, "Remarks on the Southern Religion," added to the confusion. He was ill with a high fever when he wrote the article and made five separate attempts to write its introduction. A greater difficulty, however, was that he was an atheist arguing for religious values, a man writing an essay on religion "in a spirit of irreligion."[21] No doubt because religion was the topic that confounded him the most, he reported in despair that the essay was "about everything and nothing."[22] After delaying so long that he barely made the deadline set by the publisher, he finally completed the article and mailed it.

In the essay, Tate attempted to explain why the social and cultural traditions of the Old South prevented Southerners from winning the Civil War. The South's failure, he argued, lay in its religious history. The Old South, which had been incompletely patterned after Europe, had developed into "a feudal society without a feudal religion." While Northerners wisely maintained the traditions of their colonial ancestors, who were "Protestant, aggressive, and materialistic," Southerners had mistakenly followed the same path. As "a non-agrarian and trading religion," Protestantism was not only the wrong religion for the South, but "hardly a religion at all." "Because the South never created a fitting religion," he explained, "the social structure of the South began grievously to break down two generations after the Civil War." Although Tate did not present Catholicism as the ordered, hierarchical value system that might have saved feudalism in the South, he came close to doing so. He would not convert to Catholicism for two decades, but his need for religious authority was acute even in 1930. The South, he concluded, "would not have been defeated had it possessed a sufficient faith in its own kind of God."[23]

While Tate explained the religious aspects of the Agrarian movement better than any other contributor, his essay confused readers. T. S. Eliot refused to print it in the *Criterion*. "It seems to me," he explained to Tate, "that you succeed in rejecting yourself by exhibiting that gift for abstractions you rather deprecate when employed by Northerners."[24] H. L Mencken, who had long harbored contemptuous feelings for religious movements—especially when they emanated from the South—blasted Tate for "delicately wriggl[ing] around the most pressing of all Southern questions."[25] Other critics were mystified by several lines that appeared toward the end of the essay. In answer to the question, "How may the Southerner take hold of his Tradition?" Tate had answered, "by violence." Explaining this line to John Gould Fletcher, Tate remarked, "I didn't mean to imply external force—I mean only inner compulsion." The violence he proposed, Tate further explained to Cowley, was not physical but "a sheer act of faith." But the damage was done. Critics believed he was issuing a call to arms. Many years later, Tate confessed, "A Southern Methodist bishop read my essay, and said here's a young man that doesn't know anything about religion at all!"[26]

Tate claimed that Agrarianism was a religious rather than a political or agricultural movement, but he and the other Vanderbilt men made every effort to disseminate their ideas among Southern farmers. They planned to start a country newspaper and wrote a series of letters to the editors of major Southern newspapers. Tate tried in vain to play his assigned role as a leader of farmers. He willingly added his signature to a letter Ransom wrote to the *Virginia Quarterly Review* on behalf of "the millions of Southern farmers who are ravaged and ruined by an arrogant industrial leadership at Washington."[27] Yet even as a summer drought was killing the crops on his own farm, Tate had trouble understanding the grim economic realities faced by farmers during the Great Depression. Romanticizing his new life at Benfolly, he wrote to the editor of the *Macon Telegraph*, asking "Southern farmers to think less about money and more about the dignity that is traditional in the Southern country life."[28]

Although Tate correctly guessed that *I'll Take My Stand* would never earn any royalties—ten years later only two thousand copies had sold—he was astonished to see how much publicity the book generated.[29] Just as the book was being distributed, Stringfellow Barr, editor-elect of the *Virginia Quarterly Review*, proclaimed that "Industrialization must be accepted" and attacked Southern traditionalists who were "frightened by the lengthening shadows of the smokestacks" and seeking "refuge in the good old days."[30] When the Associated Press reported on the Agrarians' official response to Barr, a debate of huge dimensions was planned. In mid-November 1930, some thirty-five hundred Americans, including the governor of Virginia, H. L. Mencken, and socialist Norman Thomas, massed in a large auditorium in Richmond for a showdown between John Crowe Ransom and Barr. Sherwood Anderson introduced the contestants. Although Tate concluded that Ransom, who made use of his usual detached tone, "won because Barr got angry," Barr got the audience to laugh at Ransom.[31] No doubt secretly frustrated not to have been the group's spokesman that night, Tate was nevertheless intoxicated by all of the publicity—he saw now the advantage of casting the Agrarian movement in political terms. Shortly after the big event, he joined Ransom, Davidson, Lytle, and Lanier in agreeing to form "an Agrarian party" that would "issue public statements, make and answer attacks."[32]

II

The attention Agrarianism received from the media was predictable given the social and political climate of the early 1930s. It was not only a time of agricultural crisis, but a period burdened by one of the greatest economic upheavals in American history, the Depression. After watching the economic delusions of the 1920s end in the stock market crash of 1929, and then observing unemployment and other misfortunes, some intellectuals began studying the Communist experiment launched in Russia after the Revolution in 1917. Many writers of Tate's generation followed the example set by Theodore Dreiser and John Dos Passos and turned to social protest.[33]

Unlike many of these writers, Tate never sympathized with the Communist Party. His aversion to Communism as a political system drew in part from his disdain for the increasingly powerful radical writers and literary critics he associated with New York City. Although V. F. Calverton, the Marxist critic who edited the *Modern Quarterly*; Waldo Frank, a critic and novelist educated at Yale; and Granville Hicks, the Harvard-educated editor of the *New Masses*, were beginning to categorize contemporary American literature according to its social content, Tate found such debates over "bourgeois" and "proletarian" literature not only tiresome, but irrelevant to his Modernist aesthetic theories.

To make matters worse, Tate's two closest friends from New York had become Communist sympathizers. Ever since 1925, Tate felt a sense of kinship with Edmund Wilson, who helped get him a grant from the Garland Fund for "writers who oppose the existing order."[34] But just as Tate was becoming preoccupied with his aristocratic lineage, Wilson was trying to divest himself of the stigma of his social class. Not long after *I'll Take My Stand* was published, Wilson announced that there was "no hope for general decency and fair play except from a society where classes are abolished."[35] If Tate admired Wilson for criticizing the status quo, he nevertheless began signing letters to him, "With best wishes for a happy Revolution, and with kindest regards to the Comrades—'I'd rather see than be one' . . . "[36] Later, he wrote a poem that mocked Wilson and his Communist friends. Titled *The Ivory Tower*, it accused them of hypocrisy and pedantry.[37]

Tate's friendship with Malcolm Cowley, who succeeded Wilson at the *New Republic*, became for a time equally strained. Tate liked to think of himself as an opponent of the establishment, and when Cowley went over to the Left, Tate looked for areas of agreement with him. But soon he concluded that Cowley's Communism was only "defeatism disguised as radicalism." Cowley was like the liberal Southern intellectuals who argued that nothing could be done to stop the industrialization of their region. "*You are going communistic,*" Tate told him in 1930, "*because you are convinced that communism is inevitable.*"[38] Fascinated by Russia since 1927, Cowley had developed his Communist sympathies a few years later, when he toured the infamous coal mines in Harlan County, Kentucky, and witnessed the degrading effects of industrialism firsthand. Afterward, under Cowley's editorship, the *New Republic* came to be known by conservatives as "a playground of the proletarian artists and critics," and Tate rightly feared that his days as a reviewer for the magazine were numbered.[39] Finally, in 1934, when Cowley published *Exile's Return*, his famous literary memoir of the 1920s—a good portion of which he wrote while visiting the Tates at Benfolly—Tate attacked him for slighting aesthetic issues. He wanted to know why Cowley had not written a chapter exclusively devoted to the literature of the period. He also demanded to know why he devoted more time to Harry Crosby, a representative of the capitalist ethos, than to Hart Crane, one of the greatest poets of their generation.[40]

When Tate and several of the Fugitive poets became Agrarians, they moved beyond the realm of aesthetics into social criticism, and brought themselves into direct competition with the Marxist critics. Tate, who had long argued for the separation of art and politics, found himself in a difficult position intellectually. In his view, prose, like poetry, was a craft in which form deserved more attention than subject matter. "If the Communists wish to put a moratorium upon literature for a certain period, until the 'revolution' is accomplished, that is all right with me," Tate said in contempt, "but there is a lack of intellectual integrity in trying to pretend that there is a Marxian aesthetic." What these writers produced was not art, but pure "propaganda."[41]

After Tate himself joined a political movement, he had to alter his notion of the artist's role in society. His Vanderbilt friends were shocked in 1931 when he asked the group to come to the defense of Dos Passos and Dreiser after the two were indicted in Harlan County on charges of criminal syndicalism. Tate had no interest in defending their efforts to help organize a Communist union for the Kentucky coal miners— and had "no sympathy with Dreiser's opinions as such."[42] He wished merely "to vindicate the right of individuals, particularly members of a professional class like writers, to investigate social problems."[43] He was undoubtedly thinking of the Agrarians. Yet while Tate defended the Agrarians' right to political activism, he later vowed to oppose any writer who agitated "through literature, whether the cause be Buddhism, Methodism, or Communism."[44] Poets, he explained to Horace Gregory, "while they may write about politics and be reformers in their odd moments, had better keep their poetry apart."[45]

Tate objected not only to the literary theories of the Communist writers, but also to their Marxist political thought. It is unclear whether Tate had ever actually read Marx. "As usual," Wilson once warned him, "when you get on the subject of Marxism, you seem to be combating opinions not of Marx, but of Marxist phonies."[46] But Tate held very definite opinions about Marx's work. "The only truth in that vast tome called Das Kapital," he insisted "is that the creation of surplus value by machinery is so rapid that power will suddenly slip from the rulers of a top-heavy system." Like many Southerners of his era, Tate stereotyped Jewish intellectuals and found "Marx's next notion, that Justice for the worker follows" to be "sheer Hebraic divination backed only by Hegelian abstraction called Historical Law. There is only one historical law—that somebody always seizes the power." Moreover, Tate's study of American history left him deeply cynical about the possibility of the Marxists gaining a foothold in Southern politics. He told Morton Zabel that the Communist Party in America "couldn't rule a rural county in Tennessee with ordinary efficiency."[47] Tate professed to "believe in but one political philosophy, and that is Jefferson modified by Calhoun."[48]

Marxism, Tate argued, was less attractive than Agrarianism because it did not insist upon the inherent evil of industrialism. "You and the other Marxians are not revolutionary enough," Tate complained to Cowley.[49] "Communism," he elaborated, "is not radicalism; it is merely a theory of efficient production and distribution of commodities"[50]—"a horror" that led eventually to Fascism. "What good would the worker's share in his labor do him if it did not give him liberty, the power to do what he pleases?" Tate asked.[51] Although he shared the Communist's hatred of wage slavery, he could see a "sole point of contact" with the Communists—a "belief in the iniquity of finance-capitalism."[52]

It was no accident that, of the many titles under consideration for *I'll Take My Stand*, Tate lobbied most stridently for *Tracts against*

Communism.[53] In the early stages of the Agrarians' work on the anthology, he told the group that they should use the book to convince Southerners that Bolshevism, as he sometimes called Communism, was simply "law and order carried to tyranny."[54] Agrarianism, on the other hand, was "a system founded in a belief in the dignity of human nature." By stressing the importance of individual property ownership, Americans could save themselves both from finance capitalism and from industrialism.[55] "The real class struggle," he explained, "now as always, is between the land and the factory. Our land has been oppressed by the factory and is revolting."[56]

Many years later, the historian David M. Potter observed that agrarian movements like the one that sprang from Nashville showed the American intellectual a way to "renounce industrial capitalism and all its works without becoming a Marxist." Agrarianism, Potter elaborated, gave intellectuals "a chance to express their dissent from the prevailing system without going outside the American tradition."[57] This explanation of the lure of Agrarianism works especially well with Tate, who, in the 1930s, fancied himself both a radical and a traditionalist. But if he had found a way to be an iconoclast without giving up his membership in the establishment, now his political views were difficult to untangle. A Frenchwoman who met him at a dinner party in the early 1930s remarked afterward, "Monsieur Tate is so conservative that he's almost radical!"[58]

III

Almost immediately after the publication of *I'll Take My Stand*, Tate's fears that the Agrarians would be misunderstood were realized. To be sure, the group found allies, most notably in hard-line Southerners like the historian U. B. Phillips or in Anglo-Catholics like T. S. Eliot. Reviewing *I'll Take My Stand* in the *Criterion*, Eliot, whose conservative Christian values were close to those of the Agrarians, applauded the "sound and right reaction which impelled Mr. Allen Tate and his eleven Southerners to write their book." Although Eliot was disappointed by the "repetition, unevenness, and incompleteness" in the anthology, he was one of the few critics to understand the real question under consideration: "how far it is possible for mankind to accept industrialization without spiritual harm."[59] A far greater number of reviewers, who seemed not to have read the anthology carefully, mocked the group as plantation farmers yearning to return to the ante-bellum era.

Judged exclusively on the basis of its reception in book review pages, *I'll Take My Stand* was a disaster. Reviewers repeatedly noted the anthologists' failure to offer any practical solutions to the industrial problem in the South. A reviewer for the *New York Times* observed of the group: "They blow the note of resistance on eloquent trumpets, but confess that they are by no means sure how that resistance could be made successful."[60] Henry Hazlitt of the *Nation* denounced the group as "typewriter agrarians" who had launched "a pitiable rearguard action in what is already a lost cause." Reading their essays, Hazlitt observed, "one almost forgets that such culture as the old South had rested on slavery" and "was confined to a small privileged upper class."[61] Even sympathetic reviewers were unable to withhold criticism. William S. Knickerbocker, by now enamored with Tate, praised the Agrarians' "magnificent courage" but noted their "economic romanticism" and their "zeal for a past that never was."[62] Similarly, a reviewer for the *Nashville Tennessean* could empathize with these "voices crying in the wilderness" but despaired over their failure to present any "practical and specific" measures.[63]

Tate and the other Vanderbilt Agrarians were especially enraged by H. L. Mencken's response to *I'll Take My Stand*. By 1930 Mencken was an immensely powerful editor and editorialist, and his damning review of the book undoubtedly helped set the tone of other reviews. If Mencken was willing to admit that the group consisted of "intelligent and earnest fellows," he said their anthology was "full of defects" and "nostalgic vapors." Since Southern industry, in Mencken's opinion, was "there to stay," these men were simply "fashioners of utopias." If they had any genuine interest in aiding their fellow Southerners, he argued, they would "stop blowing pretty soap-bubbles and devote themselves honestly and courageously to concrete evils and workable remedies."[64] Throughout the better part of the 1930s, Mencken and the Agrarians would exchange barbs.[65] In a representative attack in 1935, the Sage from Baltimore described the group as "Agrarian Habakkuks" seeking "relief for their troubled minds by discovering armies of enemies over the fence." Exasperated by such outbursts, Tate concluded of Mencken, "I doubt if he has read us."[66]

Edmund Wilson may have done more to distort Agrarianism in the public mind than anyone. Wilson never read *I'll Take My Stand*, but he came to visit the Tates at Benfolly and afterward wrote a satire based on his trip. The article, titled "Tennessee Agrarians," appeared in the *New Republic*. "Cousin Charles," Wilson wrote mockingly of one of Carolyn Gordon's relatives, "is a tobacco-planter and has fifty niggers on his place." He is a Jeffersonian democrat who "takes politics seriously" and "writes long and well reasoned letters to the papers." Obsessed with the classics, his "feeling about the depression is that it serves the 'industrialists' right." His daughter "serves rich fruit-cake and clear thin agreeable wine" to visitors.

Wilson saved his most vituperative remarks for Tate. Without identifying him by name, he lumped him with the "younger generation at Nashville" who had taken to mimicking Southerners like Cousin Charles. "After inhabiting dark basements in Greenwich Village, floating with the drift of the Paris cafés," men like Tate had returned to the South "to marry girls at home, to renovate family mansions, to do some farming with the aid of a share-cropper, to write books about the Civil War." Worse, "now they blame the ills of industrialized America on the defeat of the Confederacy." In the midst of this sarcasm, however, Wilson showed some insight into the reasons for Tate's interest in Agrarianism. Because he and the other Vanderbilt men lacked "a common ideal or religion," they were attempting "to make one of ancestor worship. They revive the old myths of the family, sustain themselves with the bravery of their fathers."[67]

Tate was furious at Wilson. He dashed off a letter accusing him of turning out "a slick piece of journalese" that made the Agrarians look like "wistful boys mooning over the past." The real villains, he told Wilson, were the "*New Republic* boys" who had placed their "faith in engineers" rather than God. These "Liberal boys," Tate wrote, were "socially and spiritually bankrupt." Privately Tate confided his fear that his "beautiful friendship" with Wilson was "ruined."[68]

Tate grew heartsick over these responses to the Agrarian movement. By the end of 1931 he warned the group that their "brand of agrarianism" was "dying fast."[69] He had always doubted the political efficacy of their protest, and admitted that they were somewhat misguided in their attempt "to make a political creed do the work of religion."[70] But it was difficult for him to understand why the group was being criticized so severely. Searching for an explanation for their failure, he wondered whether "the very word tradition in our campaign was a tactical mistake." They "should have stood flatly on the immediately possible in the South."[71] While he and the other Vanderbilt men began crafting new essays to clarify their position, they would not launch the second stage of their movement for several years.

In the meantime, Tate began to despair as "the Brethren" argued amongst themselves about the movement. Ransom, Lytle, and Tate seemed to form one faction—a faction with more philosophical purposes in mind—while Davidson and Owlsey were united by their need to view Agrarianism in terms of practical politics. There were also several who did not seem to fit into either faction. Tate thought John Donald Wade "a timid man, a very fine prose stylist, who thinks it is ungentlemanly to agitate."[72] And as much as Tate valued his friendship with Stark Young, he was distressed by his "slight taint of cotton snobbery." (Young's *I'll Take My Stand* essay, Tate explained, "makes me feel that perhaps my grandfather wasn't as high and fine as his grandfather.")[73] Others within the group questioned Red Warren's commitment to their program and wanted to force him out. "We all watch one another like Mexican revolutionists," Tate observed.[74]

Since the Agrarians served as a substitute family for Tate—just as his Vanderbilt fraternity and the Fugitive poets had in earlier years—the group's lack of cohesion alarmed him. Unlike the Fugitive group, in which Ransom emerged as the unofficial spokesman, the Agrarians seemed to have no leader. As a result, the movement failed to satisfy Tate's basic need for a father figure, a representative Southern man combining all of the virtues of the Old South while also possessing religious authority. It was probably not a coincidence that year when Tate wrote *The Twelve*, a poem about the religious struggles of the Apostles of Jesus, for the poem seemed also to describe the contributors to *I'll Take My Stand*: "Twelve ragged men, the council of charity, / Wandering the face of the earth a fatherless child."[75]

IV

In the midst of his struggle with Agrarianism, Tate began working on the biography of Robert E. Lee he had promised to write for Minton, Balch. He had wanted to write about Lee since the late 1920s when he began his research for *Stonewall Jackson: The Good Soldier*. Impressed by the sympathy between Jackson and Lee, Tate made every effort in the Jackson biography to demonstrate their loyalty to one another. "Such an executive officer," Tate's Lee said of Jackson, "the sun never shone on." Jackson likewise swore that he "would follow General Lee blindfolded." After the dying Jackson's arm was amputated, Lee lamented, "He has lost his left arm, but I have lost my right." If Jackson had been with Lee at Gettysburg, Tate argued, the two generals could have won both the battle and the Civil War.

Throughout the Jackson biography, Tate seemed hesitant to criticize Lee. If Lee "had a kind of sublime humility, a consciousness of the universal moral insufficiency, that kept him from asserting himself," he "was almost God." He was not "a completely successful soldier," but it was only his "greatness as a man" and his "Godlike omniscience" that held him back.[76] One reviewer of *Stonewall Jackson* observed that Tate's need to deify Lee obscured his analysis of Jackson. "The picture of Lee is most moving and the most original," the reviewer observed. "He stands as a God the Father over the Christ of Stonewall Jackson." As a result, the Jackson biography was more than "a tribute to the saintliness of Lee." It was "an alluring witness" to Tate's own personality and needs.[77]

Yet Tate soon grew less cautious about criticizing Lee. In his 1929 biography of Jefferson Davis, Lee still appeared as "a great leader" whom Southerners "would have followed to the death," but he now possessed a "humorless rectitude."[78] Privately, Tate began attributing Lee's failure to "the egoism of self-righteousness." Lee, Tate elaborated in a letter to Lytle, "valued his own honor more than the independence of the South." "If he had taken matters into his own hands," Tate speculated, "he might have saved the situation; he was not willing to do this. It would have violated his Sunday School morality."[79]

Setting aside such misgivings about Lee, Tate set to work on the new biography. He could not help but feel the pressure placed on him by Minton, Balch, who wanted to release the book by the autumn of 1931. Earle Balch, a partner in the firm, was by now well acquainted with Tate's inability to meet deadlines and did not mince words with him. Remembering his difficulty in completing the Jackson and Davis biographies, Balch had warned him at the outset not to let his "constitutional procrastination" interfere with the firm's promotional plans.[80] It was important that the new biography appear soon after his previous two biographies.

The Lee biography, however, soon threw Tate into total despair. He began telling friends that he was "in agony" over it. "Lee," he complained to Davidson, "is about to drive me insane."[81] Although Tate had been borrowing books from the Vanderbilt University library by mail and was making a concerted effort to learn everything he could about Lee's family,[82] he had grown bored by Lee and, as a result, began writing prematurely. He now claimed to be writing the biography only out of financial necessity. Minton, Balch had given him a generous advance of fourteen hundred dollars, but his financial condition remained dire, and he was forced to continue writing reviews for the *New Republic*. Overworked and frustrated, he realized that he had completely underestimated the quantity of research involved, not to mention the amount of prose he would have to turn out. Even if he scaled the book back in size, it would still have to meet standards—"hack work," he insisted, needed "a certain finish."[83]

By the middle of 1931, Tate predicted that the book would end in failure. Still hurting over his inability to extract from the Agrarian enterprise the feelings of familial stability he craved, he had become completely preoccupied with the subject of Southern alienation and failure. "The older I get," he explained to John Peale Bishop, "the more I realize that I set out about ten years ago to live a life of failure, to imitate, in my own life, the history of my people. For it was only in this fashion, considering the circumstances, that I could completely identify myself with them. We all have an instinct—if we are artists particularly—to live at the center of some way of life and to be borne up by its innermost significance. The significance of the Southern way of life, in my time, is failure: those Southerners who leave their culture—and it is abandoned most fully by those who stay at home—and succeed in some not too critical meaning of success, sacrifice some great part of their deepest heritage. What else is there for me but a complete acceptance of the idea of failure? There is no other 'culture' that I can enter into, even if I had the desire." What was more, Tate told Bishop, his biography of Jefferson Davis "was relatively a success, but the Lee is a failure."[84]

True to his prediction, Tate was nowhere close to completing the Lee manuscript when his deadline arrived in July 1931. Afraid of breaking the news to Minton, Balch, Tate asked Andrew Lytle, who was still in New York City and who also had a contract with the publisher, to meet with Earle Balch in person and plead for an extension, saying that he had completed a draft of the entire biography, but was dissatisfied with it. Tate also wrote out a long explanation of why he was unable to write the book. "The longer I've contemplated the venerable features of Lee," he explained, "the more I've hated him. It is as if I had married a beautiful girl, perfect in figure, pure in all those physical attributes that seem to clothe purity of character, and then had found when she had undressed that the hidden places were corrupt and diseased." Since Tate did not dare write a condemnatory biography and was equally loath to turn in "a facile discussion of Lee as the exemplar of Virginia virtues," he hoped Balch would grant him more time.[85]

After Lytle told the publisher Tate's "little prevarication," Balch had no choice but to extend the deadline.[86] But Balch, who now wrote on the letterhead of Minton, Balch's parent company, G. P. Putnam's Sons, was devastated. "I am only just beginning to recover from the body blow he rendered in your behalf," he wrote Tate after Lytle's visit. The firm, he explained, had already advertised the biography as their preeminent nonfiction book for the fall of 1931. Their salespeople were visiting bookstores all over the country to promote advance sale of the biography. Since Balch was under the false impression that Tate had completed a draft of the book, he found it difficult to understand his complicated personal reasons for putting the work on hold. He urged Tate to "snap out of this slough of despondence"—to "surmount this emotional paralysis" and put the finishing touches on the manuscript at once. To become "the property" the firm expected him to become, he needed to turn out the Lee biography before his previous two biographies faded from public memory. His reputation would be enhanced and the firm might be able to make the book into a best-seller. "Lee is our big chance," Balch insisted.[87]

Contrite, Tate returned to the manuscript and vowed to complete it. Realizing that he had no choice but to attack Lee, he planned to argue that Lee's arrogance and his unwillingness to endanger his record of personal achievement cost the South victory in the war. Tate decided to call the biography *Robert E. Lee: The Man Who Could Not Fail.*[88] By the end of July, he was writing three thousand words a day, and he optimistically predicted to be finished within a month's time. Almost as soon as this sudden burst of activity began, however, his psychological block returned.

As in his previous biographies, Tate was having trouble separating his own experiences from those of his subject. More and more, he came to fear that in writing about Lee, he was writing about himself.[89] The small portion of the book he did write made Lee's family sound more like the Tates.[90] Drawing on the Agrarian ideas he had used to explain the dissolution of his own family, Tate set out to show how Lee's family history shaped his personality. ("In every family," Tate wrote, "whatever appearance it may give to the world, there is a mysterious communion that shapes the children and gives them a characteristic stamp.") Both the Tate and the Lee families sprang from "the gentle and aristocratic tradition" of Virginia, where "order and stability, and repose" governed men's lives. It was a culture in which "the breaking up of a landed estate meant the dispersal of a family unit in the larger social system." Like Orley Tate, Robert E. Lee's father, Henry Lee III, had been the youthful master of an enormous tract of land. He was also a "notorious failure" who went from heir to a large fortune to "a ruined man." Like Orley Tate, he was "fiery, impulsive, and impractical, a very poor businessman indeed."[91]

Lee's mother might have been Nellie Tate. "Mrs. Lee," Tate wrote in the manuscript, "seems to have been one of those sweet ladies who abhor the world and who, when they are invalids, achieve a perfect and soft-spoken tyranny over their families." Like Nellie, Lee's mother was a woman "weak from child-bearing and apprehensive for the welfare of her children." Tate further established his maternal relationship to the Lee family by working in a reference to Eleanor ("Nellie") Parke Custis, Robert E. Lee's aunt and the woman for whom Tate's mother was named.[92]

But Tate found disturbing differences between his own career and Robert E. Lee's. While Lee was the youngest son in his family and had been victimized by his parents in much the same manner he had been, Lee turned out to be a tranquil person. Tate's youth consisted of a series of dislocations as his parents moved from city to city, but Lee's childhood apparently ran in a "smooth routine." Although Tate could not help identifying with a boy who had pulled himself up by his bootstraps after his father's bankruptcy scattered the "family to the winds"—a boy who had determined "to redeem his blood from the stigma that his father had put upon it"[93]—he grew annoyed by Lee's asexuality, his priggishness, and his apparent lack of a personality. Since Lee had been "the poor son of failure and sensitive poverty,"[94] Tate found it difficult to understand how he had grown up as "a perfect specimen of human integration." The same humorless preoccupation with self-control and propriety that he found grating in John Ransom, Tate found insufferable in Lee. Worst of all, he discovered that "the sympathy between Robert and his mother was perfect."[95]

No doubt realizing the extent of his preoccupation with such family themes, Tate looked for ways to free himself of the biography and to confront them directly. Arguing that he needed more money to defray the costs of researching Lee's life, he decided to secure a publishing contract for a history of his family. It was an idea that had always allured—and frightened—him. A few months earlier, he confessed to Mark Van Doren that he had long "tinkered at" an autobiography in which he was attempting to reveal his personality "very indirectly, by making the framework a piece of genealogy." His ancestors, he explained to Van Doren, "and the places they lived and the way they made their livings must have all entered into my bloodstream." Having "felt always accursed" by their actions, he was submitting himself to "a kind of Wasserman test" by telling their story.[96] But now he believed that he "could write a hundred thousand word volume" about his family.[97] Bypassing Earle Balch for obvious reasons, he wrote to Maxwell Perkins, Gordon's publisher at Charles Scribner's Sons in New York City, to offer him the new book. Perkins was intrigued by the idea of a book that would use a family "to reveal the course of social (i.e. human) history in the South in the last two centuries."[98]

But interest from Perkins could not erase the reality of Tate's contract with Balch for the Lee biography. In a desperate effort to make the October deadline, Tate offered to pay Red Warren one hundred dollars to write a portion of the biography. If Warren would draft a chapter of seventy-five hundred words treating the battles of Antietam and Fredericksburg, he would edit it so that it would match his own prose style and fit his reinterpretation of Lee. After using "scissors and paste," Tate would have the joint effort typed and turn it in. Attempting "three biographies in four years," he told Warren, had brought him to "the depths of cynicism," and he no longer cared whether the book was entirely his own product. Carolyn had also promised to write a chapter. "I need not say," Tate wrote to Warren, "that such conspiracies are usually secret."[99]

Either Tate had second thoughts about this plan or Warren declined to write the needed chapter, and Tate soon had no choice but to petition Balch for another extension. Mercifully, Balch agreed to delay the book's release date until the spring of 1932, but when the new deadline arrived in January, Tate was still unable to turn in a completed manuscript. This time, Tate asked Ulrich B. Phillips to intercede on his behalf. Phillips, who believed that Tate's biography of Jefferson Davis was marred by "hasty writing," was happy to comply. He wrote to Balch "to voice an earnest hope" that Tate might be granted the extension he needed to write a definitive biography. Tate's "high talent ought to be guarded against a squandering in diluted output," Phillips warned Balch.[100]

Yet Balch, who had now twice publicized the biography as the firm's leading book, had lost all patience. He considered the news a "bombshell." He was simply unable to understand why Tate did not finish the book in the additional six months allotted to him, especially since he had used the time to collect another volume of poetry. "My impulse," he told Tate, "is to take the next train for Clarksville, since I imagine that there is a manuscript practically completed." He implored Tate "to buckle down" and "carry it through to triumphant completion."[101] But Tate repeated his argument that he could not complete the biography without money for the research and travel expenses associated with it. ("I can't sit on Benfolly hill," he told Lytle, "and spit it out of my cocoon.") Then, when Perkins mailed Tate a contract for the ancestry book, G. P. Putnam's had no choice but to agree to Tate's plan. Seeing that there was "no possibility" he would be handing in the Lee biography by the new deadline, the firm exercised first rights on the genealogy project and took it away from Scribner's.[102]

Tate imagined an eight-chapter, semifictional book that would open in 1638, in the time of his illustrious Virginia ancestor Robert Reade and culminate in the generation of the author and his brother, whom he would model after himself and his brother Ben. The two "absolutely different" brothers would epitomize the conflict of entrepreneurial pioneer values and Virginia Agrarianism but would be complementary modern personalities "motivated by the same blood traits." Tate planned to illustrate his modernist genealogy—a complete manuscript of which he intended to submit early that summer—with pictures of the homes of his own ancestors. He would call the book *Ancestors of Exile*.[103]

V

Throughout 1931, as Tate was struggling to write the Lee biography, he complained that his head was "bursting with dozens of poems," and that he was unable to decide whether to put them on paper or get back to the biography. Trapped "like the jackass between the bales of hay," he finally chose to return to the new series of poems he had begun in 1930.[104] Far more autobiographical than anything he had ever written, many of these new poems revolved around Agrarian themes: the difficulty of religious faith, the problem of reconciling the past and the present, and the need of modern Southerners to understand their ancestors.[105] Although Tate reported optimistically that he was using the past as "a form through which to view the present," he later admitted that most of the poems were "commentaries on those human situations from which there is no escape."[106]

On one level or another, all of the poems Tate wrote during this period dealt with the spiritual crisis of modern man, a problem that began to preoccupy Tate during his Guggenheim year in Europe. After returning to the South he gathered three of his poems on the topic and submitted them to Minton, Balch, who agreed to publish them as a slim volume. Tate's *Three Poems*, which appeared in 1930, contained a slightly revised version of *Ode to the Confederate Dead*, by now well known as a poem about the difficulty of maintaining religious faith in the modern world; *The Cross*, his poem about the intellectual burdens of a twentieth-century Christian; and *Message from Abroad*, a poem he wrote shortly before he left Paris that honored Andrew Lytle. In the new poem, Tate wrote of an American expatriate in Europe haunted by his "red-faced and tall" ancestor. Because modern man inherited the restless spirit of such ancestors, as well as their disrespect for tradition, he was unable to understand his own history. Modern man's fragmented intellect and memory keep him from fully imagining the world of his ancestors.[107]

It was also during this period that Tate produced the *Last Days of Alice*, a poem that Yvor Winters heralded as "possibly the best" he had ever written.[108] In the poem, Tate used the mirror in Lewis Carroll's *Through the Looking-Glass* as a metaphor for the division between the spiritual and the material world. "I have jerked the looking-glass world into an analogy with the world of modern abstract science, which has killed the spiritual life of man," Tate explained. The modern world, Tate elaborated, one of "sheer quantity, measure, form, and size," had torn man from religion. Since the prospects were much better for a sinner than for a man incapable of religious faith, the faithless were wiser to ask "the God of our *flesh* to bless us again with damnation, i.e., to restore us to a sensuous life" of spirituality. "O god of our flesh," the poem's speaker prays,

> return to us your wrath,
> Let us be evil could we enter in
> Your grace, and falter on the stony path!

This theme, Tate told Virginia Lyne Tunstall, "runs through every poem I've written."[109]

The poems Tate wrote in the early 1930s also reflected his continuing obsession with the relationship of the living to their dead forefathers. In a three-part poem he titled *The Legacy*, written in 1931 (later renamed *Emblems*), Tate retraced the westward movement of his pioneer ancestors. He also alluded to his own family's move to the Cumberland River:

Virginia Maryland and Caroline
Pent images in sleep
Clay valleys rocky hills old fields of pine
Unspeakable and deep

Out of that source of time my farthest blood
Runs strangely to this day
Unkempt the fathers waste in solitude
Under the hills of clay

Far from their woe fled to its thither side
To a river in Tennessee
In an alien house I will stay

. . . .

There some time to abide
Took wife and child with me.[110]

More and more in his poetry, Tate superimposed the story of his own
family onto a narrative of American history. "The reason why we think
in terms of family," he soon observed of Southern writers, "is that we
define our personal identity through such a system of reference."[111]

After Tate had settled into Benfolly and furnished it with his mother's genealogical relics, he became even more obsessed by his relationship to her ancestors. *The Oath* recorded a conversation at Benfolly
between Tate and Andrew Lytle. "It was near evening, the room was
cold," the poem began,

Half dark; Uncle Ben's brass bullet-mould
And Major Bogan's eighteenth-century face
Above the fire, in the half-light, plainly said
There's naught to kill but the animated dead . . .

"Being cold," Tate continues, "I urged Lytle to the fire." Lytle asks,
"Who are the dead?" but "nothing more was said."[112] One critic explained, "They are modern men feeling the same fears and seeking the
same useless protection of the fire" that ancient men did.[113]

About the time that his father and brothers came to visit him at
Benfolly, Tate wrote a collection of sonnets intended to explore the doctrine of inherited sin and the bonds of kinship in his family. *Sonnets of
the Blood* also examined Tate's relationship with his brothers. His oldest brother, Varnell, who left Kentucky in 1912 to work out West in the
oil business, had recently come home to manage Ben Tate's coal com-

pany office in Ashland. Varnell moved in with their father, who was aging and lived alone.[114] In the sonnets, Allen explains first to Ben and then to Varnell the difficulty of getting reacquainted with a brother gone so long:

> Our elder brother, whom I had not seen
> These twenty years until you brought him back
> From the cyclonic West where he had been
> Stormed by the shaking furies in the track
> We know so well, which is these arteries —
> You, elder brother, I am a little strange
> To you . . .

Still, Tate knew that all three sons were not only "flesh and blood," but "the same true marrow and bone, contrived and seasoned in a house of strife."[115] They were united by their tumultuous childhoods and their mixed feelings for their mother. The memory of Nellie Tate's domineering presence remained so strong in the minds of her sons that even after her death, they sometimes forgot that she was dead. (Ben would catch himself walking down the street in Cincinnati thinking about her as if she were alive. "Good God," he would say, stopping in his tracks. "Mama's dead!")[116] "Our blood," Tate continued in the poem, "is altered by the sudden death / Of one who of all persons could not use / Life half so well as death." Perhaps referring to their mother's dead ancestors, Tate urged, "Let's look beneath / her life."[117]

In the *Sonnets of the Blood*, Tate was also attempting to draw a parallel between the dissolution of his own family and the industrialization of the South. Although he personally had profited from Ben's success as an industrialist, he pleaded with Ben to eschew the mindless doctrine of progress that was destroying their lineage—to renounce the "Captains of industry" whose "aimless power awakens harsh velleities of time." He warned Ben not to let the forces of abstract science harm their line of descent:

> Let you, brother, a captain in your hour
> Be zealous that your numbers are all prime
> Lest false division with sly mathematic
> Plunder the inner mansion of our blood —

Other lines in the poem were intended to suggest that the industrialization of the South had permanently alienated modern Southerners like the Tate brothers from their agrarian ancestors, who—since they were unable to imagine life in the future—were likewise exiled from their own descendants. "For evil done these last two centuries," Tate explained, "We fulminate in exile from our earth."[118] He was delighted when Ben, who was "hardly a poet or devotee of the art, saw the point immediately."[119]

Meanwhile, Horace Gregory, in a letter to the editor of the April 1931 issue of *Poetry* magazine, declared that Tate had produced all the poetry he was capable of and was "dead" as a poet.[120] Unbeknownst to Gregory, however, Tate had accumulated almost enough verse for a new book. By the summer, he had gathered together a manuscript and, since he feared Earle Balch was estranged from him, sent it to Max Perkins. Perkins, who was familiar with some of the poems, was excited about bringing them out at Scribner's. "Of course anybody would be proud to publish them," he wrote Tate.[121] After reading the new poems, Perkins thought them "very notable indeed," and Scribner's released *Poems, 1928–1931* in late February 1932.[122] It was undoubtedly Tate who supplied the somewhat exaggerated biographical sketch that appeared on the dust jacket. Here, Scribner's promised, was a new young poet who had been "denied graduate fellowships at Vanderbilt and at Yale because he lacked 'the right attitude.' "[123]

The new volume received mixed reviews. Critics continued to censure Tate for the obscurity of his verse and for his insistence on intellectualizing his emotions. While recognizing him as "a sonneteer who might easily be among today's foremost," a reviewer for the *New York Times* concluded that most of his "lines are not readily understood."[124] William Rose Benét of the *Saturday Review of Literature* believed that Tate had substituted "an obscurantist pedantry" for "the expression of genuine emotions." Because of his self-conscious intellectualism, Benét concluded, Tate wrote "like a man in a library."[125] Similarly, Eda Lou Walton, a reviewer for the *Nation*, called Tate "a very sterile poet" whose mind was completely separated from his feelings. She tried to reconstruct Tate's thoughts after he wrote the first draft of an emotionally intelligible poem. "This will not do," she imagined him thinking to himself. "I have not given record here of the modern intricacies in this idea; I have not shown the conflicting associations it must arouse, I have not abstracted from this feeling or situation its philosophical and intellectual application." This kind of "clever reasoning," Walton concluded, whether "sound or unsound, is not great poetry."[126]

Part of the problem was Tate's steadfast refusal to abandon completely his highly intellectualized Modernist ideas in favor of emotionally and historically intelligible Southern themes. After returning to the South and settling at Benfolly, he had begun to feel even more comfortable with Southern themes, and his friends noticed a new voice emerging in his poetry. "It's directer, simpler, and I think more powerful than your earlier verse," Davidson told Tate.[127] But reviewers believed Tate had not moved far enough. Reviewing *Poems, 1928–1931* for the *Yale Review*, Louis Untermeyer noted "a large stride in the progress of this vigorous and versatile Southerner," yet lamented Tate's "perverse refusal to allow a native rhetoric full play."[128] Similarly, Yvor Winters, a consistent supporter of Tate's, observed that he had yet to work out his private preoccupations with his genealogy. "We are expecting the revelation of some dark family tragedy," Winters wrote, "something known to the family group in question and to them only, but we suddenly find ourselves standing in the public garden."[129] Louise Bogan observed that many of the poems in his new volume—for instance, *Message from Abroad*, *The Oath*, and *Emblems*—demonstrated a "deep and homely pride in countryside and kin." But poems like *Sonnets of the Blood*, though "in some ways impressive," were failures because Tate was unable to "decide between his early and later methods."[130]

Tate found these reviews depressing and annoying. (He was especially appalled and hurt that Bogan, who had become a close friend of his in New York during the 1920s, would criticize him so severely. "Haven't I the right," he asked her heatedly, "to expect that your bias would be just the opposite of what it is?")[131] But he himself was confused about his changing style. Arguing that his new method departed "somewhat in method from the earlier one, but not fundamentally," he also explained that the new style was "looser and more discursive."[132] He further confused matters by describing his poetic method as that of a hawk "gradually circling round the subject, threatening it and filling it with suspense, and finally accomplishing its demise without ever quite using the ultimate violence upon it."[133]

To Tate's satisfaction, he still had many admirers. Writing for the *Bookman*, J. V. Cunningham argued that "the best poems" in the new volume "should become the texts of the next generation as Mr. Eliot's poems were of the last."[134] Morton Zabel concluded that Tate was "working toward a permanent claim" to the adjective "major."[135] Despite his criticisms of the new volume, Yvor Winters still thought Tate "the most mature poet to appear in America" since Edwin Arlington Robinson. Some of his poems "mark the highest level to which twentieth century poetry has attained."[136]

Meanwhile, Tate was perfectly willing to use his reputation as a Southern Agrarian to enhance his power as a poetry critic. By now he was known as an important contributor of book reviews and criticism to virtually every important magazine and literary journal in America and Europe. As his commitment to Agrarianism grew, he looked for ways to promote himself as an arbiter of Southern literary tastes in these publications.

Ever since its founding in 1927 at Harvard University, Tate had his eye on the *Hound & Horn*. The magazine's early contributors included T. S. Eliot, E. E. Cummings, and Conrad Aiken, poets who shared much of Tate's aesthetics. In late 1930, the magazine relocated to New York City and Lincoln Kirstein took over the editorship from Bernard Bandler and R. P. Blackmur. Tate seized the opportunity to influence the magazine's editorial policies and offered the editors his help. Kirstein was receptive to Tate's offer and eventually named him Southern contributing editor. For several years, Tate would use the editorial position not only to his own advantage, but to that of the Agrarians, who became contributors to the magazine.[137]

Tate also had designs on *Poetry*, still the most important poetry journal in America. Capitalizing on his renewed friendliness with Harriet Monroe, he suggested that he edit a special issue devoted to Southern poetry. Monroe agreed to the idea, and he began gathering up poetry from the Vanderbilt group and other Southern poets he considered worthwhile. In his introduction to the special number, he claimed that he had no interest at all in proving "what the South can do in competition with other sections." He intended "merely to get together the best poems by southern poets he could find at the moment."[138] Tate included two of his own poems, as well as brief essays on Southern poetry by Warren and Davidson. "The point of such a number," Tate told Red Warren privately, "is political, though of course we mustn't confess that to our hostess."[139]

Not everyone understood that Tate's special issue was an attempt to destroy the moonlight-and-magnolia school of Southern poetry. After reading the poems he collected, one editor in New York City remarked, "Allen Tate's sentimental Southern sectionalism is very very very silly silly silly."[140] Ezra Pound was equally disrespectful and wrote to the editor of *Poetry* complaining of "Mr. Tate's hyper-complex about the relation of his aunt's uncle to his mother-in-law's sister on the distaff side." (Tate, who was already annoyed by Pound's refusal to acknowledge Southern poetry as a separate genre, commented, "It is sad that a great poet should be such a buffoon, and lacking in the ordinary dignity of a negro field hand.")[141]

By 1932, for better or for worse, Tate was known as a Southern poet. When fifteen hundred living Confederate veterans planned a convention in Richmond, Virginia, that summer, Allen Cleaton, editor of the *Richmond Times-Dispatch*, asked Tate to write a poem in honor of the reunion. Tate was delighted by the request but refused to adhere to "the Noble Veteran but Better Off Defeated theme."[142] When Tate's typically demanding poem arrived at the newspaper, Cleaton observed that it might be "a little difficult for many of the readers, but then we have comic strips for them." In fact, he considered the poem "rather magnificent" and printed it on page one. Titled *To the Lacedemonians*, an allusion to a small ban of doomed Spartans who preferred to die rather than surrender a pass they were defending, the poem consisted of a monologue by an old Confederate soldier on the eve of the reunion. "People of my own kind . . . " the veteran explains. "I am here because the dead wear gray."[143]

Even in this occasional poem, which Donald Davidson thought should be subtitled *Fathers and Sons*, Tate revealed a preoccupation with kinship.[144] "My father," the poem's speaker explains, "said that everything but kin was less than kind."[145] A play on Hamlet's criticism of his stepfather, Claudius, the line could have been homage to Tate's own father, who was just about to celebrate his seventieth birthday. Shortly after *To the Lacedemonians* appeared in print, Tate joined his two brothers in Ashland for a family party.

VI

As Tate became increasingly obsessed with his Agrarian roots, Gordon, who now began using the first name "Caroline," was renewing her own loyalties to the South. Even before she assisted Tate in the research and writing of his Confederate biographies, she had adopted many of his theories about the Civil War, Reconstruction, and the coming of the New South. But what made her seem more Southern than ever was her blossoming career as a Southern fiction writer.[146] In November 1929, while she was still at work on her novel, Yvor Winters accepted her first short story for publication in his magazine, *Gyroscope*. The story, "Summer Dust," based on Gordon's childhood in Kentucky, was soon reprinted in O'Brien's *Best Short Stories of 1930*. On the strength of this success, Gordon applied for a Guggenheim grant to complete *Penhally*.

The Guggenheim application Gordon submitted in November 1930 suggested that she shared her husband's theories about the dissolution of the Southern family. The novel in progress she described to the Guggenheim committee followed a Kentucky family over four generations, beginning with their migration from Virginia in 1826 and ending at the onset of World War I. "The conflict in the action," she explained to the committee, "is between the European idea of the preservation of the family as a unit by the handing down of property from generation to generation and the pioneer idea of individualism." Her novel would culminate with the "grandchildren, who, caught in the tide of the new South become small town bankers and merchants and speedily rid themselves of the land which was the symbol of their fathers' victory over the wilderness."[147] Tate's Vanderbilt friends were probably not surprised to learn that Tate considered his wife's book "a masterpiece of its kind" and "the true picture at last of the 'Southern manor.' "[148] The previous year the group had considered asking her to contribute an essay to *I'll Take My Stand*.[149]

Though the Guggenheim Foundation rejected Gordon's application, she was able to complete *Penhally* without their help. (She did, however, receive some help from Tate, who wrote several of the concluding pages.) After reading the completed manuscript, Maxwell Perkins wrote to say that there was not a "false note in the whole length of it."[150] Yet when Scribner's released the book in September 1931, Perkins predicted that the book would sell poorly, for the Great Depression was causing a slump in the firm's sales. (Within the year, Scribner's earnings would drop to a seventh of what they were before the stock market crash in 1929.)[151]

Despite its commercial failure, *Penhally* met with critical acclaim and Perkins gave Gordon an advance on her second novel. By late 1932 she had begun work and hoped to have it finished by the following spring. The new book would expand on the genealogical themes in *Penhally* and examine "the main phases of life experienced by an American Southern family from the seventeenth century to the present day." Thinking of the Tates' life at Benfolly, she planned to write about "the clash between the landowning family and a family of the tenant class living on the same plantation."[152] The only problem was that her advance from Perkins was too small to improve the Tates' financial situation. They owed money to a variety of creditors in Clarksville and were having trouble making ends meet. Since Gordon had published two more short stories, she decided to reapply for the Guggenheim grant. This time she was successful.

Gordon's fellowship was scheduled to begin in July 1932 and the Tates began planning immediately for a trip to Europe. First they would sublet Benfolly and move to the Gordon family farm, Merry Mont, until their departure. Since they wanted to take their Model A Ford with them on the ship to Europe, they planned to drive north, stopping to leave Nancy with Caroline's aunt in Chattanooga, and to make a side trip to visit Andrew Lytle. When they arrived in New York, they would join their old friend Sally Wood; Lyle Lanier, his wife, Chink, and their son; and Caroline's cousins Manny Meriwether and Dorothy Ross. Since everyone was traveling to Europe, the group would divide itself between two cabins on the ocean liner. The Tates were thrilled by the prospect of having their friends along for the voyage.

Shortly after the Tates arrived in Le Havre in late July, however, they began suffering from their usual restlessness. Neither was in a particularly positive frame of mind. Tate had not wanted to return to Europe, and Gordon, who underwent both an abortion and an emergency appendectomy before leaving America, was still somewhat ill. After spending a few unsatisfying weeks in Paris, a city they found dirtier and more industrialized than in 1929, they drove with Sally Wood and the Laniers to the south of France in order to be with Ford Madox Ford, who promised to find them a villa near Toulon. Ford and his companion, Janice Biala, were lonely and insisted that they stay with them. When they finally were able to escape the Fords, they lived for a while in a beachfront pension, and then moved into the edenic villa Les Hortensias.[153] But Tate was unable to derive any pleasure from the idyllic environment. He tried working on his two books, but found that he was in "an absolute coma" intellectually.[154]

A trip Tate made in the summer of 1932 brought him temporarily out of his despondence and inspired him to write a poem that many consider his finest. In mid-August, Ford invited the Tates to go with him on a picnic on the banks of a creek in the nearby port of Cassis.[155] The outing was being organized by a friend of Ford's from Paris. With a local fisherman named Marius at the helm, the Tates and fourteen other guests sailed out of the Toulon harbor in a sardine boat until they came to a deep chasm of perfectly still, pellucid water surrounded by scarlet cliffs of three hundred feet. The group swam until eleven A.M., when they went ashore and began a seven-course dinner that included a bouillabaisse made from almost three dozen different kinds of fish. An elderly native who owned a vineyard that had been in his family for three hundred years descended from the cliffs carrying bottles of wine on his shoulders. "These people will never absorb the psychology of capitalism and the machine," Tate concluded afterward, for they were completely "pure of modern contamination."[156] He was convinced that France was a model of "perfect agrarianism."[157]

On that long day at Cassis, Tate felt closer to the land than he ever had in his life. Enveloped by green pine trees, he reaffirmed his belief in preserving "land not for profit but for enjoyment of civilized life."[158] After the picnic he felt as if he had eaten in a spot where men had been gathering since the Homeric age. He was so inspired that the following day he went into Toulon and purchased a used edition of Virgil's *Aeneid*. After reading it, he began a poem about the picnic, employing his usual strategy of merging occurrences in his own life with historical events. He tinkered with the poem for several months, sending copies to his friends under such titles as *Picnic at Cassis* and *Picnic by the Mediterranean*.[159] Finally he settled on *The Mediterranean*. The poem, first published in the *Yale Review*, began

> Where we went in the boat was a long bay
> A sling-shot wide walled in by towering stone . . .
>
> . . . .
>
> —Let us lie down once more by the breathing side
> Of ocean, where our live forefathers sleep . . .
>
> . . . .
>
> Westward, westward till the barbarous brine
> Whelms us to the tired world where tasseling corn,
> Fat beans, grapes sweeter than muscadine
> Rot on the vine: in that land were we born.[160]

Many years later, R. K. Meiners observed, "The implication is that 'we,' though citizens of a different age, are also in search of a place where we may find roots, a land that will be friendly to our endeavors, where we can establish a living tradition as did Aeneas." Although modern man, the critic continued, has difficulty imagining his past, he searches for bridges between the culture of his dead ancestors and present events.[161] In another poem written in that period, *Aeneas at Washington*, Tate conflated the ancient world with that of his childhood in Kentucky and Washington, D.C.[162]

Despite the new poems, Tate remained depressed. By autumn, he was not only "completely flat, and stale" but "utterly disgusted with the rich colors" in the French countryside.[163] John Peale Bishop was so distressed by a letter Tate wrote discussing the act of suicide that Tate had to reassure him he was not on the verge of taking his life.[164] But Tate could not find much incentive to stay inside and work. Without a good library, he found it difficult to complete the background research for the history of his family. Nor was it likely to have helped his morale when Bishop urged him complete the Lee biography even if his portrayal of Lee turned out to be "Allen Tate in a white beard."[165]

Harassed by the usual financial troubles, Tate forced himself to write book reviews and essays. He wanted to pay back the advance given him by Balch but spent everything he earned on living expenses. To make matters worse, he and Caroline suddenly found themselves leading a "very hollow and peculiar" social life in Toulon.[166] Ford Madox Ford was also sick and depressed; and neither he nor Janice Biala liked the Tates' friend Sally Wood, whose obsession with self-improvement was beginning to annoy everyone. Frank and Harriet Owsley visited, but Tate found Frank Owsley's parsimonious habits insufferable.

By the end of November, Tate could tolerate Toulon no further, and he and Caroline returned to Paris. After living for a while in an eighty-five-dollar-a-month pension on the rue Denfert-Rochereau, they relocated to the Hotel Fleurus and settled into a routine divided between writing and socializing. The Fitzgeralds and the Hemingways were no longer in Paris, so they entertained Sylvia Beach, Stella Bowen, the portrait painter, and John Peale Bishop and his wife.

Tate planned to finish *Ancestors of Exile* by the New Year, but he worked only sporadically on his manuscript. Either to distract himself or to test a new prose method, he tried writing fiction instead and that fall produced his first short story, "The Grey House."[167] He got the idea for the story before leaving for Europe. Stopping in Washington on the way to New York, he had gone to Georgetown to show Caroline the house that belonged to his mother's grandfather, or "Greatgrandpa Varnell."[168] Tate had not been to the house since he was a student at the Georgetown Preparatory School, and now finding it fascinating, he decided to use it as the setting in a story. Attempting a complicated narrative device employed by Henry James, the "trapped spectator" who sees and hears the other characters only at brief and intermittent intervals, Tate told the story through a veteran paralyzed in World War I. With little to do, the invalid, who now resides near the Georgetown campus, studies the limited movements of a mysterious old woman who appears once each year on the porch of "the old brick house on the corner across from the College gate." Below his room, he hears his aunt conversing with Mrs. "Nellie" Dulany, a neighbor who shares both the first name and the rambling conversational style of Tate's mother. Eavesdropping on the neighbor's monologue, the invalid tries to make sense of the elderly lady he observes on the porch. Although Tate never identifies the old woman, she seems "put together by all past generations." In the final scene, an energetic and affluent man modeled after Ben Tate arrives and leads "the old lady on her way." Five years later, some of the story's characters reemerged in altered form in Tate's one novel, *The Fathers*.[169]

Yet Tate was not immediately successful publishing the story. Although both Yvor Winters and Ellen Glasgow praised it, Maxwell Perkins rejected it for publication in *Scribner's Magazine*, calling it "a beautiful story, but too delicate and intricate, psychologically" for magazine readers.[170] Undeterred, Tate gave the vignette to Lincoln Kirstein, who cheerfully published it in the *Hound & Horn* under a new title, "The Immortal Woman."[171] A year later, the story was included in *O'Brien's Best Short Stories of 1934*, an honor Gordon had received in 1930—and one that undoubtedly fed Tate's interest in writing fiction.

Despite the short story, the longer Tate stayed in Europe, the harder he found it to work. By the end of January 1933, he reported being at his "lowest ebb for about seven years."[172] The genealogical book was going terribly; he had made six false starts, and had changed the title from *Ancestors of Exile* to *The Legacy* (a title he had briefly applied to his poem *Emblems*). The previous month, he admitted having "made a fundamental mistake in judgment" by taking on the book. "Perhaps under the influence of some of our agrarian abstractions," he explained, "I thought it would be easy; now I discover in myself a great reluctance in trying to make my ancestry 'illustrate' anything." It seemed to him impossible "to turn one's private resources into propaganda, even for a good cause."[173] Walter Minton and Earle Balch, still nursing their wounds inflicted by Tate's delays with the Lee biography, would soon learn that *The Legacy*, which he was to have finished the previous summer, would not be ready until the spring of 1933.

The Tates originally planned to stay in Europe for eight to ten months, but they were growing homesick. Allen missed Benfolly and hated watching the Agrarian movement dissolve from afar. France was no longer an agrarian utopia in his eyes. "The whole face of Europe has changed," he complained, "and some of the inner spirit."[174] Paris, especially, was "horrible."[175] Since the Guggenheim Foundation had appropriated only two-thirds of the three thousand dollars Caroline originally requested, the Tates were also broke. Before they left Toulon, Caroline wrote to Henry Moe at the Foundation to inform him that their financial condition was desperate—they were, in fact, "wondering where the next meal" would come from.[176] Back in Tennessee, the county had launched legal proceedings against them for failing to send in their property taxes on Benfolly. "I want to be home again," Tate wrote Davidson in despair. "I could almost hate everything I see."[177] Nor did it help matters when both he and Caroline began suffering from a variety of illnesses.

When the extra stipend from the Guggenheim Foundation had still not arrived by February 1933, the Tates returned to America immediately. Although Caroline had written a third of her new novel, she was feeling guilty for leaving Nancy with relatives, and she decided it was best for them to go home. Because the tenants at Benfolly held the lease through the summer, the Tates would have to move into Merry Mont, Caroline's grandmother's house in Trenton, Kentucky.

VII

To anyone familiar with Allen Tate's intense desire to belong to a family that lived in harmony with the land, it would seem logical to conclude that he would find contentment living on the subsistence farm where Caroline had spent her childhood and where her Meriwether relatives still lived. Situated fewer than a dozen miles from bucolic Benfolly, Merry Mont exuded a timeless pastoralism. Indeed, the Meriwethers' bond with the soil was so unconscious that they came close to qualifying as the natural Agrarian family Tate often alluded to in his writings. As auspicious a setting as the farm offered, however, Caroline and Allen's stay there produced a crisis that would alter their marriage forever.

In early March 1933, the Tates moved into the second floor of the enormous, rickety house owned by Caroline's grandmother, "Miss Carrie." Since the couple had no money whatsoever, Miss Carrie's largesse was a godsend: the farm's milk, ham, fresh fruit and vegetables were theirs for the taking.[178] Describing Merry Mont as a place "where the meat has never been known to give out," Tate summed up their dependent living arrangement in a bit of doggerel:

> What you gwine a do when the meat gives out?
> Stand in the corner with my lip poked out.
>
> What you gwine to do when the meat comes in?
> Stand in the corner with a greasy chin.[179]

Without a telephone or annoying neighbors, the Tates expected to do a great deal of writing. Yet no matter how much work they had to do, they secretly hated the prospect of not having houseguests, and they immediately set to work convincing Malcolm Cowley to come down for a visit. They knew that Cowley, a sportsman, would feel at home on the farm. Tate wanted to take him to the nearby ponds and streams where he and Caroline's father fished for bass. What was more, Tate wanted his Northern friend to see people born and raised in a genuine agrarian culture. "The Henry Meriwethers," he promised Cowley, "are the nicest people in the neighborhood—very quiet—and they live very simply and think high; but even at that, being so quiet, they neither say what they think nor what they don't think."[180]

Cowley drove down to Kentucky in early May. He was soon ensconced in Cloverlands, a second Meriwether farm adjacent to Merry Mont. Years later, he wrote about the idyllic setting he found there: "Looking northward into Kentucky and southward into Tennessee, I could see sheep meadows like immense playgrounds worn bare in patches, then wheatfields already turning a paler green, with hints of gold, then cornfields pin-striped with the first bright green shoots, and among them level tobacco fields now ready for planting, after being disk-harrowed and rolled and, it seemed to me, sandpapered as smooth as the floor of Madison Square Garden. The east and west horizons were broken lines of forest. Except for Cloverlands, there were no houses in sight, but only three or four unpainted tobacco barns standing like sentries in the fields. The only token of the twentieth century was the cloud of dust that followed a distant motor car."[181]

Cowley joined the daily writing routine. Immediately after breakfast, he would begin laboring on *Exile's Return*, his memoir of the 1920s. Gordon worked on her novel while Tate tinkered with the prospectus and opening chapter to his ancestor book. "Life is pretty dull," Caroline observed.[182] Since the weather was hot and dry, they spent a good deal of their time quenching their thirst with beer and sitting on the front porch passing time with the Meriwethers. In the late day, while Allen searched for genealogical records in local archives, Cowley and Gordon went off to swim. The two swimmers, who were becoming closer friends, soon had people gossiping; once, as Caroline was leaving to have dinner with Malcolm, Miss Carrie cut short the trip. "You run around too much with married men," she said to her granddaughter. Cowley stood by her side, mortified.[183] But the two claimed to be companions only. "We were friends," he insisted years later. "Caroline, I think, was one of the chastest women I have ever met."[184]

It took a brief time for Cowley to be accepted by the Southerners in his midst. Tate, who introduced him as "our Yankee friend,"[185] worried "lest his liberalism should not thrive in this ignorant community."[186] "The Meriwethers," Cowley remembered, "suspected me of holding strange opinions and were too polite to tempt me into making statements with which they might have to disagree. As a guest I tried to match their politeness, with the result that our conversations on the porch, though sometimes literary, were usually confined to sempiternal topics like tobacco growing, the shiftlessness of tenant farmers, and how soon it would rain."[187] Before long, Miss Carrie admitted that he was "one of the nicest *northern* gentlemen" she had ever known.[188]

Away from Merry Mont, Cowley and the Tates found other social distractions. Not far from the Meriwethers lay the farm of Caroline's cousins, the Henrys, whose telephone the Tates relied upon for communication with the outside world. After Gus Henry suffered a stroke and expired, the expansive farm continued to operate under the watchful eye of his fiercely independent daughter, Marion. The Tates were already well acquainted with Marion. Caroline remembered how she came to her aid in 1931 by proofreading *Penhally* "in a most business like way." That same year, Allen had driven Marion to Nashville and tried to get work for her at a library, but her country manner ruined her prospects. "If you don't *have* to earn your living," Caroline said afterward of her cousin's behavior, "people aren't going to do much about it."[189]

Marion was notably self-absorbed. A beautiful young woman, she once complained to Caroline that "her whole life" had been "marred" because her parents kept her in stockings long after other girls were wearing socks.[190] One day, when Cowley was alone with her, he noted that "she wanted to talk about herself." He cringed when she spoke of having abandoned her desire "to *create*" for a burning ambition to acquire land. He recalled how "she closed her fist as if she were squeezing the farms together." He was haunted by her eyes. "I want all the land that my grandfather owned," she continued—"that was more than five thousand acres, and it's all I want in the world." Cowley tactfully asked what would become of the land when she died. "I don't care," she responded, missing the irony. "I'm all there is. It all comes down to me. I don't care what happens to it after I'm gone."[191]

Caroline, Malcolm, and Allen took Marion on a sightseeing trip along the Cumberland River. The group wanted to inspect a site where one of Marion's Confederate ancestors fought in a losing battle against the Union Army. After touring the fort, however, Marion would not come into a graveyard of Union soldiers. "I wouldn't be seen alive or dead in a Yankee burying ground," she explained. Allen, who was, after all, author of *Ode to the Confederate Dead*, had to have been impressed. Caroline, though, seemed to sense the sympathy that had developed between her husband and her cousin. In protest, she said, "But they're all *dead* yankees." The day's neo-Confederate theme diminished but slightly when Cowley the "Yankee" and Tate the "Rebel" stood in front of a war monument and posed for a picture as peaceful representatives of the Union and Confederate armies.[192]

In the meantime, Tate was distracted from his goal of completing the ancestor book. He lost the entire month of May battling what Miss Carrie called "spring poisoning."[193] He read Ellen Glasgow novels and corresponded with magazine editors and friends. Looking for income wherever he could find it, he took on the usual number of book reviews. He also felt increasingly harrassed by his parenting duties and now referred to his "summer complaint," a disturbance "familiar to all fathers of small children."[194] At first, he had been looking forward to seeing Nancy again. For a mere five dollars, he purchased a Shetland pony for her as a surprise welcome-home gift. Yet he and Caroline were shocked to discover how much Nancy had changed in their absence. Not only had she become somewhat obese—"71 lbs., 20 overweight,"[195] they told friends—but her Southern accent was much more pronounced after her months in Chattanooga. When she was not petitioning them for "aahce cream," she was singing popular tunes she had learned from the radio. Her parents were especially distressed when they found that she had memorized lyrics they thought should be unintelligible to a prepubescent girl. "You go home and pack your panties," she crooned repeatedly. "I'll go home and pack my scanties and we'll shuffle off to Buffalo."[196]

Tensions mounted on the overcrowded farm. "Going to Merry Mont was a mistake . . . ," Caroline confided to a friend; "it is just too hectic and the place has a very bad influence on me and through me on Allen. The family responsibilities kept getting heavier and heavier."[197] Caroline hated the way her Uncle Rob tried to make her feel guilty for not agreeing to stay on and nurse her increasingly infirm grandmother. When Allen began escaping to make more and more research trips, Caroline was so distraught over family matters that she barely seemed to care. "You were right about Allen's library spasms," she wrote to

Sally Wood. "Violent attacks, of course, all summer. But I was so glad to get him out of the house I was rather glad he had them."[198]

In mid-June, it came out that Allen had been enjoying a fling with Marion Henry.[199] All hell broke loose. Tate, who admitted to Cowley that the affair had ended and that he was feeling "cut to pieces,"[200] abandoned Merry Mont immediately. He wanted to spend a month with Andrew Lytle at his farm in Guntersville, Alabama. But he was emotionally paralyzed and had to cancel the trip. "I have been in a state of the most harassed indecision," he wrote Lytle from Nashville. "There is no time to describe it, even if I were equal to the task. Let it be enough for me to say that I am deeply troubled, and I must stay here for a while, for reasons that I cannot explain."[201] Years later, he did explain his indecisiveness, saying that instead of having an affair, he wished he had simply left Caroline: "But I was too weak," he lamented, "and I was in love with her."[202] For the next month or so, he wandered between Tennessee and Kentucky. Caroline remained in Merry Mont without even realizing, she later observed, that she had "been in the throes of a minor nervous collapse for some weeks."[203] Not until a few weeks into July did Tate, on the way to Cincinnati to see Ben (who had been hospitalized with appendicitis), stop at Merry Mont and reconcile with Caroline. A week later, the couple rendezvoused at Andrew Lytle's farm and spent a month there.

Years later, Tate blamed the affair on the Caroline's all-consuming relationship with the Meriwethers.[204] Both Caroline and Allen had become so fascinated by genealogy and with the decline of Southern aristocracy that they had taken to denigrating the social backgrounds of each other's families. Caroline, who had long harbored doubts as to the gentility of her husband's family, felt more comfortable with her own. That summer, in the company of her old-fashioned grandmother and her manipulative Uncle Rob, she grew patronizing toward Allen. "I heard you, for two months," Tate later complained, "speak to me in the collective tone and meaning of a Sho Nuff Maywether, as if you were possessed."[205] Since Allen now thought that the Meriwether men were both illiterate and noisome, and the Meriwether women "fanatically and ritualistically clean," Caroline's adoption of the family persona annoyed him no end.[206] But Caroline knew how to shrug off her husband's hostility toward her relatives. She once told a friend that he "used to say that the Meriwethers stayed on the land because they were such louts they couldn't get along in town!" But, she added sarcastically, "He was actually jealous of them. His own family used to own part of Pennsylvania Avenue in Washington but they had a habit of selling off portions of land when one of them wanted to take a trip."[207]

It was not so much the Meriwethers that Allen detested, but Caroline's preoccupation with them at the expense of her relationship with him. He tried for years to explain the affair with Marion Henry, which he said was his only lapse in the first two decades of their marriage. Most often, he described the fateful dalliance as punishment for Caroline's rejection of him. "My infidelity," he said later, "was a result of what I considered an almost total withdrawal from me in the summer of 1933. I know now it was not *from* me, but *into* what I used to call the Merry Mont fantasy or myth." Unable to get from Caroline the "total acceptance" he craved, he "blindly struck out to find it elsewhere, even for a few weeks of my sort of make-believe with that woman."[208]

Yet Tate also recognized that, at some level, his own upbringing was partially responsible for his behavior in his marriage. Recalling the affair decades later, he said to Caroline, "I was convinced that you had withdrawn from me into what I called the Mister Rob myth, and I treated you violently and humiliated you. I think you had actually withdrawn temporarily, but instead of seeing this as your own trouble, I saw it as mine; whereas mine, like yours, went far back into my childhood and only indirectly had anything to do with what I imagined you were feeling towards me."[209]

After Tate's fling in 1933, Gordon saw him as different from the man she had married. "I became two persons"; Tate said when they divorced for the first time in 1945, "one the noble creature, a Platonic abstraction, to whom formal respect was paid—this was I as mind, as poet; the other, the reincarnation of a member of my family, *moyen et sensuel*, really low-bred if not low-born, who might at any moment be expected to betray her."[210] In effect, Caroline had cast him permanently in the role of his own father.

Chapter Seven
Orphan of the South

After a futile effort late in the summer of 1933 to borrow money from the Guggenheim Foundation, Tate and Gordon left Cornsilk and returned to Clarksville in the company of the Lytles. Being so impoverished, Tate came home with a new desire to make Benfolly productive. Yet if he marveled at the tall ears of corn that were growing on his own land, Benfolly, like most subsistence farms in the South, was generating no real income for the Tates, neither of whom had any full-time work. The passing months consisted of little more than a series of desperate telegrams asking editors for advance payments on freelance work. "The daily financial pressure is demoralizing," Tate admitted.[1] Even Ben, who had so generously purchased the farm for them, was suffering as a result of the Great Depression and could offer them little in the way of financial assistance.

What Tate called "the worst poverty" he had ever known helps to explain his frequent pleas to Earle Balch for extensions on his deadlines.[2] "There has got to be some kind of revolutionary change in our financial basis," he complained.[3] But the causes of Tate's mental block between the autumn of 1933 and the autumn of 1935 were not economic alone. He was trapped between his growing political convictions and his genealogical preoccupations, between his desire to belong to a Southern coterie and his obsession with his origins. If ideological assuredness shaped his public identity as a Southern intellectual, spiritual loneliness festered in his artistic imagination.

While he might have relieved at least the immediate source of his distress by dropping either the Lee biography or *The Legacy*—or by declining to write book reviews—he put himself under even greater pressure by agreeing to take on new work. Within a two-year period, he committed himself to more writing projects than many authors would be able to complete in a lifetime. Although he had already succeeded in persuading Scribner's to publish a collection of his critical essays, he now tried to interest them in a college textbook on modern poetry that Red Warren and he would produce in collaboration. Tate also agreed to write a history of Southern literature for Funk and Wagnall's—even as he was writing to Harper's to sell them on the idea of a sequel to *I'll Take My Stand*. Spreading himself still thinner, he tried to persuade Lovat Dickson, a British publishing concern, to bring out another collection of his poems, while he simultaneously agreed to let the Alcestis Press, an independent firm in New York, publish a special numbered edition of his recent verse.

All of these projects provided him with excuses to avoid *The Legacy*, the manuscript of which he had not worked on with enthusiasm since the summer. In June 1933, he had been so confident he could soon complete the book that he allowed Balch to release an advertising prospectus that promised "a powerful and enthralling book" that would detail "the breakdown of the aristocratic system, under the pressure of industrialism, and the breakup of the religious unity of the family." The prospectus even sported a mock up of the title page in which a new title for the book was revealed: *The Fathers*.[4]

The advertising prospectus revealed that Tate had altered his conception of the book, which now culminated not in a chapter about himself and Ben, but in one based upon their mother—a conclusion that would allow him to build upon "The Immortal Woman," the short story he had already written. Writing "not history, not biography, and yet not precisely fiction," he planned to trace the genealogy of both sides of his family, the humble pioneer Allens on his father's side and the aristocratic Virginia Bogans on his mother's. Reduced from eight to seven chapters, the story was organized around three main themes: "the growth of a family in Virginia" and its destruction during the Civil War; the parallel "wanderings and final settlement in Kentucky of a typical Scotch-Irish family"; and, finally, "the fusion of these two strains in the chaos of the Reconstruction." The book would present the life of one character in each of seven successive generations, concluding in a stream-of-consciousness monologue spoken by a woman representing the family's Scotch-Irish and Tidewater descent lines intermixed. Tate intended this woman, whom he modeled after his mother, to be a "judgment upon the modern mind." Her monologue would be a "protest against the aimless life to which she is committed without quite understanding why it is aimless."[5]

Besides "The Immortal Woman," Tate succeeded in writing only one other complete chapter of this book, a chapter he called "The Migration." Changing the name of his father's Scotch-Irish ancestors from "Allen" to "Elwin," he told the story of their journey from Virginia to Kentucky at the end of the eighteenth century. Rhodam Elwin, the narrator of the story, was supposed to be Tate's great-grandfather, Rodam Allen, but he bore some resemblance to Tate himself. Both were educated in large part by their mothers at home and instructed somewhat crudely in sex education by a tall and powerful father.

The theme of the chapter was a favorite of Tate's: family stability is ruined when one generation is no longer able to pass land on to the next. Lured by the land boom in the West, the Elwins migrate from Virginia to North Carolina and then to the Cumberland Valley, where they settle. The pioneering family is quickly "reconciled to the land,"[6] but when wealthy gentry from Tidewater Virginia begin purchasing land around them, their community begins to fall apart. After part of the family moves on to Illinois (where Nellie and Orley Tate would one day begin their family), Rhodam Elwin's father dies, but not before symbolically freeing their oldest slave.

Tate wrote the chapter in archaic English, later explaining that he was trying to "master the detail of pioneer life and give it a hint of Defoe-like verisimilitude."[7] But a significant portion of Tate's prose was not his own. Without using quotation marks or otherwise identifying it as the work of another writer, he inserted extensive passages from James Ross's *Life and Times of Elder Reuben Ross*, an obscure nineteenth-century memoir about a Baptist minister. The memoir, which contained two chapters about a family's migration over the Virginia mountains, was written by an uncle of Caroline's in Clarksville. When Tate and Gordon discovered the memoir, they were stunned by it and praised Ross's brilliant prose style to friends. Yet Tate allowed "The Migration" to appear in the *Yale Review* without including any mention of Ross in the text of the story.[8]

The reasons for Tate's apparent plagiarism are complex. Distracted by the Marion Henry affair, anxious over his dire financial straits, and desperate to finish the ancestor book, he was probably delighted to have located a source that illustrated so aptly his view of antebellum culture, and that freed him of the difficult task of re-creating an authentic ancestral monologue. Perhaps he also found it easy to borrow prose written by one of his Southern relations. Like many writers of the era, including his own wife, he believed that "public documents" existed almost to be incorporated into historical fiction. He apparently believed he was identifying sufficiently his sources for "The Migration" when he told an editor at the *Yale Review* that "the tone and character of the narrator are fictitious; but every statement in it is based upon facts, both public documents of the time and family letters."[9] Moreover, according to Tate's Agrarian schema, successful prose styles were merely the perfect expression of self-contained regional cultures—so much so that the credit-claiming ego of Southern writers ought to be restrained. "My theory of literature," he told Merrill Moore that year, ". . . holds that the author should be entirely self-effacing. It would be better if we could have literature without authorship which is one of the perplexing evils of civilization."[10] Whatever the ultimate reason for Tate's appropriation of the Ross text, he later dismissed the short story. When including it in a collected edition of his fiction, he explained, "The chronicle of the Elwins I reprint here only to let them bow themselves out."[11]

Yet his evasive struggle with the story was not without benefit: He learned that that he could not transform family lore into an objective history book. In part, the problem was logistical and economic; it was too difficult to locate genealogical records and other sources while also taking on smaller writing projects for money. But there was also a personal factor that made it impossible for him to complete the project. He was beginning to accept that neither Nellie nor Orley Tate's stories belonged in a work of nonfiction. "I soon discovered," he explained years later, "that knowledge of obscure persons in the past is not history."[12]

What was more, an event on the twenty-first of October 1933 that might have eased his worries about using living people in *The Fathers* only heightened his desire to drop both it and the Lee biography. Tate's real father, who had been bedridden since being hit by a taxi several months earlier, died of a heart attack in Covington, Kentucky. Orley Tate's death, attributed to a blood clot, was swift and painless. "He suffered none at all," Tate reported to Andrew Lytle, "and we are the more reconciled to his death because there was no hope of his ever walking again." Tate attended the modest funeral in Kentucky, and afterward his brother Varnell accompanied the coffin to Washington, D.C., for burial.[13]

"A long period of trouble reached a climax in my father's death," Tate admitted.[14] "I have," he wrote John Peale Bishop, "out of heroism or cowardice (take your choice) thrown over the ancestry book forever. The agony was great, but the peace of mind is greater. It was a simple problem that I could not solve. The discrepancy between the outward significance and the private was so enormous that I decided that I could not handle the material in that form at all, without faking either the significance or the material. A couple of years were wasted, but I learned a lesson."[15]

More for himself than for Bishop, Tate also tried to eulogize the father who had been so profligate. "He was seventy-one," Tate offered, "died in poverty after a reckless life, but gallantly; with his last words he rallied the nurse about her good looks."[16] Allen's ironic account of his father's roving eye hid more than the grief and guilt he felt upon his death. There was another casualty—at least for the time being, he had allowed Orley to take *The Fathers* with him to the grave; to continue in an effort to write a genealogy of the South would have been to bury the truth about a father who was, if nothing else, a product of the same ancestral world his son sometimes found compelling.[17]

Both motherless and fatherless, Tate was now an orphan not only in spirit but in fact. Perhaps to make himself feel better, he began writing verse recasting his relationship with his parents. Using as a model an earlier poem called *The Meaning of Life*,[18] he wrote *The Meaning of Death: An After-Dinner Speech*, a poem in which he recalled his parents' efforts to discipline him in his youth:

> . . . the year when, my time begun,
> I loitered in the backyard by the alley;
> When I was a small boy living at home
> The dark came on in summer at eight o'clock
> For little Lord Fauntleroy in a perfect frock
> By the alley; mother took him by the ear
> To show a Southern gentleman what things were
> Like.

Although Tate still harbored resentments over the way his parents treated him in his childhood, he was struggling to forgive both his mother's dominance and his father's distance. "Gentleman," the poem continued, "it is necessary that we forget the past, its related errors, the coarseness of parents."[19] Yet it was no easier, Tate soon discovered, to absolve the "Charming Lady" and her "Southern gentleman" once that they were both dead.

Just as frustrating, he still faced the unpleasant task of having to explain to everyone why he had stopped work on the Lee book. He was certain Lee was not the Southern father figure he had needed since childhood, but that seemed an inadequate excuse, and he looked for one more plausible. With some exaggeration, he began complaining that Douglas Southall Freeman, the Richmond newspaper editor whose brilliant and definitive four-volume biography of Lee would eventually win the Pulitzer Prize, had monopolized the sources.[20] When the initial volumes of Freeman's biography appeared in 1934, Tate praised it as "the most exhaustively documented biography in the entire field of Southern history."[21] When the second set of volumes appeared soon afterward, Tate called the work "one of the great American biographies on the Victorian model." But he charged Freeman with having tacitly accepted the Northern interpretation of Lee's postwar attitudes— namely, that "Lee meant that the South should become a suburb of the North, should go industrial, go modern."[22] Tate had come to see Lee so much through the lens of Agrarianism and his own family history that he was annoyed when a neutral scholarly account gained such prominence. Adopting the patronizing tone he reserved for references to his father, Tate later referred to Freeman as "a fine old gentleman" who "really didn't understand much of anything."[23]

With both of his parents gone and neither the genealogical book nor the Lee biography to write, Tate needed to find another way to transform his psychic hollowness into a politically viable idea about Southern history. The alternating feelings of submission and rejection he had felt toward his parents when they were alive remained so much a force in his life that he could find a mediating authority only in his increasingly intense relationships with other Southern conservatives. He now sought and fashioned a different kind of family, one that drew its strength from fraternity. What had previously caused him pain—the absence of family rootedness—now became a paradigm for explaining the fate of traditionalists in the South. What had begun as a search for parental authority would soon become a rallying call for his greatest hope: "a Conservative Revolution" in America.[24]

II

Tate's renewed search for a fraternity of conservatives temporarily drew him back to his Vanderbilt peers. Ever since his second trip to Europe, he had been worrying that the Agrarians had lost all interest in agitating for their cause. "What I hear from Nashville," he had written Davidson from Paris in 1932, "seems to prove that the Agrarian Movement has degenerated into pleasant poker games on Saturday night."[25] Now, however, he and the other contributors to *I'll Take My Stand* conceived a second phase to their movement in which they would launch into public debate with the New Deal strategists who had gained power when Franklin D. Roosevelt was elected president of the United States that November.[26] But the Agrarians had no official publication and no financial supporters. Even conservative editors, once reliable friends such as Lincoln Kirstein and Bernard Bandler of the *Hound & Horn*, were now more interested in the Agrarians' literary criticism than in their polemics.[27] It therefore seemed like a miracle when, in the spring of 1933, an editor appeared who wanted to help them breathe new life into the movement. What the Agrarians did not know, however, was that their prospective savior, a man named Seward Collins, would help spell their demise.[28]

Seward B. Collins was a wealthy classmate of Edmund Wilson's at Princeton University. He had purchased the *Bookman* from the George H. Doran Company in 1927 and edited it as a relatively undistinguished magazine for several years. But Collins soon abandoned his inconspicuous editorial style and became a staunch advocate of Humanism during the controversy that raged among intellectuals from 1928 to 1930. He would eventually be charged with dismissing "the whole of the 1920's, consigning poets and novelists, critics and dramatists, to one vast charnel house, and extending salvation only to the little handful of those who have accepted the gospel of More and Babbitt."[29]

Tate had published sporadically in the *Bookman* since meeting Collins in New York in 1928. But tensions developed when Collins declined to publish Tate's controversial essay "The Fallacy of Humanism." Collins was "shocked at the tone of" the article. "I won't let anybody talk like that about More and Babbitt in my magazine," he confided to another contributor.[30] After Eliot published Tate's essay in the *Criterion*, Collins retaliated by publishing "Humanism and Impudence," the work of a young professor named Robert Shafer. Accusing Tate of intentionally misrepresenting the Humanists' views of religion, Shafer mocked Tate as "the new Socrates" and likened him to Mencken and "other buffoons of the literary arena." Ultimately, Shafer concluded, Tate was " 'a mere talking mole!' "[31] Collins was absolutely delighted by the vituperative article and told Shafer that it was known as "Tit for Tate" at the headquarters of the *Bookman*.[32]

Tate, who thought that more than half of the article consisted of "personal abuse and defamation of character,"[33] was enraged. "I haven't made up my mind whether I am going to horsewhip him or not," he said of Shafer.[34] He demanded that Shafer apologize for imputing his motives and for concluding the attack on such a "wholly gratuitous" note.[35] Friends began to worry that Tate might actually throw down the gauntlet. "For the love of God," warned Yvor Winters, "don't get into any kind of muddle about him—I mean physically, legally, or psychically." Back when men still fought duels, Winters reasoned, "one technically a gentleman did not fight with one who was not technically a gentleman."[36] Likewise, Lyle Lanier urged Tate to control his "outraged feelings for the son-of-a-bitch."[37] But Tate was already into one of his favorite modes: intellectual warfare. When the apology he asked for failed to materialize, he persuaded his brother Ben to begin signing a series of letters that he himself was writing. The first such letter to Shafer began, "My brother, Allen Tate, being under the existing circumstances unwilling to communicate with you directly, has asked me to write you his opinion of your letter to him."[38] Shafer still refused to apologize, but he was frightened enough to have "Humanism and Impudence" reviewed by an attorney, who found "enough evidence to go to the jury," but thought "a libel case . . . weak."[39] Tate and Shafer continued to exchange letters for several more weeks, and both men published detailed and vigorous rebuttals. Although Tate assured brother Ben that he would "beat hell out of" Shafer if he ran into him on the street, he soon grew bored by the dispute and let it drop.[40]

Collins, however, was unwilling to let the controversy fade. In his own magazine, he wrote and published an essay in which he accused Tate of "fantastic exhibitions of pseudo-subtlety, pseudo-profundity and irresponsibility."[41] Some years afterward, he was still calling Tate "puerile" and prefaced printed references to his name with the word "even" in order to call attention to the intellectual marginality he accorded his opinions.[42] In response to the increasing radicalism of the era, however, Collins began to appreciate Tate and the Agrarians for their conservative ideology. When Collins decided at the New Deal's inception to revamp the *Bookman* as a conservative political digest, he put aside previous hostilities and contacted the Agrarians for help editing his new publication, the *American Review*.[43]

Tate had vowed never again to write anything for Collins, whom he considered "insane."[44] But in 1933 he believed he could use the editor's resources to revive the Agrarian movement. Making what turned out to be one of the more significant mistakes of his career, Tate urged Donald Davidson to "accept his offer without any reservations whatever." Knowing Davidson's tendency to vacillate, Tate implored: "For God's sake, don't use a hesitating tone . . . or make it appear that there are any difficulties whatever." Tate imagined Collins only as a figurehead who would have little control over the *American Review*; the real editors would be, besides Tate himself, the seven most compatible Agrarians: Davidson, Lanier, Lytle, Owsley, Ransom, Wade, and Warren. An inner triumvirate—Tate, Davidson, and Ransom—would monitor Collins's relationship to the group. The best way to manipulate Collins for their own purposes, Tate told Davidson, would be to invite the editor to Tennessee and to see whether he would be willing to relocate the magazine to the South. "We could control him better here, in every sense"; Tate explained. "We must remember that he is as fickle as a debutante and needs watching."[45]

Tate's mistrust was well placed, for Collins and he had different goals in mind. While Tate sought first and foremost to promote the unique aspects of Southern Agrarianism, Collins seemed to care more about right-wing European conservatives enamored with royalty. The two men also parted ways over the function of art: Collins saw it as nothing but a tool to be used for a political purpose, while Tate was more committed to the autonomy of aesthetic judgments. The truth was that Tate believed in poetry more than he ever did politics. As such, there was a strained quality to his efforts to persuade Collins that the Agrarians shared his belief in the possibility of an international conservative movement. "I think we are and were a little more aware of the world movement towards reaction than *I'll Take My Stand* indicated," he wrote Collins. "We suppressed for reasons of strategy, most of the references to a similar movement in England and France. Our reason was this: We felt that if we could present the whole case for reactionary agrarianism in Southern terms, we should make a strong appeal to those very foreign allies whom we ignored. We were not only talking about an idea; we had the concrete basis for its realization." Although Tate himself often questioned whether Agrarianism could (or should) amount to anything more than an aesthetic movement, he knew when to emphasize the movement's political possibilities. Resurrecting an idea he himself had begun with—the desirability of emulating the right-wing Action Française—he promised Collins that the group would "give full support to" the Catholic reactionaries overseas. One suspects, however, both opportunism and hyperbole in Tate's statement to Collins that "Great reactionary changes will mark the next half-century, changes so great that even their proponents do not dare to predict their full scope."[46]

On March 31, 1933, Collins gathered with the Agrarians for a week-end rendezvous at Cornsilk. Everyone agreed that the Alabama meeting was enormously successful, but the hard-drinking Vanderbilt group was perplexed by Collins's teetotaling prudishness. When Andrew Lytle's father, who hosted the event, prepared a heavy breakfast that included several meats, he was dumbfounded when Collins asked instead for a cup of "weak tea." Caroline thought Mr. Lytle "would have said 'Certainly, just a minute,' if he'd been asked for a roasted ox, but tea was too much for him." After much rummaging, he located "a package of jasmine tea left by Andrew's aunts in a remote cupboard."[47] Meanwhile, Tate was repulsed by Collins's "puritan zeal," his black-and-white morality, and "the thin, unimaginative single track" of his intellect. But he did give Collins credit for being able to keep pace with the Agrarians throughout the weekend. "He is no weak fellow," he concluded. "Any man who can stand up for seventy-two hours against eight of the hardest and most fluent talkers alive wins our admiration." Tate begrudgingly decided he was "a fine and sincere fellow."[48]

Tate also found areas of ideological agreement with Collins. He was thrilled to learn about Collins's conservative political heroes, the British Distributists Hilaire Belloc and G. K. Chesterton. Devoted proponents of the religious authority, ruralism, agriculturalism, and guild economy they and their followers admired in Catholic societies during the Middle Ages, these two Distributists abhorred modernity, monopoly capitalism, and the uncontrolled growth of government. Both Chesterton and Belloc also argued tirelessly for land redistribution to the individual as a way to protect personal liberty. "The natural action, when property has fallen into fewer hands," wrote Chesterton, "is to restore it to more numerous hands." After reading the two essayists, Tate exclaimed to Collins, "Great God, how could we have missed all this? It is all pure gospel."[49]

Tate further agreed with Collins that a coalition of conservatives ought to begin responding to the American "Radicals" both men thought were gaining power as a result of sympathy generated by the Harlan, Kentucky, coal miners' strike, by the Sacco and Vanzetti trials, and by the renewed prosecution, in 1933, of the Scottsboro defendants (in 1931, nine African American men had been accused—falsely, it was later proven—of raping two white women.)[50] Sharing Collins's tendency to see liberal conspiracies in all sectors of society, Tate and the Agrarians also accepted without qualms the anti-Semitic stereotypes the editor had acquired in part from reading *The Jews* by Hilaire Belloc. Tate was "astonished," he told John Peale Bishop, to find "that

Collins has the same idea we have on the Jewish nature of liberalism and on the Old Testament character of *Das Kapital*." Moreover, in an enigmatic combination of condemnation and endorsement, Tate added, "with the fierce, literal, Yankee logic of his, Collins has worked himself into a great froth over the Jews. Let us not discourage him."[51] (While Tate did not evince anti-Semitism in his later years, clearly he did so here.)

Tate was neither hopeful about the size of the readership of Collins's magazine nor convinced that the group's conservative ideas would ever make it to the masses, but he was soon disguising his Agrarian loyalties and praising the editor's varied tastes. In the inaugural issue of April 1933, in which work by John Donald Wade and Donald Davidson appeared in the company of essays by Belloc, Chesterton, and Paul Elmer More, Collins promised a magazine that would be populated not only by Agrarians and Distributists, but also by the Humanists and the Catholic medievalists known as "neo-scholastics." The new periodical, he hoped, would become "a forum for the views of these 'Radicals of the Right,' or 'Revolutionary Conservatives.' " Collins further assured readers that "Fascist economics" would receive "sympathetic exposition" in subsequent issues.[52] After reading the first issue, Tate told Collins (one hopes disingenuously), "It is the only magazine I've ever read every word of which I was able to agree with."[53]

Tate, who was eventually permitted to edit an *American Review* issue devoted to poetry, wrote but a fraction of the Agrarian political essays that appeared in the magazine. The political contributions he did make were consistently leveled at liberals and radicals.[54] His first contribution to the magazine, "The Problem of the Unemployed: A Modest Proposal," had been rejected several years earlier by the editors of the *New Republic*. The revised version of the satire, which appeared as the lead article in Collins's second issue, was timely in light of the extremely high rate of unemployment during the Great Depression. Intended to provoke, the article was modeled on "A Modest Proposal" (1729), Jonathan Swift's classic satire arguing that impoverished Irish children could be eliminated by being fed to the affluent. The objects of Tate's satire were in this case Communists and capitalists, both of whom, he argued, worship machines, view individuals as economic units, and idealize a world in which families are stripped of their right to own land. Both New Deal liberals and *New Republic* radicals, Tate believed, promoted their sacred idea of a planned economy without finding jobs for the unemployed and their families, who constituted the 25 million poor people in the country. One solution, he suggested, would be to make prostitutes out of unemployed women—and pimps (as well as prostitutes) out of the men. But an even better solution, Tate continued, would be to exterminate all the impoverished families! That way, the trace minerals in their corpses could be recovered and sold into the market as precious resources. "The body of the mother first," he proposed revealingly, "then the body of the father, could be valued at the current price of the carbon, nitrogen, chlorine, sodium, potassium, silicon, that each yielded, and a fund deposited to the credit of the remaining family. When the children had eaten through this fund, or when, to be exact, the last child had exhausted the total credit established by the gross weight of his kin, his time would have come."[55] The subtext of this macabre satire was a familiar one in Tate's work: modern industrialism had not only destroyed the nuclear family, but was responsible for the financial ruin—and perhaps even the death—of his own parents.

Tate also used the *American Review* as forum for criticizing Southern liberals. In the initial phase of the New Deal, federal agencies needed solutions to countless domestic problems. Since many of those problems were graphically visible in the states below the Mason-Dixon Line, Southern liberals—especially sociologists, political scientists, and journalists—were enjoying new clout. Throughout the mid-1930s, these newly prominent Southerners repeatedly crossed paths with the Agrarians. Sometimes the two groups were mentioned together in periodicals because of the tendency of Northern journalists to lump together Southerners of even the most antithetical political positions. Other times, the two groups met head on, zealously debating industrialism, the so-called Negro problem, and farming issues. Liberal southern journalists such as Gerald W. Johnson, a protégé of H. L. Mencken's whose writings appeared regularly in the *New Republic*; Virginius Dabney, author of *Liberalism in the South* (1932) and editor at the *Richmond Times-Dispatch*; and Jonathan Daniels, editor of his family's paper, the *Raleigh News and Observer*, all followed their conservative counterparts closely and made sure that the Agrarian movement appeared in the news frequently, although rarely in a favorable light.

Collins, the Agrarians hoped, would give them the means to fight such liberals. "What we've needed all along," Tate said of their new supporter, "is a zealot to sponsor a campaign against the very foundations of zealotry."[56] To Tate, all of the liberal groups represented a synthesis of everything he had come to detest: Marxism, secularism, positivism, and federalism. What was worse, they often operated out of universities, and Tate thought academicians had been co-opted in the same manner he believed the abolitionists had been; these new "liberal professors," he said in disdain, were merely the "hired men" of "the Southern industrialist."[57]

The most visible of the Southern liberals were affiliated with the progressive University of North Carolina at Chapel Hill, and they became the principal antagonists to the Agrarians. The "Chapel Hill Planners,"[58] as the group was called, committed themselves to social progress in a New South, even if such advancement entailed cooperation with the forces of industrial and scientific modernization. The group's leaders included the prolific Howard W. Odum, father of the sociology department at Chapel Hill; Rupert B. Vance, Odum's colleague and an expert on cotton tenancy; and W. T. Couch, the outspoken liberal editor at the University of North Carolina Press.[59] On the whole, these men saw the South as a problem that, while enormous in scope, could be solved by the rationality of social science and economic planning. ("We oppose to the notion of 'planned economy' the notion of 'planned society,' " Tate said in response.)[60]

The North Carolina men were not watching impassively while the Agrarians rebuilt their reputation as conservative interpreters of Southern culture. From the office of the press at Chapel Hill, which had become a clearinghouse for Southern intellectuals, W. T. Couch was organizing a full-scale response to the Nashville group. In 1933, he edited a seven-hundred-page anthology titled *Culture in the South* (1934). Although the eclectic, unwieldy symposium included contributions by three Agrarians—Donald Davidson, H. C. Nixon,[61] and John Donald Wade—it was not intended as a polemical defense of Southern tradition, but as an objective discussion of progressive solutions to the region's social and economic problems. The tone of the symposium was entirely different from that of *I'll Take My Stand*. Indeed, Couch's preface explicitly referred to the Agrarian anthology, a book he claimed made the "serious error of interpreting southern life in terms of industrialism *vs.* agrarianism." The Agrarians, he elaborated, were wrong to have romanticized Southern history, to have depicted industrialism as "a destroyer of human values," and to have glorified the lives of impoverished farmers. These men from Vanderbilt, he concluded, were apparently unacquainted with "the long drawn-out misery of over-work and undernourishment, of poverty and isolation, of ignorance and hopelessness."[62]

In an extended critique written for the *American Review*, Tate took Couch's contributors to task for colluding with industrialism. The title of the book, Tate insisted, was "misleading because culture is nowhere clearly understood . . . unless culture be the purchasing-power to buy the latest manufactured articles." Although Tate found a few essays to commend in the book—and naturally reserved his highest praise for the three Agrarians contributors—he disdained the liberal essayists' "pious zeal for reform and progress." The false message he detected in their anthology was that the South consisted of nothing more than "Uncle Sam's other province." One could, he countered, overcome the farm crisis without rejecting subsistence farming, an agricultural system criticized by Northernized liberals because "industrial capitalism wants to sell the farmer *everything he uses*." Couch's anthology was thus further proof that "Southern industrialism is the tin can rattling on the tail of the academic dog." What Americans ought ultimately to remember, Tate concluded, was that "Agriculture in the past has supplied us with our civilization."[63]

Tate's review included a reply to "The Negro in the South," Couch's own essay in *Culture in the South*.[64] Here, Tate wrote, was a typical example of "reformers who are anxious to have Negroes sit by them on street-cars, but are loath to devise a program whereby they may purchase land." Such liberals were unable to see that "there has never been social equality anywhere, there never will be, nor ought there to be." Although racial strife was "inherently insoluble," a return to subsistence farming and land ownership would at least "destroy the lynching-tension between the races by putting both races on an independent footing."

Tate did not, however, argue for social equality. "I belong to the white race," he wrote, "therefore I intend to support white rule. Lynching is a symptom of weak, inefficient rule; but you can't destroy lynching by *fiat* or social agitation; lynching will disappear when the white race is satisfied that its supremacy will not be questioned in social crises."[65] Ignoring white racism, he blamed the increased number of lynchings on "three factors: Communist agitation, which deludes the Negro into believing that he can better his condition by crime; general economic fear and instability taking the form of mob violence; and outside interference in the trials of accused Negroes."[66] Tate argued that enticing "the Negro to question this supremacy without first of all giving him an economic basis is sentimental and irresponsible. Since a majority of the Negroes are in the South, and a majority of these on the land, it is a matter of simple realism to begin the improvement of their condition as farmers."[67]

Seward Collins's *American Review* allowed Tate and the Agrarians to air views they would have been less likely to make public in liberal journals. Although they grew annoyed by the editor's inefficiency and disorganization, they were desperate to revive their movement. They, in fact, became so absorbed in their efforts to manipulate his magazine that they failed to scrutinize (or perhaps they simply rationalized away) his political views. Even as early as the second issue of the journal, Collins had confessed an affection for fascism. Liberal journalists, Collins wrote in "The Revival of Monarchy," ought to overlook German anti-Semitism and welcome Hitler as a "monarchical" enemy of communism. In a shocking failure or a blithe unwillingness to see Hitler's crimes against humanity for what they were, Collins wrote: "One would gather from the fantastic lack of proportion of our press—not to say its gullibility and sensationalism—that the most important aspect of the German revolution was the hardships suffered by Jews under the new régime. Even if the absurd atrocity stories were all true, the fact would be almost negligible beside an event that shouts aloud in spite of the journalistic silence: the victory of Hitler signifies the end of the communist threat, *forever*. Wherever Communism grows strong enough to make a Communist revolution a danger, it will be crushed by a Fascist revolution. This was indicated by the advent of Mussolini. It is now proved by Hitler." Complimenting Mussolini for possessing "a sound moral system," Collins pronounced him "the most constructive statesman of our age." If Collins soon restated the review's commitment to the redistribution of private property, he added his personal belief that only "Fascism betokens the revival of monarchy, property, the guilds, the security of the family and the peasantry, and the ancient ways of European life."[68] Tate and his fellow Agrarians failed to anticipate how the essays they published in the *American Review* would be received when those essays were printed with Collins's reactionary editorials and with essays by Europeans who supported fascism. Not until the Agrarians' relationship with Collins ended in disaster several years later would they realize that they had accepted help from the wrong quarters.

III

Distracted as Tate was by politics, it is not surprising that he failed to produce his history of Southern writers for Funk and Wagnall's. His abandonment of this project is a genuine loss to literary criticism, since he held such strong opinions about the subject. By the mid-1930s, the Southern Literary Renaissance was in full swing, and while Tate had not himself written a novel yet, he was increasingly aware that he was becoming a major figure in a movement that was being scrutinized by literary critics and academics throughout America. In the space of a decade, the Fugitive poetry movement had come to occupy an honored niche in American literary history, and many writers were aware of the leading role Tate was playing, not only as an Agrarian, but also as a prominent critic in national magazines. He was in the peculiar position of being both a member of the renaissance and a critic of it. But the role he most liked to play was arbiter: a critic crushing the literary reputations of any Southern poets or writers who still clung to the maudlin themes of the Old South—while elevating, with the collusion of the Fugitive-Agrarian critics, those writers who observed proper aesthetic rules.[69] By setting himself above the renaissance as a judge, he could not only shape the critical assessments of the Fugitives, but also issue directives to straying writers and critics. Though sometimes harsh in his admonitions, he became a powerful force in steering a new generation of Southern artists away from the saccharine tastes that had long marred the region's literature.[70]

Tate came to think that the literary renaissance was "a birth, not a rebirth,"[71] and he suggested that a more appropriate name for the movement would be "the Southern Naissance."[72] Surveying the history of letters in the South, he was appalled by the narcissistic style that had characterized it from the beginning. Nineteenth-century Southern poetry he believed was by and large a disaster. With the exception of Charleston's Henry Timrod and Georgia's Thomas Holly Chivers[73] (both contemporaries of Tate's quasi-Southern hero, Edgar Allan Poe), there were virtually no Southern poets from that era who were worth preserving. Especially dispensable, in Tate's view, was the verse of Sidney Lanier, who remained one of the most popular postbellum Southern poets. Acutely aware that Edwin Mims had written a flattering book about the Georgia poet, Tate colluded with the Agrarians to lower Lanier's reputation a few notches. When Aubrey Starke's biography of Lanier appeared in 1933, Tate wrote a denigrating review of Lanier's poetry. Lanier's principal shortcoming as a poet, he argued, was his "romantic sensibility," and critics such as Starke, who depicted Lanier as "a figure on the model of Christ," were simply unable to free themselves of lost-cause nostalgia. "Lanier's chronic ill-health," Tate elaborated, "his romantic exploits as a Confederate scout, his poverty after the war, his struggles to find a literary career in the South of the Reconstruction, blinded the next generation to all but a few technical imperfections in his verse."[74]

Except for the Fugitive group, twentieth-century Southern poetry had not fared much better in Tate's eyes. He grew increasingly critical of poets such as DuBose Heyward and Josephine Pinckney, members of the Poetry Society of South Carolina who he believed were injecting their verse with purely sectional themes.[75] He could not respect contemporary critics who perpetuated a geographically fixed view of Southern poetry. ("A magnolia is unmistakable," he observed in one mocking review of a Southern poetry anthology.)[76] Nor did he show much devotion to the increasingly visible African American writers. If he had been quick to praise the work of James Weldon Johnson and Jean Toomer, he did not think of black poets so much as Southerners but as "Negro writers."[77]

Except for Augustus Baldwin Longstreet, whose *Georgia Scenes* (1835) Tate thought contained "complete, serious human beings,"[78] and William Gilmore Simms, whom Tate considered "the *only* good Southern novelist" of the nineteenth century, Tate also rejected the novelists of that era.[79] Such writers produced what Tate and his friends from Nashville referred to as "Confederate prose."[80] This genre included the novels his mother had enjoyed reading—historical romances such as John Esten Cooke's *Surry of Eagles'-Nest* (1866) and sentimental works such as Augusta Jane Evans's *St. Elmo* (1866). No better, Tate thought, were novelists such as Thomas Nelson Page and T. S. Stribling, who enjoyed greater critical recognition. Page Tate considered one of the South's "liberal second rate minds," a typical product of the postbellum period.[81] And Stribling, whose novels he judged "inferior exercises in sensational journalism," he detested.[82]

Tate saw only slight improvement in the Southern novelists closer to his own era. What bothered him about prolific authors such as Virginians James Branch Cabell and Ellen Glasgow was that they constructed their novels, especially what he called their "apprentice works,"[83] around "a sociological thesis." Even though Tate came to believe that a few later works by Cabell and Glasgow brought realism to the literature of the South, he argued that "their social attitude, because it is muddled, distracts the creative mind into mere propaganda and ruins the work of art."[84] Only in *Jurgen* (1919) and *Figures of Earth* (1921) did Cabell succeed in escaping his didacticism to write carefully constructed, artistically successful novels.[85] Tate believed Glasgow to be similarly undistinguished. Except for her more Agrarian novels such as *Barren Ground* (1925), for which he had limited praise, and *The Sheltered Life* (1932), which he admitted was "one of the finest of all

American novels"[86]—she was "a very mediocre writer" who belonged to "the book clubs" and "semi-literary New Yorkers."[87]

Meanwhile, Tate did everything within his power to deflate the reputations of the most popular writers of his own generation, most notably Thomas Wolfe, Erskine Caldwell, and Margaret Mitchell—all three of whom, he thought, traded on the North's voyeuristic interest in Southern culture. Wolfe, Tate wrote, "was simply afflicted with 'total recall'; and was a bad writer." Erskine Caldwell, who had angered the Agrarians with the degenerate farmers in *Tobacco Road*, was "a great storyteller," but his "genius for Hogarthian caricature" prevented him from creating genuine Southern characters. "One may learn as much of the South from his books," Tate said of him, "as one would learn of geography from a study of *Gulliver's Travels*."[88] Of the immensely popular Margaret Mitchell, Tate complained, "I could not get beyond page sixty of *Gone With the Wind*, and I walked out of the movie."[89] He believed that the New York critics were commodifying the wrong kind of literature. "The Northern reviewers," he later observed bitterly, "who have always dominated the literary scene, demanded the Southern stereotype, and when they got it they ridiculed it; when they got something else they ignored it."[90] He was particularly annoyed when Scribner's did more to market Mitchell's sentimentalism and Wolfe's verbosity than they did to promote Caroline Gordon's poorly selling but genuinely Southern novels.

Of the handful of contemporary Southern novelists besides his wife that Tate found to praise, he admired few as much as he did William Faulkner, whom he called "the best novelist of his age in America."[91] Tate did not begin reading Faulkner until the publication of *The Sound and the Fury* (1929) and *As I Lay Dying* (1930), but he was struck by Faulkner's genius for constructing bizarre but believable characters. The Compsons reminded him of his own family—especially the "weak father" and "sentimental mother" in *The Sound and the Fury*.[92] Tate also praised the monologues Faulkner wrote for each of the Bundrens in *As I Lay Dying*, which he considered "a brilliant piece of technique" and "a masterpiece."[93] After reading *Sanctuary* (1931), Tate devoured virtually every book Faulkner wrote, finding in them confirmation for his own ideas about the cultural history of the South. As the decades passed, his praise for the Mississippian grew to enormous proportions.[94]

Almost all of the remaining contemporary novelists Tate liked were Agrarian, either in sympathy or in fact; these were writers who used the Southern legend not as political ideology, but as an artistic tool.

Their historically grounded, intuitive understanding of Southern culture, he thought, allowed them to render the larger problems faced by humanity as a whole. (As early as 1929, Tate had cautioned Donald Davidson that "the ideal Southern novelist is the ideal novelist anywhere.")[95] Like Faulkner, such "traditionalists" succeeded in avoiding the "provincial" outlook "which sees in material welfare and legal justice the whole solution to the human problem."[96] This group included Elizabeth Madox Roberts, the critically acclaimed author of *The Time of Man* (1926); Stark Young, author of *So Red the Rose* (1934); Andrew Lytle, whose first novel, *The Long Night* appeared in 1936; Katherine Anne Porter, whose "highly civilized instruments of perception" allowed her to produce a "fully matured art"; and Robert Penn Warren, who was on the brink of a distinguished career as a novelist.[97] By 1937, Tate could point to these authors and proclaim with pride that "the literary center of the United States is definitely in the South."[98]

Tate thought that all Southern writers should bond together in response to the condescending attitudes of Northern critics during the 1930s, but he maintained something of a love-hate relationship with the non-Agrarian writers of the renascence. Although he was himself unable to remain loyal to one group for any length of time, and while he also knew that even the Agrarians were unable to show a unified front, he felt let down when Southern writers failed to consider themselves members of a close-knit group. He managed to enjoy himself socially when he attended Southern writers' conferences, but he was disappointed to note so many antagonisms among the writers in attendance—antagonisms between sentimentalists and modernist aesthetes, between liberals and conservatives, between popular writers who accepted New York City as the capital of the publishing world and obscure regionalists who rejected it. When Tate and Gordon attended one such meeting at Louisiana State University, Gordon correctly noted that the affair "was divided quite neatly into two armed camps, the Agrarians and those who thought there were far too many Agrarians present."[99]

Tate had first observed the deep divisions that existed among Southern writers when he traveled with Caroline Gordon and Andrew Lytle to the University of Virginia for James Southall Wilson's Southern Writer's Conference in 1931. Ecstatic because the conference was not to be held in New York City, Tate looked forward to his stay in Charlottesville's Monticello Hotel.[100] He soon discovered, however, that most of the writers attending the conference were uncomfortable with the label "Southern writer" and was upset that "nobody said anything but apology for being Southerners."[101] Caroline thought "it was really sort of like a gathering of second cousins who hadn't ever seen each other before but had to admit the tie of blood."[102] Even Sherwood Anderson, who was not a native Southerner and felt like an outsider at the conference, could not help but notice that "all the writers were looking at each other a bit self-consciously." (Anderson still enjoyed socializing with the Tates, admiring Caroline as "a fine black-haired, black-eyed creature, who talked intelligently about farming.")[103]

Hoping to motivate the other writers to unite the way the Agrarians had, Tate addressed the group. "I made a little speech exhorting the brethren to become more conscious of belonging to a professional class," he explained later, "but damn it we're just like the English in this, we're always remembering that we're ladies and gentlemen first, and that it is not gentle to belong to anything but society. Needless to say, my speech was not understood."[104] Many of the authors attending the conference—writers as diverse as Josephine Pinckney, Donald Davidson, and Paul Green—were not in sympathy when it came to matters of technique and theme in the Southern novel. Only the free-flowing liquor and Southern fraternity allowed these unlikely bedfellows to preserve decorum.[105] Ellen Glasgow, deaf, carrying an ear trumpet and looking "like a worldly old French woman of the eighteenth century," acted as convivial hostess to the group and delivered the opening address. Tate discovered that he was "wholly crazy about her" personally, although he apparently shared Caroline's observation that the elderly Virginian did not have a very penetrating intellect.[106] In the meantime, Paul Green, who was imbibing liberally, offended Tate and his Agrarian comrades by reading a paper that praised industrialism; Tate decided afterward that the liberal playwright was "North Carolina poor white trash."[107] Even worse, Tate found that he had been seated at dinner next to James Branch Cabell, whose work he had criticized in at least one major periodical.

Yet Tate was, of course, fascinated by Faulkner, who appeared in a resplendent British tweed suit and bemused the conferees by drinking nonstop. Faulkner's work was already well known nationally, and the other Southerners seemed to expect erratic behavior from someone toward whom they held such wonder. Although Tate observed he "behaved like a little Rimbaud, which is like a hog," he was willing to excuse him since he admired his fiction so much and since he thought the behavior "showed how agrarian he was." And despite the fact that Faulkner accidentally spit one of his drinks onto Caroline, she thought he "was the only person who conducted himself like a real he-writer, in the best Hemingway style, with some very good touches of the old south. He remained blind drunk the whole time and when he did appear he confined his remarks to 'Ma'm?' and 'Sir' and once when he was asked 'What do you think, Mr. Faulkner?' he replied in a voice like an indifferent weasel's, "*I* think I'll shorely get a little drink in three, four minutes."[108]

As disappointed as Tate was to find only a contrived esprit de corps among the writers at the gathering, he enjoyed himself and hit upon a paradigm for identifying the factions in attendance. Shortly after the event, he was motivated to write "Regionalism and Sectionalism," a piece that categorized the differing camps in the Southern Literary Renaissance. Arguing that "a genuine tradition must on the whole be unconsciously operative" (as it had been for Faulkner), he created one of his trademark paradoxes: Southern writers must be acutely conscious of their membership in a distinct cultural group—but must not be overly conscious of the Southern myth in their art. "A self-conscious regionalism," he explained, "destroys tradition with its perpetual discovery of it; makes it clumsy and sterile. And regionalism in this sense, when it merges with sectionalism, is death to literature. Sectionalism is politics; it is aggressive and abstract, and has as its true sphere a field of action which is hostile to art." As ever, Tate was trying to harmonize his political activism as an Agrarian—his own "sectionalism"—with his commitment to objectivist literary criticism; he was also trying to find a way to make Southern literature regionally authentic without being propagandistic. True regionalism, he explained, is "the immediate, organic sense of life in which a fine artist works."[109]

How, he mused, could Southerners create an organic community of writers except by supporting one another in a group? Tate had never thought highly of Joel Chandler Harris, creator of "Uncle Remus," but after reading some of Harris's essays in 1932, he observed sympathetically, "Most probably he could not see himself as a man of letters chiefly because there was no profession of letters in the South at that time; there was no model for him to go by, no solidarity of writers for him to join."[110] Already, one of Tate's seminal essays, "The Profession of Letters in the South," was beginning to take shape in his mind. Soon he described the proposed essay to Lambert Davis, editor of the *Virginia Quarterly Review*, who had solicited an article for the journal's tenth anniversary. "In the last six months," Tate wrote, "I have gone over most of the literature of the South, Old and New, and I should like to say something about our lack of the professional instinct in literature. . . . The general point is that we can't have a literature until we have a criticism, and we can't have that until we become professional."[111]

In the essay, which Tate wrote in a single sitting and published in 1935, he attempted to explain why nineteenth-century Southern literature had been weak—and to suggest the proper course of action for twentieth-century Southern writers. The failure of nineteenth-century Southern culture to produce a lasting literature he attributed to Southern aristocrats' preoccupation with the politics and economics of the slave system, a system that prevented them from developing the relationship to the land that would have allowed art to emerge. Those few intellects who did emerge in such an environment, writers such as Poe, never found a supportive coterie of writers and were forced to leave the South. With no "literary tradition" to inherit, "no city in the South where writers may gather, write, and live, and no Southern publisher to print their books," the writers who were Tate's contemporaries had no choice but to move to New York City, a move that made them too modern, divested them of "the Southern feeling," and forced them to market Northern images of what the South ought to be—to have their literary criticism "trimmed and scattered in Northern magazines, or published in books that will be read curiously as travel literature by Northern people alone."

The Southern Literary Renaissance had thus emerged under special circumstances, and Tate was pessimistic about how long it could last. "From the peculiarly historical consciousness of the Southern writer has come good work of a special order"; he admitted, "but this consciousness is quite temporary. It is that curious burst of intelligence that we get at a crossing of the ways, not unlike, on an infinitesimal scale, the outburst of poetic genius at the end of the sixteenth century when commercial England had already begun to crush feudal England."[112] In time, as Tate became acquainted with the younger generation of authors who emerged from the Agrarian tradition—writers as distinguished as Peter Taylor and Eudora Welty—he revised this cynical forecast. As late as 1968, he thought the renaissance had "scarcely abated."[113]

Over the years, Tate also offered other explanations for the sudden agglomeration of talent that appeared in Southern culture during the late 1920s. Usually, he located the source of the renaissance in the cultural tumult that followed World War I. Between the end of the Civil War and the outbreak of the First World War, the South had been separated from the wider cultural world by a "curtain of lavender and lace."[114] But the country's involvement in the war forced Southerners to admit that "the past was being overwhelmed or had been, and that the South was going to have to take its place in the modern world."[115] Summarizing these ideas in "The New Provincialism," published in 1945, Tate wrote, "With the war of 1914–1918, the South reentered the world—but gave a backward glance as it stepped over the border: that backward glance gave us the Southern renascence, a literature conscious of the past in the present."[116]

Tate was still tinkering with this idea decades later when he wrote what is perhaps his most perceptive essay on Southern literary history, "A Southern Mode of the Imagination." According to his newest theory, a dramatic transformation had taken place not so much in the manner in which Southern writers apprehended their modernizing society, but in the manner in which they saw themselves. In the Old South, writers were accustomed to pontificating; they wrote in what Tate called "the rhetorical mode" and expected no dialogue to emerge in response to their political ideas. Yet after World War I, when they "looked around and saw for the first time since about 1830 that the Yankees were not to blame for everything," they gained the self-knowledge that allowed them to write psychologically realistic interior monologues such as the ones that made Faulkner's fiction so convincing. Although this alteration "from the rhetorical mode to the dialectical mode" had been evident in Mark Twain's *Adventures of Huckleberry Finn* (1884), which Tate now called "the first modern novel by a Southerner," it took a while for later Southerners to make the transformation for themselves. Fortunately, however, the writers of the renaissance eventually succeeded. What they ultimately learned, Tate pointed out, was something Yeats had discovered years earlier: "Out of the quarrel with others we make rhetoric; out of the quarrel with ourselves, poetry."[117]

IV

Tate's ideals about a Southern literature untainted by politics and economics could not always withstand the pressure of his own financial circumstances. Throughout the spring of 1934, he and Gordon worked hard to earn money from their art any way they could. Gordon, propelled in part by her hope that Scribner's would aggressively market *Alec Maury, Sportsman*, worked steadily on her thinly veiled account of her father's adventures as a backwoods Kentucky gentleman. "Perkins keeps writing me that I must get the novel done as soon as possible," she wrote a friend. "They actually talk as if they might advertize it and then I might have some chance of pulling out of this hole of poverty."[118]

Yet just when the Tates were growing more hopeful about their finances, misfortune befell them in April. As they were en route to Nashville in a new automobile, another vehicle ran into them so hard that their car spun over and was reduced to scrap. The force of the impact jammed metal into Tate's knee, causing it to bleed profusely. Gordon was jerked so wildly in her seat that she hurt her shoulder. But these physical injuries proved far less upsetting than the financial blow. Since the driver who caused the accident was unable to assume any of the financial liability, Tate, who was still making payments on the car, was bitter. Whenever he told the story, he made sure to mention that it had been "a negro" who had run the stop sign and hit them.[119]

With Tate's debts totaling close to two thousand dollars—most of which represented advances he had received for the Lee biography and the ancestor book—he sunk into depression. An ominous silence from Balch suggested to him that the publishing firm might even be on the verge of taking legal action to recover their money. Then, in their typical fashion, the Tates found a way at the last moment to avert financial catastrophe. Red Warren, who had been teaching at Southwestern College in Memphis, quit his post for a position at Louisiana State University, leaving Southwestern in immediate need of a literature professor with credentials matching his. Tate quickly emerged as the front-runner among the candidates being considered for the position.

Southwestern College was established in 1848 in the Tates' own hometown, Clarksville. After the campus was relocated to Memphis in 1925, it grew into a thriving Presbyterian college attended by four to five hundred students, the bulk of whom were Tennesseans. Like Vanderbilt, the university was torn between its Christian ethos and a commitment to nonsectarian scholarship. A plurality of the professors held doctorates, and many had earned prestigious degrees outside the South. "Provincialism is not a characteristic of Southwestern," the college catalog boasted. "All points of view are represented in both faculty and student body."[120]

The university ran firmly under the direction of its president, a theologically liberal Presbyterian minister by the name of Charles Edward Diehl. Diehl, who held degrees from Johns Hopkins and Princeton Universities, possesed a very definite notion of the kind of institution he was building—and of the faculty who would serve it. An Anglophile with two curly locks framing his forehead, he had imported the British tutorial system and liked to hire former Rhodes Scholars. He was a strong proponent of "Christian Education," but he was not entirely a traditionalist. Several years earlier, he had successfully defended himself against heresy charges filed against him by eleven other Presbyterian ministers.[121]

Diehl did not enforce the college policy "that the faculty be composed of men who yield whole-hearted allegiance to Christ as their Savior and Lord."[122] But he was far from disinterested in the moral character of prospective faculty. In spite of Tate's literary fame, Diehl took it upon himself to solicit letters judging "his personality, his teaching ability, and his religious attitude."[123] In a confidential inquiry to one of the directors of the college, who happened to live in Clarksville, Diehl asked about Tate's reputation there. The reply from a Mr. B. A. Patch, a manufacturer, reveals the scrutiny to which Tate and Gordon were subject in their own neighborhood. "They have taken no part in any Church activities," Patch wrote, "and are not supposed to take such things seriously. They do not seem to associate with many people and are possibly a bit 'High Hat' to the average." The Tates, he continued, were "said to have rather gay drinking parties Sunday nights, gamble, etc." Though "quite pleasant" in person, they were "unconventional in dress and mode of living." Patch warned against allowing "a couple of nuts" to come to Southwestern. "Unless there were a very decided change in habits I think they would be very incongruous in the faculty circles of a Christian college."[124]

But Diehl received glowing recommendations from Tate's supporters. "He is a warm defender of religion and orthodox theology," assured John Crowe Ransom. Ransom admitted that it is always something of a risk to appoint "an individualist not used to the academic life," but Tate would "be a brilliant and stimulating accession to a college community."[125] Red Warren praised Tate's "international reputation" and "charming personality."[126] Yet it was undoubtedly a letter written by Stark Young at the *New Republic* that pleased Diehl the most. "I regard Mr. Tate as by far the most brilliant critic of poetry that we have here in America," Young wrote. "I would even go so far as to say that he is our only poetic critic of distinction and importance." What was more, when it came to Tate's artistic ability, Young shared T. S. Eliot's opinion "that he is our best American poet."[127] These testimonials left their mark, and Diehl, who was reassured when he met Tate in person, offered him the job in August 1934.[128] Embittered to professors since his rejection from the Yale graduate school, Tate was now one himself; he would be appointed as a "Lecturer in English Literature" and receive a twenty-five-hundred-dollar-a-year salary.[129] Caroline was one of the few people who knew that he had accepted the post "chiefly for the benefit of his creditors."[130]

After living so long in rural Tennessee, returning to Memphis was a dramatic transition for the Tates. Here was a Southern city that was trying to capitalize upon its agrarian roots; each year a carnival was held to honor the industries that had grown out of the cotton economy. Though somewhat weakened by the Depression, the city was also beginning to feel the economic stimulation created in the wake of the Tennessee Valley Authority (TVA), the massive hydroelectric project of the early 1930s—a project Tate believed to be, with some reservations, "a good thing."[131] As New Deal agencies and the accompanying government funds reached the city, new businesses, mostly auto shops and restaurants, sprouted, giving the town a notably commercial atmosphere.[132] The Tates' rented home at 2374 Forrest Avenue, a brick bungalow with a carport, was also a far cry from bucolic Benfolly.[133] "We have an ugly little cottage," Caroline told her friends. "Allen calls it the Hamburger House and it does resemble a hamburger on the outside at least." Fortunately, Southwestern's campus nearby was beautifully landscaped, the Memphis Zoo was just a stone's throw away, and an adjacent park offered "acres and acres of just plain Tennessee woods to walk in."[134]

The English department at Southwestern was small, and Tate quickly made friends with two other Southerners. One was Theodore Johnson, a blond, mustachioed man who taught Spenser and Chaucer. Johnson, who received his master's degree from the University of Virginia and his doctorate from the University of North Carolina, would soon be editing an anthology with Tate—a collaboration that made for collegiality but that further propelled Tate from the books he owed Earle Balch.[135] The second professor, Samuel Holt Monk, was from Selma, Alabama. A graduate of Southwestern who had earned advanced degrees from Princeton, the bespectacled scholar looked younger than his thirty-two years. Someone meeting him for the first time might not have guessed at his accomplishments.[136]

Yet Monk, who possessed a powerful intellect, was in 1934 a rising star both at Southwestern and in the academic world at large. Within a year, the Modern Language Association would bring out the youthful professor's work, *The Sublime: A Study of Critical Theories in XVIII-Century England*, a book later heralded as a classic in the field.[137] While his early professional success was accompanied by a personal tragedy of enormous magnitude (the details of which remain obscure),[138] he evidently gained a new lease on life through his scholarship and teaching, eventually shaping a legion of English literature specialists.[139]

Monk's critical acumen fed a wit that matched Tate's own, and he became a welcome guest at the Tates' literary parties.[140] John Davis, a professor of history at Southwestern who also attended the evening gatherings—memorable for the Tates' love of dramatic readings, charades, and music—recalled making a recording of a poem Monk read to Tate. The first two stanzas of the poem, titled *Allen among the Academicians*, went:

> Allen Tate, Confederate bred,
> "Dull critter of enormous head,"
> Came to work with the professors
> To raise his pay for the tax assessors.
>
> "The life of a professor, sure,
> Is spacious, easy, not too pure."
> Thus reasoned Tate, while at Ben Folly
> He scanned his bills in melancholy.[141]

Insightful even in this playful satire, Monk understood his new colleague's discomfort as a poet in the academy. Over the years, the two men grew close, and Monk came to think of Tate as a mentor who showed him how to transform his prose "from a pedantic style to the simple style."[142]

Much as Tate grew to like his new colleagues, however, he was exasperated by their seeming insecurity in his presence. "It is curious," he observed, "that such fine fellows as Johnson and Monk should feel, not antagonism towards me (a perfectly legitimate feeling, I suppose), but antagonism for the reason that they feel it. They are afflicted with the worst sense of inferiority I ever saw; they look constantly for slights; they want me every moment to snoot them; and when I don't snoot them they like it less than if I did."[143] What was worse, Tate decided Southwestern was a "sweatshop"[144] and Memphis "a cultural desert."[145] He took his teaching very seriously, spent hours preparing for each of his courses, and was consequently unable to do any of his own writing. "I am instructing the young in a depressing Presbyterian college," he complained to Mark Van Doren. "I can't face it another year."[146] The Tates' financial condition meant they would have to accept Diehl's offer of renewal. But Tate could not resist letting him know that the course load made it impossible to do any writing, "Our schedule is from eight to twelve hours heavier than the schedule at any other first-class institution that I know. The maximum at Harvard is twelve hours; at North Carolina, ten."[147]

Throughout the remainder of the academic year, Tate avoided his book and hosted a string of prominent literary figures and Agrarians. His colleagues at Southwestern were undoubtedly impressed when Louis Untermeyer, the poet and anthologist, came to campus and publicly praised Tate as "the best critic in America today."[148] Some of the visitors took up residence in the Tates' house. A long visit from Andrew Lytle was followed by one that was mercifully brief from John Gould Fletcher, whose psychological difficulties had worsened considerably since his contribution to *I'll Take My Stand*.[149] The most distinguished visitors of all were Ford Madox Ford and Janice Biala, who came to see the Tates in April.[150] Ford was to speak at the writer's conference at Louisiana State University, where Cleanth Brooks was teaching with Red Warren. Thanks in large measure to the efforts of Louisiana's infamous Huey Long, the populist governor now serving in the United States Senate, LSU was thriving. Tate's two Vanderbilt friends, whose careers he both promoted and followed with interest, were celebrating the funding of their new magazine, the *Southern Review*. The Tates were thrilled when Diehl released Allen from his onerous teaching duties and urged him to travel to Baton Rouge and stay for the duration of the conference. "Hooray!" Caroline wrote. "The president thinks that Southwestern should be represented."[151]

V

Just when President Diehl was beginning to see the obvious value of having a writer with Tate's literary connections on the faculty, a brouhaha erupted. While the Tates were at the writer's conference, they ran into a journalist acquaintance of theirs named James Rorty, who was traveling throughout the South on a fact-gathering mission. National debate over American farm policy during the New Deal meant that Rorty and other liberal journalists were aggressively investigating social and economic problems associated with Southern agriculture. A costly research study sponsored by the Julius Rosenwald Fund had recently publicized the fact that more than half of the South's cotton farms relied upon an abusive tenancy program that had grown to disturbing proportions by the 1920s. "Half of these tenants," the study found, "are 'share croppers,' owning neither land nor capital, livestock nor tools, and wholly dependent for these on their landlords." Landowners made such items available on credit, but only with usurious interest in anticipation of highly unpredictable earnings from the sharecroppers' harvests. Consequently, a vicious circle of debt kept renters starved and desperate. Many observers were placing the blame for the sharecropper crisis on the newly created Agricultural Adjustment Administration (AAA), one of the major relief agencies to emerge during the first stage of the New Deal. It was charged that the weak enforcement policies of the AAA allowed landowners to trap sharecroppers in penury—and seemed even to condone evicting them so that the landowners themselves could collect federal funds being dispensed to owners for planting crops on fewer acres.[152]

Rorty, a Communist sympathizer and a founding editor of the radical magazine, the *New Masses*, wanted to write about the dire predicament of the tenant farmers across the river in Arkansas. After following the Tates back to Memphis, he urged them to drive him to a nearby town called Marked Tree, where the tenancy crisis had erupted into a violent clash that was dividing the townspeople and attracting the attention of journalists across the nation. White landowners in Marked Tree were up in arms over the integration of black and white sharecroppers into the Southern Tenant Farmers' Union, an organization the owners said was "Red." Norman Thomas, leader of the radical wing of the American Socialist Party and one of the union's organizers, soon reported that the sharecroppers trying to join it were victims of oppression, intimidation, and violence so great "that the Federal Government would be responsible for murder if it did not act."[153] F. Raymond Daniell was covering the crisis for the *New York Times*, and in a series of six articles he recounted the disturbing events in Marked Tree.[154] In an installment that had just appeared, Daniell reported that "a band of forty-odd masked night riders fired upon the home of C. T. Carpenter, attorney for the Southern Tenant Farmers' Union." The night ride "was the climax to a series of similar attacks upon the homes of Negro members of the union." Less than a week later, "an armed band of vigilantes mobbed a group of Negro men and women returning home from church, beating several of them with pistol butts and flashlights. That same night in the neighboring town of Lepanto nightriders shot out all the lights in a Negro church, terrorizing the women and children of the congregation."[155] Shocking events such as these were not confined to the state of Arkansas. Even as the New Deal was promising "happy days" for everyone, African Americans throughout the South—and the entire country, for that matter—were subject to brutal harassment and violence.[156]

Rorty decided to interview for himself some of the townspeople described and quoted in the *New York Times* articles. The person he most wanted to locate was "Brother" J. Abner Sage, the racist Methodist minister who was using his pulpit to proselytize for the anti-union landowners—and who was said to have hidden in a railroad car to spy on a union meeting. Only a few days earlier, Raymond Daniell reported Sage's denigration of "the share-croppers" as "a shiftless lot with only themselves to blame if they are not as well blessed with this world's goods as they would like to be."[157] Brother Sage, who approved of terrorist acts against the sharecroppers, boasted that he helped "form the Nightriders since the Ku Klux Klan had a bad reputation."[158] He told Daniell he was exercised "about the way in which Northern organizers prefixed the names of Negroes with 'Mister,' shook hands with them and 'gave them ideas about social equality.' "[159]

Tate was hesitant to bring Rorty to Marked Tree, but curiosity seems to have gotten the best of him. On the one hand, he disliked radicals and anything that suggested a Communist remedy to Southern problems. Moreover, at this stage in Tate's life, both his segregationism and his racism were pronounced—he was decidedly not a defender of black social equality. On the other hand, Tate was ashamed of the violence perpetrated by white Southerners such as the ones who lived in Marked Tree, and he was distressed by the economic difficulties endured by small farmers of both races. He also had a particular interest in tenancy since a tenant family lived on Benfolly land.[160] Some of Tate's recent writings in the *American Review* even revealed that his ideas about property ownership for families and small farmers were not at odds with those belonging to the liberal proponents of the nascent Bankhead Bill, which would have appropriated a billion dollars in mortgage money for tenant farmers and sharecroppers—and which the Agrarians, Frank Owsley maintained, had partly inspired.[161] As Daniel Singal has observed, "Tate's actual pronouncements on social policy closely resembled those of New Deal liberals, while his rhetoric often came out sounding quasi-Marxist."[162]

When Rorty and the Tates appeared in town, Brother Sage was still smarting from Daniell's damning portrait of him and was not anxious to cooperate with another journalist. "Who put me on the witness stand?" Sage demanded when confronted by Rorty. When Rorty was undaunted, Sage added, "See here, if any more of the fellows come in here asking questions there's going to be trouble and if you don't let me alone there's going to be trouble for you right now."[163] Accounts differ as to what happened next. Rorty's son recalls that "Tate was concerned that the white folks in the area weren't behaving like Southern gentlemen, and he proceeded to make a stump speech in the local courthouse square on the subject. My father claimed to have saved Tate's life by dragging him into the car and speeding back across the bridge into the next state before a mob could be organized to lynch Tate as a 'nigger-lover.' "[164] Although letters written by Tate and Gordon at the time do not corroborate this story, Sage's cronies did have a policy of jailing any individuals they labeled as "outside agitators." A new law made it "unlawful for any person to make or deliver a public speech on any street, alley, park or other public place within the corporate limits of Marked Tree without first having obtained the permission of said city."[165] The Tates' "trip back to Memphis somehow wore the quality of flight," one contemporary observer recalled. "There was a sense of violence where no real violence occurred. Only angry voices followed them across the Mississippi bridge."[166]

But Brother Sage did more than shout after the Tates and Rorty. By the time they had driven back to Memphis, President Diehl already knew about their encounter and was soon waiting in his office with Sage and three other citizens of Marked Tree. "The preacher and his cohorts," Gordon recounted shortly afterward, "threaten[ed] that if any story is written they will give a story to the A.P. saying as how this northern agitator accompanied by a Southwestern professor stopped him on the street (blocked his passage on the street) and questioned him against his will."[167] When the four visitors also promised to depict Tate as a Communist, Tate enraged them by replying that such a portrayal would be actionable. But Tate believed that any negative publicity whatsoever would ruin President Diehl's fund-raising efforts in the community, and he caved in to the delegation from Marked Tree. Firing off a series of telegrams, Tate finally succeeded in locating Rorty, who made sure to state in his article that while the Tates had come with him to see Marked Tree, they "strongly disapprove of Northern interference in Southern affairs."[168]

Although publicity generated by the Southern Tenant Farmers' Union eventually forced President Roosevelt to take action on the tenancy crisis, Tate disagreed with the union's collectivist approach to agricultural problems.[169] From that day onward, he dismissed the union as a Communist front. He continued to like Rorty, but considered him a deluded radical. "The poor fellow's mind," Tate wrote, "is a seething mass of borrowed jargon and crazy-quilt abstractions." He was a liberal journalist who "knew nothing of the actual conditions—just assumed that the landowners are bastards, as they mostly are, certainly, but he was talking about *particular* landlords about whom he knew nothing." More than anything else, Tate was irked that Rorty caused President Diehl to be drawn into a showdown with a group of violent locals from Arkansas. "It hasn't, I daresay, occurred to Jim," Tate observed afterward, "that I owed at least a personal obligation to the president not to get him on the spot, where a crowd of village idiots could blackmail him."[170]

VI

Distracted as he was by the controversies of the spring of 1935, Tate was no closer to summoning the sustained work habits required to write a full-length book of any kind. But his long period of artistic stasis was finally beginning to end. By March, he had returned to his desk to write poems and articles. Gordon, who had finished *Aleck Maury, Sportsman*, and was working on the manuscript that would become *The Cup of Fury*, relished seeing her husband productive again. "The gloom that has hung over the Tate household for almost two years now has lightened somewhat in the last week," she observed. "Allen has suddenly begun to work again—and if a paralytic had suddenly thrown away his crutch and begun to take dance steps we couldn't be more excited."[171]

Reaping the benefits of his new productivity, Tate published a few new poems, most notably *To the Romantic Traditionists*, a verse salvo aimed at the Southern sentimentalists.[172] Ironically, shortly after the poem appeared, a number of local poetry clubs, which in the South were known for their sponsorship of moonlight-and-magnolia poetry, asked Tate to deliver lectures. He accepted their invitations, but his uneasiness was manifest. As a keynote speaker for the Nineteenth Century Club during "Poetry Week," he could not resist warning the members about the self-defeating nature of the South's amateurish literary organizations. "First," he told the group, "we must reform our poetry societies, stop (most of us) trying to be poets ourselves, and devote our meetings to the study of poets who can teach us something. Secondly, we must make an effort to find out who the best critics of poetry are, and read them. Thirdly, we must discourage all groups of persons writing poetry; people cannot join a club and become poets; they must be poets to begin with."[173] The audience of poetry lovers, some of whom were reported to have "gasped" during the talk, sat in silence afterward. Despite Tate's strictures, they gave prizes to three poems submitted locally: *A Spring Artist, To a Full-Grown Leaf,* and *So Sings My Hoe.*[174] Tate thought verse such as this to be mere doggerel, especially when he was writing piercingly ironic poems such as *The Robber Bridegroom*, an Edgar Allan Poe–like piece he had recently published in the campus literary magazine at Southwestern.[175] Only the honoraria he received made him patient with the poetry dilettantes in Memphis.[176]

Tate's return to writing also yielded two important essays, both of which indirectly explored the dilemmas he and the Agrarians faced as writers operating in a marketplace that rewarded only commercially appealing Southern poetry and fiction. In "The Profession of Letters in the South," he had attacked the centralization of book publishing in the North. A second article, solicited by Brooks and Warren for the *Southern Review*, Tate titled "The Function of the Critical Quarterly." Tate was motivated to write the piece after attending the writers' conference in Baton Rouge and discovering that "the specific problems of the artist were ignored in fruitless discussion of his social function."[177] Tate's larger purpose in writing the article was to stake out a claim on the newly founded *Southern Review*, which he hoped would become the Agrarian organ over which the group would have the greatest amount of control. The secret to success in any quarterly, Tate urged, lies in "concentrated editorship functioning through a small group of regular contributors." An effective quarterly needs writers "who agree that certain fundamental issues exist and who consent, under the direction of the editor, to discuss them with a certain emphasis."[178] Brooks and Warren, both Vanderbilt men, were of course the most trustworthy editors to oversee such a publication. Seward Collins, who was not a genuine member of the Agrarian group and not even a reliable editor, could not in Tate's view be counted on to advance their cause over his.

Meanwhile, the sequel to *I'll Take My Stand*, which Andrew Lytle and he had been planning since late 1933, was coming into fruition and demanding Tate's attention. When the collection was first conceived, Tate imagined an offense of propaganda in which the Agrarians would set forth the "universal implications" of Agrarianism. Having promised publishers a symposium that would be "less specific geographically," Tate hoped to assemble a new collection that would be broader than a defense of Southern culture.[179] The best way for the Agrarians to gain new supporters, he was convinced, would be to cast the widest net possible.

Yet Tate was painfully aware of the fact that the group could not risk alienating Collins, and the Agrarians went to great lengths to mollify him as they planned the new book. "Your discussion of monarchy is in line with this program," Tate reassured the editor, "though we all thought that the terms you employed needed some popularization, if we are to make the idea palatable." The anthology, Tate wrote, "will not, as you see, be a Southern book this time; but a program for breaking capitalism in the interests of a true political state."[180]

Tate's desire to give the new anthology a broad national and international appeal motivated him to locate famous contributors who were neither Agrarians nor Southerners. He hoped that in addition to the Agrarians now publishing in the *American Review*, Christopher Dawson, a prominent Catholic theologian in England, and Eliot, an Anglophile who called himself "a New Englander," would number among the contributors. In the years following the publication of the Agrarians' first symposium, Eliot had been offering himself as a potential ally. In May 1933, for instance, in his Page-Barbour Lectures at the University of Virginia, he expressed public support for their movement. The lectures, a portion of which Eliot published in the *American Review*—and all of which he dismissed in his later years as the work of "a very sick man"—would be remembered principally for a remark he made in them about the threat posed to tradition by "any large number of free-thinking Jews." But Eliot had praised *I'll Take My Stand* and lamented "that the aim of the 'neo-agrarians' in the South will be qualified as quixotic, as a hopeless stand for a cause which was lost long before they were born." To those who were arguing that "the whole current of economic determinism" runs counter to Agrarianism, Eliot replied: "Economic determinism is today a god before whom we fall down and worship with all kinds of music." Eliot, who thought the modern world "worm-eaten with Liberalism" reported to Tate that he had begun his lectures "by referring touchingly to the Nashville Group." If the Agrarians needed any "stumping by a dambyankee," he added, they ought to let him know.[181]

It was not Eliot, however, but a prominent journalist named Herbert Agar who became Tate's principal collaborator in the new symposium. On the surface, Agar and Tate had little in common. Agar, a native of New York State who received his undergraduate degree from Columbia University, went on to Princeton for a master's and a doctorate. Following a brief stint as a teacher, he became a freelance writer in Great Britain. After being "indoctrinated by the English distributists," he served as a speechwriter for Robert Worth Bingham, whom Franklin D. Roosevelt made ambassador to Britain in 1933. Ambassador Bingham, who owned the *Louisville Courier-Journal*, grew to admire Agar so much that he put him in line to assume editorship of the influential Southern newspaper.[182]

When Collins asked Tate to review Agar's 1933 book, *The People's Choice*, a work shortly to receive the Pulitzer Prize, Tate knew nothing of the author. But after reading the conservative jeremiad about the decline of the American presidency through Harding, Tate pronounced it "the most brilliant short history of our dead Republic that has ever been written."[183] "The moral of the book," he told Lincoln Kirstein, "is the complete failure of liberalism."[184] Tate immediately wrote to Agar, advising him that he had Southern soulmates who were planning to advance similar ideas in a new book. The Agrarians, Tate told Agar, now wanted more than to answer "silly charges of romantic past-worship"—they wanted nothing less than "to investigate the possibility of the Conservative Revolution" Agar had outlined "as one of the alternatives to Marxism." Tate's letter to Agar revealed better than any other how Tate then conceived of the Agrarian movement. "We have, I think, only one dogma," Tate wrote, "against the pseudo-metaphysical dogma of capitalist-communist philosophy: that men can still make the kind of society morally that they want, and that machine-technology has not changed the political nature of man."[185]

Once Tate got to know Agar better, he worried that the journalist was too much of "an idealistic reformer."[186] But Tate quickly decided that Agar ought to be more than a mere contributor to the new symposium—that he ought to coedit the book. In late 1934, Agar and his wife, Eleanor, had come to Memphis so that he and Tate could choose the essayists. The two men got along famously and were soon discussing the possibility of founding an Agrarian newspaper and asking Seward Collins for editorial help.[187] "I have persuaded myself," Agar told Collins, "not only that there is hope for our ideas, but that we have got to do something about them. . . . I give us to the end of Mr. Roosevelt's second term. If, by that time, we have not either captured the New Deal, through capturing a big block of public opinion, or else built up a self-confident and clearly defined opposition . . . the slave state will be upon us."[188]

Agar planned for their newspaper to be published in the *Courier-Journal* printing offices. "Louisville," Agar explained to Collins, ". . . fits in with my hope of being able to interest the Ambassador, at least enough to get him to express himself in favour of our program and to recommend it to the careful consideration of some of the New Dealers, possibly of the President. We might even get some money from the Government, on the grounds of the regional-culture stuff which they talk so much about."[189] Before long, Agar had even contacted the ambassador's son, Barry Bingham, Sr., in order to request cost projections for publishing up to ten thousand papers a week.

Tate's brother Ben, apparently on the mend financially, jumped on the bandwagon and almost succeeded in persuading Virginius Hall, a wealthy Southern conservative who had married into the Taft family, to underwrite the newspaper. If the paper materialized, Ben would be one of its directors and the Tates would move to Cincinnati. Tate did not relish the idea of becoming dependent on his older brother again, but he realized that the newspaper could not come into being without him.[190] In April, he joined Ben and Agar in Cincinnati in order to promote their idea at the Mercantile Library Centennial Celebration, but the idea to the publish the paper apparently went no farther.[191]

The plans for the book of essays went ahead, however, and by the fall of 1935, Agar had signed a contract with Houghton Mifflin to publish a collection he and Tate would title *Who Owns America? A New Declaration of Independence*. Donald Davidson and Frank Owsley were incensed that Tate had taken the liberty of inviting Agar to coedit the anthology. Tate, who had grown impatient with the narrow-minded sectionalism of the two men he now referred to as "General Owsley" and "General Davidson," could not understand how "the babies in Nashville" could possibly question his tactical judgment when their movement was on the verge of collapse.[192] He implored the "brethren" to accept Agar as a national spokesperson who could transcend the provincial reputation of the movement. "Agar is a gift from the Gods," Tate insisted. "He is a born public figure; he is intelligent; and he is with us to the hilt." Moreover, Tate added, "He is a leader, and not one of us is a leader that anybody will follow. We are an army made up of generals."[193]

The truth was that Tate was beginning to feel exasperated by the dynamics that had emerged within the Agrarian group. The "brethren in Nashville"[194] might have offered him a surrogate family, but he was tired of their petty sibling rivalries, and he had begun to assume a fatherly condescension toward most of them. His frustrations were compounded by his growing cynicism about the practicability of their ideas. In a May 1935 letter to John Peale Bishop that he never mailed, Tate admitted: "The Davidson wing of the Agrarians has shown so much fraternity spirit, and so much eagerness to convert the already converted, that John Ransom and I have thought of resigning. Of course there is nothing to resign from. Nor do Ransom and I plan to form a new group. We are still convinced adherents of the agrarian doctrine. But I suppose Ransom, Warren, and myself come a little nearer being artists than the others, and we cannot feel that political programs offer us the absolutes of religion."[195]

One of the great ironies of Tate's life is that he was a fierce polemicist who did not believe ultimately in the efficacy of political protest. In the end, it would be art and religion, not politics, that gained his allegiance. More than one scholar has suggested that had Tate's conversion to Catholicism come much earlier than late 1950—say, in the mid-1930s—he might have satisfied his desire for an absolute system of authority. But such a conversion might also have relieved him of the burden of working through his family history—and thus kept him from producing what became one of the major novels of the Southern Literary Renaissance.

As entangled as he was with politics in 1935, he could not stop thinking about the genealogical book he had dropped. For a brief moment earlier in the year, he had felt as if he was about to break the artistic block he had been facing since his father's death—that he might now be able to return to the painful story of his family. "Last night," he wrote in late January, "I got the first idea I've had since we came back from France. I see how to finish The Fathers, I think, and it gives me a new lease on life. I may be able to write on it even here."[196] But the epiphany—and his euphoria—were fleeting. Trapped by the historical method he envisioned for reconstructing his genealogy, the most important work of his life remained unwritten throughout 1935. He had not yet discovered that the only way for him to gain peace of mind would be to transform *The Fathers* into a novel. And as long as he sought an identity in the realm of politics instead of art, he would continue to see himself as an orphan of the South.

Chapter Eight
Fatherless Fame

As 1936 approached, Tate was headed toward a crisis in which he would have to choose between Agrarianism and artistic ambition. He would shortly give up politics and rebel against the academy, but for a brief period in the fall of 1935 his life seemed calm and his work at Southwestern not so burdensome. Returning to Memphis after a summer at Benfolly and Cornsilk, he and Caroline moved into a small house on the same street where they had lived the previous academic year. "We have a very comfortable bungalow on the other end of Forrest," Gordon wrote Harriet Owsley, "full of golden oak and gadgets but much nicer than the place we had last year, and quite a relief after Benfolly and its stairs."[1] Taking refuge in this cozy new home, Tate nursed a lingering illness and reexamined his career as a poet and critic. Finding himself trapped in the world of New Deal politics, he looked for ways to escape.

I

As if to prepare himself for a huge creative undertaking, he began to clear the decks of some of the work that had accumulated in the previous two years. He would soon ask Cleanth Brooks to take his place as coeditor of the textbook he had been planning with Robert Penn Warren. Tate regretted abandoning the project, correctly predicting that it would "be a gold mine."[2] The book, which Warren and Brooks went on to edit as *Understanding Poetry* (1938), dominated college class-rooms for decades, influenced a generation of English majors, and be-came a definitive textbook of the New Criticism.[3] But Tate's role in the birth of the critical method scholars now believe emerged in concert with the decline of Southern Agrarianism was not eliminated. The col-lection of his own essays he had promised Scribner's also became a classic in the articulation of New Critical methods.

Since Tate had decided on a table of contents for his essay collection two years earlier, he was now able to gather the selections together relatively quickly.[4] While Caroline readied her novel for Scribner's, he made minor revisions to a group of articles and book reviews he had published previously in periodicals. When, some months earlier, Max-well Perkins had read the articles, which formed a manuscript of fewer than 250 pages, he was ecstatic. A reader "almost forgets what a fine thing critical writing really can be," he told Tate.[5] The two men debated a number of titles for the book, including *Poetry and Tradition* and *Essays in Radical Reaction*. Torn between *Reactionary Essays* and *Rev-olutionary Essays*, Tate tossed a coin with Red Warren and settled on *Reactionary Essays on Poetry and Ideas*.[6] In order for the book to be published by March 1936, Tate had to turn in the manuscript by the first of December.

Drafting and rejecting nine versions of a preface for the collection, Tate attempted to adapt his ideas about literary criticism to the end stage of Agrarianism.[7] If it is true that the Vanderbilt group's move-ment to excise social and political thought from literary criticism got off the ground only after their political program had begun to fail, *Reactionary Essays* suggests that Tate's own struggle to reconcile liter-ary criticism and political theory was not yet over. Missing the ironic implications of an Agrarian critic taking such a strategy, Tate intended the new book as an attack on American socialists who merged their roles as writers, critics, and activists. If he and the Agrarians believed that the South ought to be protected from Communist invasion, they felt equally as strong about protecting literary texts from leftist critics such as Edmund Wilson. "Modern literary critics," Tate wrote in his preface, "are reversing the procedure of the historian. They are using social theories to prove something about poetry." It was a mistake, he argued, "to make a fine art respectable by showing that after all it is only a branch of politics." Any attempt to infuse poetry with "doctrine" or to use it as a means for setting out "new programs" was a betrayal of formalist principles in art. For, in the final analysis, "Poetry does not explain our experience." Thereby rejecting a simple representational view of art, Tate could also defend his own poetry. "Modern poets," he explained, "are having trouble with form, and must use 'ideas' in a new fashion that seems willfully obscure to all readers but the most devoted."[8]

The influence of T. S. Eliot was everywhere apparent in *Reactionary Essays*. Instead of using art to engineer the future, Tate argued, poets ought to focus on "experiencing the past along with the present." Prior to the modern age, the best poets were those who simply served as unself-conscious conduits for their own cultures—for the premodern era had provided such artists with "an available source of ideas . . . imbedded in a complete and homogeneous society." With the exception of some of the Elizabethan poets—who prefigured the twentieth-century problem of employing "symbols that are too complex to retain"— premodern poets were not affected by the abstracting forces of science. Because they lived in a world in which human thought and culture were integrated, Shakespeare and Donne were able to write powerful poetry that was "neither true nor false." Even as late as the nineteenth century in the United States, such unconscious, natural poetry was still possible, Tate thought. To read the verse of Emily Dickinson, for instance, one needed "not an opinion of the New Deal or of the League of Nations, but an ingrained philosophy that is fundamental, a kind of settled attitude that is almost extinct in this eclectic age."[9]

In contrast, modern poets could neither use allegory truthfully nor will a conducive cultural background into existence. Because the modern poet has "no large scheme of imaginative reference in which he has confidence," Tate argued, he turns to Romanticism, irony, or both. Edwin Arlington Robinson, for instance, lacking an "epos, myth, or code" could produce only fragments of his "romantic ego." E. E. Cummings, though enormously talented, was able to write only the "personal poetry" so fashionable in the twentieth century. Edna St. Vincent Millay might be "the spokesman of a generation," but she was trapped in nineteenth-century poetic forms.[10]

Even Tate's favorite Modernist poets were battling "disintegration." His friend Hart Crane, a failed genius, made the mistake of thinking that he could "create a myth." As such, Tate explained, Crane's "whole career is a vindication of Eliot's major premise—that the integrity of the individual consciousness has broken down." Some Modernists, such as Ezra Pound, did not attempt to "give [themselves] up to any single story or myth." Following Eliot's philosophy of mingling the past and the present in his verse, Pound revealed himself to be "a powerful reactionary, a faithful mind devoted to those ages when myths were not merely pretty, but true." Still, however, Pound was a "rootless" Modernist consigned to write "perplexingly simple" poetry "about nothing at all."[11]

In Tate's view, only those poets who engaged with religious faith could avoid the fragmenting forces of the modern era. John Peale Bishop, who personified "our modern unbelieving belief," deserved credit simply for trying "to replace our secular philosophy, in which he does not believe, with a vision of the divine, in which he tries to believe." Even more heroic, however, was Eliot, whose new Anglo-Catholic themes were confounding the critics. Eliot's *Ash Wednesday*, Tate insisted, ought to be celebrated as "a brief moment of religious experience in an age that believes religion to be a kind of defeatism and puts all its hope for man in finding the right secular order."[12]

The revision and reappearance of his controversial "Fallacy of Humanism" essay (retitled "Humanism and Naturalism") as well as his much misunderstood *I'll Take My Stand* contribution (now titled "Religion and the Old South") in the company of purely literary essays brought to the fore a common theme in Tate's art and politics: All inhabitants of the twentieth century were victims of the abstracting forces of scientific positivism, forces that made them self-conscious about the idea of history and undermined all possibility of belief in religious authority. Poets and Southerners, who had once lived in a timeless world in which they experienced a sense of wholeness, were particularly victimized. Stripped of any genuine cultural tradition, they could either produce fragmented art like the Modernists or take the nearly impossible step of trying to recover their culture by "reactionary" measures. But whatever their approach to the modern world, they should not behave like the Humanists who, lacking any "conception of religion as preserved, organized experience," were aiding and abetting the forces of abstraction by using the premises of science to create an artificial defense of tradition, religion, culture, and myth.[13] Years later, Tate admitted, "I saw very sharply what was wrong with the neo-Humanists because I had already seen it in myself without acknowledging it: a philosophy of literature that had no validity without religious authority to sustain it. The essay, looked at from this angle, is an attack on myself; but it was easier to project it onto others."[14]

Reactionary Essays was well received by the critics. In the *New York Times Book Review*, for instance, Peter Monro Jack heralded Tate's "critical integrity," applauding him for displaying "the critical intelligence of our day in its most sophisticated academic form."[15] Writing for the *New York Herald Tribune*, Mark Van Doren called Tate "powerful, comprehensive, and acute." *Reactionary Essays*, Van Doren pronounced, "establishes the grounds upon which all of Mr. Tate's very close thinking about poetry has been built."[16] These collected essays, another reviewer observed, were "even more significant than they appeared when taken separately, for Mr. Tate's thinking is of a piece throughout; one essay is often illuminated by another, and ideas adumbrated in one place are fully developed in another.")[17] Even the reception overseas was warm. Montgomery Belgion, writing for London's *Catholic Herald*, called Tate "a critic of a calibre only too rare among us here in England."[18]

R. P. Blackmur, who wrote the review with the greatest insight into Tate's aesthetic theory, ranked Tate above Ernest Hemingway. "Mr. Tate," observed Blackmur, "has a powerful, because an unusually integrated sensibility." In the eyes of "Mr. Hemingway," he explained, "experience is unique and his own and self-created. To Mr. Tate events do not become experience until the imagination creates them in objective form. The act of experience, in the arts, transpires only in form."[19] (Obviously flattered to have been rated in such a fashion, Tate told Blackmur, "I doubt if any writer of any sort, at any time in literary history, has ever received so perfect a review.")[20]

When reviewers criticized Tate, it was to chastise him for being obscure, stylistically dense, or abstract—or to point out contradictions in his thought. He knew many of the reviewers of his book, but that did not blind them to its discrepancies. Malcolm Cowley, a personal friend and political foe, understood these contradictions best. "I doubt," Cowley was willing to admit, "that any other poet in this country is a better judge of his contemporaries than Allen Tate." But Cowley thought "it almost seems that his essays are being written by three persons, not in collaboration but in rivalry." Tate, he elaborated, "is a Catholic by intellectual conviction (though not by communion), he is a Southern Agrarian by social background, he is a man of letters trained in the Late Romantic or Symbolist tradition—and these are three positions that cannot be reconciled anywhere short of Nirvana." As a result, Tate responded to "the civil war inside his mind by the process of reducing everything to abstractions."[21]

Similarly, Gorham Munson complained that "Tate refers to religion frequently but always in terms of abstractions. We cannot locate his religion; it seems literary and is certainly peculiar."[22] Reviewing the book for the *Nation*, William Troy called Tate a "hard-pressing dialectician" who had produced "criticism that is at once stimulating and exhausting." Yet Troy found "a contradiction between the idea of tradition, which must be 'automatically operative' in order to be valid, and the main implication of the book, that tradition can and must be defended through political action."[23]

Critics continued to misunderstand and criticize Tate's infamous, ambiguous answer to the rhetorical question he had posed at the end of his essay on Southern religion. "How may the Southerner take hold of his Tradition?" he had asked. "By violence" was his perplexing reply. Cowley's response was typical: "One might ask where the Southern Agrarians will get their weapons."[24] Only Geoffrey Stone, writing for the *American Review*, understood that Tate was not suggesting Southerners plan a coup d'état: "In the liberal and communist press (those eulogists of proletarian violence) this answer has already occasioned hints that Mr. Tate may yet be the apologist of an American Hitler. It is conceivable that far worse things than this might befall him (I do not say Mr. Tate expresses the least sympathy for fascism); he might, for instance, hold that the change he seeks could be accomplished and sustained through the regular machinery of parliamentary democracy."[25]

The most severe critique of the collection was written by W. J. Cash, who was already at work on his classic, *The Mind of the South* (1941). Then a journalist writing for the *Charlotte News*, Cash seemed more interested in imitating the language of H. L. Mencken than in engaging Tate's critical theories. Tate, he had decided, "likes to fancy that if only he had been fortunate enough to have been born in those fine glamorous old times, he'd have been the Sieur Alain at least, swinging gloriously back and forth from singing in the courts of love and praying in the gorgeous twilight of Chartres or Cluny."[26]

Yet even those reviewers who took exception to aspects of the book found much to praise. "Aside from . . . the recurrent vague abstruseness on religion," Gorham Munson admitted, "Mr. Tate gives every sign of becoming an important literary critic. He is certainly one of the most interesting now practicing the art in America. Keen in his technical insights, devoted to both poetry and ideas, aware of moral and political problems, he has an incisive and firm style, modeled after Eliot's, and a critical philosophy, in part derived from John Crowe Ransom."[27] "*Reactionary Essays on Poetry and Ideas*," Geoffrey Stone wrote, "does not make easy reading, but as the work of a sensitive and brilliant mind it offers deeper attractions."[28] Cowley, too, gave Tate high marks in the end. Privately he told Tate that while he had been in "pretty violent disagreement with the political section of the book," he marveled that

". . . writing from an apparently opposite point of view, you arrived at the same sort of social judgments that a good radical critic might reach."[29] Indeed, it was not only a testament to Tate's increased clout in the field of literary criticism—but to his eclectic political theories—that even his usual antagonists were in agreement: his first book of literary criticism had been a notable critical success.

II

Yet just as *Reactionary Essays* began reaching reviewers, Seward Collins was unexpectedly interviewed by Grace Lumpkin for a periodical called *FIGHT against War and Fascism*—and the Agrarians met with catastrophe. Lumpkin, raised in Georgia and South Carolina, was a leftist attracted for a time to Communism. *Let Freedom Ring*, a stage version of her famous radical novel, *To Make My Bread* (1932), had been playing in New York since autumn. Her trip to see the volatile editor in the New York office of the *American Review* went as one would predict.[30] Lumpkin asked whether he and the Agrarians had identical goals. "Yes," Collins answered, ". . . well, economic aims." Having established this link, Lumpkin went on to ask the editor a series of direct questions about his politics. The more questions she asked, the more Collins exposed his Fascism and his anti-Semitism:

> *Lumpkin.* Some of the things you have said make me think you are a fascist. Are you?
> *Collins.* Yes, I am a fascist. I admire Hitler and Mussolini very much. They have done great things for their countries. I do not agree with everything they do, but . . .
> *Lumpkin.* Do you agree with Hitler's persecution of the Jews?
> *Collins.* It is not persecution. The Jews make trouble. It is necessary to segregate them.
> *Lumpkin.* It seems to me it is Hitler who has made the trouble.
> *Collins.* Oh no. It's the Jews. They make dissension and trouble wherever they are.
> *Lumpkin.* You said you wished to go back to medieval times. Yet for seven centuries, and especially for three centuries during medieval times, when the Moors and the Jews lived together in Spain on a basis of equal freedom, there was great intellectual development, not only in Spain, not only among the Jews, but all over Europe.

Collins. That is another question . . .

Lumpkin. You have said you wish to go back to medieval times. You wish to do away with all progress?

Collins. Yes.

Lumpkin. And do you wish to have a king and nobles, counts, dukes, etc., in America?

Collins. Yes, exactly!

Lumpkin. You wish to live as people did then?

Collins. Yes, do away with the automobile and go back to the horse.

Lumpkin. You wish to do without conveniences?

Collins. Yes.

Lumpkin. Without bathtubs?

Collins. I never use a bathtub.

Lumpkin. You don't bathe?

Collins. (dignified) I use a shower.

Lumpkin. Then you would want a shower?

Collins: I could rig up a shower.

The damage was done. "This short interview," Lumpkin added,

> can give only the superficial aspects of the movement which Mr. Collins and the Southern Agrarians represent. I felt after the interview like a person who watches a magician pulling white rabbits out of a top hat. One knows that the magic is all bluff, but the rabbits are real. People laughed at Hitler's magic until the rabbits got out of the hat and multiplied and devoured a country and a people.
>
> I think it is not necessary to say that I do not believe Fascism is already upon us. I do believe after reading a number of books like *God without Thunder, I Take My Stand* [Lumpkin's error], and copies of the *Southern Review* and the *American Review*, that in those who write for them (some of them very sensitive and fine writers) there is the beginning of a group that is preparing the philosophical and moral shirt-front for Fascism with its top hat from which the rabbits come.[31]

Although not the first time the Agrarians had been charged with Fascism, Lumpkin's accusations put the Agrarians on full-scale battle alert. Their latest inductee, Herbert Agar, urged Tate to write Lumpkin, Collins, and the *New Republic* in order to deny the charges. "I think he means well," Agar said of Collins, "has lots of good ideas, and is at heart a sweet fellow. I would always be glad to have lunch with him. But in a crisis I think he can be counted on to behave like a dirty bastard." The *American Review* editor, Agar concluded, was "a public fool" of poor moral character. The Vanderbilt group thus found themselves between Scylla and Charybdis. "If we break with Collins," Tate explained to Davidson, "we've lost his magazine,—and so has he, because he can't run it long without us. I don't know how this will strike the group. *The American Review* is a mighty convenient place to publish things. But if we're to have everything we write discredited with charges of medievalism and Fascism, all we shall get out of it is the check, and I imagine we might make more money in some other business." Tate therefore relished publishing a response to the accusations. "I am so deeply opposed to fascism," he wrote, "that I should choose communism if it were the alternative to it. Both are slave-states, but the aim of fascism must be realized by force, while the aim of communism, ideally at least, looks toward order and consent." He continued, "I do not want to restore the Middle Ages. I do not want to restore any previous age. I do not want to restore anything whatsoever. It is our task to create something; and because communism, following the line of least resistance in its acceptance of the technique of production under finance-capitalism, is not radical enough, not *creative*, I am against it."[32]

Accepting only a portion of Tate's rejoinder, which appeared in the *New Republic*, Grace Lumpkin and Seward Collins wrote in to argue as well. "Retake Southern traditions by violence?" Lumpkin sneered, alluding to Tate's misunderstood *I'll Take My Stand* essay. "Does Mussolini want more than to recapture Roman slave-owning traditions by violence? Reaction is most radical? Hitler in his fraudulent radicalism calls for a return to the pre-trust era." Lumpkin demanded more from Tate. "Any kind of honest examination of the theoretical basis of fascism by you and your group," she concluded, "should make you uncomfortable at the similarity. If you are serious in saying you are against fascism, I am sure you will be responsible enough to reconsider your beliefs to find out whether they are leading you to a real search for the truth, or into a morass of intellectual confusion." Collins, of course, thought Tate had been misguided to write in condemning Fascism on behalf of the Agrarians. "There is," Collins wrote of the Southerners, "too much similarity between their avowed ideas and those prevalent in fascist movements to escape being called fascists, were I not alive." Ultimately, however, Tate wound up looking more politically backward than Fascist. Hoping for the last word, Lumpkin remarked: "As to Mr. Tate, I leave him with genuine regret and sadness as he goes about with his butterfly net busily recapturing Southern traditions."[33]

In spite of the embarrassment, Tate was unwilling to forgo access to the *American Review*. Whether it was some perverse loyalty to Collins or simply a dislike for the leftists wagging their fingers at him, Tate neither discontinued his correspondence with Collins nor stopped sending him articles.[34] Agar, however, followed a different path and maintained that "it would be a great mistake to commit our group to an anti–New Deal stand." When radicals criticized the Agrarians' continuing affiliation with Collins, Agar began squirming. "I agree about the illogicality of people who pretend to hate fascism and who still are associated with *The American Review*," he told the *Marxist Quarterly*. "But the point is that I am not associated with the magazine. . . . It finally became clear to me, eighteen months ago, that Mr. Collins was a fascist. Since that time it has become clear to everyone who reads his magazine, but it was not clear before that time. Not only did I break off all connection with Mr. Collins' work and thought and magazine, but I have urged my friends to do likewise. Some have taken my advice; others not. But that is neither here nor there. I am not responsible for the magazines in which my friends write. I would not, now that its policies have become unmistakably clear, write a piece for *The American Review* if it were the last publication left in America—as it might become if America goes fascist!"[35]

Despite a polite correspondence in which Agar and Collins courteously restated their differing political views, they now detested one another.[36] Collins accused Agar of knowing "perfectly well that my being a 'proponent of Fascist ideas' is no recent and sudden turn on my part."[37] When Agar denied the accusation, Collins further charged him with having changed his attitude only after he realized that to the public "Fascism presents the most challenging, dynamic, explosive issue there is: that as a word it is infinitely more provocative and horrendous than Communism—that in fact it is now the strongest word in the language, beside which such ancient standbys as f——, s——, and son of a b——" no longer compare. "You had not had occasion," Collins continued, "to think out the significance of Fascism and your attitude toward it until the word became universally current following the accession of Hitler and the world-wide hysterical onslaught of the Communists and the Jews."[38] Seeking confirmation for his charge against Agar, Collins turned to Tate, whom he believed had known about—and even approved of—his Fascist sympathies. Agar, Collins complained, suffered from a mania that consisted of "a vast inner instability clothed in surface harmony, efficiency, forward drive."[39]

Warning Collins against "a split in our ranks," Tate tried to mollify the editor by professing some degree of agreement with him. "As to the question of who has changed, you or I—that is not of much real interest, is it?" Tate asked, explaining: "When I said we might well come to call ourselves fascists, I had only one definite thing in mind: that if fascism ever arrived here and provided a situation that would be useful to us—contrary to my fears—we could side with a fascist party. But I don't think that ought to be used publicly now."[40] Trying to have his cake and eat it, too, Tate further assured Collins: "The good things achieved by Fascism in Europe—I have never denied, with Herbert, that achievement—might be achieved by us on the democratic basis."[41]

As Tate attempted to pacify Collins, he kept in touch with Agar, who had begun editing a new, counter-Fascist magazine, *Free America*, devoted to "wide distribution of productive property."[42] In the first week of June 1936, in Nashville, Agar and the Agrarians had convened the Committee for the Alliance of Agrarian and Distributist Groups, during which the various members conceived the idea for the new publication.[43] Tate was excited about writing for the magazine, but he imagined it operating on certain terms only. "There is no reason why the Catholics, the cooperatives, the Homesteaders, the single-taxers cannot all be represented in our pages," he wrote Agar, "but there is no reason why they should edit the magazine or even appear in the board of directors."[44] Behind Agar's back, Tate insisted to Collins: "We are not going to sink agrarianism into the other isms."[45] The problem, he elaborated, was Agar's "Broad Church tendency, the belief that a vigorous movement can be conducted from a general average of vaguely similar views."[46]

Almost simultaneously, Tate wrote to Agar behind Collins's back reporting that the Agrarians met with the *American Review* editor "to see if he could be persuaded out of his fascism far enough to reorganize on concentrated distributist principles, so as to provide a severer organ in the background of *Free America*." Tate was unable to gauge, he told Agar, whether the Agrarians were at all effective in leading Collins away from "his fascism." Collins had merely "suggested a separate section in the magazine for the agrarian group." Yet the Agrarians concluded "that Seward, as a personal editor of a sympathetic organ, still had some claim upon us." The group, Tate explained to Agar, "agreed that we stood as potential contributors to any magazine edited in the agrarian tradition."[47]

Tate would not, however, rally behind Agar's new magazine. He was pleasantly startled when, after chastising Agar for not having offered him its editorship, Agar did. But Tate told Collins privately that he "couldn't possibly accept" the editorship of Agar's magazine in light "of the situation that exists between the two groups." After inspecting the magazine, he decided that it was "rotten"—that it was nothing more than "a liberal-eclectic hash," and he pulled out of the project for the time being.[48] The problem was that the Agrarians came to be as distressed by Agar's allegiance to the New Deal welfare state as they were by Collins's views.[49] Tate still preferred FDR over the Republicans, but he believed the president, whom he called "a sentimentalist with a pretty bad ego," was "moved largely by hatred of his own class—the well-dressed Harvard men in Wall Street." Tate found such upper-crusters equally reprehensible, explaining, "I am not of their class; I come from an entirely different society, in fact another civilization." Yet, he continued, "because I hate them I see no reason to feel sorry for the worker or the sharecropper."[50]

Tate had come to agree with his conservative friends that the Roosevelt administration was laced with Marxism. "You are quite right about Roosevelt," Tate wrote Donald Davidson. "He is going to break the South up into class-conscious groups, and make the Southern farm tenant, and I suppose even the small landholder, conscious of the class-struggle. That will be the end of the South. And the process of bringing this about is only the newest way of reconstruction. I am sorry to say to you privately that if the alternative to this is fascism I will have to become a fascist: I'd rather be a colony to Eastern capitalism on a fascist basis than a socialized hinterland of government projects." Even the TVA, a project Tate once admired, now seemed both sinister and anti-Southern. "All the TVA people are foreigners," he concluded, "contemptuous of the common people whom Roosevelt has sent them there to 'serve,' mindful only of their jobs, and anxious to impress Washington at the cost of the local situation."[51]

Ultimately, however, Tate's criticisms of the TVA and of Agar—with whom he claimed to have "diverged politically"—had no impact. Collins had to fold the *American Review*—and the New Deal developed only negligible interest in subsistence farming as a federal policy. Rexford Tugwell, a key architect of the New Deal, attributed the "literary romp" of such Agrarianism to "sentimentalists who hadn't any idea what they were talking about." Whether the Agrarians admitted it or not, their alliances had discredited them in domestic political debates.[52]

III

In light of the Fascism accusations, the publication of *Who Owns America? A New Declaration of Independence* took on added urgency to Tate, who no doubt saw the volume as an opportunity to respond. He had been busy editing the articles he solicited with Agar, and by the spring of 1936, the volume was ready for release to bookstores. "This book," the promotional literature promised, "is a rational, organized attempt to clear a path that the average reader can follow. This path leads away from both Fascism and Communism, toward a modern realization of the Jeffersonian democracy; away from centralization and economic slavery, to small-scale production and the independence of property ownership."[53]

Looking at the new book's table of contents, readers familiar with *I'll Take My Stand* might have expected a repeat performance. Of the twenty-one contributors to the volume, eight had published pieces in the first book. The four Agrarians who did not appear in the volume— John Gould Fletcher, Henry Blue Kline, Herman Clarence Nixon, and Stark Young—had left the fold. Nixon was originally to contribute an article on tenant farming, but Tate and Agar found him too sympathetic to collectivism. ("We had the impression," Tate explained of Nixon, "that he had gone somewhat cooperative, if not pink, in the last few years, and we were afraid of him.")[54] Fletcher had become so paranoid and combative that Tate had broken with him; Kline would soon be helping to administer the TVA; and Young was no doubt distracted by his work as drama critic. In their place were traditional, Vanderbilt-trained men such Cleanth Brooks and James Muir Waller.

Surprising no one, a few of the Agrarians contributed essays restating their undying loyalty to Southern culture. "From the moment of Southern defeat," Davidson wrote in his essay, "the regional imperialism of the Northeast began its effective reign." Owsley called for "a new Constitution" to "reconstruct the Federal Government from center to circumference." Lytle, whose family plantation, Cornsilk, had faced seizure by the sheriff the previous summer, and who spent the winter months living with the Tates in Memphis and working on *The Long Night* (1936), wrote a romantic tribute to "the livelihood farm." John Donald Wade lamented "the war of the city against the country." George Marion O'Donnell, a new and younger Agrarian, attacked "Big-Business planters" and endorsed a transfer of power "from the plantations working for mass production of cotton to the agrarian plantations and to the small farms operated by yeomen."[55]

But the presence of a half a dozen essayists with no previous involvement in Southern Agrarianism—and of British intellectuals such as Douglas Jerrold and Hilaire Belloc—revealed much about the editors' willingness to mute the Southern theme in Agrarianism. "Among the authors of this book," Agar wrote in his rhetorically overblown introduction, "there are Protestants, agnostics, Catholics, Southerners, Northerners, men of the cities and men who live on the land. There are professional men, editors, teachers, men of affairs, and men of letters." Indeed, the South was notably absent in *Who Owns America?* Monopoly capitalism, not Northern industrialism, was named as the enemy. And this time, it was not "the Southern way of life" that contributors hailed, but "the American dream"—which, Agar held, was being assaulted "by two groups: first, by the communists, who say that any attempt to realize it must be in vain, since the attempt would contradict the laws of Marx" and "second, by the friends of Big Business."[56]

For each Agrarian contributor who remained neo-Confederate in tone, another one wanted to nationalize their movement. Ransom, who would publicly abandon Agrarianism within the year, conceded, "Hitherto, the Agrarians have addressed themselves principally to their fellow Southerners, with the result that they have sometimes been fairly unintelligible to readers from other sections." He and his colleagues, he continued, had been "delighted to discover some unforeseen friends" in other sections of the country and now hoped "to see all these sympathetic elements combined, for the sake of power." Robert Penn Warren sounded equally unpreoccupied by the South in his essay. Now less interested in Agrarianism than he was in promulgating the New Criticism, he attacked "the proletarian writer" who sees "literature as instrument." The real literary heroes, he reasoned, are "the regional writers," who "have proposed no specific connection between a literary and a political program."[57]

Tate's essay, "Notes on Liberty and Property," suggested that he, too, was fighting to suppress his Southern concerns. When he first began thinking about his essay more than two years earlier, he planned an article titled "The Union and the Machine," in which he would attack capitalism by arguing that the American political system did not emphasize "a real Union . . . , but a vast possibility of industrial exploitation."[58] But as he adopted the tenets of the British Distributists and fell under Agar's influence, he transformed the essay into an article on real property and a plea for individual—as opposed to corporate or state—land ownership.[59] Finding the topic, which none of the other contributors was willing to take on, enormously complex, Tate turned to John R. Commons, Adolf Berle, Jr., and Gardiner C. Means for ideas about economics. He wanted to be authoritative, but he did not want to come off sounding like a social scientist. Nor did he seem to want to write an essay about the South. The essay, which Tate also published in the *American Review*, matched more closely those of Jerrold and Belloc, who made a pitch for property ownership, and those of the other non-Agrarian contributors, who, by and large, attacked corporations, centralized government, collectivism, and Fascism.[60]

Yet as was often the case in Tate's work during the 1930s, personal experience with the effects of finance capitalism in the New South shaped his highly theoretical economic arguments. A few of his remarks in the article, which Tate thought both "very bad" and "a terrible job,"[61] suggest that his concern for property was as much a product of having watched his parents' shrinking social status and growing financial imprisonment as it was his reading of the British Distributists. "To the extent to which a man or a social group controls the property by which its welfare is insured is the man or group possessed of liberty," he wrote, adding that the problem lay with "the Big Business interests today, who are trying to convince the people that there is *one* kind of property,—just *property*, whether it be a thirty-acre farm in Kentucky or a stock certificate in the United States Steel Corporation." Tate had felt keenly his father's failures in small business, his mother's inability to retain the family real estate holdings, and, more recently, his brother Ben's sometimes precarious fortunes, which were ebbing in the wake of Wall Street's manipulation of the coal industry.[62]

With so many contributors and competing motives at work, it is not surprising that some critics found *Who Owns America?* a rather a dry, choppy book. But the anthology received a great deal of attention in major periodicals, where reviewers reacted according to their own political loyalties.[63] The most prominent review appeared on page one of the *New York Times Book Review*. Illustrated with a photograph of industrial smokestacks set against one of farmers baling hay, the review bore the bold title "A Share for All in America: Mr. Agar and Mr. Tate Sponsor 'A New Declaration of Independence.' " The "two and twenty blackbirds" who contributed to the volume, John Corbin wrote, had produced a "disquieting" work reinvigorating the Jeffersonian vision of America. "Harkening to the lilt of its cadences," wrote Corbin, "even the most hard-hearted Hamiltonian must have moments in which he hopes that the dream may come true." Any American leader engaged in the debate over "self-government under national control" would "do well to reckon with this very inspiring and provocative symposium."[64] (One wonders whether FDR read the volume—Agar was convinced that the president's acceptance speech at the Democratic National Convention in 1936 "came directly out of *Who Owns America?*")[65]

Agrarian periodicals raved about the anthology. Crane Brinton, writing for the *Southern Review*, which Brooks and Warren had now been editing for a year, wrote a near-worshipful review. "The Agrarians," he insisted, "are *not* romantic lovers of unmechanical discomforts and have no wish to return to horse-and-buggy and privy." They simply "want and preach what the best people have always wanted and preached."[66] A reviewer for the *Nashville Banner* was comparably enthusiastic. "One can scarcely lay it down," he said of the book. "It's the most vital bundle of ideas we have seen in many a day!"[67] Proud of the collection and its emergence from the *American Review*, Seward Collins observed, "A third of the book was published in these pages, and all but four of the twenty-one contributors have written here."[68]

Yet Tate's friend Kenneth Burke, writing for the *New Republic*, concluded, "The project suggests a 'spoiled child' theory of politics, where the papa-government is dismissed by the proud-bearers of 'freedom' as intolerable interference, until it must be called on for help." Evidently recalling a passage in Tate's essay about the urgency of studying human welfare, Burke observed, "Those who consider social welfare as a *human* problem, rather than a *class* problem, may be disturbed that there is not so much as a single paragraph devoted to the Negro question."[69] Broadus Mitchell, whose left-leaning work Tate had attacked in the *American Review*, thought the idealistic book sounded like "the shepherd's flute."[70] Similarly, Lewis Gannett of the *New York Herald Tribune* could appreciate the Agrarians' Jeffersonian, but thought their specific proposals made them come off "like babes in the political woods."[71] Finally, a reviewer for the *Saturday Review of Literature* admitted he could "thrill to the music" in *Who Owns America?* yet warned "the Messrs. Agar and Tate" against a "crusade, which must inevitably be a tangential one leading to the very thing they deplore: fascism."[72]

IV

The renewed criticism of Agrarianism sped the collapse of the movement but gave the group publicity—which they did everything within their power to maximize. After *Who Owns America?* was released, the Agarians scheduled a Nashville debate with the Chapel Hill Planners, represented by W. T. Couch, Rupert Vance, and Howard Odum. The event proved explosive. "Odum and Vance tried to pour scientific oil upon the troubled waters," recalled a Vanderbilt graduate student sitting in the audience, who also remembered Tate being "hot for a fight."[73] Young C. Vann Woodward was also there watching nervously. "Couch had his hands full," he remembered, "since the front row was filled with Agrarians." Eventually, "voices and tempers rose to a high pitch, and the exchange ended suddenly with the dramatic withdrawal of the Agrarians led by Allen Tate. They filed from the front row up the center aisle and out the door, with Tate shouting final imprecations." Afterward, Andrew Lytle invited Woodward, later to become one of the leading historians of the South, to join a party in which the Agrarians "were celebrating their triumph over poor Couch."[74]

Another showdown between Tate and liberal Southerners took place that spring when the Southern Policy Committee (a liberal advisory group) convened on Lookout Mountain in Tennessee. The Agrarians, the Chapel Hill Planners, and representatives of the Southern Tenant Farmers' Union were all in attendance. The Vanderbilt group, Tate concluded afterward, "could convert many of the North Carolinians."[75] But what the liberals remembered was Tate's confrontation with Dr. William R. Amberson, a liberal scientist from Pennsylvania who actively supported the Southern Tenant Farmers' Union. Journalist Jonathan Daniels recounted Tate's charges against Amberson:

> "You," he said in effect, "refuse to entertain any solution of the tenant problem but collectivism. You want the tenants to become more degraded even than they are now and gathered on larger plantations even than at present so that in the end the set-up will favor Communism."
>
> Amberson flushed but he spoke wearily. "The red herring of Communism."
>
> Tate cracked at his weariness. "I'm only giving a name to what you are supporting." He relaxed and smiled, "Aren't you opposed to tenants raising their own vegetables and milking their own cows?"
>
> Amberson retorted without smiling. "Your Agrarianism sounds fine, but under its pretty-poetry foolishness it is nothing but a plan to reduce the people to peasantry."
>
> Tate snorted: "That's the stock retort of Communists to any argument in favor of small ownership."
>
> "I told you there is no Communism involved in the Southern Tenant Farmers' Union," Amberson said. "And I'm no Communist. You may not know the difference between a Communist and a Socialist but there is one."

Those who heard the argument say that Tate spoke sharply. "I know the Southern Tenant Farmers' Union in the Arkansas country across from Memphis is Communistic. I went out there and I know."

Erupting in laughter, Amberson, who had heard the story of Tate's ill-fated trip to Marked Tree with James Rorty, could not resist telling the audience that Tate had been chased away by rednecks who thought he was a radical. "Somebody laughed," Daniels continued in his account. "Even Tate's friends grinned. Amberson scored on the anecdote. It was a body blow in that particular personal combat, irrelevant as it was to the philosophies beyond the personalities of the men."[76] Years later, a Communist who helped found the Southern Tenant Farmers' Union still maintained, "This ideological clash ended Southern Agrarianism, which had sought to turn back the clock to pre–Civil War days of moonlight and magnolias."[77]

In a kind of swan song, Tate wrote a couple of essays in which he explicated Agrarianism by attacking the philosophy of liberalism. In "A Traditionist Looks at Liberalism," he argued, "In modern societies, which are rapidly moving through finance-capitalism toward collectivism—the archetype of the un-traditional life—the means of livelihood are more and more divorced from the moral agency of men."[78] In "What Is a Traditional Society?" an essay he delivered in June 1936 as the Phi Beta Kappa address at the University of Virginia, he made his oft-quoted observation that "Man has never achieved a perfect unity of his moral nature and his economics."[79]

Yet Tate displayed greater and greater independence in his statements about the Agrarian movement. By late 1936 and early 1937, he was granting newspaper interviews in which he even embraced a limited form of industrialism for the South. Readers of the *Chattanooga Times* were probably astounded when they came upon the caption below a photograph of Tate holding a lit cigarette in midair: "Allen Tate, noted author, of Clarksville and Nashville, is shown in an informal pose during an interview yesterday, in which he explained why he had recently changed his views from championship of an agrarian south to an industrial south."[80] A short time later, readers of the *Washington Post* would have encountered another such admission by Tate: "This agrarianism that we have been preaching in Nashville may or may not be the answer."[81]

Ultimately, Tate abandoned Agrarianism in order to recover his identity as a Southern writer. Writing to Donald Davidson, he explained, "I must become a creative writer once more, a mere man of letters. I thought of writing something to this effect, but not in rejection of our principles. I would reaffirm them, and go on to say that I have no political talent and prefer to write as an imaginative artist. In order to reach that position it is not necessary to repudiate agrarianism. It is a question of function and talent, of what one can do best, not of principle. The principles remain the same, the approach different.—Apart from this, I am simply tired of attending conferences and pseudo-political meetings full of third rate people whose names I can't even remember a week later."[82] Three weeks later, he wrote Edmund Wilson and announced, "I have resigned from agrarianism; that is, I have parted company with those agrarians who were rapidly converting the agrarian point of view into a pseudo-system of practical politics."[83] From that period onward, Tate argued that he had not seen Agrarianism as a political program, but as "a reaffirmation of the humane tradition."[84]

V

As Tate began distancing himself from politics, he took comfort in the new artistic friendships he was building locally. One of these friendships, with a poet named Anne Goodwin Winslow, played a significant role in his transformation to novelist. Originally from Memphis, Winslow was a dignified and learned Southern grandam who gathered literary figures at her rambling family home in Raleigh, Tennessee. She was appealing to Tate in a number of ways: not only was she an admirer of his recently published *Reactionary Essays*, she was a product of Agrarian values and trained in the classics. She was sixty years old and widowed when Tate met her, but the age difference did not prevent them from becoming fast friends. Indeed, despite addressing her as "Mrs. Winslow," he seemed a bit smitten by her. "I wish she had been younger," he later confessed.[85]

Through Mrs. Winslow, the Tates became acquainted with her son, an army officer named Randolph, and his wife, Marcella, the two of whom resided in Georgetown but traveled to Raleigh to stay at "Goodwinslow" on occasion. The friendship blossomed when Marcella, on her way to becoming a portrait painter of some renown, asked Tate to let her paint him. He assented and she produced, after many months of work, a portrait of Tate at Benfolly, surrounded by fields of tobacco and holding a copy of *Reactionary Essays*. Tate was ecstatic and ordered an enlargement—from the neck up only—of a snapshot Marcella took of the painting. Bemused, Anne Winslow confided to her daughter-in-law "that Allen, whose chief physical characteristic was a bulging cranium, did not seem to know that there was anything wrong with his conformation."[86] Both he and Caroline were too busy studying the facial expression in the portrait. "The conception of my character that you seem to be putting into the portrait pleases me vastly," Tate wrote Marcella in September 1936. "Of course I don't recognize it, but that doesn't mean it isn't true, and anyhow that's what I'd like to be. I fear I am far from callous and indifferent, or take-me-or-leave-me. It is my greatest desire to please."[87] Some weeks later, he added, "Caroline says that the eyes have the cold, not quite open expression that is exactly right. If this is so—then I marvel that you got it so right in the three days that I could sit for you."[88]

But the most important piece of art to emerge from Tate's friendship with the Winslows during the Memphis era was not the portrait, but a play he wrote with Anne Winslow. Based upon *The Turn of the Screw*, Henry James's 1898 novella about a young governess hired by an enigmatic London gentleman to look after his late brother's two orphaned children, *The Governess* was Tate's only experiment with drama. He had read the James novel when he was eighteen or nineteen and became reacquainted with—and fascinated by—the story in the winter of 1935–36. One evening when he and Gordon were socializing at Goodwinslow, he read the novella to entertain the assembled group and afterward remarked on its baffling qualities. "Let's make it into a play," urged Mrs. Winslow.[89]

Ever aware of his new fame as a "reactionary" literary critic, Tate wanted to advance a radical interpretation of *The Turn of the Screw*. In the original version, the governess is sent to an Essex estate named Bly, where she encounters Miles and Flora, a boy and a girl both beautiful and disturbingly perfect in their comportment. Miles is expelled from school, but behaves faultlessly in the governess's presence, and Flora possesses a comparably exquisite nature. When the previous governess and valet, both of whom are deceased, begin appearing to the governess, it is not clear from James's text if they are figments of her overactive imagination or ghosts who enjoy independent supernatural existence. Suspecting that the orphaned children are possessed by the evil spirits, her relationship with them becomes increasingly paranoid and controlling. She fights with the little girl and develops an intense attachment—rather erotic in tone—to the ten-year-old boy, who dies in her arms at the close of the story. In the eight-scene adaptation, which Tate wrote with Anne Winslow quickly with the hope of making money, the governess's credibility is undermined early. The dramatic version highlights her lifelong tendency to fantasize and mutes the destructive aspects of the children's behavior.[90]

Caroline bragged to Ford Madox Ford about Tate's new angle on James's work, but she worried about the play's marketability: "The idea—you may divine it—is that there never were any apparitions, they were all manifestations of let us say the governess' baser self. The children instead of being corrupted by the wicked valet and governess did nothing but learn a few bad words from them but learned instead evil from the really high minded governess who was trying to 'save' them. Whether true or false it is interesting to examine the story in the light of this opinion. Every single sentence almost is capable of a double meaning. And all of this before anybody had heard of Freud! It's the most terrible thing, I believe, I've ever read. I don't know, really, whether an audience could stand it in play form. Anyhow, it's done— of course it will have to be 'doctored' and we're going to see if anything can be done with it."[91]

For the next twenty-five years, Tate would attempt through literary agents, producers, and playwrights, and moviemakers to sell the play in London, in New York, in Princeton—and even in Hollywood to Metro-Goldwyn-Mayer. Although he almost succeeded in getting the play produced, the problem seemed to be commercial viability of the adaptation (rejected immediately by Henry James's literary executors.) Tate's dear friend, Stark Young, later to be recognized as one of America's foremost drama critics, thought some of the play's scenes too short and that its overall "stage possibilities" in need of work, but he was "astonished at the technical sense displayed."[92] T. S. Eliot offered similarly qualified encouragement after Tate forwarded the play to his office at the *Criterion*. Eliot wondered whether the audience would understand the action without having first read the novella, and he was "rather disturbed at the thought of having real children taking part in an action of such horror." ("The reply to that, of course," Tate remarked, "is that Eliot hasn't any children.")[93] Such worries aside, Eliot "liked it very much."[94]

Although Tate told Mrs. Winslow that Eliot was "the only other person besides ourselves who understands *The Turn of the Screw*,"[95] Tate was shocked when a collection of Edmund Wilson's literary criticism appeared in 1938 and it included an essay advancing a nearly identical interpretation. Even more disconcerting to Tate, an earlier version of Wilson's essay had appeared in the *Hound & Horn* in the spring of 1934. "Did I get it from you?" a chagrined Tate asked Wilson. "If I did,

I must be losing my mind; but both things are possible—the getting it from you and the loss of mind. I had always assumed, from my first reading of the novel about twenty years ago, that the spooks were not objective; but it was only towards the end of 1935, reading it again, that I tested the dialogue, and found that by subtracting the Governess' speeches as well as her commentary, what the children say, see, and do is perfectly innocent." In both versions of the essay, Wilson had argued that nobody "but the governess sees the ghosts." *The Turn of the Screw* was thus not one of James's "ghost stories," but "simply a variation on one of James's familiar themes: the frustrated Anglo-Saxon spinster." Recognizing the enormous similarity between this interpretation and his own, Tate promised Wilson "a share" of the play's earnings.[96]

Although *The Governess* would not be staged until 1962, when its five performances at the University of Minnesota sold out,[97] Tate's writing of it in 1936 was a critical event in his literary career. Not only had he learned a style of first-person narration that he would use to advantage later,[98] but he had discovered the pleasure of working with fiction. The most appealing fiction to Tate would always be that which echoed his own family history. In this sense, *The Turn of the Screw*—complete with an opening reference "to a little boy sleeping in the room with his mother"—struck home.[99] For what could be more hauntingly familiar to him than a story about orphaned children abandoned by a pseudo-father and left in the grips of a psychologically manipulative and controlling Victorian woman?

VI

In addition to Tate's many obligations in the spring of 1936—from his waning duties as an Agrarian to the collections he was publishing—he was still a full-time faculty member at Southwestern. More than a year earlier, he had alerted President Diehl that without release time "for . . . private work" his plans were to leave the college after the spring term. Having resurrected his genealogical book *The Fathers*, which Earle Balch now wanted for G. P. Putnam's Sons by January 1937, Tate carried through with the planned departure, which Diehl "accepted . . . with great regret." Tate's only problem, as usual, was how he and Gordon would get along without a regular paycheck. The solution in the short term was for Allen to stay on at Southwestern through the summer session and to deliver a series of lectures outside of Tennessee. After that, however, they prayed that Caroline's forthcoming book,

None Shall Look Back, would earn large royalties. Irked by the way Margaret Mitchell's best-selling *Gone with the Wind* was preoccupying Scribner's staff, they were counting on Max Perkins to promote Caroline's book with comparable zeal.[100]

In the meantime, basking in Tate's growing fame, they departed that July on their whirlwind tour to stockpile money. The initial stop was Michigan. Joe Brewer, a generous publisher Tate had become acquainted with in New York City during the twenties, was now presiding over Olivet College, where he had founded the Middle Western Writer's Conference. Tate enjoyed teaching in the two-week summer school with poets and writers such as Arthur Kreymbourg, Jean Untermeyer, and Dorothea Brande, who had recently authored the immensely popular self-help book *Wake Up and Live!* and who was Seward Collins's fiancée and coeditor. But Tate was especially enchanted by Carl Sandburg, whom he found to be "a great old fellow," if rather "corny."[101] Western writers, Tate found, were Agrarian soulmates. "Fine folks here," he wrote Andrew Lytle, "— real agrarianism, no factories, no rush. Dislike of East, great interest in South and eagerness to learn. Gave them a talk on South & West vs. East. Great applause."[102]

From Michigan, the Tates traveled to Columbia University in New York City, where Mark Van Doren wanted Tate to deliver a week-long lecture series.[103] Since the Van Dorens had left for their country home in Connecticut, the Tates were able to occupy their Bleecker Street flat. Relieved to have escaped the sheltered faculty members at Southwestern, Tate relished Columbia. Noting how cosmopolitan his audience was, he reported to Caroline that "two very respectable looking old colored women in gold rim specs" were attending his lectures.[104] Also in attendance was John Berryman, a brilliant young man not yet the major American poet he became decades later. Berryman, who was Mark Van Doren's protégé, warmed to Tate as soon as he learned how highly Tate thought of Van Doren.[105] Capping off the heady Columbia poetry lectures with a recuperative week at the Van Dorens's Cornwall, Connecticut, estate, the Tates returned South in mid-August.

Their first priority was to find inexpensive housing. Although they had maintained ownership of Benfolly throughout their residence in Memphis, their financial resources did not allow them to reoccupy their beloved home in Clarksville. With winter approaching and no money to heat the old farmhouse, they chose to let the Normans, a family of impoverished tenant farmers who lived in an adjacent structure on their land, look after it. Fortunately, Andrew Lytle had invited the Tates to come live with him and his sister, Polly, in their family's summer cottage in Monteagle, Tennessee. Depositing Nancy in Chattanooga to attend school and live with her aunt, the Tates made their way to Monteagle, bringing along Vili Von Isanthal, a tiny, high-strung dachshund given to them by Charles Sanborn, Allen's eccentric professor from Vanderbilt.[106]

A lovely vacation village nestled in the mountains, Monteagle was not far from the University of the South at Sewanee. The cabin was thus situated close enough to a library and an intellectual community to allow the Tates to preserve their sanity. Equally attractive to the them, the accommodations in Monteagle—including food—were entirely free. On Saturdays, Andrew's father drove from Alabama to supply them with fresh vegetables and dairy products from Cornsilk. Mr. Lytle was sometimes accompanied by the African American servants who worked for them. Caroline, whose racism was more naked than her husband's, spoke of the workers as little more than objects. Bragging to a friend that Mr. Lytle "keeps us in Negroes," she described them as if slavery were still in existence. "All the negroes on the plantation have been trained to make wonderful muffins and biscuits," she told one friend, adding "and that, after all, is all that you can ask of any Negro cook."[107] Writing to Red Warren, Gordon referred to the African American servants who came to the cabin with Mr. Lytle as "niggers." She added, "When one cook has to go home to pick cotton he sends another to take her place."[108]

While Caroline, who rarely had difficulty with writer's block, found in the quaint, fireplace-heated cabin an extremely conducive workplace, Tate sunk into deep depression. That fall, he wrote an essay or two, but could not seem to touch the manuscript of *The Fathers*.[109] Obsessed by his debts, he described his predicament in labored detail to friends, as in a letter he wrote to Seward Collins in October: "I'm indebted to one publisher to the amount of $1500.; to another, $300. These amounts were originally and respectively $2100. and $600. but in the last two years I've paid them back and reduced them. The balance of $300. I expect to pay back in cash; I never expect to go forward with the history of Southern literature for which the original $600. were advanced. But the $1500. I expect to pay back with a book to Putnam."[110] Tate knew that his career was on hold until he got *The Fathers* to Earle Balch at Putnam's, but he was agonizing over it exactly as he had the aborted Robert E. Lee biography. One day he would vow completion of *The Fathers* "not merely because I feel it morally, but because the book is one that I am tremendously interested in finishing."[111] The very next day, he would describe it as "a book that I've never really wanted to write." What was worse, he knew that it was impossible to complete the project he had originally described. "I could have written it when it first occurred to me," he confessed to John Peale Bishop, "but four years have done something to my conception of the material; and there's little left that I can go on."[112]

Tate's problem seemed to be that the genealogy he was constructing had grown remote to his own experience. "Each chapter of the book," he explained to Seward Collins, "is the autobiography of a man or a woman of a certain generation; the two families are brought down to the present in alternating chapters until they are united in marriage, and the merely historical experience is converted into a personal dramatic experience."[113] Because these characters were not genuine ancestors in his mind's eye, he had come to see the project as more of a history book to be written than a novel to be imagined. Struggling in this effort to write objective generational history, he soon realized that he was violating his own principles—that to complete the book, he must abandon positivism and fictionalize the persons and events in his own family history.

VII

Aggravating Tate's book-writing block, he had been unable to write any new poetry—and was incensed by the total failure of the Alcestis Press to distribute copies of *The Mediterranean and Other Poems*, the thin collection of his poems published just a few months previously. The collection had appeared after what seemed to him an interminable string of delays by the press, an independent firm owned by an exasperating man Tate eventually concluded was "a fly-by-night opportunist."[114] The publisher, who went by the name J. Ronald Lane Latimer and who was engaged in bringing out a series of small (and costly) books by contemporary poets such Wallace Stevens and William Carlos Williams, did not solicit the manuscript Tate sent him. He was reported to have said that he accepted "it because Tate had 'so much influence.' "[115]

Latimer's firm was to have produced *The Mediterranean* in November 1935, but when the agreed-upon date came and went, Tate concluded that Alcestis, a firm "of a most mysterious and vanishing nature," was engaged not in the publishing of books, but in "very fishy business." Latimer's disappearance was especially upsetting to Tate since, some years previously, a publisher named Leippert had vanished in the same way after successfully soliciting Tate and others for hand-written copies of their poetry and promising to publish them in holograph form. Now Tate confirmed a distressing fact: Latimer and Leippert were the same person! The publisher, whom Tate now called "Leippert-Latimer," had numerous addresses, it turned out, and had accrued so many debts that publication of *The Mediterranean* seemed doubtful—even though it was already in proof. When, at last, Tate received a letter on Alcestis letterhead from an H. T. Stuart ("another *alias*," Tate speculated) promising the book's imminent release, Tate had grown so frustrated that he referred to the book as "the damned thing." The final blow came when Latimer failed to market the volume to booksellers. Two years later, 100 of the 165 copies published (30 of which were presentation copies) remained unsold—a maddening situation to Tate since he had expected to earn several hundred dollars from the venture.[116]

Because the book was never distributed, only a few reviews appeared, most of which praised Tate's technical skill and erudition. Yet if the new volume included some of Tate's finest work—critics hailed poems such as *Shadow and Shade* and *The Mediterranean*—his new reputation as a "reactionary" made them evaluate the poetry through the lens of his Agrarianism exclusively. All but one of the poems in *The Mediterranean* had made their first appearances in periodicals between 1932 and 1936 and some of them—such as *To the Lacedemonians* (narrated by "A Confederate on the night before the veterans' reunion") and *Aeneas at Washington*—were therefore written during peak years of Tate's commitment to Agrarianism. Those poems that did not take up specific themes from Southern history took their inspiration from the philosophical values of Agrarianism, attacking positivism or bemoaning the decline of Western civilization. "The only real thing below this distinguished verbal epidermis," a *New York Times* reviewer wrote, "is Mr. Tate's passionate preoccupation with the South; but even here is a network of reveries and reminiscences, contradictions and indecisions, nostalgias, indirections, meditations, and monologues."[117] Even Tate's friends thought the Southern theme was undermining his poetry. Kenneth Burke found the work "exceptionally penetrating," but he concluded: "No purely contemplated South, I believe, no sanctioned and cherished ancestry, no refurbished feudalism however humane, even no 'progressive' solution, can be the antidote to . . . abstraction."[118] Tate's mentor, John Crowe Ransom, himself on the verge of renouncing Agrarianism, issued a similar warning. True, Ransom wrote, Tate was "one of the most distinguished living American men of letters"—indeed, the Paul Valéry of the United States. But Tate's "lyricism" had become "somewhat choked" by politics. "Perhaps Mr. Tate suffers from a fate which has befallen other Fugitives," Ransom explained. "Some of these gentleman have fed their imaginations on a way of life that is nearly departed, a cause that is so nearly lost that it has to be fought for, and consequently they have turned belligerent. But belligerence consumes the poetic impulse . . . . A Jeremiah is a great asset, but as a poet he can author only Jeremiads."[119]

Tate despaired over such criticisms. "I am always both annoyed and amused," he wrote some months later, "when people accuse me of writing 'Agrarian poetry' or of approving only of the same thing in others. I feel sure that the only effect that agrarianism has had on my verse or on my view of it in other people's verse, is the growth of a steady aversion to agrarian propaganda in poetry, or any other kind of propaganda." He was therefore simply sick and tired of "being judged on the basis of a program."[120]

Nevertheless heeding the advice of Ransom and others, Tate determined to bring closure to the Southern stage of his artistic development by bringing out a selection of all of the poems he had written in that era. "I shall never write the sort of thing again," he observed of his Southern-sounding poetry, "and like most authors I want to make as much of what I've done in a certain phase as I can."[121] What was more, with his coffers empty and his writing blocked, Tate collected the poems as a way fighting what had become "the blackest fit of depression" of his life. "I am in the desperation that all writers know when they are in that state," he wrote Stark Young, explaining that gathering the poems provided a welcome distraction. At the very least, the book might allow him to book more of the lucrative readings and talks that he had been asked to do the previous summer.[122]

The obvious publisher to turn to was Max Perkins. Recognizing that Perkins published him not for profit, but for prestige, Tate knew to be modest when approaching him. "I want to use the verse I've written so far to enhance my reputation as much as possible," he wrote the editor, "and I feel that the publication of my essays last spring has made it possible to give the little reputation that I have as much significance as the work will allow."[123] Yet Perkins hesitated, keeping the poems a long time and referring to their publication as "a hard question."[124] Worried, Tate wrote offering to forgo the modest royalties he was already receiving from Scribner's in exchange for publication of the new collection. The appeal was unnecessary. As usual, Perkins, whom Tate believed "the most remarkable publisher in America," had conceived a plan:

defer publication of the volume until late 1937. "I believe that a book of poems, particularly a selection," he explained to Tate, "is likely to have a better sale in that season anyway, and it would still be out in time to be a candidate for the Pulitzer prize of '37,—and I should think a likely candidate."[125]

Tate thought the possibility of winning a Pulitzer slim, but he finished revising the poems in Monteagle in early November and dedicated the manuscript to Mark Van Doren.[126] Although the new collection, in which Tate gathered virtually all of *The Mediterranean and Other Poems* and *Poems, 1928–1931* and thirteen verses published in his first volume, *Mr. Pope and Other Poems* (1928), contained no new poetry, he was able to make extensive revisions to individual poems. *Ode to the Confederate Dead*, for instance, which he had been revising for ten years, received a final round of tinkering. He overhauled his *Sonnets of the Blood*.[127] But once he had completed assembling and editing the collection in the autumn of 1936, he had nothing to do but wait, for it would be a full year before it was published.

In the meantime, *The Fathers* lay largely unwritten. It was one thing to edit poems he had already written and quite another to write a prose book from the top of his head. Suffering from cabin fever and frustrated by his inability to imagine in his mind's eye the "fathers" whom he had irrevocably made the title of the book, Tate sought distraction— anything that might help him to regain his artistic imagination. Gordon seemed to find her greatest period of artistic productivity when she was writing in the midst of a routinized domestic space such as the Monteagle cabin. By contrast, Tate's greatest productivity came when he could wander from and then return to such settings. His own mother had shuttled him around the South so often during his childhood to avoid his father, Tate had apparently grown accustomed to the thought of impending trips followed by returns to safe havens. To stop the familiar cycle of restlessness actually aggravated both his depression and artistic paralysis.

It was therefore with anticipation that Tate, not yet aware that his mood was about to improve dramatically, made plans for a nostalgic trip. He was already scheduled to meet some of the Agrarians in Richmond, Virginia, in late December for the Modern Language Association convention, but now he decided to make a detour afterward and revisit Alexandria, Virginia, and Georgetown. Of the many towns Nellie Tate had taken him to in his boyhood, these were most central to her romantic fantasies about their ancestors. Conveniently for him, Marcella Winslow, the portrait painter, still lived there—and he immediately alerted her of his plans. "In the book I'm trying to write now," he wrote her in October, "Prospect Avenue and the [Georgetown] University get a long section; I want to observe more closely than I've ever done some of the physical details of the scene." Alluding to the character he had invented in "The Immortal Woman," Tate explained, "If Mrs. Dulany is walking down the street I've got to know what she sees every step of the way. That's the trouble about a writer with no imagination; he can't make it up.' "[128] He even wondered again about his great-grandmother's "old red brick house," known to him from family lore as the place where she "sewed her intoxicated consort into a sheet, applied the horse-whip and said years later, after his death, that 'he never touched another drop.' "[129]

Knowing what he must do, on December 17, 1936, Tate packed Caroline, Nancy, and their frenzied dachshund into their car and set off for Virginia. The MLA meeting, which took place over several days immediately following Christmas, signaled Tate's reclamation of an aesthetic imagination. Not only would New York friends such as Mark Van Doren be in Richmond, but Davidson, Ransom, Warren, and Cleanth Brooks were congregating in the city to join Tate in delivering papers on poetry. Although the Vanderbilt panel would later publish the panel in the *American Review*, the content of the papers was more reminiscent of the Fugitive era than of the Agrarian movement. Tate was looking forward to a gathering of his Vanderbilt friends in which the mood would be distinctly literary, not political. His paper, "Modern Poets and the Convention," while resurrecting his favorite themes, suggested how much his focus had moved from politics to language and aesthetic formalism. It was still "the task of poetry . . . to comprehend its awareness of the past in the experience of the present," Tate argued, but "the constant aim of serious poetry—exists in a new order of language."[130]

At the time of the conference, Tate was still enjoying the favorable publicity that followed publication of *Reactionary Essays*, and his fame among other writers was, for now, greater than that of his Vanderbilt friends. The difference was made clear when Ellen Glasgow, who was to give a keynote address to the conferees but had come down with laryngitis, chose him to read the paper for her. She had been trying for some years to get Tate to write a long article about her work, and there was an obvious degree of professional calculation in her choice. Privately Tate held reservations about her work, but he could not turn down the opportunity to appear as the public representative of a major American novelist. The address, in fact, received a great deal of publicity, including coverage by the *New York Times*.[131] Afterward, Glasgow was pleased to learn from members of the audience that Tate delivered the speech "beautifully."[132]

Tate had known he would see Glasgow, but it was a complete surprise when he encountered Thomas Wolfe, whose latest autobiographical novel, *Of Time and the River* (1935), was rocketing his fame to heights far greater than Tate's. Like his fellow Agrarians, Tate disdained Wolfe's confessional style of fiction and was perturbed that Max Perkins thought so much of the North Carolina author. For his part, Wolfe neither understood nor cared a wit about Agrarianism. But one thing he and Tate shared was a love of social gatherings; and, as in most face-to-face interactions among Southern writers, conviviality muted their artistic rivalries. Wolfe, distraught over irreconcilable political differences with Perkins and on the verge of abandoning Scribner's as a publisher, had been drinking heavily even before joining the Agrarians for cocktails in a Richmond hotel room. By the time Wolfe reached Ellen Glasgow's holiday party, he was even more gregarious. Inebriated and rambling, he kept telling Caroline, "Mrs. Gordon, Max Perkins thinks you're wonderful."[133]

The festive literary atmosphere at the MLA meeting was the tonic Tate needed. Being surrounded by so many Southern novelists, especially ones whose artistic imagination he believed inferior to his own, not only brought him out of his despair, but helped revive his literary ambitions—indeed, he had evidently begun to imagine that he, too, could be a novelist. Having made his dramatic decision, he appeared in Georgetown that New Year's Eve in the highest spirits he had been in for years—and seemed to the Tates' hostess, Marcella Winslow, to be oozing charisma. Marcella and her husband, who maintained a comfortable home on P Street, installed the Tates in the guest room, acceding to their request that Vili be squeezed into the room, too. Vili, however, who had a habit of growling and generally making a nuisance of himself, failed to charm Marcella the way Tate had.[134]

But not even his misbehaving dachshund could mar Tate's magical visit to Georgetown. Tate could still remember the addresses of homes owned by his ancestral fathers during the Civil War era, and he was soon touring the neighborhood to locate and inspect them. His celebrity followed him to Georgetown, where the *Washington Post* caught wind of his new plan and published a prominent feature article. Accompanied by a photograph of Tate—pensive, smoking a pipe, and looking very much the formidable fiction writer he planned to become—the article reported on the "noted Southern poet, who is visiting here preparatory to writing a novel on life in old Georgetown and Fairfax county." Tate, the author of the article reported, "went to the old home yesterday at Prospect and Thirty-fifth streets northwest, to find it completely closed and possessing something of a reputation in the neighborhood as a 'mystery house.' "[135]

Enjoying such publicity and surrounded by the enigmatic physical evidence of his family history—the details of which could only be left to the imagination—Tate's spirits soared. He even experienced an epiphany that allowed him to convert his euphoria into action. Several days earlier, Seward Collins and Dorothea Brande, newly married, had arrived in Washington. Socializing with the couple, Tate—no doubt happily telling them about the ancestral homes he had come to see— was still unable to conjure the people who lived in them. Then Brande shared an image that came to her. Tate later described it, cryptically, as "her vision of the house on the ridge and the row of trees . . . of the fat man with the pear-shaped head."[136] Tate himself had been haunted by a similar vision, for in 1931 he had published *A Dream*, a poem in which a "boy-man"—undoubtedly Tate himself—imagines himself to be his mother's grandfather and then, as he walks on a path lined by "scrub pines," encounters "a tall fat man with stringy hair."[137] But it was Brande's vision, Tate admitted to Collins a few weeks later, that "actually made it possible for me to write my book. I can't explain it precisely, except that the Vision gave those vanished places and persons a sudden violence of new life in my mind, or perhaps gave me some guarantee that they have never ceased to exist. If you all hadn't been across the room from me, who was out of the light, you would have seen that I was so excited that I was almost in tears!"[138] Tate finally had both fame and a mental picture of "the fathers" he had been unable to imagine for four years. When the image finally presented itself, he crushed in an instant the massive emotional block that had diminished his productivity and thrown him into despair for so long. He was finally ready to make peace with his family history.

Chapter Nine

A Family Reconstructed

Haunted by the lingering memories of his Georgetown perambulations—and by the recurrent images of two anonymous men—"one young, the other old, in 1850 costume," Tate went back to Monteagle, where his imagination exploded.[1] Within a month, he had written fifteen thousand words. Observing her husband's record-breaking productivity, Gordon spread the news of his artistic conversion. "Speaking of novelists," she wrote a friend, "we have a new one in our midst. Allen started on what he now openly calls 'my novel' right after Christmas. He has been working every day since we got back and shows all of the signs of a genuine seizure." She had witnessed such behavior from him in the past, but this time he was maintaining both his frenetic pace and his interest in what he was writing.[2]

Years of frustration over his inability to write any kind of family history seemed to evaporate in an instant. "It took Allen five years to get the first paragraph of *The Fathers*," Gordon recollected. "Once he got that, it went forward like an express train!"[3] Tate himself confirmed this observation: "The nucleus of my book came to me unexpectedly, as a first sentence. From that sentence, I developed the plot, the locale, motive, and characterization."[4] The sentence, which he crafted on the very day he returned to Monteagle, evoked his childhood days in Georgetown: "It was only today as I was walking down Fayette Street towards the river that I got a whiff of salt fish, and I remembered the day I stood at Pleasant Hill, under the dogwood tree."[5] Now Tate had only "to decide who had written the sentence and why he was under the tree, and how he would get away."[6]

Tate was certain that he wanted to tell the entire story in the first person. ("Omniscience would compel me to know more about the past than I do know," he explained.)[7] Having written very little fiction in his career, he turned for models to novelists whose techniques in narration he most admired. He especially liked Marcel Proust and Henry James for the way "they both put the narrator or the 'observer' inside the story as the central intelligence."[8] Remembering *The Turn of the Screw*, Tate decided to experiment again with the Jamesian use of first-person narration "as a device for disguising commentary."[9]

Tate found further evidence of such narration by a "trapped spectator" in Ford Madox Ford, whose novel *The Good Soldier* he read over and over—and "imitated . . . in the way Johnson imitated Juvenal in *London*." Tate thought the way Ford controlled the perspective of his character John Dowell brilliant—"as if *Oedipus Rex* were a novel told in the first person by Creon. The action would be the same, but our access to the action would be delayed by Creon's limited perception."[10] It was Ford, Tate told Anthony Hecht decades later, who taught him "how to use the first person narrator"—how "to keep the proper distance in action, and yet have the narrator sufficiently involved to make him seem like a real character, as if he were in the drama himself."[11]

First-person narration also came readily to Tate since he derived so much of the story and the characters in *The Fathers* from his family history. Altering the names of his mother's ancestors, the Bogans, to the Buchans, he was able to generate an immediate and extensive genealogical background for the novel's principal characters. Tate's great-grandfather on his mother's side, a Virginia secessionist named Major Benjamin Lewis Bogan (1795–1870), became Major Lewis Buchan, one of the novel's protagonists—but Bogan was now a Unionist. Susan Bogan Varnell (1834-1909), Tate's grandmother, who became estranged from her husband (and to whom Tate dedicated his early poem *Obituary*), became Susan Buchan Posey, the daughter of Major Buchan.[12] Tate did not even bother to change the name of the Bogans' estate in Virginia—the Buchans would also live on Pleasant Hill.[13]

Tate planned to contrapose the Buchan family with the Posey family. He made the Poseys Catholic Marylanders and based them on the other maternal line in own family, the Varnells. George Posey, the hero of the story, he modeled in part after Nellie Tate's father, an unhappily married timber baron and former Confederate Army captain named George Henry Varnell (1833–89). Tate made Varnell into a tall, dashing man who has recently become precariously joined to the Buchan family by marrying Susan Buchan. The ambitious George Posey, like his real-life counterpart, pursues business interests his in-laws consider rather vulgar.[14] Yet by also basing Posey on his own brother Ben, Tate tried to make the character sympathetic as well. As Caroline Gordon told Tate years later, Ben was "the man you'd like to be, the man of action you had to give up being in order to function as a poet."[15]

At first, Tate had envisioned using the character of George Posey to illustrate "how the modern American rose in unfavorable surroundings, the conservative background of Virginia at that time."[16] "Posey," Tate explained to his brother Ben, "was the prototype of you and all other 'big business' men of our day."[17] Yet Tate grew increasingly leery of using fictional characters to express historical "forces." Had he been satisfied to turn out a purely factual, "historical novel," he explained later, his two major characters would have been reduced to "mere instances of forces and movements of which they consciously knew little." He wanted them instead to be unaware of their moment in history. "I knew that 'George Posey,'" Tate said, "— knew it by family tradition—was different from the 'Buchans,' but so feeble is the historical sense of ordinary people who live by a rigid code, I could never make out from the legend just what the quality of this difference was." The novel, Tate continued, was "perhaps the effort to fix that quality, not as it 'really' was, but as it might have been."[18]

The largest problem remaining for Tate was creating the narrator. He knew that he could heighten the "conflict of manners" between the Buchans and Posey by keeping the first-person narrator he wanted to use confined "inside the situation" and subject to "the same social inhibitions that the other people felt."[19] Yet where in the Tate family tree would he find the model for such a narrator? The obvious choice, Tate soon realized, was himself. Not until years later did he admit that Lacy Gore Buchan, the major's son, who narrates the novel in retrospect as a retired physician, was an autobiographical "projection."[20] Anyone who knew Tate's own family would have seen the similarities between the character and his creator. Lacy has two older brothers, Charles and Semmes (all three Buchan sons are based loosely on actual Bogans),[21] and, like Tate, a sister who died in infancy. The older Buchan boys are as unintellectual in comparison to Lacy as Varnell and Ben Tate were in relation to their younger brother. While Tate admitted Semmes Buchan represented "one side of" his own personality, he intended the character to be "*simple*"[22]—and for Lacy's other brother, Charles, to be both "conventional and unimaginative."[23] Thus, Tate could further explore his relationship with his own siblings.[24]

Lacy Buchan's narrative, which consists of a series of flashbacks he shares with readers, begins in Fairfax, Virginia, in April 1860, when he is but fifteen. The Buchan family and some of their Posey relatives have gathered for the burial of Lacy's mother. The funeral, the precocious boy recollects as a man, was "the last time" he ever witnessed the "whole family assembled" at Pleasant Hill. Soon, they would, "either out of violence in themselves or the times," be "scattered into the new life of the modern age." "Why," he muses, "cannot life change without tangling the lives of innocent persons? Why do innocent persons cease their innocence and become violent and evil in themselves that such great changes may take place?"[25]

The violent people Lacy Buchan describes are his own kin—for an ominous friction was evident that day between Major Buchan and George Posey. Modern by comparison, Posey suffers from a personal worldview that the Major, whom Tate constructed in part as a symbol of the culture he associated with the antebellum South, has never experienced. ("If either Posey or the Major had known the meaning of the other," Tate explained later, "there could have been no story. That meaning is the body of the plot."[26] The novel's "general theme"—"loyalty versus individualism, the personal ego versus the code," he elaborated, is "the essence of the modern problem.")[27] The Major is alienated by Posey's tendency to ignore the Southern code of manners, to act as if all people were engaged in business relationships. "My father," Lacy observes of the Major, "knew the moves of an intricate game that he expected everybody else to play."[28] By comparison, Lacy idolizes Posey, who gives him a gun against the Major's wishes, thus supplanting him as a father.

Tate had a reason for exaggerating young Lacy's unbridled affection for Posey. When John Peale Bishop complained that Lacy lacked "enough distance from the scene he describes," Tate replied that the boy, "as a Virginian of his time, has the Virginian lack of historical perspective—a lack that permits him to see in George Posey mystery and excitement; whereas you and I know that Posey is only the American dream, which you've often called the American nightmare. I hope my moral is clear—that the Dream is not naive and vital, but disorderly, coming out of a background of decadence."[29]

Having transformed his mother's father into George Posey and her grandfather into Major Buchan, Tate turned the tables on Nellie Tate by dramatizing her endless reminiscences of their family on Pleasant Hill, in Georgetown, and in Alexandria. He devoted pages to a jousting match that was "exactly" the same as the ones Nellie "attended as a girl in the 1880s in Fairfax and Prince William Counties, Virginia."[30] Family lore about a duplicitous ancestor who arrived inebriated to fight "the last duel in Virginia" made it into the novel as a showdown between Posey and a cowardly minor character named John Langton.[31] Tate even used physical mementos he had inherited from his mother, hanging pictures of her family around the desk where he wrote. A pair of Benjamin Lewis Bogan's gold cufflinks helped him to imagine the character of Major Buchan.[32] An inscribed manuscript Nellie's grandfather received from his cousin George Washington Parke Custis, a playwright, made it into one scene.[33] Yet the family stories were being told to suit his purposes, not Nellie Tate's.

Yet as much as Tate attempted to gain control over his mother's version of the family history, even in the unfettered world of his imagination he could not seem to escape the shame he felt over his ambiguous feelings for her. Much is revealed about Tate when Lacy announces, "The death of my mother is a suitable beginning for my story." Only after his mother's death could Lacy—who is repeatedly referred to as a "motherless boy"—allow himself to see that his mother was a woman with a "physical body" who had once been pregnant with him. After she died, he learned that "the little boy's fiction, that grown women were only neck and head set above a mysterious region that did not exist, was a fiction of death." Indeed, he confessed, "in the conviction of guilt that harasses children I saw myself responsible for my mother's death."[34]

Like Tate, Lacy discovers that even after his mother's death, his fear of her sexuality affects his relationships. Lacy makes this alarming discovery on the day of his mother's funeral when he has a groping encounter with George Posey's younger sister. Jane Posey is a half-girl, half-woman adored by Lacy's brother Semmes; but Lacy loves her, too, and he kisses her after bringing her into—of all places—his dead "mother's dressing room."[35] Alone afterward in the room, Lacy picks up a perfumed silk petticoat that belonged to his mother. Grief-stricken and lonely, he longs for Jane Posey to return and comfort him. Yet when he tries to summon the image of the young girl, she appears in his mind's eye as his mother! He imagines seeing Jane "standing over me, in these grown-up clothes, the small feet in the satin slippers and an edge of red below her hoops, but the hands were not hers, the wide gold band on the long left ring-finger being too familiar; the delicate blue veins above the knuckles were on my mother's hand." Realizing that his mother was once nubile, he grows "terrified as the smell of the petticoat blotted out the room."[36]

Haunted by the ghost of his own mother and her family, Tate worked on the novel like a man possessed. He turned out a minimum of three hundred words a day, sometimes, his friends learned, "rising in the middle of the night to put down a speech or an idea."[37] He planned to complete three hundred manuscript pages by June 1937, and by March he had drafted the opening section of the novel.[38] In that first part, titled simply "Pleasant Hill," Tate introduced the members of the Buchan and Posey families, established the character of his narrator, of Major Buchan, and of George Posey, introduced their individual slaves, and foreshadowed the crisis that was to erupt later. Yet Tate was doubtful whether Earle Balch would find the work-in-progress acceptable, and he began worrying after sending it to the publisher for approval. "I reckon he don't like it," Tate wrote Andrew Lytle when he did not get an immediate reply. "If that's the case," he added, "I'll give it to Perkins and feel very pleased."[39]

II

Eager to continue writing, Tate and Gordon reclaimed Benfolly as their headquarters for the late spring and summer of 1937. As impecunious as the Tates were, African American domestic workers in Clarksville earned such a pittance that Caroline was able to hire two servants named Electra and Ida (a mother and her daughter) to help with the farm's endless upkeep. The grounds around the house were verdant and alluring, but the Tates stayed inside and wrote. While Gordon typed out yet another novel, *The Garden of Adonis*, and oversaw Ida in the kitchen, Tate hammered out part two of his manuscript. Their routine established, the Tates began summoning literary friends to Benfolly. Before long, the farm was as crowded as an artists' colony.[40]

Tate's reputation as a poet had grown so much in recent years that other writers now sent aspiring poets to the literary mecca at Benfolly. The most important of these poets was an emotionally immature college student named Robert Lowell. A Harvard undergraduate from a distinguished Boston family, Lowell had just suffered a falling-out with his puritanical and protective parents over a socialite he planned to wed. After his father wrote a letter to the woman's father condemning the couple's dormitory-room trysts, Lowell was so incensed that he punched his father in the face. Lowell's mother saw this episode as a worsening of her son's psychological troubles. But young Lowell, not yet a junior at Harvard, was spared being placed in a mental institution by the intervention of Merrill Moore, the former Fugitive poet who was now a psychiatrist in New England. For some time, Mrs. Lowell had sought help from Moore in handling her son's wild behavior. Recognizing the poetic genius in Lowell, Moore talked Mrs. Lowell into letting her son leave for Tennessee to become a student of Ransom and to meet Tate.[41] Moore was encouraged in this scheme by Ford Madox Ford, who passed through town and pronounced Lowell "the most intelligent person he'd met in Boston."[42] "Young man," Ford commanded Lowell, "go south and learn how to write."[43]

No doubt acting on the advice of Moore, Lowell buried his nose in Fugitive poetry during the train ride to Nashville. "Allen Tate," he concluded, "is very topnotch, a painstaking tecnician [sic] and an ardent advocate of Ezra Pound."[44] Borrowing a car for the drive to Clarksville, the windblown Lowell appeared in the Tate's driveway dramatically: emerging from his auto, he urinated on the side of the road.[45] The unkempt genius, whose friends called him "Cal" (short for Caliban and Caligula both) made a frightening sight. Caroline was horrified. "When Cal Lowell walked up the hill towards Allen and me," she recalled, "and I saw him for the first time in my life, something inside me said that he was mad, so urgently that I repeated the words to Allen."[46] Tate likewise "saw him as a badly unadjusted boy"[47] but invited him in anyway—thereby inaugurating one of the most powerful and volatile mentor-protégé relationships in American literary history.[48]

Lowell's first impressions of Benfolly stayed with him for life. "The Tates were stately yet bohemian," he remembered, "leisurely yet dedicated. A schoolboy's loaded twenty-two rifle hung over the Confederate flag over the fireplace. A reproduced sketch of Leonardo's *Virgin of the Rocks* balanced an engraving of Stonewall Jackson." Off the back of the compound, "the deadwood-bordered Cumberland River was the color of wet concrete, and Mr. Norman, the token tenant, looked like slabs of his unpainted shack padded in work-clothes." But it was the conversation that impressed Lowell the most. "After an easy hour or two of regional anecdotes, Greenwich Village reminiscences, polemics on personalities," he remembered, "I began to discover what I had never known. I, too, was part of a legend. I was Northern, disembodied, a Platonist, a puritan, an abolitionist. Tate handed me a hand-printed, defiantly gingersnap-thin edition of his *The Mediterranean and Other Poems*."[49]

Bowled over, Lowell reveled in being near such a powerful and erudite critic. "All the English classics," he recalled, "and some of the Greeks and Latins were at Tate's elbow. He maneuvered through them, coolly blasting, rehabilitating, now and then reciting key lines in an austere, vibrant voice. Turning to the moderns, he slaughtered whole Chicago droves of slipshod Untermeyer Anthology experimentalists." Lowell was further amazed by the certainty with which Tate approached every aspect of his literary work. "He said that he always believed each poem would be his last," Lowell recalled. "His second pronouncement was that a good poem had nothing to do with exalted feelings of being moved by the spirit. It was simply a piece of craftsmanship, an intelligible or *cognitive* object." To make Lowell understand such craftsmanship, "Tate brought forward Mr. Norman, the hand-printed edition of *The Mediterranean*, and finally a tar-back cabinet with huge earlobe-like handles." Tate, using walnut felled on his own land, had made the cabinet himself.[50]

Recognizing that his own poetry thus far amounted to juvenilia, Lowell tried to seize the opportunity before him. Returning to the Tates as soon as he could, he screwed up his courage and suggested that he might not mind spending the summer living with them. But in the brief time since Lowell had returned to Nashville, Ford Madox Ford had come to town with Janice Biala and an in-law, Mrs. "Wally" Tworkov, for their own extended visit. While there was plenty of room in the house for Lowell, Tate was not keen on the troubled young poet, whom he believed "potentially a nuisance."[51] Hoping to send Lowell back to Nashville, Tate joked, "If you came you'd have to live in a tent. I'm sorry, I wish we could have you."[52] Lowell, as wide-eyed as he was wild, drove to Sears and Roebuck, purchased an olive-colored camping tent, and pitched it on the grounds at Benfolly. Prying eight dollars weekly from his mother to defray expenses, he was able to live there for the summer after all.[53]

Trying hard to please Tate, Lowell wrote "grimly unromantic poems—organized, hard and classical" and read them aloud first before bringing them indoors for criticism.[54] Thus Lowell realized every aspiring poet's dream—to have each poem he produced receive immediate review by a leading American poet—thereby getting an early start on a career that would end in critical acclaim and celebrity alike. But Lowell got much more than a poetic voice from Tate. A friend later observed that Lowell "had left home and camped on the property of the parents he would like to have had, Caroline and Allen."[55] "Like a torn cat," Lowell later admitted, "I was taken in when I needed help."[56] He later annoyed his host by calling him "Father Tate,"[57] but Tate treated him like a son, even enlisting his help with some woodworking projects. Before long, Tate and Gordon had grown both "very fond" and protective of Lowell. "There was a great effort to get him to tie his shoe laces, tuck in his shirt tails and take baths," Nancy Tate recalled.[58]

Meanwhile, Ford, who was suffering a variety of physical ailments— aggravated by the greasy Tennessee food—found the immature young man grating and accurately speculated that several decades down the road Lowell would write embarrassing lyrics about him.[59] Ford had not dreamed, Caroline observed, that Lowell would do exactly what he had commanded and come South. But Ford was making great headway on *The March of Literature* and let neither his health nor Lowell ruin his visit. Day after day, he would either translate the Roman poets or walk the length of Benfolly and dictate passages for transcription by Wally Tworkov, his amanuensis.[60]

Tate called Benfolly that summer a "precariously balanced *ménage*"—but the word *menagerie* would have been just as appropriate.[61] Lowell had to share the lawn with a cow named Uncle Andrew who had a habit of leaning too close to his tent. Yet Lowell remained a city slicker. Much to Tate's amusement, the naive Bostonian looked at some mules and said, "I've never seen so many donkeys."[62] Nancy, home for the summer with a friend from school, was given a pony and was struck by equestrian fever. Even Caroline was preoccupied by animals—she spoiled Vili the dachshund more than ever. But she spent most of her time helping the servants cook. Thinking back on the era, she noted, "It was a wonder I even got any writing done in those days. What I spent my time doing was feeding poets."[63]

III

Tate allowed his writing and hosting duties at Benfolly to be interrupted only for one of his favorite pastimes: a literary battle. The episode began late that spring when Kenyon College tried to lure John Crowe Ransom to Ohio to teach and to found a literary magazine.[64] An underpaid English professor at Vanderbilt—in a department now chaired by the Fugitives' arch enemy, Edwin Mims—Ransom was heavily in debt and mulled over the offer. Tate, taking hold of an opportunity to honor mentor Ransom at the expense of nemesis Mims, laid plans for a full-scale attack. Late that May, he disseminated a public censure of Vanderbilt to the local papers. Calling Ransom's imminent departure "a calamity," Tate chastised Vanderbilt Chancellor James H. Kirkland for undervaluing "one of the most distinguished men of letters in the world." Reminding Kirkland of the Fugitives' central role in the Southern Literary Renaissance, he added, "I can only ask you to imagine Harvard University, at the height of the New England revival, letting Charles Eliot Norton go to a small college in the Middle West." The letter also included a condescending attack on Kirkland. "If you, as the head of a great university," Tate wrote, "are indifferent to the grounds of this expostulation, then I can only pity you."[65] Puzzled by Tate's public form of communication with him, Kirkland replied, "I am not ignorant of Mr. Ransom's distinction in letters, and I am not indifferent to the grounds of your expostulations, so that I do not deserve either your censure or your pity." Either feigning ignorance or missing Tate's implicit point that Vanderbilt ought immediately to duplicate or exceed the offer to Ransom, Kirkland professed to have heard from a third party "that the financial conditions attached to the offer in Ohio are so favorable that Mr. Ransom cannot afford to decline the invitation."[66] The press followed up the story with an editorial sympathetic to Ransom's plight and a series of prominently placed articles. "One more distinguished southerner is to be lost to the south," Tate told the papers.[67]

While Ransom said that Tate's letter left him "embarrassed," the members of their Vanderbilt coterie were thrilled by such public humiliation of the university. Calling the letter "a masterpiece" in the genre, Lytle thought Tate would never do better "in letters of this nature."[68] Davidson wrote to say, "I felt like throwing up my hat and giving the rebel yell."[69] Such reactions were indicative of the long list of grievances that the Fugitives had accumulated against Vanderbilt, the first of which was Kirkland's refusal to purchase a subscription to the *Fugitive* magazine years earlier.[70] But it was Edwin Mims who figured most prominently in their complaints. They had not forgotten how the jealous professor had taken them to Nashville's Commercial Club for lunch in an attempt to discourage them from publishing the magazine in the first place.[71] Mims, they speculated, had grown even more competitive as their fame grew—and he wanted nothing more than to free Vanderbilt of them forever. Robert Penn Warren, they observed, was dropped from the department during Mims's tenure. Next, John Donald Wade quit the department, telling his friends, "Mims treated me like a grocer's clerk."[72] Finally came the evidence that Mims, who had requested that Ransom not make public Kenyon's offer, wanted him to move on, too. Tate, who never stopped believing that Mims had blocked his own admission to the Yale graduate program in classics, concluded that their former professor was "making a final heroic effort to disperse our group."[73]

Since Donald Davidson and Lyle Lanier remained on the Vanderbilt faculty, Tate received a continuous series of communications reporting on actions taken by Mims, who was, in response to Tate's maneuvering, "about to have a calf."[74] Although Mims had told the press "that he would do everything 'in reason' to keep Ransom," Tate "heard from two authentic sources the quoted words of Mims that they intended to do nothing."[75] (Mims, indeed, had written a letter to Kirkland in which he halfheartedly praised Ransom, yet advised that the university "should not match the offer" from Kenyon.)[76] In a conciliatory meeting with Davidson, however, Mims blamed Tate for the university's inaction, suggesting that the letter had backed them into a corner. "Oh, if Allen had only waited," Davidson reported Mims saying, "—if he had only talked to me first!"[77] Egged on, Tate drafted a chilly letter to Mims, in which he vowed, "I shall reprehend strongly and publicly any attempt of the authorities of Vanderbilt University to place upon me the slightest degree of responsibility should John Ransom leave you, under the pretense that I have forced your hand and that the dignity of the University will not allow you to compete with Kenyon College."[78] Shifting the entire thrust of his attack from Kirkland to Mims, Tate then sent newspaper accounts of the controversy and a letter to the editors of *Time* magazine in which he imposed an ultimatum: "I am asking Professor Edwin Mims, head of the English Department at Vanderbilt, to wire you his official decision by Monday, June 1st," Tate wrote.[79] Meanwhile Lyle Lanier, who believed the entire episode "exposed Mims in all of his tortuous duplicity and intellectual emptiness," was summoned by the professor "to 'make peace,' " Rejecting Mims's overture, however, Lanier went to his office and "let him have it full blast for about an hour." Merciless, Lanier then gleefully "arranged to have other people drop in and take pot shots at the deformed torso."[80]

Ransom, initiating his own strategy, told Vanderbilt officials in a meeting that while he did not demand that they reproduce Kenyon's terms, he would be pleased by "the payment of a cash bonus by the University (entirely privately) in recognition of past services."[81] But then the rumor emerged that, during the course of the discussion, Mims had "reminded Ransom that he had done him a favor all those years in keeping him without a Ph.D."—and had even suggested patronizingly that Vanderbilt "would take up a collection in Nashville to pay [his] debts." Recognizing the opportunity to further embarrass Mims, Tate wrote to another Vanderbilt official and to the *Chattanooga Times* exposing the plan "to pass the hat to rich men and then to hand the charity to one of the most distinguished men in America."[82]

When it began to appear that Vanderbilt would not bid what Kenyon had for Ransom, and that he would have no choice but to leave, Tate hatched another plan. Merging his own literary clout with that of Ford Madox Ford, Tate succeeded in getting the *Virginia Quarterly Review*, the *Southern Review*, the *Sewanee Review*, the *Saturday Review of Literature*, and *Poetry* to hold an elaborate party in celebration of Ransom.[83] Assisted by Andrew Lytle, George Marion O'Donnell, Ford, and Mrs. Tworkov, Tate mailed printed invitations to prominent literary figures asking them either to be present or to send letters for dissemination to the press.[84] While Tate told guests that "Vanderbilt need not be mentioned at all in the speeches,"[85] the unstated purpose of the function was to make the institution look as foolish as possible. Tate meanwhile mailed his diploma back to Vanderbilt, explaining to Kirkland that "it is no longer an honor to be one of her alumni." Tate likened the institution to a business school. "You have done honor to industrialists, economists, and politicians," he wrote. "But you have not been publicly aware that men of letters exist, even when from time to time, following the conditions of migratory labor, they have appeared on your faculty. Your institution has been the center of an important intellectual revival, but you have ignored it."[86] Privately, Tate worded this accusation even more frankly. "To urge the claims of literary distinction among such people," he said of the administration at Vanderbilt, "is like delivering a lecture on chastity in a whore house."[87]

The dinner party, held in Nashville on the tenth of June 1937, not only made it obvious that Vanderbilt University had grossly misjudged Ransom's fame, but made for a grand evening. Huffing and puffing, the obese Ford Madox Ford, wearing "white duck trousers, a beat-up dinner jacket, and shod in espadrilles," hosted the event.[88] Ransom, overwhelmed by emotion at least once during the testimonials, expressed enormous gratitude to Tate afterward—but he could not resist teasing his former student about his love of crisis. "You are a fire horse," he told Tate before departing for Kenyon, "and when the smoke begins to smell you can't keep out of the harness." Tate, who had worried that his grandstanding would permanently alienate Ransom, was undoubtedly relieved by Ransom's good-natured reaction to the public spectacle he had manufactured.[89] Ultimately, however, it was the devastating consequences for Edwin Mims that pleased Tate the most. When the beleaguered Mims was heard to utter, "My world is crumbling about me," that comment alone, Caroline Gordon observed, "gave Allen as much joy as he is likely to get in this life."[90]

IV

Tate's joy was ephemeral, however. As the remainder of 1937 sped by, everything seemed to conspire against his efforts to complete *The Fathers*. Much of the time, it was the help he extended to other writers that kept him from his work. In mid-July, he and Caroline departed for Michigan to teach once more at the Olivet conference. This time, they took along not only Ford, Biala, and Robert Lowell, but Nancy and Vili. The group headed north for Urbana, Illinois, where they would stay overnight with Frank and Harriet Owsley. Wedged like sardines into the Tates' little car, none of the passengers found the trip a happy one. Exasperated by the Fords' difficulties adjusting to life in the South, Tate realized that he would not mourn their departure. Nor were the Fords, who were not pleased to be traveling in such close proximity to Lowell, feeling any more sentimental. When they arrived in Urbana, they decided to hop on a train to Michigan.[91]

Tate, however, could abandon neither his old nor his new literary friends for very long. During the conference, which was not especially memorable, he took in yet another student under his wing. Ted Roethke, who had come to Olivet "to meet 'writers' " began sharing his poetry with him daily.[92] When Tate was finally ready to go home, he and Gordon insisted that Katherine Anne Porter, whom they had called to the conference, join them for the long car trip back. Tate made them take a detour to Virginia so he could inspect another family estate for *The Fathers*, but once he was home in Clarksville, his friends again took precedence over his writing. Although Lowell, the Fords, and Mrs. Tworkov had long ago left for New York City, new visitors appeared. When Cleanth and Tinkum Brooks came, they found only Robert Lowell's abandoned tent "flapping in the breeze." But Brooks's youthful colleague at the *Southern Review*, Albert Erskine, soon showed up and fell head over heels in love with Porter, a married woman almost twenty-five years older. The mismatched couple stayed up flirting long into the night. Unable to sleep, Tate heard their entire conversation and found himself "thinking they ought to go off to New Orleans together and have an affair."[93]

Battling such distractions, Tate lost a great deal of momentum on his manuscript that summer—even as his wife, who rarely allowed even the most trying of social circumstances to impede her work, succeeded in completing yet another novel. While he had that September come up with "a new idea" for *The Fathers* that he believed would "simplify the whole thing from now on," he was still not turning out the number of pages he had the previous winter and spring.[94] By October, he was fighting off despair again. "I'm still at my novel," he wrote Davidson. "Some of it is fair, but on the whole I'm convinced that fiction was not meant for me. The inventions of poetry are credible, but the inventions of fiction seem to me to be monstrous and unbelievable."[95]

Tate's despair worsened after the appearance of his *Selected Poems* that fall. While the book's publication should have been a cause for celebration, he could not "bear to look at it." "I haven't written a poem in nearly three years," he explained, "and the book places the fact squarely before me."[96] Once he had held high hopes for the physical appearance of the book, even planning to have a bust of himself by a newly prominent sculptor named Harold Cash photographed for the frontis piece. But financial realities at Scribner's, he lamented, "chiselled it away until only a cheap looking thing appears in the end."[97]

Tate's friends and many reviewers, however, recognized *Selected Poems* as the work of a major poet. "If you don't receive the Pulitzer prize for this book," Donald Davidson assured Tate, "it will be only for the same reason that an Agrarian Law could not pass the Supreme Court."[98] Reviewers such as Cudworth Flint praised the collection as a book "no one who cares for the health and high estate of poetry in America can afford to overlook."[99] Comparing Tate to Yeats, a reviewer for the *Boston Transcript* hailed the collection as "the ultimate best of a poet whose hard and active mind makes a deep impression on the thinking of the times, and the poetry of the future."[100] Morton Zabel wrote in the *New Republic* that some of the poems in *Selected Poems* were "among the finest American poems of our time."[101] Likewise, Carl Sandburg, who befriended Tate at the Olivet Writer's Conference, was thrilled to receive the collected poems of "a man familiar with several lost causes, a man with imagination and music and sudden capacity for horse laughter—with enough of bitterweed and salt humor to be content if his book is highly companionable and is kept in a corner among the repeatedly used books."[102]

Yet *Selected Poems* failed to win Tate a Pulitzer. For all the accolades the book earned, the old charge of obscurity cropped up in most of the reviews. Eda Lou Walton of the *New York Times Book Review* announced: "In Allen Tate obscurity is due definitely, I think, to a lack of poetic ability, a lack of any deep passion or intuitive grasp of life."[103] A British reviewer praised Tate's "underlying force of feeling," but taunted him by quoting back one of his own lines of poetry: "High in what hills, by what illuminations / Are you intelligible?"[104] A more respectful reviewer for *Time* magazine could not resist adding that "Tate's poems . . . conduce to the racking of brains in private."[105] Even Tate's admirers had grown impatient with the difficulty of deciphering his verse. "Tate has been," one observer of this impatience wrote, "and to a lesser extent still is, the most highly praised poet of his generation with the exception of Hart Crane. It is true that more recently he has had his share of condemnation, not only from the Left, but rather surprisingly, from what one would suppose to be congenial quarters."[106] Tate tried to make sense of the new criticism he was receiving from old admirers. "All the reviewers," he concluded years later, "turned several flips and made numerous obeisances to some superior quality, and even assumed that the author of these poems must be one of the few really good living poets; and then proceeded to pick at the edges."[107]

Such qualified admiration may have stemmed in part from Scribner's overzealous marketing of a volume they knew would have a limited audience. (While T. S. Eliot thought it "a volume which stands up extremely well," he declined publishing the book in England simultaneously because of the difficulty in selling copies.)[108] In an effort to cash in on the *Gone with the Wind* mania that was sweeping America, Scribner's misled buyers to believe that Tate's "best poetry is a reflection of the Southern soul filled with sad memories of a story popularly conceived as having ended at Gettysburg." He and "the true sons and daughters of the Old South," one promotional review maintained, "continue to add their own dreamy postlude, and this contact with the receding beauty of other days has in it the very essence of poetry."[109] Yet readers expecting to find a Southerner weeping below the moonlight and magnolias found instead a poet who continued to renounce direct emotional statements in favor of Eliot's "objective correlative." "As a poet, I have never had any experience," Tate explained in the book's preface. ". . . my concern is the experience that I hope the reader will have in reading the poem."[110] Behind Tate's "objective" verse, however, lay experiences and emotions too powerful for public revelation. (It would be for Robert Lowell, years later, to speak the truth about Tate's verse: "His poems, all of them, even the slightest, are terribly personal.")[111]

By November 1937, the upbeat mood that had permeated Benfolly and made the Tates so happy had evaporated. Caroline's new book, *The Garden of Adonis*, had come out, but it was being panned. Licking his wounds over his *Selected Poems*, Tate dropped his personal correspondence and tried to work on *The Fathers*, but he was getting nowhere. Then he learned that Catherine Wilds, Gordon's cousin whom they had entertained at the Van Dorens's apartment just the previous year, committed suicide. Tate and Gordon were left with the funeral arrangements for Wilds, who had fallen into a tailspin when the man whom she loved would not get married to her. To make matters worse, the object of her unrequited love was Harold Cash, the sculptor who had recently made the bust of Tate.[112]

One tragedy followed another that fall. Next, when Tate and Gordon went to Vanderbilt for a football game on Thanksgiving, Vili the dachshund ran away. While they were at the game, a maid came to clean the apartment they had borrowed; the unpredictable dachshund bolted through the door and onto West End Avenue, never to be seen again. Gordon stayed up through the night waiting for Vili and then wandered through town "for days calling like a banshee" until Tate made her come home. The little dachshund had appealed to her deepest instincts as a nurturer, and she was heartsick.[113]

In the midst of their pain, the Tates found themselves standing at yet another professional crossroads. In early December, a letter had arrived from W. C. Jackson, dean of Administration at the Woman's College of the University of North Carolina, Greensboro, inviting them to campus to discuss the possibility of a joint appointment to teach creative writing. When the discussion resulted in an offer, the Tates faced an agonizing decision. Since Gordon was planning another novel that happened to be set in North Carolina, she favored the move. But Tate remembered all too well the ill effects of the Southwestern teaching load on his writing. The officials at Greensboro, he insisted, "must not hire us as Chinese jugglers and then expect us to cook."[114] Dean Jackson, however, not only promised a far lighter teaching load, but full professorial rank for both of them and separate salaries of twenty-four-hundred dollars apiece annually. Tate thought the money "fabulous"—even "perfectly incredible."[115] There was, of course, no choice but to accept.

Since they were expected to be in residence by the first of February, Tate returned to his manuscript and tried his best to complete it before

Christmas and the move to Greensboro. If he finished the book, he and Caroline could even take a holiday trip without guilt. Ben had given them a brand new Plymouth during a recent visit, and they wanted to drive to it to the Gulf of Mexico on vacation. But the Tates' bad luck returned in December: Nancy fell ill and had to undergo a tonsillectomy. Taking in no visitors, the Tates tried to cheer up their sick daughter by decorating a tree and passing "a very quiet Christmas" with the Normans, their tenant family.[116]

V

Greensboro, known as the "Pivot of the Piedmont," was the inverse of Clarksville, Tennessee. With cotton mills, colleges, thriving retail districts, tall hotels and corporate buildings, railroads, and more than ten thousand industrial workers, it was no farm town.[117] Fortunately for the Tates, they were able to secure the short-term rental of a fully furnished "nine room house in a beautifully wooded section quite near the college." The landlord at 112 Arden Place, Gordon told friends, "reserves two rooms but the rest of the house is ours from cellar to attic." Built of brickface and wood, the large, comfortable home was only ten years old. There would be ample room for the Tates, for Nancy, and even for Hans, a dachshund puppy they recently acquired from Dr. Sanborn as a replacement for Vili.[118]

While the Tates had hoped to keep a low profile, local writers soon learned of their arrival and began extending social invitations. Since North Carolina's thriving intellectual community tended to be liberal politically and thought little of the conservative Tennessee milieu that produced the Agrarians, the Tates did not know what to expect from the tarheels. Before long, however, the Tates were socializing, albeit awkwardly, with prominent liberals such as Jonathan Daniels, the editor of the *Raleigh News and Observer*, W. T. Couch, editor of the press at Chapel Hill, and Rupert Vance, one of the university's progressive sociologists.[119] While such gatherings caused Tate to relive a number of the Agrarians' hostilities with the Chapel Hill crowd, his discomfort was now more often literary than political. After being invited to Chapel Hill to deliver a talk, Tate complained to Marion O'Donnell that "they've never heard of the modern poets who to us are the basis of all discussion," concluding, "I suppose we don't appreciate the atmosphere of Nashville till we get away from it."[120] To Tate's surprise, however, he was greeted warmly when he gave the talk. "There is no hostility to us at Chapel Hill," he observed in astonishment. "Even Couch is most friendly."[121]

Encouraged, the Tates reached out to the writers who lived nearby. A typical evening was the sort they spent with the liberal playwright Paul Green, whom they had met some years earlier at a Southern writers' conference. "Paul Green came over last night and read his play on the lost colony," Gordon reported. "It was pretty dreadful and Paul got carried away with his own eloquence and went on for nearly two hours. I never see Paul without thinking of what Andrew said: 'He looks like the kind of man that would burn your barn.' "[122] Tate now referred to Green patronizingly as "a good Carliny country boy."[123]

The Tates were also ambivalent in their feelings toward the faculty at Greensboro, but they soon discovered that they liked most of their well-educated colleagues. The college, created in 1891 by New South progressives such as Charles Duncan McIver, had grown quickly under the direction of Dean Jackson, who assumed control shortly after it was subsumed by the University of North Carolina in 1932. Heralded as a model of liberal educational reform, the institution had attracted many academicians trained in the Ivy League. While only a handful of the nineteen members of the English department held doctorates, almost half had earned advanced degrees from Columbia or Harvard. Tate noted that faculty morale was much better among the high-paid Greensboro faculty than among the overburdened professors at Southwestern.[124]

When Tate and Gordon began teaching at Greensboro in 1938, almost two thousand young women attended the college—although the institution seemed to assume that all women would marry and raise children. "Educate a man," the college's founder told people, "and you educate an individual; educate a woman and you educate a family."[125] Nevertheless, Gordon, both a mother and a thriving professional, seems to have been worshiped at the college. Indeed, readers of newspaper accounts at the time of the Tates' appointment to the faculty might easily have concluded that her fame was greater: her name, photograph, and works were described before Tate's—sometimes preceded by headlines such as "Kentucky Novelist and Poet Husband to Join Faculty of University of N.C."[126]

While Gordon taught a year-long course called the Writing of Fiction, Tate taught two one-semester courses, the Writing of Verse and the Writing of Literary Criticism. Teaching the fields he knew best, selecting his own students, and meeting with them only on alternate days, he was able to work on *The Fathers* practically every day. Even on the days when he did have to appear in the classroom, he was not due on campus until two in the afternoon to teach "seven girls for an hour."[127] Asked by a correspondent whether he delivered lectures to his students, Tate replied that his job was merely to "read the essays and reviews that the girls write, and tell them to do better next time."[128] He even had time in the afternoons to lift weights at the Greensboro YMCA gymnasium. Proud to see his "muscles . . . hardening after fifteen years of disuse," Tate was happy again.[129] At this rate, he could complete his novel in June.

In mid-February, however, Tate could not resist taking a break from his work in order to appear at Harvard University. Robert Hillyer had invited him to deliver one lecture in a prestigious series sponsored by the Morris Gray Poetry Fund. Like most of his public lectures, Tate wrote "Tension in Poetry" with a view to publishing it as an essay.[130] Completing it several days before delivering it, the essay was both a defense of his own poetic technique and an early example of the New Criticism—both of which explored the "tension" between a poem's internal language and its "literal statement." Endorsing poetry based upon "a configuration of meaning" rather than one based upon "the fallacy of communication," Tate argued "whatever the poet's 'philosophy,' however wide may be the extension of his meaning—like Milton's Ptolemaic universe in which he didn't believe—by his language shall you know him; the quality of his language is the valid limit of what he has to say."[131]

After being introduced by the poet Ted Spencer, Tate delivered the lecture on February 17, 1938. Accustomed as he now was to the Woman's College in North Carolina, Tate found the experience in Massachusetts rather unpleasant. "The atmosphere of that auditorium and the sour New England faces," he admitted to Donald Davidson, "were too much for me."[132] Fortunately, the intimate social gathering that followed the lecture was far more pleasurable. Passing the evening in Eliot House with literary critics F. O. Matthiesson, R. P. Blackmur, Philip Horton, who had recently written a biography of Hart Crane, and poet Richard Eberhart, Tate charmed the small crowd. Eberhart, later to become a major poet himself, was transfixed. "Tate has a winning way about him," he wrote the next day; "is a true American; has a fascinating Southern accent, and tells quaint tales of the South. He is not at all formidable personally; rather the reverse, and seems hardly the man, being so animated and eager, to have written his 'dry' poetry." As he joined the debate over Hart Crane's poetry, Eberhart was also assessing Tate's famed head. Noting the "enormous frontal part of that organ" on Tate, Eberhart was nevertheless surprised by his "slight" build. Having seen Tate only in photographs, he admitted, "I thought I must shudder should I see him, so formidable did that cranium appear. But in fact he has a fine lean and active face, is oddly bald on one side but not the other, so that when you see him from the left as he lectures you think he is forty." While distracted by his appearance, Eberhart decided that he "liked Tate immensely."[133]

Tate felt out of place at Harvard, but the visit did not alienate him totally from New England. While he and Gordon stopped in New York to visit Mark and Dorothy Van Doren, the couple invited them to join them in Cornwall, Connecticut, for the summer. The Tates were enthralled by the idea of spending July and August in the pastoral northern village. Tate had not been looking forward to all of the distractions that would come his way if they returned to Benfolly for the summer, and Gordon was equally worried about being so close to Merry Mont and her family, a constant drain on her time and energy. Willing and eager to forsake the South for a few months, the Tates accepted the Van Dorens's proposal and investigated renting a cottage in Cornwall.[134]

VI

Pleased to have made summer plans, Tate finally began a steady routine of work on *The Fathers*. Except for making another visit to New York City to deliver lectures during his spring vacation, he stayed in Greensboro to write. Part of the new motivation he felt that spring stemmed from the positive response he had gotten from the friends he let read his work in progress. Cleanth Brooks had been called upon to comment on the first section of the book and had pronounced it "mighty impressive." Robert Penn Warren offered more specific criticisms, but he, too, thought the book consisted of "the real stuff." He particularly liked its "strong narrative drive," telling Tate he was "fine at managing the leads and holding suspense." Caroline called the book "swell" and was every bit as supportive about his work as he had been about hers for so many years.[135]

Tougher critics, of course, would be Tate's Northern friends. The Van Dorens, whose literary judgment Tate treasured, had always been somewhat intimidating to him. When he finally built up the courage to show what he had written to Dorothy Van Doren, his fears were borne out. "I know exactly what the reviewers are going to say about my book . . . ," he said when she criticized the narrative technique. "They will say that the narrator beats about the bush for a hundred thousand words but never comes to grips with the characters." He knew that Dorothy Van Doren "was right." Nevertheless, he asked, "What could I do without having the patience and gifts of Flaubert?" While Flaubert "would have thrown it all away and started again," Tate confessed that he minded "just enough about the book to finish it as it is, not enough to rewrite it."[136]

It was Mark Van Doren, however, his friend since the 1920s, whose approval Tate craved the most. "If, after reading what I sent you, you wish to see how it ends," Tate wrote him of *The Fathers*, "I shall be confirmed in my determination to finish it. But if you *aren't* interested in the fortunes of the people, I am depending on you to say so. That wouldn't keep me from finishing it; it might make me take a new inventory, and think of improvements."[137] Fortunately, Van Doren liked what he read so much that he "felt badly cheated when the MS. broke off." He praised Tate for opening "the second part in a way which is especially tantalizing to one who hasn't the whole before him—that pool of blood, and George Posey changing his clothes!" Calling the manuscript "very subtle work, of which H[enry] James would have been proud," Van Doren urged, "Decidedly you must go on."[138] Encouraged, Tate wrote another large chunk of manuscript in April and vowed he would complete the book by June.[139]

Tate opened part two of *The Fathers*, which he titled, "The Crisis," in May 1861, about one year after the events in part one. Following the death of Lacy's mother, the Buchans had relocated temporarily to Alexandria, Virginia, to live in the house of their cousin John. Lacy's physical description of the view from the brick house is a tribute to the lengths to which Tate went in order to reconstruct historical settings. "From the top of the house where my room was," Lacy recollects, "I could see over the roofs on bright days far up the river into Washington, six miles as the crow flies: the unfinished dome of the Capitol, the truncated obelisk which later became the Washington monument, and off to the right a little, the flag-pole in the White House yard."[140] On the other side of the river lay the Poseys' Georgetown home, which Tate had already described in his short story "The Immortal Woman." Revisiting the brick-and-stone house during his stay at Marcella Winslow's, he had discovered that the 1797 structure was boarded up.[141] But his genealogical knowledge made it easy for him to reinhabit the structure with his forebears.

Starting a new section of the manuscript also allowed Tate to delineate the separate attitudes of George Posey and Major Buchan toward property. While the Major sees no monetary value in anything having to do with the functioning of Pleasant Hill, Posey sees a cash value in everything from land to slaves.[142] With the Major easing into retirement, Posey acquires the title to "all the landed property, including besides Pleasant Hill some two thousand 'undeveloped' acres" owned by Lacy's mother. After buying out the interests of Lacy's brothers, Posey takes actions that will mean the dissolution of Pleasant Hill, but that will avert a bankruptcy. Posey insists that the land produce a cash crop, and he sells an entire slave family to a Georgia slave trader in order to pay down the Major's debts. Meanwhile, the Major, who is unable to fathom the idea that Pleasant Hill might be an asset, appears to be oblivious to Posey's maneuvers.[143]

Long after writing *The Fathers*, Tate described the shock he felt in locating, once he had already begun the novel, hard evidence for a rift between Major Benjamin Lewis Bogan, the man on whom he based Major Buchan, and George Henry Varnell, the man on whom he based Posey. The evidence, a deed Tate unearthed during a research trip to the Fairfax County courthouse, showed how little Bogan thought of Varnell. Finding the document, Tate recalled, "gave a sort of historical reality to a plot already forming in my mind."[144] Yet the novelist in Tate was willing to depart from history in order to widen the gulf between the two men. For instance, despite the fact that Major Buchan's historical counterpart had professed a desire to join the Confederate military, Tate explained, he "made him a Unionist for the sake of the plot, history seldom being as dramatic as one would like it to be."[145]

Such poetic license also allowed Tate to dramatize the disagreements that developed when his ancestors were forced to choose sides during the early days before the Civil War. Lacy's narrative recounts the growing political tensions between his father and George Posey in the months prior to Lincoln's inauguration. When South Carolina secedes from the Union in December 1860, Posey observes of President Buchanan, "The damned old fool ought to reduce Charleston to ashes!"[146] The remark is appalling to Major Buchan, who, while a Unionist, possesses a blind faith in the capacity of the federal government to resolve the crisis in an orderly manner. Even after the attack on Fort Sumter, the old Major can only ask, "War? . . . How can there be a war?"[147]

Major Buchan sees neither his family's deep distrust of the Union nor their need for independence. After Posey's loyalties move toward the Confederacy, for whom he becomes an arms smuggler, the Major watches helplessly as Semmes, who he believes has been influenced by Posey, announces that he is a Rebel. Lacy, despite watching his father disown Semmes, realizes that he, too, has become a secessionist. The two brothers idolize Posey—and are each infatuated with his young sister, Jane. Encouraged by their own sister Susan, however, Lacy ignores his brother's feelings and allows himself to fall even more for Jane Posey, thinking, "How nice it would be to be married to Brother George's sister!"[148]

VII

As Tate continued reshaping his family history for the plot of *The Fathers*, he did not fail to explore the history of enslaved African Americans owned by his ancestors.[149] Hoping to illustrate his new theories about the effects of slavery on antebellum families, he added a number of slave characters to the novel. When he had written about slavery in his biographies during the 1920s, he defended the institution by arguing that the plantation system was less heinous than modern industrialism.[150] In 1929, for instance, he told Mark Van Doren that while he was "an abolitionist . . . at heart, and could not by any stretch of casuistry bring [himself] to own a slave," he believed "that the end, agrarian rule, would justify the means, slavery, if no other means were at hand."[151] But now that the Agrarian movement had ended in failure, Tate's interest in slavery was less that of a polemical historian of the Confederacy than that of a novelist who wanted to explore his own genealogy.[152]

It was by conscious design, then, that *The Fathers* reached a climax in a piece of family history about a slave Tate fictionalized as Yellow Jim, George Posey's "mulatto" brother. In order to illustrate Posey's tendency to quantify everything in his environment, Tate has him sell Yellow Jim for fifteen hundred dollars to procure a large horse—which Posey rides in the jousting match. In Jim's place, Posey keeps a slave named Blind Joe, whom he considers less valuable. When Jim attempts to explain his master's choice to Major Buchan's slave Coriolanus (a third slave character whose "yassir[s]" and "respectful obstinancy" Tate clearly meant for readers to admire), Jim can only report that Posey had to have the cash.[153]

But the Buchans do not approve of Posey's assignment of monetary value to slaves. "I had heard it said," Lacy observes, "that it wasn't much worse to sell negroes than to buy them."[154] The old Major keeps a copy of Hinton Rowan Helper's *The Impending Crisis* (1857) "locked up in the secretary so that no other member of the family could read it." He tells his family that it is "a dangerous book. . . with the little truth in it that slavery was an evil." Yet Lacy finds his father's (and Posey's) view of slavery alien to his own view, concluding, "slavery was a great evil only to the slaveholders themselves." (Neither Lacy, his father, nor Posey is able to see that the institution's greatest wrong was the denial of liberty and safety to fellow human beings.)[155]

Tate thought that his three male slave characters—impetuous Yellow Jim, passive Blind Joe, and loyal Coriolanus—showed that the demeanor of slaves was determined by each master's attitude toward the institution. But the tale of Yellow Jim revealed more about the Southern slaveholders' legendary mythologizing of white women. In the third and final part of the novel, Jim, having run away from an overseer who was making him work in the fields, reappears to live with the Poseys after a hiatus of three years. He picks up his old duties with a bizarre devotion, and with the exception of beating the independent-minded mare for which George Posey sold him, Jim impresses Lacy as "a gentleman in every instinct." He especially dotes on Lacy's beloved Jane, whom he once served as a constant companion and nursemaid. Jim's constant attention is disconcerting to Jane, who is no longer a dependent child, and at length she confesses to Lacy, "I am afraid of that man."[156] When Yellow Jim overhears her remark, he disappears, ominously, from the house.

Meanwhile, Semmes Buchan, who is now a Confederate Army surgeon with Virginia's Thirty-third Regiment at Harper's Ferry, shows up. Having turned against both his sister Susan and George Posey, Semmes wants to leave with Jane and marry her. Lacy continues to keep his feelings for Jane from his brother Semmes but is devastated. Retiring for the evening, he can only lie in bed hating Semmes and thinking the worst of their family and its future. In lines that have become some of Tate's most-frequently cited, Lacy steps back into his role as trapped spectator and observes: "Nobody today, fifty years after these incidents, can hear the night; nobody wishes to hear it. To hear the night, and to crave its coming, one must have deep inside one's secret being a vast metaphor controlling all the rest: a belief in the innate evil of man's nature, and the need to face that evil, of which the symbol is the darkness, of which again the living image is man alone." Refusing to "pity" the Posey and Buchan families, Lacy concludes, "none of them was innately good. They were all, I think, capable of great good, but that is not the same thing as *being* good."[157]

Lacy is woken from his dreamlike meditations later in the evening when he hears "a door slam like a gunshot." Investigating, he discovers

Yellow Jim huddled in the hallway outside Jane's room. Entering the room, Lacy and Susan find Jane catatonic on the floor by her bed. Her "mouth was open. Her skin was tight and chalky, like pressed muslin." What "a shame," thinks Lacy, "that any girl should be lying there humiliated, so young." Observing the "torn" sleeve of Jane's gown and then her arm, Susan finds "four shallow scratches about an inch apart and an inch long." Lacy concludes that Jane was "clawed as she had drawn away."[158]

Not merely because she is no longer the emblem of white womanhood so worshiped by the Confederate South, but because Susan wants to stop her marriage to Semmes, Jane is placed in a convent.[159] A Catholic priest concludes solemnly, "There's no other way. The girl can never be the bride of any man." The consequences for Yellow Jim are even more severe. "Take him up the river," Susan demands. Professing his innocence, Jim protests, "I didn't do nothin', I didn't mean to tech Miss Jane either. Hit was when she hollered. That's when I done it. Hit come over me."[160]

But Jim's fate is sealed, even after Susan has changed her mind and encouraged him to flee. Lacy, aware of the wrong that is about to be committed, concludes, "Yellow Jim had been used by us all; by Brother George, to get a bay mare and to cut a big dash among strangers; by sister, to prevent a marriage that out of some deep and, to me, barely discernible level of her being, she hated; by me even, who had lacked the imagination to take Jim the night before up the river and, instead of shooting him, to turn him loose and make him run away; and I had used him again today, boasting of my fault before him as if I expected, as I no doubt did secretly expect, him to applaud the confession; and then by Jane herself, in some obscure but still culpable impulse of shallow hysteria that had impelled her to dramatize her fear of sister into the perpetual fear of women—negro men."[161] Despite his misgivings, Lacy joins Semmes and George Posey as they bring Jim to the banks of the Potomac, where instead of being freed he is shot dead by Semmes. The commotion continues when Posey suddenly fires at and kills Semmes, apparently in defense of his "mulatto" brother, whom he only wanted to help escape.[162]

The fact that Yellow Jim was a "mulatto" shot for an alleged sexual crime against a white woman proved distressing to conservative Southern readers of the novel, who believed that the character would serve to confirm Northerners' belief that antebellum Southern men had sexual relations with their female slaves and then turned into violent vigilantes who claimed that white women were threatened by black males.

Donald Davidson, for instance, admitted being "troubled somewhat by the final incident of Yellow Jim's doings, & what immediately followed." He thought *The Fathers* magnificent, but he warned Tate, that "you seem here to play into the hands of our Yankee torturers just a little. I don't so much mind Susan's monstrous connivance. I do mind the (to me) unnecessary blood-kinship of Yellow Jim & *his own* white folks. And certain other things, possibly—because they will be misunderstood." Another reader, Davidson added, "assures me that Yellow Jim did *not* rape the girl. I got the impression he did. Maybe you have been a little too subtle there for me to follow you."[163]

Tate, however, believed that the Yellow Jim incident proved that fear governed the relationship between blacks and whites. "I knew that you would question at least the Yellow Jim aspect," he wrote Davidson, adding that he ". . . was perhaps led too far by certain actual circumstances pertaining to a negro in my grandfather's family. After the war he killed another negro, and was sent to the Maryland state prison. My grandfather got him paroled and took him into the family. He tried to assault one of the ladies after he had heard her say she was afraid of him. I followed that tale pretty literally because I knew that it contained a profound truth of the relation of the races. I wouldn't have felt so secure with an invented incident. The actual negro was not so closely related as half-brother, but he was at least a first cousin of the lady he attacked.—On the other hand Coriolanus seems to me to strike the balance—the best effects of slavery, Yellow Jim the worst, Blind Joe the average."[164] Tate evidently believed that Coriolanus was somehow less like an enslaved man than Yellow Jim because Major Buchan did not view his slaves as marketable units the way George Posey did.[165] Although Tate thought his portrayal of slavery unsentimental, he was rather surprised when *The Fathers* won the praise of leftist critic Lionel Trilling, who wrote of the novel, "Here, too, is slavery understood in all its human aspects, and hated—seen in the apocalyptic vision of George [Posey] riding in the 'tournament' on the back of his mulatto half-brother: in effect, of course; actually he had only sold the man for the price of a good mare."[166] As insightful as Tate thought Trilling's review, he was distressed whenever he believed a critic had reduced *The Fathers* to social critique. "I've been trying to see why Trilling thinks my fable an indictment of the Old South," Tate wrote to Philip Rahv. "I think it may as easily be seen as a justification of it, quite apart from the style. It is an indictment only in the sense that it is an indictment of the necessary limitations of human nature."[167]

Tate saw the critical dispute over the social message of the novel as a vindication of the formalistic principles that had governed his writing of it. Admitting a revulsion for the popular "naturalistic novel, with its hocus-pocus of 'background' and 'motivation,' " he believed only a handful of formalist critics understood that *The Fathers* was not intended as a sociological study of an epoch. He expressed particular gratitude to R. P. Blackmur, who he decided had recognized "the central intention I am aware of in myself both as a poet and prose writer." Blackmur had extended him the ultimate compliment, Tate explained, in expressing the "feeling that I had led you to *what* was in that age, not to *how* it got there." The fact that Trilling, who was "concerned with the *how*, took the novel as an 'indictment' of the Old South" while "another [saw it] as a 'vindication' " demonstrated, Tate thought "how irrelevant the naturalistic approach to any art probably is."[168]

Tate would have been even more shocked by the way recent critics have focused on the novel's social philosophy instead of on its aesthetic strategy. While critics writing during his lifetime more often wrote with a goal of interpreting *The Fathers* as he himself viewed it, contemporary observers have been more interested in the novel not merely for its depiction of slavery, but for its window into Tate's views of gender and race relations. Other modern critics have used the novel to explore white Southerners' fears of "miscegenation" and have pointed to the novel's stereotypes: black males as potential rapists, black females as oversexed, and "mulattos" as tragic.[169]

It is true that Tate had always been fascinated by those slaves in his family who were of mixed racial ancestry. In his adolescence, his mother and he visited a very elderly former slave named Martha Jackson in Washington, D.C. "Aunt Martha Jackson," Tate was told, was the half-sister of Major Bogan and had apparently been willed to the Major by his father and hers, John Armistead Bogan. When Tate's mother sat him down before the aged blind woman, he recalled, "she ran her bird-like claws over my forehead, my ears, my nose, my chin" and remarked, "He favors his grandpa." Her remark, which Tate thought a welcoming into the family, remained vivid to him, and he used the meeting as a motif in his truncated memoirs. "If the sense of a past," he told readers, "comes less from parish registers, old houses, family Bibles, old letters, county records, and tombstones, than from the laying on of hands from one generation to another, then what sense of a living past I may have goes back through the bird-claws of an ancient female slave, my blood-cousin who, ironically enough, in family authority seemed to take precedence over my mother."[170]

Despite the apparent pride Tate took in having African American relatives, he had a deep-seated fear of "miscegenation." The extent of his fears, and of his racism during the 1930s, were revealed in an infamous letter he wrote during that decade. In 1933, also the year Tate began *The Fathers*, Lincoln Kirstein requested that he write an essay for the *Hound & Horn* clarifying the Agrarians' position on the race issue, and he had responded with a lengthy letter that included his views on interracial sex. "The negro race is an inferior race," Tate wrote, adding that "miscegenation due to a white woman and a negro man" threatened the white family. "Our purpose," he continued, "is to keep the negro blood from passing into the white race." Unwaveringly, he concluded, "The psychology of sex says that a man is not altered in his being by sexual intercourse, but that the body of a woman is powerfully affected by pregnancy. A white woman pregnant with a negro child becomes a counter symbol, one of evil and pollution." Written at a peak moment in his Agrarian fervor, the racist letter represents Tate at his worst.[171]

Nor was Tate's desire to limit white interaction with blacks confined to paper during the 1930s. He refused to socialize with black writers in any situation that might challenge the rigid code of segregation he had learned as a child. His relationship with the writers of the Harlem Renaissance was especially troubled. It was not so much their verse that left him cold, for he was an admirer of the poetry of Jean Toomer,[172] but rather the prospect of having to interact with them on an equal plane socially. In 1929, for instance, Tate would sometimes rendezvous with Countée Cullen, who was also in France as a Guggenheim Fellow.[173] Yet when Cullen suggested on one occasion that he would like to join Tate and the poet Léonie Adams for conversation, Tate blanched at the thought of bringing a lady to a public gathering with "a negro."[174]

Another such episode took place in 1932 when Langston Hughes came to Nashville to read poetry. Loudly protesting a party planned to honor Hughes and his host James Weldon Johnson, Tate attempted to coerce Tom Mabry, of the Vanderbilt English Department, not to hold the event. "Johnson and Hughes are both very interesting writers and as such I would like to meet them," Tate wrote in an open letter to Mabry. "This would be possible in New York, London, or Paris," he explained, "but here such a meeting would be ambiguous. My theory of the racial relations is this: there should be no social intercourse between the races unless we are willing for that to lead to marriage." Although Tate agreed that it was "unfortunate that we live in a civilization which makes it impossible for writers of two races to meet socially," he was not planning to tamper with folkways. Such segregation, he continued, would end "only in heaven where there are no distinctions of color and no marriage or giving in marriage." Tate signed the letter, "Yours for realism and a proper respect for the colored race." When Mabry issued a strong rebuke—in which he called Tate's ideas "not only indicative of an entire lack of respect for the negro race but a shocking example of intellectual dishonesty"—Tate claimed to have had only noble intentions: "My refusal to meet these colored men is due, in part, I hope, to a desire not to create a situation which might eventually humiliate them." He was willing to agree that they were his "intellectual equals," yet he feared that the "casual people" they would encounter would insult them.[175]

Tate found opposition to neither his segregationist nor his paternalistic race attitudes among Agrarian comrades such as Robert Penn Warren, who often made equally disturbing statements. After Mabry accepted a job at all-black Fisk University, for instance, Warren wrote to say that "Mabry has definitely decided to commercialize his talent for nigger-loving."[176] When Warren wrote his segregationist essay for *I'll Take My Stand* in 1930, Tate praised his friend's ideas, which he believed were in the best interests of blacks. Warren's "views of negro education," Tate told Davidson, "seem to me to be sound: if we don't educate the negro into a self-sufficient agrarianism, the industrialist will propagandize him into the factory. . . . The salvation of the negro lies in sticking to the land."[177]

If Tate shared Warren's halfhearted interest in the education and economic plight of Southern blacks, he believed such aid was endangered by Northern reformers challenging the Southern race hierarchy.[178] When it came to his disdain for these reformers, Tate's views on race relations during the Agrarian period were indistinguishable from those of the fire-eating Agrarian, Frank Owsley. Like Owsley's, Tate's remarks about race issues were often accompanied by attacks against "Eastern liberals" and Communists. The Agrarians, Tate argued in the early 1930s, might have been able to join forces with radical writers when they protested labor conditions in Harlan, Kentucky, but in a case such as the Scottsboro trial, the Nashville group's views on race relations would make it impossible. "Not because," he wrote the Harvard-trained John Brooks Wheelwright, "the nine, or is it ten, colored boys are guilty, or if not guilty ought to be hanged anyhow, but because the unfortunate negro, when your compatriots paid us a four year visit in the last century, was turned over to the mercies of the poor white mob. It has always been an impossible situation, and there's nothing we can do short of presenting the negro agitators with the case they most desire: defense of ten negroes would be defense of the whole race. Rather than that, I will shut my eyes, and see the colored boys executed. You have no idea what it is to live—and not merely sympathize from Boston or New York—with another race; and for that and all the complicating reasons I see the negro question in terms of power. When there are two unassimilable races one of them must rule; and being white I prefer white rule, and I will not give up the slightest instrument of white rule that seems necessary. It's too bad that the negro has no interested protector—for example, an owner—and is at the mercy of the mob. I see no solution."[179]

Flickers of a pained conscience did occasionally appear in poetry Tate wrote during the Agrarian movement. The African American poet and anthologist Arna Bontemps recognized that, even in the 1930s, when Tate wrote *Sonnets at Christmas*, he was ashamed of his behavior toward blacks.[180] "Ah, Christ, I love you rings to the wild sky," the second sonnet began.

> And I must think a little of the past:
> When I was ten I told a stinking lie
> That got a black boy whipped . . . .
> Therefore with idle hands and head I sit
> In late December before the fire's daze
> Punished by crimes of which I would be quit.[181]

But such confessional moments in Tate's poetry, or elsewhere, were rare during the 1930s. Indeed, his views on race issues, as well as his belief in segregation, remained relatively unchanged through the 1940s. He would make no public amendments to his views until the 1950s, by which time his expatriation from the South—and a long series of charges that he was undemocratic—made him more self-conscious about his social pronouncements.[182]

Tate startled many critics by writing, in 1950, an introduction to the poetry of Melvin Tolson that Tolson called the "literary Emancipation Proclamation" for black American writers.[183] Readers who had a view of Tate as an unreconstructed Southerner were equally surprised when they read his terza rima poem *The Swimmers*. Written after he experienced a flashback, in 1951, to the sight of a lynched man he had come upon in Kentucky some forty years earlier, Tate recalled seeing the "limber corpse" and pondered the actions of his townsmen. "Alone in the public clearing," he wrote in the poem's final stanza, "This private thing was owned by all the town, / Though never claimed by us within my hearing."[184]

Before the 1950s were over, Tate participated in a two-day civil rights forum titled "The Sectional Crisis of Our Time." Martin Luther King delivered the keynote address and Tate's lecture, given on the same day—the centennial of the raid on Harper's Ferry—consisted of an attack against the radical abolitionist John Brown. Tate told the audience he would rather adopt "a more recent strategy—the example of Dr. Martin Luther King, whose leadership in the non-violent resistance of his people in the now famous boycott of the bus system in Montgomery is to my mind a model of the kind of action that should be undertaken all over this country." Tate called King's model "an imperfect one, not inherently imperfect, but rather incomplete" and appeared to be supporting integration for reasons of practicality as much as for anything else. "The political and social welfare of all Americans," Tate said, "and not only justice to the Southern Negro, demands that the Negro everywhere be given first-class citizenship."[185]

Tate's support of voting rights for African Americans and his begrudging endorsement of integration was accompanied by a growing impatience with the segregationist tirades of his more conservative friends like Davidson, who joined the White Citizens Council at Vanderbilt during the 1960s. Davidson's "Southernism," Tate complained to Robert Penn Warren, "for all its cunning and learning, is now at the level of mere White Supremacy."[186] Yet Tate remained a gradualist who preferred that integration, which he supported largely because it was inevitable, be overseen by Southerners.[187] "If you can't lick 'em, join 'em, might well be the Southern slogan," he wrote Davidson; "that is, take over integration and do it gradually the Southern way."[188]

Once Martin Luther King's movement began to triumph, however, Tate found it difficult to maintain any loyalty to Southern diehards such as Davidson. For a while, Tate tried to walk a tightrope between his Southern and Northern friends. He told Anthony Hecht that blacks might have gained their civil rights without so much difficulty had they delayed their early push for educational integration, which he believed had "aroused the deepest prejudices of . . . the ignorant Southerner."[189] Praising King's voter registration drive as a more practical starting point, Tate perhaps thought he had found a way to support the campaign for civil rights without endorsing integration across-the-board.

Yet the more Tate observed the actions of those Southerners violently opposed to King's movement—and the nation's horrified response to them—the more self-conscious he became. Finally, he seized an opportunity to publicly disassociate himself from the Southern segregationists. Writing for the *Spectator* on April 9, 1965, the anniversary of the confederate surrender at Appomattox, he denounced the segregationist governors George Wallace and Ross Barnett—as well as the "half literate Red Necks" at sporting events who were unfurling the Confederate flag. "An elegiac devotion to the Confederate flag," he argued, "can have a dignified propriety. There is no dignity in displaying it as a symbol of the oppression of the Negro. It once stood for the best of the South; it now stands for the worst." He had seen the flag "diminished to a small emblem set in the helmets of the Alabama State Troopers" who appeared "on television beating Negroes, who were trying to register to vote, with clubs, wet ropes, and cattle prods." Although Tate continued to express cynicism about the chances for producing social equality in the South by educating people, he restated his belief that "the vote is the fundamental political reality, from which other liberties must come or not at all."[190] He was proud of having veered away from neo-Confederates such as Davidson and told Robert Penn Warren (who was undergoing a political conversion of sorts and publishing more liberal, while no less paternalistic, work on Southern race relations) that his piece on Appomattox was "a personal confession which might have been subtitled 'Up from Segregation.'"[191]

In the meantime, as Tate's early statements about slavery were becoming known to literary critics, he began referring critics to *The Fathers*, which he believed came closer to presenting his views. When Matthew Josephson published his 1962 memoir, *Life among the Surrealists*, in which he wrote that "Allen Tate and John Crowe Ransom abandoned all hope in the Machine Age and planned to return as Southern Agrarians to the provincial traditions and the 'racial myth' of the Old South," Tate was incensed. After contacting his attorney, he wrote an angry letter to Josephson's publisher. "In the climate of opinion of our time," Tate maintained, "this is defamatory. I challenge Mr. Josephson to cite in the entire range of my writings, over a period of some forty years, a statement which would support his accusation. The delineation of the Negro hero, 'Yellow Jim,' of my novel *The Fathers*, would prove conclusively that I did not subscribe to any belief remotely resembling a 'racial myth.'"[192]

Embarrassed by charges such as Josephson's, Tate took every opportunity to renounce and, if possible, to suppress publication of his racist letters of the 1930s. For instance, he engaged his attorney to block distribution of a 1966 book about the *Hound & Horn* that reprinted his diatribe to Kirstein about white supremacy and "miscegenation."[193]

The racist letter, Tate told Malcolm Cowley, "could be quoted out of context by enemies to my very great damage. I wasn't born with virtue in these matters; I have had to acquire it."[194] But the book made it into people's hands anyway, and ten years after its distribution, Tate was still mortified when people read it. When his friend Daniel Aaron, a professor at Harvard, used it as a source for *The Unwritten War*, a literary history Tate thought brilliant, Tate was especially distressed. "You certainly pinned me to the wall about Blacks," he wrote Aaron. "Frankly," Tate added, "I had hoped that no one would dig up my early opinions for I have not held them for about forty years." Alluding to "a certain experience" that produced "a complete reversal" in his views, Tate later explained to Aaron that he had an experience "not unlike that of the man who saw the black at Smyrna and realized that he was a human being."[195]

Moving up the date of the experience to 1936—when it apparently occurred in 1931, *before* he wrote the letter to Kirstein—Tate told the Harvard professor the story of his friendship with an African American teacher named Joseph Kezee, who spent part of each year running a farm near Benfolly. Kezee, who Tate said conversed in "aristocratic" English unlike anything he had heard from other Southern blacks, offered to undertake some groundskeeping work in exchange for grammar lessons. Tate spent a month or so tutoring Kezee, and before long the two men were addressing each other by their first names. Yet even in recounting a story Tate hoped would rehabilitate him, his attitude toward interracialism was evident. "I remember asking him one day if he approved of miscegenation," Tate wrote approvingly of Kezee. "He said no, neither in cattle nor in human beings."[196] In the end, Tate neither overcame his prejudices nor kept them from being known publicly.[197] In this regard, he was in larger measure than he either anticipated or realized, his father's son.

VIII

Distracted as he was by the plot of *The Fathers*, Tate barely seemed to care when *America through the Essay*, the reader for college freshmen that he began coediting in 1936, was published by Oxford University Press in May.[198] While the five-hundred-page textbook was largely the work of A. Theodore Johnson, a former colleague of his in the English Department at Southwestern, the reader made it plain how much Tate's resentment of the North had softened since the late 1920s. While reminding readers of the existence within America "of regions or sections with diverse conditions, needs, and aspirations," Tate and Johnson nevertheless stated their wish not "to impose upon students a point of view inimical to any section, race, or creed." In fact, the editors professed their conviction that "sectional ill-will may be diminished through wider knowledge of conditions in all regions of America."[199]

Along with Herbert Agar, merely four Vanderbilt Agrarians—Davidson, Tate, Ransom, and John Donald Wade—appeared in the book. The remaining twenty-five essays were by presidents such as Abraham Lincoln and Theodore Roosevelt; by historians such as Henry Adams, Frederick Jackson Turner, and Arthur Schlesinger, Sr.; by men of letters the likes of T. S. Eliot, Sinclair Lewis, Sherwood Anderson, Edgar Allan Poe; and Walt Whitman; and by the philosopher George Santayana. With the exception of the brief preface and an appendix titled "Biographical Notes and Study Questions" (in which only flickers of Tate's earlier social philosophy were evident), the book was more American than Southern.

Explaining the book's nationalism to Davidson, a regionalist whose essay was excerpted from a new book he had written lamenting centralized power in America, Tate blamed Oxford University Press. "When it came to dropping four or five pieces," he explained "the regional work was the first to suffer."[200] But the fact was that Tate and Johnson were eager to market the textbook nationally and knew that a sectionalist book would never be taken up in American literature courses. Despite Tate's willingness to mute Agrarianism, the book was not a commercial success. Except for fleeting attention in the Greensboro papers, where one reviewer pronounced it "thoroughly acceptable," it was by and large ignored.[201] The book's commercial failure was a moot point to Tate, who, having already recognized what a small role he played in its editing, let Johnson keep the bulk of its earnings. The one consolation to Tate was confirmation of his suspicion that Americans preferred Southern writers to stick to Southern topics—he could have predicted that an eclectic work titled *America through the Essay* would be both the least known and the least appreciated of his books.

Sensing correctly that *The Fathers*, and not a mere college textbook, would be the crowning achievement of his career, Tate pushed ahead with his novel. Yet as the summer of 1938 approached, he began encountering problems again. Rereading what he had written, he found that the second part, which he had begun writing after a lengthy hiatus, did not match the first. "I can't reproduce the tone of Part One," he wrote Davidson. "The break will be obvious to the most innocent reader. The only thing I can do is to try to make the change of tone seem calculated."[202] Nervous about solving the problem in such a contrived fashion, he went ahead and wrote for another month straight—until he encountered an even greater problem. He had thought he could speed his work by reducing the book from three sections to two. But as was his habit, the closer he got to the conclusion, the more complex his design became. "I find that I am putting in all sorts of fancies and mixed devices towards the end," he admitted to Mark Van Doren. "I simplified the plan, but instead of shortening the book it has lengthened it."[203] Once again, however, he decided to ignore the problem and, by mid-June, he had written everything but the concluding fifty pages of the book.

Lacking the time and energy to repair what he called the "sagging place in the middle"[204]—and eager to honor the June deadline—he mailed the seventy-two-thousand-word manuscript to Balch and pondered what to do about the missing conclusion. By adding as much as he had to the book in the previous two months, he had exhausted his material without bringing the story to a close. What was worse, he was beginning to feel the claustrophobia that came upon him whenever his writing was blocked. Eager for a change in environment, he decided that he and Caroline would leave for Connecticut early. That way, he explained to her, he could think about the conclusion during their drive. Although Caroline found the abrupt change of plan somewhat disconcerting, she saw that her husband was "tak[ing] writing a novel hard." No doubt thinking back upon all of his patience with her during comparable moments, she assented, admitting, "I never realized before what it is to be married to a novelist."[205]

IX

To the Allen Tate of the early Agrarian era, the unspoiled rural village of Cornwall might have seemed edenic—had it not been situated in northwestern Connecticut. But to the Tate of July 1938, who no longer insisted that he live or write below the Mason-Dixon line, Cornwall served his purposes well. Indeed, that he would choose a classic New England village as the setting in which to finish reconstructing his origins suggested that he was almost at peace with his Southern identity, if not yet with the parents who imposed it upon him. Both of his parents, he evidently still did not know, were born in Illinois. Yet now that he had made himself the narrator of their history and converted it to fiction, he was beginning to let go of what the historian C. Vann Woodward, inspired by Robert Penn Warren, would decades later call "the burden of southern history." And like Woodward, Warren, and Cleanth Brooks, all of whom eventually left the south for Yale University, Tate was about to accept the fate of many Southern writers in the twentieth century. Several times during the previous several years, he had allowed Max Perkins to inquire about a job for him at Princeton University—and the Northern appointment would soon materialize.[206]

Arriving exhausted in Cornwall on the eighth of July 1938, Tate noted with irony that the cottage he and Gordon had rented a few miles from the Van Doren house was owned by a descendant of Henry Ward Beecher, the famed antislavery minister. As Tate surveyed the tiny rooms in the rundown house, which had no utilities and but a single kitchen faucet, he perused the library of books. There he found the works of Frederick Law Olmsted, the landscape architect who wrote Southern travelogues but was a native of Connecticut, and of Fanny Kemble, the British diarist who wrote *Journal of a Residence on a Georgian Plantation*.[207] "At any other time," Tate joked to Lytle, books about the South by those potentially inimical to it "would give me a feelin' of snakes, but I don't have no feeling at all."[208]

Tate set to work almost immediately upon his arrival. Earle Balch lived forty miles from Cornwall and had warned him that he would be dropping by in a just few days to inspect the manuscript. If Balch had appeared during any other summer since Tate began the book, he would have found very little to inspect. "For the first time in five years," Tate admitted of his relationship with Balch, "I can see him with conscience." Excited by the portion of the manuscript he had read, Balch had already begun a major advertising campaign for the book. When the publisher arrived, he brought the welcome news that five thousand copies of the novel had been ordered. Promising him the completed mansucript within the week, Tate forced himself to rise every day at five o'clock to write. Ignoring for now the allure of Cornwall's "fine lake, tennis courts, and fishing," he assured Balch that he would deliver the complete manuscript to him "even if a few details aren't what they ought to be."[209]

His word on the line, Tate had no choice but to speed the pace of the narrative dramatically in order to bring the story to a close. Up to the moment of his departure for Cornwall, he had not known where to take his plot, which he worried reached its climax abruptly.[210] After recounting the deaths of Yellow Jim and Semmes, Tate had transported Lacy Buchan back to Georgetown, where, looking across the river into

Arlington, the fast-aging boy observes that the the flag of the Confederacy has been lowered. Making it to Alexandria, only to learn that the town has suffered its first Civil War casualties, Lacy manages to get to the house the Buchans had occupied, but he discovers its doors are locked.[211] Here, Tate had broken off the manuscript. "I was up against it," he told an interviewer later. "I didn't know what I was going to do." He wanted to put Lacy back on Pleasant Hill but could not contrive a way to dramatize the trip.[212]

Shortly before Tate's departure from Greensboro, however, evidently while he was stopped at Benfolly on the way to Cornwall, he hit upon the idea of superimposing onto his narrative the story of Jason and the Golden Fleece.[213] Enthusiastically launching into a new section of the conclusion, he invested Lacy's return trip through the fields and rural roads of Virginia with the qualities of a dream. Puzzled, distraught, and exhausted, the young Buchan observes of the landscape: "It is an old country . . . powdered by the sun; an old country, and too many people have lived in it, and raised too much tobacco and corn, and too many men and women, young and old, have died in it." Half imagining, half-hallucinating, Lacy conjures up the image of a dead ancestor. Lacy could not escape, he confesses, "the face of my grandfather Buchan in the portrait hanging in the front parlor at Pleasant Hill. His black silver-buckled shoes printing the brown dust; the black stockings below the tight broadcloth knee-breeches, black too; the buff waistcoat under the bottle-green tail-coat and, impossibly high, the white linen stock rising to the pompus and kindly face that radiated the correct, habitual mixture of warmth and indifference." Delerious, Lacy begins conversing with the ghost. "He didn't mean to do it," Lacy insists, referring to George Posey. "No," Lacy's grandfather replies, "it was not the intention of your brother-in-law to kill your brother. It is never, my son, his intention to do any evil but he does evil because he has not the will to do good." In this sense, the ghost continued, Posey resembled Jason, who was preoccupied by "the Golden Fleece and the like impossible things, while at the same time getting himself involved with the humanity of others, which it was not his intention but rather of his very nature to betray."[214]

Lacy's encounter with the specter of his grandfather, later critics recognized, derived from Tate's poem *A Dream*.[215] Tate resurrected the hallucination of the grandfather as "a trick" to include the Golden Fleece story as "an external commentary on the action" without undermining Lacy's "narrational 'point of view.' "[216] Having even considered titling the book *The Golden Fleece*, Tate was proud of the way he adapted the myth. *The Fathers*, he explained to R. P. Blackmur, was "a study in the relation between order and violence" and "the expressed meaning of violence must always be myth." Tate concluded that "the only way to identify the action and the mythical order in which violence becomes arrested and knowable, was to present the myth at a moment of hallucination."[217]

But the Golden Fleece story did not end Tate's novel. When his narrator Lacy finally locates Pleasant Hill, he is barely able to distinguish reality. Seeing his father, he tries to follow an argument the old Major is having with Mr. Higgins, the overseer. But Lacy soon realizes that they are fighting over the mechanization of the plantation, and he loses consciousness. Remaining in a state of delirium for weeks, he awakes to find Coriolanus nursing him back to health as the family is disintegrating around them. Lacy's sister Susan has lost her senses; her hair turned white, she paces and stares at everyone blankly. (Later admitting that the behavior of Susan and every female character in *The Fathers* was incomprehensible, Tate tried to defend their improbable reactions. Perhaps thinking of his mother, he admitted, "I feel that the Virginia women *should* have behaved as Susan did upon the destruction of their order.")[218]

Meanwhile, Major Buchan, wracked by guilt, frail and deluded, is preoccupied by a barely suppressed fury against George Posey. When Posey suddenly appears at the estate, the old man can only wonder aloud, "Why has that young man done this thing to me?"[219] But Posey has no intention of staying. Donning a Confederate uniform, he departs Pleasant Hill in the company of Lacy and the slave Blind Joe to join General Longstreet's brigade at the Battle of Bull Run. (Remembering the exhaustive military history in his biographies of Stonewall Jackson and Jefferson Davis, Tate resolved to include in the novel but "one battle: first Manassas.") Yet Posey's participation in the battle is cut short when he shoots and kills John Langton, his adversary, who has reappeared and denounced him before their colonel.[220]

George and Lacy return to Pleasant Hill, but they find that it has been burned to the foundation by Union army soldiers. The scene, Tate later wrote, was based upon the actual destruction of the Bogan estate "by General [Louis] Blenker's New York 'Dutch' Brigade on July 17, 1861, as the Union Army advanced."[221] Tate now had a way to make use of the image of Pleasant Hill in ruins that had been haunting him since his mother took him to inspect it when he was a boy. (He never did learn that Nellie Tate was not, as she may have led him to believe, born there.) "The foundations," he recalled of the visit, were "overrun with honeysuckle and . . . poisonous jimson weed," obscuring every-thing but "the stump of a large, crumbling brick chimney."[222] In the novel, Tate brought the ruins back in time to the moment of their cre-ation, adding to the lone chimney the freshly "charred end of a beam." The slaves have fled, and Major Buchan, unwilling to evacuate, has hung himself with a rope. Putting his druggist's outfit on, George Posey decides to go back to Georgetown. Lacy determines to remain behind and fight. "It won't make any difference if I am killed," he says in the novel's concluding lines. Unable to escape the influence of George Posey, he vows, "If I am killed it will be because I love him more than I love any man."[223]

This concluding line proved so ambigious to readers that Tate was forced eventually to clarify it: "I wrote it very fast, without calculation, because I was convinced it would be right. Critics have wondered how Lacy could love a man who had killed his brother, run his sister crazy, and hated the life of Pleasant Hill." Interpreting his closing for the critics, Tate wrote, "Lacy, scarcely more than a boy, has the instinct of survival, regardless of principle; yet at the same time 'principle' is back of his decision to return to the army. He affirms the principles that George scorns, and in a sense, as his surrogate, attributes them to George. George will permit Lacy to survive in a new world in which not all the old traditions, which Lacy partly represents, are dead."[224]

Critics would also debate the degree to which Tate intended to build his story around opposing fathers, one an inexpressive Southern gentle-man to whom young Lacy is made to profess every day "God bless you, papa," and another, Posey, a rude and spontaneous representative of the South as it might become. There has been further disagreement over which of these potential fathers was the hero and which the anti-hero.[225] Ultimately, however, the novel's conclusion served Tate more than his readers. In selecting as a narrator a boy who quietly revolts against "the perfection of [his] father's character," and who aligns himself with the man who destroys the old Major, Tate was at last dis-placing his own father, Orley Tate, who may have been as capricious as George Posey, but whose emotional distance from his sons matched Major Buchan's. If one accepts John Peale Bishop's suggestion that Tate was more critical of Major Buchan than he was of the culture that made him, one could say that Tate found a way to attack Orley Tate without rejecting the South.[226]

Tate thought Posey a man "without conviction," whose most danger-ous delusion was his unconscious belief in progress. Yet as at least one critic has observed, Tate also possessed a jealous admiration and love for Posey, a hero who could accept modernity.[227] If Tate came to believe that *The Fathers* was "about the destruction of the Family," he could not blame Posey for the downfall of the Buchans. The Agrarian in Tate attributed a portion of their downfall to modernizing forces that disrupted "an ordered society" in the South. Even without the actions of Posey, who "was trying to be a capitalist," Tate later explained, "the Buchans would have been destroyed then or later in some other way by the same historical pressures." In the final analysis, however, Tate came to believe that the Buchans—and his own family—had been ruined not only by external forces, but by their limited worldview. The true theme of *The Fathers*, to use Tate's own words, was "the moment when order decays from within."[228] The failings of the South, he had come to realize, were those of his own mother and father. In this sense, the book was as matricidal as it was patricidal.[229]

Tate spent much of his life, he explained some years later, "wondering why the people and families I knew—my own family particularly—had got to be what they were, and what their experience had been."[230] As early as 1932, he explained to a Northern critic that he and other Southerners "think in terms of family" because "we define our personal identity through such a system of reference." In his own case, he explained, "The character of the older members of my family, their casual prejudices, the intensive family life, in which four or five generations seemed to exist simultaneously, and though long dead still controlled our lives in as much as they were the chief materials of speculation and imagination." Because that family history, he concluded, was "both a part of me and something that is dead, something that survives physically in society in a debased form, it is at once the object of love and hate."[231] Indeed, for most of his conflicted childhood, Tate possessed a family history but not a family.

X

Caroline Gordon always thought "the real motif" of *The Fathers* was her husband's "deep sense of insecurity" over "something that his family has lost" that her own closeknit Meriwether relatives had not.[232] The historian Henry Steele Commager put it less gingerly when he described *The Fathers* as "a psychological horror story" with the message: "Man cannot live alone, but only as part of a family, a community, part of something larger than himself."[233] It was perhaps only to be expected then that as Tate dashed off the ending to the book, he would begin thinking about reconstructing his own family. In having been so preoccupied by the parents that produced him, he had given little thought to the daughter that he and Gordon had created. But now he had the wherewithal to reexamine his relationship to Nancy, whom he had been ignoring and casting off on relatives for much of her life. Only a few years previously, he thought the decision he and Caroline had made to leave Nancy with a great aunt in Chattonooga was "much better for her and us."[234] He rarely if ever even mentioned Nancy in the thousands of letters he wrote, and now it almost seemed as if he was realizing, for the first time, that he had a daughter.

Nancy had undergone as much a transformation as her father had during the years he had been at work on *The Fathers*. It had never been easy for her as the child of writers, especially of those whose fame went hand in hand with transience and penury. Early in her childhood, she had adopted her parents' technique for survival: a bitingly sarcastic sense of humor. Having learned to call anything typewritten "a living," she once took a manuscript from her father's desk and asked, "Is this my living, Daddy?" Indeed, it was, Tate replied. "It's mighty thin, Daddy" she retorted.[235] She was equally willing to tease her mother. When the Tates were living in Monteagle, she had accompanied her mother to shop for Christmas presents. Mortified by Gordon's frenetic interactions with salesclerks in the stores, she implored, " 'Mama, don't tell them your mind is going. They know it, anyhow.' "[236]

But Nancy had begun to gain new respect for her father. As recently as a year or two before, she was subject to requests such as the one put to her by the headmistress at her school in Chattanooga. "Now, Nancy, can't you recite one of your father's lovely poems?"[237] Neither bookish nor particularly interested in poetry, she probably would not have been able to comply even if she had wanted to. But Tate was shocked in February 1937, when Nancy began showing interest in his novel. "She has heard so much about books and the writing thereof," he reported, "and has progressed so satisfactorily out of her shame for her parents' trade, that she asked me to dedicate *The Fathers* to her! There is nothing like being honored by one's children."[238] Nancy, who came to think of Tate as a good father "within his means," seemed to have begun accepting the fact that he was an artist first and a father second.[239]

By the summer of 1938, Nancy was a blossoming twelve year old who liked to listen to Bing Crosby and ride horses. Although she had put on weight when she was about eleven and wore glasses that made her look "deceptively scholarly,"[240] her mother thought the pigtails she wore made her look "saintly." Often permitted by her parents to bring friends to their various residences for extended stays, Nancy this time enjoyed the companionship of "little Dot Arnett," whose father taught in the history department at the Woman's College in Greensboro. "Dot is as thin as Nancy is fat—" Caroline observed, "they look like Laurel and Hardy. And Dot's brow is as high as Nancy's is low."[241] Tate marveled that Nancy had a friend "who breeds white rats and discusses socialism at the age of twelve." Dot had a schoolgirl's crush on her friend's father, and she reveled in each bit of praise she received from Tate.[242]

Tate even seemed to win the admiration of the Van Doren children. Charlie Van Doren, the older of two boys, was especially taken by the charismatic Southern gentleman in their midst. Only twelve years old that summer, he could not answer a military history question posed by Tate. The following day, Tate gathered everyone together, dragged a blackboard out to the sun-drenched lawn, and delivered a lengthy lecture on the Battle of Gettysburg.[243] Indelibly impressed, Charlie wrote a book on one of the battle's war heroes years later.

Lecturing the Yankee Van Dorens on the Civil War, no doubt playfully hamming up his Southern persona, Tate seemed not to take himself quite so seriously. Surrounded by children, relaxed and happier than he had ever been, he was playing a role that he was unaccustomed to playing. He was even able to revise his bitter childhood memories, calling the summer of 1938 "the happiest I've had since I was a boy."[244] Perhaps such a revision was possible because he brought a symbolic end to that childhood when he completed *The Fathers*. Having written a book that exposed the delusions of his mother and father both, he was poised to let go of his obsession with his family history. His mood in the skies, he wrote friends, "I finished the novel the night of the 21st: the last incident was on July 21st 1861. Nancy became a woman on the 21st. The book will appear on Sept. 23rd, her birthday. The moon seems to favor it."[245] Looking forward rather than backward, Allen Tate was no longer an orphan but a father.

A Note on the Text
and Abbreviations
Used in the Notes

In the interests of readability, I have silently eliminated most ellipses and altered capitalization, spelling, and punctuation within quotations, taking special care not to change meaning. When I have made informed speculations, I have tried to minimize the use of qualifying phrases such as "in all probability" and "it is likely that."

I use the abbreviations listed below for commonly cited manuscript collections in public repositories and in private hands, cited in this book by permission. (The following list does not include the many essays, reviews, interviews, newspaper and journal articles, individually published poems, theses and dissertations, miscellaneous published and unpublished primary and secondary sources cited in full in the notes.)

AB   Ashley Brown, Private Collection
AG-VHS   Armistead C. Gordon Papers, Virginia Historical Society
AGW-UM   Anne Goodwin Winslow Papers, Mississippi Valley Collection, University of Memphis Libraries
AM-VU   Arthur Mizener/Allen Tate Correspondence, Special Collections, The Jean and Alexander Heard Library, Vanderbilt University.
AT-PU   Allen Tate Papers, Manuscripts Division of the Department of Rare Books and Special Collections, Princeton University Library
AT-VU   Allen Tate Collection, Special Collections, The Jean and Alexander Heard Library, Vanderbilt University
AW   Ann Waldron, Private Collection

BC-NYPL   Berg Collection of English and American Literature, The New York Public Library, Astor, Lenox and Tilden Foundations

BC-VU   Brainard ("Lon") and Frances Neel Cheney Papers, Special Collections, The Jean and Alexander Heard Library, Vanderbilt University

CB-YU   Cleanth Brooks Papers, Yale Collection of American Literature, Beinecke Rare Book and Manuscript Library, Yale University

CG-PU   Caroline Gordon Papers, Manuscripts Division of the Department of Rare Books and Special Collections Princeton University Library

DA   Daniel Aaron, Private Collection

DDF   Donald Davidson Family Private Collection

DD-VU   Donald Davidson Papers, Special Collections, The Jean and Alexander Heard Library, Vanderbilt University

DES-STN   Donald E. Stanford Papers, Department of Special Collections, Stanford University Libraries

EG-UVA   Ellen Glasgow Papers (#5060), Special Collections Department, University of Virginia Library

EW-YU   Edmund Wilson Papers, Yale Collection of American Literature, Beinecke Rare Book and Manuscript Library, Yale University

FB   Ferman Bishop, Private Collection

FLO-VU   Frank Owsley Papers Special Collections, The Jean and Alexander Heard Library, Vanderbilt University

FMF-CNL   Ford Madox Ford Collection (#4605), Division of Rare Book and Manuscript Collections, Cornell University Library

GMOD-WU   George Marion O'Donnell Papers, Special Collections, Washington University Libraries, St. Louis.

HC-CU   Hart Crane Papers, Rare Book and Manuscript Library, Columbia University

HCS-VU   Herbert Charles Sanborn Papers, Special Collections, The Jean and Alexander Heard Library, Vanderbilt University

HD   Harry Duncan, Private Collection

HG-SYR   Horace Gregory Papers, Syracuse University Library, Department of Special Collections

H&H-YU   *Hound & Horn* Papers, Yale Collection of American Literature, Beinecke Rare Book and Manuscript Library, Yale University

HLM-NYPL   H. L. Mencken Papers, Manuscripts and Archives Division, New York Public Library, Astor, Lenox and Tilden Foundations

JBW-BRN   John Brooks Wheelwright Papers, Manuscripts Division, Brown University Library

JG   John Goetz, Private Collection

JGF-UAF   John Gould Fletcher Papers, Special Collections Division, University of Arkansas Libraries, Fayetteville

JH-YU   Josephine Herbst Papers, Yale Collection of American Literature, Beinecke Rare Book and Manuscript Library, Yale University

JLS   John L. Stewart, Private Collection

JPB-PU John Peale Bishop Papers, Princeton University

JSGMF John Simon Guggenheim Memorial Foundation, New York City

JW-VU Jesse E. Wills Papers, Special Collections, The Jean and Alexander Heard Library, Vanderbilt University

LA-YU Léonie Adams Papers, Yale Collection of American Literature, Beinecke Rare Book and Manuscript Library, Yale University

LB-AC Louise Bogan Papers, Archives and Special Collections, Amherst College Library

LDR-SHC Louis D. Rubin Papers, #3899, Southern Historical Collection, Wilson Library, The University of North Carolina at Chapel Hill

LDR-2 Louis D. Rubin, Private Collection

LT-CU Lionel Trilling Papers, Rare Book and Manuscript Library, Columbia University

LU-UD Louis Untermeyer Papers, University of Delaware Library, Newark, Delware

MA-RC Monroe Goodbar Morgan Archives, Rhodes College, Memphis, Tennessee

MC-NL The Malcolm Cowley Papers, Special Collections, The Newberry Library, Chicago

MDZ-CHI Morton D. Zabel Papers, Department of Special Collections, University of Chicago Library

MJ-YU Matthew Josephson Papers, Yale Collection of American Literature, Beinecke Rare Book and Manuscript Library, Yale University

MM-LOC Merrill Moore Papers, Manuscript Division, Library of Congress

MVD-CU Mark Van Doren Papers, Rare Book and Manuscript Library, Columbia University

PG-SHC Paul Green Papers, #3693, Southern Historical Collection, Wilson Library, The University of North Carolina at Chapel Hill

PM-CHI *Poetry* Magazine Papers, Department of Special Collections, University of Chicago Library

RCB-VU Richmond Croom Beatty Papers, Special Collections, The Jean and Alexander Heard Library, Vanderbilt University

RK Robert Kent, Private Collection

RPB-PU R. P. Blackmur Papers, Manuscript Division of the Department of Rare Books and Special Collections Princeton University

RPW-YU Robert Penn Warren Papers, Yale Collection of American Literature, Beinecke Rare Book and Manuscript Library, Yale University

RS-WU Radcliffe Squires Papers, Special Collections, Washington University Libraries, St. Louis

RVT Robert Varnell Tate, Private Collection

SC-YU Seward Collins/*American Review* Papers, Yale Collection of American Literature, Beinecke Rare Book and Manuscript Library, Yale University

SR-YU *Southern Review* Papers, Yale Collection of American Literature, Beinecke Rare Book and Manuscript Library, Yale University

SY-PM   Stark Young Papers (MA 4560), The Pierpont Morgan Library, New York

TAU   Thomas A. Underwood (letters written to author)

VLT-UVA   Virginia Lyne Tunstall Papers (#8606-G), Special Collections Department, University of Virginia Library

VQR-UVA   *Virginia Quarterly Review* Archives (#RG-24/3), Special Collections Department, University of Virginia Library

WD-SHC   Ward Dorrance Papers, #4127, Southern Historical Collection, Wilson Library, The University of North Carolina at Chapel Hill

WTB-VU   William T. Bandy Papers, Baudelaire Studies Center, Central Library, Vanderbilt University

YR-YU   *Yale Review* Papers, Yale Collection of American Literature, Beinecke Rare Book and Manuscript Library, Yale University

YW-STN   Yvor Winters Papers, Department of Special Collections, Stanford University Libraries

I use the following abbreviations for commonly cited secondary works, editions of correspondence, interviews with, and works by, Tate.

Aaron-1961   Daniel Aaron, *Writers on the Left* (1961; repr., New York, 1965)

Aaron-1975   Daniel Aaron, *The Unwritten War* (1975)

"ACI"   Edward S. Shapiro, "American Conservative Intellectuals, the 1930s, and the Crisis of Ideology," *Modern Age: A Quarterly Review* 23 (Fall 1979): 370–80

Brushes   Marcella Comès Winslow, with a foreword by Louis D. Rubin, Jr., *Brushes with the Literary: Letters of a Washington Artist, 1943–1959* (Baton Rouge, La., 1993)

Clippings   Merrill Moore, *The Fugitive: Clippings and Comment* (Boston, 1939)

Collected Poems   Tate, *Collected Poems, 1919–1976* (New York, 1977)

Cowan-1959   Louise Cowan, *The Fugitive Group* (Baton Rouge, La., 1959)

DD-AT   John Tyree Fain and Thomas Daniel Young, eds., *The Literary Correspondence of Donald Davidson and Allen Tate* (Athens, Ga.: 1974)

EFD   Tate, *Essays of Four Decades* (Chicago, 1968)

Fable   Lewis P. Simpson, *The Fable of the Southern Writer* (Baton Rouge, La., 1994)

Fathers-1938   Tate, *The Fathers* (New York, 1938)

Fathers-1960   Tate, *The Fathers* (New York, 1938; repr. Denver, 1960)

Fathers-1977   Tate, *The Fathers* (New York, 1938; repr., Baton Rouge, La., 1977)

Gentleman   Thomas Daniel Young. *Gentleman in a Dustcoat* (Baton Rouge, La., 1976)

Hammer-1993   Langdon Hammer, *Hart Crane and Allen Tate: Janus-Faced Modernism* (Princeton, 1993)

Hemingway: Selected   Carlos Baker, ed., *Ernest Hemingway: Selected Letters, 1917–1961* (New York, 1981)

ITMS   Twelve Southerners, *I'll Take My Stand: The South and the Agrarian Tradition* (New York, 1930; repr. with an intro. by Louis D. Rubin, Jr., and biographical essays by Virginia Rock (Baton Rouge, La., 1977)

JD:R&F   Tate, *Jefferson Davis: His Rise and Fall* (New York, 1929)

Jonza   Nancylee Novell Jonza, *The Underground Stream: The Life and Art of Caroline Gordon* (Athens, Ga., 1995)

Jonza-ms.   Nancylee Novell Jonza, "The Underground Stream: The Life and Art of Caroline Gordon" (typescript, 672 pp)

King   Richard H. King, *A Southern Renaissance: The Cultural Awakening of the American South, 1930–1955* (New York, 1980)

Kreyling   Michael Kreyling, *Figures of the Hero in Southern Narrative* (Baton Rouge, La.,: 1987)

M&O   Tate, *Memoirs and Opinions, 1926–1974* (Chicago, 1975)

Makowsky   Veronica A. Makowsky, *Caroline Gordon: A Biography* (New York, 1989)

Mandarins   Sally Wood, ed., *The Southern Mandarins: Letters of Caroline Gordon to Sally Wood, 1924–1937* (Baton Rouge, La., 1984)

Mims/O'Brien: "The Correspondence of Edwin Mims," ed. Michael O'Brien (Master's thesis, Vanderbilt University, 1972)

Mr. Pope   Tate, *Mr. Pope and Other Poems* (New York, 1928)

O'Brien-1979   Michael O'Brien, *The Idea of the American South, 1920–1941* (Baltimore, 1979)

Poets   Eileen Simpson, *Poets in Their Youth: A Memoir* (1982; repr., New York, Vintage Books, 1983)

Republic   Thomas Daniel Young, and John J. Hindle, eds., *The Republic of Letters In America: The Correspondence of John Peale Bishop and Allen Tate* (Lexington, Ky., 1981)

Reunion   Rob Roy Purdy, ed., *Fugitives' Reunion: Conversations at Vanderbilt* (Nashville, Tenn., 1959)

Robber Rocks   Susan Jenkins Brown, *Robber Rocks: Letters and Memories of Hart Crane, 1923–1932* (Middletown, Conn., 1969)

Saddest   Arthur Mizener, *The Saddest Story: A Biography of Ford Madox Ford* (New York, 1971)

"SA-HLM"   Edward S. Shapiro, "The Southern Agrarians, H. L. Mencken, and the Quest for Southern Identity," *American Studies* 13 (Fall 1972): 75–92

Southern Agrarians   Paul K. Conkin, *The Southern Agrarians* (Knoxville, Tenn., 1988)

Squires-1971   Radcliffe Squires, *Allen Tate: A Literary Biography* (New York, 1971)

SJ:GS   Tate, *Stonewall Jackson: The Good Soldier* (New York, Company, 1928)

Sullivan-1988   Walter Sullivan, *Allen Tate: A Recollection* (Baton Rouge, La., 1988)

Surrealists   Matthew Josephson, *Life among the Surrealists* (New York, Holt, Rinehart, 1962)

Tate-Broughton   Irv Broughton, "An Interview with Allen Tate," *Western Humanities Review* 32 (Autumn 1978): 317–36.

Tate-Forsyth et al.   James Forsyth, Tom Speight, and Dan Williams, "Allen Tate Interview," *Rebel Magazine* 9 (Winter 1966): 2–17

Tate-Hecht   Anthony Hecht, Interview with Allen Tate (New York, 1965), 54-page typed transcript in possession of author

Tate-McDonnell   Thomas P. McDonnell, "Interview with Allen Tate," *Ramparts* 2 (Winter 1964): 33–41

Tate-Millgate   Michael Millgate, "An Interview with Allen Tate" *Shenandoah* 12 (Spring 1961): 27–34

TDY-L   Thomas Daniel Young, and Elizabeth Sarcone, eds., *The Lytle-Tate Letters: The Correspondence of Andrew Lytle and Allen Tate* (Jackson, Miss., 1987)

Tillers   Alexander Karanikas, *Tillers of a Myth: Southern Agrarians as Social and Literary Critics* (Madison, Wisc. 1969)

Voyager   John Unterecker, *Voyager: A Life of Hart Crane* (New York, 1969)

Waldron   Ann Waldron, *Close Connections: Caroline Gordon and the Southern Renaissance* (New York, 1987)

War Within   Daniel Joseph Singal, *The War Within: From Victorian to Modernist Thought in the South, 1919–1945* (Chapel Hill, N.C. 1982)

Wary Fugitives   Louis D. Rubin, Jr., *The Wary Fugitives: Four Poets and the South* (Baton Rouge, La., 1978)

Notes

Introduction
"My Terrible Family"

1. *M&O*, ix.
2. Stark Young to Tate [undated], AT-PU [Allen Tate Papers, published with permission of Manuscript Division, Department of Rare Books & Special Collections, Princeton University Library] AM 19629; Young to Dr. Charles Diehl, 1 Sept. 1934, MA-RC.
3. Thomas A. Underwood, "A Bard among Bibliographers: Allen Tate's Washington Year," *Southern Literary Journal* 24 (Spring 1992): 36–48; see also William McGuire, *Poetry's Catbird Seat: The Consultantship in Poetry in the English Language at the Library of Congress, 1937–1987* (Washington, D.C., 1988.)
4. See George Core, "Remaking the *Sewanee Review*," *Chattahoochee Review* 8 (Summer 1988): 71–77; and Robert E. Bonner III, " 'The Purer Half of the Modern Dilemma': Allen Tate's Editorship of *The Sewanee Review*" (undergraduate thesis, Princeton University, 1989), esp. 105.
5. *M & O*, ix. For thought-provoking interpretations of Tate's reasons for quitting the memoir, see Lewis Simpson, who suggests that Tate quit it because of the difficulty of writing Southern autobiography without facing the truth about slavery and racial oppression in Southern history (*Fable*, 24–53). Pointing out that Tate's productivity declined precipitously before he amassed the honors of his later years, Simpson also suggests that Tate quit the book out of a Christian "need to subject the willful self to the authority of a culture rooted a great moral and religious tradition" (*Fable*, 114–115, 115). An equally plausible explanation, I believe, was Tate's unwillingness to relive the painful feelings of orphanhood he endured in his early years.

6. Tate to Robert Penn Warren, 6 April 1969, RPW-YU.
7. *M&O*, 3–23.
8. *M&O*, 7, 17.
9. Tate, Essays, Misc. 3-page typescript, p. 2, AT-PU.
10. Ibid.
11. There is ample evidence that Tate knew he was born in Kentucky long before his mother died in July 1929. As early as 1923, he wrote, "I suppose I'm a Kentuckian only by the accident of birth; I have hardly been in the state for over ten years, and that long ago I was little past the stage of being a small boy; so, although I spring from the Blue Grass, people back there now find it hard to believe" (Tate to Virginia Lyne Tunstall, 3 Nov. 1923, VLT-UVA). In April 1929, he again told Tunstall, "I am fated to remain a Kentuckian from a small town" (Tate to Tunstall, 15 April 1929, VLT-UVA). Yet in his application for a 1928–29 Guggenheim Fellowship, which he filed on 13 December 1927, Tate reported that he was born in Fairfax County, Va. (JSGMF) No doubt using information supplied by Tate, the author of a biographical profile published in 1931 listed Tate's birthplace as Virginia, adding, "He was brought up in Kentucky and Tennessee. . . . He tells Kentuckians he is a Tennessean, and he tells Tennesseans he is a Kentuckian" (*Living Authors: A Book of Biographies*, ed. "Dilly Tante" [New York, 1931], 400). By the time the sketch appeared, Tate was telling his correspondents, "I am a Kentuckian by adoption, in the last ten years resident in Tennessee, except for a brief period in New York and abroad" (Tate to John Wilson Townsend, 19 May 1931, Special Collection and Archives, University Libraries, University of Kentucky).

After these prevarications entered other dictionaries, Tate spent years trying to explain them. In 1937, he wrote Morton D. Zabel, "Before I forget it I want to place somewhere in the back of your mind a correction of my birthplace in case you ever have occasion to revise your notes in the back of *Literary Opinion in America* [New York, 1937, 635]. I was born in Winchester, Clark County, Kentucky. The Virginia confusion started ten years ago out of a conversation misapprehended by my first publisher. I remarked that my mother's family were Fairfax County people and when he wrote the blurb for *SJ:GS* [1928], he said I was born there. Louis Untermeyer copied it for my first appearance under his satrapy, and it has spread ever since" (Tate to Zabel, 24 Sept. 1937, MDZ-CHI).

The anecdote Tate relates in *M&O*, 5–8 (for a MS. version, see "Essays: Miscellaneous," AT-PU, AM 19629, 1:11) may have had its origins in a story he told in 1964 after returning from a motor tour through his native Kentucky. "When I arrived in Winchester," he wrote, "I was informed by Cousin Belle, aet. 86 and widow of Cousin Ed Tate, as follows: 'Young man (me being 64), you were not born in the house you think you were born in' " (Tate to Warren, 17 Oct. 1964, RPW-YU).

12. *M&O*, 39. Despite including the apocryphal birthplace story, Singal analyzes astutely Tate's description of his "terrible family" and its effects on him *(War Within, 232–33)*.

13. See, for instance, *Wary Fugitives*, 323–26; and *War Within*, 259–60.

Chapter One
"Mother Wanted Me at Home"

1. An in-depth history of Tate's childhood is unavailable in any published, chronologically arranged source. Although my account is based primarily on unpublished sources, I have drawn some material from *M&O*, 3–23. To rearrange the story in a linear fashion, and to correct Tate's errors, I have supplemented the brief and haphazard sketch in *M&O* with the fuller MS version in AT-PU, with interviews and with information gleaned from stray references, newspapers, correspondence, secondary school transcripts, and local history sources (some of these minor sources are not cited here). On Tate's youth and family history, I have also drawn from Cowan-1959, 36–37; *War Within*, esp. 232–33; and Squires-1971, 13–26.

2. W. M. Beckner, *Hand-book of Clark County and the City of Winchester* (Chicago, 1889), 30. See also Lucien Beckner, *Winchester: Its Remarkable Growth* (n. p. 1906), Winchester Public Library; Judge James Flanagan, "Winchester" (1901), typescript, University of Kentucky Library; A. Goff Bedford, *Land of Our Fathers* (n. p., 1958), Winchester Public Library.

3. Tate to Squires, 2 Feb. 1969, RS-WU; I have made extensive use of a chronology appended to this letter (and of Tate's MSS in Essays: Misc. AT-PU, 1:11).

4. Interview with Robert Varnell Tate, 17 Oct. 1988, Wayne, Pa.

5. Interview with Nancy Tate Wood, San Cristóbal de Las Casas, Mexico, 30 March 1987.

6. Essays: Misc., AT-PU, 1:11.

7. Allen Tate to Robert Varnell Tate, 27 Jan. 1971, RVT. I have also drawn from Allen Tate to Robert Varnell Tate, 22 Feb. 1973 (ibid.); and undated genealogical charts (ibid.).

8. *Twelfth Census of the United States , 1900, Clark County, Kentucky.*

9. Tate, "Several Thousand Books," University of Minnesota Commencement Address, 18 March 1967, AT-PU, 1:9.

10. Orley's mother, Josephine Allen, descended from a slaveowning planter named Rodam Allen. Orley's father, James Johnston Tate, who came to Kentucky to tutor the Allen family, was vociferously anti-slavery and

broke with his father-in-law over seccession. One of Orley's rebel grand-fathers was mobbed and attacked by Louisville Unionists in 1861.

11. Tate, Essays: Misc., 3-page typescript, p. 2, AT-PU.

12. Essays: Misc., AT-PU, 1:11.

13. Ibid.

14. Interview with Helen H. Tate, Waco, Texas, 1 Feb. 1987.

15. *Wary Fugitives*, 1.

16. For background material on Nashville, I have drawn from *Nashville, 1900–1910*, ed. William Waller (Nashville, Tenn., 1972).

17. Tate quoted in *Poets*, 195.

18. Essays: Misc., AT-PU, 1:11. Years later, Tate said that he had measles "three times—all before I was ten!" Tate to Edmund Wilson, 8 Feb. 1926, EW-YU.

19. Tate quoted by Bob Lundegaard, "University of Minnesota's Poet Tate: 'I Am Out of Tune with the Times,' " *Minneapolis Tribune*, 24 Jan. 1965, p. 1.

20. Essays: Misc., AT-PU, 1:11.

21. Andrew Lytle quoted in Sullivan-1988, 4.

22. Caroline Gordon to Lon [Brainard] and Frances Cheney, [21 April 1947], BC-VU.

23. Gordon to Ward Dorrance [ca. 1946], WD-SHC. After Tate and Gordon were remarried, the problem appeared. As their second marriage disinte-grated, Gordon observed, "When a man succeeds in persuading his wife to play the role of his mother he inevitably does one of two things: rebels against or deceives her" (Gordon quoted in Dora Bernhard to Tate, 18 March 1956, AT-PU, 11:32). Struggling to mend the marriage, Tate's Jungian analyst urged him to "quit the last ties of dependence on a de-structive forbidding powerful mother" (Dora Bernhard to Tate, 6 Dec. 1955, AT-PU, 11:32).

24. Julia Cherry Spruill, *Women's Life and Work in the Southern Colonies* (Chapel Hill, N.C., 1938), 60–61; undated typescript with annotation in Tate's hand, AT-PU, box 48.

25. Essays: Misc., AT-PU, 1:11.

26. Tate to Andrew Lytle, 16 June 1929, TDY-L, 31.

27. Adam G. Adams to Tate, 21 April 1975, AT-PU, box 1.

28. Waller, 169, 172–76, 230–34; Jack Norman, Sr., *The Nashville I Knew* (Nashville, 1984),103–4; *A Bicentennial Chronicle* (Metropolitan Nash-ville–Davidson County Public Schools, 1976), 149–50.

29. Tate, "A Dream," *Scribner's Magazine* 90 (October 1931): 400; repr. as part of "Records" in *Poems, 1928–1931* (New York, 1932), 24; and in *Collected Poems, 1919–1976* (New York, 1977), 61.

30. Marjorie Taylor, "Veteran Teacher Faces Ouster from Home," *Louisville Courier Journal*, 25 July 1941.

31. "Cross School Tests Advanced Methods," *Louisville Courier Journal*, 15 Aug. 1937.

32. Essays: Misc., AT-PU, 1:11.

33. Irving Kalin, "Kentucky-Born Educator Advocates Stress on Humanities In Schools," *Louisville Courier Journal*, 8 Aug. 1956.

34. *A History of Ashland, Kentucky, 1786 to 1954* (Ashland Centennial Committee, 1954); Arnold Hammers, *Ashland Past: A Pictorial History* (Ashland, 1976); Hammers, *Ashland's Pictorial Past* (Ashland, 1986.)

35. Tate quoting his father, unpublished interview with Anthony Hecht, New York, 1965, p. 34 (copy courtesy of Mr. Hecht).

36. Essays: Misc., AT-PU, 1:11.

37. Tate to Warren, 9 Aug. 1977, RPW-YU; Warren to Tate, 18 Aug. 1977, AT-PU, IIc, 9:10.

38. Interview with Nancy Tate Wood, 30 March 1987.

39. Squires correctly calls Tate's father a "rather dreamy orphan, untrained for any practical pursuit." See Squires-1971, 20–21, 21.

40. Tate to Van Doren, 22 Dec. 1933, MVD-CU.

41. Interview with Ben E. Tate, Jr., Cincinnati, Ohio, 28 Aug., 1988; Biographical sketch, "Allen Tate," SC-YU.

42. Tate to Van Doren, 23 July 1943, MVD-CU.

43. Tate to Van Doren, 22 Dec. 1933, MVD-CU.

44. There is some question whether they received their undergraduate degrees. Vanderbilt lists both Ben and Varnell as members of the class of 1910 and the law school class of 1912, but no transcripts survive. Ben apparently left the law school in 1911.

45. *M&O*, 40.

46. Interview with Ben E. Tate, Jr.

47. Ibid.

48. James Varnell Tate to Robert Varnell Tate, 11 Nov. 1937, RVT.

49. Interview with Robert Varnell Tate, Wayne, Pa., 17 Oct. 1988.

50. "Ben and Allen," Varnell wrote, "are outstandingly successful in their widely different fields, while I have at least shown that I am capable of doing something in life, due to the important and responsible positions I have held" (James Varnell Tate to Robert Varnell Tate, 11 Nov. 1937, RVT).

51. Helen Barron Tate to Robert Varnell Tate, undated, RVT.

52. Tate, "Several Thousand Books," 3–4.

53. "Variety and Fullness Mark Poet's Growth," *Greensboro Daily News*, Nov. 7, 1971, D1.

54. Donald Davidson, *Southern Writers in the Modern World* (Athens, Ga., 1958), 10–11; Cowan-1959, 36n.

55. *The Works of the Late Edgar Allan Poe, with A Memoir by Rufus Wilmot Griswold and Notices of His Life and Genius by N. P. Willis and J. R. Lowell*, 4 (vols. New York, 1856–57).

56. Information about Tate's early exposure to Poe is from Tate, "Our Cousin, Mr. Poe," repr. in *EFD*, 385–87. The engraving of Poe attached to the edition cited above shows a pleasant-looking man rather than someone "desperate and asymmetrical."

57. *M&O*, 17.

58. "A Lost Traveller's Dream," AT-PU, 1:28.

59. Tate to Ellen Glasgow, 24 May 1933, EG-UVA.

60. Tate to Davidson, 4 April 1952, DD-VU. The biographical sketch Tate referred to appeared in a manuscript version of Cowan-1959.

61. Tate-Broughton, 320.

62. *Evansville City Directory* (Evansville, 1915); *At the Bend in the River: The Story of Evansville* (n. p., Windsor Publications, 1982); and James E. Morlock, *The Evansville Story: A Cultural Interpretation* (1956); Theodore Dreiser, *A Hoosier Holiday* (New York, 1916), 454–64. See also Darrel E. Bigham, *We Ask Only A Fair Trial: A History of the Black Community of Evansville*, Indiana (Bloomington, 1987).

63. On Cincinnati, I draw from *Williams' Cincinnati Directory* (Cincinnati,1915); Charles R. Hebble and Frank P. Goodwin, eds., *The Citizens Book* (Cincinnati, 1916); Iola Hessler Silberstein, *Cincinnati Then and Now* (Cincinnati, 1982.)

64. Henry A. Meyer, *Central High School: Its First Hundred Years* (Evansville,1954); Ruth K. Kilbert, *Central High School, Evansville, Indiana: Its History* (Evansville, 1932); *Central High School, Evansville: Session 1919–1920, Sixty-fourth Year* (Board of Education, n.d.)

65. David Artland Hilton, "The History of Walnut Hills High School" (master's thesis, Teachers College, University of Cincinnati, 1947), esp. 9–10, 16, and 22; *The Remembrancer* (1914, 1915, and 1917); "Highlights in the History of Walnut Hills High School, 1891–1976," in *Walnut Hills High School Teacher's Manual*.

66. On the Conservatory, I draw from John Lewis, "An Historical Study of the Origin and Development of the Cincinnati Conservatory of Music" (Ph.D. diss., Teachers College, University of Cincinnati, 1943), p. 156 and passim.

67. *Sharps and Flats: Published Quarterly by Students of the Conservatory of Music* [hereafter, *S&A*], 8 (March 1917): 24.

68. Stanley Sadie, ed., *The New Grove Dictionary of Music and Musicians* (London, 1980), 20:582–83; Warren Ramsey, *Jules Laforgue and the Ironic Inheritance* (New York, 1953), 72.

69. Broughton-Tate, 332.

70. "Music is not understood, it is felt; it emanates from the heart and the soul" (quoted in Marie Brunfaut, *Jules Laforgue Les Ysaÿe et Leur Temps* [Brussels, 1961], 110); Harold Morris, "Tribute To Ysaÿe," *S&A* 10 (April 1919): 10–11; "Ysaÿe's Master Class," *S&A* 10 (March 1919): 28–

29. Eugene Ysaÿe, "The Tools of Violin Mastery," *S&A* 9 (Oct. 1918): 5–8, 8.

71. Eric Bentley to TAU, 24 May 1987 (letter in possession of author).

72. "In Print, Allen Tate: Man of Letters in Minneapolis," unidentified clipping, University of Minnesota, University Relations Office files.

73. Tate, "Mere Literature and the Lost Traveller," AT-PU, 1:29. On Georgetown Preparatory School, I have drawn from William S. Abell, *Fifty Years at Garrett Park, 1919–1969* (Garrett Park, Md., 1970), ix–18; *Bulletin of the Georgetown Preparatory School* (Garrett Park, Md., 1917); quotations appear on p. 4; Joseph Deharbe, S.J., *A Full Catechism of the Catholic Religion*, trans. Rev. John Fander (New York, 1889.)

74. Tate to Herbert Charles Sanborn, 22 July 1960, HCS-VU. See also Jesse E. Wills, who recalls Tate saying, "If my family had not been in straightened circumstances, I might have gone to Princeton. Instead, I came here where my brothers had been" (Wills, "Reminiscences of the Class of 1922," 8-page typescript, JW-VU, p. 8).

75. Interview with Dorothy Bethurum Loomis, Nashville, Tenn., 21 July 1987.

76. Essays: Miscellaneous, AT-PU, AM 19629, 1:11.

Chapter Two
"Unlike a Natural Mother"

1. Tate, "Literary Criticism and the Humanities," p. 1, AT-PU, 1:25. I am indebted to Helen Tate for authorizing the Vanderbilt Registrar to release Tate's academic transcript and to the Vanderbilt graduates I thank by name in my acknowledgments section. Except for direct quotations, I have not attributed everything told to me by these individuals. Nor have I attributed anything but quotations to the 1918–22 editions of the Vanderbilt yearbook, *The Commodore*. I also draw from the *Register of Vanderbilt University for 1917–1918, 1918–1919, 1919–1920, 1920–1921*, and *1921–1922* (Nashville, Tenn., 1918, 1919, 1920, 1921, and 1922); and from the *Vanderbilt Alumnus* 4 (Nov. 1918): 3–7; and 4 (Jan. 1919): 37.

2. Eve Zibart, "The Literary Kingmaker: Allen Tate, Champion of the Southern Renaissance, and Reflections on a Golden Age," *Washington Post*, 29 Oct. 1978, H1, H4–5, H5.

3. Here and throughout, I have drawn from Paul K. Conkin's monumental study *Gone with the Ivy: A Biography of Vanderbilt University* (Knoxville, Tenn., 1985) (hereafter referred to as *Ivy*).

4. William S. Vaughn, "Some Recollections of a Fugitive Sort," *Vanderbilt Magazine* 72 (Fall 1987): 12; "Summary of Students by schools and States," *Register of Vanderbilt University for 1922–1923* (Nashville, Tenn., 1923), 225.

5. Jesse E. Wills, *"Reminiscences of the Class of 1922,"* 8-page undated type-script, 5. JW-VU. I have drawn from this memoir throughout.
6. Interview with Dorothy Bethurum (Mrs. Roger Sherman Loomis), 21 July 1987.
7. Leland L. Sage to TAU, 1 Nov. 1988.
8. "Britons Honor Steele," *Vanderbilt Alumnus* 8 (1922–23): 50; "Dr. R. B. Steele Dies," *Vanderbilt Alumnus* 30 (1944–45): 6; "The Giants of 1915," *Vanderbilt Alumnus* 51 (1965–66): 30.
9. *Reunion*, 111–12, 114; Tate to Frank Owsley, 14 April 1941, FLO-VU.
10. Tate, Essays: Misc., AT-PU, 1:11.
11. [Tate], *Profs (with Apologies to Mr. Rudyard Kipling)"* (unsigned poem) *Commodore* 13 (1921): 270.
12. Interview with Ivar L. Myhr (Mrs. Edgar H. Duncan), Nashville, 14 July 1987.
13. Ella Puryear Mims, '34, "My Father Remembered," undated 5-page type-script (copy courtesy of Ella P. Mims), 2; Wills, *Reminiscences*, 5.
14. Interview with Dorothy Bethurum.
15. Interview with Ivar L. Myhr (Mrs. Edgar H. Duncan), 14 July 1987.
16. Mims to Clara Mims, 25 August 1919, Mims/O'Brien, 432.
17. Sullivan-1988,19.
18. I am grateful to Michael O'Brien for correcting me on Mims's career, on his stature in 1912, and on Kirkland's relationship to him.
19. On Tolman, I draw from "Dean H. C. Tolman Dies," *Vanderbilt Alumnus* 9 (Nov. 1923): 39–44.
20. Tate, "Te Saluto!" *Vanderbilt Alumnus* 9 (Nov. 1923): 42.
21. [Tate], *Profs*; *Register of Vanderbilt University for 1918–1919*, 87.
22. Copy of James Turney Allen, *The First Year of Greek* (New York, 1918), annotated in Tate's hand, Fugitive Room, Heard Library, Vanderbilt University.
23. Tate, "Te Saluto!"
24. Tate, "Several Thousand Books," University of Minnesota Commencement Address, 18 March 1967, AT-PU, AM 19629, 1:9, p. 7.
25. [Tate], *Profs*; Sullivan-1988, 112.
26. *Ivy*, 296.
27. Leland L. Sage to TAU, 1 Nov. 1988.
28. Tate-Broughton, 317.
29. Wills, 7 *Reminiscenses*; Tate to Nancy Tate Wood, 15 Sept. 1963, AT-PU, IIc., 10:IIA.
30. Tate, "*The Fugitive, 1922–1925: A Personal Recollection Twenty Years After*," *Princeton University Library Chronicle* 3 (April 1942): 75–84, 82. Throughout this chapter, I draw extensively from this article—hereafter referred to as "Personal Recollection."
31. Interview with Robert Varnell Tate, Wayne, Pa., 17 Oct. 1988.
32. Wills to Orlém [Allen Tate], 10 July [1919], AT-PU, AM 19629, 46.

33. Ibid.
34. Alice Lee (Mrs. Stanislaw J.) Makielski to Allen Tate, April 9 [no year], AT-PU, IIc., 5:16.
35. Wills to Orlém.
36. Permanent Record Card, University of Virginia Summer School," for O. A. Tate.
37. Curtis Hidden Page, *The Chief American Poets* (Boston, 1905); *Southern Prose and Poetry*, ed. Edwin Mims and Bruce R. Payne (New York, 1910), v.
38. Tate, letter to the editor, 24 Jan. 1941, *Vanderbilt Alumnus* 26 (March 1941): 15.
39. Mims to William H. Glasson, 18 March 1918, Mims/O'Brien, 427.
40. Richmond C. Beatty, "Notes on a Retired VU Scholar," *Nashville Tennessean*, 13 March 1960, 6c; *Essays in Honor of Walter Clyde Curry*, Editorial Committee, Dept. of English, Vanderbilt University (Nashville, 1954).
41. *Reunion*, 116.
42. Blurb for *American Poetry Magazine* 1 (July 1919).
43. Tate, Essays: Misc., AT-PU, AM 19629, 1:11.
44. Tate, *Impossible, American Poetry Magazine* 2 (March 1920): 5.
45. *American Poetry Magazine* 1 (July 1919): 28.
46. Curry to *American Poetry Magazine* 1 (August 1919): 35.
47. "Personal Recollection," 77.
48. Sanborn to Tate, 12 Feb. 1927, AT-PU, 38:24. Sanborn later took to breeding dachsunds to prove the importance of heredity over environment and began insisting that international bankers had conspired to bring on the Civil War. Sanborn to Tate, 27 Feb. 1941; 15 Sept. 1952, AT-PU, 38:24.
49. *Register of Vanderbilt University for 1919–1920*, 98.
50. Tate to Sanborn, 22 July 1960, HCS-VU; "At 69 He Still Bests His Vandy Fencers," *Louisville Courier Journal*, 8 March 1942.
51. *Reunion*, 108.
52. Probably George Boole, *Collected Logical Works* (Cambridge, 1854; repr. Chicago, 1916).
53. *Ivy*, 232.
54. William S. Vaughn '23, "Some Recollections of a Fugitive Sort," *Vanderbilt Magazine* 72 (Fall 1987): 14. I have drawn on this memoir throughout.
55. Unpublished MS by Donald Davidson, quoted in Cowan-1959, 56.
56. Tate to Louis Rubin, 16 January 1967, LDR-SHC.
57. *Commodore*, ser. 12, Comet Ser. 34 (1920): 265.
58. Interview with Madison S. Wigginton, [Vanderbilt '22], Nashville, July 29, 1987.
59. Interview with Nancy Tate Wood, 30 March 1987.

60. *M&O*, 39–40.
61. Tate quoted in Howard Nemerov to Tate, 7 January 1977, AT-PU, IIc.
62. Interview with Wigginton; Interview with William Waller [Vanderbilt '18], Nashville, 29 July 1987.
63. Tate to Professor C. B. Wallace [carbon copy; no date], AT-PU, AM 19629, 44:14.
64. Tyree Fain to Tate, 2 April 1957, AT-PU, AM 19629, 20:24; J. D. Tyner, "Allen Tate: We Have Lost a Great Mind," *Nashville Banner*, 23 Feb. 1979, 10.
65. Tate-Broughton, 320–21.
66. Edwin M. Yoder, Jr., "Tar Heel Talk: An Interview with Allen Tate" [Fall 1966] unidentified clipping, UNC-Greensboro Archives.
67. Mrs. Mary Lynn (Dobson) Armistead to TAU, [16 May 1988].
68. Interview with Wigginton.
69. Tate-Broughton, 317.
70. Vaughn, "Some Recollections of a Fugitive Sort," 15.
71. Tate to Mark Van Doren, 29 Oct. 1931, MVD-CU.
72. Interview with Nancy Tate Wood.
73. Louise Davis, "The Cerebral Mr. Tate," *Nashville Tennessean Magazine*, 12 Sept. 1965, p. 8.
74. Telephone Interview with William Bandy, 26 Oct. 1987.
75. Davis, "The Cerebral Mr. Tate," 8. I have merged Davis's version of this anecdote with a slightly variant account told to me by William Bandy, 26 Oct. 1987.
76. Tate to Dorothy Bethurum, 26 March 1969, Fugitive/Agrarian Collection, Vanderbilt University.
77. Interview with Bethurum.
78. " 'Fugitive' Tate Hailed as Giant among Writers" *Nashville Tennessean*, 10 Feb. 1979, 6.
79. On Tate and Ella Mai Wilson, I am indebted to A. E. Chester to TAU, 21 May 1988.
80. Unsigned [by Tate], *Girls (Many Thanks to Mr. Poe)*, *Commodore* 13 (1921): 65.
81. Interview with Myhr (Duncan).
82. Ralph McGill, *The South and the Southerner* (1959; repr. Boston, 1964).
83. [Tate], *Profs*.
84. Tate to Davidson, 24 Feb. 1941 [carbon], AT-PU, 6:14. Some tensions did, however, develop between Tate and Sanborn; see Sanborn to Tate, 16 Dec. 1926, AT-PU, 38:24.
85. On Ransom's manner of speech, see Sullivan-1988, 28.
86. On Tate's first meeting with Ransom, I have drawn from Tate, "Gentleman in a Dustcoat," *Kenyon Alumni Bulletin* 26 (April/June 1968): 36.
87. John Crowe Ransom, *Poems about God* (New York, 1919); I have drawn from Young's richly informative *Gentleman*. "English Writers Praise 'The

Fugitive,' " unidentified clipping, *Nashville Tennessean* [July–Aug.? 1922], AT-PU.

88. Ransom, *In Amicitia, Sewanee Review* 67 (Autumn 1959): 531.
89. Tate-Forsyth et al., 11.
90. *Reunion*, 90.
91. Tate, "Gentleman in a Dustcoat: Honors Day Address at Kenyon College in Celebration of John Crowe Ransom's Eightieth Birthday, April 30, 1968," AT-PU, AM 19629, 1:5, pp. 7–8.
92. Tate, "Reflections on the Death of John Crowe Ransom, 1974," *M&O*, 39. While I cannot agree with Makowsky's judgment that "the portraits of cold and controlled father figures [in Tate's assessments of Ransom and of his father] suggest that Tate's subconscious version of God the Father was a deity so indifferent to man that he would not even acknowledge his postlapsarian identity as a sinner"—Tate, I believe, *wanted* (more than he feared) a God to save both him and the South—she makes intelligent use of Tate's interpretation of his oedipal patterns with Ransom and his parents, and recognizes that Tate located a surrogate family in the Fugitive group (Makowsky, 47–55, 54).
93. Mencken, "The Sahara of the Bozart," in *Prejudices: Second Series* (New York, 1920), 136–54, 136. I have also drawn from Fred C. Hobson, Jr., *Serpent in Eden: H. L. Mencken and the South* (Baton Rouge, La., 1974.) See also SA-HLM, 75–92, 76.
94. *Reunion*, 92, 132.
95. Tate to Virginia Lyne Tunstall, 23 March 1932, VLT-UVA; Tate to Mark Van Doren, 4 Feb. 1937, MVD-CU.
96. Tate, *Red Stains, American Poetry Magazine* 3 (Autumn 1921): 13.
97. Tate, *A Ballade of the Lugubrious Wench, Jade* 3 (12 Nov. 1921): 17.
98. Tate, "Literary Criticism and the Humanities," 1, AT-PU, 1:25.
99. Here and elsewhere, I have drawn heavily from William T. Bandy, "Allen Tate's Juvenilia," 9-page, undated typescript of an essay published in *Southern Review* 25 (Jan. 1989): 86–94 (photocopy of typescript courtesy of Professor Bandy); the quotation appears on p. 8.
100. Interview with Dorothy Bethurum.
101. Ransom, *In Amicitia*, 530.
102. In my discussion of the Fugitives, I have appropriated information and ideas from Cowan-1959. I have also drawn freely from accounts in John M. Bradbury, *The Fugitives: A Critical Account* (Chapel Hill, N.C., 1958; repr., New Haven, 1964); John L. Stewart, *The Burden of Time: The Fugitives and Agrarians* (Princeton, 1965); William Pratt, "Introduction: In Pursuit of the Fugitives," *The Fugitive Poets* (New York, 1965), 13–46; Squires-1971; *Wary Fugitives*; and *Southern Agrarians*.
103. Ella Puryear Mims, "My Father Remembered," 2.
104. *Reunion*, 145, 121.
105. Ransom, "In Amicitia," 533.

106. Ibid.
107. *Reunion*, 86.
108. Ibid. 102; "Personal Recollection," 78.
109. Tate to Merrill Moore, 21 Nov. 1929, MM-LOC.
110. Tate, Letter to the Editor, 24 Jan. 1941, *Vanderbilt Alumnus* 26 (March 1941): 15.
111. Hawthorne, "Feathertop: A Moralized Legend," in *Tales And Sketches* (repr. New York, 1982), 1103, 1105, 1117, 1121, 1123. For intelligent discussions in somewhat different contexts of Tate's association between Feathertop's mother and his own, see Makowsky, 48–49; and Hammer-1993, 24.
112. "Personal Recollection," 80.
113. [Tate], *Fugitive* 1 (April 1922):16.
114. [Tate], "To Intellectual Detachment" *Fugitive* 1 (April 1922): 9.
115. Tate to H. L. Mencken, 15 April 1922, HLM-NYPL.
116. Quoted in *Clippings*, 7.
117. Mencken to Tate, 23 May [1922], AT-PU, AM 19629, 30:13.
118. Quoted in *Clippings*, 16.
119. All quoted in *Clippings*, 13, 14–15.
120. Tate, Letter to the Editor. It is true that the Fugitives were praised in Great Britain; see "English Writers Praise 'The Fugitive' " (unidentified clipping), *Nashville Tennessean* [July–Aug.? 1922], AT-PU.
121. Tate, "Euthanasia" *Double Dealer* 3 (May 1922): 262.
122. John McClure, ed., *Double Dealer*, to Tate, 20 May 1922, AT-PU, AM 19629, 19:26.
123. Tate to Virginia Lyne Tunstall, 15 April 1929, VLT-UVA.
124. Vaughn, "Some Recollections of a Fugitive Sort," 15.
125. For a photocopy of the bound volume presented to Eleanor Hall, I am indebted to Ms. Marice Wolfe, Head of Special Collections, and to Ms. Joan Sibley of the Fugitive Room, Heard Library, Vanderbilt University; all lines quoted in my text are from that copy. Here again, I have made extensive use of Bandy's, "Allen Tate's Juvenilia," 7–9.
126. An interview with Thomas Daniel Young, Rose Hill, Mississippi, 11 Aug. 1987. Professor Young was present when Tate, instead of having copies transcribed, tore the pages from this edition in order to provide Farrar, Strauss, and Giroux with copies of his juvenilia for *Collected Poems, 1919–1976* (New York, 1977).
127. Here and elsewhere, I have drawn from Thomas F. Heffernan, "Allen Tate in the Fugitive Years" (Ph.D. diss., Columbia University, 1970; Ann Arbor, Mich.: University Microfilms, 1971), who concludes that Tate's early poetry had a common theme: "the artist with conspicuous ego encounters the woman and treats her as an object or point of reference for his own aggrandizement, a treatment which is usually violent" (3).

128. Tate to Donald Davidson, 12 July 1922, DD-VU. Another insightful assessment of Tate's early poetry is Martha E. Cook, "Allen Tate in the Jazz Age," in *The Vanderbilt Tradition: Essays in Honor of Thomas Daniel Young*, ed. Mark Royden Winchell (Baton Rouge, La., 1991), 47–58, esp. 48, 50–51.
129. Tate to Jesse Wills, 12 Jan. 1969, JW-VU.
130. *Commodore 1922* (Published by the Students of Vanderbilt University), ser. 14, Comet Ser. 36, p. 6 in a special supplement titled *The Vandy Vulture*, following p. 298.

Chapter Three
"O Poet, O Allen Tate, O Hot Youth!"

1. "A Short History of Valle Crucis," mimeographed 2-page typescipt, 2 pp., n.d., Valle Crucis Mission School, N.C.; *The Heritage of Watauga County*, vol. 1 (Winston-Salem, N.C., 1984), 73–76; Tate to Davidson, 28 June 1922, DD-VU.
2. Quoted in Jesse E. Wills to Tate, 10 July 1922, AT-PU, 46.
3. Tate to Davidson, 20 June 1922, DD-VU.
4. Wills to Tate, 10 July 1922 and 20 June [1922], AT-PU, 46.
5. Tate, "From My Room: Valle Crucis, North Carolina, Aug., 1923" [apparently misdated] *Fugitive* 2 (Oct. 1923): 132.
6. Tate to Davidson, 8 Aug. 1922, DD-VU.
7. Merrill Moore to Tate, 2 July 1922, AT-PU, 31:21.
8. Davidson to Tate, 15 July 1922, AT-PU, 18:1.
9. "Current Magazines," *New York Times Book Review and Magazine* 16 July 1922, 28; quoted in "A Poem by Allen Tate," *Vanderbilt Alumnus* 9 (Nov. 1923): 150; "Exploding a Vulgar Error," *Double Dealer* 4 (July 1922): 2.
10. Tate to Davidson, 5 July 1922, DD-VU.
11. Here and throughout my text, I have profited by the excellent discussions of Modernism in Hammer-1993; in *War Within*, 232–60 and passim; and in Houston A. Baker, Jr., *Modernism and the Harlem Renaissance* (Chicago, 1987); read together, the three accounts suggest the aesthetic dispute over literary Modernism in the United States masked a debate over cultural power. (I comment more fully on Hammer-1993 in an endnote for my next chapter.) I also draw throughout from Rubin's important chapter, "Allen Tate: The Poetry of Modernism" (*Wary Fugitives*, 64–135).
12. Tate-Broughton, 325; see also Hammer-1993, ix.
13. Tate to Davidson, 8 Aug. 1922, DD-VU. Hammer argues that Crane and Tate later fell out over Eliot's Modernism: Eventually embracing "a modernism that opposes 'everything modern,' Tate turned away from Crane, and Crane turned away from Tate. Tate came to see Crane as a Romantic

poet whose mystical claims to personal 'vision' seemed naive and reckless beside the learned skeptcism of Eliot" (Hammer-1993, xii).

14. Tate to Davidson, 5 July 1922, DD-VU.
15. Tate to Davidson, 8 Aug. 1922, DD-VU.
16. Tate to Merrill Moore, 11 July 1922, MM-LOC.
17. Tate to Davidson, 31 July 1922, DD-VU.
18. Davidson to Tate, 8 July 1922, AT-PU, 18:1.
19. Tate to Davidson, 20 June 1922, DD-VU.
20. Tate to Davidson, 17 Aug. 1922, DD-VU; Tate to Hart Crane, 13 July 1922, HC-CU.
21. Tate to Davidson, 5 July 1922, DD-VU.
22. Tate to Hart Crane, 13 July 1922, HC-CU.
23. Kenneth Burke to Malcolm Cowley, 2 Sept. 1922, in *Selected Correspondence of Kenneth Burke and Malcolm Cowley, 1915–1981*, ed. Paul Jay (New York, 1988), 124.
24. Moore, *Clippings*, 15.
25. Ibid., 16.
26. Tate to Davidson, 7 Dec. 1922, DD-VU.
27. Davidson to Tate, 13 Aug. 1922, AT-PU, 18:1.
28. Wills to Tate, 20 June [1922], AT-PU, 46.
29. Eliot, *The Sacred Wood : Essays on Poetry and Criticism* (London, 1920; repr., 1928), 100.
30. Tate to Davidson, 17 Aug. 1922, DD-VU.
31. Cowan-1959, 65.
32. For a useful discussion of the influence of the philosophy of Immanuel Kant on Tate and his circle, see William J. Handy, *Kant and the Southern New Critics* (Austin, Tex., 1963), esp. 72.
33. Tate to Davidson, 8 Aug. 1922, DD-VU.
34. Tate to Davidson, 17 Aug. 1922, DD-VU.
35. Tate to Davidson, 7 Dec. 1922, DD-VU.
36. Tate to Davidson, 17 Aug. 1922, DD-VU.
37. Tate to Davidson, 21 July 1922, DD-VU.
38. Cowan-1959, 75–76. I draw from Cowan's excellent work throughout this chapter.
39. W. J. Cash, *The Mind of the South* (1941; repr., New York, n.d.), 52.
40. Rubin makes the fascinating observation that the other Fugitives, who were less conscious of their Southern lineage than was Tate's mother, saved Tate from allowing a preoccupation with lost aristocracy turn him into a writer such as Cabell or Glasgow, characterized by "personal evasion of withdrawal and satire" (*Wary Fugitives*, 74). When Rubin says that Tate's family made him "potentially more receptive to the literary forms and attitudes of modernism" (73), he evidently means that the Tate family's less provincial roots and their downward social mobility produced a son more accepting of the cultural instabilities associated with

Modernism. My somewhat different take on Tate's attraction to Modernism is that the psychological style he learned from his parents made him want to hide both his emotions and his Southern identity in a literary technique based upon indirection. Rubin may be correct that the Fugitives eventually made Tate face "the inevitability of grappling with the problems of one's personal identity in society" (73) and that Ransom misunderstood both Tate's and Eliot's modernism as "a surrender to passion" (87). Yet Tate ignored the Fugitives' objections to his Modernism, which he continued to use in that period and afterward to disguise his Southernness.

41. Thomas F. Heffernan, "Allen Tate in the Fugitive Years" (Ph.D. dissertation.: Columbia University, 1970; Ann Arbor, Mich.: University Microfilms, 1971), 2. George Core points out that while Tate's "poetry usually does not embody an emotional dimension which is equal to the burden of its ideas," his finest poetry was rooted in "experience" and that his later work "regularly explored the theme of love" ("Mr. Tate and the Limits of Poetry," *Virginia Quarterly Review* 62 [Winter 1986]: 110, 109).

42. Tate, *The Date*, undated typescript, Heard Library, Vanderbilt University. Martha Cook has observed that this poem, which "develops the theme of sex without love" treats an "emotionless relationship." "Allen Tate in the Jazz Age," in *The Vanderbilt Tradition: Essays in Honor of Thomas Daniel Young*, ed. Mark Royden Winchell (Baton Rouge, La., 1991), 53.

43. Tate to Davidson, 17 Aug. 1922, DD-VU.

44. Tate to Davidson, 12 July 1922, DD-VU.

45. Tate to Davidson, 21 July 1922, DD-VU.

46. Tate to Davidson, 31 July 1922, DD-VU.

47. Alec Stevenson to Tate, 12 Nov. 1922, AT-PU, 40:53.

48. Davidson to Tate, 15 July 1922, AT-PU, 18:1.

49. Tate to Davidson, 7 December 1922, DD-VU.

50. Tate, *First Epilogue to Oenia*, typescript, HC-CU.

51. Tate to Alec B. Stevenson, 14 Nov. 1922, quoted in Cowan-1959, 81.

52. Tate, "Personal Recollection," 81.

53. Tate to Davidson, 31 Aug. [1922], DD-VU.

54. Ibid.

55. Tate-Broughton, 328.

56. Tate to Davidson, 18 Nov. [1922], DD-VU.

57. Tate to Davidson, 29 Nov. [1922]; 18 Nov. [1922], DD-VU.

58. Tate to Davidson, 21 Nov. 1922, DDF.

59. Tate to Davidson, 7 Dec. 1922, DD-VU; *Mary McDonald*, first published in the *Fugitive* 2 (Feb–March 1923): 3.

60. Babette Deutsch, "Help for a Young German Author," *New Republic* 33 (13 Dec. 1922): 71; Tate, "Our Struggling Writers," *New Republic* 33 (10 Jan. 1923): 177.

61. Tate to Merrill Moore, 21 Nov. 1929, MM-LOC; Wills to Tate, 7 Feb. 1923, AT-PU, 46.

62. Cowan-1959, 81, 87–88.

63. Stevenson to Tate, 12 Nov. 1922, AT-PU, 40:53; Davidson to Tate, 8 Nov. 1922, AT-PU, 18:1.

64. Davidson to Tate, 23 Jan. 1923, AT-PU, 18:1.

65. The poem *Calidus Juventa*? table of contents, and epigraph from Horace all accompany Tate to Davidson, 1 Jan. 1923, DDF.

66. Tate to Davidson, 11 Feb. [1923?], DD-VU.

67. Davidson to Tate, 12 Jan. 1923, AT-PU, 18:1.

68. Tate to Davidson, 10 Nov. [1922] & 3 Feb. [1923], DD-VU.

69. Tate to Davidson, 16 Jan. 1923, DD-VU.

70. Ibid.

71. Ransom to Tate, [Feb.? 1923], AT-PU, 36:26.

72. Davidson to Tate, 23 Jan. 1923, AT-PU, 18:1.

73. Biographical sketch, *Twentieth Century Authors : A Biographical Diction-ary of Modern Literature*, ed. Stanley J. Kunitz and Howard Haycraft (New York, 1942), 1386.

74. Jesse Wills to Tate, 7 Feb. 1923, AT-PU, 46.

75. Biographical sketch in *Twentieth Century Authors : A Biographical Dic-tionary of Modern Literature*, ed. Stanley J. Kunitz and Howard Haycraft (New York, 1942),1386. See also *Current Biography*, ed. Maxine Block (New York, 1940), 790.

76. William S. Vaughn [Vanderbilt '23] to TAU, 17 Jan. 1989.

77. Tate, "Personal Recollection," 81.

78. Tate to Crane, 30 May 1923, HC-CU.

79. To reconstruct the story of Tate's first meeting with Warren, I have merged the account in Tate, "Personal Recollection," 81–82, with that told by Sullivan-1988, 31.

80. Quoted by Sullivan-1988, 31.

81. On Ridley Wills, I draw from Cowan-1959, 77–78, and Tate, "Personal Recollection," 82.

82. Tate to Hart Crane, 28 June 1923, HC-CU.

83. Tate, "Personal Recollection," 82; Warren to TAU, 10 March 1987.

84. Warren to TAU, 10 March 1987.

85. Ibid.

86. Tate to Davidson, 31 July 1923, DD-VU.

87. Tate to Crane, 14 May 1923, HC-CU; Tate to Davidson, 31 July 1923, DD-VU.

88. In my discussion of *The Golden Mean and Other Poems* ([Nash-ville],1923), I also draw from "Personal Recollection," 82; Cowan, 109–10; Robert Buffington, "High Jinks in Nashville, 1923" *Sewanee Review* 87 (Spring 1979): xxx, xxxii; and Sandra Roberts, "Allen Tate's First Book Reprinted," *Tennessean*, 21 Oct. 1979, P11. See also William S.

Knickerbocker's curious article, "Friction of Powder-Puffs: Tatian Eso-
terics," *Sewanee Review* 48 (July–Sept. 1940): 315–21.

89. Tate, *In Defense of Suicide, Golden Mean*, 21.
90. Wills, *Tercets of the Triad, Golden Mean*, 27.
91. Wills, *Life of Allen Tate, Golden Mean*, 31.
92. Tate, *Life of Ridley Wills, Golden Mean*, 32.
93. Tate to Crane, 16 April 1923, HC-CU.
94. Davidson to Tate, 9 Feb. 1923, AT-PU, 18:1.
95. Wilson to Tate, 3 Jan. 1923, AT-PU, 46:5.
96. Tate to Davidson, 7 Jan. 1923, DD-VU.
97. Tate to Crane, 28 June 1923, HC-CU.
98. Tate to Davidson, 31 Aug. [1922], DD-VU.
99. Ransom, "In Amicitia," *Sewanee Review* 67 (Autumn 1959): 532.
100. William S. Vaughn, "Some Recollections of a Fugitive Sort," *Vanderbilt Magazine* 72 (Fall 1987): 15, 16.
101. Tate-Broughton, 328; Tate, "Personal Recollection," 82.
102. Tate to Davidson, 31 July 1923, DD-VU.
103. Tate to Hart Crane, 14 May 1923, HC-CU.
104. Warren to TAU, 10 March 1987.
105. Vaughn, "Some Recollections of a Fugitive Sort," 16.
106. Tate to Crane, 30 May 1923, HC-CU.
107. Tate to Crane, 30 May 1923, HC-CU.
108. Tate to Crane, 14 May 1923, HC-CU.
109. Davidson to Tate, 26 June 1923, AT-PU, 18:1.
110. Tate to Crane, 28 June 1923, HC-CU.
111. Tate to Crane, 14 June 1923, HC-CU.
112. Tate to Davidson, 22 June 1923, DD-VU.
113. Tate to Crane, 16 April 1923, HC-CU.
114. Vaughn [Vanderbilt '23] to TAU, 17 Jan. 1989.
115. For information on Lanier, I am indebted to C.F., "Lyle Lanier: Still Taking His Stand," *Vanderbilt Alumnus* 59 (Summer 1974): 26–27.
116. Catherine Mims [Vanderbilt '24] to TAU, 20 Aug. 1987.
117. Wills, from a typescript on Tate's letterhead, annotated by Tate, "notes left in W. C. Curry's room in Kissam Hall, Vanderbilt, summer 1923, by Laurence Blair, Alec B. Stevenson, and Jesse E. Wills," AT-PU, 49.
118. Tate to Davidson, 31 July 1923, DD-VU.
119. Wills to Davidson, 24 July 1923, quoted in Cowan-1959, 112.
120. Tate to Crane, 28 June 1923, HC-CU.
121. *Clippings*, 40.
122. Tate to Davidson, 31 July 1923, DD-VU.
123. [Morley], "The Literary Lobby," *Literary Review*, published by the *New York Evening Post* 3 (7 July 1923): 824.
124. Ibid., 904. See also Cowan-1959, 119–20.
125. Tate to Davidson, 14 July 1923, DD-VU.

126. Ransom, "Waste Lands," *Literary Review*, published by the New York *Evening Post* 3 (14 July 1923): 825–26.

127. Tate, "Waste Lands," *Literary Review*, published by the *New York Evening Post* 3 (4 Aug. 1923): 886.

128. See Ransom to Tate, 30 July [1923], in T. D. Young and George Core, eds. *Selected Letters of John Crowe Ransom* (Baton Rouge, La., 1985), 119–20, and Ransom to the editor of *Literary Review* [holograph, undated], AT-PU, 36:26; Ransom evidently sent Tate the handwritten draft of the letter to Morley. "Mr. Ransom Replies," *Literary Review*, published by the New York *Evening* Post 3 (11 Aug. 1923): 902.

129. Tate to Davidson, 18 Aug. 1923, DD-VU. Cowan (Cowan-1959, 118–27) and Rubin (see esp. "Eliot and Ransom as Models," *Wary Fugitive*, 75–87) are helpful on the Tate-Eliot-Ransom triangle, a notable achievement since all three poets were still living when those accounts were written. When, for instance, Tate read a MS version of Cowan-1959, he wanted, but evidently was not successful in getting her "to omit, or merely glance at, the row between John and me in 1923" because a "reader, not knowing anything about the friendship that developed afterwards and that has now run without interruption for more than 25 years, would get entirely the wrong emphasis" (Tate to Davidson, 4 April 1952, DD-VU). What I've tried to do in this chapter, by quoting numerous hostile remarks about Ransom that Tate expurgated from *DD-AT* (and which, to my knowledge, have not been published previously), is to show that Tate's animus toward Ransom in 1923 was far more personal than Tate would admit to himself or to critics. An insightful assessment of the more collegial and nonrebellious Tate-Ransom relationship in later years is in the introduction by Young and Core to the *Selected Letters of John Crowe Ransom*, 1–15.

130. Davidson to Tate, 14 Aug. 1923. AT-PU, 18:1.

131. Davidson to Tate, 30 Aug. 1923, AT-PU, 18:1.

132. Tate to Davidson, 22 June 1923, DD-VU.

133. Tate to Davidson, 7 Sept. 1923, DD-VU.

134. Tate to Davidson, 27 Aug. 1923, DD-VU.

135. Davidson to Tate, 22 Aug. 1923, AT-PU, 18:1.

136. Interview with Dorothy Bethurum, Nashville, 21 July 1987.

137. *Clippings*, 20, 22.

138. Tate to Davidson, 7 Sept. 1923, DD-VU.

139. Davidson to Tate, 10 Sept. 1923, AT-PU, 18:1.

140. Tate, "Te Saluto!" *Vanderbilt Alumnus* 9 (November 1923): 42.

141. William Y. Elliott to Donald Davidson, 11 Oct. 1923, quoted in Cowan-1959, 131.

142. Lyle H. Lanier to TAU, 13 Oct. 1988; telephone interview with Lanier, 12 Dec. 1988.

143. Warren to Tate [early Spring 1924], AT-PU, 44:28; shortly before his death, Warren dismissed Mrs. Tolman's charges; see Joseph Blotner to TAU, 9 Nov. 1988.

144. "A Poem by Allen Tate," *Vanderbilt Alumnus* 9 (Nov. 1923): 150; Minutes of the Vanderbilt Chapter of Phi Beta Kappa, 5 Dec. 1923, Heard Library, Vanderbilt University; "Phi Beta Kappa Roll," *Vanderbilt Alumnus* 9 (1923–24): 76, 80. In a list of graduating seniors whose names are followed by cum laude, magna cum laude, or summa cum laude, Tate's name appears with nothing afterward; "Degrees and Honors, 1922–1923," *Register of Vanderbilt University for 1923–1924* (Nashville, 1924), 231. Yet an updated copy of his Vanderbilt transcript (dated Jan. 29, 1924 and attached to his 1928–29 Guggenheim application) suggests that the designation magna cum laude was added to his record sometime after his graduation (JSGMF).

145. Ransom to Tate, 5 Nov. [1922], quoted in Cowan-1959, 80.

146. Tate to Hart Crane, 18 March 1923, HC-CU.

147. *Fugitive* 1 (April 1922): 1.

148. Moore, *Clippings*, 30.

149. Ibid., 30–31.

150. Ibid., 8.

151. Ibid., Moore, 35, 25.

152. Tate to Davidson, 29 June 1923, DD-VU. On Mencken's retrograde and divisive role in the early stages of the renaissance, see *War Within*, 83–87.

153. Tate to Virginia Lyne Tunstall, 3 Nov. 1923, VLT-UVA.

154. Tate to Davidson, 29 June 1923, DD-VU.

155. Tate to Crane, 9 April 1923, HC-CU.

156. Tate to Crane, 18 March 1923, HC-CU.

157. *Clippings*, 18. Tate quoted in "A Poem by Allen Tate," 150.

158. Tate to Davidson, 29 June 1923, DD-VU.

Chapter Four
"They Used to Call Me 'the Yankee' "

1. Tate to Radcliffe Squires, 21 July 1969, RS-WU.

2. George Hemphill has observed, "True to the geography of his birth, Tate is a Borderer, a man who seems torn between conflicting loyalties but who has managed to find a coherent set of values" (*Allen Tate*, University of Minnesota Pamphlets on American Writers [Minneapolis, 1964], 5–6).

3. On West Virginia, I have drawn some information from Dorothy Davis, *History of Harrison County, West Virginia* (Clarksburg, W.V. 1970), 214–15 (hereafter referred to as *Harrison County*).

4. On Lumberport, I draw from *Harrison County*, 359–66; Lumberport Heritage Committee, *History of Lumberport and Surrounding Communi-*

ties (Salem, W.V., 1977), 10–25, 28–29, 34–37; Randal Strother, ed., *Clarksburg Exponent*, "Memo To TAU," 16 July 1987, 3 pp. typescript; Randal Strother to TAU, 6 Oct. 1987; *The Eaglet*, 1st ed. (Lumberport, W.V., 1924), 34–35 (hereafter *Eaglet*).

5. Tate to Davidson, 21 Feb. 1924, DD-VU.
6. *Eaglet*, 35.
7. Tate to Davidson, 21 Feb. 1924, DD-VU.
8. *Poem for My Father, Voices* 3 (March–April 1924): 47; repr. as *A Pauper* in *Mr. Pope*, 20–21.
9. Interview with Mrs. Henrietta Vincent, 6 July 1987, Lumberport, W.V.
10. Interview with Mr. Lawrence Brooke, 6 July 1987, Lumberport, W.V.
11. Interview with Mrs. Henrietta Vincent.
12. Tate to Davidson, 8 March 1924, DD-VU.
13. Eaglet, 36.
14. Interview with Mr. Lawrence Brooke; Tate to Davidson, 27 Feb. 1924, DD-VU.
15. See John Tyree Fain, "Fifty Years Have Come and Gone," *Nashville Tennessean*, 8 Sept. 1974, 6-F.
16. Tate to Bill Bandy, 21 April [1924], WTB-VU. Some of Tate's reviews from the *Tennessean* have been reprinted in Ashley Brown and Frances Neel Cheney, eds. *The Poetry Reviews of Allen Tate, 1924–1944* (Baton Rouge, La., 1983.) Years later, Tate still dismissed everything he wrote during this period (see Tate to Davidson, 21 April 1963, DD-VU).
17. Tate to Davidson, 13 March [1924], DD-VU.
18. Tate, "E. E. Cummings' Poetry Perfection, within Limitations, Tate Believes," *Nashville Tennessean*, 23 March 1924; Tate to Davidson, [1924], DD-VU.
19. Tate, "E. E. Cummings' Poetry Perfection."
20. Tate, "Whose Ox," *Fugitive* 1 (Dec. 1922): 99–100; "Evaporation," *Double Dealer* 6 (Jan. 1924): 32–33.
21. Ransom to Tate, 6 May [1924], AT-PU, 36:26.
22. Tate to Davidson, 14 April 1924, DD-VU.
23. Tate, "E. E. Cummings' Poetry Perfection."
24. Tate, "One Escape from The Dilemma," *Fugitive* 3 (April 1924): 34–36.
25. Tate to Davidson, 13 March [1924], DD-VU.
26. Tate to Davidson, 14 March 1924, DD-VU.
27. Tate to Davidson, 3 March [1924], DD-VU.
28. Tate to Davidson, 14 April 1924, DD-VU.
29. Tate to Davidson, 3 March 1924, DD-VU.
30. Tate to Davidson, 26 April [1924], DD-VU.
31. Tate to Davidson, 16 April 1924, DD-VU.
32. Davidson to Tate, 23 April 1924, AT-PU, 18:1.
33. Tate to Davidson, 16 April 1924, DD-VU.
34. Carbon copy of Tate to Sidney Mttron Hirsch, 26 April 1924, DD-VU.

35. Ransom to Tate, 6 May [1924], AT-PU, 36:26.
36. Tate to Davidson, 28 May [1924], DD-VU.
37. Tate to Davidson, 16 April 1924, DD-VU. Over the years, the story of Mims's interference in his career grew more elaborate in Tate's memory. A story developed that Tate, after being notified that he had received the scholarship from Yale, charged into Mims's office announcing his victory and proclaiming, "And I wanted to point out that I got it without any recommendation from you." The tale concluded with Mims using his clout in academic circles to have the Yale offer rescinded. There is no evidence that Mims did any such thing, but Tate terrorized him for decades, taking every opportunity to criticize him publicly. Only forty years later, as Tate lay on his deathbed, did he confess to Mims's daughter, "I was not fair to your father" (Sullivan-1988, 19; Ella Puryear Mims, '34, "My Father Remembered," 5-page undated typescript [copy courtesy of Ella P. Mims], p. 4).
38. Warren to Tate, undated [early spring 1924], AT-PU, 44:28.
39. Tate to Davidson, 26 April 1924, DD-VU.
40. Warren to Tate, undated [early spring 1924], AT-PU, 44:28.
41. Warren to Tate, undated [late spring 1924], AT-PU, 44:28.
42. Sanborn to Tate, 16 Dec. 1926, AT-PU, 38:24.
43. Tate to Davidson, 26 April 1924, DD-VU.
44. Tate to Davidson, 7 May [1924], DD-VU.
45. Tate to Davidson, 11 October 1924, DD-VU.
46. Tate to Davidson, 5 June 1924, DD-VU.
47. Tate to Davidson, 7 May [1924], DD-VU.
48. Tate to Davidson, 16 April 1924, DD-VU.
49. Tate to Davidson, 7 May [1924], DD-VU.
50. Tate to Davidson, 7 May [1924], DD-VU.
51. For a useful discussion of Cowley's complex attitudes toward Modernism, see James Michael Kempf, *The Early Career of Malcolm Cowley: A Humanist among the Moderns* (Baton Rouge, La., 1985.)
52. Tate to Davidson, 14 May [1924], DD-VU.
53. On Warren's suicide attempt, I draw from Davidson to Tate, 21 May 1924, AT-PU, 18:1; Jesse E. Wills to Tate, 22 May 1924, AT-PU, 46:4; Lyle Lanier to Tate, 24 May [1924], AT-PU, 27:8; Robert Penn Warren to Tate, 16 Nov. 1978, AT-PU, IIc.
54. Davidson to Tate, 21 May 1924, AT-PU, 18:1.
55. Lanier to Tate, 6 May 1924, AT-PU, 27:8.
56. Tate to Davidson, 24 May 1924, DD-VU.
57. Typescript enclosed with Tate to Hart Crane, 15 Sept. [1924], HC-CU; published as *Advice to a Young Romanticist, Nation* 120 (14 Jan. 1925): 45; repr. as *To a Romanticist* in *Mr. Pope*, 43.
58. Warren to Tate, [late spring 1924], AT-PU, 44:28.
59. Tate to Davidson, 28 May [1924], DD-VU.

60. Tate to Davidson, 15 June [1924], DD-VU.
61. Tate to Davidson, [8 June 1924?], DD-VU.
62. Ibid.
63. Tate to Davidson, 15 June [1924], DD-VU.
64. Cowley, "Two Winters with Hart Crane," *Sewanee Review* 67 (Autumn 1959): 547–56, 547. I draw from this memoir throughout.
65. Tate to Davidson, 15 June [1924], DD-VU.
66. Tate to Davidson, [8 June 1924?], DD-VU.
67. Cowley to Burke, 24 June 1924, in *Selected Correspondence of Kenneth Burke and Malcolm Cowley*, ed. Paul Jay (New York, 1988), 161.
68. Tate to Davidson, 15 June [1924], DD-VU.
69. Crane to Gorham Munson, 9 July 1924, quoted in Squires-1971, 52.
70. Tate to John Brooks Wheelwright, JBW-BRN, I. Correspondence. MS. 79.1, 3:15.
71. Tate to Davidson, 11 July [1924], DD-VU.
72. To make emendations throughout this chapter, I have drawn where necessary from Waldron and from Makowsky.
73. Gordon used her given name, "Carolyn," until late 1929 and early 1930, at which time she began using "Caroline" (see Jonza, 71, 77, and 85).
74. Ransom to Tate, 11 February [1923], AT-PU, 36:26.
75. Gordon, *Chattanooga News*, 10 Feb. 1923, magazine section, 11.
76. Danforth Ross, "Memories of Allen Tate," 13 March 1980, unpublished memoir, 15 page typescript (copy courtesy of Mr. Ross), 8.
77. Warren to TAU, 10 March 1987.
78. Dora Bernhard to Tate, 30 October 1955, AT-PU, 11:32.
79. Tate to Bill Bandy, 7 April 1924, WTB-VU.
80. Tate to Davidson, 26 April [1924], DD-VU.
81. Tate to Hart Crane, 10 September [1924], HC-CU.
82. James Edward Tobin, "Tate's Mr. Pope" *Explicator* 15 (March 1957): [35]. For an alternate reading, see Margaret Morton Blum, "Allen Tate's 'Mr. Pope': A Reading," *Modern Language Notes* 74 (Dec. 1959): 706–8. Louis D. Rubin, Jr., has observed, "His poem on Pope—he was writing about himself, or an ideal of himself! The hunchback, the little guy who kept the world at bay through his wit and ferocity" (Rubin to TAU, 31 Jan. 1989). "Mr. Pope" first appeared in the *Nation* 121 (2 September 1925): 258; repr. in *Mr. Pope*, 3.
83. Tate to Davidson, 8 March 1924, DD-VU.
84. Tate to Davidson, 15 June [1924], DD-VU.
85. Carbon copy of Tate, "To the Editor of *Poetry: A Magazine of Verse*," 5 Oct. 1924, with annotation to Davidson in Tate's hand, DD-VU.
86. Quoted in Martin Seymour-Smith, *Robert Graves: His Life and Work* (London, 1982), 125 (hereafter Seymour-Smith). On Riding, I am indebted to Seymour-Smith, 122–30; Joyce Piell Wexler, *Laura Riding's Pursuit of Truth* (Athens, Ohio, 1979), esp. 6–16. Although I do not use

Deborah Baker's *In Extremis: The Life of Laura Riding* (New York, 1993) as a source, Ms. Baker and I shared leads by mail. After I wrote this section, I was pleased to be asked by her to criticize several excellent chapters of that book in manuscript form.

87. Tate to Davidson, 7 May [1924], DD-VU.

88. Quoted by Laura [Riding] Jackson, "The Fugitives, etc." *London Magazine* 16 (Aug.–Sept. 1976): 91.

89. Tate to Davidson, 21 February 1924, DD-VU.

90. Tate to Bill Bandy, 7 April 1924, WTB-VU.

91. Laura [Riding] Jackson, "To the Editors," *New York Review of Books* 30 (22 Dec. 1983): 61.

92. Tate to Davidson, 2 June [1924], DD-VU.

93. Waldron, 32; Ward Dorrance to Tate, 19 Aug. [1971?], AT-PU, IIc.

94. Tate to Davidson, 6 Aug. 1924, DD-VU.

95. Wills to Tate, 12 Aug. [1924], AT-PU, 46.

96. Tate to Davidson, 25 Aug. [1924], DD-VU.

97. Tate to Hart Crane, 10 Sept. [1924], HC-CU. Tate claimed to have forgiven Mims, but it was clear that he neither had nor could. "I do think," he observed of Mims, "he is doing both himself and me a wrong in elevating a plain personal hostility into the realm of retributive justice." Such behavior, Tate concluded was "nothing else than presuming to the performance of the business of God." Tate to Davidson, 4 Sept. 1924, DD-VU.

98. Tate to Davidson, 8 Dec. [1924], DD-VU.

99. Tate to Hart Crane, 15 Sept. [1924], HC-CU.

100. Tate to Bill Bandy, 13 Oct. [1924], WTB-VU.

101. Tate to Davidson, 31 October [1924], DD-VU.

102. Tate to Ben E. Tate, 21 Dec. 1960, AT-PU, IIc.

103. *Death of Little Boys, Nation* 121 (9 Dec. 1925): 663; reprinted in *transition* 3 (June 1927): 138; and in *Mr. Pope*, 4. Tate later explained that the poem was inspired by Rimbaud's *Les Chercheuses de Poux* ("The ladies who look for lice"), a short poem about a feverish and pain-ridden little boy taken in by nuns; see Roy Harvey Pearce, "A Small Crux in Allen Tate's 'Death of Little Boys': Postscript" *Modern Language Notes* 75 (March 1960): 214. In *The Last Alternatives: A Study of the Works of Allen Tate* (Denver, 1963), R. K. Meiners has called the poem "one of the clearest examples in all of Tate's poetry of the presentation of bogus experience" (105). Yet in *Rumors of Mortality: An Introduction to Allen Tate* (Dallas, 1969), M. E. Bradford observes of the poem, "More than other 'rumors of mortality' (the phrase itself well describes the body of Tate's verse), the passing of children scandalizes the positivist's expectation of secular beatitude, challenges his sense of total power over his condition" (12). Throughout my text, I have profited by the discussions of this and other Tate poems in Bradford's and Meiners's studies.

104. Tate to Davidson, 9 Nov. [1924], DD-VU.
105. Tate to Davidson, 17 Dec. [1924], DD-VU.
106. Tate to Davidson, 8 Dec. [1924], DD-VU.
107. Tate to Davidson, 30 Dec. [1924], DD-VU.
108. Tate to Davidson, 22 Nov. [1924], DD-VU.
109. Tate, "American Poetry since 1920," *Bookman* 68 (Jan. 1929): 506.
110. Tate to Davidson, 17 Dec. [1924], DD-VU.
111. Tate, "Edmund Wilson," 2-page typescript enclosed in Tate to Frances Steloff, 13 Nov. 1939, BC-NYPL.
112. *Surrealists*, 253.
113. *Voyager*, 358.
114. *Twentieth Century Authors*, ed. Stanley J. Kunitz and Howard Haycraft (New York, 1942), 734.
115. Tate to Donald E. Stanford, 17 Dec. 1975, DES-STN.
116. *Surrealists*, 252–53.
117. Tate, "A Farewell to Stark Young," typescript, AT-PU, 47:10.
118. Tate to Davidson, 5 May 1925, DD-VU.
119. Tate to Davidson, 9 Feb. [1925], DD-VU.
120. Quoted in Tate to Davidson, 3 Nov. [1924], DD-VU.
121. Tate to Davidson, 9 Nov. [1924], DD-VU.
122. Tate to Davidson, 16 Jan. 1925, DD-VU. "Don't think these people are an organized group of aesthetes," Allen warned the Fugitives. "They're the simplest and least given to 'organization' of all people I've seen; and are far less conscious of being 'poets' than we are as a group" (Tate to Davidson, 15 June [1924], DD-VU).
123. Quoted in Waldron, 39.
124. Tate, *Prothesis for Marriage*, *Double Dealer* 6 (Aug.–Sept. 1924): 214. Tate to Davidson, 21 May 1925, DD-VU. Accounts by the Gordon biographers of the period between the conception of the baby and the Tate's marriage differ, but all agree that the marriage took place 15 May 1925 (see Waldron, 39–41; Makowsky, 57–60; Jonza, 43–45).
125. Jean [probably Catel] to Tate, 14 July [1925], AT-PU, 6:9.
126. Tate to Wilson, 23 Sept. 1925, EW-YU.
127. Tate to Wilson, 24 Sept.1925, EW-YU.
128. Tate to Davidson, 30 Sept. 1925, DD-VU.
129. Tate to Davidson, 15 Oct. 1925, DD-VU.
130. Tate to Davidson, 30 Sept. 1925, DD-VU.
131. Quoted in Seymour-Smith, 127; Jackson, "To the Editors," 61.
132. Tate to Horace Gregory, 4 Oct. 1944, HG-SYR.
133. Tate to Davidson, 14 May 1926, DD-VU.
134. Tate to Davidson, 3 Jan. 1926, DD-VU.
135. See, for example, the excellent work of O'Brien-1979, 136–61, esp. 143; Singal's influential chapter "The Divided Mind of Allen Tate," in *War Within*, 232–60; and *Fable*, 26. I can appreciate Singal's claim that Tate's Modernism blocked his "identification" with the South (*War*

Within, 238) and Hammer's conclusion that "Tate's Southernism" became "a style" in which he used Southern "props" as "the machinery of
a particular modernist drama" (Hammer-1993, 104), but I suggest here
and in other chapters that Tate was more a Southerner who attempted
to use Modernism than a Modernist who attempted to use the South.
Using different definitions of Modernism (Hammer is a poetry critic, and
Singal a cultural historian), the two scholars are more persuasive on the
interaction of Tate's Southernism and his Modernism. To Hammer, the
interaction limited Tate's definition of literary Modernism; to Singal,
the interaction impeded Tate's conversion to modern cultural thought.
(Similarly, Rubin's claim that Tate was a modernist for whom "the antebellum, aristocratic South" was merely "an instrument of strategy"
[*Wary Fugitives*, 96] applies more to Tate's attitude toward the Old
South, I would suggest, than it does to the highly personal Southern
identity Tate avoided via Modernism, attempted to reclaim via Agrarianism, and resolved via *The Fathers*.)
136. Tate to Davidson, 6 Aug. 1924, DD-VU.
137. Tate to Davidson, 8 Dec. [1924], DD-VU. Tate may have harbored resentments toward Mencken for another reason: ever since the first issue
of *The Fugitive* appeared, Tate had been submitting poetry to Mencken,
which he repeatedly turned down.
138. Tate to Paul Green, 8 Jan. [1925], PG-SHC.
139. See Fred C. Hobson, Jr., *Serpent in Eden: H. L. Mencken and the South*
(Baton Rouge, La., 1974.) I have especially profited by Hobson's superb
chapter, "Beyond Mencken: The Agrarians and the South," 147–84. "In
many ways," Hobson concludes, "the Dayton trial was a prototypic
event, the single event that more than any other of the 1920s brought
to the surface all the forces and tensions that had characterized the postwar South, the event that most forcefully dramatized the struggle
between Southern provincialism and the modern, secular world; and
finally, the event that caused Southerners to face squarely the matter
of the South and their own place in it" (148). Shapiro argues that
Mencken's attacks moved the Fugitives' toward Southern Agrarianism
("SA-HLM").
140. Tate, "Last Days of the Charming Lady," *Nation* 121 (28 Oct. 1925):
485–86.
141. DuBose Heyward, quoted by Tate in Tate to Malcolm Cowley, 30 March
1926, MC-NL.
142. Tate, "Last Days of the Charming Lady."
143. Tate to Davidson, 29 July 1926, DD-VU.
144. Ibid.
145. I continue to draw, as I have throughout this chapter, from *War Within*,
232–60.
146. Tate to Davidson, 9 Nov. [1924], DD-VU.

147. Quoted in Bob Lundegaard, "University of Minnesota's Poet Tate: 'I Am Out of Tune with the Times,' " *Minneapolis Tribune*, 24 Jan. 1965, 1.

148. *Robber Rocks*, 40–41. I have made use of this memoir throughout.

149. Tate to Davidson, 26 Nov. 1925, DD-VU.

150. Tate to Paul Green, 13 Jan. [1925], PG-SHC.

151. Sullivan-1988, 18–19.

152. Quoted in *Robber Rocks*, 31.

153. *Voyager*, 420. Throughout this section I draw from *Voyager*, esp. 417–35. I have further profited by accounts in the Caroline Gordon biographies.

154. Interview with Mr. William Slater Brown, 12 May 1988, Rockport, Mass.

155. Tate to Davidson, 3 Jan. 1926, DD-VU.

156. Tate to Hart Crane, 9 Dec. [1925], HC-CU.

157. Tate to Davidson, 3 Jan. 1926, DD-VU.

158. Tate to Edmund Wilson, 9 Dec. [1925], EW-YU.

159. Tate to Davidson, 3 Jan. 1926, DD-VU.

160. *Robber Rocks*, 57.

161. Crane to Grace Hart Crane, 18 April [1926], in *Letters of Hart Crane and His Family*, ed. Thomas S. W. Lewis (New York, 1974), 478, 482.

162. Crane to Wilbur Underwood, [July 1926], quoted in *Voyager*, 444. Hammer argues that "Crane's [financial] extravagance aggravated Gordon in particular, who may have felt his intrusion as a specifically sexual threat to her marriage with Tate" (Hammer-1993, 34).

163. Crane to Grace Hart Crane, 18 April [1926], *Letters of Hart Crane and His Family*, 479, 480.

164. Hammer has published both rediscovered letters and Crane's reply as "Caroline Gordon, Allen Tate, and Hart Crane: An Exchange," *Sewanee Review* 106 (Winter 1998): 140–45, 142. I have also profited from Hammer's fair-minded introduction to these letters.

165. Tate to Morton D. Zabel, 2 May 1932, MDZ-CHI.

166. Tate, "Foreword," *White Buildings: Poems by Hart Crane* (New York, 1926); repr. in Tate, *M&O*, 110–14. In recent years, a few scholars have questioned the authorship of the introduction Tate published, and have ascribed much of it to a draft by Eugene O'Neill, who was originally to have written it. O'Neill's biographer states, "For more than a year O'Neill, who found nondramatic writing difficult, had procrastinated about the introductory piece; an article of any length cost him nearly as much thought and effort, he has said, as a play. Shortly before leaving Bermuda, though, he wrote a foreword of some eight hundred words, but he was so dissatisfied that he never sent it to Crane or even told him about it" (Louis Sheaffer, *O'Neill: Son and Artist* [Boston, 1973], 207). Although the existence of a typescript version similar in content to the one Tate published, but with O'Neill's byline and handwritten corrections (BC-NYPL), supports Sheaffer's conclusion that O'Neill actually

wrote a draft introduction, one equally plausible explanation is that Tate wrote the piece for O'Neill, signing O'Neill's name to it, only to have O'Neill reject it after trying in vain to make the prose sound more like his own. Matthew Josephson, for instance, concludes that when O'Neill "found himself unable to write even a brief critical foreword, Allen Tate undertook to 'ghost' it for him, which was a most generous action. In the end, O'Neill insisted that Allen's foreword, an analytical study of Crane's poetic method, sounded so unlike his, O'Neill's, writing that Allen should sign it himself" (*Surrealists*, 298). (Josephson's account is probably a derivation of Malcolm Cowley's in "Two Winters with Hart Crane," 554–55.)

Certainly the language and argumentation in the published version suggest Tate as the author. And while the typescript version opens with O'Neill's personal recollection of his first meeting with Crane, it is entirely conceivable that Tate, who socialized with both O'Neill and Crane, had heard the story and incorporated it in order to make the foreword sound like the work of O'Neill. (For further references, see *Voyager*, 448; Tate to Virginia Lyne Tunstall, 18 July 1926, VLT-UVA; Tate to Donald Davidson, 29 July 1926, DD-VU; Hart Crane to Grace Hart Curtis, 30 July [1926], in *Letters of Hart Crane and His Family*, 507; Tate to Edmund Wilson, 4 Aug. 1926, EW-YU; Hammer-1993, 49–50, 242n).

167. Tate to Morton D. Zabel, 2 May 1932, MDZ-CHI. After writing my account of the relationship between Tate and Crane, my friend Langdon Hammer published his book (Hammer-1993), a small portion of which I was privileged to read in early manuscript form. Using as a motif the argument that broke out between Tate, Crane, and Gordon in 1926, Hammer sets out to explore the antagonistic definitions of Modernism that governed the literary and, in Hammer's view, homoerotic relationship between Tate and Crane. The version of Modernism Tate learned from Eliot, and that Crane abandoned to Tate's disapproval, Hammer argues, was antiromantic, antimodern, homophobic, paternal, professionalized, and exclusive. Taking on the "masculine" role of "poet-critic," Tate relegated Crane to a "feminine" or "mystical" role, thus denying Crane the role he preferred as "fraternal," visionary, poetic "genius." Robert Lowell, Hammer argues in his conclusion, never escaped Tate's Eliotic standard and mimicked, in *Life Studies*, Tate's use of it to measure Crane's poetic style.

Both my methodology as a historian of Southern literature and my perspective as a Tate biographer are naturally different from those of Hammer, who writes in powerful sympathy with Crane's interests, point of view, and critical reputation, and who reaches many of his conclusions based upon close analysis of poetic diction. Hammer is, in my view, too critical of Tate's poetry, and he invests Tate the critic with more control over the careers and self-perceptions of his peers and protégés than he possessed. Yet in certain aspects of Hammer's argument, I find support for my own interpretation of Tate as an orphan. For instance, I share Hammer's conclusions that "Tate felt unmanned by the 'sentimentalism' of the genteel South—a world he found soft, entrapping, feminine" and which he correlated with his mother (Hammer-1993, 61, 24), and that the version of Modernism Tate found so appealing in Eliot depended upon "patriarchal authority vested in tradition" (11). I cannot, however, agree that "Tate's appeal to Crane seeks an alternative to the Oedipal struggle Tate staged in the Fugitive group" (62). With the exception of Tate's relationship to Ransom, about which I agree with Hammer, Tate's relationship to the Fugitives, and later to the Agrarians, was, I argue, as fraternal as it was oedipal. Of Tate's initial affection for Crane, Hammer observes, "It is as if Tate's combat with the Father had disclosed, on the other side of the coin, an exhilarating, erotically-charged bond with a brother" (58). I may not be contradicting Hammer when I suggest that Tate's search for "male comradeship" (58) was not unique to his relationship with Crane. On the whole, I see the soured relationship between the two poets somewhat differently, as one in which Tate endured as much pain as Crane. If one accepts Tate's view that Crane felt "a kind of personal betrayal" once he realized that Tate (who was a *Southerner* trying to reconstruct a nuclear family) was heterosexual, Tate's loss of a surrogate brother deserves as much sympathy as the pain Crane felt when Tate remained loyal to Eliot over him. True, Tate's suggestion to Morton Zabel that "homosexuals" suffered from "a malady" may reveal more than a simple acceptance of the destructive psychological interpretation of the era. It seems to me, however, that one can accept much of Hammer's argument without believing that Tate was insensitive to Crane's sexual preference as a matter of policy. Indeed, Stark Young and other friends of Tate who were gay (they would not, of course, have used this modern word to describe themselves) seemed to feel that Tate accepted them without judgment. To whatever degree sexual orientation governed the Tate-Crane relationship, I am extremely grateful to have found myself in discourse with Hammer, who is both a brilliant and a formidable critic of poetry. His learned book offers a thought-provoking critique of the conventional definition of Modernism and has helped me to make a number of emendations to my own, variant account of an important literary friendship.

168. Van Doren to Allen Tate, 13 February 1936, AT-PU, 43:8.
169. Tate to Davidson, 8 July 1925, DD-VU.
170. Handwritten sheet with tabulations in Tate's hand, "Earnings from reviews and articles in the years indicated, A.T.," AT-PU, 49.
171. Tate to Davidson, 2 April 1926, DD-VU.
172. Tate to Malcolm Cowley, 30 March 1926, MC-NL.
173. Tate to Davidson, 8 Dec. [1924], DD-VU.

174. Wills to Tate, 29 April [1926], AT-PU, Box 46.
175. Tate to Wilson, 4 Aug. 1926, EW-YU.
176. Eliot, *New Criterion*, to Tate, 22 June 1926, AT-PU, 19:53.
177. Tate to Davidson, 29 July 1926, DD-VU.
178. Cowley to Burke, 26 July 1926, *Selected Correspondence of Kenneth Burke and Malcolm Cowley, 1915–1981*, ed. Paul Jay (New York, 1988), 176.
179. Quoted in Waldron, 53.
180. Tate to Davidson, 8 July 1925 and 25 July 1925, DD-VU.

Chapter Five
God the Father and the South

1. Tate to Davidson, 1 Aug. 1931, DD-VU. I share Robert Brinkmeyer's observation that "southern writers eventually find something missing from their lives . . . the society of their childhoods, or at least their conception of that society as they interpret it as adults" (*Three Catholic Writers of the Modern South* [Jackson, Miss., 1985], xiii).
2. Quoted in *Surrealists*, 306.
3. Tate to Yvor Winters, 5 Feb. 1927, Hart Crane Collection., Banc, Mss. 74/134z, Courtesy of Bancroft Library, University of California at Berkeley.
4. Quoted in *Saddest*, 359.
5. *Surrealists*, 306–7; Tate to Josephson, 11 Jan. 1962, MJ-YU.
6. On Nov. 8, 1936, Tate wrote Stark Young, "I began the poem ten years ago next month" (SY-PM). I quote from what Tate called "the first typed copy" (courtesy of American Academy of Arts and Letters, New York City), which includes Tate's Bank Street address—and which was annotated by Ransom, Tate states in the appended note, "some time in December 1926." The *Ode* was first published in *The American Caravan: A Yearbook of American Literature*, ed. Van Wyck Brooks, Alfred Kreymborg, Lewis Mumford, and Paul Rosenfeld (New York, 1927), 792–94, and would change greatly over time. I have profited by reading the following discussions of the poem: Lawrence Kingsley, "The Texts of Allen Tate's 'Ode to the Confederate Dead,' " *Papers of the Bibliographical Society of America* 71 (1977): 171–89; David A. Hallman, "Donald Davidson, Allen Tate, and All Those Falling Leaves," *Georgia Review* 27 (Winter 1973): 550–59 (hereafter "Falling Leaves"); Thomas Daniel Young, "Introduction" to *The Fathers*-1977, xiii; and Lillian Feder's "Allen Tate's Use of Classical Literature," *Centennial Review* 4 (Winter 1960): 89–114.
7. Tate, "Narcissus As Narcissus," *Virginia Quarterly Review* 14 (Winter 1938): 108–122, 113, 111, 114.
8. Feder, "Allen Tate's Use of Classical Literature," 89–114, 103. I have found Feder's article helpful here and elsewhere; on an offprint of it, Tate

wrote a note to his daughter: "The best thing ever written about Daddo!" (AT-PU, IIc, Additional Correspondence).

9. Tate to Davidson, [12–24 April] 1928, DD-VU.
10. Tate to John Gould Fletcher, 31 May 1933, JGF-UAF.
11. Tate, *Ode to the Confederate Dead (1861–1865)*, *American Caravan: A Yearbook of American Literature*, 792–794, 794.
12. Here I quote from the final version (repr. in Tate, *The Swimmers and Other Poems* [New York, 1970], 17–20, 19–20.
13. Davidson to John Gould Fletcher [original held by VU], no date given, quoted in "Falling Leaves," 555.
14. Davidson to Tate, 15 Feb. 1927, AT-PU, AM 19629, 18:2.
15. Warren to Tate, 6 Feb. 1926 [apparently misdated], AT-PU, 44:28.
16. Here and below, I draw from Lytle, "A Journey South" *Kentucky Review* 1 (Spring 1980): 3–10.
17. Tate, "Distinguished Minor Poetry," *Nation* 122 (3 March 1926): 237–38.
18. Lytle, "Allen Tate: Upon the Occasion of His Sixtieth Birthday," *Sewanee Review* 67 (Oct.–Dec. 1959): 542–44, 542.
19. Tate to Davidson, 5 Sept. 1927, DD-VU; Lytle, "A Journey South," 4.
20. Lytle, "Allen Tate: Upon the Occasion of His Sixtieth Birthday," 542–44, 544.
21. Gordon to Sally Wood, [late winter 1928], *Mandarins*, 36.
22. Tate to James Southall Wilson, 23 May 1927, *VQR*-UVA.
23. Tate to Davidson, 31 May, 1927, DD-VU.
24. *Surrealists*, 306.
25. Tate to Yvor Winters, 14 March 1927, YW-STN.
26. Tate to Davidson, [12–24 April] 1928, DD-VU.
27. Tate, *Obituary in Memoriam: S.B.V. 1834–1909*, *The American Caravan: A Yearbook of American Literature*, ed. Van Wyck Brooks et al. (New York, 1927), 794; repr. in *Mr. Pope*, 7. See also Tate to Virginia Lyne Tunstall, 5 July 1926, VLT-UVA.
28. Tate to Varnell Tate, 26 March 1927, RVT.
29. Tate to Louise Bogan, 11 February 1927, LB-AC, IV:1.
30. Tate to Davidson, 5 Jan. 1927, DD-VU.
31. Tate to Varnell Tate, 26 March 1927, RVT.
32. Fletcher's diary is quoted in Ben Johnson, " 'A Strange and Lonely Figure': John Gould Fletcher and Southern Modernism," 40-page typescript, 18, a superb essay to which I am heavily indebted regarding Fletcher, his poetic career and theories, and his relationship with Tate. See also Tate to Davidson, 17 March 1927, DD-VU: and *War Within*, 239–40.
33. Tate to Davidson, 24 March 1927, DD-VU.
34. Tate to Fletcher, 24 Dec. 1927, JGF-UAF.
35. Tate to Wills, 1 June 1927, JW-VU.

36. Tate to Fletcher, 27 Aug. 1927, JGF-UAF; Tate to Davidson, 19 Jan. 1928, DD-VU.
37. Tate to Davidson, 1 March 1927, DD-VU. In the original letter, the second "was" appears as "which." I have silently corrected this error in my text.
38. Tate to Jesse E. Wills, 1 June 1927, JW-VU.
39. Tate to Armistead Gordon, 8 Feb. 1927, AG-VHS.
40. Tate to Virginia Lyne Tunstall, 4 June 1927, VLT-UVA.
41. Tate to Davidson, 26 Feb. 1928, DD-VU.
42. Tate to Fletcher, 20 July 1927, JGF-UAF.
43. Tate to Davidson, 17 July 1927, DD-VU.
44. Tate to Yvor Winters, 23 July 1927, YW-STN.
45. Tate to Davidson, 11 April 1928, DD-VU.
46. Tate to Davidson, 27 Nov. 1927, DD-VU.
47. Roy Bird Cook, *The Family and Early Life of Stonewall Jackson* (Richmond, Va., 1924); G. F. R. Henderson, *Stonewall Jackson and the American Civil War*, 2 vols. (London, 1898); Mary Anna Jackson, *Memoirs of Stonewall Jackson* (1891; repr., Louisville, Kentucky, 1895).
48. Clarence C. Buel and Robert U. Johnson, eds., *Battles and Leaders of the Civil War*, 4 vols. (New York, 1884–87).
49. Tate, *SJ:GS*, 321.
50. Unsigned review, *Bookman* 68 (Oct. 1928): xxxviii.
51. Tate to Davidson, 13 May 1927, DD-VU.
52. Emily Simms Bingham, "Where Are the Dead? Three Agrarians in Search of the Southern Past, 1920–1940" (senior thesis in history, Harvard University, 1987), 85. I draw throughout from Bingham, who analyzes Tate's published biographies on pp. 81–90 (hereafter "Where Are the Dead?"). In my discussion of Tate's *SJ:GS*, I have also appropriated ideas from Aaron-1975, 285–309; Max Webb, "The Self, Fortune, and Providence: Allen Tate on Stonewall Jackson," *Mississippi Quarterly* 30 (Spring 1977): 249–58; and Steve Davis, "Turning to the Immoderate Past: Allen Tate's *Stonewall Jackson*," *Mississippi Quarterly* 32 (Spring 1979): 241–53. I have also profited by Ferman Bishop's chapter, "Tate the Biographer," in *Allen Tate* (New York, 1967), 47–60.
53. *SJ:GS*, 214.
54. Tate to Davidson, 5 May 1927, DD-VU.
55. *SJ:GS*, 107.
56. Ibid., 25.
57. Tate to Fletcher, 24 December 1927, JGF-UAF.
58. Tate to Davidson, 28 April 1927, DD-VU.
59. Singal calls the biography "a psychological portrait of the sort of man Tate secretly wished he could be" (*War Within*, 240). Yet Tate's Jackson was much the man Tate already was.
60. *SJ:GS*, 282.

61. *SJ:GS*, 281, 10. As Bingham observes, "The similarity of this delusive cloud of former familial riches and glory to the one that hovered over Tate's childhood can hardly be missed" (Bingham, "Where Are The Dead?" 84).

62. *SJ:GS*, 48. Rubin did not need to know that Nellie Tate was born in Illinois to make a persuasive case that Tate's Jackson was affected by the disparity between his mother's attachment to Virginia's elite and the family's descent into shabby gentility (see *Wary Fugitives*, 68–69, 296–97.)

63. *SJ:GS*, 27.

64. Brickell, "The Literary Landscape," *North American Review* 225 (June 1928): [n.p.]; Daniel Robert Maué, "Each to His Hero," *Outlook* 149 (16 May 1928): 113.

65. Unsigned review, *Bookman* 68 (Oct. 1928): xxxviii.

66. Holden, "Stonewall Jackson," *Nation* 126 (23 May 1928): 593; Vernon, "Stonewall Jackson Appears among Us Moderns," *New Republic* 54 (16 May 1928): 404–5, 404.

67. William E. Dodd, "Old Jack," *New York Herald Tribune Books*, 22 April 1928, sec. 12 pp. 1–2, 2.

68. Dodd to Tate, 27 April 1928, AT-PU, AM 19629, 6:9.

69. Tate to Davidson, 11 April 1928, DD-VU.

70. Davidson, "Stonewall Jackson's Way," *Nashville Tennessean*, 29 April 1928, 7.

71. *SJ:GS*, 127.

72. Tate to Davidson [12–24 April 1928], DD-VU; Steve Davis, "Turning to the Immoderate Past: Allen Tate's *Stonewall Jackson*," 248–49.

73. Davidson, "Stonewall Jackson's Way," 7.

74. Tate to Fletcher, 25 February 1928, JGF-UAF.

75. Lytle, "A Journey South" *Kentucky Review* 1 (Spring 1980), 8.

76. Ibid., 8–9; Tate to Van Doren, 15 June 1928, MVD-CU.

77. Lytle, "A Journey South," 8.

78. Ibid., 8–9, 10.

79. Tate to Edmund Wilson, 9 Aug. 1928, EW-YU.

80. Tate to Malcolm Cowley, 10 July 1928, MC-NL.

81. Tate to Virginia Lyne Tunstall, 19 Aug. 1928, VLT-UVA.

82. Tate to Davidson, 1 March 1927, DD-VU.

83. Tate, "Poetry and the Absolute," *Sewanee Review* 35 (Jan. 1927): 41–52, 49, 50.

84. Putnam to Tate, 17 May 1927, AT-PU, 35:28. See Knickerbocker's "The Fugitives of Nashville," *Sewanee Review* 36 (April–June 1928): 211–24, 222.

85. Tate to Yvor Winters, 5 Feb. 1927, Hart Crane Collection, Banc. Mss. 74/1342, Courtesy of Bancroft Library, University of California at Berkeley.

86. *Surrealists*, 307.

87. Eliot, "Tradition and the Individual Talent," in *The Sacred Wood: Essays on Poetry and Criticism* (London, 1928), 47–59, 49; see also J. A. Bryant, Jr., Introduction to Lytle, "A Journey South," 3.
88. Tate to Davidson, 20 Feb. 1927, DD-VU.
89. I continue to profit, throughout this chapter, from *War Within*, 232–60; and O'Brien-1979, 136–61.
90. Tate to Davidson, 12 Aug. 1926, DD-VU.
91. Tate to Malcolm Cowley, 15 April 1929, MC-NL.
92. Tate to Edmund Wilson, 1 March 1928, EW-YU; *Causerie, Calendar of Modern Letters* 3 (Oct. 1926): 205–6; repr. as "Retroduction to American History," in *Mr. Pope*, 30–32. "Causerie II" was printed under the title *Causerie* in *transition* 3 (June 1927): 139–42.
93. Tate, Guggenheim Fellowship Application Form, 1928–29 (JSGMF).
94. Tate, *Causerie, transition* 3 (June 1927): 142, 141. Cook's discussion of *Causerie* is insightful ("Allen Tate in the Jazz Age," in *The Vanderbilt Tradition: Essays in Honor of Thomas Daniel Young*, ed. Mark Royden Winchell [Baton Rouge, La., 1991], 55–57).
95. Cowan-1959, 115.
96. Tate to Davidson, 17 Feb. [1927], DD-VU.
97. *Fugitives: An Anthology of Verse* (New York, 1928.)
98. Wilson, "The Tennessee Poets," *New Republic* 54 (7 March 1928): 103–4.
99. Tate, "American Poetry since 1920," *Bookman* 68 (Jan. 1929): 503–8.
100. *Mr. Pope and Other Poems* (New York: Minton, Balch and Co., 1928).
101. Eliot to Tate, 6 May 1927, AT-PU, 19:53.
102. Waldron, 61. I have used Waldron as a supplemental source for minor factual details throughout.
103. Tate to Davidson, 16 March 1928, DD-VU.
104. Editorial correspondence, Putnam's, AT-PU, AM 19629, 35:29.
105. Morton Zabel, "A Critic's Poetry," *Poetry: A Magazine of Verse* 33 (Feb. 1929): 281–84. Several years later, J. V. Cunningham said that *Mr. Pope* contained "outside of its four or five great poems, more bad poetry than any other volume of the century—but 'bad' through ambition, because, no matter how poor the writing was, the attitude was always the serious one of traditional morality" ("*Poems: 1928–1931*," *Bookman* 75 [April 1932]: 84).
106. Fletcher, "Fierce Latinity," *Nation* 128 (3 April 1929): 404–5.
107. Tate to Malcolm Cowley, 29 Aug. 1928, MC-NL.
108. Tate to Davidson, 1 April 1973 and 27 Nov. 1927; both in DD-VU.
109. Tate, Guggenheim Fellowship Application Form, 1928–29, dated 13 Dec. 1927 (JSGMF).
110. Tate to Virginia Lyne Tunstall, 14 Sept. 1928, VLT-UVA, Makowsky, 77. I also use Makowsky as a supplemental source for minor factual

details throughout. Jefferson Davis, *The Rise and Fall of the Confederate Government* appeared in 2 vols. (New York, 1881).

111. Tate to Andrew Lytle, 2 Oct. 1928, TDY-L, 12.
112. Gordon to Sally Wood, 8 Oct. 1928, *Mandarins*, 41–42; Tate to Edmund Wilson, 12 Nov. 1928, EW-YU; Tate to Mark Van Doren, 6 Nov. 1928, MVD-CU.
113. Tate, "American Poetry since 1920" appeared in *Bookman* 68 (Jan. 1929): 503–8. Tate was at work revising a very early version of the essay that appeared under the title "Emily Dickinson" in *Outlook* 149 (15 Aug. 1928): 621–623. The revised essay would eventually appear as "New England Culture and Emily Dickinson," *Symposium* 3 (April 1932): 206–26, and would be reprinted over the years as "Emily Dickinson."
114. Tate to Cowley, 23 May 1928, MC-NL.
115. Tate to Davidson, 24 October 1928, DD-VU.
116. Tate, "Introduction to a Reading of Poems by T. S. Eliot," U. of Minn., 15 Feb. 1965, 4-page typescript, AT-PU, 19:53.
117. Tate, "Foreword," *Selected Writings of Herbert Read* (London, 1963), 7.
118. Tate, "Inner Weather: Frost as Metaphysical Poet," 3-page handwritten MS, AT-PU, 1:20; apparently a draft of a lecture delivered at the Library of Congress on 26 March 1974; repr. as "Robert Frost as Metaphysical Poet," in *M&0*, 95–109.
119. Quoted in *M & 0*, 97.
120. Tate, "Introduction of Robert Frost At the U. of Minn., 1961," AT-PU, 1:6.
121. Tate to Davidson, 1 Aug. 1931, DD-VU.
122. Tate to Van Doren, 29 January 1929, MVD-CU.
123. Gordon to Josephine Herbst, [Fall 1929], JH-YU.
124. *The Official Records . . . War of the Rebellion : A Compilation of the Official Records of the Union and Confederate Armies*, 128 vols. (Washington, D.C., 1880–1901).
125. Tate, untitled typescript pages numbered 2, 3, and 4 at top (AT-PU, AM 19629, 1:11).
126. Tate to Virginia Lyne Tunstall, 15 April 1929, VLT-UVA.
127. Tate, "Miss Toklas' American Cake," *M&0*, 46–66, 48; page references here are to the repr. of the memoir in *M&0*, and not to its original publication in *Prose*, no. 3 (1971): 137–61. I have drawn from this memoir throughout.
128. Tate to Fletcher, 19 Oct. 1928, JGF-UAF.
129. Tate to Davidson, 12 Dec. 1929, DD-VU.
130. Tate, "Good Prose," *Nation* 122 (10 Feb. 1926): 160–62.
131. Tate, "The Spirituality of Roughnecks," *Nation* 123 (28 July 1926): 89–90.

132. Tate, "Hard-Boiled," *Nation* 123 (15 Dec. 1926): 642, 644.
133. Tate to Davidson, 12 Dec. 1929, DD-VU.
134. Tate to Carlos Baker, 2 April 1963, Gen. MSS [misc.] "TA-TAU": 23, Princeton University Library.
135. Tate to Arthur Mizener, 26 Aug. 1969, AM-VU.
136. Tate to Davidson, 12 Dec. 1929, DD-VU.
137. Tate to Carlos Baker, 2 April 1963, Gen. MSS [misc.] "TA-TAU": 23, Princeton University Library.
138. Tate, *The Pit*, typescript enclosed with Tate to Edmund Wilson, 22 Oct. 1929, EW-YU; later published as *The Cross*, *Saturday Review of Literature* 6 (18 Jan. 1930): 649; Tate to Wilson, 19 Nov. 1929, EW-YU.
139. Hemingway to Perkins, 21 Dec. 1926, *Hemingway: Selected*, 239.
140. Tate, "Hard-Boiled," *Nation* 123 (15 Dec. 1926): 642; Hemingway to Perkins, 14 Feb. 1927, *Hemingway: Selected*, 246.
141. Tate to Carlos Baker, 2 April 1963, Gen. MSS [misc.] "TA-TAU": 23, Princeton University Library.
142. Hemingway to Malcolm Cowley, 14 Nov. 1945; Hemingway to Perkins, 12 Aug. 1930 and 15 Dec. 1929, *Hemingway: Selected*, 605, 327, 316.
143. Tate to Carlos Baker, 2 April 1963, Gen. MSS [misc.] "TA-TAU": 23, Princeton University Library.
144. Tate, "Miss Toklas' American Cake," *M&O*, 60.
145. On Tate's friendship with Fitzgerald, I draw from James R. Mellow, *Invented Lives: F. Scott and Zelda Fitzgerald* (Boston, 1984), 332, 346–47, 350–51; Tate "Miss Toklas' American Cake," *M&O*, esp. 61–63 (for a variant account of Tate's interactions with Fitzgerald and Hemingway, see Matthew J. Bruccoli, "Interview with Allen Tate," *Fitzgerald/Hemingway Annual* [1974]: 101–13).
146. Tate, "Miss Toklas' American Cake," *M&O*, esp. 62.
147. Quoted in Mellow, *Invented Lives: F. Scott and Zelda Fitzgerald*, 347.
148. Tate, "Miss Toklas' American Cake," *M&O*, 62–63.
149. Ibid., 66; Tate to Carlos Baker, 2 April 1963 and 19 April 1963, Gen. MSS [misc.] "TA-TAU": 23, Princeton University Library.
150. André LeVot, *F. Scott Fitzgerald*, trans. by William Byron (Garden City, N.Y., 1983), 235.
151. Tate, "Miss Toklas' American Cake," *M&O*, 65.
152. Tate to Mark Van Doren, 29 January 1929, MVD-CU.
153. Tate to Carlos Baker, 19 April, 1963, Gen. MSS [misc.] "TA-TAU": 23, Princeton University Library.
154. Garry Mitchell, "Allen Tate Says Southern Writing Still Distinct," *Minneapolis Star*, 17 April 1974, 8C.
155. Tate, "Miss Toklas' American Cake," *M&O*, 55.
156. Jefferson Davis: His Rise and Fall (New York: Minton, Balch, and Company, 1929).
157. Tate to Davidson, 9 Nov. 1929, DD-VU.

158. *JD:R&F*, 303; William E. Dodd, *Jefferson Davis* (Philadelphia, 1907); Hamilton James Eckenrode, *Jefferson Davis: President of the South* (New York, 1923.)

159. Frank L. Owsley, *State Rights in the Confederacy* (Chicago, 1925); Tate to Owsley, 2 July 1928, FLO-VU; *JD:R&F*, 303, 305; Tate to Lytle, 5 July 1928, TDY-L, 11.

160. Chesnut, *A Diary from Dixie* (New York, 1906); Jones, *A Rebel War Clerk's Diary*, 2 vols. (Philadelphia, 1866; repr. ed. Howard Swiggett, New York; 1935); William E. Dodd, *The Cotton Kingdom: A Chronicle of the Old South* (New Haven, 1919.)

161. Tate to Davidson, 22 Oct. 1929, DD-VU; this letter and Waldron, 69, would suggest that Gordon wrote chapter 6, "The Confederacy Abroad" (*JD:R&F*, 154–76). I am grateful to Jonza, who shared her note on an undated letter from Gordon to Sally Wood (CG-PU) in which Gordon admitted: "I put the famous story about Aunt Emily marrying the young nigger to cut the stove wood, in the part of Allen's book that I wrote." Since that anecdote appears in chapter 8, "The People" (*JD:R&F*, 207–30, 214–15), Gordon evidently wrote that chapter as well. Gordon's third chapter remains a mystery.

162. See Tate to Lytle, 16 June 1929, TDY-L, 31–33, 31; Varina Howell Davis, *Jefferson Davis, Ex-President of the Confederate States of America: A Memoir by His Wife*, 2 vols. (New York, 1890).

163. Tate to Davidson, 9 Nov. 1929, DD-VU.

164. *JD:R&F*, 60, 80, 27, 5, 67, 7, 8, 12. Departing from an observation by Singal (*War Within*, 240), Bingham maintains, "Stonewall Jackson represents the unflinching Southerner, secure of his identity, Tate would have liked to be, while Jefferson Davis is the modern Southerner, unable to act decisively—the failure Tate feared he was" ("Where Are the Dead?" 90).

165. *JD:R&F*, 197, 148.

166. Allan Nevins, "Lincoln and Davis," *New Republic* 61 (15 Jan. 1930): 229–30.

167. Henry Steele Commager, "The Man and the Hour," *New York Herald Tribune Books*, 29 Sept. 1929, sec. p. 26.

168. Owsley, untitled review, *Mississippi Valley Historical Review* 16 (March 1930): 570–72.

169. Dr. Sam Small, "Jefferson Davis," *Atlanta Constitution*, 16 Feb. 1930 .

170. Mrs. [?] Patterson, *Books*, quoted by Tate in a letter to Mark Van Doren, 19 Nov. 1929, MVD-CU.

171. Warren to Tate, [Fall 1929], AT-PU, AM 19629, 44:28.

172. Charles Mercer, G. P. Putnam's Sons, to Tate, 12 March 1969, AT-PU, IIC, 7:10.

173. *SJ:GS*, 22, 188.

174. *JD:R&F*, 35, 37, 215.

175. Ibid., 39.
176. Madison Grant, *The Passing of The Great Race, or the Racial Basis of European History* (New York, 1916); Tate to Andrew Lytle, 1 April 1929, TDY-L, 21.
177. Ulrich Bonnell Phillips, *American Negro Slavery: A Survey of the Supply, Employment, and Control of Negro Labor as Determined by the Plantation Régime* (1918; repr., New. York, 1940). Tate, who listed both *American Negro Slavery* and Phillips's subsequent work, *Life and Labor in the Old South* (Boston, 1929), in the bibliography to *JD:R&F* (306), told Mark Van Doren, "If you want to see the sum of all evil in action, read Phillips' Life and Labor in the Old South" (Tate to Van Doren, 26 May 1929, MVD-CU). Shortly after making this comment, Tate wrote, "Professor Phillips' volume is one of the most distinguished additions to the new history, and in its particular field it is without an equal." From the book, Tate concluded that slaves' "condition was not different from that of other laboring classes except that it bore the stigma of a word hateful to the nineteenth century and that they were certain of care, often affectionate, to their graves" (Tate, "Life in the Old South," *New Republic* 59 [10 July 1929]: 211–12).
178. See, for example, David Brion Davis, "Slavery and the Post–World War II Historians," *Daedalus* 103 (1974): 1–16; and Carl N. Degler, "Why Historians Change Their Minds," *Pacific Historical Review* 45 (1976): 167–84.
179. Essays by Thomas R. Dew and William Harper appear in *The Pro-Slavery Argument* (Charleston, 1852), which appears in the bibliography to *JD:R&F*, 306 (although Michael O'Brien has warned me that Tate was not likely to have read Dew and Harper in the original); Tate to Davidson, 10 Aug. 1929, DD-VU; see also *JD:R&F*, 44–45.
180. George Fitzhugh, *Cannibals All! or, Slaves Without Masters* (Richmond, 1857; repr. Cambridge, Mass., 1960.) In 1930, Tate referred to Fitzhugh as a "brilliant but neglected writer," whose *Sociology for the South; or, The Failure of Free Society* (Richmond, Va., 1854) showed "that Marxism is only the extreme form of any Capitalistic Industrialism, a form that we are arriving at in this country" (Tate to Davidson, 9 Feb. 1930, DD-VU). For a discussion of the proslavery writers, see David Donald, "The Proslavery Argument Reconsidered," *Journal of Southern History* 37 (Feb. 1971): 3–18.
181. *SJ:GS*, 39, 291, 59.
182. *JD:R&F*, 55.
183. Anne Ward Amacher has shown that both Tate and Lytle drew heavily from the ideas of Calhoun and sometimes distorted his arguments to conform to their purposes; "Myths and Consequences: Calhoun and Some Nashville Agrarians," *South Atlantic Quarterly* 59 (Spring 1960): 251–64. Alexander Karanikas shows the influence of Calhoun and of

Christopher Hollis (*The American Heresy* [London, 1927]) on Tate's ideas about race; see *Tillers*, 28–30.

184. *SJ:GS*, 39.

185. *JD:R&F*, 72, 43.

186. Although Tate said he was "an abolitionist . . . at heart, and could not by any stretch of casuistry bring myself to own a slave," he also argued "that the end, agrarian rule, would justify the means, slavery, if no other means were at hand." Tate to Van Doren, 26 May 1929, MVD-CU.

187. *SJ:GS*, 25.

188. On Tate's reactions, I draw from Tate to Percy Wood, 9 March 1956, AT-PU, IIc, 10:IIa.

189. Tate to Lytle, 31 July 1929, TDY-L, 33.

190. Quoted in Waldron, 61.

191. *Mother and Son* appeared eventually in *New Republic* 64 (27 Aug. 1930): 42; Untermeyer to Tate, 21 Feb. 1929, AT-PU, 42:70; Essays, Misc., AT-PU, 1:11. Years later, Tate was angered by John L. Stewart's reading of *Mother and Son* in *The Burden of Time: The Fugitives and Agrarians* (Princeton, 1965), 314. "The inferences you draw from my Mother and Son about the character of my mother I find disconcerting," Tate wrote Stewart. "Even had she been a 'dominating woman,' I do not see how this would in any way aid the critic in elucidating the poem: the poem speaks for itself" (Tate to Stewart, 28 May 1965, JLS). Stewart, Tate elaborated to Louis Rubin, "infers from 'Sonnets of the Blood' and 'Mother and Son' that my mother was a 'dominating woman' who created tension in the family difficult for a sensitive boy to deal with. And from 'A Vision' he infers that my mother was 'proud of her ties with this group'—meaning Tidewater Virginia. I simply had to write him a letter of protest about this. What is his evidence for it? You know what Southern women of that generation were like: they took their family connection for granted." (Tate to Rubin, 4 June 1965, LDR-SHC). Although Tate also complained to Warren and Davidson about Stewart's reading (see Tate to Davidson, 29 May 1965, DD-VU; and Tate to Warren, 8 June 1965, RPW-YU), he would soon make similar criticisms of his mother in his aborted memoir.

Tate found Ferman Bishop's reading of the poem (in *Allen Tate* [New York, 1967], 93–96) much more satisfactory, and told Bishop, "Nobody before you has ever done much with Mother and Son, which I consider one of my best pieces. Your analysis has a rightness and precision that astonish me" (Tate to Ferman Bishop, 4 Jan. 1968, FB).

192. *Voyager*, 38–39.

193. Tate to Wilson, 2 April 1929, EW-YU.

194. Tate to Malcolm Cowley, 14 June 1929, MC-NL.

195. Tate to Fletcher, 24 Dec. 1927, JGF-UAF; Hollis, *The American Heresy* (London, 1927). Tate told Davidson that Hollis was "the ablest defender

the South has had since Dew, Harper, and Calhoun" (Tate to Davidson, 12–24 April 1928, DD-VU). In his bibliography to *JD:R&F,* Tate remarked, "In so far as the general point of view of this volume is not the author's—in so far as it is indebted to influences too minute or too remote to be acknowledged—it is that of a book called *The American Heresy,* by Christopher Hollis. The book is incomplete and inaccurately documented, but it is the first effort to comprehend the supposedly mixed forces of American history under a single idea" (*JD:R&F,* 303). On Hollis and Tate, I draw from Paul H. Buck's illuminating review essay, "American Heresies," *Hound & Horn* 6 (Jan.–March 1933): 357–67.
196. *JD:R&F,* 301.
197. Tate to Van Doren, 23 March 1929, MVD-CU.
198. Tate to Lytle, 4 May 1929, TDY-L 26.
199. Tate to Fletcher, 21 Nov. 1928, JGF-UAF.
200. Tate to Davidson, 18 Feb. 1929, DD-VU. Brinkmeyer argues that Tate deferred converting to Catholicism "in 1929, mainly because he came to see such a step as a repudiation of his . . . southern identity" (*Three Catholic Writers of the Modern South* [Jackson, 1985], 25). Rubin observes that Tate may have waited "because he realized that for him at this time it would be *only* a strategy, an intellectual act" (*Wary Fugitives,* 125).
201. On *The Cross,* first published in the *Saturday Review of Literature* 6 (18 Jan. 1930): 649, I have drawn from Richard J. O'Dea's "Allen Tate's 'The Cross,' " *Renascence: A Critical Journal of Letters* 18 (Spring 1966): 156–60; and from Charles C. Walcutt, "Tate's THE CROSS," *Explicator* 6 (March 1948): [41].
202. Tate to John Crowe Ransom, 27 July 1929, in DD-VU. Here and in subsequent chapters, I have profited from Leonard Greenbaum's discussion of humanism in *"The Hound & Horn": The History of a Literary Quarterly* (The Hague, 1966), 77–95.
203. Tate, "The Fallacy of Humanism," *Criterion* 8 (July 1929): 661–81, 678. Tate made revisions to the article for its inclusion in *The Critique of Humanism: A Symposium,* ed. G. Hartley Grattan (New York, 1930), 131–66.
204. Eliot to Tate, 5 March 1929, AT-PU, 19:53.
205. Tate to Edmund Wilson, 29 July 1929, EW-YU.
206. Tate to Davidson, 10 Aug. 1929, DD-VU.
207. Tate to Lytle, 31 July 1929, TDY-L, 33–34, 34.
208. Tate to Malcolm Cowley, 14 June 1929, MC-NL; Tate to John Crowe Ransom, 27 July 1929, in DD-VU.
209. Davidson to Tate, 29 Dec. 1929, AT-PU, 18:2.
210. Tate to Edmund Wilson, 29 July 1929, EW-YU.
211. *SJ:GS,* 56.
212. *JD:R&F,* 87.

213. Tate to Ransom, 27 July 1929, in DD-VU.
214. Tate to Fletcher, 5 March 1929, JGF-UAF.
215. Tate to Andrew Lytle, 31 July 1929, TDY-L, 34.
216. Tate to John Crowe Ransom, 27 July 1929, in DD-VU.

Chapter Six
An Agrarian and "the Brethren"

1. Gordon to Léonie Adams, [early 1930], LA-YU.
2. *Sewanee Review* 38 (Oct.–Dec. 1930): 479–83, 480.
3. Gordon to Armistead Gordon, 28 Sept. 1931, AG-VHS.
4. Tate to Cowley, 3 May 1930, MC-NL; Waldron, 81.
5. On Benfolly and Nellie Tate's possessions, see Gordon to Adams, undated, LA-YU; Tate to Cowley, 8 April and 3 May 1930, both in MC-NL; Gordon to Herbst, [n.d.] JH-YU; Tate to Untermeyer, 8 July 1930, LU-UD; and Tate to Wilson, 30 July 1930, EW-YU. I am also grateful to the owners of the estate, who gave me a tour in 1987.
6. Tate to Untermeyer, 8 July 1930, LU-UD.
7. Mark Van Doren to Tate, 14 Feb. 1931, AT-PU, 43:8.
8. Tate to John Gould Fletcher, 4 Nov. 1930, JGF-UAF.
9. Tate to Wilson, 30 July 1930, EW-YU.
10. Mrs. Ursula S. Beach, Clarksville, Tenn., to TAU, 3 Aug. 1987.
11. Tate to Davidson, 5 June 1930, DD-VU.
12. Tate to Davidson, 9 June 1930, DD-VU.
13. Tate to Davidson, 5 June 1930, DD-VU.
14. Throughout my discussion of the Agrarians, I have drawn heavily from *Southern Agrarians*; and, while I disagree with many of its conclusions, from *Tillers*. I also draw from Virginia J. Rock, "They Took Their Stand: The Emergence of the Southern Agrarians," *Prospects* 1 (1975): 205–95; and from William C. Harvard and Walter Sullivan, eds. *A Band of Prophets: The Vanderbilt Agrarians after Fifty Years* (Baton Rouge, La., 1982.)
15. William C. Havard, "The Politics of *ITMS,*" *Southern Review* 16 (Oct. 1980): 757–75, 760.
16. Tate to Donald Davidson, 3 Feb. 1930 and 5 July 1930, both in DD-VU.
17. Warren to Tate, 19 May 1930, AT-PU, 44:28.
18. Tate to Davidson, [late summer? 1930], DD-VU.
19. Tate, "Remarks on the Southern Religion," in Twelve Southerners (Donald Davidson, John Gould Fletcher, H. B. Kline, Lyle H. Lanier, Stark Young, Allen Tate, Andrew Nelson Lytle, H. C. Nixon, F. L. Owsley, John Crowe Ransom, John Donald Wade, and Robert Penn Warren), *I'll Take My Stand: The South and the Agrarian Tradition* (New York, 1930) reprinted, with an introduction by Louis D. Rubin, Jr., and biographical essays by Virginia Rock (Baton Rouge, 1977), 155.
20. *ITMS*, xxxvii, xxxix, xlii, xlvii, xxxix, xxxvii, xlvii, xlv.

21. Tate, "Remarks on the Southern Religion," *ITMS*, 155.
22. Tate to Davidson, 18 July 1930, DD-VU.
23. Tate, "Remarks on the Southern Religion," *ITMS*, 166, 167, 168, 174. For a useful explication of this essay, see O'Brien-1979, 147–49.
24. T. S. Eliot to Tate, 28 Oct. 1930, AT-PU, 19:53.
25. Mencken, "Uprising in the Confederacy," *American Mercury* 22 (March 1931): 380.
26. Tate, "Remarks on the Southern Religion," *ITMS*, 174; Tate to John Gould Fletcher, 3 Dec. 1930, JGF-UAF; Tate to Cowley, 19 Dec. 1930, MC-NL. Some years later, however, Tate told Cowley, "Only two readers of that essay in the past five years have seen the intention of that statement. It is irony. If the question were put otherwise: How shall the Southerner, along with you in New York, restore or create a dignified life for men, the answer would be (for me) by reviving the institution of property through the use, if necessary, of violence.—The irony lay in the fact that a tradition as such cannot motivate men. The desire for an improved life, in concrete terms, can motivate them violently" (Tate to Cowley, 26 April 1936, MC-NL). In his later years, Tate told Louis Rubin, "Except for the last two pages I'd like to 'repudiate' my essay in *ITMS*" (Tate to Rubin, 14 Nov. 1973, LDR-2). "I don't like your essay at all," Yvor Winters wrote Tate. "It seems to me that you took a terrifically long way around to something not very difficult to get down, and the end is obscure to me. By violence do you mean a reopening of the Civil War, an Evangelical campaign, or an act of the will? I could believe any one of you, and all three seem to me wholly impracticable" (Winters to Tate, 29 Dec. 1930, AT-PU, 46:17; Tate-Hecht, 13).
27. Tate and John Crowe Ransom to Stringfellow Barr, 20 Sept. 1930 [draft or copy], DD-VU.
28. Tate "To the Editor, *Macon Telegraph*" [29 November 1930, draft or copy], DD-VU.
29. Tate to Davidson, 27 Feb. 1930, DD-VU.
30. Stringfellow Barr, "Shall Slavery Come South?" *Virginia Quarterly Review* 6 (Oct. 1930): 481–494, 490, 488.
31. Stringfellow Barr to Michael F. Plunkett, 10 March 1975, Papers of the *Virginia Quarterly Review* (MSS 292-i), Special Collections Department, University of Virginia Library; Tate to Cowley, 19 Dec. 1930, MC-NL; Shapiro, "SA-HLM," 84, 91n; M. Thomas Inge, "Richmond's Great Debate: Agrarians Sought a Simpler Life," *Richmond Times-Dispatch*, 6 Dec. 1970; *Gentleman*, 217–23.
32. "*Memorandum of Organization*, Drawn up on Nov. 22, 1930, by five members of an Agrarian Party: Donald Davidson, Lyle H. Lanier, Andrew Nelson Lytle, John Crowe Ransom, and Allen Tate; at Nashville, Tenn.," AT-PU, 18:4.

33. Throughout this section, I have drawn from Aaron-1961; and Marshall Van Deusen, "Criticism in the Thirties: The Marxists and the New Critics," *Western Humanities Review* 17 (Winter 1963): 75–85.

34. Tate to Edmund Wilson, 24 Sept. 1925, EW-YU.

35. Edmund Wilson, *The American Jitters: A Year of the Slump* (New York, 1932), 307. For Tate's reaction to this book, see Tate to Wilson, 23 March 1932, EW-YU.

36. Tate to Edmund Wilson, 26 March 1932, EW-YU.

37. *The Ivory Tower* [carbon copy of MS version], with Tate to Mark Van Doren, 2 July 1934, MVD-CU; first published in *Mediterranean*; repr. in *Collected Poems*, 83–84.

38. Tate to Cowley, 19 Dec. 1930, MC-NL.

39. Lillian Symes, quoted in Aaron-1961, 347.

40. *Exile's Return: A Literary Odyssey of the 1920's* (1934; repr., New York, 1951). For Tate's indictment of *Exile's Return*, see Tate to Mark Van Doren, 2 July 1934, MVD-CU. I have also drawn from Cowley's *The Dream of the Golden Mountains: Remembering the 1930s* (New York, 1980.)

41. Tate to Horace Gregory, 7 Feb. 1933, HG-SYR. "For the purposes of poetry," Tate later told Cowley, "Communism *on principle* is no better than Mesmerism or Fourierism, or Hitlerism or Fascism or Agrarianism." Tate to Cowley, 9 May 1934, MC-NL. An excellent explication of Tate's anti-Marxist aesthetic is Richard H. Pells, *Radical Visions and American Dreams: Culture and Social Thought in the Depression Years* (New York, 1973), 184–86.

42. Tate to Donald Davidson and Robert Penn Warren, 10 Dec. 1931, DD-VU.

43. Tate to John Crowe Ransom, 17 Dec. 1931 [carbon], AT-PU, AM 19629, 6:14.

44. Tate to Josephine Herbst, 1 Nov. 1935, JH-YU.

45. Tate to Horace Gregory, 20 Dec. 1932, HG-SYR.

46. Wilson to Tate, 22 July 1936, AT-PU, 46:5.

47. Tate to Morton D. Zabel, 2 Feb. 1933, MDZ-CHI.

48. Tate to Edmund Wilson, 10 June 1933, EW-YU.

49. Tate to Cowley, 9 May 1934, MC-NL.

50. Tate, *Democratic Bulletin*, 31 Dec. [1931?], quoted by Isabell Howell in "Vanderbilt Books and Authors," *Vanderbilt Alumnus* 17 (Jan. 1932): 75.

51. Tate, MS of "Relief for the Unemployed," with Tate to Mark Van Doren, 20 Feb. 1931, MVD-CU. Later published as "The Problem of the Unemployed: A Modest Proposal," *American Review* 1 (May 1933): 129–49.

52. Tate to Malcolm Cowley, 26 April 1936, MC-NL.

53. Lytle to Tate, [June 1930], TDY-L, 38–40, 40n.

54. Tate to Donald Davidson, 9 Feb. 1930, DD-VU.

55. Tate to Edmund Wilson, 23 March 1932, EW-YU.

56. Tate to Horace Gregory, 7 Feb. 1933, HG-SYR.

57. Potter, "The Enigma of the South," *Yale Review* 51 (Oct. 1961): 142–51, 149.

58. Adrienne Monnier, quoted in Waldron, 119.

59. Eliot, "A Commentary," *Criterion* 10 (April 1931): 481–85, 485, 483–84.

60. Arthur Krock, "Industrialism and the Agrarian Tradition in the South: Two Forces Are at War for Control of the Future below the Mason and Dixon Line," *New York Times Book Review* 4 (Jan. 1931): 3.

61. Henry Hazlitt, "So Did King Canute," *Nation* 132 (14 Jan. 1931): 48–49.

62. Knickerbocker, "Back to the Hand [*sic*]," *Saturday Review of Literature* 7 (20 Dec. 1930): 467–68.

63. James I. Finney, "Southern Agrarians Protest Industrialism's Encroachment," unidentifed clipping from *Nashville Tennessean* [late 1930?], AT-PU.

64. Mencken, "Uprising in the Confederacy," *American Mercury* 22 (March 1931): 379–81.

65. Here and throughout, I am indebted here to Shapiro, "SA-HLM." Ultimately, Shapiro concludes, "Mencken and the Agrarians misunderstood each other" ("SA-HLM," 89).

66. Mencken, "The South Astir," *Virginia Quarterly Review* 11 (Jan. 1935): 47–60, 53, 57; Tate to Lambert Davis , 10 March 1935, *VQR*-UVA.

67. Wilson, "Tennessee Agrarians," *New Republic* 67 (29 July 1931): 279–81.

68. Tate to Wilson, 28 July 1930, [carbon] SY-PM; Tate to Robert Penn Warren, 16 Aug. [1931], RPW-YU.

69. Tate to Davidson, 17 Dec. 1931, DD-VU.

70. Tate to John Gould Fletcher, 3 Dec. 1930, JGF-UAF.

71. Tate to Donald Davidson, 10 Dec. 1932, DD-VU.

72. Tate to John Gould Fletcher, 3 Dec. 1930, JGF-UAF.

73. Tate to John Gould Fletcher, 4 Nov. 1930, JGF-UAF.

74. Tate to Malcolm Cowley, 19 Dec. 1930, MC-NL.

75. Tate, *The Twelve*, MS version with Tate to Louis Untermeyer, 11 January 1931, LU-UD; later published in *Adelphi* 2 (May 1931): 118; repr. in *Collected Poems*, 44.

76. *SJ:GS*, 227, 314, 285, 254, 272.

77. A. W. Vernon, "Stonewall Jackson among Us Moderns," *New Republic* 54 (16 May 1928): 404–5.

78. Tate, *JD:R&F*, 271, 62.

79. Tate to Lytle, 1 April 1929, TDY-L, 21.

80. Earle Balch to Tate, 28 May 1930, AT-PU, 35:29.

81. Tate to Davidson, 16 April 1931 and 14 July 1931, both in DD-VU.

82. See Tate to Will Ella [Smith?], 17 March 1931, Heard Library, Vanderbilt University, in which Tate expresses his desire to see "the vast tome on the Lee Family."

83. Tate to Davidson, 16 April 1931, DD-VU.

84. Tate to Bishop, [early June 1931], *Republic*, 33–37, 34, 36. Here I have drawn from Lewis Simpson, who observes, "The underlying rationale of Tate's biographical ventures, the . . . letter [to Bishop] suggests, was the establishment of the three great leaders of the Confederacy—Jackson, Davis, and Lee—as exemplary figures of a culture he had conceived in his search to find his own identity. . . . Establishing the exemplary figures of this culture was a way of establishing his own identity" (*Fable*, 32–33, 33). Kreyling, whose insightful work on the trajectory of Tate's work from the biographies to *The Fathers* Simpson endorses and amplifies, argues that Tate was annoyed that Lee, unlike Davis, seemed immune to the psychological effects of modernity. "The hero that Tate would eventually represent in his own life and work," Kreyling concludes, "would be an amalgam of the southern hero of the narrative tradition and the modern man of fragmentation" (103–24, 112). I would only add to the compelling remarks of both scholars that one should not lose sight of the fact that Tate interpreted his quest in concrete terms via the real lives of, and his actual relationship to, his own parents.

85. Tate to Lytle, 16 July 1931, TDY-L, 46.

86. Tate to Lytle, 31 July 1931, TDY-L, 49.

87. Balch to Tate, 24 July 1931 and 28 July 1931, AT-PU, 35:29.

88. Bibliographic references typed by Tate at the bottom of Henry Allen Moe [to Tate], 27 July 1931 (JSGMF). See also Balch to Tate, 28 July 1931, AT-PU, 35:29.

89. On Tate's autobiographical entanglement, I am indebted to Squires-1971, 127–28; Tate to Bishop, 19 Oct. 1932, *Republic*, 64–65. See also Kreyling, who defines Tate's withdrawal from the Lee project as the "discovery of an ideological abyss between himself and the font of southern heroic" (116–117, 116); and *Fable*, esp. 31–34. While Tate, Simpson observes, knew "that he could not accommodate Lee to the southern culture of failure," his Southern readers were expecting "a Lee who could be mounted on the pedestal formerly occupied by George Washington as a southern father figure. . . . The spiritual confederacy that arose after the military defeat of the South required another symbolic father, a hero of victory in defeat." Ultimately, Simpson concludes, "Tate was overwhelmed by his sensitivity to the problem of writing a life of Lee that would be at the same time his own self-biography and, so to speak, an autobiography of the South" (*Fable*, 33–34). Rubin advances the thesis that Tate abandoned the book because, of the three Southerners whose biographies he took on, only "Lee was a Virginian," a fact that caused

Tate to find his mother's Old South state wanting (*Wary Fugitives*, 296–99, 297).

90. Years later, a newspaper reporter asked Tate why the book appeared on a bibliography of his work issued by the Library of Congress. Tate replied, " 'I never finished it. . . . I was feeling very optimistic many years ago when I filled out the form for 'Who's Who' and said I did. I burned the manuscript many years ago. It was very poor' " (see Paul Sampson, "Poet Tate Admits He Padded Own Biography for No Rhyme or Reason," *Washington Post*, 13 Jan. 1959, clipping, Manuscript Division Library of Congress). It is unclear whether there was ever a full manuscript for Tate to destroy. Fifty-four pages of a manuscript survive at Princeton: "Unfinished biography of Robert E. Lee," AT-PU, 1B (hereafter referred to as *R.E.L.*).

91. Tate, *R.E.L.*, 27, 5, 10, 23, 19, 16.

92. Ibid., 8, 19, 35. "Apparently," Tate told Louis Rubin, "my mother got her elaborate name not because she was *blood* kin to the famous 'Nelly Custis,' but because *her* mother had, as a child, known Eleanor Parke Custis Lewis (d. 1850); her husband, Lawrence Lewis of 'Woodlawn,' was my grandmother's great-uncle; and Lawrence Lewis was Geo. Washington's nephew" (Tate to Rubin, 22 Jan. 1974, LDR-SHC).

93. Tate, *R.E.L.*, 29, 16, 30.

94. Ibid., unpaginated fragment.

95. Ibid., 31, 28.

96. Tate to Mark Van Doren, 23 March 1931, MVD-CU.

97. Tate to Donald Davidson, 16 April 1931, DD-VU.

98. Perkins to Tate, 9 July 1931, AT-PU, 38:58.

99. Tate to Warren, 9 Aug. 1931, RPW-YU.

100. Draft of Ulrich B. Phillips to Earle Balch, 25 Jan. 1932, with annotated note to Tate at bottom, AT-PU, 35:29.

101. Balch to Tate, 28 Jan. 1932, AT-PU, 35:29.

102. "Scribner's," Tate told Lytle, "have done sent me a check to do this new book on, but [Walter J.] Minton is being a dog in the manger—doesn't want the book himself and don't want anybody else to git [*sic*] it" (Tate to Lytle, 16 April 1932, TDY-L, 54–55); Lynn Carrick, G. P. Putnam's Sons, to Tate, 11 April 1932, AT-PU, 14:37.

103. Tate to Bishop, 11 Feb. 1932, JPB-PU, AM 79–31, 23:1; Balch to Tate, 28 Jan. 1932, AT-PU, 35:29 (see also Squires-1971, 128–29). Although I do not agree with Lewis Simpson's theory that Tate may have given up *Ancestors of Exile* because he was, unconsciously or otherwise, avoiding the issue of "miscegenation" (I argue instead that the genre of genealogy did not allow him to fully reconstruct—and thereby lay to rest—the biography of his own parents), I have found Simpson's discussion of "the autobiographical impulse" behind Tate's "family history" helpful (*Fable*, 34–38, 34).

104. Tate to Warren, 16 Aug. 1931, RPW-YU.
105. Throughout this section, I have freely appropriated from the brilliant readings in Robert S. Dupree's, *Allen Tate and the Augustinian Imagination: A Study of the Poetry* (Baton Rouge, La., 1983).
106. Tate to Mark Van Doren, 13 May 1931, MVD-CU; Tate, "Elegy," n. d., Essays: Miscellaneous, AT-PU, 1:11.
107. Tate, *Message from Abroad*, in *Three Poems* (New York, 1930); reprinted in *Collected Poems*, 40. Years later, Tate wrote that he "intended the 'red-faced man' to be a tidewater planter" (see Tate to Louis D. Rubin, 2 Feb. 1974, LDR-SHC).
108. Yvor Winters to Tate, 20 Jan. 1930, AT-PU, 46:17.
109. Tate to Virginia Lyne Tunstall, 23 March 1932, VLT-UVA; Tate, *Last Days of Alice*, *New Republic* 66 (13 May 1931): 354; reprinted in *Collected Poems*, 38.
110. Tate, *The Legacy*, early typescript version, MC-NL. A later typescript version is enclosed with Tate to Mark Van Doren, 29 April 1931, MVD-CU. Tate published the revised version of *Legacy*, together with a second poem, originally titled *Emblems II*, under the title *Emblems*, in *New Republic* 68 (30 Sept. 1931): 182. (A MS copy of *Emblems II* accompanies Tate to Mark Van Doren, 13 May 1931, MVD-CU.) The final version of *Emblems*, to which Tate added a third part (which he had previously published as *Pioneers* in *New Republic* 64 [24 Sept. 1930]: 152), first appeared in *Poems, 1928–1931* (New York, 1932) and is reprinted in *Collected Poems*, 36–37. My reading of *Emblems* also draws from David Schiff, *The Music of Elliott Carter* (New York, 1983), 84–88. Many years later, Elliott Carter would set *Emblems* to music after John Berryman told him about the poems.
111. Tate to Morton D. Zabel, 4 March 1932, MDZ-CHI.
112. Tate, *The Oath*, typescript of early version, with Tate to Louis Untermeyer, 11 Jan. 1931, LU-UD; first published in the *Virginia Quarterly Review* 7 (April 1931): 228, and repr. in *Collected Poems*, 43.
113. J. B. Roberts, "On Allen Tate's 'The Oath,' " *Comment: The University of Alabama Review* 4 (Spring 1966): 31–35, 35.
114. Memorandum prepared by Mr. Robert Varnell Tate for TAU, 4 Sept. 1989.
115. Tate, *Sonnets of the Blood*, published in a series titled "The Rooftree," *Poetry: A Magazine of Verse* 39 (Nov. 1931): 59–69, 62, 60; repr. in *Collected Poems*, 49–53.
116. Ben Tate quoted by Nancy Tate Wood, interview, 30 March 1987.
117. Tate, *Sonnets of the Blood, Poetry: A Magazine of Verse* 39 (Nov. 1931): 62–63. My discovery that Tate himself lied about his Kentucky birthplace and that his mother was born in Illinois complicates Rubin's reading of *Sonnets of the Blood* in which he observes that Tate, by admitting

Nellie's bloodline was tainted, had situated, for the first time, *"within the Virginia legacy the potentiality for disorder"* (*Wary Fugitives*, 302–4, 304).

118. Tate, *Sonnets of the Blood*, 65, 64.
119. Tate to Davidson, 1 Aug. 1931, DD-VU.
120. Gregory quoted in "Correspondence," *Poetry: A Magazine of Verse* 38 (April 1931): 51–53, 53.
121. Perkins to Tate, 27 June 1931, AT-PU, 38:58.
122. Perkins to Tate, 1 July 1931, AT-PU, 38:58
123. Dust jacket blurb, *Poems, 1928–1931* (New York, 1932).
124. Unsigned review under "New Books of Poetry," *New York Times Book Review*, 10 April 1932, p. 16.
125. William Rose Benét, "Round about Parnassus," *Saturday Review of Literature* 8 (23 April 1932): 685.
126. Eda Lou Walton, "Dry Hollows of the Mind," *Nation* 134 (4 May 1932): 519.
127. Davidson to Tate, 11 May 1931, AT-PU, 18:3.
128. Untermeyer, "Five Notable Poets," *Yale Review* 21 (June 1932): 811–17, 812, 813.
129. Yvor Winters, "Poets and Others," *Hound & Horn* 5 (July–Sept. 1932): 675–86, 676.
130. Louise Bogan, "Allen Tate's New Poems," *New Republic* 70 (30 March 1932): 186–187, 187. In her private notebook, Bogan wrote, "My thorough dislike for this particular book may sound like an obsession, but I am often confronted by people who cannot see what I mean when I condemn it as bad writing, bad thinking, bad approach and completely lacking in intuitive flow. . . . Allen stands for ideas, for philosophic bases, for moral values. . . . I shall never be able to understand how such fakery goes down with really sensitive people" (quoted by Elizabeth Frank, in *Louise Bogan: A Portrait* [New York, 1985], 149; also see 142, 372–74).
131. Tate to Louise Bogan, 29 March 1932, LB-AC, IV:1.
132. Tate to Morton D. Zabel, 16 August 1931, MDZ-CHI.
133. Tate quoted in *Living Authors: A Book of Biographies*, ed. "Dilly Tante" (New York, 1932), 401.
134. J. V. Cunningham, "The New Books," *Bookman* 75 (April 1932): 83–85, 83.
135. Morton Zabel, "The Creed of Memory," *Poetry: A Magazine of Verse* 40 (April 1932): 34–39, 37.
136. Yvor Winters, "Poets and Others," *Hound and Horn* 5 (July–Sept. 1932): 677, 679.
137. On the *Hound and Horn*, I have drawn from Frederick J. Hoffman, Charles Allen, and Carolyn F. Ulrich, *The Little Magazine* (Princeton,

1947), 206–10; from Bernard Bandler, *Hound and Horn*, to Tate, 11 Jan. 1932, AT-PU, 24:72; and (esp. regarding Tate's relationship to the magazine) from Leonard Greenbaum, *"The Hound & Horn": The History of a Literary Quarterly* (The Hague, 1966), esp. chapter 7.

138. Tate, "Comment: Editorial Note," *Poetry: A Magazine of Verse* 40 (Southern number, ed. Tate) (May 1932): 90.

139. Tate to Robert Penn Warren, 19 Jan. 1932, RPW-YU.

140. Quoted by Morton D. Zabel in a letter to Tate, 16 Jan. 1933, AT-PU, Box 47.

141. "Mr. Pound Replies to Mr. Tate," *Poetry: A Magazine of Verse* 41 (Jan. 1933): 231–32; Tate to Morton D. Zabel, 6 June 1932, MDZ-CHI.

142. Here I have drawn from Donald Davidson, "The Meaning of War: A Note on Allen Tate's 'To the Lacedemonians," *Southern Review* 1 (Summer 1965): 720–30; Tate to Lytle, 14 June 1932, TDY-L, 59–60.

143. Cleaton to Tate, 23 June 1932, AT-PU, 6:8; Tate, "To The Lacedemonians . . . *The old Confederate, on the Night before the Re-union, speaks, partly to himself, partly to Imaginary Comrades,*" early typescript version, with Tate to Mark Van Doren, 17 June 1932. The poem was first published in the *Richmond Times-Dispatch*, 21 June 1932, 1; repr. in *New Republic* 85 (8 Jan. 1936): 250; repr. in *Collected Poems*, 85–88.

144. Davidson, "The Meaning of War," 724.

145. Tate, *To The Lacedemonians*.

146. Throughout this chapter, and in this section especially, I continue to draw material from Waldron and from Makowsky.

147. Caroline Gordon Tate, John Simon Guggenheim Memorial Foundation Fellowship Application Form, 1931–32, submitted 12 Nov. 1930 (JSGMF).

148. Tate to Davidson, 1 Aug. 1931, DD-VU.

149. Conkin, *Southern Agrarians*, 94.

150. Quoted in A. Scott Berg, *Max Perkins: Editor of Genius* (New York, 1978), 207.

151. Ibid.; see also Tate to Armistead Gordon, [28 September 1931], AG-VHS.

152. Caroline Gordon Tate, John Simon Guggenheim Memorial Foundation Fellowship Application Form, 1932–33, submitted Oct. 28, 1931 (JSGMF).

153. Tate to Arthur Mizener, 3 Oct. 1968, AM-VU.

154. Tate to Don Davidson, 9 Oct. 1932, DD-VU.

155. In order to reconstruct this important day in Tate's life, I have drawn from: Tate to Andrew Lytle, 22 Aug. 1932, TDY-L, 62–64, 63–64; Tate to Frank MacShane [ca. 1961], quoted in MacShane to Tate, 2 May 1963, AT-PU, 29:12; and *Saddest*, 412–13.

156. Tate to Davidson, 9 Oct. 1932, DD-VU.

157. Tate to Lytle, 22 Aug. 1932, TDY-L, 62–64, 63.
158. Ibid, 64.
159. *Picnic at Cassis*, typescript version with Tate to Mark Van Doren, 6 Dec. 1932, MVD-CU; *Picnic by the Mediterranean*, typescript version with Tate to Louis Untermeyer, 28 Dec. 1932, LU-UD. In another account, Tate reports buying the book shortly *after* he wrote the poem. Tate to Bishop, 31 Oct. 1932, *Republic*, 68–69, 69.
160. *The Mediterranian, Yale Review* 22 (Spring 1933): 474–75; repr. in *Collected Poems*, 66–67.
161. R. K. Meiners, "A Reading of 'The Mediterranean,'" *University of Kansas City Review* 27 (Dec. 1960): 155–59, 155.
162. Tate, *Aeneas at Washington, Hound and Horn* 6 (April–June 1933): 445–46. See Lillian Feder's discussion of both this poem and *The Mediterranean* in "Allen Tate's Use of Classical Literature," *Centennial Review* 4 (Winter 1960): 93ff.
163. Tate to Morton D. Zabel, 3 October 1932, MDZ-CHI.
164. For the suicide discussion, Tate to Bishop, 26 Oct. 1932, Bishop to Tate, 2 Nov. 1932 and [Autumn 1932], and Tate to Bishop, 7 Nov. 1932, all in *Republic*, 67–71.
165. Bishop to Tate, [19–26 Oct. 1932], *Republic*, 65–66.
166. Tate to Lytle, 2 Nov. 1932, TDY-L, 69–71, 69.
167. "The Grey House." 19-page typescript with annotation in Tate's hand, "Final version, May 15, 1933," in Tate to Lincoln Kirstein, 17 May 1933, *H&H*-YU. See also Squires's excellent reading of the story in relationship to narrative style and characterization in *The Fathers* (Squires-1971, 130–33).
168. Tate to Lytle, 2 Nov. 1932, TDY-L, 69–70, 70.
169. Tate, "Note on 'The Migration' and 'The Immortal Woman,' with a Glance at Two Scenes in *The Fathers*," in *The Fathers*-1977, 311–14 (hereafter referred to as "Note"). Tate, "The Immortal Woman" [formerly titled "The Grey House"], *Hound & Horn* 6 (July–Sept. 1933): 592–609, 593, 603, 599, 609; repr. in *The Fathers*-1977, 351–70.
170. Tate, "Note," 312; Perkins to Tate, 24 Oct. 1932, AT-PU, 38:58.
171. Kirstein to Tate, 8 Dec. 1932, AT-PU, 24:72.
172. Tate to Mark Van Doren, 28 Jan. 1933, MVD-CU.
173. Tate to [Robert Penn Warren?], p. 2 of an undated [Dec. 1932] letter, RPW-YU.
174. Tate to Harriet Monroe, 10 Dec. 1932, PM-CHI.
175. Tate to Donald Davidson, 10 Dec. 1932, DD-VU.
176. Caroline Gordon to Henry Allen Moe, 2 Nov. 1932 (JSGMF).
177. Tate to Donald Davidson, 9 October 1932, DD-VU.
178. Gordon to Henry Allen Moe, 23 March 1933, JSGMF.
179. Tate to Mark Van Doren, 13 March 1933, MVD-CU.

180. Tate to Cowley, 22 April 1933, MC-NL.
181. Malcolm Cowley, "The Meriwether Connection," *Southern Review* 1 (Jan. 1965): 46–56, 46–47. I draw from this memoir throughout this section.
182. Gordon to Ford Madox Ford, [June? 1933], FMF-CNL.
183. Gordon to Sally Wood, 6 June 1933 [apparently misdated], *Mandarins*,143–47, 145.
184. Cowley quoted in Thomas Daniel Young, *Conversations with Malcolm Cowley* (Jackson, Miss., 1986), 195.
185. Cowley, "The Meriwether Connection," 46–56, 52.
186. Tate to Lincoln Kirstein, 30 April 1933, *H&H*-YU.
187. Cowley, "The Meriwether Connection," 46–56, 48.
188. Tate to Lytle, 2 June 1933, TDY-L, 82–84, 84.
189. Gordon to Sally Wood, 21 Aug. 1931, *Mandarins*, 84–86, 85.
190. Gordon to Sally Wood, [early autumn 1931], *Mandarins*, 86–90, 88.
191. Cowley, "The Meriwether Connection," 46–56, 51.
192. Ibid., 46–56, 52–53.
193. Tate to Ellen Glasgow, 24 May 1933, EG-UVA.
194. Tate to Mark Van Doren, 15 June 1933, MVD-CU.
195. Tate to Lytle, 2 June 1933, TDY-L, 82–84, 84.
196. Gordon to Ford Madox Ford, [June? 1933], FMF-CNL.
197. Gordon to Sally Wood, 6 June 1933 [apparently misdated], *Mandarins*, 143–47, 144.
198. Ibid.
199. I am grateful to have been able to supplement my own account of Tate's affair with Marion Henry with some material gleaned from Waldron, 94, 127–29; Makowsky, 118–21; and Jonza-ms., 200–205. My account quotes directly Tate's remarks on the affair.
200. Cowley, quoted by Makowsky, 120.
201. Tate to Lytle, 27 June 1933, TDY-L, 85–86.
202. Tate to Sally Wood Kohn, 1 Nov. 1945, Gen. MSS [misc.], TA-TAU, Folder 22, Princeton University Library.
203. Gordon to Sally Wood, 6 June 1933 [apparently misdated], *Mandarins*, 143–47; 143–44.
204. Jonza observes that "the greatest strain on their marriage resulted from Allen's increasing dislike of the Meriwethers, and his feeling that Caroline was becoming too immersed in their lives" (Jonza-ms., 201).
205. Tate to Gordon, 10 May 1954, CG-PU, 37:9, AM 20562.
206. Tate to Sally Wood Kohn, 22 Nov. 1945, Gen. MSS [misc.], TA-TAU, Folder 22, PU.
207. Gordon to Floyd C. Watkins, 27 July 1977, Watkins Papers, MS. 534, Special Collections Department, Robert W. Woodruff Library, Emory University.

208. Tate to Sally Wood Kohn, 31 March 1959, Gen. MSS [misc.] , TA-TAU, Folder 22, Princeton University Library.
209. Tate to Gordon, 18 Jan. 1958, AM 20562, 37:10, CG-PU.
210. Tate to Sally Wood Kohn, 1 Nov. 1945, Gen. MSS [misc.], TA-TAU, Folder 22, Princeton University Library.

Chapter Seven
Orphan of the South

1. Tate to Robert Penn Warren, 17 Oct. 1933, RPW-YU.
2. Tate to Morton D. Zabel, 20 Oct. 1933, MDZ-CHI.
3. Tate to Robert Penn Warren, 17 Oct. 1933, RPW-YU.
4. *The Fathers*, a prospectus printed by Minton, Balch and Co., 1933; including a blurb, flyleaf, title, and contents pages, foreword (dated 23 May 1933), and pp. 3–6 of chapter 2, "The Migration," 1757–1820. AT-PU, 1:14 (bookstore buyers were undoubtedly puzzled when the material accompanying the prospectus continued to refer to the book as "Legacy"). "THE FATHERS grows on me as the title for your book," Balch wrote. "I think its implications are good. Thank God we didn't use LEGACY if it conveyed to many people the idea it conveyed to you!" (Balch, Putnam's, to Tate, 13 June 1933, AT-PU, 35:29).
5. *The Fathers*, prospectus; Tate to Ellen Glasgow, 31 May 1933, EG-UVA. Despite errors and gaps in his account, Squires is still helpful about the evolution of the ancestor book and its relationship to "The Immortal Woman" and *The Fathers*, (Squires-1971, 128–33). Using it to support his speculations about Tate's reasons for dropping the ancestor book, Simpson sees Tate's new ideas for the book as fateful: "Once he allowed the mixing of bloodlines [the Scotch-Irish and the Tidewater] to become a theme . . . he had opened his story up to the most sensitive issue in southern culture, that of the blood relation between black and white" (*Fable*, 36–37). True, Tate was evading *something*—and he did take up the issue of "miscegenation" in *The Fathers*—but the changes he made at this stage may merely reflect his effort to document the union of his paternal (Scotch-Irish) and maternal (Tidewater) descent lines.
6. Tate, "The Migration," *Yale Review* 24 (Autumn 1934): 83–111, 105; reprinted in Tate, *The Fathers*-1977, 317–47.
7. Tate, *The Fathers*-1977, 311.
8. James Ross, *Life and Times of Elder Reuben Ross*, with an introduction and notes by J. M. Pendleton (Philadelphia, [1882]); see esp. 78–98. Danforth Ross, James Ross's great-grandson, explains, "Allen read this book while at Benfolly and particularly admired James Ross's style, which reflected his classical education and a simplicity of approach. He told me time and again that James Ross was one of the finest stylists America had produced and that *Life and Times* should be republished. He himself

wanted to edit the book but could not find a publisher. He did persuade Stark Young to include three excerpts in a *Southern Treasury of Life and Literature* (1937) [New York, 78–85] and grounded, not entirely without plagiarizing, an eighteen-page story, 'The Migration,' on the chapters narrating the Ross family's migration from North Carolina to Tennessee" (Danforth Ross, "Memories of Allen Tate," 15-page typescript, 13 March 1980, p. 3, copy courtesy of Mr. Ross). Gordon praised James Ross in a letter to Josephine Herbst, [1931], JH-YU. See also Gordon to Red and Cinina Warren, [August 1932], RPW-YU.

9. Tate to Helen McAfee, 22 Nov. 1933, *YR*-YU.

10. Tate to Merrill Moore, 24 Dec. 1933, MM-LOC.

11. Tate, *The Fathers* - 1977, 311.

12. Tate, "A Note on THE FATHERS by the Author," Essays: Misc., AT-PU, 1:11.

13. Tate to Andrew Lytle, 25 Oct. 1933 [misdated 1937], TDY-L, 116.

14. Tate to Morton D. Zabel, 27 Oct. 1933, MDZ-CHI.

15. Tate to Bishop, 30 Oct. 1933, JPB-PU, AM 79–31, 23:1.

16. Ibid.

17. I suggest this theory in response to the fleeting observation of Singal, who concludes Tate's rejection of the book after his father's death was "probably not coincidental" (*War Within*, 255). Rubin theorizes that the death was "of some significance" to "The Migration" (*Wary Fugitives*, 311).

18. For early typescript versions, see: Tate to Mark Van Doren, 6 Dec. 1932, MVD-CU; Tate to Virginia Lyne Tunstall, 14 Jan. 1933, VLT-UVA; and Tate to Morton D. Zabel, 11 April 1933, MDZ-CHI. First published in *New Verse* 2 (March 1933): 9–10; repr. in the *Hound and Horn* 7 (Oct.–Dec. 1933): 42; and in *Collected Poems*, 74. For a useful explication of this poem, see R. K. Meiners, "Tate's THE MEANING OF LIFE," *Explicator* 19, no. 62 (June 1961).

19. Tate, "THE MEANING OF DEATH (An After-Dinner Speech)," early typescript version in Tate to Mark Van Doren, 22 Dec. 1933, MVD-CU. First published in *The Magazine: A Journal of Contemporary Writing* 2 (Sept.–Oct. 1934): 80–81; repr. in *Collected Poems*, 75–76.

20. In Tate's later years, he claimed, "I gave up Lee for reasons Radcliffe Squires sets forth. . . . I came to *detest* him! And besides, Freeman had a monopoly on the 'materials' " (Tate to Louis D. Rubin, 24 Feb. 1975, LDR). It is not clear when Tate began to make this charge. Even in 1936, Balch had not lost hope that Tate would someday return to the Lee biography. "I am relieved also to hear that the LEE is still working itself around in the back of your mind and to have your explanation of why the delay, from the standpoint of adequate interpretation, was necessary. It would have helped me enormously to know this before; for instance, not until I read your letter did I realize that Freeman had cornered documents no one else had access to. Had I known this I should have felt much less mystified than I was. Now, after his monumental work, I can see the great

chance you have to do a work of superlative literary excellence that will be a real interpretation of Lee's character" (Balch to Tate, 19 May 1936, AT-PU, IIc, Box 1). A year later, the following account appeared in an unsigned magazine article: "When Allen Tate, critic and poet, had written most of a long-planned life of Robert E. Lee, Douglas Southall Freeman's four-volume, definitive *R.E. Lee* . . . appeared, blew his house down before the roof was on" ("After the Big Wind," *Time* 29 [1 March 1937]: 70,72; 70). A variant account of Tate's abandonment of the biography appears in Waldron, 132–33. In an intelligent explication of Tate's problems with the book, Bingham argues that Tate's abandonment of it was "closely linked to his struggle to defend Agrarianism" (see "Where Are the Dead?" 90–99). For a brilliant comparison of Freeman's flattering Lee to Tate's censorious rendering, see Kreyling, 103–24.

21. Tate, "The Definitive Lee," *New Republic* 81 (19 Dec. 1934): 171–172, 171.

22. Tate, "R. E. Lee Complete," *New Republic* 82 (10 April 1935): 255.

23. Tate to Davidson, 16 March 1965, DD-VU. Freeman was born only thirteen years before Tate's birth and was not elderly in the 1930s.

24. Tate to Herbert Agar, 9 Sept. 1933 [carbon copy], AT-PU, 6:14.

25. Tate to Davidson, 10 Dec. 1932, DD-VU.

26. Edward S. Shapiro demonstrates that while the Agrarians (Southern and otherwise) entertained the belief after the first and second FDR presidential wins that monopoly capitalism in America was finally going to be undone, they grew unhappy when they discovered that the New Deal liberals were not necessarily committed to this and other goals of Agrarianism. For this point, and on the Agrarians' evolving reactions to and strategies vis-à-vis FDR and the New Deal, I have drawn (in this chapter and subsequently) from Shapiro's impressive: "The Southern Agrarians and the Tennessee Valley Authority," *American Quarterly* 22 (Winter 1970): 791–806; "Decentralist Intellectuals and the New Deal," *Journal of American History* 58 (March 1972): 938–57 (which condenses Shapiro's Ph.D. dissertation, "The American Distributists and the New Deal," Harvard University 1968); "Catholic Agrarian Thought and the New Deal," *Catholic Historical Review* 65 (Oct. 1979): 583–99; and "American Conservative Intellectuals, the 1930s, and the Crisis of Ideology," *Modern Age: A Quarterly Review* 23 (Fall 1979): 370–80 (from which I learned much about the Agrarians and the *American Review*). I share neither Shapiro's conservative views nor all of his appraisals, but I admire greatly his careful historical scholarship and insight, as when he sketches out the ideological paradoxes of Agrarianism. He demonstrates that the Agrarian group, on the one hand, intended their "decentralist" (to use his terminology) ideas to remedy those of the New Deal collectivists. On the other hand, as he observes, their "criticisms of the New Deal for merely tinkering with capitalism and for failing to recognize the need for drastic reforms were

suprisingly similar to the complaints of collectivist individuals" ("Decentralist Intellectuals," 955–56). I also learned much during my work with Emily Bingham, coediting and introducing our forthcoming collection, *The Southern Agrarians and the New Deal: Essays after "I'll Take My Stand"* (Charlottesville, Va.).

27. Leonard Greenbaum, *The Hound & Horn: The History of a Literary Quarterly* (The Hague, 1966), 153. On the Agrarians' attempt and failure to make the *Hound & Horn* their mouthpiece, as well as on the humanism and Shafer episodes, I have again found Greenbaum useful, particularly chapters 7 and 5. In December 1933, Tate would resign formally as Southern editor for the *Hound & Horn* (see esp. 154–58).

28. As Albert E. Stone, Jr., observes, "the Southern Agrarians needed a national sounding board for their economic and political doctrines; the *Southern* and *Sewanee Reviews* were chiefly literary organs and could not reach the audience Collins was in touch with." See Stone's "Seward Collins and the *American Review*: Experiment in Pro-Fascism, 1933–1937," *American Quarterly* 12 (Spring 1960): 3–19, 13. On the Agrarians' involvement with the Fascist Collins, with Collins's *American Review*, and with Herbert Agar, I have throughout chapters 7 and 8 drawn much from this article by Stone and from Shapiro's "American Conservative Intellectuals." Although Shapiro could have discussed even more fully the implications of the Agrarians' failure to separate themselves at the outset from Collins's Fascist views—views that, Shapiro shows, were evident almost immediately (see "American Conservative Intellectuals," 379n–380n)— he nevertheless makes a strong case for the argument that a reaction to capitalism and not dreams of a Fascist state in America propelled the Agrarian program. "In truth," Shapiro concludes, "the Agrarians were anti-fascist as well as radical critics of the New Deal. When they criticized the New Deal it was for failing to move more vigorously against high finance and big business, and for neglecting the small businessman and the small farmer" ("Southern Agrarians and the Tennessee Valley Authority," 805). Both Stone ("Seward Collins," 13–14) and Shapiro ("The American Distributists," 54) make the point that Agrarian and Fascist tenets differed in critical areas.

29. Unsigned, "The Embattled Humanists," *New Republic* 61 (12 Feb. 1930): 315.

30. Seward Collins to Robert Shafer, 26 Nov. 1929 [carbon], SC-YU.

31. Robert Shafer, "Humanism and Impudence," *Bookman* (Jan. 1930): 1–10, 10, 8. See also Greenbaum, "*Hound & Horn*," 88ff. & 128–29.

32. Collins to Shafer, 26 Nov. 1929 [carbon], SC-YU.

33. Tate to Seward Collins, 25 Jan. 1930, SC-YU.

34. Tate to William Skinkle Knickerbocker, 29 Jan. 1930, William S. Knickerbocker Papers, Rare Book and Manuscript Library, Columbia University.

35. Tate to Seward Collins, 22 Jan. 1930, SC-YU.

36. Yvor Winters to Tate, 23 Jan. 1930, 46:17, AT-PU.
37. Lyle Lanier to Tate, 25 Jan. 1930, 27:8, AT-PU.
38. Ben E. Tate [Allen Tate] to Robert Shafer, 27 Jan. 1930 (typescript copy), SC-YU; see also Allen Tate to Ben Tate, 23 Jan. 1930, 7:10, AT-PU.
39. "I.M.B.," 3-page typescript, dated 29 Jan. 1930, and titled, "QUESTION: Whether the article by Robert Shafer on Humanism and Impudence is actionable libel," SC-YU.
40. Tate, "The Same Fallacy of Humanism: A Reply to Mr. Robert Shafer," and Shafer, "In Wandering Mazes Lost," both in *Bookman* 71 (March 1930): 31–36, 37–39; Allen Tate to Ben Tate [carbon], 4 Feb. 1930, 7:10, AT-PU.
41. Seward Collins, "Criticism In America: II, The Revival of the Anti-Humanist Myth," *Bookman* 71 (July 1930): 400–415, 403.
42. Caroline Gordon to Ford Madox Ford, [Dec. 1931], FMF-CNL.
43. See Shapiro, "American Conservative Intellectuals," 370.
44. Tate to Donald Davidson, [late summer or fall 1930], DD-VU; see also Tate to Bernard Bandler, 5 Feb. 1930, *H&H*-YU.
45. Tate to Davidson, 14 March 1933, DD-VU.
46. Tate to Collins, 26 March 1933, SC-YU. On the Action Française, see Eugen Weber, *Action Française: Royalism and Reaction in Twentieth-Century France* (Stanford, Calif., 1962); and Paul Mazgaj, *The Action Française and Revolutionary Syndicalism* (Chapel Hill, N.C., 1979).
47. Caroline Gordon to Janice Biala, [April 1933], FMF-CNL.
48. Tate to Davidson, 8 April 1933, DD-VU.
49. G. K. Chesterton, *The Outline of Sanity* (1926; repr., New York, 1927), 145. Tate had apparently read both this book and Hilaire Belloc's *The Servile State* (1912). Tate to Collins, 14 April 1933, SC-YU. On Distributism, I have drawn from an excellent study by Jay P. Corrin, *G. K. Chesterton and Hilaire Belloc: The Battle against Modernity* (Athens and London, 1981). Corrin, who shows how the movement became increasingly tainted by Fascism and anti-Semitism, also charts the Distributist presence in the *American Review* and reports on Collins's early support of Fascist ideas and authors.
50. Tate to Collins, 5 April 1933, SC-YU; Dan T. Carter, *Scottsboro: A Tragedy of the American South*, rev. ed. (Baton Rouge, La., 1979); see also James Goodman, *Stories of Scottsboro* (New York, 1994).
51. Tate to John Peale Bishop, 5 May 1933, AM 79–31, 23:1, JPB-PU. On Collins's anti-Semitism, see Stone, "Seward Collins," 11–12.
52. "Editorial Notes," *American Review* 1 (April 1933): 122–27, 125–27; see also Corrin, *Chesterton and Belloc*, 163.
53. Tate to Collins, 14 April 1933, SC-YU.
54. Tate published a total of five essays and two book reviews in the *American Review*.

55. "The Problem of the Unemployed: A Modest Proposal," *American Review* 1 (May 1933): 129–49, 147–48.
56. Tate to Davidson, 8 April 1933, DD-VU.
57. Tate to John G. Fletcher, 19 Jan. 1934, JGF-UAF.
58. See Marion D. Irish's (now-dated) article, "Proposed Roads to the New South, 1941: Chapel Hill Planners vs. Nashville Agrarians," *Sewanee Review* 49 (Jan.–March 1941): 1–27.
59. The most incisive discussion of these Southern liberals (a discussion to which I am indebted) is contained in *War Within*.
60. Tate to Eugene F. Saxton, [carbon copy], 17 Nov. 1933, VU.
61. Although Tate thought H. C. Nixon's contribution "one of the best essays in the book" ("A View of the Whole South," review of *Culture in the South*, ed. W. T. Couch, *American Review* 2 [Feb. 1934]: 414), tensions were developing between Nixon and the rest of the Agrarians, who were distressed by his growing interest in collectivism and other measures associated with New Deal liberals. Nixon would soon be virtually indistinguishable from the Chapel Hill Planners; see Sarah Newman Shouse's marvelous biography, *Hillbilly Realist: Herman Clarence Nixon of Possum Trot* (University, Ala., 1986.)
62. W. T. Couch, ed. *Culture in the South* (Chapel Hill, N.C., 1934), vii–xi, vii, viii.
63. Tate, "A View of the Whole South," 411–32; 411, 421, 422, 429, 432. Couch replied to Tate in "An Agrarian Programme for the South," *American Review* 3 (Summer 1934): 319–26.
64. W. T. Couch, "The Negro in the South," in Couch, *Culture in the South*, 432–77. David M. Potter has made the compelling observation that the Chapel Hill Planners did not, as many assume, greatly aid the cause of African Americans in the South: "Like the doctrinal agrarians with whom they disagreed, they presented an image of the South which emphasized the plight of farmers rather than the plight of Negroes" (*The South and the Sectional Conflict* [Baton Rouge, La., 1968], 8).
65. Tate, "A View of the Whole South," 424.
66. Ibid., 426; Tate was responding to "The Pattern of Violence," H. C. Brearley's entry in Couch, *Culture in the South*, 678–92.
67. Tate, "A View of the Whole South," 424–25.
68. Seward Collins, "Editorial Notes: The Revival of Monarchy,"*American Review* 1 (May 1933): 243–56, 246–48, 253; Collins, "Editorial Notes: *The American Review's* First Year," *American Review* 3 (April 1934): 118–28, 124; Shapiro, "American Conservative Intellectuals," 379n–380n; Corrin, *Chesterton and . . . Belloc*, 163, 180. On Seward Collins's anti-Semitism, see also Stone, "Seward Collins," pp. 11–12.
69. Susan V. Donaldson argues that the model Tate created "of the modern southern writer" was "white, male [and] conservative"—thus producing "a southern literary canon cast largely in the self-image of the Fugitive-

Agrarians" ("Gender, Race, and Allen Tate's Profession of Letters in the South," in *Haunted Bodies: Gender and Southern Texts*, ed. Anne Goodwyn Jones and Susan V. Donaldson [Charlottesville, Va., 1997], 492–518, 506).

70. George Core makes an important point about Tate's long-term contribution as editor and critic to all Southern writers: "More than any other writer but William Faulkner, Tate made it possible for the Southern renascence to have an informed critical reception" (see "Mr. Tate and the Limits of Poetry," *Virginia Quarterly Review* 62 [Winter 1986]: 106).

71. Tate, "A Southern Mode of the Imagination," repr. in *Collected Essays* (Denver, 1959), 554–68, 554.

72. Tate, "Faulkner's *Sanctuary* and the Southern Myth," 1968; repr. in *M&O*, 144–54, 146.

73. See Tate, "The Lost Poet of Georgia," review of *Thomas Holly Chivers: Friend of Poe*, by S. Foster Damon, *New Republic* 63 (23 July 1930): 294–95.

74. Tate, "A Southern Romantic," review of *Sidney Lanier*, by Aubrey H. Starke. *New Republic* 76 (30 Aug. 1933): 67–70. Starke, a Harvard professor fiercely committed to Lanier's poetry, fought back. He first sent a sarcastic rejoinder to the letters column of the *New Republic* (A. H. Starke, "More about Lanier," *New Republic* 76 [1 Nov. 1933]: 337–38). Tate's equally sarcastic reply appeared below Starke's letter. Starke then wrote "The Agrarians Deny a Leader," a defense of Lanier intended for the approving eyes of the United Daughters of the Confederacy (see "From Massachusetts to Nashville 'Inkpot Storm' Rages over Poet Lanier," *Nashville Tennessean*, 16 March 1934). Years later, however, Tate continued to insist that "Lanier was a windbag" (Tate-Forsyth et al., 9).

75. Tate, "Regionalism and Sectionalism," *New Republic* 69 (23 Dec. 1931): 159. Before Tate's Southern conversion, he wrote much more favorably of Heyward; see "DuBose Heyward Proves Looked for Interpreter in 'Sky lines and Horizons,' " *Nashville Tennessean*, 20 April 1924.

76. Tate, "Mr. Hibbard and Col. Telfair." review of *The Lyric South*, ed. Addison Hibbard, *Herald-Tribune*, 16 Sept. 1928, 13.

77. Tate, "Negro Poet Depicts Simple Life of Race," review of *Cane*, by Jean Toomer, *Nashville Tennessean*, 24 Feb. 1924; "New Authology [*sic*] Gives Verse of Negro Writers," review of *An Anthology of Negro Poetry*, ed. Newman Ivey White and Walter Clinton Jackson, *Nashville Tennessean*, 3 Aug. 1924. On Tate's attempt to write African American writers out of the Southern Literary Renaissance, see Donaldson, "Gender, Race, and Allen Tate's Profession," esp. 493, 499, 505.

78. Tate, "Faulkner's *Sanctuary* and the Southern Myth," 147.

79. Tate to Malcolm Cowley, 6 Dec. 1944, MC-NL.

80. Tate to Malcolm Cowley, 2 June 1966, MC-NL; Tate, "A Southern Mode of the Imagination," 556.

81. Tate to Davidson, 26 June 1926, DD-VU.
82. Tate, "T. S. Stribling," review of *Unfinished Cathedral*, by T. S. Stribling, *Nation* 138 (20 June 1934): 709–10, 709.
83. Tate, "Faulkner's *Sanctuary* and the Southern Myth," 146.
84. Tate to Davidson, 12 Dec. 1929, DD-VU. Donaldson argues that "it was in the name of [a] unified white male sensibility that Tate . . . excoriate[d] . . . Glasgow and James Branch Cabell" ("Gender, Race, and Allen Tate's Profession," 504). On the Tate-Glasgow relationship, I draw from two talented critics who are in disagreement. Ellen M. Caldwell has argued that "the influence of Allen Tate encouraged Glasgow in mid-career to look again at the richness of her own literary tradition and, ultimately, to take her stand with the Southern Agrarians"; ("Ellen Glasgow and the Southern Agrarians," *American Literature* 56 [May 1984]: 203–13, 203–4). In contrast, Ritchie D. Watson, Jr., of Randolph-Macon College, argues that: "In spite of Caldwell's forcefully argued thesis, the extent of Allen Tate's influence on Glasgow's literary development and, indeed, the extent of her conversion to Agrarian principles remains debatable" ("Ellen Glasgow, the Nashville Agrarians, and the Glasgow–Allen Tate Correspondence," 19-page typescript, copy courtesy of author).
85. Tate, "Mr. Cabell's Farewell," review of *The Way of Ecben*, by James Branch Cabell, *New Republic* 61 (8 Jan. 1930): 201–2. Years earlier, before his Agrarian phase, Tate wrote of "the profoundly serious comedy of James Branch Cabell"; Tate, "Cabell's New Book Is Bitterness Overtone in His Ironic Symphony," review of *The High Place*, by James Branch Cabell, Nashville *Tennessean*, 16 March 1924.
86. Tate to Lincoln Kirstein, 6 Feb. 1933, *H&H*-YU.
87. Tate to Malcolm Cowley, 7 March 1945, MC-NL.
88. Tate to the editor of *North American Review*, 21 March 1939 [carbon copy], DD-VU; see Tate's remarks on *God's Little Acre* in "Techniques of Fiction," *Sewanee Review* 52 (April–June 1944): 210–25, 214.
89. Tate-McDonnell, 35.
90. Ibid., 36.
91. Tate to the editor of *North American Review*.
92. Tate to Arthur Mizener, 15 June 1971, AM-VU.
93. Tate-Forsyth et al., 12.
94. Along with Malcolm Cowley, Tate became an important promoter of Faulkner's work (see Tate, "William Faulkner, 1897–1962," 1962; repr. in *M&O*, 82–86). Although I find fault with some of Lawrence H. Schwartz's conclusions, and question in particular his downplaying of Tate's pre–World War II appreciation for Faulkner, Schwartz has written an important book entitled, *Creating Faulkner's Reputation: The Politics of Modern Literary Criticism* (Knoxville, Tenn., 1988.)
95. Tate to Davidson, 12 Dec. 1929, DD-VU.

96. Tate, "The New Provincialism: With an Epilogue on the Southern Novel," 1945; repr. in *EFD*, 535–46, 545.

97. Tate, "A New Star," review of *Flowering Judas*, by Katherine Anne Porter, *Nation* 131 (1 Oct. 1930): 352–53.

98. Eugene Warner, "South Is U.S. Literary Center, Asserts Allen Tate, Noted Poet," *Washington Post*, 5 Jan. 1937, 13.

99. Caroline Gordon to Sally Wood, [Spring 1935], repr. *Mandarins*, 182–87, 185. Tate discusses the conference in a letter to Stark Young dated 14 April 1935, SY-PM.

100. Tate to James Southall Wilson, 4 Sept. 1931, *VQR*-UVA.

101. Gordon to Léonie Adams, [late Oct. 1931], LA-YU; Tate to Mark Van Doren, 29 Oct. 1931, MVD-CU.

102. Gordon to Ford, Madox Ford, [Dec.? 1931], FMF-CNL.

103. Anderson to Laura Lou Copenhaver, 24 Oct. 1931, in *Letters of Sherwood Anderson*, ed. Howard Mumford Jones in association with Walter B. Rideout (Boston, 1953), 250–53. On the conference, I am indebted in part to Joseph Blotner's magisterial, *Faulkner: A Biography*, vol. 1 (New York, 1974), 705–16, although I do not believe that the event was quite as successful as Professor Blotner has it. It was in my judgment a misstatement when Emily Clark observed afterward that the conferees "learned to like one another's personalities so well that they resolved henceforth to tolerate their books" (quoted in Watson, p. 4).

104. Tate to Virginia Lyne Tunstall, 23 March 1932, VLT-UVA.

105. On the contradictory relationships among Southern writers, I am indebted to David Herbert Donald, *Look Homeward: A Life of Thomas Wolfe* (Boston, 1987), 359–62.

106. Tate to Virginia Lyne Tunstall, 31 Oct. 1931, VLT-UVA; Gordon to Léonie Adams [late Oct. 1931], LA-YU. Watson writes that while Glasgow and Tate achieved an "instantaneous personal rapport" at the conference, before meeting "they probably had no desire to know each other or to make more than the most superficial of social exchanges." Watson also correctly observes that, after the conference, one could see in their letters "a clearly detectable element of mutual ego-stroking" (Watson, "Ellen Glasgow, 3, 7).

107. Tate to Mark Van Doren, 29 Oct. 1931, MVD-CU.

108. Stingfellow Barr to Plunkett, 10 March 1975, UVA; Tate to Van Doren, 29 Oct. 1931, MVD-CU; Gordon to Léonie Adams, [late Oct. 1931] and [late 1931], both in LA-YU.

109. Tate, "Regionalism and Sectionalism," *New Republic* 69 (23 Dec. 1931): 158–61; Tate explained to James Southall Wilson, "I believe we should have regionalism for literature, but sectionalism in politics; they are different methods of getting at the same ends. A consciously sectional politics alone will tend to preserve the regional situation that writers must have in order to do their best work: politics is inevitably abstract while

literature must be concrete and pursued unconsciously" (Tate to Wilson, 29 Oct. 1931, *VQR*-UVA). In his introduction to *Sanctuary*, Tate wrote, "Faulkner, in a letter to [Malcolm] Cowley while Cowley was getting together the *Portable Faulkner*, said that he was not conscious of a legend. That was as it should be if the legend was to be imaginatively effective. For it was more than a legend, it was a myth; and it was every Southerner's myth from 1865 to about 1940, or up to World War II" (150–51). Like Tate, T. S. Eliot maintained "that a *tradition* is rather a way of feeling and acting which characterises a group throughout generations; and that it must largely be, or that many of the elements in it must be, unconscious" (*After Strange Gods: A Primer of Modern Heresy*: *The Page-Barbour Lectures at the University of Virginia.*, 1933 [New York, 1934], 31.) I am indebted to Singal's insightful and contextualizing discussion of the paradoxes built into Tate's intellectual worldview (see *War Within*, esp. 247–54).

110. Tate, "The Cornfield Journalist," review of *Joel Chandler Harris, Editor and Essayist*, ed. Julia Collier Harris, *New Republic* 71 (3 Aug. 1932): 320–21, 320.

111. Tate to Lambert Davis, 24 Oct. 1934, *VQR*-UVA.

112. Tate, "The Profession of Letters in the South," *Virginia Quarterly Review* 11 (April 1935): 161–176, 165, 173, 175–76. Donaldson observes, "If Tate yearned, in this essay and elsewhere, to find an image of what he thought of as the ideal southern tradition *and* writer—white, male, conservative, rooted to time and place, and unified in sensibility—he nonetheless had the integrity to acknowledge, albeit with very bad grace, the possibility that such an image would always prove chimerical or, at the very least, radically unstable" ("Gender, Race, and Allen Tate's Profession," 493).

113. Tate, "Faulkner's *Sanctuary* and the Southern Myth," 149.

114. Tate-Forsyth et al., 11.

115. Tate-Millgate, 33.

116. Tate, "The New Provincialism, *EFD*, 535–546, 545.

117. Tate, "A Southern Mode of the Imagination," repr. in *Collected Essays* (Denver, 1959), 554–568, 560, 568, 567. For Tate on Faulkner's interior monologues, see Tate to Andrew Lytle, 4 Dec. 1954, TDY-L, 237–39, 238.

118. Gordon to Sally Wood, 22 May 1934, repr. *Mandarins*, 164–65, 164.

119. Ibid., 164–65; Tate to John Peale Bishop, 4 June 1934, JPB-PU, AM 79–31, 23:1; Tate-Broughton, 324; Tate to Mark Van Doren, 9 May 1934, MVD-CU.

120. On Southwestern, I have drawn from: Waller Raymond Cooper, *Southwestern at Memphis, 1848–1948* (Richmond, Va., 1949), 114–40; James E. Roper, *Southwestern at Memphis, 1948–1975* (Memphis,

1975), 2; "The Faculty of Southwestern: Christian Teachers in a Christian College," *Southwestern Bulletin* 21 (Sept. 1934): 3–21, 4.

121. "The Faculty of Southwestern," 6; "The Official Report of the Hearing of the Charges Preferred by Eleven Presbyterian Ministers against President Charles E. Diehl, Held on Tuesday, February 3rd, 1931, by the Board of Directors of Southwestern," *Southwestern Bulletin* 18 ("Extra") (March 1931).

122. "The Faculty of Southwestern," 5.

123. Diehl to B. A. Patch, 9 Aug. 1934 [carbon copy], MA-RC.

124. B. A. Patch to Diehl, 10 Aug. 1934, MA-RC.

125. Ransom to Diehl [telegram], 25 Aug. 1934, MA-RC.

126. Warren to Diehl, 8 Aug. 1934, MA-RC.

127. Young to Diehl, 1 Sept. 1934, MA-RC.

128. Diehl to Patch, 25 Aug. 1934; Diehl to J. C. Ransom, 25 Aug. 1934, both carbon copies in MA-RC.

129. Diehl to Tate, 25 Aug. 1934 [carbon copy], MA-RC.

130. Gordon to Léonie Adams, [1934], LA-YU.

131. Quoted by Shapiro in "The Southern Agrarians and the Tennessee Valley Authority," 791–806, 792. Donald Davidson aside, writes Shapiro, the Agrarians "were generally favorable to the project" (791).

132. On Memphis in the Great Depression and the New Deal, I draw from Charles W. Crawford, *Yesterday's Memphis* (1976), 111.

133. I am grateful to Jameson Jones, Ralph Hon, and Goodbar Morgan for help identifying the Tates' Memphis homes, both 2374 Forrest Avenue, described above, and 1531 Forrest Avenue, described in the next chapter. Mr. Jones was kind enough to take photographs of both houses for me.

134. Gordon to Léonie Adams, [1934], LA-YU.

135. A. Theodore Johnson and Allen Tate, eds., *America through The Essay: An Anthology for English Courses* (New York, 1938.)

136. For a better understanding of Monk, I am grateful to Professors Robert Kent, Earl Miner, and Lillian Feder.

137. Howard Anderson and John S. Shea, eds., *Studies in Criticism and Aesthetics, 1660–1800: Essays in Honor of Samuel Holt Monk* (Minneapolis, 1967), 3–7; I have also drawn from Charles E. Diehl's "Foreword" to Monk's "Colleges and Freedom of Opinion in a Revolutionary Era," *Southwestern Bulletin* 34 (July 1947).

138. Through the grapevine, Monk's friends and graduate students heard different stories about the tragedy; the most common version had his wife drowning after a boating mishap on the Gulf of Mexico. Monk himself alludes to the tragedy in a letter to Allen and Helen Tate, 18 Aug. 1968, AT-PU, IIc.

139. On Monk's legacy as a teacher, see Earl Miner, "Samuel Holt Monk, 1902–1981," *Eighteenth-Century Studies* 15 (Spring 1982): 365; Anderson and Shea, *Studies in Criticism and Aesthetics*, 6–7.

140. "Prof. John H. Davis, Southwestern at Memphis, April 1967," 4-page typescript introduction AT-PU, IIc, Box. 3, p. 2.

141. Ibid, 2–3.

142. Samuel Holt Monk to Robert Kent, 10 May 1979, RK.

143. Tate to Robert Penn Warren, [fragment, early 1935], RPW-YU.

144. Ibid.

145. Tate quoted by Peter Taylor (interview with Taylor, Gainesville, Fl., 10 Jan. 1988).

146. Tate to Mark Van Doren, 16 January 1935, MVD-CU. Van Doren invited Tate to come teach at Columbia, but Tate had become too much of an Agrarian to consider returning to New York City. But it was a painful decision. "If Columbia had been in the South," he explained, "I think I would have taken the offer" (Tate to Robert Penn Warren, [fragment, early 1935], RPW-YU.

147. Tate to Charles Diehl, 20 Feb. 1935, MA-RC.

148. "Allen Tate Called Best Critic in America Today," *Sou'wester* 16 (1 March 1935): 4.

149. "Education, Past and Present," *ITMS* (New York, 1930; repr., Baton Rouge, La., 1980), 92–121; also see Virginia Rock's appended profile of Fletcher, *ITMS* (1980) 375–79. After leaving Memphis, Fletcher wrote a flurry of paranoid letters to Tate and the rest of the group, accusing them of colluding with the enemy by continuing to publish in the *Virginia Quarterly Review* after the journal editors rejected an essay by Donald Davidson. Tate, who had said little during a number of scenes Fletcher created when he visited Memphis, had lost patience. He replied with his characteristic genius for turning the tables on correspondents. "I think I am a little tired of you," he wrote to Fletcher. "I assure you that I accept your breaking off of our friendship with a regret the less sharp for its having been chiefly on my side." Accurately predicting Fletcher's demise, Tate added, "If you don't get a little more feeling for your reality, I foresee, I regret to say, some sort of dire calamity in your life." (Tate to Fletcher, 14 March 1935 [copy], DD-VU). The very next month, Fletcher found himself in a mental hospital. In 1950, he committed suicide (see Ben Johnson " 'A Strange and Lonely Figure:' John Gould Fletcher and Southern Modernism," 40-page typescript 25–27).

150. *Saddest*, 426–27.

151. Gordon to Red and Cinina Warren, [late Jan 1935], RPW-YU.

152. "South's Land Evils Assailed in Report," *New York Times*, 21 March 1935, 25; "Thomas Says AAA Is Lax," *New York Times*, 21 March 1935, 25. Franklin D. Roosevelt's secretary of agriculture admitted, "We recognize that the operation of the cotton program has probably added

to the immediate difficulties, just as relief policies have injected additional complications into the usual tenant and farm-labor relationships. It is inevitable in a period of emergency that such disturbances should occur. But we should realize that neither the AAA programs nor any relief program can really come to grips with the fundamentals of these conditions" (see "Wallace Points To Dangers of Tenancy," *New York Times Magazine*, 31 March 1935, 4, 21). Throughout this section, I also draw from Donald H. Grubbs, *Cry from the Cotton: The Southern Tenant Farmers' Union and the New Deal* (Chapel Hill, N.C., 1971); from H. L. Mitchell, *Mean Things Happening in This Land: The Life and Times of H. L. Mitchell, Co-Founder of the Southern Tenant Farmers' Union* (Montclair, N.J., 1979); and from the F. Raymond Daniell articles cited in n. 154.

153. "Socialists Avoid Party Link to Idle," New York *Times*, 24 March 1935, sec. 1, p. 12.

154. Perhaps because Daniell was trying to maintain some objectivity, his articles—when read as a unit—reveal certain contradictions in argument. Nevertheless, I have drawn from all six *New York Times* articles: "AAA Piles Misery on Share Croppers," 15 April 1935, 6; "Arkansas Violence Laid to Landlords," 16 April 1935, 18; "Tenant Law Clash Roils Cotton Belt," 18 April 1935, 24; "Farm Tenant Union Hurt by Outsiders," 19 April 1935, 18; " 'Run off Farms,' Tenants Declare," 20 April 1935, 5; "AAA Seen Hurting The Tenant Farmer," 21 April 1935, sec. 2, p. 1. I also draw from two subsequent articles by Daniell in the *New York Times*: "AAA Aims at an End to Share Cropping," 22 April 1935, 7; and "The Share-Cropper: His Plight Revealed," *New York Times Magazine*, 5 May 1935, 4, 19.

155. Daniell, "Arkansas Violence Laid to Landlords," 18.

156. Roosevelt's labor and civil rights record has long been the subject of historiographical debate. Of FDR's failure to denounce the Arkansas landowners, Donald Grubbs has asked, "Could this be the president who was claiming to lead a bold New Deal for the Forgotten Man seventy-three years after the Emancipation Proclamation?" (*Cry from the Cotton*, 107).

157. Daniell, "Arkansas Violence Laid to Landlords," 18.

158. Mitchell, *Mean Things*, 72.

159. "Arkansas Violence Laid to Landlords," 18.

160. Since renting Benfolly had proven impossible prior to the Tates' departure for Southwestern, they closed some rooms, including those with plumbing, and permitted their tenants, the Normans, to live in the main house (Gordon to Ford Madox Ford and Janice Biala, [1934], FMF-CNL).

161. See "Billion Farm Aid Passed By Senate," *New York Times*, 25 June 1935, 1–2. Henry A. Wallace endorsed the bill ("Wallace Points to Dan-

gers of Tenancy," *New York Times Magazine*, 31 March 1935, 4, 21). The Bankhead-Jones Farm Tenancy Act, a remarkably weaker version of the original bill, would be passed in 1937. A lucid history of the bill's passage and legacy appears in chapter 7 of Grubbs, *Cry from the Cotton* 136–61; Shapiro, "Decentralist Intellectuals and the New Deal," 949n.

162. *War Within*, 250–51, 250.
163. Caroline Gordon to Sally Wood, [spring 1935], in *Mandarins*, 182–87, 183.
164. Richard Rorty to TAU, 16 July 1993. In another version, Richard Rorty, who cannot vouch for the truth of either account, has written, "Tate undertook to address a gang of rednecks in a village square on how they should stop trying to lynch the local black radical leaders, and had to be hastily dragged off the stump in order not to himself be lynched" (see note quoting Richard Rorty to Ann Waldron, 21 May 1985, AW). Although I believe Waldron could have made different use of the sources on the Marked Tree episode, I am very grateful to her for her characteristic generosity in sharing a number of those sources, including copies of *New York Times* articles and a letter to her from Hon. Don Pryor, U.S. Congress, 24 Jan. 1985, AW. Her account appears in Waldron, 149–51. A brief account also appears in Makowsky, 126–27.
165. Quoted in "Arkansas Violence Laid to Landlords," 18.
166. Jonathan Daniels, *A Southerner Discovers the South* (New York, 1938), 86–87, 86.
167. Caroline Gordon to Sally Wood, [spring 1935], *Mandarins*, 182–87, 184.
168. Quoted ibid.
169. On 3 May 1935, Tate wrote to John Brooks Wheelwright, "I have been teaching this year and doing little else except brief excursions into Arkansas to look things over. I don't agree that socialist collectivism is the solution" (JBW-BRN).
170. Tate to Mark Van Doren, 17 Jan. 1936, MVD-CU.
171. Gordon to Ford Madox Ford, [early spring, 1935], FMF-CNL.
172. Tate, *To the Romantic Traditionists*, *Virginia Quarterly Review* 2 (April 1935): 254–55; Tate refers to the poem in Tate-McDonnell, 35.
173. "POETRY WEEK, by Allen Tate, a Paper Read before the Nineteenth Century Club, Memphis, May 25, 1935," 6-page typescript, AT-PU, 1:11, p. 5.
174. William Thomas, "An Echo of Fugitive Days," *Memphis Commerical Appeal* n.d., Feb. 1979.
175. *Southwestern Journal* 15 (Winter 1935): 36.
176. A few months later, Tate entered into an eight-month agreement with the "Scribblers' Club" in order to earn money for his real estate taxes. He "nearly fainted" when "a hard-faced, bedizened huzzy, with the kept-woman air" produced a line of poetry more to his liking. "She must

have stolen it," he concluded. Tate to Lytle, 27 Oct. 1935, TDY-L, 98–99, 99.

177. Tate to John Peale Bishop, 6 May 1935 [not sent], AT-PU, 6:14.

178. Tate, "The Function of the Critical Quarterly," *Southern Review* 1 (Winter 1936): 551–59, 559.

179. Tate to Eugene F. Saxton, 17 Nov, 1933 [carbon copy], VU; Tate to Saxton, 14 Oct. 1933 [never mailed], 6:14, AT-PU.

180. Tate to Seward Collins, 9 Sept. 1933, SC-YU.

181. Peter Ackroyd, *T. S. Eliot: A Life* (New York, 1984), 200–202; Eliot, *After Strange Gods*, 16, 15, 20, 17–18, 12 (see also Eliot, "Tradition and Orthodoxy," *American Review* 2 [March 1934]: 513–528); Eliot to Tate, 18 May 1933, 19:53, AT-PU.

182. Agar to Tate, 7 Nov. 1933, AT-PU, 9:20; Tate to Gilbert Seldes, 29 April 1935, 39:8, AT-PU; Agar to Tate, 15 Jan. 1935, AT-PU, 9:20; Susan E. Tifft and Alex S. Jones, *The Patriarch: The Rise and Fall of the Bingham Dynasty* (New York, 1991), esp. 161–62; Marie Brenner, *House of Dreams: The Collapse of an American Dynasty* (1988; rpt., New York, 1989), esp. 139; and Shapiro, "American Conservative Intellectuals," 371 (Shapiro mistakenly identifies the ambassador as Barry Bingham).

183. Tate to Collins, 9 Sept. 1933, SC-YU. "Under the first six Presidents," Agar wrote in his preface, "the Government was an oligarchy, dominated by a little group of privileged and public-spirited men. About the time of Andrew Jackson, the seventh President, the country became a democracy, or rather three separate democracies: a thorough-going social and political democracy in the new Western States, where conditions of life reduced inequality to a minimum; a Greek democracy in the South, based on slave labor and accepting the leadership of the educated class; and lastly, in the Northeast (where the new industrialism had brought wealth and power), a democracy of city mobs bossed by politicians who took their orders from the rich. The last Presidents of this second period were Lincoln and Jefferson Davis, representatives of the Western and Southern forms of democracy . Both forms were destroyed by the Civil War, which left the country in the hands of the plutocrats." *The People's Choice, from Washington to Harding: A Study in Democracy* (Boston and New York, 1933). Agar's thesis is not sustainable by modern scholarship. Revisionist scholars have overturned much of the notion of "Jacksonian Democracy" while the New Western Historians have exposed the gross inequities of life on the "frontier." The notion that the antebellum South was in any remote sense democratic is, of course, preposterous. Yet blaming the country's ills on the Civil War naturally appealed to Tate, who wrote a review praising Agar, while indicting Communism and "capitalist 'democracy' " (see "Where Are the People?" review of *The People's Choice*, by Herbert Agar, *American Review* 2 (Dec. 1933): 231–37, 235. Tate was equally fond of Agar's essay "The

Task for Conservatism" (*American Review* 3 [April 1934]: 1–22), in which Agar attacked "capitalism in economics and plutocracy in politics" (11) and endorsed "the widest possible distribution of property" (13).

184. Tate to Lincoln Kirstein, 16 Sept. 1933, *H&H*-YU.
185. Tate to Herbert Agar, 9 Sept. 1933 [carbon copy], 6:14, AT-PU. Singal observes that Tate's new willingness to define Agrarianism "in terms of a general traditionalism with little or no mention of the South" grew more pronounced after he met Agar (*War Within*, 250).
186. Tate to Andrew Lytle, 14 Feb. 1935, TDY-L, 93.
187. Shapiro's account demonstrates the misjudgment Agar showed in embracing Collins ("American Conservative Intellectuals," esp. 371, 372).
188. Agar to Collins, 10 Dec. 1934, SC-YU.
189. Ibid.
190. Gordon to Robert Penn Warren, undated [late Feb. 1935?], RPW-YU.
191. "Political Weekly Plans to Be Made," *Louisville Courier-Journal*, 31 March 1935.
192. Tate to Andrew Lytle, 28 Sept. 1935, TDY-L, 97–98.
193. Tate to Davidson, 28 Sept. 1935, DD-VU.
194. Tate uses this term in a letter to Donald Davidson of 18 Nov. 1935, DD-VU.
195. Tate to John Peale Bishop, 6 May 1935 [not sent], AT-PU, 6:14.
196. Tate to Robert Penn Warren, 27 Jan. 1935, RPW-YU.

Chapter Eight
Fatherless Fame

1. Gordon to Harriet Owsley, undated [1935], FLO-VU.
2. Tate to Brooks, 5 April 1937, CB-YU. See also Brooks to Tate, 7 April 1937, AT-PU, 13:33; and Tate to Brooks, 19 April 1937, CB-YU.
3. Brooks and Warren, *Understanding Poetry*, 3d ed. (1938; repr. New York, 1960).
4. See the preliminary table of contents appended to Tate to Zabel, 20 Nov. 1933, MDZ-CHI. See also *"Reactionary Essays,"* AT-PU, AM 19629, 3:10.
5. Maxwell Perkins to Tate, 24 May 1935, AT-PU, 38:58.
6. Perkins to Tate, 22 Dec. 1933, AT-PU, 38:58; Bob Lundegaard, "University of Minnesota's Poet Tate: 'I Am Out of Tune with the Times,' " *Minneapolis Tribune*, 24 Jan. 1965, 1.
7. Tate to Van Doren, 10 Nov. 1935, MVD-CU. A couple of drafts of the preface survive; see Tate, MS, *Reactionary Essays on Poetry and Ideas*, MS Am. 1334, Houghton Library, Harvard University (cited by permission); and Tate to Stark Young, 13 Oct. 1935, SY-PM.
8. Tate, *Reactionary Essays on Poetry and Ideas* (New York, 1936), ix–xii.

9. Ibid., xii, 19, 79, 107, 3.
10. Ibid., xi–xii, 200, 194, 231, 221.
11. Ibid., 26, 35, 39, 49, 50, 48, 46.
12. Ibid., 63, 214.
13. Ibid., 135.
14. *M&O*, xi.
15. Peter Monro Jack, "Allen Tate's Critical Integrity," *New York Times Book Review* (12 April, 1936), sec. 6, pp. 4,11, 4.
16. Van Doren, "An Interpretation of Poets," *New York Herald Tribune Books*, 12 April 1936.
17. S.C.C., "Reactionary Essays From Mr. Tate on Poetry and Ideas," unidentified clipping, AT-PU, IIc.
18. Belgion, "A Rare Critic," *Catholic Herald*, 4 Sept. 1936, AT-PU, 5:5.
19. R. P. Blackmur, "The Experience of Ideas," *Columbia Review*, 29–32, 29, 30, AT-PU, 5:5.
20. Tate to Blackmur, 5 May 1936, RPB-PU, 8:11.
21. Cowley, "A Game of Chess," *New Republic* 86 (29 April 1936): 348–49, 348. For Tate's response to the review, see Tate to Cowley, 26 April 1936, MC-NL.
22. Gorham Munson, review of *Reactionary Essays*, by Allen Tate, *North American Review* 242 (Winter 1936–37): 394–400, 398–99.
23. William Troy, "Tradition for Tradition's Sake," *Nation* 142 (10 June 1936): 747–48.
24. Cowley, "A Game of Chess," 349.
25. Geoffrey Stone, "It Is the Virile Part to React," *American Review* 7 (Summer 1936): 341–52, 350.
26. See Bruce Clayton, *W. J. Cash: A Life* (Baton Rouge, La., 1991), 127–28, 128. I reviewed Clayton's excellent book in "The Mind (and Physiology?) of the South," *Southern Literary Journal* 24 (Fall, 1991): 110–14.
27. Munson, review of *Reactionary Essays*, 399.
28. Stone, "It is the Virile Part to React," 352.
29. Cowley to Tate, 23 April 1936, AT-PU, 16:29.
30. Albert E. Stone, Jr., "Seward Collins and the *American Review*: Experiment in Pro-Fascism, 1933–1937," 3–19, esp. 14ff.; and Shapiro, "American Conservative Intellectuals, the 1930s, and the Crisis of Ideology" (hereafter "ACI"), 370–80, esp. 372ff. Throughout sections II and III of this chapter, my narrative of events again draws much from these indispensable articles by Stone and Shapiro (although my account makes a number of corrections and interpretive departures based upon my own reading of the archival sources and periodical literature I quote from below). Stone is especially valuable for his explication of the Fascist ideas published in the *American Review*, for his analysis of Collins's fascism, and for his assessment of the Agrarians' entanglement with him. Shapiro's account, to which my narrative is also greatly indebted, includes compel-

ling analysis of the competing conservative ideologies and strategies of Collins, Agar, and Tate, and of the complex relationship between the three men.

On Lumpkin, I have profited from Suzanne Sowinska, "Introduction," *To Make My Bread* (1932; repr., Urbana, Ill., 1995), vii–xliii; Jane A. Bowden, ed., *Contemporary Authors* (Detroit, 1978), vols. 69–72: 388; and Lillian Barnard Gilkes, afterword to *The Wedding*, by Grace Lumpkin (1939; repr., Carbondale and Edwardsville, Ill., 1976), 309–19. Cyrilly Abels's favorable review of *To Make My Bread* appeared in Collins's *Bookman* 75 (Nov. 1932): 739–40.

31. I quote from a portion of Lumpkin's "I Want a King" (*Fight* 3 [Feb. 1936]) excerpted by Stone, "Seward Collins," 14–16.

32. "Our enemies," Tate wrote even in 1935, "charge us with Fascism for the very reason that you point out: we don't believe in Communism" (Tate to Gilbert Seldes, 8 March 1935, 39:8, AT-PU); Agar to Tate, 15 Feb. 1936, 9:20, AT-PU (in a stern but tactful tone, Agar also wrote to Collins on 15 Feb. 1936, SC-YU); Stone, "Seward Collins," 16–17; "ACI," 372–73; Tate to Davidson, 23 Feb. 1936, DD-VU; "Fascism and the Southern Agrarians," *New Republic* 87 (27 May 1936): 75.

33. "Fascism and the Southern Agrarians," 75–76, 76. Albert Stone points out, however, that "Agrarian regionalists opposed not only the monarchist aspect of fascism, but its nationalism as well" ("Seward Collins," 13). Collins, Lumpkin, and "THE EDITORS," "The Sunny Side of Fascism," *New Republic* 87 (10 June 1936): 131; "ACI," 373, 380n.

34. Collins was both relieved and grateful when Tate sent "What Is a Traditional Society?" (*American Review* 7 [Sept. 1936]: 376–87); Collins to Tate, [Summer 1937], AT-PU, AM 19629, 15:45. Tate later sent him "Modern Poets and Convention," a paper he delivered at the 1936 Modern Language Convention. (*American Review* 8 [Feb. 1937]: 427–35.) Ben Johnson observes that "fascism undeniably pervaded the *American Review* before 1935, and the Agrarians continued to appear in its pages after that year" (" 'A Strange and Lonely Figure': John Gould Fletcher and Southern Modernism," 24). Shapiro argues that Tate and his friends "refused to boycott the *American Review* because they remained grateful to Collins for opening up the pages of his review to them" ("ACI," 376).

35. Agar to Chard Powers Smith, 13 April 1936, SC-YU; Agar, as quoted by Bern Brandon, "Metaphysics of Reaction," *Marxist Quarterly* 1 (Jan.–March 1937): 125–33, 129n; Stone, "Seward Collins," 18; "ACI," 373.

36. On Agar's previous optimism about Collins, see "ACI," 371, 372.

37. Collins to Chard Powers Smith, 12 Dec. 1936 [carbon copy], SC-YU.

38. Collins to Agar, 23 Dec. 1936 [carbon], AT-PU, AM 19629, 15:45.

39. Collins to Tate, 19 Dec. 1936 [carbon], SC-YU.

40. Tate to Collins, 23 May 1936, SC-YU.

41. Tate to Collins, 17 Dec. 1936, SC-YU.

42. Agar, "Free America," *Free America* 1 (Jan. 1937): 2. In addition to the exchange of letters I cite below, on *Free America* I draw from "ACI," esp. 374–77; and William E. Leverette, Jr., and David E. Shi, "Agrarianism for Commuters," *South Atlantic Quarterly* 79 (Spring 1980): 204–18, 215–16, an article I have found useful in general.

43. "ACI," 374.

44. Tate to Agar, 9 Dec. 1936 [carbon], AT-PU, 9:20. On Tate's initial enthusiasm for *Free America*, see Tate to Davidson, 17 Oct. 1936, DD-VU.

45. Tate to Collins, 12 Dec. 1936, SC-YU.

46. Tate to Collins, 17 Dec. 1936, SC-YU. Shapiro reports that "[Donald] Davidson, for his part, was prepared to break with Agar if it came down to a choice between Collins and Agar" ("ACI," 376).

47. Tate to Agar, 7 Jan. 1937 [carbon copy], AT-PU, AM 19629, 9:20.

48. On Tate's request for the editorship, see Tate to Agar, 7 Jan. 1937 [carbon] , AT-PU, 9:20. Tate to Collins, 27 Jan. 1937, SC-YU; Tate quoted in Gordon to Ford Madox Ford [early 1937], FMF-CNL. According to Shapiro, however, "Despite Agar's fervent entreaties, no Agrarian ever became officially associated with *Free America* except for Tate, who, for a few months in 1939 and 1940, was book review editor" ("ACI," 376). (For an example of Agar's lobbying, see Agar to Tate, 17 Oct. 1937, AT-PU, 9:20.) Shapiro concludes, "The quarrel between *Free America* and the *American Review* ultimately involved the attempt to develop a relevant conservatism for the America of the 1930s" ("ACI," 377).

49. While I believe that Albert Stone overstates the case when he claims that Tate and the Agrarians "did not hesitate to repudiate fascism," I agree with his observation that they were "caught between Agar's [New Deal] Democracy and Collins' pro-fascism" ("Seward Collins," 18).

50. Tate to Desmond-Hawkins, 19 Feb. 1937 [copy], AT-PU, IIc, 8:4. According to Albert Stone, Seward Collins grew disillusioned with FDR because he thought "that Roosevelt's objective was not the Corporate State but rather to save capitalism" ("Seward Collins," 8).

51. Tate to Davidson, 30 March 1937, DD-VU. This letter, which is neither reprinted in (DD-AT) nor listed in the "Register" of correspondence prefixed to the volume (xxix–lxx), was apparently not available to the collection's editors. According to Albert Stone, "While at first applauding President Roosevelt for his forceful leadership, Southern Agrarians opposed in theory a strong central government" ("Seward Collins," 13). On the TVA, see Shapiro, "The Southern Agrarians and the Tennessee Valley Authority."

52. Tate to Davidson, 30 March 1937, DD-VU; Stone, "Seward Collins," 18–19. Stone also concludes that Collins could not keep on schedule after the Agrarians "withdrew their support" (12). Tugwell (as quoted in Leverette and Shi's helpful article, "Agrarianism for Commuters," 211) was also referring to Ralph Borsodi; Leverette and Shi examine Borsodi's subsis-

tence agrarianism, its reception during the New Deal, and its relationship to southern Agrarianism. On the rise and fall of the Agrarian movement during the 1930s, I have also been influenced by Conkin, *Southern Agrarians*, which I reviewed in *American Literature* 61 (March 1989): 115–17. See also *The Southern Agrarians and the New Deal: Essays after "I'll Take My Stand*," the collection I edited and introduced with Emily Bingham for University Press of Virginia, and which is forthcoming.

53. "WHO OWNS AMERICA?" mimeographed typescript, Box D174, Subject File, "Tate, Allen," MM-LOC.

54. Tate to Frank Lawrence Owsley, 26 Sept. 1935, FLO-VU. On Nixon's relationship with the Agrarians, I have found indispensable Sarah Newman Shouse's *Hillbilly Realist: Herman Clarence Nixon of Possum Trot* (University, Ala., 1986.)

55. Herbert Agar and Allen Tate, *Who Owns America? A New Declaration of Independence* (Boston, 1936), 118, 58, 248, 251, 162, 169 (hereafter referred to as *WOA*).

56. Ibid., ix, viii.

57. Ibid., 180, 274, 275.

58. Tate to Eugene F. Saxton, [carbon copy] 17 Nov. 1933, VU.

59. "It is no longer possible to hold property in small quantities," he told Gilbert Seldes. "That is the point at which the American tradition went off the track" (Tate to Gilbert Seldes, 8 March 1935, 39:8, AT-PU).

60. Tate, "Notes on Liberty and Property," *American Review* 6 (March 1936): 596–611; repr. in *WOA*, 80–93.

61. Tate to Davidson, 14 Jan. 1936, DD-VU.

62. *WOA*, 80, 82.

63. On *WOA* and the reaction to it (and especially for sending me to all but three of the book reviews I cite below), I am indebted to "ACI," 373–74, and 380n.

64. John Corbin, "A Share for All in America: Mr. Agar and Mr. Tate Sponsor 'A New Declaration of Independence,' " *New York Times Book Review*, 10 May 1936, sec. 6, pp. 1, 13.

65. Agar quoted in "ACI," 373.

66. Crane Brinton, "Who Owns America?" *Southern Review* 2 (1936): 15–21, 16, 21.

67. M. Lanning Shane, "Corporations vs. Human Beings," *Nashville Banner Magazine*, 26 April 1936.

68. Seward Collins, "Three Important Books," *American Review* 7 (Oct. 1936): 601–4, 604.

69. Kenneth Burke, "Property as an Absolute," *New Republic* 87 (1 July 1936): 245–46.

70. Broadus Mitchell, " 'O Time in Your Flight,' " *Nation* 142 (24 June 1936): 813–14.

71. Quoted in "To Make America Free" [unsigned review], *Commonweal* 24 (8 May 1936): 30.

72. John Chamberlain, "Agrarianism, American Style," *Saturday Review of Literature* 14 (25 July 1936): 17.

73. Danforth Ross, "Memories of Allen Tate," 13 March 1980, addendum, 4-page typescript.

74. "Some embarrassment followed my identification as a friend of the foe," Woodward remembered, "but good manners prevailed and despite some awkwardness the door was opened to some relationships of lasting importance and meaning to me" (C. Vann Woodward, *Thinking Back: The Perils of Writing History* [Baton Rouge, La., 1986], 18–19).

75. Tate to Davidson, 11 May 1936, DD-VU; *Southern Agrarians*, 117–18.

76. Jonathan Daniels, *A Southerner Discovers the South* (New York, 1938), 81–88, 85–87.

77. H. L. Mitchell, *Mean Things Happening in This Land: The Life and Times of H. L. Mitchell, Co-Founder of the Southern Tenant Farmers' Union* (Montclair, N.J., 1979), 124–27, 127.

78. "A Traditionist Looks at Liberalism," *Southern Review* 1 (Spring 1936): 731–44, 743–44.

79. "What Is a Traditional Society?" *American Review* 7 (Sept. 1936): 376–87, 376, 386.

80. "Noted Author Visions South as Industrial," *Chattanooga Times*, 4 Nov. 1936, 12.

81. Tate quoted by Eugene Warner, "South Is U.S. Literary Center, Asserts Allen Tate, Noted Poet," *Washington Post*, 5 Jan. 1937, 13.

82. Tate to Davidson, 30 March 1937, DD-VU.

83. Tate to Edmund Wilson, 20 April 1937, EW-YU.

84. Tate to Davidson, 4 Dec. 1942, DD-VU. See also Tate to Thomas H. Carter, 11 March 1952 [carbon], AT-PU, 14:46.

85. Interview with Marcella Comès Winslow, 21 Feb. 1988, Washington, D.C.; Helen White, ed., *Anne Goodwin Winslow: An Annotated Check List of her Published Works and of Her Papers* (Memphis, Tenn., 1969), 7–9; Marcella Comès Winslow, with a foreword by Louis D. Rubin, Jr., *Brushes with the Literary: Letters of a Washington Artist, 1943–1959* (Baton Rouge, La., 1993), esp. xix, 1, 4, 5.

86. Brushes with the Literary, xix–xx, 1–3, 3.

87. Tate to Winslow, 17 Sept. 1936, repr. in *Brushes with the Literary*, 2.

88. Tate to Winslow, [Nov. 1936], quoted in *Brushes with the Literary*, 3.

89. Playbill, "University Theater: Studio Theater, 1961–1962, The Governess," AGW-UM.

90. Here I work from an 81-page typescript of the play with handwritten annotations (RS-WU) that is apparently a later or revised copy of the original by Tate and Winslow. I have exercised caution in using this MS to make judgments about Tate's alteration of James, since "The Govern-

ess" was revised prior to its May 1962 production. In a blurb written for the playbill, Tate wrote, "My wife, the poet Isabella Gardner, a professional actress as well as a poet, rewrote the first two scenes and touched up parts of the dialogue throughout" (Playbill, AGW-UM). Nevertheless, one can safely conclude that Tate would not have approved any revisions contrary to his interpretation of James's story. I have profited in this section from Squires's commentary on *The Governess* and from his observation that the play prefigures Tate's work on *The Fathers*, esp. in its treatment of the theme of evil (see Squires-1971, 133–35). I am equally grateful to my friend Prof. Michael Anesko of Penn State University for discussing James with me.

91. Gordon to Ford and Janice Biala, [Dec. 1935 and Jan. 1936], FMF-CNL.

92. Young to Tate, [ca. 1936], AGW-UM. On Tate's attempt to sell the play, see Tate to Anne Winslow, 18 Sept. 1936, 31 March 1937, 16 April 1937, 22 March 1938, and 24 Aug. 1950 (all in AGW-UM), Tate to Marcella Winslow, 27 Nov. 1936, Princeton University Library, Gen. MSS [misc.] AM 85–87; Tate to Andrew Lytle, 24 March 1937, TDY-L, 104–6, 105; Tate to Paul Green, 16 Aug. 1944, PG-SHC; Tate to Bernice Baumgarten, Brandt and Brandt, 28 Oct. 1946 [unsigned carbon copy], AT-PU, AM 19629, 13:9.

93. Tate to Edmund Wilson, 19 May 1938, EW-YU.

94. Eliot to Tate, 12 April 1938, AT-PU, AM 19629, 19:53.

95. Tate to Anne Winslow, 22 March 1938, AGW-UM.

96. Tate to Wilson, 19 May 1938, EW-YU. Squires, who was probably not familiar with this letter, goes a bit astray when he observes "that in 1936 *The Turn of the Screw* was not encircled by excesses of scholarship and interpretation. Edmund Wilson's notorious naturalistic interpretation had appeared. Little else. Tate's insights were original" (Squires-1971, 134). Wilson, *The Triple Thinkers: Ten Essays on Literature* (New York, 1938), 122–64, 125, 130, 131–132; Wilson, "The Ambiguity of Henry James," *Hound and Horn* 7 (April–June 1934): 385–406, 387, 390, 391.

97. Tate to Mary Winslow, 3 May 1962, AGW-UM; Playbill, AGW-UM.

98. After *The Fathers* appeared, Tate wrote R. P. Blackmur, "I suspected that you would remind me of James' warning against the first person narrator. Yet curiously, James' own practice in *The Turn of the Screw* persuaded me of its value as a device for disguising commentary and the biased personal view with the look of action, of actuality, of what happened. . . . But James on the whole was right. The first person is useful for special tasks, but dangerous if used as a maid of all work" (28 Nov. 1938, RPB-PU, AM 21403, 8:11). After reading Andrew Lytle's *A Name for Evil* (1947), Tate told Lytle he was "a little too conscious of the close parallel to *The Turn of the Screw*. . . . There are echoes of James' rhythms, some of his mannerisms, and even his phrases. In *The Turn of the Screw* James never lets the Governess reflect philosophically; all her observations bear

upon her defense and support her 'version'; I think you somewhat overdo this phase of your story" (Tate to Lytle, 29 July 1947, TDY-L, 212–13).

99. Henry James, *The Turn of the Screw and Daisy Miller* (repr., New York, 1978), 7.

100. Tate to Diehl, 20 Feb. 1935, MA-RC; Ross, "Memories of Allen Tate," 13 March 1980, p. 6; Balch to Tate, 19 May 1936, AT-PU, Box 1, IIc; Diehl to Tate, 11 Sept. 1936, AT-PU, AM 19629, 6:6; Tate to Seward Collins, 22 Oct. 1936; and Gordon to Leonie Adams, [early summer 1936], both in SC-YU. On the competition with *Gone with the Wind* and Gordon's desire for royalties, see Gordon to Ford Madox Ford [Summer 1936]; Gordon to Ford Madox Ford and Janice Biala, [Dec. 1936], both FMF-CNL. See also "After the Big Wind," an unsigned review of *None Shall Look Back* in *Time* 29 (1 March 1937): 70, 72.

101. Dorothea Brande, *Wake Up and Live!* (New York, 1936). Tate to Mark Van Doren, 20 July 1936, MVD-CU; Tate-Forsyth et al., 16. On Brewer and his conference, see Tate to Arthur Mizener, 29 Jan. 1969, AM-VU; and *Saddest*, 438.

102. Tate to Lytle, 29 July 1936, TDY-L, 102.

103. See E. H. Wright, Columbia, to Tate, 17 and 25 Oct. 1935, both in AT-PU, 6:2; Tate to John Peale Bishop, 18 Nov. 1935, JPB-PU, AM 79–31, 23:1.

104. Gordon to Ford Madox Ford [Summer 1936], FMF-CNL.

105. Tate to Van Doren, [5 Aug. 1936], MVD-CU; see also Tate to Berryman, 20 Sept. 1936, John Berryman Papers, MSS Division, University of Minnesota Libraries, Twin Cities.

106. Tate to Bishop, 23 Oct. 1936, JPB-PU, AM 79–31, 23:2; Gordon to Ford Madox Ford, [Summer 1936], FMF-CNL.

107. Gordon to Léonie Adams, [Dec. 1936?], LA-YU.

108. Gordon to Robert Penn Warren, [Nov. or Dec. 1936?], SR-YU.

109. Tate to Mark Van Doren, 10 Nov. 1936, MVD-CU.

110. Tate to Seward Collins, 22 Oct. 1936, SC-YU.

111. Ibid.

112. Tate to John Peale Bishop, 23 Oct. 1936, JPB-PU, AM 79–31, 23:2.

113. Tate to Seward Collins, 22 Oct. 1936, SC-YU.

114. Tate to Ashley Brown, 19 July 1977, AB.

115. J. R. L. Latimer to Willard Maas [undated], Maas Papers, Brown University; Horace Gregory to Jack Wheelwright, 4 Aug. 1936, JBW-BRN, 9:26. (Gregory adds that the "wholly bad" book would "decrease Tate's 'influence' measurably.")

116. Tate to Maxwell Perkins, 12 Nov. 1936, AT-PU, 38:57; Tate to Mark Van Doren, 30 Sept. 1935, 19 April 1936, 18 June 1936, all in MVD-CU; H. T. Stuart, The Alcestis Press, to Tate, 6 June 1938, AT-PU, AM19629, 6:7.

117. Tate, *The Mediterranean and Other Poems* (New York, 1936); Peter Monro Jack, "A New Collection of Poems by Allen Tate," *New York Times*, 16 Aug. 1936.

118. Kenneth Burke, "Tentative Proposal," *Poetry* 50 (May 1937): 96–100, 97, 99.

119. John Crowe Ransom, "Allen Tate's New Poetry," *Nashville Banner Magazine* [ca. 1936], 6. Ford Madox Ford, to whom Tate dedicated the volume, wrote praising it, but never wrote a review; see Ford to Tate, 6 Sept. 1936, AT-PU, AM 19629, 21:16.

120. Tate to Lawrence Lee, 26 Feb. 1937, Lee Papers, Special Collections Department, University of Pittsburgh Library System.

121. Tate to Mark Van Doren, 10 Nov. 1936, MVD-CU.

122. Tate to Stark Young, 8 Nov. 1936 and 26 Nov. 1936, both SY-PM.

123. Tate to Maxwell Perkins, 12 Nov. 1936, AT-PU, 38:57.

124. Quoted in Tate to Stark Young, 26 Nov. 1936, SY-PM.

125. Tate to Stark Young, 26 and 30 Nov. 1936, both in SY-PM; Perkins to Tate, 10 Dec. 1936, AT-PU, 38:58.

126. Tate to Van Doren, 10 Nov. 1936 and 5 April 1937, both in MVD-CU. Some months after submitting the manuscript that autumn, Tate wrote Perkins with instructions on reordering the poems and sent a final revision of the *Ode to the Confederate Dead*. See Tate to Perkins, 3 April 1937, General MSS, Misc. Collection, Princeton University Library.

127. Tate, "Preface," *Selected Poems* (New York, 1937), vii–ix. On Tate's remorse over his lack of poetic productivity, see Tate to Marion O'Donnell, 24 Sept. 1937, GMOD-WU.

128. Tate to Marcella Comès Winslow, 29 Oct. 1936, quoted in *Brushes with the Literary*, 7 (Princeton University Library, Gen. MSS [misc.] AM 85–87).

129. Tate to Marcella Comès Winslow, 17 Sept. 1936, quoted in *Brushes with the Literary*, 2 (PU-Gen. MSS [misc.] AM 85–87).

130. "Modern Poets and Convention," *American Review* 8 (Feb. 1937): 427–35, 434–35.

131. " 'Empty Novels' Hit by Ellen Glasgow," *New York Times*, 1 Jan. 1937, col. 8, p. 21.

132. Glasgow to Tate, 2 Jan. 1937, AT-PU, AM 19629, 22:44.

133. On Wolfe and the Agrarians, I am indebted to David Herbert Donald, *Look Homeward: A Life of Thomas Wolfe* (Boston, 1987), 359–62. I have also explored this topic in "Thomas Wolfe's Trip to Richmond: Détente at the 1936 MLA Meeting," *Virginia Magazine of History and Biography* 95 (July 1987): 353–62; and in "Autobiography and Ideology in the South: Thomas Wolfe and the Vanderbilt Agrarians," *American Literature* 61 (March 1989): 31–45. Tate wrote John Peale Bishop, "Last fall Caroline was competing with Stark [Young], this spring you suffered Thomas Wolfe, and both of you met reverses. Wolfe sells, and there is

no answer to that argument; but I can't quite forgive Perkins for thinking him good. I can't read him. I have no interest in a novelist's personal philosophy at best; it is positively boring at its worst in Wolfe." Tate to Bishop, 3 July 1935, JPB-PU, AM 79–31, 23:1; Gordon to Sally Wood, 8 Jan. 1937, *Mandarins*, 202–5, 205.

134. Winslow, *Brushes with the Literary*, 7; Marcella Winslow to Anne Goodwin Winslow, 4 Jan. 1937, *Brushes with the Literary*, 8–9. Of Vili, Caroline observed, "He can't bear anybody but me and growls whenever Allen comes in the room" (Gordon to Ford Madox Ford and Janice Biala, [Dec. 1935–Jan. 1936], FMF-CNL.

135. Warner, "South Is U.S. Literary Center, Asserts Allen Tate, Noted Poet," 13.

136. Tate to Seward Collins, 27 Jan. 1937, SC-YU.

137. On the partial origins of *The Fathers* in "Records I. A Dream II. A Vision," I am indebted to Squires-1971, 142–43. The two-part poem is reprinted in Tate's *Poems, 1928–1931* (New York, 1932), 24–25.

138. Tate to Seward Collins, 27 Jan. 1937, SC-YU.

Chapter Nine
A Family Reconstructed

1. Tate to Bill Troy, 7 Oct. 1938, LA-YU.
2. Tate to Seward Collins, 27 Jan. 1937, SC-YU; Gordon to Lon Cheney, 28 Jan. 1937, VU; Gordon to Stark Young, [1937], SY-PM. See also Gordon to Ford Madox Ford, [early 1937], FMF-CNL; and Jonza-ms, 272–73.
3. Gordon to Radcliffe Squires, 4 Jan. 1977, RS-WU.
4. Tate quoted in "Mr. Allen Tate Speaks to Club at Chapel Hill," *Carolinian* [newspaper of Women's College of UNC], 25 Nov. 1938, p. 4.
5. Tate to Lytle, 22 March 1939, TDY-L, 135; Tate, *The Fathers*-1938, 3. Throughout this chapter, I have tried to keep my discussion of *The Fathers* (the literature on which has grown too large to be cited here in its entirety) focused on Tate's own psychological relationship to the novel. I am therefore indebted not only to Tate's own explications (as contained in primary sources), but also to those critics who he thought came closest to understanding his artistic intent. Tate most liked the readings by Arthur Mizener and Howard Baker. As such, I am especially indebted to Mizener, " 'The Fathers' and Realistic Fiction," *Accent* 7 (Winter 1947): 101–9; revised as "The Fathers," *Sewanee Review* 67 (Autumn 1959): 604–13 (the version I cite below), and reprinted as "Introduction" to *The Fathers*-1960, ix–xix. Baker concludes that the novel, in which "the Buchans are equivalent to the Old South" and Posey to "modern progressivism or . . . capitalism," is a debate over "the innate evil of man" ("Grand Tour of Fiction," *Southern Review* 4 [Spring 1939]: 801–24, 821, 823). Other critics understanding Tate's intent (and to whose excel-

lent work I am indebted) are Aaron-1975, esp. 301–4, 305n-306n; Ford Madox Ford, "The Fathers by Allen Tate" undated typescript, UNC-Greensboro Archives; Thornton H. Parsons, "The Education of Lacy Buchan," *Quarterly Journal of the Library of Congress* 36 (Fall 1979): 365–76; Lionel Trilling, "Allen Tate as Novelist," *Partisan Review* 6 (Fall 1938): 111–13; Louis D. Rubin, *Wary Fugitives*, 95, 316–25; and Thomas Daniel Young, "Introduction" to *The Fathers*-1977, ix–xx.

Among the most sympathetic readings are those of Radcliffe Squires (Squires-1971, 123–46, most of which appeared first as "Allen Tate's 'The Fathers,' " *Virginia Quarterly Review* 46 [Autumn 1970]: 629–49) and of Lewis P. Simpson (*Fable*, 38–44), both of which I have found useful. Squires, who calls Mizener's interpretation "fundamental" (127), is helpful on the structure and narrative technique of the novel—and especially on its genesis in Tate's Lee biography, genealogical book, two short stories, play, and poem, *Records*. Like Squires, Simpson is correct surmising that Tate's novel and the work leading to it were autobiographical in their impetus (*Fable*, 38.)

On the themes of race and slavery in *The Fathers*, I have profited from those critics of the novel I cite in the notes to section VII of this chapter. I am also indebted to Katie Gunther Kodat's brilliant feminist critique of the novel and to her review of the critical reception to it (see " 'You Have Your Ma's Eyes': Modernity, Narration, and the Feminine in Allen Tate's *The Fathers*," 31-page typescript courtesy of Professor Kodat, now of Hamilton College, who delivered a similar version of the paper on 29 Dec. 1992 at the MLA convention in NYC). Rejecting what she terms the "homogeneous critical reception" (1) launched by Mizener, in which "all tensions arising from the events of the story are subsumed under the 'conflict' between Major Buchan and George Posey" (4), Kodat sees the novel not as a contest between the Old South's code and the New South's violence of change, but as a "confrontation with modernization in terms of anxieties about the feminine" (5), as a patriarchal ideology obscuring itself as a modern text. Although I am unwilling to dismiss Mizener's compelling reading—the biographical evidence in support of it is too great—I am indebted to Kodat, who understands, if not the biographical source, the artistic manifestations of Tate's fear of women. What Kodat calls "anxieties about the feminine" I would translate as Tate's ambivalence toward his mother; what Kodat views as "a story about the triumph of patriarchal tradition," I view as Tate's supplanting of his father. Finally, while Kodat views the novel as "a phoenix-like rebirth of patriarchy under the sign of modernism," I view the novel as Tate's effort to wrest himself from and to answer the historical narrative and psychological identity foisted upon him by both of his parents. From the perspective of a biographer, I can therefore see the readings by Mizener and Kodat as complementary rather than mutually exclusive; Mizener's reading suggests more about Tate's relationship with his father, Kodat's more about Tate's relationship with his mother. My own view of the novel is as a model for understanding Tate's relationship to his parents and his immediate family. As such, I find that Richard H. King's paradigm for the novel, while not a perfect fit with the facts of Tate's life, is compelling structurally. Without knowing much about the genealogy on which Tate based *The Fathers*, King understands Tate's familial preoccupation in the novel, which he identifies as a "Southern family romance" (King, 7), a genre in which "Culture and civilization are seen as literally and symbolically *of the father*" (110). In the family romance, white Southerners struggle with an "idealized" (27) appraisal of their parents while nurturing a "fear of the family's dissolution" (29). I have also been influenced throughout my discussion by Singal's analysis in *War Within*, 254–60, although I disagree with his main conclusion (see notes below).

6. Tate to Bill Troy, 7 Oct. 1938, LA-YU.
7. Tate to Mark Van Doren, 4 Feb. 1937, MVD-CU. Tate further explained his justification for using the first person over omniscience in a letter to Mizener, 17 Nov. 1939, AM-VU.
8. For the suggestion that Tate drew on Proust for the *The Fathers*, I am grateful to Ashley Brown (Brown to TAU, 13 April 1990), who also referred me to Tate's discussion of Proust's *Swann's Way* in Huntington Cairns, Tate, and Mark Van Doren, *Invitation to Learning* (New York, 1941), 169–80, 178–79. John Peale Bishop also saw similarities between Proust and Tate; see an insightful letter about *The Fathers* Bishop wrote on 6 Sept. 1938 (*Republic*, 143–45, 144). Simpson has pointed out that Tate's later work, *M&O*, demonstrated "a Proustian coalescence of memory and history" (*Fable*, 28).
9. Tate to R. P. Blackmur, 28 Nov. 1938, RPB-PU, AM 21403, 8:11.
10. Tate, "FMF," in *Selections from the First Two Issues of "The New York Review of Books,"* ed. Robert B. Silvers and Barbara Epstein (New York, 1988), 74, 75, 76. Squires-1971 correctly calls *The Fathers* "a triumph of the Jamesian viewpoint as extended by Ford Madox Ford" and further "extended by Tate" (145).
11. Hecht-Tate, 28. To Frederick K. Sanders, Tate wrote, "I had known *The Good Soldier* since 1929. Ford taught me a great deal—much of it intangible but indispensable. What I learned from *The Good Soldier* was both simple and enormously difficult to apply; that is, how to give the narrator sufficient involvement in the action to keep him from being a mere observer, and at the same time not to involve him to the extent that his own interests would cloud his view of the *whole*" (Tate to Sanders, 20 July 1962, quoted in Sanders to Tate, 13 Dec. 1963, AT-PU, 38:28). In a 1964 interview, Tate said, "Ford's *The Good Soldier* had a direct influence upon

The Fathers. Any success I may have had with my first-person narrator is due to Ford's example" (quoted in Tate-McDonnell, 36). See also Tate's remarks about Ford quoted in Tate-Forsyth et al., 6.

12. Tate, *Mr. Pope and Other Poems* (New York, 1928), 7.

13. On Tate's genealogy and on his use of it in *The Fathers,* I draw much, here and throughout, from: Tate to Varnell Tate, 26 March 1927; Tate to Robert Varnell Tate, 27 Jan 1971, both in RVT.

14. Ibid.

15. Ben Tate "came of a family almost as nutty as the Poseys," Tate wrote John Peale Bishop, 28 Sept. 1938, JPB-PU, 23:2. Gordon to Tate, [1957], CG-PU, AM 20562, 37:11.

16. Tate to Mark Van Doren, 4 Feb. 1937, MVD-CU.

17. Allen Tate to Ben Tate, 28 Oct. 1938, AT-VU.

18. Tate, "A Note on THE FATHERS by the Author," 2-page typescript, AT-PU, 1:11 (largely identical to statement by Tate reprinted in "North Carolina Novelist Discusses His New Book," *Charlotte Observer,* 7 July 1938.

19. Ibid.

20. Tate quoted in Tate-Millgate, 28.

21. Three of Benjamin Lewis Bogan's sons were physicians; one, a Dr. Joseph Lacy Bogan, fought for the Confederacy in the same company with his brother-in-law, George Henry Varnell (see Tate to Robert V. Tate, 27 Jan. 1971, RVT). But Joseph Lacy Bogan lived, according to Tate, from 1836 to 1867, a lifespan that does not match that of Lacy Buchan in *The Fathers.*

22. Tate to John Peale Bishop, 28 Sept. 1938, JPB-PU, 23:2.

23. Tate, *The Fathers*-1938, 81.

24. One gets a sense of the dramatic differences between Tate and his brothers—as well as their affectionate recognition of those differences—in a letter Varnell Tate wrote after hearing about his younger brother's novel in progress. "I understand that it is serious fiction," Varnell told his son, "and will be quite different from the regular run of present day stuff. Yes, Allen is a top-liner in the writing business, and is one of the real highbrow writers of this age. I think that his is the type that will last, and not be read and thrown into the corner and sink into oblivion" (Varnell Tate to Robert V. Tate, 11 Nov. 1937, RVT).

25. The Fathers-1938, 4, 5.

26. Tate to R. P. Blackmur, 28 Nov. 1938, RPB-PU, AM 21403, 8:11. "It was not that Posey and the Major saw things differently," Tate wrote Marion O'Donnell. "They saw different things" (Tate to O'Donnell, 27 Sept. 1938, GMOD-WU).

27. Tate quoted in "North Carolina Novelist Discusses His New Book."

28. The Fathers-1938, 44; here I am indebted to Mizener, "The Fathers," 609–10.

29. Bishop to Tate, 6 Sept. 1938, *Republic*, 143–44; Tate to Bishop, 28 Sept. 1938, JPB-PU, 23:2 (Tate's letter responding to Bishop was not included in *Republic*).

30. Tate to Jay B. Hubbell, 22 Feb 1961, Hubbell Papers, Rare Book, Manuscript and Special Collections Library, Duke University.

31. Tate to Mizener, 17 Nov. 1939, AM-VU. In "Recent Criticism" (*Southern Review* 5 [Autumn 1939] 376–400, 380n-381n), Mizener had written, "One of the crucial incidents in which George Posey's world is posed against the Buchans's . . . is the scene in which, on the field of honor, George punches John Langton (John Langton is temporarily drunk; George Posey is permanently intoxicated with the terrible wine of his impulses and is in constant danger of losing altogether his sense of his own existence)." Tate was so intrigued by Mizener's brief analysis that on 30 Oct. 1939 (AM-VU), he wrote asking him to elaborate. On 17 Nov., Tate wrote Mizener again, praising his "fine commentary on the Posey-Langton affair," adding, "I feel certain that you must be the only person living—persons dead a hundred years might join you, or even Henry James—who understands my novel." The exchange between Tate and Mizener marked the beginning of their long friendship.

32. In later years, Tate began attributing the inspiration for the image of Major Buchan not to Dorothea Brande's vision in Georgetown, but to a practitioner of psychometry. Tate reported being stunned when the psychic described both Benjamin Bogan and a stand of cedar trees at Pleasant Hill merely by examining the major's "gold studs." Tate, "A Lost Traveller's Dream," *Michigan Quarterly Review* (Autumn 1972): 225–36, 229. After reading Tate's difficult-to-believe account of this event, Mizener wrote him, "Then I could see that that studs episode was—as it now began to seem, glaringly—emblematic: authentification by specificity (those cedars) is not just a characteristic of a psychometrist's convincingness but of poetry's and of the whole realm of which poetry is a part (credo quia impossibile). And so this episode 'inspires' *The Fathers*, not just in the sense of starting you off but of being in some deep sense analagous in nature to it" (Mizener to Tate, 9 Sept. 1972, AT-PU, IIc, 5:28).

33. Tate to Varnell Tate, 26 March 1927, RVT; *The Fathers*-1938, 41.

34. *The Fathers*-1938, 4, 86, 104, 43. According to Kodat, when Lacy Buchan calls his mother's death "a suitable beginning for my story," he is "evoking what Alice Jardine calls the 'founding fantasy' of Western patriarchal history, 'the active negation of the Mother' " (Kodat, " 'You Have Your Ma's Eyes,' " 6.) King argues that the death of Mrs. Buchan typifies the white family romance, in which the woman is both "subordinate . . . to the powerful and heroic father" (34) and "the asexual mother of the Southern male hero" (King, 34–36, 34, 35).

35. *The Fathers*-1938, 93. Parsons observes that "Lacy struggles with competing emotions within himself—grief over his mother's death and erotic

attraction toward Jane," and is compelled to kiss Jane because he begins to identify himself with the impetuous George Posey (Parsons, "Education of Lacy Buchan," 366). Kreyling observes that the "kiss brings guilt and emotional turmoil; Lacy seizes Jane's slipper and a piece of his mother's petticoat at the same time, thus conflating the objects of his desire" (Kreyling, 122).

36. The Fathers-1938, 95–96.
37. Mark Van Doren to Tate, 11 Feb. 1937, AT-PU, 43:8.
38. Tate to MVD, 4 Feb. 1937, MVD-CU; Tate to Zabel, 19 March 1937, MDZ-CHI; Tate to MVD, 8 March 1937, MVD-CU.
39. Tate to Andrew Lytle, 19 May 1937, TDY-L, 108–9, 109.
40. Gordon to Sally Wood, May 1937, *Mandarins*, 205–10; Tate to Mizener, 29 Jan. 1969, AM-VU.
41. In addition to the primary sources I cite, in this section I draw from Ian Hamilton, *Robert Lowell: A Biography* (New York, 1982), esp. 28–52; from *Poets*, esp. 123–25; and from *Saddest*, 439–41.
42. Quoted in Hamilton, *Robert Lowell*, 43.
43. Gordon to Anne Winslow, [Summer 1937], AGW-UM.
44. Quoted in Hamilton, *Robert Lowell*, 43.
45. Tate-Forsyth et al., 4; Gordon to Sally Wood, May 1937, *Mandarins*, 209, 210n. Throughout this section, I also draw from Robert Lowell, "Visiting the Tates," *Sewanee Review*, 67 (Oct.–Dec. 1959): 557–59.
46. Gordon to Léonie Adams, "St James' Day," 1962, LA-YU.
47. Tate to Mrs. R. T. S. Lowell, 17 April 1940, Caroline Gordon–Allen Tate Correspondence, McFarlin Library, University of Tulsa.
48. A perceptive study of that relationship is William Doreski's *The Years of Our Friendship: Robert Lowell and Allen Tate* (Jackson, Miss., 1990), which I reviewed in *American Literature* 63 (June 1991): 351–53. See also Hammer's provocative chapter, "Robert Lowell's Breakdown," Hammer-1993, 211–32.
49. Lowell, "Visiting the Tates," 557.
50. Ibid., 558; Tate-Forsyth et al., 4.
51. Tate to Andrew Lytle, 19 May 1937, TDY-L, 108–9, 108.
52. Tate-Forsyth et al., 4.
53. "Notes by A.T. on trivial inaccuracies" for Arthur Mizener, p. 3, AM-VU.
54. Lowell, "Visiting the Tates," 559.
55. Simpson, *Poets*, 131.
56. Lowell, "Visiting the Tates," 559.
57. Simpson, *Poets*, 132.
58. Tate-Forsyth et al., 4; Nancy Tate Wood to Alfred Bush, 30 June 1991, photocopy courtesy of Alfred Bush.
59. Tate to Mizener, 29 Jan.1969, AM-VU.
60. Gordon to Anne Winslow, [Summer 1937], AGW-UM; Tate, "FMF," 73.
61. Tate, "FMF," 73.

62. Tate-Forsyth et al., 4.
63. Gordon quoted by Simpson, *Poets*, 125.
64. For an account of Kenyon's interest in Ransom, see Roberta T. S. Chalmers, "The Founding of the *Kenyon Review*," 2-page typescript dated 14 March 1988; photocopy courtesy of Waldron. President Chalmers apparently did not broach the topic of a magazine with Ransom until Oct. 1937; see Ransom to Tate, 29 Oct. [1937] and [undated], both in AT-PU. In the undated letter, Ransom asks Tate, "Would Scribner's be interested in backing a Review if you and I were its editors?"
65. Tate to James H. Kirkland, 24 May 1937, VU; repr. as "Appendix G2" in TDY-L, 376–77.
66. Kirkland to Tate, 25 May 1937, AT-PU, 7:6.
67. "Faculty Loss at 'Vandy' Hit," unidentified clipping, VU; "Vanderbilt's Dilemma," *Chattanooga Times*, 27 May 1937; Tate's remark appears in "Head of Vandy Answers Tate," 27 May 1937, unidentified clipping, VU. The executive editor of the *Chattanooga Times* told Tate "the story was a splendid one." Nevertheless, he added, "your letter was couched in terms so frank that you rather closed the door on any move on the part of the Chancellor or the trustees to reconsider" (Julian LaRose Harris to Tate, 1 June 1937, AT-PU, 7:6).
68. Lytle to Tate, [May 1937], AT-PU, AM 19629, 28:24.
69. Davidson to Tate, 26 May 1937, AT-PU, 18:3.
70. See Cowan-1959, 47.
71. *M&O*, 28.
72. Tate to Richmond ("Dick") Croom Beatty, 7 Feb. 1941, RCB-VU. On the Agrarians' relationship to Mims and on Ransom's crisis with Vanderbilt, I draw from the preceding letter and from Tate to Robert Penn Warren, 4 June 1937 [carbon], AT-PU, 7:6; Tate to Charles Cason, 1 June 1937 [draft], AT-PU, 7:6; Tate to Mark Van Doren, 26 June 1937, MVD-CU; Tate to Seward Collins, 7 July 1937, SC-YU; Tate to Stark Young, 6 Oct. 1937, SY-PM.
73. Tate to Robert Penn Warren, 4 June 1937 [carbon], AT-PU, 7:6.
74. Lyle Lanier quoting Davidson in Lanier to Tate, 27 May 1937, AT-PU, 7:6.
75. Lytle to Tate, [May 1937], AT-PU, AM 19629, 28:24; Tate to Robert Penn Warren, 4 June 1937, AT-PU, 7:6.
76. Mims quoted in *Gentleman*, 276. Young is mistaken when he concludes, "There is no evidence that Kirkland ever talked to Ransom or that Ransom and Mims conferred at all after Ransom told him that he had been 'approached by President Gordon Chalmers of Kenyon'" (278)—see Lyle Lanier to Tate, 27 May 1937, AT-PU, 7:6. Nevertheless, I have been able to emend my account throughout this section by comparing Young's otherwise helpful version of the affair (272–90). I am also indebted to Marian Janssen, *The Kenyon Review, 1939–1970: A Critical History* (Baton

Rouge, 1990), 10–16. Ian Hamilton's brief account (*Robert Lowell*, 45–46, 48, 53) focuses on the effects of the episode on Lowell.

77. Quoted in Davidson to Tate, 26 May 1937, AT-PU, 18:3.
78. Tate to Mims, 28 May 1937, DD-VU, apparently never mailed (see Mims/O'Brien, 542n–543n).
79. See Tate to Davidson, 28 May 1937, V.U.; and Tate to "The Editors, TIME MAGAZINE," 28 May 1937 [copy], AT-PU, 7:6.
80. Lanier to Tate, 27 May 1937, AT-PU, 7:6.
81. Lanier to Tate, 1 June 1937, AT-PU, 7:6.
82. Tate to Beatty, 7 Feb. 1941, RCB-VU. Tate to the Editor of the *Chattanooga Times*, 1 June 1937, AT-PU, 7:6. See also Tate to Charles Cason [draft], 1 June 1937, AT-PU, 7:6. Young quotes a letter Tate also wrote on 1 June 1937 to O. C. Carmichael, Kirkland's successor (see *Gentleman*, 281 and 494n).
83. "Ransom Given Time on Offer," *Chattanooga Times*, [early June 1937?], pp. 1, 11, 1; Tate to Lambert Davis, 28 May 1937 [c.c.], AT-PU, 7:6, and 4 June 1937, *VQR*-UVA. Young reports that while Kirkland would eventually consider raising Ransom's salary significantly, he left it to Mims to prepare a proposal for the trustees. Mims, while not opposed to the idea of a bonus, ultimately refused to recommend a permanent salary for Ransom equal to that proposed by Kenyon, (see *Gentleman*, 284–86). Yet Mims seemed unwilling to dismiss Ransom and the Agrarians entirely and wrote Kirkland: "Waving aside all that Allen Tate and his zealous friends have said—and I strongly resent their tactics and spirit—I should say that he [Ransom] has won a distinct place for himself among creative writers in America and England. . . . . While I do not agree with many of the ideas and methods of the so-called Agrarian group, I feel that they have had something to say and said it well" (Mims quoted in *Gentleman*, 284–85.)
84. Tate to O'Donnell, [28 May 1937 postmark], 3 June 1937, and [ca. June 1937]; O'Donnell and Tate to Bernard De Voto [fragment—draft], all in GMOD-WU; Zabel to Tate, 27 May 1937, and two letters of 4 June 1937 [carbon copy], Tate to Zabel [telegram] 9 June 1937, all in MDZ-CHI.
85. Tate to Robert Penn Warren, 4 June 1937 [copy], AT-PU, 7:6. Tate made an exception for Seward Collins, to whom he wrote, "We shouldn't object at all if your message took a pot-shot at Vanderbilt and Mims." See note by Tate on "Homage to John Crowe Ransom" [invitation], SC-YU.
86. Tate to Kirkland, 7 June 1937 [carbon copy], AT-PU, 7:6.
87. Tate to Mark Van Doren, 26 June 1937, MVD-CU.
88. Tate to Mizener, 29 Jan. 1969, AM-VU; *Saddest*, 440.
89. Ransom to Tate, 17 June 1937, AT-PU, 36:26. "I hope in spite of my high-handed methods," Tate had written Lytle, "to retain one of my dearest friends" (29 May 1937, TDY-L, 111–13, 112).

90. Gordon to Anne Winslow, [summer 1937], AGW-UM Not long after the dinner, Tate wrote Marion O'Donnell, "Mims just doesn't realize what he has done—the old fool still thinks he's the main show" (26 June 1937, GMOD-WU). Some months later, however, a satisfied Tate wrote Lambert Davis, "Mims knows he is defeated, and even thinks of going to the University of California" (25 Oct. 1937, *VQR*-UVA). When Tate met Ransom's replacement, he triumphantly described him as "a nice fellow, would make a good sexton in a Methodist Church" (Tate to Davidson, 9 Oct. 1937, DD-VU).

   Once the planning began for the *Kenyon Review*, Ransom asked Tate to consider serving as coeditor. Although Tate found the prospect alluring, he ultimately declined, fearing that the quarterly would have a rocky beginning. See Tate to Lambert Davis, 17 and 26 Dec. 1937, both in *VQR*-UVA.

91. Tate to Mizener, 29 Jan. 1969, AM-VU; Nancy Tate Wood to Alfred Bush, 30 June 1991, photocopy courtesy of Alfred Bush; Tate to Lytle, 28 July 1937, TDY-L, 114. On Ford and Lowell, see Hamilton, *Robert Lowell*, 50–52; on Ford and the Tates, see *Saddest*, 441.

92. Tate, "In Memoriam: Theodore Roethke, 1908–1963," page proof from unidentified publication, AT-PU.

93. Cleanth Brooks, untitled memoir, *Quarterly Journal of the Library of Congress* 36 (Fall 1979): 352. "The Tates," Brooks observed, "were genuinely and generously hospitable" (352). Joan Givner, *Katherine Anne Porter: A Life* (New York, 1982), 304–5, 305. (Misdating and misreading a letter of Tate's, Givner mistakenly concludes on page 304 that Porter and Tate had an affair.) Erskine and Porter were soon wed and divorced (310–15).

94. Tate to Lytle, [10 Sept. 1937], TDY-L, 114–15, 115.

95. Tate to Donald Davidson, 7 Oct. 1937, DD-VU.

96. Tate to Marion O'Donnell, 24 Sept. 1937, GMOD-WU.

97. Tate to Stark Young, 26 Nov. 1936, SY-PM; Tate to Zabel, 18 Sept. 1937, MDZ-CHI.

98. Davidson to Tate, 7 Oct. 1937, AT-PU, 18:3. For more on Tate's feeling about the Pulitzer, see Tate to Davidson, 9 Oct. 1937, DD-VU.

99. F. Cudworth Flint, "A Poet Makes Austere Demands," unidentified clipping, Library of Congress.

100. *Boston Transcript*, 31 Dec. 1937.

101. Zabel, "Reactionary Poems," *New Republic* 92 (20 Oct. 1937): 315–16, 315. Privately, Zabel wrote Tate, "I find myself so deeply involved in your problems and view point that I can hardly get enough distance for comfort" (28 Sept. 1937, AT-PU, Bx. 47).

102. Sandburg to Tate, 9 Dec. 1937, AT-PU, 38:27.

103. Walton, "On Analyzing Allen Tate's Poetry," *New York Times Book Review*, 5 Dec. 1937; *Current Biography: Who's New and Why, 1940,* ed. Maxine Block (New York, 1940), 790.
104. "Critic as Poet," [London] *Times Literary Supplement,* 26 Feb. 1938.
105. "E Pluribus Duo," *Time,* 1 Nov. 1937, 81–82, 81.
106. Samuel French Morse, "Second Reading," *Poetry* 51 (Feb. 1938): 262–66, 262.
107. Tate to Harry Duncan, 29 April 1945, HD.
108. Eliot to Tate, 12 April 1937, AT-PU, 19:53.
109. "Allen Tate," *Bookbuyer* (Nov. 1937), 9.
110. Tate, "Preface," *Selected Poems* (New York, 1937), ix.
111. Robert Lowell, "Visiting the Tates," 559.
112. Waldron, 173; Tate to Davidson, 20 Nov. 1937, DD-VU; Tate to Mark Van Doren, 8 Dec. 1937, MVD-CU.
113. Gordon to Anne Winslow, [late 1937?], AGW-UM.
114. Ibid.
115. W. C. Jackson to Tate, 16 Dec. 1937, AT-PU, AM 19629, 6:6; Tate to John Peale Bishop, 27 Dec. 1937, JPB-PU, AM 79–31, 23:2; Tate to Lambert Davis, 22 Dec. 1937, *VQR*-UVA.
116. Gordon to Anne Winslow [late 1937?], AGW-UM
117. Greensboro *City Directory,* 1938, 11–19.
118. Gordon to Harriet Owsley, [Feb. 1938], FLO-VU; J. Stephen Catlett, Archivist, Greensboro Historical Museum, to TAU, 13 Oct. 1987.
119. Gordon called Daniels "a mealy mouthed fathead" (see Gordon to Owsley, [ca. March 1938], FLO-VU); Tate to Davidson, 5 March 1938, DD-VU.
120. Tate to O'Donnell. 29 March 1938, GMOD-WU.
121. Tate to Donald Davidson, 12 April 1938, DD-VU.
122. Gordon to Harriet Owsley, [Feb. 1938], FLO-VU.
123. Tate to Davidson, 12 April 1938, DD-VU.
124. On the university and the Tates' courses, I draw from *The Woman's College of the University of North Carolina Bulletin,* 1937–38, esp. 15–16, 29, 106, 220; Virginia Terrell Lathrop, *Educate a Woman: Fifty Years of Life at the Woman's College of the University of North Carolina* (Chapel Hill, N.C., 1942), xi-xiii, 72–73; Tate to Lytle, 9 Feb. 1938, TDY-L, 116–17. Citing Dean Jackson's deep affection for each individual connected with the college, Lathrop wrote: "He loves them all, regardless of race, or creed, or color" (72). Jackson, however, ran a racially-segregated institution.
125. Lathrop, *Educate A Woman,* xii.
126. "Kentucky Novelist and Poet Husband to Join Faculty of University of N.C.," *Louisville Courier-Journal,* 8 Jan. 1938; "Noted Writers Will Teach at Woman's College," *Carolinian,* 14 Jan. 1938, p. 5; 2-page typescript "For Release Sunday, January 2," University of North Carolina–

Greensboro Archives. An exception is an undentified clipping titled "Two Writers Are Becoming Members of College Faculty: Allen Tate, Poet and Critic, and Wife, Who Writes under Name of Caroline Gordon, Will Teach Courses in Writing at Woman's College." According to Makowsky, "at this time Caroline was regarded as more or less Allen's equal as a writer. At the Woman's College, this was also the case since they both held the rank of professor and had equal teaching loads. In later years, Caroline regarded this situation with longing and bitter regret since she was soon to be demoted [at Princeton] to the rank of faculty wife; similarly, her reputation would decline while Allen's skyrocketed during the 1940s" (152).

127. Tate to Marion O'Donnell, 8 March 1938, GMOD-WU.

128. Tate to Desmond Hawkins, 15 April 1938 [copy], AT-PU, IIC, 8:4.

129. Tate to Lytle, 9 Feb. 1938, TDY-L, 116–117;117.

130. "Tension in Poetry," *Southern Review* 4 (Summer 1938): 101–15; the paper was originally titled "Tension in Poetic Imagery"; see Tate to John Peale Bishop, 11 Jan. 1938, JPB-PU, AM 79–31, 23:2.

131. Tate, *EFD*, 64, 56, 58, 67.

132. Tate to Davidson, 21 March 1939, DD-VU.

133. Richard Eberhart to Michael Hulme, 18 Feb. 1938, quoted in Mrs. Michael (Janet) Roberts, London, to Tate, 7 Oct. 1960, AT-PU, 37:32.

134. Tate to Mark Van Doren, 22 Feb. 1938, MVD-CU; Tate to Davidson, 6 March 1938, DD-VU; Tate to Folger Frost, 4 March 1938 (accompanies a letter of the same date from Tate to Dorothy Van Doren), MVD-CU.

135. Brooks, untitled memoir, 352; Brooks to Tate, [Summer 1938?], AT-PU, 13:33; Warren to Tate, [spring 1937], AT-PU, 44:28; Gordon to Warren [1937], *SR*-YU.

136. Dorothy Van Doren to Tate, [undated], AT-PU, 43:8; Tate to Mark Van Doren, 2 June 1938, MVD-CU.

137. Tate to Van Doren, 26 March 1938, MVD-CU.

138. Mark Van Doren to Tate, 29 March 1938, AT-PU, 43:8.

139. Tate to Cleanth Brooks, 30 April 1938, CB-YU.

140. The Fathers-1938, 117. Throughout my discussion of *The Fathers*, I have been aided by J.H., "*The Fathers*: A Pictorial Introduction," *Quarterly Journal of the Library of Congress* 36 (Fall 1979): 357–64; and by the illustrations accompanying Parsons insightful article, "The Education of Lacy Buchan," published in the same issue.

141. Tate-McDonnell, 36; Eugene Warner, "South Is U.S. Literary Center, Asserts Allen Tate, Noted Poet," *Washington Post*, 5 Jan. 1937, 13. See also an unattributed but annotated photograph of the house, UNC-Greensboro Archives.

142. Mizener is persuasive on this topic ("The Fathers," 610).

143. The Fathers-1938, 131–36, 132 (see again Mizener, " 'The Fathers' and Realistic Fiction," 109n).

144. Tate, "Note" appended to *The Fathers*-1977, 313; Tate, "A Note on THE FATHERS by the Author," 2-page typescript, AT-PU, 1:11, p. 2. See also Tate to Varnell Tate, 26 March 1927, RVT, in which he discusses "the feud that exists to this day" between the Varnells and the Bogans.

145. Tate, "A Lost Traveller's Dream," *Michigan Quarterly Review* (Autumn 1972): 225–36, 230 (repr., in *M&O*, 3–23, 11.)

146. The Fathers-1938, 122.

147. Ibid., 140.

148. Ibid., 183.

149. A portion of the following section I delivered as a paper titled " 'Punished by Crimes of Which I Would be Quit': The Racial Thought of Allen Tate, 1899–1979," Southern Historical Association, 1990. In the significant revisions I made to those remarks for inclusion here, I have attempted to respond to the excellent unpublished critiques delivered at the conference by Robert H. Brinkmeyer, Jr., and by Dan Singal. I am also indebted to Prof. Brinkmeyer for pointing out a number of my oversights about *The Fathers*. (For a fascinating explication of Tate's attitude toward Catholicism in the novel, see Brinkmeyer's *Three Catholic Writers of the Modern South* (Jackson, Miss., 1985), 42–47).

I have also profited from "Memories and Opinions of Allen Tate" (*Southern Review* 28 [Oct. 1992]: 944–64, 954–57, 963), an excellent article in which my friend and former colleague Lem Coley reaches similar conclusions about Tate's racism and feelings of guilt. Coley may overstate the case when he concludes "that Tate's poetic impotence was related to guilt about racism" (955), but is persuasive in his argument that "Tate felt guilty for behaving dishonorably, not for racism" (954). (Another possible explanation for the guilt expressed in Tate's poetry is proposed by Brinkmeyer, who argues that it "has less to do with specific acts than with humanity's fallen condition, the ongoing taint of original sin" [Brinkmeyer critique, 7].) Although not aware of all of Tate's public and private utterances about race, Coley is well versed in the sources and is insightful about the race themes in poems such as *Sonnets at Christmas* and *The Swimmers*.

150. Karanikas (*Tillers*, esp. 28–30), and Anne Ward Amacher ("Myths and Consequences: Calhoun and Some Nashville Agrarians," *South Atlantic Quarterly* 59 [Spring 1960]: 251–64) have shown that Tate and other Agrarians adapted such arguments from John C. Calhoun and Christopher Hollis.

151. Tate to Mark Van Doren, 26 May 1929, MVD-CU.

152. In an unpublished paper, Dan B. Miller contends that *The Fathers*, because Tate was responding to the attack against *ITMS* launched by liberals, "represents a progressive racial awareness that leaves traditional Agrarian ideology far behind" ("The Liberal Critique of *I'll Take My Stand* and a Reevaluation of Major Buchan and George Posey in Allen

Tate's *The Fathers*," 13 Jan. 1989, 25-page typescript copy courtesy of Mr. Miller, p. 13).

153. The Fathers-1938, 50, 54. Brinkmeyer observes that "Pleasant Hill . . . with its ordered life and well-treated slaves embodies just about all of the attributes of the Southern myth. The Major's flaw is not that he owns slaves but that he cannot adapt to changing times; it is George Posey, the embodiment of modern individualism, who sees slaves as 'liquid capital' and treats them as such. . . . In the emerging new world order, as opposed to the paradigm of the Old South, liquid capital is all that matters" (Brinkmeyer critique, 6–7). Seeing the sale of Jim as further evidence of the family romance motif, King observes, "What is 'wrong' in the transaction [to Tate] is not the enslavement and sale of a human being," but "the separation of the slave from his black family and . . . his white family" (King, 108).

154. The Fathers-1938, 19; Mizener, "The Fathers," 610.

155. The Fathers-1938, 31. Tate had held for some time before writing *The Fathers* the belief that the presence of African American slaves had kept white Southerners from developing strong ties to their own land and culture. See *Tillers*, 89–90. See also Lewis P. Simpson in Louis D. Rubin et al., eds., *The History of Southern Literature* (Baton Rouge, La., 1985), 174n.

156. The Fathers-1938, 205, 208.

157. Ibid., 218–19.

158. Ibid., 223, 226.

159. Reading the Yellow Jim episode and its aftermath as an instance of what W. J. Cash called the South's "gyneolatry" (*The Mind of the South* [New York, 1941; repr., Vintage Books], 89) and as illustrative of "gender relations under paternalism," Kodat reaches the novel conclusion that while George Posey is reaffirming "Southern patriarchal privilege," Susan Posey, "in staging a 'rape' in order to prevent a marriage, exhibits an opposition to paternal order nearly terrorist in its intensity" (Kodat, " 'You have Your Ma's Eyes,' " 16–24; 18, 19, 21). Mizener argues that Susan grew so disillusioned by the Poseys that she "determined to prevent her brother's marrying Jane" ("The Fathers," 612–613, 613).

160. The Fathers-1938, 236, 227, 230.

161. Ibid., 244–45.

162. Tate's intent in the denouement, Tom Wicker concludes, is to demonstrate that "Semmes shoots Yellow Jim as a necessary act to sustain a society built on the subjugation of a race; but George shoots Semmes as an immediate personal reaction to the murder of his black brother" "On Allen Tate's *The Fathers*," in *Classics of Civil War Fiction*, ed. David Madden and Peggy Bach (Jackson, Miss., and London, 1991), 174–80, 178.

163. Davidson to Tate, 3 Oct. 1938, *DD-AT,* 317–18, 318; in the original letter Davidson underlined the words "his own," as they appear above (AT-PU, 18:3). See also Glenn Cannon Arbery, "Victims of Likeness: Quadroons and Octoroons in Southern Fiction," *Southern Review* 25 (Jan. 1989): 52–71, 65–66. R. P. Blackmur also "felt dissatisfied at not knowing just what Yellow Jim did" (Blackmur to Tate, Thanksgiving Day [1938?], AM 19629, AT-PU, 12:6). Even after the 1960 reprint of the novel, readers were still puzzled over Yellow Jim's actions. Wondering what Jim "is supposed to have done to Jane . . .," Nevill Coghill asked, "What on earth did he do it for? I cannot believe he would want to rape his half-sister, yet there are the marks on her wrist" (Coghill to Tate, 13 Sept. 1962, AT-PU, AM 19629, 15:36).

164. Tate to Donald Davidson, 6 Oct. 1938, DD-VU (critics interpreting Tate's remarks in this letter usually overlook his theory about fear and violence). Some time later, Tate wrote Davidson, "I remember that you questioned in *The Fathers* my use of the Yellow Jim episode, on the ground that 'our enemies' would misunderstand it. They *did* misunderstand it; but if I had suppressed it, I should have been doing exactly the same thing our enemies do when they exaggerate such things in Southern life. I wasn't writing *The Fathers* as a representative of the South; I was simply writing my understanding of what I knew best" (7 Jan. 1940, DD-VU). It is difficult to determine at what point in the writing of *The Fathers* Tate added the Yellow Jim episode. A portion of an outline, which sketches scenes that appear in the final two sections of the novel— but which makes no mention of Yellow Jim—suggests that the story was not a part of Tate's early conceptions of the book (see Tate, untitled fragment of an outline of *The Fathers,* AT-PU, 1:12).

165. See *The Fathers*-1938, 19. Wicker observes, "Note the disparity in the names Mr. Tate gives to the 'good slave' Coriolanus, who accepts, and the bad slave [Yellow Jim], who transgresses." Calling Tate's "portrayal of southern slavery . . . romanticized," "soft-edged," and "roseate," Wicker comments, "I don't make much distinction between a willingness to own human beings and a willingness to sell them" ("On Allen Tate's *The Fathers,*" 177, 178).

166. Tate to George Marion O'Donnell, 22 Nov. 1938, GMOD-WU; Trilling "Allen Tate as Novelist," 112. Miller argues that Tate was admitting via Posey's treatment of Yellow Jim that "traditional Southern society had always rested *on the backs* of black labor"—and that Tate was stressing through Lacy's narrative "the shared culpability of all elements within Southern society . . . for the shame of a racial iniquity" (Miller, "The Liberal Critique of *I'll Take My Stand,*" 12, 13.)

167. "Allen Tate on 'The Fathers' " *Partisan Review* 6 (Winter 1939): 125– 26, 125. The Trilling papers contain a typescript version of the afore-

mentioned publication; see *"Letter from Allen Tate to Ph. Rahv. Novem-ber 22, 1938,"* LT-CU. (For comment on the letter, see Irving Howe, *A Margin Of Hope: An Intellectual Autobiography* [New York, 1982], 149.) In regard to the Old South, Aaron concludes, "Tate seems to be saying: 'Let us appropriate what is beautiful and true about the Old Order without being beguiled by its self-deceptions.'" (Aaron-1975, 303).

168. Tate to R. P. Blackmur, 28 Nov. 1938, RPB-PU, AM 21403, 8:11. Tate wrote a similar letter about *The Fathers* to Arthur Mizener: "Your per-ception that the whole structure is an artifice is the central point. In so far as I had a theory before I wrote the novel, it was this: that I wished to retain the great gains in sensuous immediacy won by the Jamesian or impressionist branch of the naturalistic tradition, and to eliminate its hocus-pocus of 'motivation' and cause and effect, along with its reliance upon 'recognition' or mere detailed photography of the scene for effect upon the reader. In short I wanted to retain realism without naturalism" (17 Nov. 1939, AM-VU).

169. Katie Gunther Kodat ("'You Have Your Ma's Eyes,'" 11n, 22–23) and Susan V. Donaldson have argued that race and gender relations in *The Fathers* are interrelated. According to Donaldson, "Lacy's hallucination [of Posey riding on Yellow Jim as if he were his new horse] serves, in a sense, as an apt and fleeting figure of the power dynamics of southern literary history. . . . A white man is forever linked in conflict with a black man, a contest determining the masculinity of each. And the centrality of that contest necessiates the marginalization of anything remotely sub-ordinate or feminine, including white and black women" (Susan V. Don-aldson, "Gender, Race, and Allen Tate's Profession of Letters in the South," in *Haunted Bodies: Gender and Southern Texts*, ed. Susan V. Donaldson and Ann Goodwyn Jones [Charlottesville, Va., 1997], 492–518, 510–511, 511). Arbery, whose excellent article about Southern novelists and "miscegenation" includes an etymology of the word (Ar-bery," "Victims of Likeness," 53) and anaylsis of Tate (57, 65–67, 69–70), calls Tate's inclusion of "a half-grown mulatto girl with kinky red hair and muddy green eyes in a pretty, Caucasian face" (*The Fathers*-1938, 60) "the living sign of her mother's concubinage and her owner-father's adultery" (57). Wicker calls the subsequent passage in which the "mulatto wench" (*The Fathers*-1938, 73) is willing to have sex with Lacy at the jousting tournament one of only "two points [in the novel when] the harsher reality of slavery comes savagely into focus" (Wicker, "On Allen Tate's *The Fathers*, 179). The family romance genre, King argues, made African Americans into "illegitimate children" of the white family (36), and steroytyped black women as sexual seductresses or mammies and black men as sexual predators or Uncle Toms. "The ulti-

mate challenge to the family romance," King argues, "was the sexual relationship of black men and white women, a violation of the incest and the miscegenation taboos" (37).

Also calling "the real violence of the novel the convergence of incest and miscegenation," Arbery reaches the fascinating conclusion that Tate "habitually comes to terms with the ideas and stances he most abhors by taking them into his family, knowing them, as it were, in his own blood. Looking back on slavery, for which he accepts an ancestral responsibility, he faces its darkest abuses through the intuitive medium of kinship, which will not allow it to be abstracted and disowned" ("Victims of Likeness," 66–67). From a somewhat different angle, Lewis Simpson has suggested in *Fable* that Tate failed to complete "Ancestors of Exile" because he was unable to confront (either in his own genealogy or in Southern history as a whole) the issue of white slaveholders' miscegenation. Picking up on Tate's later life suggestion that Posey's murder of Semmes was a form of symbolic redemption for that "miscegenation," Simpson concludes that *The Fathers* was "the autobiography that would fulfill [Tate's] quest for the paternity of the South and of himself," a Trojan horse containing the "appalling story of himself and of his family—a story of slavery, race, and America" (*Fable*, 40, 43–44, 52). While I share wholeheartedly Simpson's conclusions about the paternal resolution Tate achieved by writing the novel, the resolution in 1938 may have come not with contrition over the sins of his fathers disguised as fiction, but in the reclamation of his own role as a father in a nuclear family.

170. Tate, "A Lost Traveller's Dream," *Michigan Quarterly Review* (Autumn 1972): 225–36, 230–31, repr. in *M&O*, 12–14). See also the annotations about Martha Jackson, in Tate's hand, on the reverse of a photograph in AT-PU, 48:6. On Tate's inclusion of the anecdote in his memoirs, see *Fable*, 29–31, 37–40, 53.

171. Tate to Lincoln Kirstein, 10 May 1933, *H&H*-YU. Tate argued in the same letter that he and other white Southerners would want control over race relations "even supposing that we had a superior race like the Chinese in our midst." While admitting that Tate was "imprisoned by a conviction of black inferiority," neoconservative historian Eugene Genovese has argued that Tate's remark is evidence that his main concern was "not some presumed superiority [of whites] but the defense of a discrete culture" (Genovese, *The Southern Tradition: The Achievement and Limitations of an American Conservatism* [Cambridge, Mass., 1994], 88). Genovese's argument about the remark does not erase the stark fact that Tate's letter to Kirstein was thoroughly racist in its assumptions and that it endorsed white supremacy.

172. Tate, "Negro Poet Depicts Simple Life of Race," *Nashville Tennessean*, 24 Feb. 1924, 12; Tate, "New Anthology Gives Verse of Negro Writers," *Nashville Tennessean*, 3 Aug. 1924. See also Frederik L. Rusch, "Meet-

ings of Allen Tate and Jean Toomer," *American Notes and Queries* 17 (Dec. 1978): 60.

173. Michael Fabre, *From Harlem to Paris: Black American Writers in France, 1840–1980* (Urbana, Ill., 1991), 83.

174. Tate to Mark Van Doren, 29 Jan. 1929, MVD-CU.

175. I am indebted here to three slightly variant accounts: Eugene Levy, *James Weldon Johnson: Black Leader, Black Voice* (Chicago, 1973), 326–28; Arnold Rampersad, *I, Too, Sing America: The Life of Langston Hughes*, vol. 1, *1902–1941* (New York, 1986), 231; and John Egerton, *Speak Now against the Day: The Generation before the Civil Rights Movement in the South* (New York, 1994), 68–69. For the exchange of letters, see Tate to Tom Mabry, 20 Jan. 1932 [carbon copy], Records of the NAACP, Administrative Files, Box C-102, Personal Correspondence: White, Walter, Library of Congress; Mabry to Tate, 22 Jan. 1932, AT-PU, Box 28; Tate to Tom Mabry, 25 January 1932 [copy] , Records of the NAACP, Administrative Files, Box C-102, Personal Correspondence: White, Walter, Library of Congress.

176. Warren to Tate, fragment [ca. 1931], AT-PU, 44:28.

177. Tate to Davidson, 22 July 1930, DD-VU. Both Davidson and Lyle Lanier thought Warren's essay too liberal! See Davidson to Tate, 21 July 1930, AT-PU, 18:2; Lanier to Tate, 1 Aug. 1930, AT-PU, 27:8. For a Southern liberal's reaction to the treatment of race issues in *ITMS*, see Ralph McGill, *The South and the Southerner* (1959; repr. Boston, 1964), 82.

178. See Tate to Lytle, 2 June 1933, TDY-L, 82–84, 83.

179. Tate to John Brooks Wheelwright, 25 Feb. 1932, JBW-BRN. Tate attempted to conflate such white supremacist thinking and Agrarian paternalism in his review essay, "A View of the Whole South," *American Review* 2 (Feb. 1934): 411–32, 423–25, 426.

180. Arna Bontemps to Langston Hughes, 10 November 1966, in *Arna Bontemps–Langston Hughes Letters, 1925–1967*, ed. Charles H. Nichols (New York, 1980), 477.

181. Tate, *Sonnets at Christmas, Collected Poems*, 103. Tate explained to Anthony Hecht: "I told a lie to escape punishment that got a negro playmate of mine punished, and I didn't have the courage to confess the lie. . . . [A]t the age of 65 I am still rather haunted by that occasionally. Because this boy Henry was about a year older than I am and he was drafted in the first World War and he was killed in Japan, I never had a chance to apologize to him" (Tate-Hecht, 34).

182. During World War II, Tate continued to harbor hostility toward Northern race reformers. In 1943, for instance, he wrote a letter to the governor of Tennessee in which he urged "responsible Southern leaders" to take action lest "irresponsible and ignorant people in the North" begin to "take over the leadership of the negro." Along with the letter, in which he defended segregation, Tate forwarded some literature he had received

in the mail, describing it to Cooper as "the most recent specimen of Eastern racial agitation." The literature, Tate told the governor, was "well within the historic pattern of abolitionist feeling, an attitude that may be defined as the desire to improve the morals of people at a distance with no cost to oneself" (Tate to Gov. Prentice Cooper, 17 Sept. 1943 [carbon copy, unsigned: "fc/at"] AT-PU, AM 19629, 16:13). In Tate's wartime correspondence with Frank Owsley and Donald Davidson, he also expressed agreement with the race attitudes of the two most reactionary Agrarians. (See Tate to Owsley, 18 Nov. 1943, FO-VU; Tate to Davidson, 4 Aug. 1944, 13 Oct. 1944, & 27 Jan. 1945—all in DD-VU; and Davidson's segregationist diatribe, "Preface to Decision," in the *Sewanee Review* 53 [July–Sept. 1945]: 394–412, written at the request of, and privately praised by, Tate, who was then editing that journal.) When Tate published a partly critical editorial responding to Davidson's article, he warned that "any responsible leader who ignores Mr. Davidson's central argument ignores it at the peril of the south and the country." ("Mr. Davidson and the Race Problem," *Sewanee Review* 53 [Oct.–Dec. 1945]: 659–60, 660.) Nevertheless, Tate simultaneously professed to hold more moderate and pragmatic views than Davidson, with whom he expressed impatience and some disagreement when writing to other friends (see Tate to Brainard Cheney, 18 Oct. 1945, BC-VU; and Tate to F. O. Matthiessen, 16 Oct. 1945, Yale Collection of American Literature, Beinecke Rare Book and Ms. Library, Yale University).

Coley has written of the postwar Tate, "As a citizen of a wider world, Tate felt, I think, that southern racism and the exploitation of blacks made him and his intellectual position vulnerable. I think he wanted to somehow ease the situation of blacks without altering the structure of southern society, not a rare stance for educated southerners before the Civil Rights movement. Over the years he made gestures that later seemed patronizing or fainthearted to some, such as his foreword to Melvin B. Tolson's *Libretto for the Republic of Liberia*; but they meant something to him" ("Memories and Opinions of Allen Tate," 954).

183. Tolson to Tate, 15 March 1950, AT-PU, AM 19629, 42:21.

184. Tate, "Speculations," *Southern Review* 14 (April 1978): 226–32, 232; *The Swimmers, Collected Poems*, 132–35, 135. Of this final line, Coley observes, "Tate closed the poem with a home truth most southern writers couldn't manage." Such authors, Coley adds, "presented racial terrorism as the work of cranks and rednecks, people marginal to the community" ("Memories and Opinions of Allen Tate; 955).

185. Program, "American Studies Conference on Civil Rights" (photocopy courtesy of Mrs. Lucy Bowron); Tate, untitled typescript of speech delivered at the University of Minnesota, 16 Oct. 1959, 6 pp., with corrections in Tate's hand (photocopy courtesy of Mr. Paul Collinge, Heartwood Books, Charlottesville, Va.), 2, 4.

186. Tate to Warren, 5 Oct. 1960, RPW-YU. See also Tate to Lytle, 9 Sept. 1959, TDY-L, 284, and Dan Ross, "Memories of Allen Tate," 13 March 1980, 15-page typescript, 4–5.
187. See Tate to Jesse Wills, 18 May 1962, JW-VU; Tate to Davidson, 19 Oct. 1962, DD-VU; Tate-Hecht, 38–40, 38.
188. Tate to Davidson, 23 Nov. 1962, DD-VU.
189. Tate-Hecht, 38–40, 38.
190. Tate, "April 9, 1865: *A Peroration a Hundred Years After,*" 5-page typescript, AT-PU, 3:6. See also "Appomattox, April 9, 1865: A Peroration a Hundred Years After," *Spectator* (April 1965): 467–68.
191. Referring to Warren's *Who Speaks for the Negro?* (New York, 1965), Tate wrote, "Your general point of view I share completely, and I hope it will have some effect on Negro leadership as well as upon white people, North and South." Tate to Warren, 8 June 1965, RPW-YU.
192. Tate to Daniel Aaron, [ca. 1976], DA; *Surrealists*, 356; Tate to Stanley Burnshaw, 24 Feb 1962, typescript copy, AT-PU, 25:66.
193. The author and book were Leonard Greenbaum, *The Hound and Horn: The History of a Literary Quarterly* (The Hague, 1966); the letter is quoted on 145–48. For the story of Tate's effort to block distribution of the book, see Tate to John Goetz, 23 Nov. 1966, 25 Nov. 1966; Tate to Greenbaum, 27 Nov. 1966 [carbon copy]; Simon Silverman, Humanities Press, to Tate, 1 Dec. 1966; Donald Gallup, Beinecke Library, to Tate, 2 Dec. 1966; Goetz to Tate, 3 Dec. 1966 [carbon copy]; Tate to Goetz, 5 Dec. 1966; Greenbaum to Tate, 6 Dec. 1966; Gallup to Greenbaum, 8 Dec. 1966 [carbon copy]; Tate to Greenbaum, 12 Dec. 1966 [copy]; and Tate to Goetz, 14 Dec. 1966—all in JG. See also Tate to Yvor Winters, 27 Nov. 1966 [c.c.], AT-PU, 46:18; Kirstein to Tate, 30 Nov. 1966, AT-PU, 22:49; Tate to Cowley, 1 Dec. 1966, MC-N; Tate to Winters, 6 Dec. 1966, YW-STN; and Silverman to Tate, 12 Sept. 1968; and Tate to Silverman, 16 Sept. 1968 [carbon copy]—both in AT-PU, IIc, 4:6.
194. Tate to Cowley, 1 Dec. 1966, MC-N.
195. Tate to Aaron, [ca. 1976], and Tate to Aaron, 1 April 1976, DA. Aaron had argued, "On miscegenation . . . Tate hardly differed from Thomas Nelson Page" (Aaron-1975, 299–300, 299).
196. Tate to Aaron, 1 April 1976, DA. The following passage in a 1931 letter by Caroline Gordon evidently refers to Tate's relationship with Kezee: "We have the most remarkable milker, a negro school teacher. He and Allen have long talks. He seems to have thought on all the problems of the day and has a long, considered answer. The problem of race equality he dismisses by saying he has no use for any animal that isn't thoroughbred. He is rather moony and finally confessed that he sometimes wrote poems. He brought Allen one called 'Sorrow' that wasn't bad, sort of Biblical in phrasing" (Gordon to Sally Wood, 21 Aug. 1931, *Mandarins,* 84–86, 86). Gordon, whose letters are replete with racist remarks, was

given to making comments such as, "Niggers are unfathomable" (see Gordon to Cinina Warren, undated, RPW-YU). In the 1932 letter to Tom Mabry in which Tate insisted that "there should be no social intercourse between the races unless we are willing for that to lead to marriage," he added, "This interesting theory is not original with me. It was expounded to me by the colored man who milks our cow." Tate to Mabry, 20 Jan. 1932 [carbon copy], Records of the NAACP, Administrative Files, Box C-102, Personal Correspondence: White, Walter, Library of Congress.

197. Even after solemnly renouncing his earlier views, Tate's letters periodically contained racist jokes—and his views on race hardened when the 1960s turned radical. His support of King cooled considerably when the civil rights leader became involved in protests against the Vietnam War, an involvement Tate thought opportunistic. Whatever support Tate had shown for the civil rights movement as a whole diminished during urban rioting and the Black Power and student protest movements of the 1960s. In late 1967, Tate wrote his daughter, Nancy, "The Negro revolt could not have taken place had the Negro been really *oppressed* today; he is rebelling because he has got more than he has ever had and now demands more: he demands *all*, far more than the Southern Red Necks are getting. . . . I am not moved by the Negro's demand for social justice and equality (worthy as those causes may be); I am interested in order and civilization, which in a crisis take precedence over all other aims; for without civilized order the Negro's justice will be mere vengeance" (Tate to Nancy Tate Wood, 25 Oct. 1967, AT-PU, IIc, 10:2b). Tate seemed almost to be echoing his 1933 letter to Kirstein in which he had argued "not social justice but social order is the key. . . . Once the power is established, there is legal justice for the ruled race—but that is very different from social justice. It is the outside interference that frightens the South so terribly that we get hysterical and deny the negro what we are really willing to give him: legal justice" (Tate to Kirstein, 10 May 1933, *H&H*-YU).

Tate did not approve of busing. "Of course, I believe in civil rights," he said in a 1971 newspaper interview. "This busing thing, though, is awful. It is villainous for politicians to play with the schools and the children in that way" (Tate quoted in "Defender of Southern Faith, Tate Is a Citizen of the World," *Greensboro Daily News*, 7 Nov. 1971, D1).

198. A. Theodore Johnson and Allen Tate, *America through the Essay: An Anthology for English Courses* (New York, 1938.)

199. "Preface" (ibid.). Tate's own contribution was his essay on Emily Dickinson, repr. on 312–27.

200. Tate to Donald Davidson, 4 May 1938, DD-VU. See Davidson's *The Attack On Leviathan: Regionalism and Nationalism in the United States* (Chapel Hill, N.C., 1938.)

201. S.S., "Allen Tate Is Co-Editor of New Volume of Essays," *Greensboro Daily News*, [15 May] 1938; "Mr. Allen Tate Has New Book Published," *Carolinian*, 20 May 1938, 1.

202. Tate to Davidson, 4 May 1938, DD-VU. Tate later said that he had changed the tone intentionally. "The labor in the book was the prose-rhythm and the tone," he wrote Bill Troy. "I still don't know whether I got by with the shift of tone after Lacy reaches the Posey house: it was necessary but I wanted it imperceptible" (Tate to Troy, 7 Oct. 1938, LA-YU).

203. Tate to Mark Van Doren, 2 June 1938, MVD-CU.

204. Tate to Van Doren, 18 June 1938, MVD-CU.

205. Gordon to Janice Biala, [Summer 1938], FMF-CNL. See also Gordon to Elizabeth Green, [ca. June 1938], PG-SHC.

206. Woodward discusses the Agrarians and the Southern literary renaissance writers (including Tate, Faulkner, and Warren) in *The Burden of Southern History*, 3d ed. (1960; rpt. Baton Rouge, La., 1993), x, 8–9, 24–39, 265–88 (and analyzes his own book in *Thinking Back: The Perils of Writing History* [Baton Rouge, La., 1986]), 101–19, 109). Here I have also been influenced by King, who speaks of the Southern family romance writers' Freudian "attempt to to tell [their] story and be freed of the burden of the past" (10). Yet I believe King underplays the many traditionalist features in the work of Woodward and Warren when he concludes that the two Yale professors "articulated a transcending vision of the southern past" (277). Singal may be correct in asserting that "the god of the Old South had failed" for Tate by 1938, but I cannot agree that "the South had never been the real focus of Tate's concern" or that he merely "used" his Southernism as a "healing" agent for modern angst (*War Within*, 259, 260). Instead I see Tate as having at last acquired permanent comfort with the regional identity he acquired in childhood.

207. On Olmsted in the South, see Victor A. Kramer, *Encyclopedia of Southern Culture*, ed. Charles Reagan Wilson and William Ferris (1989; repr., New York, 1991) 2:509–10.

208. Tate to Lytle, 10 July 1938, TDY-L, 123–24, 124. Caroline, often more critical of Northerners than Tate, said of the Beecher affiliation, "I hope his spirit does not haunt the mound" (see Gordon to Janice Biala, [Summer 1938], FMF-CNL).

209. Tate to Lytle, 10 July 1938, TDY-L, 123–24; Gordon to Janice Biala, [July 1938], FMF-CNL. Tate's hastiness did result in quite a few mistakes. "The book is full of errors owing to the rush of getting it through," he admitted. "There's one very bad misstatement of dates on page 117" (Tate to Lytle, 14 Sept. 1938, TDY-L, 126–27). Over the years, a variety of readers located other anachronisms. On Tate's misuse of the 1928 *Book of Common Prayer*, see Nicholas Phillips, "A Note on Allen Tate's *The Fathers*," *American Notes & Queries* 21 (Jan.–Feb. 1983): 74–75.

Upon reading Aaron-1975, 303n–304n, Tate admitted, "I am sorry I flubbed Mr. Jackson at the Marshall house. You're right: Major Buchan would not have known him" (Tate to Aaron, 1 April 1976, DA). For a list of emendations Tate made for the 1960 reprint, see AT-PU, 20:20.

210. Tate later wrote Lytle, "I felt that the scene of the killings—Yellow Jim and Semmes—was too brief, in actual reading time; but then it had to be all action, and I decided that anything else added would be padding" (10 Oct. 1938, TDY-L, 130).

211. The Fathers-1938, 258–62.

212. Tate-Forsyth et al., 5.

213. It is uncertain when Tate decided to use the story of the Argonauts to dramatize Lacy's return trip. In 1966, Tate recalled, "I got to that particular place [in the MS] and the boy had to get home. . . . Well, I couldn't do anything for about a month and finally the Jason thing popped into my head one morning and I rushed to the Vanderbilt Library and got out *The Argonauts* by Apollonius of Rhodes and read it" (Tate-Forsyth et al., 5). But an outline Tate apparently drafted before he wrote the Yellow Jim episode mentions "A day at school with the Argonauts affair" (untitled frag., outline of *The Fathers*, AT-PU, 1:12).

214. The Fathers-1938, 266–68. King, who observes that the "family romance . . . pitted son against father and often joined grandson and grandfather," points out that Lacy nevertheless ignores his grandfather's evaluation of Posey (King, 35, 109).

215. See Squires-1971, 142–43. "One takes the poem as a whole," Squires concludes, "as a vision of the intensity of Tate's feeling about his ancestors: their secret bond with each other; the way that one generation dies into the birth of the next; and the way all of the generations are bound together by love . . . and evil" (143). Tate explained, "It had occurred to me that I could also use a part of a poem I had written long before . . . about a boy walking along a road with an old man who's evidently his grandfather; and so the myth of Jason, plus this walk with the apparition, gave me the suggestion about the device of using the myth. I couldn't just let it occur in Lacy Buchan's mind. I wanted somebody else to tell *him*. So I had the apparition of his grandfather, and the boy was hallucinated" (Tate-Forsyth et al., 5). But other evidence suggests that Tate may not have been consciously aware of echoing his poem. In 1963, for instance, he told Davidson, "I *think* that Arthur Mizener spotted the relation of my Records I to Lacy's vision; but I'm not sure. In a sense that early poem was the spring-board for *The Fathers*" (Tate to Davidson, 10 Jan. 1963, DD-VU).

216. Tate to Desmond Hawkins, 9 May 1939 [carbon copy], AT-PU, IIC, 8:4.

217. Tate to R. P. Blackmur, 28 Nov. 1938, RPB-PU, AM 21403, 8:11.

218. The Fathers-1938, 272–79; Tate to Bishop, 28 Sept. 1938, JPB-PU, 23:2.

219. The Fathers-1938, 284.
220. The Fathers-1938, 289–301. Gordon to Robert Penn Warren, [1937], *SR*-YU.
221. Tate to Robert V. Tate, 29 Jan. 1971, RVT.
222. Tate, "A Lost Traveller's Dream," *Michigan Quarterly Review* (Autumn 1972): 225–36, 228.
223. The Fathers-1938, 302–6, 303, 306.
224. Tate, "Note" appended to *The Fathers*-1977, 314. Responding to critics, Tate revised the concluding lines in that edition to "fifty years later I remembered how he restored his wife and small daughter and what he did for me. What he became in himself I shall never forget. Because of this I venerate his memory more than the memory of any other man." The changes, Tate wrote, produce "two heroes: Major Buchan, the classical hero, whose *hubris* destroys him; George Posey, who may have seemed to some readers a villain, is now clearly a modern romantic hero" (*The Fathers*-1977, 306–7, xxi). For the critical role Cleanth Brooks played in Tate's revision of the ending, see Brooks to Tate, June 9 [1976?], AT-PU, IIc, Box 2. Assessing the two versions, Simpson argues that Lacy's attitude toward Posey in both is made believable by Posey's symbolic reclamation of Yellow Jim as a family member (*Fable*, 41–43). Kodat argues that the revised ending "makes explicit the tribute to modernization and resurrection of patriarchy hitherto mostly implicit in the 1938 version" (Kodat, " 'You Have Your Ma's Eyes,' " 24–25, 25.) For an intelligent query about the first version, see Nevill Coghill to Tate, 13 Sept. 1962, AT-PU, AM 19629, 15:36. Thornton Parsons, in "The Education of Lacy Buchan" (cited above), builds one of the most persuasive interpretations of the evolved reasoning behind Lacy's final judgment of Posey.
225. The Fathers-1938, 126; Young, "Introduction," xviii–xix. Rubin argues that Posey "*meant* well" but helped the "abstract," passionless Major Buchan destroy his family. Pointing to the plural in Tate's title, Rubin concludes that Posey, whose "modernity" Lacy recognizes in himself, "is, equally with Major Buchan, Lacy's spiritual father" (*Wary Fugitives*, 317, 321, 322, 323). Brinkmeyer argues that Lacy, "hoping to forge his own vision of wholeness," learns from both fathers but picks Posey in the end (*Three Catholic Writers of the Modern South*, 46–47). Kreyling argues that Tate reenacted his rejection of Robert E. Lee through Lacy, who sees Major Buchan the way Tate saw Lee, as an "an impregnable whole" possessing a "seamless selfhood." Lacy, according to Kreyling, is more like Tate's Jefferson Davis, fractured, deracinated, and modern. While Lacy "is called to both models of the self," ultimately he commits "patricide" such as that committed when Tate withdrew from Lee. Nevertheless, Kreyling concludes, Lacy forgoes Major Buchan's tradition-bound "character" only to inherit Posey's self-conscious "personality"

and its modern "replica of hell" where "there are to be no answers" (Kreyling, 120–24). Miller, who argues "that Posey and Buchan are not best understood in their opposition, but rather, in their convergence" ("The Liberal Critique of *I'll Take My Stand*" 5), criticizes "efforts to understand Posey as a simple agent for the destruction of traditional Southern society" (18) and suggests that Tate based the characters on Ransom and Eliot (22–25). From another angle altogether, Kodat rejects "the traditional view of the novel as only, or even primarily, the story of a conflict between two fathers" (" 'You Have Your Ma's Eyes,' " 14).

King believes Tate was only partly successful in his effort to escape his history. "Tate's work, beginning with 'Ode to the Confederate Dead' and culminating in *The Fathers*," he argues, ". . . ends in a tragic confusion between past and present" in which "neither repetition nor recollection can triumph" (18). King understands the novel's "deep ambivalence toward both Buchan and Posey as representatives of two distinct ways of life" (310n), but he treats the novel as more irresolute than it is. What is missing from his interpretation is Tate's personal psychological resolution, a reintegration revealed indirectly in Lacy's "love" for Posey—which King finds "a mystery" (109). "The loss of the father," King observes, "signals the destruction of an ordered world" (110). But one could argue that Tate found another world in losing his father.

226. The Fathers-1938, 43. This emotional distance is what Rubin calls Major Buchan's "freezingly polite disdain" (*Wary Fugitives*, 95). On Bishop's suggestion, see *Republic*, 146n.

227. Tate, untitled fragment of an outline of *The Fathers*, AT-PU, 1:12. Parsons argues that, at the novel's conclusion, "Lacy is entering upon great danger and uncertainty by himself, and in doing so he is emulating his hero and his father-elect, George Posey." Yet he warns readers against viewing "Posey primarily as the New Southerner" (Parsons, "The Education of Lacy Buchan," 373). Although I agree with Squires that Lacy, whom he believes may be Tate's real hero, picked the living Posey over the dead, "foolish" Major, Squires may overstate the case by arguing that Tate meant to expose "the antebellum plantation order [as] imperfect and somehow silly . . . to a contemporary mind" (Squires-1971, 144–45). Asked about Mizener's prediction ("The Fathers," 607) that "Tate may become very unpopular in The South, for he knows he is not Major Buchan and never can be, knows that he is as completely excluded from the world of Pleasant Hill as George Posey was, and therefore shares George's sense of its radical absurdity," Tate responded, "What Mr. Mizener apparently does not know is that the entire modern South is 'as completely excluded from the world of Pleasant Hill as George Posey was'—quite as excluded as I am" (Tate-McDonnell, 37). After selling his papers to Princeton for a large sum, Tate admitted, "I'm a grandson of G. Posey, and have business and money in the blood. . . . I

did it just to please the ghost of Grandpa" (Tate to Mizener, 25 Oct. 1967, AM-VU).

228. Tate to Lytle, 6 July 1959, TDY-L, 278. (Numerous critics have noticed Tate's creation of an inherent problem in the Buchan family and their world, with some suggesting that Posey accelerated events—see Baker, "grand Tour of Fiction," 821; Young, "Introduction," xiv, xvii, xix; Rubin, *Wary Fugitives*, 317, 320, 322; and King, 110). In a perceptive reading of the novel as "the work of a writer who was drenched in Southern history and who viewed that history against the private history of his own family," George Core sees Posey as an "intruder who wanders into a dying conventional society," one that was destroying itself "before 1861." Core points out many of the novel's technical flaws, such as "characters [who] occasionally lapse into stereotypes," but concludes that the book nevertheless succeeds by virtue of "the cogency of its style, the authority of its tone" (see "Mr. Tate and the Limits of Poetry," *Virginia Quarterly Review* 62 [Winter 1986]: 110–11, 112, 113; Tate-McDonnell, 37, 34, 37). Tate added, "I was not so much concerned with an 'idea of the South' as with the age-old conflict between individual power and social order. The germ of the novel was in my own antebellum family history, and this fact gave the conflict a local habitation and a name. When Frank Kermode reviewed *The Fathers* in *Encounter*, he discussed it along with *The Leopard*, pointing out that both novels were centered in the moment of violent change from order to chaos" (Tate-McDonnell, 33–34). (Kermode's review, "Old Orders Changing," *Encounter* 15 [Aug. 1960]: 72–76, which I have found helpful on a number of points, is glowing.) Bingham concludes, "*The Fathers* did not resolve Tate's divided loyalties, but the novel's mode of criticism struck a more balanced view of the South by emphasizing the Southern past as an expression of the universal human condition" ("Where Are the Dead?" 99–107,106.)

229. Simpson points out that between the genealogy book and the novel, Tate dropped the Scotch-Irish bloodline and kept only the "the Virginia bloodline." (*Fable*, 38) Yet one should remember that Tate had modeled that Scotch-Irish line after his paternal ancestors. Further bearing in mind Makowsky's observation that Tate's mother "managed to replace the Tates with the Bogans as Allen's imaginative fathers" and that Tate's connection to Major Buchan (Bogan) therefore existed "through 'the mothers' " (45), the "species of patricide" Kreyling attributes to Tate-as-Lacy (Kreyling, 124) is thus directed toward a man who is descended from Tate's mother and who acts like Tate's father. Singal is right that the novel's "original filiopietistic impulse had become transmuted" (255) in the period leading to its creation, yet because he finds Tate's Modernism half-trapped in Victorianism, he suggests the patricidal impulses were aimed more toward Posey than Major Buchan. But in the 19

Nov. 1938 letter to Bishop that Singal cites as evidence, Tate intended his exclamation "All honor to Major Buchan" more as a defense against the "Marxist" critique of the Old South by Trilling (*Republic*, 146). Like Richard King, who makes Robert Penn Warren the true Modernist and liberal over Tate, Singal finds it hard to believe that Tate could have admired Posey, whom he calls "a rootless modern liberal" and "a Victorian's nightmare" (*War Within*, 257).

230. Twentieth Century Authors, ed. Stanley J. Kunitz and Howard Haycraft (New York, 1942), 1386.
231. Tate to Zabel, 4 March 1932, MDZ-CHI.
232. Gordon quoted in Jonza-ms., 389.
233. Commager, "Conflict of Ways of Life in the Old South," *New York Herald Tribune*, 25 Sept. 1938.
234. Tate to Lytle, 13 Sept. 1936, TDY-L, 102–3, 103.
235. Gordon to Sally Wood, [late winter 1928], *Mandarins*, 34–36; 35.
236. Gordon to Léonie Adams, [late 1936?], LA-YU.
237. Gordon to Léonie Adams, [June 1936?], LA-YU.
238. Tate to Mark Van Doren, 4 Feb. 1937, MVD-CU.
239. Interview with Nancy Tate Wood, 31 March 1987.
240. Gordon to Léonie Adams, [late 1936?], LA-YU; Gordon to Anne Winslow, undated [very late Dec. 1937 or early Jan. 1938], AGW-UM.
241. Gordon to Elizabeth Green, [ca. June 1938], PG-SHC.
242. Tate to Mark Van Doren, 2 June 1938, MVD-CU; Waldron's account of the summer has also proved helpful (180–81).
243. Interview with Charles Van Doren, 28 Feb. 1988, Cornwall, Conn.
244. Tate to Van Doren, 2 Oct. 1938, MVD-CU.
245. Tate to Bishop, 24 July 1938, JPB-PU, AM 79–31, 23:2. Kodat interprets these lines, with their initial allusion to Tate's book and then to the Battle of Bull Run, as evidence of his unconscious ranking of "masculine history" before "a woman's history," i.e., Nancy's. It may be true, as Kodat suggests, that Tate's words here contribute to a "subterranean feminine effect," but his remarks might just as easily be read as a dimunition of male egocentrism: as a sign of Tate's new acceptance of his personal responsibilities as a father. Kodat is close to getting at this transformation when she observes, "Most *Fathers* hope for a son, but this one wants a moon" (Kodat, " 'You Have Your Ma's Eyes,' " 14) I would argue that Tate, by finding a way to escape his mother's version of Southern history, and thereby his feelings of orphanhood, was finally able to love his own daughter.

Sources and Acknowledgments

Although no comprehensive biography of Tate is yet available, over the years there have been four attempts besides my own to write one.[1] One of those attempts has been abandoned, two are pending, and one was published. The obstacles to Tate biographers include the huge volume of sources, the multiplicity of approaches available, and the contemporaneity of the topic (Tate died in 1979). Any potential biographer encounters the additional difficulty of discussing the details of Tate's unpredictable personal life, especially during his later years. Although he was as often loyal and reliable, he quarreled with many of his closest friends, engaged in extramarital affairs, and was married four times: twice in a row to Caroline Gordon (1895–1981), once to the poet Isabella Gardner (1915–81),[2] and finally to Helen Heinz. The number of marriages puts any Tate biographer attempting to write his entire life into the unusual position of having to satisfy the stipulations of three different literary executors—not to mention having to respond to the concerns of Tate's living friends and acquaintances. In the late 1960s, Tate himself began worrying that some eager literary scholar would come along and open doors he preferred

---

[1] Here and below, I revise and reprint a number of passages from my article, "Mr. Tate and His Biographers: The New Criticism and the Problem of Literary Biography," *Princeton University Library Chronicle* 50 (Spring 1989): 206–19. I also use portions of the "Preface and Acknowledgments," i–viii, in my "Orphan of the South: A Life of Allen Tate" (Ph.D. diss., Harvard University, 1990), which examined Tate's life between 1899 and 1933.

[2] Marian Janssen, of the Katholieke Universiteit in the Netherlands, is preparing a biography of Isabella Gardner.

were kept closed. Not long after he had sold some thirty cubic feet of his papers to the Princeton University Library, he wrote to the University Librarian in a slight panic worried that someone without discretion would examine his personal letters.[3]

Yet the first person to show an interest in writing Tate's biography was the well-known historian of Southern literature, Louis D. Rubin, whose interest in Tate lay mainly in Tate's literary career. Rubin, University Distinguished Professor Emeritus at the University of North Carolina at Chapel Hill and author of a series of important books about the Southern Literary Renaissance, formerly edited the *Johns Hopkins Review* and the *Southern Literary Journal.* He struck up a professional friendship with Tate in 1953, and shortly afterward Tate supported his application for a *Sewanee Review* fellowship. "Eventually somebody is going to write your biography; you know that," Rubin warned Tate in 1965. "And if that somebody is any good . . . he is going to try to show you not simply as poet and novelist and essayist, but also as a man of letters." For the next decade, Rubin would continue discussing the project with Tate, who respected Rubin's ability but came to fear that Rubin knew him too well to write an impersonal account of his life.[4]

Meanwhile, in 1967, a few years after Rubin had made his initial proposal, a poet named Radcliffe Squires wrote to Tate asking permission to write a literary biography. Squires, who received his doctorate from Harvard University, went on to become a professor of English at the University of Michigan and published a number of volumes of poetry and criticism. When he wrote for permission to begin the project, Tate replied with some enthusiasm; he told Squires that he had complete confidence both in his prowess as a textual critic and in his ability to be discreet with personal information. It did not matter, Tate added, that Squires was not a Southerner, for the lives of French writers are not always told by their countrymen.[5]

Before long, Squires was immersed in the research. "I have been steeping myself lately in Tate materials, catching up on books and articles," he reported to Tate. "I also spent several days in Princeton making a dent in the deposit there. I'll have to go back later. It was simply too formidable."[6] Although Squires faced restrictions imposed on him by Tate and by an editorial deadline, in 1971 he produced an admirable study, focusing mostly on Tate's poetry and criticism. In the preface to *Allen Tate: A Literary Biography,* he alluded to

[3] Tate to William S. Dix, 28 June 1967, Princeton University Library, Vertical File.

[4] Rubin to Tate, 5 May 1965, AT-PU, Box 37; Tate to Rubin, 17 Dec. 1973, LDR-SHC. For an account of Rubin's effort to write the biography, I have drawn from Louis D. Rubin, Jr., to TAU, Dec. 1988. See also Walter Sullivan, *Allen Tate: A Recollection* (Baton Rouge, La., 1988), 85–86.

[5] Tate to Squires, 6 Aug. 1967, RS-WU.

[6] Squires to Tate [carbon copy], 3 May 1968, RS-WU.

certain difficulties he had encountered in working on the project: "Writing about a living contemporary," he commented, ". . . is a delicate matter. It requires a gentlemanly contract whose stipulations are all the more strict for being unstated."[7] When Caroline Gordon read the finished product, she immediately wrote to Squires: "Working all that stuff up must have been an immense labour. I am somewhat handicapped, though, in reading the narrative part of your book. It is a miracle of tact but what you have written often contradicts facts. I suspect that you have been misled by Allen's habit of writing his friends accounts of his daily life which did not tally with what happened. . . . It all strengthens me in my conviction that people shouldn't have their biographies written while they are still alive. There is a certain sifting of events which only posterity can accomplish. . . . I cannot believe, however, that any critic who comes along will surpass you in the reading of Allen's poems."[8] (My work has been made easier by the existence of this groundbreaking biography of Tate, and I am further grateful to have had the encouragement of a critic as able as the late Professor Squires, who warned me more than ten years ago that Tate "could be charmingly naughty.")[9]

Despite the publication of Squires's book, Louis Rubin maintained his interest in writing a biography. But he was discouraged by the restrictions Tate seemed to insist on, and he tried to persuade him that he needed a freer hand. "There is no way that I could write the biography you deserve unless I am given full authority," he argued. "I could not simply *exclude* portions of your experience relevant to your life and art. If *I were* to attempt that, someone else would point them out. All I could and would assuredly do would be to keep the narrative focused on the main show."[10] Rubin evidently knew then what he correctly observed after Tate's death—that "almost all that [Tate] wrote is drawn either directly from his own situation or from that of his immediate forebears"—and he saw that an impersonal biography would shed little light on Tate's work.[11] Tate balked, and Rubin abandoned the biography.

Professor Rubin was generous enough to allow me to interview him, to share photocopies of letters he received from Tate, and to write me accounts of his efforts to write a biography. What he would have argued had he written one, he once wrote to me, was that in Tate's poem *Mr. Pope*, he "was writing about himself, or an ideal of himself! The hunchback, the little guy who kept the world at bay through his wit and ferocity." I also share Professor Rubin's

[7] Squires-1971, preface.

[8] Gordon to Squires, 7 June 1971, RS-WU.

[9] Squires to TAU, 12 Dec. 1988.

[10] Rubin to Tate, 1 Jan. 1976, AT-PU, Box 7.

[11] Louis D. Rubin, Jr., "Allen Tate, 1899–1979," *Sewanee Review* 87 (Spring 1979): 267–273, 270. The obituary was reprinted in Rubin, *A Gallery of Southerners* (Baton Rouge, La., 1982).

insight that Tate was "really a very vulnerable person."[12] (Rubin, I should add, is author of an excellent critical study, *The Wary Fugitives: Four Poets and the South* (1978), which has influenced this biography in a number of ways. Rubin, for instance, is one of the critics who understands Tate's struggles with religious faith, with the world of Nellie Tate, and with Tate's view of himself and his work before and after her death. Yet I seem to make a friendly departure from Rubin and several others who argue that Tate's Southernism was more of an accessory to than it was a cause of his Modernism; I believe Tate's much-discussed "persona" was not his Southernism but his Modernism. Perhaps Professor Rubin, to whose work I owe a substantial debt, would agree with me that Tate used Modernism to keep his emotions as a Southerner at bay.)

Once Rubin abandoned his biography, Tate grew concerned that someone would write an unauthorized life, so he attempted to find an official biographer. He asked John Crowe Ransom's biographer, Thomas Daniel Young at Vanderbilt, if he would undertake the project, but Young turned him down.[13] Finally, Tate contacted a talented writer named Robert Buffington, a Vanderbilt Ph.D. in English. Buffington, whose dissertation on John Crowe Ransom's poetry was brought out by the Vanderbilt University Press at Tate's recommendation, published a complimentary review essay on Tate in 1973.[14] He had since become an editor at the University of Georgia Press, where he helped bring out the correspondence between Tate and Donald Davidson.[15] Not long after Louis Rubin withdrew from the biography, Tate designated Buffington as his "authorized" biographer. Under the auspices of a grant from the National Endowment for the Humanities, Buffington spent an uninterrupted year researching the book. He was sensitive to Tate's wish not to be relegated to the status of a regional poet, and during an early stage of his research he assured Tate that he was building a portrait of him as one of the most important writers

[12] Rubin to TAU, 31 Jan. 1989. Rubin explicates the poem more fully in *Wary Fugitives*, 88–92.

[13] My work would have been far more complicated without the assistance of Professor Young, whose *Gentleman* has not been supplanted, and whose intelligently introduced editions of Tate correspondence are essential sources (see *DD-AT*, *Republic*, and TDY-L). Professor Young and his family were kind enough to entertain me in Rose Hill, Mississippi, in August 1987.

[14] Robert Buffington, *The Equilibrist: A Study of John Crowe Ransom's Poems, 1916–1963* (Nashville, Tenn., 1967); "'The Directing Mind': Allen Tate and the Profession of Letters," *Southern Literary Journal* 5 (Spring 1973): 102–15. In the essay, Buffington makes the valuable observation that "much of Tate's practical criticism is literary biography in brief: the essays on Emily Dickinson, Keats, Hart Crane, Hardy" (105)—and that it thus contradicts the stereotyped definition of New Critical principles.

[15] See *DD-AT*; and Thomas Daniel Young and M. Thomas Inge, *Donald Davidson: An Essay and a Bibliography* (Nashville, Tenn., 1965).

in this century.[16] But Buffington apparently became alienated when his knowledge of the subject began to exceed the official parameters of the project, and before long he had "publicly declared his independence, saying that if he left out all of the names he had been pressed to leave out, there would not be much left to write."[17]

Caroline Gordon had never been excited about the prospect of another biography being written while her former husband was still alive. "Allen Tate," she told Buffington, "has played an important part in the history of American Literature. And anybody who has published *a book is, of course, fair game for any contemporary critic*. . . . I feel, however, that I would not be according him his just due if I broke my rule and furnished you or any other contemporary biographer information about his life. Posterity is, after all, the inevitable judge of every life!"[18] Although I do not know Mr. Buffington, I have come to appreciate some of the frustrations he endured. Nor can I help feeling anything but a bond with a biographer who has devoted so much energy to Tate. Mr. Buffington, who is the author of a number of articles on Tate and remains one of his biographers, is a poetry critic who was merely trying to do his job.[19]

About the time that Mr. Buffington suspended work on his biography, a fourth biographer entered the picture. Ned O'Gorman, a friend of Caroline Gordon and of Isabella Gardner, brought to the project an established reputation as a poet; already he had published numerous volumes of verse with Harcourt Brace and Alfred A. Knopf. O'Gorman also served formerly as a State Department American Studies specialist in South America. In 1979 Simon and Schuster invited him to sign a contract to write a biography of Tate. He immediately began writing to individuals who knew Tate, explaining, "I have decided to do [the biography] though I am simply scared to death at the thought of it but I am driven on by a great kind of delight and excitement."[20] To Radcliffe Squires he wrote, "I am not a scholar nor am I a critic, I am a poet. I have published some books, poetry and others, but this landscape of scholarship and letters is a strange one for me. But I am increasing in courage."[21]

[16] Buffington to Tate, 1 Dec. 1978, AT-PU: Additional, 2:15.

[17] Sullivan-1988, 102.

[18] Copy of Gordon to Buffington, 14 April 1977, AT-PU, Box 4.

[19] Although I did not use the following two articles as sources, I reach, working from Tate's letters, a few conclusions similar to those drawn by Mr. Buffington in "Young Hawk Circling," *Sewanee Review* 87 (Fall 1979): 541–56; and I think Mr. Buffington's "Allen Tate: Society, Vocation, Communion," *Southern Review* 18 (Jan. 1982): 62–72, a wonderful celebration of Tate's total devotion to letters. (In my third chapter, I do make use of Mr. Buffington's review, "High Jinks in Nashville, 1923." *Sewanee Review* 87 [Spring 1979]: xxx, xxxii.)

[20] O'Gorman to Margaret Mills, 13 May 1979 (courtesy of American Academy of Arts and Letters, New York City).

[21] O'Gorman to Squires, 1 Aug. 1979, RS-WU.

Although Mr. O'Gorman enjoyed the benefits of already knowing many of Tate's friends, and even succeeded in recording an interview with Caroline Gordon, he soon began running into the same problems faced by Squires, Rubin, and Buffington. In a prospectus he delivered before Aileen Ward's biography seminar at New York University, O'Gorman described some of these problems: "So one day the biographer has enough to begin. And he begins to write and discovers, as I have discovered, that lies, deceptions, half truths, fake truths, family loyalties, friendships, literary feuds get in the way and render even a birth date suspect."[22] "The difficulty," he explained, "after all the literary feuds are ironed out is how we will deal with Allen's erotic life. It was not a phase, a period, a flash of libidinous fever. It was a quality in his life that assumed in his marriages a fragmenting power and dealt to his creative life a sundering loss of energy. He lived out a literary 'soap opera'; the tales are infinite, all of them true, most of them scandalous. Many of the ladies with whom Allen slept are alive. Many of them are distinguished, and some of them are 'celebrities.' . . . I must find a way to deal with this erotic 'element' and to do it with charity—but unless it is dealt with there is no biography."[23] Mr. O'Gorman, who has now retired from his post as headmaster of the Children's Storefront School in Harlem, may still have a contract with Simon and Schuster. But Helen Tate has threatened to take him to court if he publishes his unauthorized life of Tate.

This is how the field looked in 1985 when I began working on a biography of Tate. Although I have completed all of the research for a full life of Tate, this book ends in 1938, by which time Tate had helped define the Southern Literary Renaissance, had founded and abandoned the Agrarian movement, and had written *The Fathers*. As an American Studies scholar who specializes in Southern history and literature, I have focused on that phase of Tate's career in which he attempted to reconcile his art and his ancestry. By 1938, he had resolved many of his feelings of regional and personal orphanhood.[24] (While I have not avoided any sensitive topics in writing this biography, I hasten to explain to those readers expecting more salacious detail that most of Tate's philandering occurred after 1938.)

I here acknowledge only those individuals and institutions whose assistance helped me to write Tate's life prior to 1939. Although I have not written an "official" biography, my greatest debt is to Mrs. Helen Heinz Tate, Tate's widow and literary executrix, who has consistently offered her full cooperation and encouragement; she has required me to expurgate nothing from my account. I am also grateful to her two sons, John and Benjamin Tate, whose

[22] O'Gorman, untitled typescript, n.d., p. vi.

[23] O'Gorman, untitled typescript, p. vii.

[24] In my title and throughout, I refer to the "psychic, emotional, or spiritual orphanhood" discussed by Eileen Simpson in *Orphans: Real and Imaginary* (New York, 1987), 218–33, 220.

418 • Sources and Acknowledgments

intelligence, wit, and sensitivity brought their father to life for me. Mrs. Nancy Tate Wood, Allen Tate's daughter by Caroline Gordon, and Dr. Percy Wood, Mrs. Wood's husband, not only entertained me in two different countries, but allowed me to record hours of interviews and wrote access letters to a variety of archives. Mr. Ben E. Tate, Jr., of Cincinnati, Ohio; Mr. Robert Varnell Tate, of Wayne, Pennsylvania (the sons of Allen Tate's two older brothers); and Mr. Allen W. Tate (Robert Varnell Tate's son) were equally generous with their time.

This is a fully and painstakingly documented book based primarily upon exhaustive research in manuscripts libraries. The Tate Papers, housed in the Firestone Library at Princeton University, are among the several most important collections of literary correspondence in the United States. The collection contains letters to Tate from T. S. Eliot, Robert Lowell, Ernest Hemingway, William Faulkner, and dozens of other important American and European authors. Of this collection, the late Willard Thorp, Tate's former colleague at Princeton, observed, "Any scholar who wishes to write about [Tate's] life and work or the condition of poetry and criticism in his lifetime will have to see these papers. They fill 57 boxes."[25] As far as I know, I am the only scholar to have read the entire collection. After spending the summer of 1986 exploring the voluminous collection, it quickly became clear to me that I would be spending many more months in the Firestone Library. To facilitate my work, I spent the 1987–88 academic year as an Exchange Scholar in the Princeton University History Department—and then passed three additional summers working in the archives.

In Firestone, I benefited from the expert guidance of Miss Jean F. Preston, Curator of Manuscripts; from her successor, Mr. Don C. Skemer; and from the late Mr. Alexander Wainwright, Ms. Jane Moreton, Ms. Ann Van Arsdale, Ms. Margrethe Fitzell, Ms. Dolly Pinelli, Mr. Charles Green, Keeper of the Reading Room, Ms. Margaret M. Sherry, Reference Librarian and Archivist, and Ms. Annalee Pauls, Photoduplication Coordinator. For help negotiating my way through the library system, and for never-ending encouragement, I owe special thanks to my dear friend Mr. Alfred Bush, Curator of the Western Americana Collection. The late Professor Arthur S. Link of the Princeton University History Department and Editor-in-Chief of the Woodrow Wilson Papers, my interim adviser in 1987–88, helped me in more ways than I can recount. Several members of the Princeton English Department extended courtesies: the late Professor Wilbur Samuel Howell, Professors A. Walton Litz, Richard M. Ludwig, Thomas P. Roche, Jr., and the late Willard Thorp. Highly literate Prince-

---

[25] Thorp, "Allen Tate at Princeton," *Princeton University Library Chronicle* 41 (Autumn 1979): 1–21; 1. Citing the observation of Young and Hindle that Tate's letters to John Peale Bishop are a window into "Tate's search for an authoritative source to give order, direction, and meaning to his personal life" (*Republic*, 7), Lewis P. Simpson suggests that Tate's letters as a whole constitute an autobiography (*Fable*, 31n.).

tonians such as Kim and Loraine Otis, Howard and Paola Greenfeld, and Professor Bruce Redford enlivened my research by merging the intellectual, the social, and the culinary. My editors at Princeton University Press have shown the patience of Job with me. I am especially grateful to Mr. Robert E. Brown, who negotiated my contract and served as my first editor, to Ms. Mary Murrell, my editor since 1994, and to Ms. Cindy Crumrine, my copy editor.

In addition to my years of work at Princeton, I corresponded with and, in many cases, worked in, a total of some ninety additional manuscript libraries, out of which I amassed more than ten thousand photocopies of Tate letters or manuscripts. Although it is not possible for me to list all the reference and manuscripts librarians throughout the country who helped me, I can at least mention a few. Mr. Steve Love, Reference Librarian at the Hilles Library, Radcliffe College, seemed actually to enjoy fielding my endless and obscure bibliographic questions. Mr. Nathaniel Bunker of the Widener Library at Harvard University graciously purchased numerous dissertations for my use. In the Beinecke Rare Book and Manuscript Library of Yale University, I received the generous assistance of Ms. Christa Sammons, Acting Curator; Mr. T. Michael Womack, Processing Archivist; Mr. William R. Massa, Jr., Public Services Archivist; and Mr. Donald Gallup (who helped me research the authorship of Tate's introduction to *White Buildings*.) At the Butler Library of Columbia University, staff members Mr. Bernard R. Crystal, Ms. Jane Rodgers, and Mr. Hugh Wilburn were kind enough to help me. Mr. Jon Reynolds, University Archivist, Georgetown University Library and Archives, and his assistant, Ms. Lisette C. Matano, helped me to piece together Tate's time at the Georgetown Preparatory School. Ms. Patricia A. DeMasters, Records Supervisor, Office of the University Registrar, University of Virginia, was kind enough to dig out Tate's "Permanent Record Card" from his enrollment in the 1919 summer school session. It would have been impossible to reconstruct Tate's Vanderbilt connections without the aid of a number of affiliates of that university, most notably Ms. Marice Wolfe, Head of Special Collections & University Archivist; Ms. Joan Sibley, her able assistant; Ms. Strawberry Luck, photographic archivist; Mr. R. Gary Gibson, University Registrar; Ms. Susie C. Archer, Associate University Registrar; Jan Gardner, Office of Alumni and Development; Mr. Thomas Russell, Student Assistant, Office of Alumni Publications; and the late Professor William T. Bandy of the W. T. Bandy Center for Baudelaire Studies. The Rhodes College alumni office, Ms. Martha H. Shepard, editor of *Rhodes Today*, and Mr. William M. Short, Head of Information Services in the Burrow Library at Rhodes, helped me to locate materials related to Tate's tenure at Southwestern. For information on Valle Crucis, North Carolina, I am indebted to Mr. H. G. Jones and Ms. Alice R. Cotten of the North Carolina Collection, University of North Carolina Library. Ms. Emilie Ward Mills, Special Collections Librarian, and her staff at the University of North Carolina at Greensboro, and Mr. J. Stephen Catlett, Archivist at the Greensboro Historical Museum, helped me with the Greensboro era. For help researching Tate's years in Ashland, Kentucky, I am grateful to Mr. Arnold Hanners.

Since this biography also attempts to synthesize the primary sources with the existing secondary literature in multiple fields, I have also read extensively from (but I am sure not all of) the published works by and about Tate. Fortunately, five excellent bibliographical guides to a vast number of works are available to scholars. The first of the guides was prepared by Willard Thorp. Though now superseded, Mr. Thorp's work ("Allen Tate: A Checklist," *Princeton University Library Chronicle* 3 [April 1942], 85–98) remains useful for its manner of arrangement. The next bibliography did not appear for twenty-five years, when a former student of Tate's, Mr. James Korges, prepared "Allen Tate: A Checklist Continued" (*Critique* [Summer 1968]: 35–52). Mr. Korges's checklist is helpful but was shortly dwarfed by an entire volume of citations, Mr. Marshall Falwell's *Allen Tate: A Bibliography* (New York, 1969). More than a hundred pages long, Mr. Falwell's bibliography is exhaustive, intelligently arranged, and easily navigated. To update this fine listing, I have turned to two briefer but more recent bibliographies: one is appended to *Allen Tate and His Work: Critical Evaluations*, ed. Radcliffe Squires (Minneapolis, 1972); the other is contained in Philip Lee Carman's massive dissertation, "A Bibliographical Study of the Major Fugitive Poets: Donald Davidson, John Crowe Ransom, Allen Tate, and Robert Penn Warren" (University of Tulsa, 1977). Sources not generally included in bibliographies include newspaper articles, tape recordings of Tate readings, lectures, interviews, and dissertations on Tate in microfiche.

While it is impossible to cite every single source I have read in my study of all seventy-nine years of Tate's life, readers will find in the copious endnotes that precede this bibliography full citations to all sources that I have used in the preparation of this volume. My policy has been to construct my narrative from primary sources first, enriching the story with detail from secondary sources whenever necessary. It should then be obvious that I could never have written this book without the previous work and personal assistance of other scholars and critics, many of whom have become friends. I have attempted to exercise the highest standards whenever I made direct use of their work. Although I have not thought repetitious citations necessary each and every time I drew minor factual details from these secondary sources, I have taken the utmost care in attributing fully those sources from which I have drawn any ideas, conclusions, quotations, or from which I have used an extensive amount of material. Some similarities to those works are, of course, unavoidable due to shared use of primary sources. I have nevertheless worked hard to make my account differ in vocabulary, tone, and interpretation from all other accounts; if any unconscious echoes of other biographical or secondary sources have crept into my narrative, I hereby acknowledge the authors of those works and thank them.

While I thank many more Tate and Gordon scholars in the exhaustive end-notes to this book, I single out for special mention here Professor Ashley Brown of the University of South Carolina English Department;[26] Professor Lewis P. Simpson, editor emeritus of the *Southern Review* and author of *The Fable of the Southern Writer*;[27] Professor Joseph Blotner, the authorized biographer of Robert Penn Warren;[28] the late Professor Ferman Bishop, author of *Allen Tate*;[29] Professor John L. Stewart, author of *The Burden of Time: The Fugitives and Agrarians*;[30] and Professor Langdon Hammer, of the Yale English department, author of *Hart Crane and Allen Tate: Janus-Faced Modernism*.[31] At the annual meeting of the Southern Intellectual History Circle (SIHC) at Emory University in Atlanta, Georgia, in April 1989, I profited from discussions with Professor Daniel Joseph Singal, Department of History, Hobart and William Smith Colleges, whose excellent work on Tate's struggle with cultural modernism has been indispensable in the preparation of this volume.[32] I am equally grateful to the organizer of that conference, Professor Michael O'Brien, Department of History, Miami University, whose incisive Tate criticism has also

[26] Ashley Brown is editor, with Frances Neel Cheney, of *The Poetry Reviews of Allen Tate, 1924–1944* (Baton Rouge, 1983).

[27] Over the years, I have profited by much conversation and correspondence with my valued friend Lewis Simpson, who also has shared copies of his compelling articles and books. Although I disagree with a number of specific interpretations he advances in *The Fable of the Southern Writer* (Baton Rouge, La., 1994), I have found it a brilliant analysis of "Tate's lifelong struggle to come to terms with the self-reflective, the autobiographical, impulse" (31) and share wholeheartedly his recognition that Tate's "scheme to write autobiography as family history" (35) lay at the center of his life and work (see *Fable*, esp. 24–53). Yet while Simpson understands Tate's search for paternity, he defines Tate's "family history" projects more abstractly as genealogical, autobiographical, or historical projects; I use the term differently to mean Tate's psychological obsession with the idea of recasting the biography of his own parents and thus reconstructing his nuclear family. Only then, I argue, was Tate able to shed his identity as a Southerner orphaned by region and family alike. Nevertheless, Simpson's work has influenced this biography.

[28] Professor Blotner was kind enough to answer a number of my queries over the years. I have decided to refrain from reading his *Robert Penn Warren: A Biography* (New York, 1997) until my Tate biography appears, but I here cite for interested readers what is probably the definitive Warren biography.

[29] (New York, 1967.) Professor Bishop graciously shared photocopies of the letters he received from Tate.

[30] (Princeton, 1965.) Professor Stewart was generous enough to share photocopies of his letters from Tate.

[31] (Princeton, 1993). Professor Hammer offered helpful comments on two passages from my manuscript and made me think more about the aesthetic disagreements among modernist poets such as Tate and Crane.

[32] "The Divided Mind of Allen Tate," in *The War Within: From Victorian to Modernist Thought in the South* (Chapel Hill, N.C., 1982), 232–60.

influenced me.[33] Professor O'Brien helped me in innumerable ways and read an early version of my manuscript for Princeton University Press. Professor Michael Kreyling of the Vanderbilt University English Department served as a second reader for the press and offered equally valuable criticisms and suggestions.[34] Professor Fred Hobson, coeditor of the *Southern Literary Journal*, helped in innumerable ways. Professor Lem Coley of Nassau Community College (State University of New York), author of an insightful essay on Tate, engaged me in stimulating conversation and correspondence.[35] The late Professor M. E. Bradford, whom I also met at the SIHC conference, was kind enough to give me a copy of his helpful monograph on Tate.[36] Although I never got a chance to speak with his colleague at the University of Dallas, Professor Robert S. Dupree, I have profited by his excellent study of Tate's poetry.[37] (The University of Dallas is evidently teeming with Tate scholars, for its faculty also includes Professor Louise S. Cowan, whose classic on the Fugitives has been of immeasurable value to me.)[38]

My task was also made easier by a decade of intellectual dialogue with Caroline Gordon's three biographers. Gordon's first biographer,[39] Mrs. Ann Waldron, who cheerfully tolerated my contrary theories about the relationship between Tate and Gordon, generously opened her files to me. Professor Veronica A. Makowsky of the University of Connecticut English Department, author of the second Gordon biography to appear, aided me during my visit to Louisiana State University.[40] Dr. Nancylee Novell Jonza, author of the third biography, and I answered each other's queries; later I was pleased to read her manuscript for the University of Georgia Press and urge its publication.[41] I was also happy to have chaired "Caroline Gordon and Allen Tate Reconsidered," an April 1996 Society for the Study of Southern Literature panel in Richmond, Virginia, where the three Gordon biographers appeared together for the first

[33] Michael O'Brien, "Allen Tate: 'The Punctilious Abyss,'" in *The Idea of the American South: 1920–1941* (Baltimore, 1979), 136–61.

[34] Professor Kreyling, whom I got to know through our numerous conference panels, is author of *Figures of the Hero in Southern Narrative* (Baton Rouge, La., 1987), which contains a brilliant examination of Tate's aborted biography of Robert E. Lee (103–24).

[35] "Memories and Opinions of Allen Tate," *Southern Review* 28 (Oct. 1992): 944–64.

[36] *Rumors of Mortality: An Introduction to Allen Tate* (Dallas, 1969).

[37] *Allen Tate and the Augustinian Imagination: A Study of the Poetry* (Baton Rouge, La., 1983).

[38] *The Fugitive Group* (Baton Rouge, 1959).

[39] *Close Connections: Caroline Gordon and the Southern Renaissance* (New York, 1987).

[40] *Caroline Gordon: A Biography* (New York, 1989).

[41] *The Underground Stream: The Life and Art of Caroline Gordon* (Athens and London, 1995). In my notes, I cite the manuscript version of this book as Jonza-ms.

time. The existence of these Gordon biographies, all three of which naturally take Gordon's point of view over Tate's, has not only allowed me to make a number of emendations to my account of the Tate-Gordon years but has given me the luxury of keeping my own book centered on Tate.

During my years of studying Southern Agrarianism, I have amassed a significant debt to scholars of that movement. Professor Emily S. Bingham, whom I met at Harvard in 1986 when she was at work on her excellent undergraduate thesis on the Agrarians, has since become a valued colleague and friend. During the long period she and I spent coauthoring the introduction to and editing our forthcoming collection *The Southern Agrarians and the New Deal: Essays after "I'll Take My Stand"* for the Southern Texts Society and the University Press of Virginia, I profited from our countless discussions about the movement.[42] Although I have never met Professor Edward S. Shapiro of Seton Hall University, I have cited his excellent journal articles so frequently that I feel as if I have; I am especially indebted to his persuasive scholarship on Tate during the *American Review* era. Professors Paul K. Conkin, whose book *The Southern Agrarians*[43] I have found quite helpful, and Professor Dewey W. Grantham, another distinguished member of the Vanderbilt University History Department, were kind enough to share their thoughts about the Agrarians and to entertain me at the Vanderbilt faculty club. While I did not use Professor Mark G. Malvasi's recent book on the Agrarians in the preparation of this biography, I believe his well-written book adds to our understanding of the Agrarians' anticapitalism.[44] In December 1998, I was pleased to have chaired a well-attended Society for the Study of Southern Literature session at the San Francisco MLA meeting, in which Professors Virginia J. Rock, Susan V. Donaldson, and Gene Bell-Villada delivered the thought-provoking papers that constituted *"I'll Take My Stand* at Fin de Siècle: The Southern Agrarians Reconsidered" and Professor Michael Kreyling served as respondent.[45] While I look at the Agrarian movement (and the Southern Literary Renaissance) in different terms than does Professor Richard H. King, I have found his theory

[42] I am also indebted in a number of ways to Emily Simms Bingham, "Where Are the Dead? Three Agrarians in Search of the Southern Past, 1920–1940" (senior thesis in history, Harvard University, 1987), esp. 68–109.

[43] (Knoxville, Tenn., 1988); I reviewed Conkin's book for *American Literature* 61 (March 1989): 115–17.

[44] *The Unregenerate South: The Agrarian Thought of John Crowe Ransom, Allen Tate, and Donald Davidson* (Baton Rouge, 1997); I reviewed Malvasi's book for *American Literature* 70 (Dec. 1998): 911–12.

[45] I have profited by Professor Rock's "They Took Their Stand: The Emergence of the Southern Agrarians," *Prospects* 1 (1975): 205–95, and by the biographical sketches she wrote for Twelve Southerners, *I'll Take My Stand: The South and the Agrarian Tradition* (1930; repr., with an introduction by Louis D. Rubin, Jr.; Baton Rouge, La., 1977.)

of the "southern family romance" compelling as cultural-historical context for the biographical model I employ in my final chapter, which explores Tate's effort to "reconstruct" his actual family.[46]

During a visit to Sewanee, Tennessee, I was grateful for the stimulating conversation of Mr. George Core,[47] editor of the *Sewanee Review*, whose advice to slow down and to focus on the early portion of Tate's career ultimately proved correct. Mr. Core and his wife, Susan, were also kind enough to introduce me to Mr. Monroe Spears, editor emeritus of the review, and to Mr. Don Keck Dupree. I also owe a great debt to the many Tate scholars on whom I have tested my ideas at conference panels devoted to southern literary history; Professor Robert H. Brinkmeyer, Jr., of the University of Mississippi Department of English, gave me some valuable criticisms of a paper I delivered at the Southern Historical Association meeting in 1990.[48] Professor Bertram Wyatt-Brown of the University of Florida chaired that panel and gave me encouragement in the early days of my work. Professor Katie Gunther Kodat of Hamilton College was kind enough to share a copy of her work on *The Fathers*. Professor Martha E. Cook, also a fine Tate scholar, has graciously attended my Tate and Gordon panels for years.[49] Professor James M. Kempf gave me valuable leads into Tate's relationship with Malcolm Cowley. Professor Al Filreis, of the University of Pennsylvania Dept. of English, directed me to a number of primary sources. Professor Brom Weber, of the University of California at Davis Department of English, shared his valuable advice about the Tate's relationship with Hart Crane. Professor Ben Johnson of Southern Arkansas University, who was kind enough to share a copy of his early work on John Gould Fletcher, made

[46] Richard H. King, *A Southern Renaissance: The Cultural Awakening of the American South, 1930–1955* (New York, 1980.)

[47] With T. D. Young, Mr. Core edited the *Selected Letters of John Crowe Ransom* (Baton Rouge, La., 1985), the introduction to which I admire for its recognition of Tate's attempt to define himself against (and without) his family and for its assessment of the friendship between Tate and Ransom—whom I agree "were southern gentlemen of an older time, regardless of their relation to modernism" (1–15, 4, 5). Mr. Core's fine work on Tate includes "Mr. Tate and the Limits of Poetry," *Virginia Quarterly Review* 62 (Winter 1986): 105–14, an article notable for its understanding of Tate's "search for authority" and "a compensatory discipline and order in his writing" (109); and "Remaking the *Sewanee Review*," *Chattahoochee Review* 8 (Summer 1988): 71–77.

[48] Professor Brinkmeyer's *Three Catholic Writers of the Modern South* (Jackson, Miss., 1985), a valuable sequel to this book, suggests that Tate wrestled with "the pain of unbelief" (33) in the 1930s and would not transform his "spiritual homelessness" (xiv) into "spiritual wholeness" (34) until his conversion to Catholicism in 1950.

[49] See Cook's "Allen Tate in the Jazz Age," in *The Vanderbilt Tradition: Essays in Honor of Thomas Daniel Young*, ed. Mark Royden Winchell (Baton Rouge, La., 1991), 47–58.

me think much more about Tate, Fletcher, Southern Modernism, and the depressions to which both poets were subject.[50]

Two Tate scholars whose books I did not have the opportunity to read until after the completion of my manuscript, and whose specific conclusions I cannot at this stage address in my text or in my notes, ought to be recognized for their important contributions to Tate studies. While Peter A. Huff's monograph, *Allen Tate and the Catholic Revival: Trace of the Fugitive Gods* (New York and Mahwah, N.J., 1996), engages themes that are largely outside the chronology and the thematic focus of my book, Huff's work, along with Robert Brinkmeyer's, sheds light on Tate's early attraction to Catholicism (which I discuss in chapter 5) and on the complex evolution of Tate's search for religious authority. While I disagree with some of Professor Huff's conclusions, and sometimes think he excises the South from Tate's identity, he does an excellent job of placing Tate within the context of the international Catholic Revival. It seems to me that the revival figures with whom Tate associated formed a fraternity similar to those Tate found in, and rebelled against, in the Fugitive and Agrarian groups—but perhaps dissimilar to the genealogical family he reimagined for *The Fathers*. Reading Huff's book as a sequel of sorts, I also cannot help but wonder whether Tate at times translated his father-son struggle into submission to and rebellion against the Catholic Church.

The other Tate scholar I want to mention is Gale H. Carrithers, Jr., author of *Mumford, Tate, Eiseley: Watchers in the Night*, a dense comparative study best read by specialists in rhetoric, semiotics, and the history of ideas. Professor Carrithers, who focuses on Tate's "prophetic" essays (which he points out correctly were often delivered first as speeches), rewards patient readers with genuine insight into Tate's recognition of "the discrepancy between oral and literate" and his engagement with "structures of authority." Most exciting to me, the book demonstrates Tate's family paradigm was echoed in the very structure of his thought. Assessing the "psychic roots in family" of Tate's "*in between*" intellectual style, "both allied and adversarial," Carrithers asks, "Did the Dark Father/Surrogate Mother/Surrogate Self stand in the way of maturity?" Carrithers's answer is powerfully true: "Tate could not endure having the South or his genealogical family as a failure that was the center for his life. Both had to be decentered or redefined." Having once feared "engulfment by family," Tate became "profoundly a man of family," who "invested himself heavily in an extended quasi family of longtime intellectual companions."[51]

The search for Tate's family, actual and surrogate, took me from Chiapas, Mexico, throughout the continental United States, where I tape-recorded

---

[50] Ben Johnson, " 'A Strange and Lonely Figure': John Gould Fletcher and Southern Modernism," 40-pp. typescript. Professor Johnson has since published *Fierce Soltitude: A Life of John Gould Fletcher* (Fayetteville, Ark., 1994), which I have not yet had the opportunity to read.

[51] (Baton Rouge, La., 1991), x, 109, 131, 111, 108, 111, 112n, 143, 174, 151.

interviews with more than eighty-five people and corresponded with many others. Among those whose recollections helped me in narrating Tate's life up to 1938, I am especially grateful to Mrs. Ursula S. Beach, Mr. Eric Bentley, the late Mr. Cleanth Brooks, Dr. and Mrs. Jameson Jones, the late Mr. Lyle H. Lanier, the late Mr. Danforth Ross, Mr. Randal Strother, the late Mr. Peter Taylor, Mr. Charles Van Doren, and Mrs. Marcella Comès Winslow. Mr. Anthony Hecht generously supplied me with a transcript of (and granted me permission to quote from) his unpublished interview with Tate. The late Mr. Harry Duncan supplied me with photocopies of his Tate letters. I am also grateful to the following Vanderbilt graduates for sharing their recollections in interviews: William Waller '18, Dorothy Bethurum Loomis '19, Madison S. Wigginton '22, William T. Bandy '22, Ivar L. Myhr (Mrs. Edgar H. Duncan) '24. Others helped me through the mail: Mr. A.E. Chester '18, Ms. Mary Lynn Dobson (Mrs. H. H. Armistead) '22, Mr. Leland L. Sage '22, Mr. William S. Vaughn '23, the late Mr. Robert Penn Warren '25, and Mrs. Ella Puryear Mims '34.

A number of people at Harvard University were kind enough to read portions of my manuscript: I owe an enormous debt, intellectual and personal, to Mr. David Herbert Donald, Charles Warren Professor of History, Emeritus, Harvard University;[52] and to Mr. Daniel Aaron, Victor S. Thomas Professor of English, Emeritus, Harvard University, both of whom read an earlier and shorter version of this biography.[53] Professor Alan Brinkley (now a member of the Columbia University Department of History) and Professors Robert Gorham Davis, David Riesman, and Caldwell Titcomb read and criticized my work in the earliest stages. Professor David Blight of Amherst College was visiting Harvard in 1988 and offered some helpful criticism after I delivered a talk. Professor Robert Warren Kent, now retired from the Harvard University Graduate School of Business Administration, shared his insight into Samuel Holt Monk as well as his Monk and Tate letters. Other Harvard-affiliated critics were Mr. Peter Anagnostos, Professor Heather C. Richardson, Professor Gil Troy, and Dr. William A. Braverman. Five Harvard undergraduates helped me by photocopying journal and magazine literature: Mr. Michael Alterman, Ms. Allison Hagood, Mr. Carlos Mendoza, Ms. Julia McDonald, and Mr. John Murphy. For translations from Greek to English, I was fortunate to have the help of Mr. Seth Fagen, a teaching fellow in the Harvard University Classics Dept. Professor Stephan Thernstrom presided over a prospectus I delivered at Harvard, and Ms. Ruth DiPietro helped arrange the event. Professor Werner Sol-

[52] I have been greatly inspired by Professor Donald's two Pulitzer Prize–winning biographies: *Charles Sumner and the Coming of the Civil War* (New York, 1960; repr., 1989) and *Look Homeward: A Life of Thomas Wolfe* (Boston, 1987).

[53] It would have been difficult to undertake this biography without *The Unwritten War* (New York, 1975) and *Writers on the Left* (New York, 1961; repr., Avon Books, 1965).

lors and Professor James Engell have helped me professionally throughout my work on this project.

A number of institutions helped underwrite the costs of my research, travel, and writing. Due to the generosity of an anonymous donor to the History of American Civilization Program at Harvard, I received funding for my work during the summers of 1986 and 1988. The Mrs. Giles Whiting Foundation in New York City was kind enough to award me a Whiting Fellowship in the Humanities for the 1988–89 academic year, which allowed me an uninterrupted year in which to work on my manuscript. Dr. Cynthia Verba, Director of Fellowships for the Graduate School of Arts and Sciences at Harvard, made it possible for me to attend the SIHC meeting mentioned above. Some portions of the manuscript I wrote while summering in Middlebury, Vermont, where Professor James Ralph of the Department of History at Middlebury College provided housing, scholarly discourse, and friendship. Professor Mark Witkin of the Middlebury Department of Classics loaned me an office during his absence from the college. Professor Timothy B. Spears, of the American Literature and Civilization program at Middlebury, was kind enough to invite me to test some of my ideas in a public lecture there in February 1997.

Allen Tate's words appear by permission of Mrs. Helen H. Tate (copyright © by the Estate of Allen Tate). I am also grateful to the following individuals for permission to quote from and/or cite unpublished, published, and copyrighted letters and writings. Daniel Aaron's words and/or letters from Tate and/or Gordon appear by permission of Professor Aaron; William T. Bandy's by his family; Ferman Bishop's by Ms. Audrey Bishop; Louise Bogan's by Ms. Ruth Limmer, Literary Executive of Louise Bogan; Cleanth Brooks's by John Michael Walsh for the Estate of Cleanth Brooks; Kenneth Burke's by Michael Burke, Co-Trustee, Kenneth Burke Literary Trust; Brainard and Frances Neel Cheney's by Roy M. Neel; Malcolm Cowley's by Mr. Rob Cowley (copyright © by the Literary Estate of Malcolm Cowley); Donald Davidson's by his family; Harry Duncan's by Ms. Nancy K. Duncan; Richard Eberhart's by Richard B. Eberhart, POA; T. S. Eliot's by the Eliot Estate and Faber & Faber; Caroline Gordon's by Nancy Tate Wood; Ernest Hemingway's in Carlos Baker, ed., *Ernest Hemingway: Selected Letters, 1917–1961*, copyright © 1981, the Ernest Hemingway Foundation, Inc., by Scribner, a Division of Simon and Schuster; Josephine Herbst's by Hilton Kramer for the Estate of Josephine Herbst; Matthew Josephson's by Carl Josephson; Robert Lowell's by Elizabeth Hardwick and the Lowell Estate; Andrew Lytle's by George Chamberlain for the Estate of Andrew Lytle; H. L. Mencken's by the Enoch Pratt Free Library of Baltimore in accordance with H. L. Mencken's will; Arthur Mizener's by Rosemary Mizener Colt for the Estate of Arthur Mizener; Frank Owsley's by Margaret O. Seigenthaler; Maxwell E. Perkins's by Scribner, a Division of Simon & Schuster; John Crowe Ransom's by Helen Ransom Forman, Executrix, Ransom Literary Estate; the late Danforth P. Ross's "Memories of Allen Tate" by Mrs. Dorothy Ross; Louis D. Rubin, Jr.'s by Professor Rubin; John L. Stewart's by

Professor Stewart; Eileen Simpson's in *Poets In Their Youth: A Memoir* (New York: Random House, 1982; repr., Vintage Books, 1983) and in her *Orphans: Real and Imaginary* (New York: Weidenfeld and Nicolson, 1987), copyright © by Eileen Simpson, by permission of Georges Borchardt, Inc.; Robert Penn Warren's by Professor John Burt for the Estate of Robert Penn Warren; Jesse Wills's by Ridley Wills II; and William Ridley Wills's by John Thad Wills.

Finally, I would like to express my deep gratitude to the people who have made my world over the years. My many former students, who have studied with me in a range of courses at a variety of institutions, kept me on my toes intellectually. My lifelong friends—they know who they are—helped me to stay motivated over the years. My brother, Walter, my sister, Elizabeth, my father (who continues to teach at the age of eighty-six), and my late mother—Texans all—ensured that I myself never felt orphaned by the South. And to Suzanne Rivitz, who cheerfully listened to me read portions of this book aloud, I owe more than these mere words.

Thomas A. Underwood

Index

Johnson, Stanley, 52, 67, 79, 125
Johnson, Theodore, 221
Jones, Howard Mumford, 39
Josephson, Matthew, 56, 63, 108, 122–23,
 126, 136, 295, 339n.166
Joyce, James, 63, 144

Kant, Immanuel, 64, 94
Keats, John, 40, 62
Kemble, Fanny, *Journal of a Residence on a
 Georgian Plantation*, 299
Kenyon College, offer of teaching position
 to John Crowe Ransom, 272–76,
 393nn.64, 67, 72, 76, 394n.83
Kenyon Review, 395n.90
Kezee, Joseph, 296, 405–6n.196
King, Martin Luther, 294, 406n.197
Kirkland, James, 31, 34, 35, 54, 273,
 394n.83
Kirstein, Lincoln, 183, 189, 202, 230, 291,
 295, 296
Kline, Henry Blue, 156, 245
Knickerbocker, William S., 135, 158–59,
 169
Kreymbourg, Arthur, 255

LaForgue, Jules, 24, 62
Lamar, L.Q.C., *Eulogy on Charles Sumner*,
 38
Langton, John (character), 268, 301,
 391n.31
Lanier, Chink, 186
Lanier, Lyle, 79, 85, 98, 125, 156, 186,
 203, 274
Lanier, Sidney, 38, 160, 211
Latimer, J. Ronald Lane, 257–58
Lee, Alice, 37
Lee, Robert E., 8, 148, 154
Lewis, Eleanor Parke Custis, 357n.92
Lewis, Sinclair, 297
Lieber and Lewis (publishing firm), AT's
 efforts to publish *Calidus Juventa*, 70,
 74, 93
Lieber, Maxim, 74, 94
Literary Review, 81
Little Review, 50, 63
Longstreet, Augustus Baldwin, 156;
 Georgia Scenes, 212
Lost Generation, 142–43, 146–47
Lowell, Amy, 127; *Tendencies in Modern
 American Poetry*, 34
Lowell, James Russell, 18

Lowell, Robert "Cal," 269–72, 276,
 278–79
Lumpkin, Grace, 239–42; *To Make My
 Bread*, 239
Lytle, Andrew
 and Agrarian movement, 171, 249
 death of Orley Tate and, 199
 friendship with Tates, 134, 152, 179,
  186, 194, 255–60
 on AT's letter on Ransom's offer from
  Kenyon College, 273
 and Southern symposium, 154
 support for AT's Lee biography, 173–
  74, 177
 visit to Southwestern College, 223
 works: contributor to *Who Owns
  America?*, 228, 245; *The Long
  Night*, 214, 245

Mabry, Tom, 291–92
McDonough, Rev. Vincent S., 27
McGill, Ralph E. "Mac," 44, 46
McIver, Charles Duncan, 281
Macmillan and Company, 118
McNeilly, Robert, 36, 42
Marxism, 167, 244
Mather, Cotton, 128
Matthiesson, F. O., 282
Maué, Daniel Robert, 132
Means, Gardiner C., 246
Meiners, R. K., 187
Mencken, H. L.
 AT's animosity toward, 112, 114
 compliments for the *Fugitive*, 55–56
 criticism of Southern literature and
  culture, 49, 87, 112, 137
 as editor of: *American Mercury*, 112;
  Smart Set, 55–56, 87
 response to *I'll Take My Stand*, 169
 response to Southern religious
  movements, 163
 writer of rank, 62
 works: *The Sahara of the Bozart*, 49
Meriwether family, 126, 186, 191–95, 303,
 362n.204
Merry Mont (Gordon farm, Kentucky),
 102, 158, 190–95
Middle Western Writer's Conference, 255,
 276, 277
Mims, Edwin "Eddie"
 and AT's and Warren's sexual conduct,
  96
 awarding AT Phi Beta Kappa, 85

New York Times reviews
  of AT's poetry in *Double Dealer*, 61
  of AT's *The Mediterranean and Other
    Poems*, 258
  Fugitive, first issue of, 56
  of *I'll Take My Stand*, 169
  of MLA meeting (1936), 262
  of *Reactionary Essays*, 236
Nichol, Katherine, 85
Nixon, Herman Clarence, 156, 208, 245,
  368n.61
North American Review, 132
North Carolina, University of (Chapel Hill),
  Chapel Hill Planners, 208, 368nn. 61,
  64
North Carolina, University of (Greensboro),
  Woman's College, Tates teaching at, 279,
  280–83, 396–97n.126

Oak Grove (Allen family estate, Ken-
  tucky), 8
O'Donnell, George Marion, 245, 280
Odum, Howard W., 208, 248
O'Gorman, Ned, 417–18
Olivet Writer's Conference, 255, 276, 277
O'Neill, Eugene, 107, 338–39n.166
Ott, William Pinkerton, 33, 77
Owsley, Frank, 147, 149, 156, 171, 188,
  225, 231, 245, 276, 292
Owsley, Harriet, 188, 276

Page, Thomas Nelson, 113, 212
Page, Walter Hines, 38
Peabody Teachers' College, AT as student,
  77–79
Pelham, John, 11
Perkins, Maxwell, 176, 181, 185, 189, 218,
  234, 255, 259–60, 262, 299, 386–
  87n.133
Phillips, Ulrich Bonnell
  Agrarian supporter, 168
  interceding with Balch on AT's biograph-
    ies, 176
  works: *American Negro Slavery*, 150–51,
    349n.177
Pinckney, Josephine, 212, 215
Pleasant Hill (fictional place), 265,
  299n.153, 301–2
Pleasant Hill (Varnell ancestral home,
  Virginia), 8, 19
Poe, Edgar Allan, 18–19, 211, 297,
  318n.56

works: *Eureka* (essay), 19; *Marginalia*,
  19
Poetry (magazine), 50, 103, 138, 181, 183
Poetry Review, 141
Poetry Society of South Carolina, 139, 212
Pope, Alexander, 103
Porter, Katherine Anne, 125, 134, 154,
  276–77, 395n.93
Posey, George (character), 265–68, 284–
  86, 300–303, 391n.31, 399nn.159, 162
Posey, Jane (character), 268, 268–69, 286,
  288, 391–92n.35
Posey, Susan Buchan (character), 265–66,
  301, 399n.159
Potter, David M., 168
Pound, Ezra
  criticism of Southern poetry, 183
  editing of Eliot's works, 70
  Fletcher rejection of, 127
  influence on AT, 3, 50, 270
  as Modernist poet, 62, 235–36
Proust, Marcel, 265
Putnam, Phelps, 135

Race relations
  and the Agrarian movement, 291–92
  AT's racist letters to *Hound & Horn*,
    291–92, 295–96, 398n.149
  AT's remarks on white supremacy, 209,
    293, 402n.171, 403–4n.182
  AT's views on civil rights movement,
    294, 406n.197
  civil rights forum, 294
  gender and, 401–2n.169
  and "miscegenation" issue, 288–96,
    405–6n.196
  racial terrorism and lynchings, 293–94,
    404n.184
  Scottsboro trial, 292–93
  and sharecroppers' incident at Marked
    Tree, 225–27
  and slavery, 149–52, 286–87, 349n.177,
    399n.153
  voting rights, 294
Rahv, Philip, 289
Ransom, John Crowe
  and Agrarian movement, 164–65, 171,
    231, 246, 258
  AT's competition and jealousy of, 57,
    81–82, 94–95, 323n.92, 330n.129
  AT's poetry, critique of, 258–59
  debate on Agrarianism with Barr,
    164–65

Starke, Aubrey, biography of Sidney Lanier, 211
Steele, R. B. "Tootsie," 28–29, 32
Stein, Gertrude, 142, 146–47
Stevenson, Alec, 52, 66, 67, 69
Stevens, Wallace, 257
Stone, Geoffrey, 238
Stowe, Harriet Beecher, *Uncle Tom's Cabin*, 152
Swift, Jonathan, 206
Symbolist movement, 50, 62, 70
Symons, Arthur, 70

Tate, Allen. *See* Tate, John Orley Allen
Tate, Annie Josephine (sister), childhood death of, 10
Tate, Benjamin (brother)
  birth of, 7
  as college student, Vanderbilt, 9, 29, 52, 317n.44
  financial support for family, 28, 43, 77–79, 96, 105, 159
  health of, appendicitis attack, 194
  letters to Shafer on behalf of AT, 203
  relationship with AT, 17, 82, 97, 179–81
  relationship with mother, 17
  role in founding Agrarian newspaper, 231
  as successful businessman, 18, 68, 72, 179–80, 317n.50
Tate, Benjamin (son), 418
Tate, Bessie (wife of Benjamin), 43
Tate, Carolyn/Caroline (wife). *See* Gordon, Carolyn/Caroline
Tate, Eleanor "Nellie" Custis Parke Varnell (mother)
  ancestors and family history, 8, 19
  birthplace of, 8
  death of, 152
  education at Georgetown finishing school, 8
  health declining, 36, 50, 78
  inheritance from, 160
  last meeting with AT, 151–52
  marriage and relationship with husband, 6–9, 15–16
  move to Washington, D.C. (1924), 105–6
  personality and characteristics of, 4, 7–8
  reading interests, 8
  relationship with AT, 19–20
  relationship with sons, 4–5, 17, 65
  religious piety, 7–8
  traveling lifestyle of, 9, 14, 17, 19

Tate, Helen Heinz (wife), 413, 418
Tate, James Johnston, 127, 315n.10
Tate, Jane, 141
Tate, John Orley Allen
BIOGRAPHY
  ancestors and family history, 19, 126–28, 179
  marriages, 110, 413
  birthplace of, 4, 6, 127, 314–15n.11, 358–59n.117
  childhood, 315n.1; with mother, 10–14; reunion with family, 14–15; moving with family, 21
  as schoolboy: at Tarbox grammar school in Nashville, 11–12, 36; at Cross School in Louisville, 12–14, 27–28; in Ashland, 18–19
  high school years: at Central High School in Ashland, 20; at Evansville High School, 23, 25; at Walnut Hills High School in Cincinnati, 23; at Cincinnati Conservatory of Music, 23–25
  student at Georgetown Preparatory School, 26–29
  college student: Vanderbilt, *see under* Vanderbilt University; University of Virginia summer school, 36–37
  job at Ford Motor plant, 43–44
  job at United Collieries (coal firm), 68, 72
  college student, Peabody Teachers' College, 77–79
  teaching position, Lumberport High School, West Virginia, 89–92, 97
  college student, Yale University graduate fellowship rejected, 84, 333n.37
  visiting Hart Crane in NYC (1924), 99–101
  visiting Red Warren in Guthrie (1924), 101–6
  application to George Washington University rejected, 105
  assisting mother with move to Washington, D.C., 105
  job at Climax Publishing Company, NYC (1924), 106, 114–15
  literary and social life in NYC, 107–14
  marriage to Carolyn Gordon, 110
  move to writers' colony in Patterson, New York (1925), 115–19
  job as janitor in NYC, 122
  job as manuscript reader for Minton, Balch, and Company, 122

Tate, John Orley Allen *(cont.)*
   return to Greenwich Village, NYC, 122
   tour with Carolyn of Shenandoah Valley
      (July 1927), 129
   Southern tour with Carolyn and Nancy
      (1928), 134–35
   trip to Europe (1928), 139–47
   living in New York City (1930), 158
   return to the South, 158
   trip to Europe (1932), 186–90
   living at Merry Mont, 190–95
   return to Benfolly, 196
   teaching position at Southwestern Col-
      lege, 219–23, 233, 254
   lecture tour (summer 1936), 254–55
   teaching position at Middle Western Writ-
      er's Conference, 255
   visit to Lytle's in Monteagle (1936),
      255–60
   publication of *The Mediterranean*, 257–
      58
   trip to Virginia and Modern Language As-
      sociation meeting, 260–63
   return visit to Monteagle and writing of
      The Fathers, 264–69
   return to Benfolly and writing of *The
      Fathers*, 269–75
   controversial letter on Ransom's offer
      from Kenyon College, 272–76
   trip to Michigan for Olivet Writer's Con-
      ference (1937), 276–77
   teaching position at Woman's College of
      the University of North Carolina, 279,
      280–83, 396–97n.126
   Harvard University Morris Gray Poetry
      Fund lecture series, 282–83
   summer in Cornwall, Connecticut, with
      Van Dorens, 283–84, 298–99, 303–5
   return to Benfolly (1937), 279–80
   divorce from Carolyn Gordon (1945),
      195; remarried, 316n.23
   death of (1979), 5, 413
   PERSONALITY, TRAITS, HABITS
   anti-Semitism of, 205–6
   appearance of, 10, 31, 108, 252, 282–83
   confrontations with authority figures, 71
   conservative politics of, 205–6, 230, 232;
      at Nashville Debate with Chapel Hill
      Planners, 248–49; a Southern Policy
      Committee meeting, 249–50
   drinking of: at Vanderbilt, 45; while in
      Europe, 142

   family relationships: with brothers, 17,
      82, 179–81; with daughter, 304–5;
      with father, 4–5, 15–16, 199–200;
      with mother, 4–5, 10–14, 17, 19–20,
      30, 32, 191n.350; with mother after
      her death, 180, 200, 269
   fears: of being orphaned or abandoned,
      85; nightmare of father dying, 16–17
   health of: childhood illnesses, 10–11, 12;
      and cigarette smoking, 57, 60; conva-
      lescing at Valle Crucis, North Carolina,
      60–68; depression and talk of suicide,
      187, 256, 259; hospitalization at Vand-
      erbilt, 57; while in Europe, 141, 142,
      190; withdrawal from Vanderbilt, 59
   musical studies, 23–25
   nicknames for, 16, 36
   racism of: guilty feelings about,
      398n.149; and "miscegenation" issue,
      288–96, 405–6n.196; racist letters to
      Hound & Horn, 291–92, 295–96; and
      segregation, 294–95; and sharecrop-
      pers' incident at Marked Tree, 225–27;
      social avoidance of black writers, 291–
      92; supporting white supremacy, 209,
      293, 402n.171; views on African
      Americans and slavery, 149–52, 286–
      87, 294, 295, 349n.177, 399n.153,
      403–4n.182; views on civil rights
      movement, 294, 406n.197
   reading of, 68; classical studies, 13, 26,
      27–29, 35; during school years, 13,
      26–27; poetry, 13, 27; private family li-
      brary, 18–19
   religious beliefs: conversion to Catholi-
      cism, 27, 154, 351n.200; instruction
      in Christian doctrine, 27; as religious
      atheist, 157, 163; search for belief sys-
      tem, 154–55
   routine and habits: daily routine at Pea-
      body, 79; daily routine in writers' col-
      ony, Patterson, NY, 116; daily writing
      routine at Marry Mont, 191; prolific
      writer, 68
   sexuality: allusions in poems by, 66–67;
      cynicism about women, 102–3, 109–
      10; father's facts of life lecture, 15–16;
      feelings about love and sex, 66; He-
      mingway's advice on orgasms, 144; ho-
      mophobia, 339–40n.167; phallic sym-
      bol in poems by, 47, 58

sexual relationships, 418; affairs with
Carolyn Gordon, 101–2, 104, 109–10;
affair with Eleanor Hall, 51, 57–58,
59, 61, 66, 79, 102; affair with Marion
Henry, 192–95; with coeds at Vander-
bilt, 46–47, 85, 96; coed scandal at
Vanderbilt, 79–80, 96; flirtation with
school girl, 20; friendship with Laura
Riding, 80, 103–4, 111; romance with
Alice Lee, 37

AS CRITIC
for book reviews and magazine articles,
92, 105, 118
defense of Eliot, 70–71
lack of experience, 93–94
Malcolm Cowley's views on, 237
for the *Nation* and the *New Republic*,
122
and New York literary politics, 118
of poetry, 182–83
reputation of, 117–18, 182

AS EDITOR
book review editor for *Free America*,
381n.48
of *Fugitive*, 69
for *Sewanee Review*, 3

AS POET
Chair of Poetry at Library of Congress, 3
critical reviews of poetry of, 258–59, 278
Fugitives critical support of, 61
marketing to publishers, 61, 118–19,
138, 259–60
mixed reviews of poetry, 181
Modernist influence on, 63, 64, 69, 76,
135–36, 138, 181
modern vs. Southern, 135–36
obscurity of style, 63–64, 138
sexual allusions in poems, 66–67
themes in, 324n.127, 327n.41
youthful arrogance, 72

AS PROFESSOR/TEACHER
North Carolina University Woman's Col-
lege (Greensboro), 279, 280–83, 396–
97n.126
Princeton University, Resident Fellow in
Creative Writing, 5
Southwestern College, 219–23, 233, 254
University of Minnesota, 5
Wallace University School, 43

AS WRITER
attraction to Modernism, 326–27n.40
awards and honors, 3–4, 139

contributor to the *American Review*,
202–9
Guggenheim Fellowship, 139, 140, 142,
158
influences on, of Davidson, 61
lack of experience, 92–93
pseudonym, Henry Feathertop, 54–55
Southern Writers' Conference (1931),
AT's speech at, 214–15
style: first-person narration, 254, 384–
85n.98; Modernist influence on, 135–
36; obscurity of, 63–64, 138; skills as
prose stylist, 68–69
technique: narrative device of the
"trapped spectator," 188, 265; narrative models, 265; Ransom criticism of,
48–49
themes in his work: Agrarian themes,
177; American in the industrial age,
136–37; fear and human mortality, 58;
female innocence and decadence, 56,
58, 66; kinship bonds, 179, 182, 184;
loss of virginity, 51; loyalty vs. individualism, 267; modern world in conflict
with spiritual life of man, 178; from
politics to language, 261; separation
and abandonment, 58–59, 66; Southern history and traditions, 136; writer's block, 256–57; writing projects,
197

WRITINGS, BIOGRAPHIES, 356n.84
Jefferson Davis: His Rise and Fall, 139,
142, 147
of Robert E. Lee unfinished project, 154,
171–76, 177, 188, 200–201, 256,
356–57nn. 89, 90, 364–65n.20,
409n.225–26
sources for, 129–30, 147, 148
Stonewall Jackson: The Good Soldier,
128–33, 151, 171–72

WRITINGS, ESSAYS
on arts and letters in the South, 112–14
on Emily Dickinson, 140
"American Poetry since 1920," 140
"The Fallacy of Humanism" (retitled
"Humanism and Naturalism"), 155,
202
"The Function of the Critical Quarterly,"
228
"Humanism and Naturalism," 236
"Last Days of the Charming Lady," 113–
14

Winslow, Anne Goodwin, 251–52
Winslow, Marcella
    portrait of Allen Tate by, 251–52
    visit from Tates, 260–62, 284
Winslow, Randolph, 251
Winters, Yvor, 136, 178, 182, 184, 189,
    203, 353n.26
Wolfe, Thomas, 74, 213, 386–87n.133;
    Of Time and the River, 262
Wood, Nancy Tate. *See* Tate, Nancy Susan
    (daughter)
Wood, Sally, 186, 188, 194
Woodward, C. Vann, 249, 299,
    383n.74
Wordsworth, William, 18, 62

Yale Review, 182, 187, 198–99
Yale University, AT's graduate fellowship
    denied, 84, 89, 95, 333n.37
Young, Stark, 156, 171, 220, 259,
    340n.167
    critique of AT's play *The Governess*,
        253
    as drama critic for *New Republic*,
        156, 245
    So Red the Rose, 214
Young, Thomas Daniel, 416n.13,
    416
Ysaÿe, Eugéne, 24, 25

Zabel, Morton, 138, 167, 182, 277

WITHDRAWN